Identities
and Issues
in Literature

Identities
and Issues
in Literature

Volume 1

Abbey, Edward – *Emergence of Green, An*

Editor

David Peck

California State University, Long Beach

Project Editor

Eric Howard

Salem Press, Inc.
Pasadena, California   Englewood Cliffs, New Jersey

Managing Editor: Christina J. Moose
Project Editor: Eric Howard   *Production Editor:* Joyce I. Buchea
Acquisitions Editor: Mark Rehn   *Proofreading Supervisor:* Yasmine A. Cordoba
Research Supervisor: Jeffry Jensen   *Page Layout and Graphics:* James Hutson
Photograph Editor: Karrie Hyatt   *Data Entry:* William Zimmerman

Library of Congress Cataloging-in-Publication Data

Identities and issues in literature / editor, David Peck; project editor, Eric Howard.
    p.   cm.
    Includes bibliographical references and index.
    ISBN 0-89356-920-8 (set : alk. paper). — ISBN 0-89356-921-6 (v. 1 : alk. paper)
    1. American literature—Minority authors—Dictionaries.   2. Literature and society—North America—Dictionaries. 3. Canadian literature—Minority authors—Dictionaries.   4. Social problems in literature—Dictionaries.   5. Group identity in literature—Dictionaries.   6. Ethnic groups in literature—Dictionaries.   7. Minorities in literature—Dictionaries.   8. North America—Literatures—Dictionaries.   I. Peck, David R.   II. Howard, Eric, 1961-   .
PS153.M56I34   1997
810.9'920693—dc21
                                           97-11951
                                             CIP

First Printing

PRINTED IN THE UNITED STATES OF AMERICA

Publisher's Note

North America has never had a homogeneous culture. Native American tribes were and are richly varied in language and custom; explorers from Europe arrived who served different, often rival, nations and religions; settlers of various national, linguistic, and religious backgrounds came; slaves from Africa were imported; immigrants from all nations and all political, economic, and cultural groups arrived from Africa, the Americas, Asia, and Europe.

For immigrants, assimilation was not merely allowed to happen; it was impressed upon them in schools and in other social institutions, public and private. For slaves and their descendants, on the other hand, assimilation was deliberately slowed or withheld; difference was preserved. One effect of this practice was that differences among people of European origin did not seem so great as they did in Europe. Therefore, even the issues of difference and assimilation were also experienced differently by different people in America. Some arrived with great hope, some as refugees, others by force; some arrived at Ellis Island from Eastern Europe in the late nineteenth century, others at Los Angeles International Airport from Korea in the late twentieth century. Although some forms of assimilation—for example, linguistic assimilation—have typically been consistent and rapid in the United States, North America was heterogeneous and remains so. Furthermore, patterns of immigration and population growth by native birth since 1965 have contributed to America's becoming more heterogeneous. By the mid-2000's, according to forecasts by the U.S. Bureau of the Census, most Americans will be of non-European origin.

In recognition of this, literature and history, which often have been taught with the intent of establishing a homogeneous, patriarchal, Eurocentric view of American life, have begun to be taught in the context of ethnic and cultural diversity, of women and women's issues, and of the identity of marginalized peoples. This change, the result of social upheavals of the 1960's and 1970's—including the Civil Rights movement, the women's movement, and the gay rights movement—has brought controversy, as evidenced by the numbers of books on the topic, whether they are about the validity, or lack thereof, of the canon, and what works belong in it; about diversity; about race and ethnicity; about women; about homosexuality; about religious diversity; about the university's role in promulgating this social change; or about what effects this social change has brought.

Identities and Issues in Literature concentrates, as the title implies, on how this great social change can be traced in the literature of North America. Its three volumes explore authors, works, and subjects related to North American and world literatures—of people of African, Asian, Canadian, European, Gay, Jewish, Latino, Lesbian, and Native American identity, for example. Issues regarding religion, disease, and regions are also addressed. Topics covered, which can be searched by means of the Category List in volume 3, include abortion and birth control, African American identity, appearance and identity, Asian American identity, Catholicism, diaries and journals, ethnic composition of universities, feminism, the Harlem Renaissance, the Korean War, mixed race and identity, Native American identity, popular culture, and violence. The set's focus on issues that both unite and divide Americans encourages readers to compare, assess, and appreciate multiple perspectives. With 809 articles and more than 550,000 words, the set encompasses a comprehensive selection of the literature that has described the experience of the many who make up North America.

One definition of identity is what one is called; the editors of this set have made strong efforts to avoid racist, sexist, or otherwise biased language. Decisions about group names were based on the emerging consensus among scholars and within the group itself. Acceptable group names are in flux, and reflect changing group identity; some alternates are allowed in text; for example, "black" and "African American" are used interchangeably, as are "American Indian" and "Native American." Other terms used include "Asian American," "Asian Canadian," "Chicano," and "Latino." Immigrants are, in appropriate contexts, referred to by country of origin, for example "Mexican American." A limited and consistent set of group names is used at the top of each article, when appropriate, after the "Identities" heading; this is done so that the Category List, provided at the end of volume 3, may be, for those who wish to research by topic or category, more comprehensive. Greater ethnic awareness, including awareness of multiple ethnic backgrounds, has led to changes in the way, in the United States, the ten-year census is taken; many have suggested that people be allowed to check off all that apply from a list of racial and ethnic categories, rather than be obliged to pick only one. The "Identities" groups were created with this concept in mind; they provide the researcher a few threads on which to tug, rather than pigeonhole given authors and titles. Hence, the "Identities" line allows for multiple listings, and the same article may be found in the Category List under different category headings.

The 809 entries in the three volumes of the set are arranged alphabetically, using by-word (not by-letter) alphabetization rules. In all articles, the text focuses on the identity theme or relates the topic to the identity theme, thus providing the reader with a single source for recent scholarship on a large, complex issue in literature and literary criticism. There are three types of entry: author, subject, and title. All articles have bibliographic entries under a "Suggested readings" header and cross-references under a "See also" header. Longer subject articles have annotated bibliographic entries. Author and title articles are 500 words long; subject articles vary in length from 500 to 4,000 words. Author articles contain the name of the author, with the surname by which the author is alphabetized first, and other name, if any, following in parentheses. Information about place and time of birth and death follows, then a list of principal works, in order of publication. The "Identities" line that follows describes identities most associated with the author and the author's work. For example, under "Allen, Paula Gunn," after the "Identities" header are listed "family," "gay, lesbian, and bisexual," "Native American," and "women." Allen's works have been concerned with all these identities; the text of the article describes her multicultural, multilingual upbringing in more detail. After the "Identities" line is "Significant achievement," a short, one-sentence description of the author's literary contribution.

Subject articles have the "Identities" header when there is a specific group to which the article pertains; often, an article (for example "Urban life" or "Poverty") pertains to all groups; in such cases, no "Identities" list is given. In longer subject articles, subheads indicate which sections of the article treat a given topic.

Title articles cover major literary works that address the identity theme. Title articles begin with the title, list the author (with birth name, if different, and years of birth and death in parentheses), year first published (with additional information, such as foreign-language title or year of production for drama, when needed), and an "Identities" line. For example, the "Identities" line for the article on *The Diary of Frida Kahlo* lists "disability," "Latino," and "women."

Identities and Issues in Literature contains eighteen articles on Canadian writers, works, and issues; eleven articles on Caribbean writers, works, and issues; twenty-four articles on gay, lesbian, and bisexual authors, works, and issues; six regional surveys; eleven articles on religious issues; sixteen articles on women's issues; and sixty-five subject articles treating general issues such as the canon, divorce, and World War II. More than three hundred articles are about women authors or their works. Two hundred sixty-four authors are represented, and 424 articles about particular works (selected to provide a comprehensive representation of the many identities of North American writers and readers) are to be found in *Identities and Issues in Literature*. Six hundred eighty-nine articles (all the articles on specific works or on authors) are five hundred words in length. Seventy-two articles 2000 words or longer address such topics as adolescent identity, the *Bildungsroman* and *Künstlerroman*, the nontraditional family, and religious minorities.

Volume 3 contains research aids for further study of the many faces of North American literature. For those seeking additional information outside the set, there is a mediagraphy listing films, recordings, and other media by identity category. Additionally, a 10,000-word bibliography lists recent scholarly works by category. For those seeking information inside the set, the Category List groups the articles under the identity categories. Finally, a comprehensive index lists names, titles, and other keywords alphabetically, with page numbers.

The contributors to this encyclopedia, who are listed in volume 1, represent a variety of academic and cultural backgrounds as well as multiple academic approaches. They present clear, objective information on topics that are often controversial. David Peck, the Editor, worked to create a balanced, inclusive list of entries, and other editors worked diligently to polish and illustrate the text. The efforts of all are greatly appreciated.

— Eric Howard

Introduction

In the last quarter of the twentieth century, the cultural map of the United States was redrawn. The very notion of an American literature was lost in the recognition of the fluidity of the borders within North America and the profound influences on that literature from Canada, Mexico, and South America. Students began to speak more accurately of the "literatures of North America"; the older monolithic model of a coherent and unified "American literature" has gone. Within the boundaries of the United States, any sense of a unitary, homogeneous national literature—which prevailed in the United States at least through the 1950's in company with the equally incomplete concept of the melting pot—was destroyed by the discovery of dozens of new literary identities created through a deeper understanding of the importance of gender, race, and ethnicity in American culture. The emergence of a truly multicultural and multiethnic North America has been the result of women, gays, and ethnic groups demonstrating the uniqueness of their voices and declaring the importance of their histories. The essentially European American concept of the melting pot of the 1950's was replaced in the 1980's by a patchwork quilt.

Identities and Issues in Literature documents the numerous forms these changes have taken in North American literature. Textbooks at all levels have been shifting to reflect the discovery of the new and emergent literatures, but reference works have been slow to undertake a full range of writers, works, and themes that this revolution in consciousness has created. *Identities and Issues in Literature* collects, in one resource, the full depth and breadth of American literatures.

Literature has always given readers a sense of their identity and the issues that involve them. What can teach more about social class than the novels of Edith Wharton and John Galsworthy, more about alienation than Franz Kafka's "The Metamorphosis" (1915) and J. D. Salinger's *The Catcher in the Rye* (1951)? While knowledge of human behavior often comes from scientists of all stripes—Sigmund Freud and Carl Jung in psychology, for example—intimate understanding of any subject may first come from poets and novelists: Fyodor Dostoevski and Theodore Dreiser on the psychological consequences of crime, for example. Literature is often in fact the leading light that reveals most sharply the essential issues of human life and behavior. To know about the legacy of Puritanism, one may read Nathaniel Hawthorne. To learn about the values and ideals of the American South, one should read William Faulkner, Carson McCullers, Flannery O'Connor, or Harper Lee. To learn about environmental issues, one may read the literature of Edward Abbey or Wendell Berry, *Walden* (1854) and *The Grapes of Wrath* (1939).

What makes *Identities and Issues in Literature* so necessary is the radical change that has taken place in the canon of American literature. The formal study of the literatures of North America started only at the beginning of the twentieth century, when writers and critics freed themselves from the hold of British dominance. For its first half century, at least, American literary study was strictly historical, and focused mainly on the major figures of the second half of the nineteenth century: from Hawthorne and Herman Melville through William Dean Howells and Stephen Crane. The only woman granted canonical status was Emily Dickinson; ethnic writers were notable only by their absence.

This academic distortion lasted at least through the 1940's. While women (from Anne Bradstreet to Katherine Anne Porter) and ethnic writers (from Frederick Douglass to Luis Valdez) had been making important contributions to the literatures of North America all along, they were nearly always relegated to a secondary, noncanonical literary status. They were outsiders, exceptions to the rule of white male literary supremacy.

Identities and issues identified in literature during this time reflected this monolithic European American canon. Critics and historians talked about regionalism in literature (the influence of the idea of the frontier, for example) or about immigration (and acculturation)—about any social, historical, or psychological issue, in other words, that assumed the notion of a mainstream American literature. Some topics that imply, or were thought to imply, such a notion include the American Dream (from Benjamin Franklin through F. Scott Fitzgerald's *The Great Gatsby*, 1925) or the rural-urban split in America. Economics was a safe subject, geography even safer. Any issue or writer outside the bounds of this linear, homogeneous literary model was marginal and thus unrepresentative.

Furthermore, discussions of any issue tended to be elitist and patriarchal, because the model was male and white. Discussions of adolescence and initiation before 1960, for example, usually described white male protagonists (Thomas Wolfe's Eugene Gant, or Salinger's Holden Caulfield), and only rarely women or people of color (Sylvia Plath's Esther Greenwood, or Zora Neale Hurston's Janie from *Their Eyes Were Watching God*, 1937). Models of psychosexual development were nearly always heterosexual.

Soon after World War II, critics and scholars were obliged to abandon that model. Symbolically, at least, it may have been the Beat generation of writers in the 1950's—Allen Ginsberg, Jack Kerouac, and others—who helped to break the mold. In their writings and in their public recitations, the Beats challenged all the assumptions of the European American melting pot. They were writers who wrote and spoke openly about drugs, homosexuality, Eastern religions, jazz music and its black performers, and the Beats made all these subjects sound attractive and liberating rather than corrupting, as the older Puritan-influenced literary model would have.

At the same historical moment changes were occurring in the foundations of American society. Beginning with Martin Luther King, Jr., and the Civil Rights movement of the 1950's, through the Chicano and feminist revolutions of the 1960's and 1970's, the white and patriarchal assumptions and social codes of the United States were being challenged and destroyed. Whole groups of Americans who had contributed to the history—but who had been left out of the history books— came forward with their stories. Ethnic groups (Native American, Latino, and Asian American, as well as African American) reclaimed their history and demanded political representation. Women and other gender groups (most notably gays and lesbians) claimed their space and recited their sometimes painful, often joyful histories. The consequences of this social revolution for literature were enormous. On one hand, it meant the rediscovery of works and writers that had been ignored in the monolithic American literary history of the past century. In the 1970's and 1980's, figures from the past emerged to take their rightful places in the canon. To cite one example, the American Realist movement at the end of the nineteenth century—dominated by Mark Twain and Henry James for decades—was transformed by the addition of Kate Chopin (*The Awakening*, 1899) and Charlotte Perkins Gilman ("The Yellow Wallpaper," 1892). This process went on for every group claiming recognition and proclaiming its history. Scholarly journals and international conferences were quickly filled with analyses of Valdez's *Zoot Suit* (1978) and Hisaye Yamamoto's *Seventeen Syllables* (1949) and with discussions of Rudolph Fisher and Lorraine Hansberry. Anthologies of American literature suddenly discovered slave narratives, poems from the Chinese immigrants who wrote on the walls of the barracks of Angel Island, accounts of the Harlem Renaissance of the 1920's, and stories of Japanese American internment during World War II.

This transformation meant the emergence of whole new lists of issues, for the rediscovered writers brought with them new themes and new questions of their own. The canon and its central concerns were expanding, and readers were suddenly talking about issues such as pluralism versus assimilation, mixed race and identity, and racism and ethnocentrism in literature. A truly diverse and pluralistic American literature had been discovered, its issues were being hotly debated, and its growth was exponential.

One example of this complex social and literary development was that by the 1980's, a number of different American writers had become widely popular, and their issues had become essential

American issues. Alice Walker's *The Color Purple* (1982) won the Pulitzer Prize in fiction in 1983, for example, and Toni Morrison's *Beloved* (1987) took the same prize in 1988. Other ethnic American writers—Amy Tan and Richard Rodriguez, Oscar Hijuelos and Louise Erdrich, James Welch and Isabel Allende, T. Coraghessan Boyle and Cynthia Ozick, writers, in short, from every ethnic and racial group in America—gained similar popularity in the 1980's and 1990's. The issues they were raising, from ageism to incest, poverty to homelessness, slavery and affirmative action, patriarchy and matriarchy, were the issues all Americans were discussing.

Two of the most important playwrights of the postwar American theater—to take one genre example—were gay: Tennessee Williams and Edward Albee. Their sexuality was veiled, however, and came out only obliquely in character and theme. The theater since the 1960's, in contrast, has been dominated by openly gay dramatists (notably Harvey Fierstein and Tony Kushner) and by women (such as Beth Henley and Wendy Wasserstein) and ethnic writers (including August Wilson and David Henry Hwang), and their inclusion has meant a broadening of dramatic interests and themes. Unlike the pre-1960's theater, American drama since then has been exploring the identities and issues of all of its citizens. A similar process has been taking place in every genre of the literatures of North America.

At the same time, American literature has finally been living up to its name, and the borders of North America have been breached. Canadian writers (including Margaret Atwood and Alice Munro) have been as popular in the United States as in their native country. The interaction along the southern U.S. borders is even more profound. Caribbean writers (including V. S. Naipaul and Jamaica Kincaid) have become widely popular across the North American continent. The Caribbean Derek Walcott was awarded the Nobel Prize in Literature in 1992. Since the 1970's, some of the most significant literary influences in North America have been coming from Mexico and Latin America, not only in the popularity of individual writers such as Carlos Fuentes (*The Death of Artemio Cruz*, 1962) and Gabriel García Márquez (*One Hundred Years of Solitude*, 1967) but in movements they created, such as Magical Realism, which have influenced North American literature.

The job facing students and teachers is certainly a daunting one. Not only do new American writers and works emerge in great numbers when the white, male, middle-class canon is abandoned but also the list of themes and issues they address seems overwhelming. Even the most knowledgeable readers are constantly learning new issues: the AIDS crisis, for example, or addictions and twelve-step programs, or nontraditional families, or physical disabilities and identity. These are just a few of the themes that American writers—or American textbooks, syllabi, and reference books—rarely mentioned even as late as the early 1970's.

The range of writers and works looks equally immense to the student and to the teacher of the literatures of North America. The informed reader knows that Jesús Colón and Nicholasa Mohr came from Puerto Rico, for example, and that Evelyn Lau and Joy Kogawa are Canadian writers. *Identities and Issues in Literature* informs readers of Native American writers such as Michael Dorris and Joy Harjo, of African American writers such as John Edgar Wideman and Audre Lord, of Asian American writers such as Garrett Hongo, Bharati Mukherjee, and Cynthia Kadohata, of Latino writers such as Sandra Cisneros, Gary Soto, and Rudolfo Anaya, and of European American writers such as Carolyn Forché, Raymond Carver, Joyce Carol Oates, and Edmund White. It is not easy being an informed reader in a time of expanding canons, but the rewards are great.

The reader who is aware of the literatures of North America is better able to see the world through new eyes: not only with the perspective of an individual ethnicity and gender but with the vision of all Americans in a truly multicultural world. *Identities and Issues in Literature* certainly makes the job easier.

—David Peck

Contributors

Editor
David Peck
Department of English
California State University, Long Beach

Ann Marie Adams
Bowling Green State University

A. Owen Aldridge
University of Illinois

John Allen
University of Wisconsin—Milwaukee

Amy Allison
Independent Scholar

Eleanor B. Amico
Independent Scholar

Gerald S. Argetsinger
Rochester Institute of Technology

Angela Athy
Bowling Green State University

H. C. Aubrey
Independent Scholar

Lisa R. Aunkst
Independent Scholar

Charles Avinger
Washtenaw Community College

Michelle A. Balée
College of Dupage

RoseLee Bancroft
Alice Lloyd College

Jack Vincent Barbera
University of Mississippi

Paula C. Barnes
Hampton University

Henry J. Baron
Calvin College

David Barratt
Independent Scholar

Margaret W. Batschelet
University of Texas, San Antonio

Rosemarie A. Battaglia
Morehead State University

Michael L. Bazemore
Independent Scholar

Carol F. Bender
Alma College

Jacquelyn Benton
Edgewood College

Cynthia A. Bily
Adrian College

Margaret Boe Birns
New York University and The New School for Social Research

Denise Blue
University of Phoenix

Sandra F. Bone
Arkansas State University

Bernadette Lynn Bosky
Independent Scholar

Virginia Brackett
East Central University

Jane D. Brady
Brigham Young University

Muriel W. Brailey
Wilberforce University

Harold Branam
Savannah State College

Gerhard Brand
California State University, Los Angeles

Wesley Britton
Grayson County College

Michael Broadway
State University of New York—Geneseo

Faith Hickman Brynie
Independent Scholar

Jeffrey L. Buller
Georgia Southern University

Cherelyn Bush
Independent Scholar

Susan Butterworth
Independent Scholar

Linda Costanzo Cahir
Centenary College

Dowling G. Campbell
Northern Arizona University

Jeff H. Campbell
Midwestern State University

Thomas J. Campbell
Pacific Lutheran University

Peter A. Carino
Indiana State University

Emmett H. Carroll
Seattle University

Linda M. Carter
Morgan State University

Caroline Carvill
Rose-Hulman Institute of Technology

Leonard Casper
Boston College

Russ Castronovo
University of Miami

Christine R. Catron
St. Mary's University

Susan Chainey
Sacramento City College

Laurie Champion
Sul Ross State University

Nancy L. Chick
University of Georgia

Balance Chow
San Jose State University

C. L. Chua
California State University, Fresno

J. Robin Coffelt
University of North Texas

David Conde
Metropolitan State College of Denver

Helen O'Hara Connell
Barry University

Holly Dworken Cooley
Independent Scholar

Virginia M. Crane
California State University, Los Angeles

Jeff Cupp
Independent Scholar

Shira Daemon
Independent Scholar

Susan Jaye Dauer
Austin Community College

Clark Davis
Northeast Louisiana University

Delmer Davis
Andrews University

Jo Culbertson Davis
Williams Baptist College

Joyce Chandler Davis
Gadsden State Community College

Barbara Day
City University of New York

Frank Day
Clemson University

Mary Jo Deegan
University of Nebraska—Lincoln

Seodial Deena
East Carolina University

Frenzella Elaine De Lancey
Drexel University

Bill Delaney
Independent Scholar

Michael Dickel
University of Minnesota

Matts G. Djos
Independent Scholar

Susan R. Dominguez
Michigan State University

Joyce Duncan
East Tennessee State University

Mary Dunn
College of Lake County

Stefan Dziemianowicz
Independent Scholar

Philip Uko Effiong
University of Tennessee—Martin

Harry Edwin Eiss
Eastern Michigan University

Don Evans
Trenton State College

Thomas H. Falk
Michigan State University

Grace Farrell
Butler University

Tom Feller
Independent Scholar

Edward A. Fiorelli
St. John's University

T. A. Fishman
Clemson University

Anne Fleischmann
University of California, Davis

Robert Frail
Centenary College

D. Douglas Fratz
Independent Scholar

Tom Frazier
Cumberland College

Chris Freeman
St. John's University

Janet Fujimoto
California State University, Fresno

Patricia H. Fulbright
Clark College

Constance M. Fulmer
Pepperdine University

Joe Boyd Fulton
Dalton College

Amy Carolyn Fuqua
Independent Scholar

Keith Fynaardt
Northwestern College

Greg Garrett
Baylor University

Victoria Gaydosik
East Central University

Jill B. Gidmark
University of Minnesota

Craig Gilbert
Portland State University

Joyce J. Glover
Independent Scholar

Marc Goldstein
Independent Scholar

Lucy Golsan
Independent Scholar

Lewis L. Gould
University of Texas

Charles A. Gramlich
Xavier University of Louisiana

James B. Graves
Independent Scholar

James Green
Arizona State University

John L. Grigsby
Tennessee Technological University

Dana Anthony Grove
Indian Hills Community College

Morris Allen Grubbs
University of Kentucky

Robert Haight
*Kalamazoo Valley Community
College*

William T. Hamilton
*Metropolitan State College of
Denver*

Betty L. Hart
University of Southern Indiana

Stephen M. Hart
University of Kentucky

Peter B. Heller
Manhattan College

Terry Heller
Coe College

Diane Andrews Henningfeld
Adrian College

Holly K. Henson
University of Central Oklahoma

Peter J. Higgins
University of Tennessee—Knoxville

Kay Hively
Independent Scholar

Arthur D. Hlavaty
Independent Scholar

W. Kenneth Holditch
University of New Orleans

John R. Holmes
*Franciscan University of
Steubenville*

Jane Hoogestraat
Southwest Missouri State University

Joan Hope
Indiana University at Bloomington

Pierre L. Horn
Wright State University

Kenneth L. Houghton
Independent Scholar

Patricia J. Huhn
Trinidad State Junior College

Mary Hurd
East Tennessee State University

Andrea J. Ivanov
Azusa Pacific University

Maura Ives
Texas A&M University

John Jacob
Northwestern University

Martin Japtok
University of California, Davis

Helen Jaskoski
Independent Scholar

Doris O'Donnell Jellig
Tidewater Community College

Bill Jenkins
University of Central Arkansas

David Johansson
Brevard Community College

Jeff Johnson
Brevard Community College

Andrew O. Jones
University of California, Davis

Jane Anderson Jones
Manatee Community College, South

Anne K. Kaler
Gwynedd-Mercy College

Theresa M. Kanoza
Eastern Illinois University

Leela Kapai
*University of the District of
Columbia*

Ludmila Kapschutschenko-Schmitt
Rider University

Daven M. Kari
California Baptist College

Steven A. Katz
State Technical Institute at Memphis

John F. Keener
University of Kentucky

Douglas Keesey
*California Polytechnic State
University*

D. G. Kehl
Arizona State University

Steven G. Kellman
*The University of Texas at San
Antonio*

Howard A. Kerner
Polk Community College

Mabel Khawaja
Hampton University

Jacquelyn Kilpatrick
Governors State University

Christine H. King
University of California, Davis

Vincent Allan King
University of South Carolina

Cassandra Kircher
Elon College

Elaine L. Kleiner
Indiana State University

Laura L. Klure
Independent Scholar

Lynne Klyse
Independent Scholar

Grove Koger
Boise Public Library

Chris LaLonde
North Carolina Wesleyan College

Mary L. Otto Lang
Del Mar College

Gregory W. Lanier
The University of West Florida

Douglas Edward LaPrade
University of Texas—Pan American

Arlene Larson
Casper College

William Laskowski
Jamestown College

William T. Lawlor
University of Wisconsin—Stevens Point

Jacqueline Lawson
University of Michigan—Dearborn

Ray Leadbetter
Andrews University

Linda Ledford-Miller
University of Scranton

Richard M. Leeson
Fort Hays State University

Elisabeth Anne Leonard
Kent State University

Leon Lewis
Appalachian State University

Thomas Lisk
North Carolina State University

Donna Joyce Litherland
North Dakota State University

Jun Liu
California State University, Los Angeles

Janet E. Lorenz
Independent Scholar

Bernadette Flynn Low
Dundale Community College

R. C. Lutz
University of the Pacific

Robert J. Lysiak
Appalachian State University

Joanne McCarthy
Tacoma Community College

Gina Macdonald
Loyola University, New Orleans

Grace McEntee
Appalachian State University

Mara Lynn McFadden
State University of New York—Brockport

Ron McFarland
University of Idaho

S. Thomas Mack
University of South Carolina—Aiken

Joseph McLaren
Hofstra University

Jane Helm Maddock
Western Montana College of the University of Montana

Mary Mahony
Wayne County Community College

Thomas A. Maik
University of Wisconsin—LaCrosse

Anne B. Mangum
Bennett College

Barry Mann
Independent Scholar

Lois A. Marchino
University of Texas at El Paso

Chogollah Maroufi
California State University, Los Angeles

R. A. Martin
Lausanne Collegiate School

Charles E. May
California State University, Long Beach

Kenneth W. Meadwell
University of Winnipeg

Warren L. Meinhardt
Southern Illinois University

Julia M. Meyers
North Carolina State University

Michael R. Meyers
Shaw University

Sharon Mikkelson
El Centro College

B. Diane Miller
Independent Scholar

Paula M. Miller
Biola University

Anuradha M. Mitra
The Union Institute

Christina J. Moose
Independent Scholar

Robert A. Morace
Daemon College

Geneviève Sanchis Morgan
University of California, Davis

Charmayne Richardson Mulligan
East Tennessee State University

Roark Mulligan
Christopher Newport University

C. Lynn Munro
Independent Scholar

Russell Elliott Murphy
University of Arkansas at Little Rock

John M. Muste
Ohio State University

William Nelles
University of Massachusetts—Dartmouth

Adele S. Newson
Florida International University

Joe Nordgren
Lamar University

Rafael Ocasio
Agnes Scott College

Max Orezzoli
Florida International University

William Osborne
Florida International University

Cynthia Packard
University of Massachusetts—Amherst

Janet Taylor Palmer
Caldwell Community College

Matthew Parfitt
Boston University

Sandra J. Parsons
Independent Scholar

David Partenheimer
Truman State University

G. A. Toks Pearse
Hunter College

David Peck
California State University, Long Beach

Thomas D. Petitjean, Jr.
Louisiana State University—Eunice

Marion Boyle Petrillo
Bloomsburg University

Lela Phillips
Andrew College

Allene Phy-Olsen
Austin Peay State University

J. Scott Plaster
Independent Scholar

Andrew B. Preslar
Lamar University, Orange

Victoria Price
Lamar University

R. C. S.
Independent Scholar

Brian Abel Ragen
Southern Illinois University—Edwardsville

Nefretete S. Rasheed
New York University

Erik Rasmussen
Independent Scholar

Ralph Reckley, Sr.
Independent Scholar

Peter J. Reed
University of Minnesota

Rosemary M. Canfield Reisman
Independent Scholar

Barbara Cecelia Rhodes
Central Missouri State University

Martha E. Rhynes
East Central University, Ada

Janine Rider
Mesa State College

Christy Rishoi
Michigan State University

Larry Rochelle
Johnson County Community College

Carl Rollyson
Baruch College

Lois Roma-Deeley
Independent Scholar

Robert L. Ross
University of Texas at Austin

Mark Sanders
College of the Mainland

Richard Sax
Madonna University

Eric Schocket
Stanford University

Robert H. Schwarz
Fayetteville High School

Daniel M. Scott III
Rhode Island College

Lisa Seale
University of Wisconsin Marathon Center

Helen Shanley
Independent Scholar

Chenliang Sheng
Northern Kentucky University

Amy Beth Shollenberger
Independent Scholar

Debra Shostak
The College of Wooster

R. Baird Shuman
University of Illinois at Urbana-Champaign

Thomas J. Sienkewicz
Monmouth College, Illinois

Charles L. P. Silet
Iowa State Unversity

Amy Sisson
Independent Scholar

Joseleyne Ashford Slade
Michigan State University

Marjorie Smelstor
University of Wisconsin—Eau Claire

Pamela J. Olubunmi Smith
University of Nebraska—Omaha

Virginia Whatley Smith
University of Alabama—Birmingham

Traci S. Smrcka
University of Southern Louisiana

Brian Stableford
Independent Scholar

August W. Staub
University of Georgia

Joshua Stein
University of California, Riverside

Judith L. Steininger
Milwaukee School of Engineering

David Stevens
The Pennsylvania State University

Geralyn Strecker
Ball State University

Trey Strecker
Ball State University

Sonja H. Streuber
University of California, Davis

Irene Struthers
Independent Scholar

Charlene E. Suscavage
University of Southern Maine

Roy Arthur Swanson
University of Wisconsin—Milwaukee

J. K. Sweeney
South Dakota State University

James Tackach
Roger Williams University

James T. F. Tanner
University of North Texas

Philip A. Tapley
Louisiana College

Australia Tarver
Texas Christian University

Judith K. Taylor
Northern Kentucky University

Julie Tharp
*University of Wisconsin Center—
    Marshfield Wood College*

Lorenzo Thomas
University of Houston—Downtown

Konny Thompson
Gonzaga University

Jonathan L. Thorndike
Lakeland College

Tony Trigilio
Northeastern University

Richard Tuerk
East Texas State University

Paul Varner
*Oklahoma State University—
    Oklahoma City*

William Vaughn
Independent Scholar

Arnoldo Carlos Vento
University of Texas

Martha Modena Vertreace
Kennedy-King College

Emil Volek
Arizona State University

Steven C. Walker
Brigham Young University

Gary P. Walton
Northern Kentucky University

Qun Wang
*California State University,
    Monterey Bay*

Dennis L. Weeks
University of Great Falls

Gary Westfahl
University of California, Riverside

Jennifer Westmoreland
Independent Scholar

Annemarie Koning Whaley
East Texas Baptist University

James S. Whitlark
Texas Tech University

Albert E. Wilhelm
Tennessee Technological University

Thomas Willard
University of Arizona

Donna Glee Williams
*North Carolina Center for the
    Advancement of Teaching,
    Western Carolina University*

Michael Witkoski
Independent Scholar

James A. Wren
Niigata University

Qingyun Wu
*California State University, Los
    Angeles*

Robert E. Yahnke
University of Minnesota

Aiping Zhang
California State University, Chico

Abby Zidle
University of California, Davis

Gay Zieger
Santa Fe Community College

Alan Ziskin
Independent Scholar

Contents

Identities
and Issues
in Literature

Abbey, Edward

BORN: Home, Pennsylvania; January 29, 1927

DIED: Wolf Hole, Arizona; March 14, 1989

PRINCIPAL WORKS: *Desert Solitaire*, 1968; *Slickrock*, 1971; *Appalachian Wilderness*, 1973; *Cactus Country*, 1973; *The Monkey Wrench Gang*, 1975; *The Hidden Canyon*, 1977; *The Journey Home*, 1977; *Abbey's Road*, 1979; *Good News*, 1980; *Down the River*, 1982; *Beyond the Wall*, 1984; *Slumgullion Stew*, 1984; *Confessions of a Barbarian*, 1986; *One Life at a Time, Please*, 1988

IDENTITIES: European American; West and Southwest

SIGNIFICANT ACHIEVEMENT: In his essays and novels, Abbey is an advocate for the environment and a champion of the American West.

Edward Abbey is one of the most outspoken nature writers and defenders of the West. His writing, whether fiction, nonfiction, or essays, is angry, blunt, and without apologies. He is not afraid to criticize those whom he feels have damaged or destroyed the country he loves, and in his writing he attacks organizations, such as the government and big business, and individuals, including lazy, thoughtless tourists and greedy landowners. This attitude has earned him critics and followers. Many environmentalists, in fact, consider Abbey a hero, a spiritual adviser who is not afraid to say what needs to be said.

A transplanted Easterner, Abbey lived in the West from age twenty-one until his death. He received two degrees from the University of New Mexico and worked fifteen years in western national parks. His profession was writing; his subject matter was almost always the Western United States.

One of Abbey's political messages is defined in his popular novel *The Monkey Wrench Gang*. In this book an unruly gang consisting of three men and one woman destroy man-made structures that they feel are ruining the West. At the book's end they blow up a bridge spanning the Colorado River. The point of the book is that violence and destruction are warranted if they stop harmful development. Abbey's nonfiction, especially *Desert Solitaire* and *Abbey's Road*, places Abbey in the American literary tradition of nature writing, a tradition begun by Henry David Thoreau. In his essays and longer works of nonfiction, Abbey's political anger is often muted and replaced with quick, impressionistic descriptions of the natural world molded from figurative language and literary allusion. This technique makes the natural places about which Abbey writes come alive in his writing and reveals his love for a world that he thought was worth defending.

Edward Abbey's works have championed the environment, especially that of the desert Southwest. (Michael Hendrickson)

SUGGESTED READINGS

Bishop, James, Jr. *Epitaph for a Desert Anarchist: The Life and Legacy of Edward Abbey*. New York: Atheneum, 1994.

Loeffler, Jack. "Edward Abbey, Anarchism and the Environment." *Western American Literature* 28, no. 1 (1993): 43-49.

Sandlin, Tim. "Nightmare Abbey." *The New York Times Book Review*, December 11, 1994, 11.

—Cassandra Kircher

See also American identity: West and the frontier; Environment and identity

Abolitionist movement. *See* Slavery

Abortion and birth control

IDENTITIES: Women

DEFINITION: An abortion is the artificial termination of a pregnancy.

For centuries, abortion was one of the few ways to prevent the birth of an unwanted child. In the late eighteenth and the nineteenth centuries, researchers made tremendous progress in understanding the physiology of reproduction, and other methods of birth control gradually became available. Abortions are still practiced as a means of birth control, but people also have access to a wide variety of reliable birth control methods, such as condoms, diaphragms, IUDs, birth control pills, and surgical sterilization.

At issue
During the last two hundred years a controversy has arisen between proponents of birth control, who emphasize its beneficial effects, and its enemies, who oppose birth control on moral, religious, or political grounds. Birth control advocates argue that it benefits society at large because it limits population growth and therefore helps to ensure against widespread starvation and political unrest. Advocates also argue that birth control benefits families because it gives them the ability to control the number and spacing of offspring, and hence maximize the family's economic resources and ensure the greatest amount of personal freedom for parents, particularly mothers, by making parenthood a choice. Opponents of birth control contend, however, that it encourages lax standards of sexual behavior, and that these in turn undermine the strength of the family and trigger a general decay in public morality. Conservative Christians and others have opposed the use of abortion—and in some cases other means of birth control—on religious grounds as an unjustifiable deprivation of an unborn infant's God-given right to life.

History
The modern debate over birth control first took written form with the publication of *An Essay on the Principle of Population* (1798) by the English clergyman and economist Thomas Malthus. Malthus argued that population always increases faster than the food supply, so that every society must eventually face overpopulation. For the human species, overpopulation results in civil unrest, disease, and warfare. Thus Malthus was the first to describe the correlation between human population growth and human misery. Malthus himself, as a clergyman, did not advocate contraception or abortion as a means of dealing with this problem, but others in Europe and America did. Partly as a result of their efforts, birthrates fell in the industrialized countries of the West throughout the nineteenth century. Even so, knowledge of the various means of birth control were largely confined to the upper and middle classes, and information about it spread slowly, by word of mouth. In Great Britain, for example, it was illegal to publish or distribute information about birth control devices and techniques until after 1875, while in the United States it remained illegal until the twentieth century had begun.

In the early twentieth century Margaret Sanger finally broke the long-standing American silence about birth control. Working as a trained nurse among poor women in New York City in the early 1900's, Sanger became convinced that they could have economic and social equality with men—as well as a far greater amount of personal happiness—if the women were free from unwanted pregnancies. Sanger successfully challenged the laws against the public dissemination of infor-

Abortion and Birth Control
Ten Important Dates

1798　*An Essay on the Principle of Population*, by Thomas Malthus.

1823　Francis Place distributes handbills on birth control.

1831　Robert Dale Owen publishes *Moral Physiology*.

1832　Charles Knowlton publishes *Fruits of Philosophy*, a book on birth control, and is subsequently prosecuted and convicted.

1912　Margaret Sanger's *What Every Girl Should Know*, a pamphlet on birth control, is confiscated by U.S. postal authorities.

1917　Emma Goldman is deported from the United States for radicalism, including advocacy of birth control.

1968　Paul R. Ehrlich's *The Population Bomb* renews public awareness of the overpopulation problem, as first described by Malthus.

1977　With *Carey v. Population Services International* the U.S. Supreme Court upholds the rights of lay providers to supply contraceptive education to minors.

1985　Margaret Atwood's novel *The Handmaid's Tale* describes a bleak future in which fertility is a government resource and in which doctors who have performed abortions are executed.

1991　Abortion gag rule: an amendment to Title X of the Public Health Service Act forbids discussion of abortion by federally funded agencies. In *Rust v. Sullivan* the U. S. Supreme Court rules that the prohibition is constitutional. After Bill Clinton becomes president of the United States in 1993, he signs an executive order nullifying the controversial regulation.

mation about birth control, set up clinics, and founded the American Birth Control League, the organization which eventually became known as Planned Parenthood. Sanger wrote an important series of books that influenced public opinion in favor of birth control. Perhaps the most important of these was *Woman and the New Race* (1920), a powerful argument for the "necessity of setting the feminine spirit absolutely free" to enjoy a "voluntary motherhood," by using an appropriate method of birth control and without having to suffer the negative physical side effects of surgically or chemically induced abortions. This in turn, Sanger argues, "implies a new morality—a vigorous, constructive, liberated morality . . . [that will] prevent the submergence of womanhood in motherhood."

Thus, unlike Malthus, Sanger puts the rights and freedoms of the individual at the center of her argument. She makes it clear, however, that society—indeed the entire world—will eventually benefit from the enhanced individual status of women. In effect, Sanger was reiterating the English philosopher John Stuart Mill's view of the importance of the individual as the motive force of historical change, and especially of social and technological progress. She was reiterating it with an important difference, for she claimed that universal access to birth control would enable women, for the first time in history, to act fully as individuals rather than merely wives and mothers. Birth control would enable women to become individuals in Mill's sense, and thereby to become a motive force in the making of human history.

Later in the century the American biologist Paul R. Ehrlich returned to the arguments of Malthus in his influential book *The Population Bomb* (1968). For Ehrlich the rights of individuals pale before their responsibilities, particularly in reproductive matters. Unless every family on earth manages to limit itself to producing two children to replace the parents, Ehrlich argues, the original Malthusian trajectories of rapid population growth and slow food production growth would soon prevail in the developing countries of the world. By the 1970's, he predicted, this pattern would trigger international epidemics and armed conflicts that would engulf and destroy even those developed countries that had managed to tailor their population to their food supply. Ehrlich called for a massive worldwide program of birth control education and medical clinics staffed with specialists in birth control methods and techniques. He helped found Zero Population Growth, an organization that promotes this philosophy throughout the world.

3

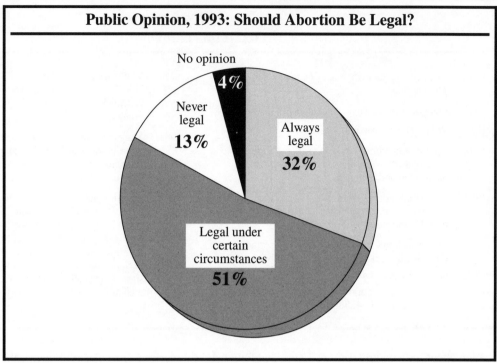

Public Opinion, 1993: Should Abortion Be Legal?

No opinion 4%

Never legal 13%

Always legal 32%

Legal under certain circumstances 51%

Source: U.S. Department of Justice, Bureau of Justice Statistics, *Sourcebook of Criminal Justice Statistics—1993.* Washington, D.C.: U.S. Government Printing Office, 1994. Primary source, *The Gallup Poll Monthly*, April, 1993.
Note: The question asked was, "Do you think abortions should be legal under any circumstances, legal only under certain circumstances, or illegal in all circumstances?"

Ehrlich's Malthusian doomsday did not arrive as planned, but his powerful vision of crisis and collapse resulting from overpopulation stimulated a positive response, in the late 1960's and early 1970's, to the idea of birth control, including the legalization of abortions. At the same time feminists, including Germaine Greer (*The Female Eunuch*, 1971), argued that women could only achieve individual identity if they were free, whether they were married or not, to make motherhood the product of a conscious choice rather than the result of biology. Taking up Margaret Sanger's vision of setting the feminine spirit free through the prevention of unwanted pregnancies, feminists sought to extend that quest for freedom by advocating a woman's right to terminate an unwanted pregnancy. Women began to promote legal abortion as an important means of guaranteeing a woman's social, economic, and personal freedom. Groups interested in social and political reform promoted acceptance and use of all forms of birth control, and as a result in the 1970's many countries—including the United States—liberalized their abortion laws.

The legalization of abortion as a means of birth control catalyzed an intense public controversy in the last decades of the twentieth century. Typically, liberals and feminists supported abortion on the grounds that it benefited and empowered the poor, minorities, and women, while political and religious conservatives opposed it on the ground that it was a form of murder and therefore unconscionable. The idea of birth control through contraception (that is, the prevention of pregnancy rather than its termination) is not an issue in the abortion debate. The abortion debate does, however, engage the issue of personal freedom versus social responsibility that has marked discussions about birth control since the time of Malthus.

In literature   Although abortion and birth control have constituted an important theme in relatively few mainstream works of literature, extreme forms of birth control have figured prominently in three of the twentieth century's most important and controversial novels of social criticism: Aldous Huxley's *Brave New World* (1932), George Orwell's *Nineteen Eighty-Four* (1949), and Margaret Atwood's *The Handmaid's Tale* (1985). Central to the vision of each of these novels is the issue of direct societal intervention and control of individual sexuality. *Brave New World*, a critique of modern Western culture, depicts a world state that has succeeded in completely separating sexuality and reproduction. Lower-caste women have been sterilized, while upper-caste women have been trained always to use contraceptives. All fetuses are produced through artificial fertilization of eggs, which are then placed by the state in huge, assembly-like incubators until gestation is complete. The newborns are "decanted" and raised in state-run nurseries and schools. The family has ceased to exist. Only the individual human being remains, freed from the physical and emotional pain that has always marked the traditional family. This new individual is ready to enjoy physical and sensual pleasure to the fullest, through government-sponsored games, entertainments, and orgies. Ironically, the price of this individual freedom is a striking lack of individuality: The members of each caste are conditioned and trained from the time of conception onward to feel and think alike. Huxley then introduces a character, John Savage, who was born to his own mother, has lived in a traditional society, and has taken part in religious rites. Savage is alienated from the carefree, sexually unrepressed, and materially affluent life of the world state. Savage, horrified by the lack of individuality and sickened by the moral and spiritual degradation of those around him, eventually commits suicide. In effect Huxley argues that individual sexual freedom without the counterbalance of reproductive responsibilities requires the extinction of true individual identity, for identity is developed only through the individual's engagement with societal and familial limits on the gratification of desire.

In contrast, *Nineteen Eighty-Four* envisions a socialist totalitarian state devoted to the destruction of individuality rather than to its preservation and exaltation. Everything in *Nineteen Eighty-Four* is controlled for the benefit of the state rather than for the benefit of the individual. The state must erase the individual identity of each of its subjects in order to control them completely and to harness all their energies for the ends of the state. Since sexuality lies at the core of identity and is a powerful energy source, it must be controlled by the state as well. In *Nineteen Eighty-Four*, however, the method of control is not physical control of sexuality and reproduction through technology and conditioning, as in *Brave New World*. The control is repressive rather than too freeing; the citizens of Oceania are constantly told that human reproduction is a duty owed to the state, but that it should be mechanical and joyless. Sexual pleasure is considered evil and dangerous, and it is actively suppressed by the state-sponsored Anti-Sex League. Making love is an act of political rebellion, and Orwell's hero, Winston Smith, seeks to rebel against the state through a love affair. He and his lover are caught, brainwashed, and finally freed when they love only Big Brother and no longer have any interest in each other or in sex. As in *Brave New World*, the separation of sexuality and reproduction becomes the means whereby individual identity is made vulnerable and capable of being destroyed.

The Handmaid's Tale makes extensive and searching analysis of the connections between sexuality, gender, and individual identity. The novel has little to say about the mechanics of birth control or abortion. As in the two preceding novels, however, the central theme is the preservation of individual identity in a world in which reproduction and sexuality have been officially separated by the state that seeks to control its populace. In contrast to the total annihilation of individual identity depicted by Orwell, or the severe diminution of it envisioned by Huxley, Atwood's heroine, Offred, preserves her sense of her specifically female individuality through a passionate love affair. As do Smith and his lover, Offred and her lover risk death for their transgression. Moreover, the Commander himself turns out to need sexual and personal intimacies he officially deplores, suggesting that the forms of female bondage that the Republic of Gilead officially promotes and countenances as healthy, sane, and moral ways to free women from sexual exploitation and sex crimes are unnatural. The novel does not let readers know whether or not Offred and her lover escape from Gilead, but their attempt is suggested at the novel's end. Thus Atwood, like Orwell and Huxley, sees state-sponsored separation of sexuality and reproduction as inimical to the existence of personal identity and freedom. She is more optimistic, however, about the inability of such repressive states to succeed in the long run.

SUGGESTED READINGS

Cozic, Charles P., and Stacey L. Tipp. *Abortion: Opposing Viewpoints.* San Diego: Greenhaven Press, 1991. A representative sampling of the arguments put forth on both sides of the abortion controversy.

Ehrlich, Paul R., and Anne H. Ehrlich. *The Population Explosion.* New York: Simon & Schuster, 1990. A review of trends in world population growth since the publication of *The Population Bomb,* followed by projections of food crises in the twenty-first century and emphasis on the continuing need to curb population growth.

Greer, Germaine. *The Female Eunuch.* New York: McGraw-Hill, 1971. Argues that sexual and reproductive autonomy for women is necessary for the advancement of society as a whole.

Meunsch, Elizabeth, and Alan Freeman. *The Politics of Virtue: Is Abortion Debatable?* Durham, N.C.: Duke University Press, 1993. An attempt to break new ground in the controversy over abortion.

Mitchell, Juliet. *Woman's Estate.* New York: Pantheon, 1971. Part 1 is a history of the woman's movement of the 1960's; part 2 presents classic feminist discussions of work, reproduction, sexuality, and the socialization of children.

Sanger, Margaret. *Woman and the New Race.* New York: Eugenics Publishing Company, 1920. Argues for the benefits for women and for society as a whole of using birth control methods to separate sexuality and reproduction.

—*R. A. Martin*

See also Erotic identity; Feminism; Fertility and identity; *Handmaid's Tale, The*; Women and identity

Absalom, Absalom!

AUTHOR: William Faulkner (1897-1962)

FIRST PUBLISHED: 1936

IDENTITIES: African American; European American; family; South

Three men struggle to define their identity in William Faulkner's novel, *Absalom, Absalom!* The first is Thomas Sutpen, the son of poor whites from West Virginia, who arrives in Mississippi with a group of Haitian slaves and a dream: to carve a hundred square miles of plantation out of wilderness and create a new identity for himself. As a boy, Sutpen was refused entry to a rich landowner's home by a black slave. Now he seeks to become that landowner, with wealth, a house, slaves, and a son to establish his dynasty.

Sutpen's Haitian marriage was annulled when he discovered that his wife and their son, Charles Bon, had African blood. His second marriage in Jefferson produces a son and a daughter. Still, the town considers him an interloper and refuses to accept him. Years later, when Sutpen's white son Henry meets Bon, who passes for white, at the university, they become friends. Bon charms Henry and his sister Judith. Unaware that he is her half-brother, Judith agrees to marry Bon.

Charles Bon is a few years older and a man of the world, with an octoroon mistress and infant son in New Orleans. He appears mildly amused at the situation in which he finds himself. Once he realizes that Sutpen is his father, he waits four years to tell the others. Bon wants Sutpen to acknowledge his identity as a legitimate son, warning Henry he will call off the marriage only if Sutpen acknowledges him. What they all understand is that Sutpen will never acknowledge a son who is not white. At last Henry is forced to murder Bon, whom he adores, to prevent an incestuous union. Ironically, the last survivor of Sutpen's line is a slow-witted black youth, his great-grandson through Bon.

The story of Sutpen and Bon is told to Quentin Compson, whose grandfather, a Civil War hero, attempted to befriend Sutpen. Quentin, a student at Harvard, struggles to piece together the story, as if through the anguished history of these people and their region he can come to understand his own legacy. Faulkner's novel, its title echoing the lament of King David for his dead son, reveals the tragedy of a family blighted by racism and fear of miscegenation, and a father who cannot weep.

SUGGESTED READINGS

Backman, Melvin. *Faulkner, the Major Years: A Critical Study*. Bloomington: Indiana University Press, 1966.

Brooks, Cleanth. "History and the Sense of the Tragic." In *William Faulkner: The Yoknapatawpha Country*. New Haven, Conn.: Yale University Press, 1963.

Ladd, Barbara. " 'The Direction of the Howling': Nationalism and the Color Line in *Absalom, Absalom!*" *American Literature* 66, no. 3 (September, 1994): 525-551.

Poirier, Richard. " 'Strange Gods' in Jefferson, Mississippi: Analysis of *Absalom, Absalom!*" In *Twentieth Century Interpretations of "Absalom, Absalom!": A Collection of Critical Essays*, edited by Arnold Goldman. Englewood Cliffs, N.J.: Prentice-Hall, 1971.

—*Joanne McCarthy*

See also Alienation; American identity: South; Faulkner, William; *Intruder in the Dust*; *Light in August*; Mixed race and identity; Racism and ethnocentrism; *Sound and the Fury, The*

Acculturation

DEFINITION: Acculturation is a process whereby individuals or groups modify their culture by adapting to another culture.

"Acculturation" is not a common term in literary studies; it has been used mainly in sociological and anthropological studies. The term did not find its way into *The Oxford English Dictionary* until 1989; it first appeared in the writings of an American geologist and ethnologist, John Wesley Powell, in 1880. Despite the fact that study of cultural modifications is international, the term is still primarily American. The study of acculturation has gone beyond the realm of cultural anthropology, and numerous studies have been conducted to define and conceptualize cultural adaptations between a subculture and the dominant culture. In a sense, acculturation is not a recent phenomenon in human history, nor is it a rare theme in literature. With the rise of the multidisciplinary approach to research and, particularly, the development of the concept of multiculturalism, acculturation has been a constant theme in scholarship.

Overview

Scholars and critics differ in defining the types, levels, and aspects of acculturation, but agree that acculturation occurs on two levels, individual and group. There are also three types of operation. In the first type, people of different cultures voluntarily adopt culture traits from one another because of prolonged contact. In the second type, the dominant culture imposes its ideas and values upon the people of nondominant cultures. In the third type, people from different cultures respect and appreciate one another's cultures. It is essential, however, to make a clarification between "acculturation" and "assimilation." "Acculturation" means a voluntary or forced acquisition of the culture of the dominant group. "Assimilation" indicates the disappearance of group identity through such actions as friendship and marriage outside the subgroup; such actions require a mutual effort of the dominant group and the subgroup. Although the term "acculturation" is often thought to refer to cultural modification, it more specifically refers to a process of cultural adaptation by minority people toward the majority people's culture.

It is true both in sociocultural studies and literary writings that acculturation is seldom, if ever, explored in reference to European American acculturation into a culture not their own. People of non-European American origin, however, are typically expected, in North America, to acculturate themselves to the American way of life. As a literary theme, therefore, acculturation has always been explored within the context of Americanization.

Acculturation and identity

Writers dramatize the contrasts and tensions of people, cultures, and societies manifested in the process of acculturation. The literary works that pursue the theme of acculturation can be grouped into three categories.

The first category is the acculturational experiences depicted by writers such as James Fenimore

Cooper and Herman Melville. These experiences are based on encounters between colonized natives and European colonizers. What is unique about this type of acculturation is that, as part of the Western overseas expansion, such acculturation was a unidirectional imposition of the minority but dominant culture upon the "host" but conquered society, and that such acculturation was a confrontation between two different racial and cultural identities. Disgusted with attempts to justify colonization by means of stereotypes such as that of the savage, Cooper and Melville were more keenly interested in the encounter, and interplay between the representative of indigenous culture and the representative of what may be called an advancing civilization. Even though both writers used some clichés of the time in portraying their "uncivilized" characters, critics generally believe that neither Cooper nor Melville was inherently hostile toward the Indians. While the acculturative process in Cooper's Leatherstocking series and in Melville's *Typee* (1846) and *Omoo* (1847) mostly occurs in the form of natives learning to conform to European American standards, the European Americans do appropriate certain traits of native culture, typically some practical skills that prove useful under colonial conditions. In *The Pioneers* (1823), one of the five novels in the Leatherstocking series, John Mohegan is portrayed as a character who embodies the best qualities and upholds the best traditions of the Mohicans. His switch from a "savage" appellation to the common English name of John, his altered appearance, and his conversion to Christianity indicate a considerable degree of acculturation. The portrayal of Natty Bumppo, Cooper's archetypal character of cultural synthesis in all five Leatherstocking novels, shows an acculturation from the opposite direction. Natty is by no means a loafing, uninterested colonist or even the descendant of such. As an effective agent of acculturation, he interprets, mediates, and appropriates both white and native practices.

Unlike Cooper, however, what Melville implies in his novel is the assertion that white men such as Tommo in *Typee* or Lem Hardy in *Omoo* lack the sincerity and capability to acculturate themselves to the native culture. As the Western visitors gone native, they are only hybrids, unable to achieve the authentic identity of a Natty Bumppo. To neutralize the polarization between cultures, as Melville illustrates in *Omoo*, both the "savage" and the civilized should meld through a reciprocal acculturation. Similar concerns and issues regarding the acculturation between the colonized and the colonizer appear in some British novels of the same era, such as Joseph Conrad's *Heart of Darkness* (1902), Rudyard Kipling's *Kim* (1901), and E. M. Forster's *A Passage to India* (1924).

Acculturation and choice

The second category is the depiction of the two-directional acculturation between Europeans and Americans. Around the turn of the century, a substantial number of Americans, many of whom were writers and artists, lived in Europe. At the same time America itself experienced a tremendous influx of immigrants from Europe. Works such as Henry James's *The American* (1877) and *The Portrait of a Lady* (1881) present adventures of Americans who acculturate themselves to the codes and customs of the Old World in order to maintain a niche in its upper-class circle. For the generally poor immigrants to America, acculturation was not easy either. The nostalgia, deprivation, and hardship of immigrant acculturation are vividly featured in works such as Willa Cather's *O Pioneers!* (1913) and *My Ántonia* (1918) and Arthur Miller's *A View from the Bridge* (1955). One work of this category that is particularly noteworthy is the trilogy written by William Carlos Williams: *White Mule* (1937), *In the Money* (1940), and *The Build-Up* (1952). In this trilogy, Williams offers readers a close look at the ambivalent feelings the immigrants had toward, and the hard choices they made between, the Old and New Worlds. What the Stetcher family goes through represents a standard Americanization story, an acculturational process full of dreams, conflicts, hard choices, compromises, and frustrations.

Acculturation and ethnicity

The third category is the exploration of a more mutual acculturation between European American and non-European American cultures, with the issue of ethnicity as the focus. Readers may also find the literary treatment of similar themes in other regions' literature, especially in postcolonial writings. Chinua Achebe's *Arrow of God* (1964), Salman Rushdie's *The Satanic Verses* (1988), Samuel Selvon's *The Housing Lark* (1990), and Simi Bedford's *Yoruba Girl Dancing*

(1991) are examples of this category of acculturation stories. No country, however, has produced more literary works addressing ethnic identity as a dimension of acculturation than the United States. Considering the United States' identity as a melting pot and the fact that the life of most of its citizens is affected in one way or another by acculturation, there is nothing surprising about the volume, diversity, and intensity in the literature of acculturation in the United States. After 1965, there was a sharp increase of minority population in America. This increase has been the result of immigration: Immigrants bring languages and customs that differ from the values of the dominant population. The act of immigration turns people into "ethnics" and leads to cultural disorientation. There is a duality in immigrant identity that is based on the doubling of social realms. Immigrants have to deal, typically, from an economic, social, and political position inferior to that of the dominant group, with the dilemma of straddling both the old and the new culture. A broad range of literary works explore this theme with ethnic concerns and sensitivities, from the Jewish American novels by Henry Roth, Saul Bellow, Bernard Malamud, and Philip Roth to novels, poems, plays, and autobiographies by African American, Asian American, and Latino American writers.

Henry Roth's *Call It Sleep* captures the fear and pain in Jewish acculturation by dramatizing the trauma of David Schearl, a Jewish boy, who lives with his newly arrived immigrant parents in New York and tries desperately to belong, to choose between the values of the old and the new, and to master his own destiny in his adopted country. This seems to be a cruel test for many boys and girls in writings of what might be called the American ethnic *Bildungsroman*, such as José Antonio Villarreal's *Pocho* (1959) and Maxine Hong Kingston's *The Woman Warrior* (1975). One novel that has attracted much critical acclaim is John Okada's *No-No Boy* (1957), which portrays two Nisei brothers of a Japanese American family struggling with tough choices in their acculturation during World War II. One brother, Ichiro, is put in jail and, consequently, becomes an outcast, simply because he chooses his Japanese heritage and refuses to fight the Japanese on the American side. The younger brother, Taro, does the opposite, joining the U.S. Army, but, as a result, he loses all his ties with his family.

For years, people have been led to believe that to be successful in America one must be acculturated to the European American culture and that maintaining one's culture impedes the process and one's subsequent success. Many writers contend, however, that this has not held true for minority people. In their view, even when minority people have the desire and capacity for acculturation, the society prevents it. Carlos Bulosan's *America Is in the Heart* (1943) and Ralph Ellison's *Invisible Man* (1952) describe the endless ordeal of minority people who are subject to discrimination, abuse, and injustice. Their emotional state is characterized by confusion, anxiety, alienation, loss of identity, and resistance to contact with society.

SUGGESTED READINGS

Buenker, John D., and Lorman A. Ratner, eds. *Multiculturalism in the United States: A Comparative Guide to Acculturation and Ethnicity*. Westport, Conn.: Greenwood Press, 1992. A detailed study of how American culture was shaped from the cultures of all the major ethnic groups in America.

Gates, Henry Louis, Jr. *Loose Canons: Notes on the Culture Wars*. New York: Oxford University Press, 1992. An illuminating book on the issues of African American literature and multiculturalism.

Gordon, Milton M. *Assimilation in American Life: The Role of Race, Religion, and National Origins*. New York: Oxford University Press, 1964. A source book for the definitions of key terms in the study of acculturation.

Gutmann, Amy, ed. *Multiculturalism: Examining the Politics of Recognition*. Princeton, N.J.: Princeton University Press, 1994. Presents diverse views on the importance of recognition and the tensions between personal and ethnic identities.

Herskovits, Melville J. *Acculturation: The Study of Culture Contact*. Gloucester, Mass.: Peter Smith, 1958. Widely regarded as a landmark book on this subject, defining the basic concepts and patterns in the study of acculturation.

Said, Edward W. *Culture and Imperialism*. New York: Vintage Books, 1993. An insightful view of the acculturational interactions between cultures.

Sollors, Werner, ed. *The Invention of Ethnicity*. New York: Oxford University Press, 1989. A collection of interdisciplinary essays, discussing the cultural construction of ethnicity in American literature.

—Aiping Zhang

See also *Bildungsroman* and *Künstlerroman*; Cather, Willa; Emigration and immigration; Kingston, Maxine Hong; Melting pot; Miller, Arthur; Multiculturalism; Okada, John; Villarreal, José Antonio

Acquired immune deficiency syndrome. *See* AIDS

Adams, Henry

BORN: Boston, Massachusetts; February 16, 1838

DIED: Washington, D.C.; March 27, 1918

PRINCIPAL WORKS: *Democracy: An American Model*, 1880; *History of the United States of America*, 1889-1891; *Mont-Saint-Michel and Chartres*, 1904; *The Education of Henry Adams*, 1907

IDENTITIES: European American; family

SIGNIFICANT ACHIEVEMENT: Adams, in his autobiography and historical writings, argued that scientific and technological progress comes at the expense of traditional human values and identities.

Henry Adams says at the beginning of his autobiography, *The Education of Henry Adams*, that he was "distinctly branded" by the legacy of his famous family. Adams felt an obligation to maintain a family tradition of public service established by two presidents (his great-grandfather, John Adams, and his grandfather, John Quincy Adams). American politics was in his blood. When his father, Charles Francis Adams, a congressman, was appointed minister to England in 1861, Adams became his private secretary in London, where he learned the complexity and intrigues of international politics. When Adams returned to the United States in 1868, he became a newspaper correspondent and wrote articles exposing political and social corruption for major newspapers and magazines. In the tradition of his family, Adams was a reformer. For example, he worked for civil service reform and a reformed Republican Party. When he and the other reformers failed, he expressed his disappointment with American politics in a novel, *Democracy*. Adams became disillusioned with politics and never ran for an elected office, but he lived across the street from the White House, where he built his home and associated with political, social, and intellectual leaders until his death.

In addition to an intimidating political heritage, Adams acquired a love of knowledge from his family, who were published scholars in many areas of the humanities. He felt driven to understand the complexity of life at its core. This lifelong ambition, which he called his education, is traced in *The Education of Henry Adams*. His formal career as a scholar began in 1870, when he was appointed assistant professor of medieval history at Harvard. In 1877, he resigned to devote more time to his study of American history, in particular the administrations of Jefferson and Madison, resulting in his nine-volume *History of the United States of America*.

Gaining acclaim as an American historian was not enough to satisfy Adams' search for understanding. After 1893, Adams studied modern science for more conclusive knowledge. The electric generator, also called the dynamo, became a symbol for him of modern American society, powerful yet indifferent to human beings and human values. Adams realized that his family's values were especially threatened by a modern technological society. He found reassurance in the Virgin Mary of the Middle Ages as a symbol of protection, pardon, and love, as illustrated in his *Mont-Saint-Michel and Chartres*.

SUGGESTED READINGS

Samuels, Ernest. *The Young Henry Adams*. Cambridge, Mass.: Harvard University Press, 1948.

_____. *Henry Adams: The Middle Years*. Cambridge, Mass.: The Belknap Press of Harvard University Press, 1958.

_____. *Henry Adams: The Major Phase*. Cambridge, Mass.: The Belknap Press of Harvard University Press, 1964.

—*David Partenheimer*

See also American identity: Northeast; *Education of Henry Adams, The*

Addiction

IDENTITIES: Disease

DEFINITION: An uncontrollable craving for a substance or chemical, characterized by a painful withdrawal when the drug is removed.

Defining addiction remains a daunting task for the medical and academic communities. An uncontrollable craving for a substance or chemical, characterized by a painful withdrawal when the drug is removed, forms the most common definition of addiction, yet this definition falls short of describing the place of drugs in the minds of those who use them for inspiration. Several Native American cultures, for example, employ psychoactive drugs such as peyote and magic mushrooms in religious rituals. Such use can hardly be called that of the addict. Many writers have experimented with altered states of consciousness, however, until they have become addicts. The literature of addiction may therefore be thought of as literature that seeks to render the intense psychological states wrought by drugs, whether euphoric, epiphanic, hellish, or insane. Writers have revealed the immense pain brought about by addiction on the user and the user's family. A last aspect of addiction, recovery, is also chronicled in many literary works.

History

Addiction in North American literature begins with tobacco. Early woodcuts and colonial literature depict settlers smoking, for example, a peace pipe with the leaders of Native American tribes. Often overlooked was the addictive and destructive nature of the tobacco inside the pipe. Tobacco became one of the largest cash crops in the New World and continues to appear throughout literature. The poet T. S. Eliot, for example, refers to a "tobacco trance" in one of his ironic poems about urban life.

Addiction to other drugs appears in literature written after the Civil War. Many Civil War veterans became addicted to laudanum, a mixture of opium dissolved in alcohol. The warm, mind-numbing effect of the opium created a sense of well-being, warding off the agony of everything from amputated limbs to abscessed teeth. The snake oil salesmen who appear throughout U.S. literature of the post-Civil War period, hawking their cure-all potions, were not working crowds as naïve as might be supposed, especially when a few swallows from one of their bottles appeared to cure whatever ailed the patient, temporarily. Opium addiction influenced the life and the work of nineteenth century writer Edgar Allan Poe. The terror and hysterical ravings rendered in Poe's short stories may be read as a metaphor for the agony of opium addiction and withdrawal. The various governmental antidrug campaigns have been seen by some writers as failures whose purpose from the start was not the elimination of drug addiction but the erosion of civil liberties, allowing unlawful searches and seizures. The antidrug forces often saw the war on drugs as a kind of holy war, with its roots in the American Puritan tradition of sin and punishment.

In literature

Dominant in the literature of addiction is the writing of the Beats. The Beats took their name from Jack Kerouac's famous novel *On the Road* (1957), which tells of young people who have exiled themselves from the mainstream culture. To be Beat was to be open to all experience. To be Beat was to live the life of the artist and the philosopher. Specifically, to possess the red eyes of the marijuana user was to have "philosopher's eye." Also included in this counterculture were certain legal drugs, most notably Benzedrine, or "speed," which could be purchased at a drugstore and which was said to have fueled the three-week frenzy during which Kerouac typed *On the Road*, which mentions addiction to speed.

Following on the heels of the Beats came the hippies, whose own counterculture movement grew much stronger and more visible than that of the Beats. A mix of environmental, free love, and equal rights philosophies, the hippie movement also spawned more literature of addiction. Many hippies practiced elements of Eastern religion, including Yoga and Zen Buddhism. As a shortcut or alternative to the enlightenment attained through meditation, the counterculture used LSD, magic mushrooms, and other psychedelic drugs. Drug use, then, was seen not as merely recreational but as one way of opening a door to a higher consciousness. The pursuit of this chemical bliss is chronicled in Tom Wolfe's *The Electric Kool-Aid Acid Test* (1968), a work of creative nonfiction that depicts the exploits of drug guru Ken Kesey and his band of Merry Pranksters as they traveled across America in a wildly painted bus.

By the 1970's the casualties of the drug culture had risen. Many casualties—of drugs and violence—also returned from Vietnam to the United States. Fusing the promise of the counterculture and the horror of the war, Robert Stone's novel *Dog Soldiers* (1974) renders heroin addiction in vivid, startling detail. The summer of love reached a winter of disillusionment.

In the 1980's the greed of bankers, stockbrokers, and lawyers was fueled by cocaine, as portrayed by the characters in Jay McInerny's *Bright Lights, Big City* (1984).

Social strata

Addiction is not limited to one economic level or to the young. Chemical dependency requires only that its victims be human and that they indulge in a chemical to the point that their lives are seriously harmed. Depending on social standing, however, the drug of choice may vary from Valium to crack cocaine. In the novels of John Cheever, for example *Bullet Park* (1969), many of the characters, who are middle-class suburbanites, are addicted to legal drugs prescribed by their doctors. Legal addiction is no less damaging than the illegal variety and has dire consequences for all who use, whether it be amphetamines (speed) or tranquilizers (downers). In either case, prescription drugs help Cheever's characters survive a world of bleak business trips made between the prosperous suburbs of Connecticut and the offices of New York, a concrete enclave where Cheever's characters work at mind-numbing jobs devoid of personal fulfillment. At home, their lives are no better, with failed dreams and unsatisfying sex lives driving them to the refuge of the pill bottle.

At another level of the social strata, far from Wall Street, African American writer James Baldwin depicts the life of heroin users in Harlem, most notably in *Going to Meet the Man* (1965). Attempting to escape from their bleak reality, Baldwin's characters turn to addiction in order to give themselves a sense of control and purpose. Baldwin's "Sonny's Blues," the story of a recovering heroin user, concerns a young man who finds a healing substitute in music, specifically in the blues. For only the blues can adequately convey the suffering of not merely an individual but of a whole people. When Sonny plays and the crowd applauds, the sensation is like being on heroin, and therefore he—and the reader—achieve a kind of transcendence, traveling upward from heroin through art and finally to God.

Implications for identity

Identity is a crucial issue within the experience of addiction since often users indulge in a chemical either to escape their identities or to forge new ones. If the aim is recreational, the user may simply want to try on a series of different identities, much like one might try on a variety of disguises at a costume shop. Given the particular chemical, whether it be nitrous oxide, cocaine, heroin, amphetamines, or even nicotine and caffeine, the user will see different faces in the mirror, some more to his or her liking than others. The possibility of becoming another self has always been a strong lure. In some senses it may even represent the desire to experience death and the journey into heaven.

Recovery

The nature of addiction contains another dichotomy, an extrapolation of its fundamental property, which is that pleasure and pain are two sides of the same coin. While the addict is using, he or she vacillates between the intense good feeling generated by the high and the guilt and sickness generated by "coming down." If this crash is intensified through family or legal problems, the lows sink even further. A tenet of recovery is that the addiction does not end until the addict "hits bottom," or realizes complete defeat, usually after losing such things as health, home, or family. The addict who hits bottom experiences a lonely misery quite foreign to nonaddicts, a solitary confinement made all the more bleak because the sufferer can expect little sympathy.

Yet at this point, ironically, the addict is open to the experience of spiritual and physical resurrection. The addict who recovers breaks through to the other side of addiction to bask in the dazzling light of sobriety. The recovering addict is thus allowed a second chance in life, something denied to all but a lucky few. Many works describe recovery; examples include testimonials in books intended to help other addicts recover.

SUGGESTED READINGS

Fiedler, Leslie A. "The Alteration of Consciousness." In *Waiting for the End*. New York: Stein and Day, 1964. A derisive summary of William Burroughs' early work, asserting that he is naïve "aesthetically, philosophically, and intellectually."

Holmes, John Clellon. *Representative Men: The Biographical Essays*. Vol. 2. Fayetteville: University of Arkansas Press, 1988. Includes essays on Ginsberg, Kerouac, and Neal Cassady.

Kherdian, David. *Six Poets of the San Francisco Renaissance: Portraits and Checklists*. Fresno, Calif.: Giligia Press, 1967. Character sketches and bibliographies of psychedelic writers.

Marks, Jeannette. *Genius and Disaster: Studies in Drugs and Genius*. New York: Adelphi, 1926. Examines the use of opium and other drugs by prominent nineteenth century writers, including Poe.

Porterfield, Kay Marie. *Sleeping with Dionysus: Women, Ecstasy and Addiction*. Freedom, Calif.: The Crossing Press, 1994. Explores the relationship in literature between substance abuse and the sexual behavior of women, paying particular attention to women authors.

Stephenson, Gregory. *The Daybreak Boys: Essays on the Literature of the Beat Generation*. Carbondale: Southern Illinois University Press, 1990. Critical essays focusing on the works of Allen Ginsberg, Burroughs, Gregory Corso, and Lawrence Ferlinghetti. Also includes an overview of the development of the Beat movement.

—David Johansson

See also Alcoholism; Drugs; Psychological theories of identity; Twelve-step programs

Adolescent identity

IDENTITIES: Adolescence and coming-of-age

DEFINITION: Adolescence, the age between the onset of puberty and maturity, is a critical period in the formation of personal identity.

All humans experience adolescence, so it provides a focus for much literature. All genres, including fiction, nonfiction, poetry, and drama may be used to focus on the changes between childhood and adulthood. In this stage, individuals develop a strong concern for self, seeking affirmation through peers. Psychological theories, such as those of Abraham Maslow, contend that adolescence is part of the normal progression in the search for the basic human needs of belongingness, love, and esteem. These needs must be met before one becomes a productive adult. Adolescent literature deals with the meeting of such needs.

Importance

The German word *Bildungsroman* refers to a novel in which a youth breaks away from family to seek independence. The word is associated with the adolescent experience in literature. Another word used to refer to such literature is "coming-of-age." The experience an adolescent undergoes in literature generally leads to an epiphany, or life-changing realization. Through such a change, the character becomes rounded. Realizations signal the maturity of the adolescent, who gains a new outlook on some aspect of life. This allows the character to develop a personal identity, causing a movement toward adulthood. In literature the search for identity grows out of the tradition of the quest, such as that embarked upon in Homer's *Odyssey* (c. 800 B.C.) by Odysseus' son, Telemachus. In traditional stories, males journey abroad and females travel about within the domestic sphere (from one residence or school to another), searching for identity. In modern stories, both genders move about freely in their environments. Usually these stories reflect aspects of the character's social, economic, and social surroundings. Thus, while all main characters search for identities, their means of discovery may differ widely. All adolescent characters face some type of conflict, either within themselves, with another person, or with their environment. The meeting and overcoming of this conflict leads to the discovery of an aspect of identity.

History

In American literature, Benjamin Franklin's *The Autobiography of Benjamin Franklin* (1791) is generally considered the first *Bildungsroman*. Franklin tells the story of rejecting his father's trade as a soap boiler, his apprenticeship to his brother as a printer, and his eventual disagreement with his brother leading him to search, as a youth, for a new life. Franklin's running away from Boston to establish himself in Philadelphia symbolizes the many changes taking place in America at that time. Franklin matures along with his country. He attempts to pass along the wisdom he has gained to help his readers in finding their own identities. This is a major purpose of many autobiographies discussing the adolescent experience. Another well-known American autobiography is that of Frederick Douglass. His *Life and Times of Frederick Douglass* (1881, 1882) saw five different revisions and publications. Douglass relates his slavery experience from childhood through adulthood.

Following autobiography came novels, including those written by Horatio Alger, Jr. Alger wrote tales of young men who made their fortunes through hard work. His books have been labeled inspirational adventures; they taught his readers that hard work pays. Louisa May Alcott wrote some of the first American coming-of-age fiction for girls. Her most well-known novel, *Little Women* (1868, 1869), tells of four sisters who mature during the Civil War. Her books are termed autobiographical because, while not completely factual accounts of her life, they contain much detail from the Alcott household. She wrote several other works, including *Eight Cousins* (1874), in which an orphan girl is raised in what would later be called a nontraditional family. Her uncle encourages her to try experiences not usually recommended for girls. Reflecting the culture of the mid-nineteenth century, the book focuses upon the restrictive clothing, lack of education, and poor diets forced upon American females. Laura Ingalls Wilder also wrote fiction based upon the experiences of her family on the prairie. Her series of "Little House" books shows the maturation of Laura and her sisters through their experiences in the western part of the United States. Mark Twain's *The Adventures of Tom Sawyer* (1876) and *Adventures of Huckleberry Finn* (1884) are known as classics among works of adolescent literature. The rebellious Tom, an orphan, and Huck, the runaway child of an abusive alcoholic father, each search for their place among their small-town neighbors and their friends. Twain's books also deal with larger issues of racism, bigotry, and cruelty. When Huck takes a trip up the Mississippi River with the escaped slave, Jim, he must choose between obeying the laws of humanity, which proclaim that some are not free, and the laws of nature, under which all are born free. Thus, Huck's conflict is with his culture, or environment. When he chooses to support Jim's freedom, he develops a new outlook on life's priorities. Stephen Crane's *The Red Badge of Courage* (1895), about the Civil War, examines the psychological effects of battle upon a young combatant. Its protagonist is a teenage boy who discovers the meaning of courage when he reluctantly becomes part of the Union Army. His struggle against his own fears and the "red beast" of war serves as a prototype of the adolescent conflict novel.

The twentieth century

Some classic novels dealing with adolescence include Marjorie Rawlings' *The Yearling* (1938), in which a boy must sacrifice his pet deer to save his family's crops; J. D. Salinger's *The Catcher in the Rye* (1951), focusing upon a young boy's sexual maturing; William Golding's *Lord of the Flies* (1954), which tells of the behavior of a group of boys when stranded on an island together; and Harper Lee's *To Kill a Mockingbird* (1960), a story of young people's experience with racial prejudice in the Depression-era South.

Langston Hughes, a famous black poet, began writing seriously when he was in high school. Much of his poetry emits a spirit of pride in his race and protest against discrimination. His "Mother to Son" features one generation seeking to inspire another. Joyce Carol Oates captured adolescence in "Insight," a poem about love and recklessness, while John Updike examines life after high school basketball in "Ex-Basketball Player." Themes of multiculturalism surface in "Indian Children Speak," a poem by Pima Indian poet Juanita Bell. As multiculturalism became more acceptable, literature focusing upon the experiences of adolescent minorities appeared in greater quantity.

A change of public attitude in the twentieth century allowed the acceptance of subjects for adolescents which were previously considered taboo. Previous to about 1960, authors could not publish writing for young people that dealt with such realistic subjects as divorce, alcoholism, physical abuse, teen pregnancy, mental illness, or drug abuse among teenage characters. Today, these subjects often provide focus for popular novels, even for younger teens.

Adolescent fiction may be classified by genre. Social realism features teens who feel out of step **Classification** with society. They discover, through experience, ways by which they may come to terms with conflict. Such books may lack a happy ending, and they may contain profanity and scenes that may shock readers. In Robert Cormier's *The Chocolate War* (1974), when a youth at an all-boys' school goes against a school tradition, his actions result in his being attacked by other boys and by an abusive instructor. The tone of this novel remains pessimistic, as the main character finds no solution for his problem. Paula Danziger's books, such as *The Cat Ate My Gymsuit* (1974) and *There's a Bat in Bunk Five* (1980), use humor and an optimistic tone to follow the experiences of an overweight teen who finds her niche as a camper and later as a camp counselor. Adolescent characters may also find themselves caught up in problems of worldwide import. In *Summer of My German Soldier* (1973), Bette Greene writes of a mistreated Jewish girl who befriends an escaped prisoner in Arkansas in the 1940's, discovering her own identity by helping a person who should, according to society, be her enemy. Prolific writers of popular social realism novels depicting adolescents include Richard Peck, Cynthia Voigt, and Lynn Hall. Hall's book, *The Solitary* (1986), tells of a teenager who must cope with the fact that her mother killed her abusive father. Judy Blume, a popular writer, has produced books dealing with sexual maturing, religion, and death. Her books have, from time to time, been banned from some schools and libraries. The ethnic backgrounds of characters and authors may vary widely. In Mari Sandoz's novel *The Story Catcher* (1963), a young Sioux brave named Lance hopes to show his people that he is worthy of their confidence, and an interracial friendship causes problems for the characters in Virginia Hamilton's *A White Romance* (1987). One black writer popular for his themes of the value of understanding to all ethnic groups is Walter Dean Myers.

Sports stories have been made popular by authors such as Chris Crutcher, who wrote *Running Loose* (1983). In this novel, a high school senior football player obeys his coach and injures a rival black quarterback, then finds he can no longer play. Mysteries first gained popularity with series featuring teens such as Nancy Drew and the Hardy brothers. Later the aspects of suspense and horror were added to mysteries by writers such as Lois Duncan. Duncan's teen characters confront drugs, sex, divorce, and crime as they juggle peer relationships and identity crises. Romances are also of interest for teens. Eileen Gouge and Suzanne Rand are among many authors who have written entire series based upon the challenges of young love. Fantasy stories ask readers to believe other worlds might exist. Ursula K. Le Guin's Earthsea books, *Wizard of Earthsea* (1968), *The Tombs of Atuan* (1971), *The Farthest Shore* (1972), and *Tehanu* (1990), connect to form a continuous coming-of-age story. Closely related to fantasy are those books called science fiction. Poul Anderson and Karen Anderson have together written dozens of science-fiction books that stress scientific laws and technological inventions and depict adolescents facing the same struggles as those in more traditional literature. Historical fiction is based on fact. These works incorporate factual people, places, and times into fictional plots. In Ann Rinaldi's *The Last Silk Dress* (1988), a fourteen-year-old Confederate girl in the midst of the Civil War confusion discovers she is the illegitimate daughter of a Yankee. The novel deals with her attempt to overcome the resulting internal conflict.

All these genres have in common the facing of conflicts by teens placed in difficult situations.

As is true with adult-themed books, works about adolescent experience must endure for years before being singled out as fine representatives of their respective genres.

SUGGESTED READINGS

Beetz, Kirk H., ed. *Beacham's Guide to Literature for Young Adults*. Washington, D.C.: Beacham, 1994. Eight volumes of analyses of popular works and their authors; includes project suggestions.

Kardux, Joke. "The Politics of Genre, Gender, and Canon-Formation: The Early American *Bildungsroman* and Its Subversions." In *Rewriting the Dream: Reflections on the Changing American Literary Canon*, edited by W. M. Verhoeven. Atlanta: Rodopi, 1992. Discusses Franklin's autobiography as the first American *Bildungsroman*.

Lukens, Rebecca J. *A Critical Handbook of Children's Literature*. 4th ed. Glenview, Ill.: Scott, Foresman, 1990. Discusses narrative elements of literature and its many genres suitable for young readers. Contains lists of award winners.

Nakamura, Joyce, ed. *High-Interest Books for Teens: A Guide to Book Reviews and Biographical Sources*. 2d ed. Detroit: Gale Research, 1988. Serves as guide to 2,000 authors and 3,500 titles of fiction and nonfiction for junior and high school readers. Especially helpful for teens with learning disabilities or underdeveloped reading skills.

Reed, Arthea J. S. *Reaching Adolescents: The Young Adult Book and the School*. New York: Holt, Rinehart, and Winston, 1985. Scholarly but readable information about literature for young adults. Examines approaches to teaching literature and supplies ample bibliographic materials.

Sutherland, Zena, and May Hill Arbuthnot. *Children and Books*. 8th ed. New York: HarperCollins, 1991. Discusses the development of reading materials for the young; supplies abundant bibliographical listings.

—*Virginia Brackett*

See also *Bildungsroman* and *Künstlerroman*

Adultery

IDENTITIES: Family; men; women

DEFINITION: Adultery is the intimate relationship of a couple, one or both of whom are committed to others.

Terminology

Discussion of adultery in literature must recognize a far-reaching network of terms and categories into which the term "adultery" fits, and in which it must be differentiated. On the one hand, there are terms such as "desire," "passion," "sexuality," and "sexual liaison." Taken by themselves, such terms could be encompassed by a category such as the erotic in literature, or even pornography. The identity involved is the individual's alone. On the other hand, however, lie such terms as "marriage," "family," "social contract," and "religious covenant." These point to the fact that adultery (sexual relations with someone other than one's spouse) is a social act, and literature deals with the social or socioreligious repercussions of unfaithfulness in marriage as well as with questions of individual identity. Shifts in the social identity of the adulterer or adulteress are ultimately shown to be of more significance than the personal in certain literary genres and historical periods.

Background

It has been claimed that adultery is central to Western literature. For example, Tony Tanner, in his groundbreaking study, *Adultery in the Novel: Contract and Transgression* (1979), suggests that it is "the unstable triangularity of adultery rather than the static symmetry of marriage that is the generative form of Western literature as we know it." This is too large a claim: The classic nineteenth century novel, for example, deals with an unmarried hero or heroine and the revealing of a true identity in marriage. It is certainly true, however, that the plot of adultery has been mythically generative from ancient times: The Trojan war, centered on Helen's unfaithfulness, inspired Greek epic and drama. The Arthurian cycle contains as a central feature Guinivere's adultery with Sir Lancelot, leading to the fall of the Round Table. Such transgressions are heroic not only in that are they of highborn heroes and heroines but also in that they cause their society to become tragically uprooted.

Several other literary traditions have developed and form part of the ongoing treatment of adultery in literature. One is the comic tradition of the cuckold, often an older man with a young wife, as in Geoffrey Chaucer's *The Canterbury Tales* (1387-1400) or in Giovanni Boccaccio's *Decameron* (1349-1351; English translation, 1620). These are tales in which adultery has relatively little moral, religious, or social implication. Some of the earliest novels picked up on this, as did Restoration drama of the late seventeenth century, in which sex is a social game. In *Moll Flanders* (1722) by Daniel Defoe, the genre of the confession is employed to give a very loose moral framework to Moll's sexual misdemeanors, possibly because females have been expected to be chaster than men. Henry Fielding's novel *Tom Jones* (1749) has no such repentant libidinous hero.

Another literary tradition in the treatment of the theme of adultery developed in the nineteenth century novel and might be termed the Protestant tradition. It is heralded by Fielding's eighteenth century contemporary, Samuel Richardson, and deals primarily with the psychological aspects of adultery, so that seduction and temptation, rather than romance and heroism, are central. The New Testament defines adultery as being in the mind and links it with the body, the "Temple of the Holy Spirit." It is in this faith that Richardson's heroine Clarissa Harlowe withstands sexual control over her body by Robert Lovelace. Charlotte Brontë's Jane Eyre similarly withstands Rochester's blandishments. Both prefer death or exile to inner defilement; they insist on marriage.

In the light of this discussion, certain key American texts stand out in their unique development, **American identity** especially of this last tradition. Nathaniel Hawthorne's *The Scarlet Letter* (1850) has an unremitting Protestant and patriarchal society as its setting. There is no interest at all in Hester's physical act of adultery: The whole romance is quite unerotic. The stress is on the inner states of Hester Prynne and Arthur Dimmesdale. The attempt to flee society by going into the forest or overseas is thwarted by the sense of inner violation rather than social pressure. In the end, confession, death, and atonement are the necessary price to be paid for redemption. In romance, the hope for a less legalistic, more graceful social identity for the sexually fallen is a common theme.

Kate Chopin's *The Awakening* (1899) likewise appeals to a society in transition from patriarchy to female self-determination. A contemporary, Henry James, uses traditional American themes of innocence in *What Maisie Knew* (1897) to make a child's identity central to the novel of adultery. The ironies generated are rich and complex: What Maisie knows is not the knowing of a sophisticated adult society accustoming itself to adultery and divorce, but its falsity, its breaking of all its vows and promises. Adultery becomes, as in much of the modern American novel, a sign of a society losing its values and descending into meaningless personal relationships. John Updike's *Couples* (1968) is a good example of this: In the novel, the social and sexual games of the Restoration comedy returns. In an attempt to find new plots, the old games are constantly replayed.

Arthur Miller makes perhaps the last expression of family values, in which adultery is significant transgression. In *Death of a Salesman* (1949) and *The Crucible* (1953), single acts of adultery form defining moments, not in their action, but in their confession or denial, making protagonists take on new authentic or inauthentic identities that, for Miller, become American archetypes. Pioneering psychologist Sigmund Freud pointed out that the price of civilization is repression; much modern

---

Adultery
Five Key Works

c. 800 B.C.	Homer's *The Iliad*. A ten-year war results from the abduction of Helen, wife of Menelaus.	1850	Nathaniel Hawthorne's *The Scarlet Letter*.
		1857	Gustave Flaubert's *Madame Bovary*.
c. 1469	Sir Thomas Malory's *Le Morte d'Arthur*, one of the countless works about King Arthur.	1956	*Peyton Place*, by Grace Metalious, explicitly describes diverse sexual misconduct.

American literature prefers the anarchy of undifferentiated sexual libido, with the result that adultery in literature no longer signifies.

SUGGESTED READINGS

Ariès, Philippe. *Centuries of Childhood: A Social History of Family Life*. Translated by Robert Baldick. New York: Alfred Knopf, 1962.

Belsey, Catherine. *Desire: Love Stories in Western Culture*. Cambridge, Mass.: Blackwell, 1994.

Girard, René. *Deceit, Desire, and the Novel: Self and Other in Literary Structure*. Translated by Yvonne Freccero. Baltimore: The Johns Hopkins University Press, 1965.

Rougemont, Denis de. *Love in the Western World*. Garden City, N.Y.: Doubleday, 1957.

Tanner, Tony. *Adultery in the Novel: Contract and Transgression*. Baltimore: The Johns Hopkins University Press, 1979.

—David Barratt

See also *Awakening, The*; *Crucible, The*; *Death of a Salesman*; Erotic identity; Freud, Sigmund; *Scarlet Letter, The*

Adventures of Augie March, The

AUTHOR: Saul Bellow (1915-   )
FIRST PUBLISHED: 1953
IDENTITIES: Jewish

The Adventures of Augie March is an autobiographical *Bildungsroman* covering a Jewish American's struggle to find himself, through trial and error, from the 1920's through the 1940's. Saul Bellow's hero-narrator Augie March is bewildered by the freedom and opportunities available to Jews in America after centuries of persecution and segregation in other lands.

Augie is a resilient but not a strongly motivated character. Not knowing what he wants, he allows himself to be misguided by a succession of domineering personalities, beginning with the family's tyrannical boarder, Mrs. Lausch, a refugee from Czarist Russia, who tries to make him an Old World gentleman.

Augie and his older brother Simon have to go to work while still children to supplement the meager family income. Both quickly become hardened by the streets of Chicago. Criminal acquaintances involve Augie in felonies that nearly get him sent to prison. Augie, however, has a love for education and self-improvement because they offer hope of finding self-realization and escape from the ghetto. The combination of slang and erudite diction Augie uses in telling his story is an outstanding feature of the novel.

Simon is another domineering personality who tries to run Augie's life. Ruthless, money-hungry Simon cannot understand his younger brother's indifference to materialism and despises his bookworm mentality. They have a dynamic love-hate relationship throughout the novel.

Simon marries into a wealthy family and becomes a millionaire, but Augie sees that his unhappy brother is suicidal. Augie wants more from life than money and a loveless marriage. He tries shoplifting, union organizing, smuggling illegal immigrants, managing a punch-drunk boxer, and other fiascos. He experiences many changes of fortune. He plunges into love affairs with women who try to redirect his life. The most formidable is a huntress who collects poisonous snakes and trains an eagle to catch giant iguanas in Mexico.

When World War II comes, Augie joins the Merchant Marine and barely survives after his ship is torpedoed. After the war, he and his wife move to Europe, where he grows rich trading in black-market merchandise. At novel's end he has still not found himself. Augie finds that he has settled for a comfortable but shallow existence, but he realizes that other people have no better understanding of who they are or what they want than he does himself.

During the 1950's and 1960's *The Adventures of Augie March* was popular with young readers because they identified with a protagonist who rejected traditional values and sought self-realization in a world seemingly doomed to atomic annihilation.

SUGGESTED READINGS

Dutton, Robert R. *Saul Bellow*. New York: Twayne, 1982.

Gerson, Steven M. "The New American Adam in *The Adventures of Augie March*." *Modern Fiction Studies* 25 (Spring, 1979): 117-128.

Harper, George Lloyd. "Saul Bellow." In *Writers at Work: The Paris Review Interviews*, edited by George Plimpton. New York: Penguin, 1977.

Kiernan, Robert F. *Saul Bellow*. New York: Continuum, 1989.

—*Bill Delaney*

See also Bellow, Saul; *Bildungsroman* and *Künstlerroman*; Jewish American identity

African American identity

IDENTITIES: African American

In the eighteenth century, when the empirical theories of English thinkers John Locke and Isaac Newton were shaping American literature generally, the African American presence in America added a new dimension to the cultural identity of American literature. Since African Americans were involuntarily transported into a new environment, their cultural transition became the source of their literary creativity as well as a historical contribution. With the passage of time, African American writers infused new perspectives into the literary canon through experimentation and through revisions of existing conventions.

Biographical accounts

Personal accounts of slaves' journeys to and bondage in America produced a new genre, the slave narrative. The genre borrows from the autobiography, travelogue, and captivity narratives that were already common forms of writing among the early settlers. Slave narratives include complaints about a forced journey to America. While most Puritans and Pilgrims expressed faith in their God and hope in their journey to a new land, the African American narratives convey extremes of alienation and suffering.

Among the pioneer African American writers of slave narratives is Gustavas Vassa, who narrates his experiences in America. His account contains a description of the terrible journey by sea. He attributes magical powers to slaveholders, illustrating how human imagination can be limited by the boundaries of one's cultural heritage and background. In his autobiography, titled *The Interesting Narrative of the Life of Olaudah Equiano, or Gustavus Vassa, the African, Written by Himself* (1789), Vassa mentions how his first exposure to horses made him think that they, too, were magical creatures. Gradually, the opportunity to communicate with other slaves and his experiences enabled him to realize that horses were a species of animals that were common in Africa and North America. Vassa's realization not only confirms that there has long been great diversity in America but also indicates the fact that African Americans came from diverse regions of Africa. Slaves were perceived in America as members of a single race, so their diversity of heritage was overlooked and their regional differences were ignored by slave owners, who defined them in terms of their functions.

For African Americans, the slave narrative became a means of protest against mistaken perceptions. From 1830 to 1865, with the exception of one poet, James H. Whitfield, all black authors wrote autobiographies or were subjects of biographical works. *Scenes in the Life of Harriet Tubman* (1869, revised as *Harriet the Moses of Her People*, 1886) is the biography of a runaway slave who became a conductor on the Underground Railroad; at great risk to her life, she assisted slaves in fleeing to the northern states and freedom.

Frederick Douglass

The most famous African American in the antislavery movement was Frederick Douglass. He wrote three autobiographies during various phases of his life. He reports his early interest in learning how to read and write, his confrontation with his inhumane owners, and his ultimate freedom. He urged President Abraham Lincoln to enlist blacks in the Union Army. Dedicated to a vision of transforming the oppressed state of his race, Douglass shared his story to inspire others.

Madame Keckley   A slave narrative written from a woman's perspective is Madame Keckley's *Behind the Scenes* (1868). It gives a personal account of her life as a slave for thirty years and four years as a resident of the White House. This is a story of a woman whose talent as a dressmaker helped support her owners and whose savings from her own labor permitted her to buy her freedom and that of her son. A tragic blow came to her when her son died as a Union soldier. She rose to professional heights, serving as Mrs. Lincoln's dressmaker. She enjoyed the respect of the Lincolns, and President Lincoln referred to her as Madame Keckley. The publication of the book, however, with its description of her interracial connections at the highest levels of post-Civil War society, strained her relations with the first family. Abandoned, in poverty, Keckley died in the House for Destitute Women and Children in Washington, D.C.

African American Identity Milestones

1720?	Jupiter Hammon, a slave whose poems were published and widely praised in his lifetime, born (d. 1800?).
1746	Lucy Terry's "Bars Fight," a short poem about an Indian raid, written; published 1893.
1753	Phillis Wheatley, poet, born in Africa.
1760	First slave narrative, the dictated *A Narrative of the Uncommon Sufferings, and Surprising Deliverance of Briton Hammon, a Negro Man,—Servant to General Winslow of Marshfield, in New-England*.
1760	First American publication of literature written by an African American: "An Evening Thought: Salvation by Christ with Penetential Cries," by Jupiter Hammon.
1773	Phillis Wheatley's *Poems on Various Subjects, Religious and Moral* published in London with a note—from white men who had examined Wheatley and the work—vouching that she had indeed written the poems. Thomas Jefferson considered the work beneath the dignity of criticism. First book published by an African American in America—in 1786.
1778	Jupiter Hammon's *A Poetical Address* praises Phillis Wheatley.
1787	Jupiter Hammon's *Address*, a religious poem.
1789	Olaudah Equiano's *The Interesting Narrative of the Life of Olaudah Equiano, or Gustavus Vassa, the African, Written by Himself*, a celebrated, widely read, and often-reprinted slave narrative.
1800's	High period of slave narratives, often published with the aid of abolitionists. Some conventions of the slave narrative are whippings, separation of families, rape or seduction, lack of food, shelter, or other necessities, religious exhortation, denunciation of slaveholders, and the suspenseful escape attempt. Slave narratives written by the slaves themselves typically contain "written by himself" or "written by herself" in the title and letters from prominent white citizens guaranteeing the authenticity of the account. Disbelief or ignorance of the conditions of slavery was common; slaveholders promoted false images of slavery. Slave narratives are successful in their aim of arousing public opinion against slavery.
1820-1821	*King Shotaway* produced at the African Grove Theatre in New York. Probably the first play written and produced by African Americans. White vandals force closure of the theater in 1822.
1829	David Walker's *Appeal in Four Articles; Together with a Preamble, to the Colored Citizens of the World, But in Particular, and Very Expressly, to Those of the United States of America*, an antislavery essay.
1829	George Moses Horton's *The Hope of Liberty*.
1831	Maria Stewart's *Religion and the Pure Principles of Morality, the Sure Foundation on Which We Build*, an antislavery essay.
1836	Jarena Lee's *The Life and Religious Experience of Mrs. Jarena Lee, a Coloured Lady, Giving an Account of Her Call to Preach the Gospel, Revised and Corrected from the Original Manuscript, Written by Herself*.
1845	Frederick Douglass' *Narrative of the Life of Frederick Douglass, an American Slave, Written by Himself*.
1847	William Wells Brown's *Narrative of William. W. Brown, a Fugitive Slave, Written by Himself*.
1852	*Uncle Tom's Cabin: Or, Life Among the Lowly*, by Harriet Beecher Stowe, first serialized in the antislavery journal *The Nation* from 1851

After the Civil War, biographical narratives remained a popular genre among African American writers. These narratives integrate the art of storytelling and history telling and allow the authors to address the theme of racial discrimination within personalized contexts of economic and social challenges.

The autobiography of Booker T. Washington, *Up from Slavery: An Autobiography* (1901), is a personal testimony of success which is in many ways comparable to Benjamin Franklin's famous autobiography. As a native son of Virginia, Washington realized the importance of education. He worked at odd jobs and had $1.50 when he came to Hampton Normal, which later became Hampton University. He organized the first night school for black and Native American students. Washington became an advocate of the development of practical and technical skills; many of his

Booker T. Washington

African American Identity Milestones — CONTINUED

	to 1852. The antislavery book is a best-seller and is credited with hastening the Civil War. A dramatization by George Aiken is also widely popular.	1923	*Cane*, by Jean Toomer.
		1925	Alain Locke's *The New Negro*, the leading anthology of the Harlem Renaissance.
1853	William Wells Brown's *Clotel: Or, The President's Daughter*, published in London. American publication 1864. First African American novel.	1926	Montgomery Gregory's *Plays of Negro Life*, an anthology of African American drama. In the 1920's and 1930's, white playwrights (Eugene O'Neill, Paul Green, DuBose Heyward and Dorothy Heyward) are producing successful plays with African American themes on Broadway, but black playwrights find little opportunity to publish or to produce their works.
1855	Frederick Douglass' *My Bondage and My Freedom*.		
1859	Harriet Nelson's *Our Nig: Sketches from the Life of a Free Black, in a Two-Story White House, North, Showing that Slavery's Shadow Falls Even There*. Tells of Frado, of mixed race, a servant for a family of abolitionists who are nevertheless bigoted. First African American novel published in America.		
		1928	Nella Larsen's *Quicksand*.
		1929	Wallace Thurman's *The Blacker the Berry*.
		1929	Nella Larsen's *Passing*.
		1931	Jessie Redmon Fauset's *The Chinaberry Tree*.
1861	Harriet Jacobs' *Incidents in the Life of a Slave Girl*.	1932	Rudolph Fisher's *The Conjure-Man Dies: A Mystery Tale of Dark Harlem*, a mystery novel.
1868	Elizabeth Keckley's *Behind the Scenes: Or, Thirty Years a Slave, and Four Years in the White House*.	1932	Sterling Brown's *A Southern Road*.
		1936	Arna Bontemps' *Black Thunder*.
1869	Paul Laurence Dunbar's *Lyrics of Lowly Life*, a collection of poetry.	1937	Zora Neale Hurston's *Their Eyes Were Watching God*.
1899	Charles Waddell Chesnutt's *The Conjure Woman*, a novel.	1939	William Attaway's *Let Me Breathe Thunder*.
		1940	Richard Wright's *Native Son*.
1901	Booker T. Washington's *Up from Slavery: An Autobiography*, beginning with his slavery and ending with his presidency of Tuskegee Institute.	1942	Zora Neale Hurston's *Dust Tracks on a Road*.
		1942	Margaret Walker's *For My People*.
1903	W. E. B. Du Bois' *The Souls of Black Folk*.	1945	Richard Wright's *Black Boy: A Record of Childhood and Youth*.
1905	Charles Waddell Chesnutt's *The Colonel's Dream*, a novel.	1945	Chester Himes's *If He Hollers Let Him Go*.
1912	James Weldon Johnson's *The Autobiography of an Ex-Coloured Man*.	1945	Gwendolyn Brooks's *A Street in Bronzeville*.
		1946	Anne Petry's *The Street*.
1919	"If We Must Die," by Claude McKay.	1950	Alice Childress' *Florence*.
1921	"The Negro Speaks of Rivers," by Langston Hughes.	1952	Ralph Ellison's *Invisible Man*.

(continued)

African American opponents criticized him for his excessive loyalty to whites in a laboring capacity. His use of anecdotes in his biography invites a diversity of interpretations; however, it is clear that he offers African Americans practical advice for survival under severely adverse economic conditions.

W. E. B. Du Bois   W. E. B. Du Bois is another black author who was concerned about the survival of African Americans in America; he advocated democratic rights for his race. He was conscious of the diversity among African American cultural experiences. Unlike Washington, who was born a slave, Du Bois was born free and grew up in the cosmopolitan culture of Massachusetts. He attended Fisk University in Nashville, Tennessee, then went to Harvard and was graduated magna cum laude. He recorded impressions of his complex experiences in *The Souls of Black Folk* (1903). In

---

African American Identity Milestones — CONTINUED

1953	James Baldwin's *Go Tell It on the Mountain*.		*considered suicide/when the rainbow is enuf: a choreopoem*.
1953	Anne Petry's *The Narrows*.		
1953	Claude McKay's *Selected Poems*.	1977	Toni Morrison's *Song of Solomon*.
1955	Ted Shine's *The Bats out of Hell*.	1978	*I've Been a Woman: New and Selected Poems*, by Sonia Sanchez.
1959	Paule Marshall's *Brown Girl, Brownstones*.		
1959	Lorraine Hansberry's drama *A Raisin in the Sun*.	1980	*Blues People: Negro Music in White America*, nonfiction, by Amiri Baraka.
1959	*The Selected Poems of Langston Hughes*, by Langston Hughes.	1981	*A Soldier's Play*, by Charles Fuller.
1960	Gwendolyn Brooks's *The Bean Eaters*, poetry, wins a Pulitzer Prize, the first for an African American.	1982	Alice Walker's *The Color Purple*.
		1982	Gloria Naylor's *The Women of Brewster Place*.
1961	*Purlie Victorious: A Comedy in Three Acts*, by Ossie Davis, is successful on Broadway.	1983	Rita Dove's *Fifth Sunday*, fiction.
		1984	Octavia Butler's *Clay's Ark*.
1962	James Baldwin's *Another Country*.	1985	*Healing Songs for the Inner Ear*, by Michael Harper.
1964	Malcolm X's *The Autobiography of Malcolm X*.		
1964	Amiri Baraka's *Dutchman*.	1987	Morrison's *Beloved*, a novel, winner of the Pulitzer Prize.
1965	Claude Brown's *Manchild in the Promised Land*.	1988	*Joe Turner's Come and Gone*, by August Wilson.
1966	*Selected Poems*, by Robert Hayden.		
1968	Nikki Giovanni's *Black Feeling, Black Talk*.	1990	*Devil in a Blue Dress*, by Walter Moseley.
1968	Anne Moody's *Coming of Age in Mississippi*.	1990	Jamaica Kincaid's *Lucy*.
1970	Ida B. Wells's *Crusade for Justice: The Autobiography of Ida B. Wells*.	1990	August Wilson's *The Piano Lesson* awarded the Pulitzer Prize in drama.
1970	Maya Angelou's *I Know Why the Caged Bird Sings*.	1991	*Black Ice*, by Lorene Cary.
		1991	Stephen L. Carter's *Reflections of an Affirmative Action Baby*.
1970	Julius Lester's *To Be a Slave*.	1992	*Waiting to Exhale*, by Terry McMillan.
1972	Ishmael Reed's *Mumbo Jumbo*.	1993	Toni Morrison awarded the Nobel Prize in Literature.
1974	Angela Davis' *Angela Davis: An Autobiography*.		
1975	*Dhalgren*, by Samuel R. Delany.	1994	Nikki Giovanni's *A Collection of Essays*.
1976	*Roots*, by Alex Haley.	1995	*The Collected Essays of Ralph Ellison*, by Ralph Ellison.
1977	Ntozake Shange's *for colored girls who have*	1996	*How Stella Got Her Groove Back*, by Terry McMillan.

this work, he makes a case for a racial bond among African Americans despite their varied backgrounds. He explains that Washington's advice in *Up from Slavery* stems from his rural agrarian background; however, the future of the African American race called for a more uniform approach to democratic rights. Du Bois was aware of the psychological tensions linked to segregation; therefore, he predicted the color line as the problem of the twentieth century. He advocated that the talents and skills of African Americans must not be developed in contempt for other races, but rather in conformity to the greater ideals of the American republic. He proposed that double consciousness or pride in African heritage and pride in American citizenship was better than a divided self. There was no need for African Americans to seek assimilation in America at the cost of their African heritage. Although Du Bois' influence remains significant throughout the twentieth century, he expressed his own disillusionment with the lot of African Americans in his autobiographies.

Some African Americans resorted to collaborative writing for biographical narrative. An example is *The Autobiography of Malcolm X* (1964), written in collaboration with Alex Haley. It blends the dramatic conventions of narration with first-person reporting. The book captures America's cultural landscape of the 1950's and 1960's, while highlighting the turning points in Malcolm X's life. The biography records his criminal activities, prison experiences, and conversion to the Nation of Islam. After his release from prison, Malcolm X's pilgrimage to Mecca led to the realization that the message of religion is to foster peaceful relations among all races. Therefore, upon his return to America, he renounced his allegiance to Elijah Muhammad, who was preaching hatred toward the white race. Malcolm X remained active in the struggle for equality of African Americans and became a popular black leader; he was assassinated in 1965. **Malcolm X**

African American writers have used the genres of poetry and fiction to express their identity in America. The legacy of folk literature enabled them to connect with their cultural origins despite their harsh experiences in America. With the passage of time, folk literature became a vehicle for blending the reality of their experiences in America with their nostalgia for the African past. The emotional experience of African American slaves inspired them toward artistic creativity, generating an international mix of poetic rhythms and sounds. As a result of their designated role in a laboring capacity, slaves were not allowed to get a formal education and were generally perceived as unfit for intellectual activities. Only a few slaves had their owners' permission to read and write, and their literacy centered on the reading and interpretation of the Bible. **Poetry and fiction**

Among such privileged and literate slaves was the first African American poet, Phillis Wheatley, who was known as "a sable muse" among European educated circles. Wheatley was faced with the dual challenge of writing as an African American as well as a woman. She blended the literary conventions of her time, such as heroic couplets, with innovative zeal. For example, many of her poems depict the speaker as "an Ethiop," announcing her claim to a black heritage. In many of her elegies, she addresses the subject of death in the metaphorical context of Christian hope for salvation, implying rescue from a state of bondage. It was her love of liberty that prompted her to write the poem "To His Excellency General Washington" for leading the forces of independence. Unfortunately, poverty and domestic hardship squelched her poetic voice. Wheatley's literary work was primarily accepted as testimony of African American ability to participate in American literature. Even though Wheatley's African American identity separates her from other early American writers, the devout religious trend in her poetry is in common with other colonial poets, such as Anne Bradstreet and Edward Taylor. Her personal awareness of the bondage of slavery, however, gives Wheatley's biblical allusions a special poignancy. **Phillis Wheatley**

Religious overtones in African American poetry are also present in the poetry of George Moses Horton. He was moved by hymns, so he learned to read and write in order to create his own poetry. In his collection *The Hope of Liberty* (1829), he makes free use of the ode, blank verse, heroic couplet, and stanzaic patterns. He was eventually successful in buying his freedom by selling his poetry, which was popular among the abolitionists.

Another source of inspiration to African American writers was folk music. In fact, the African

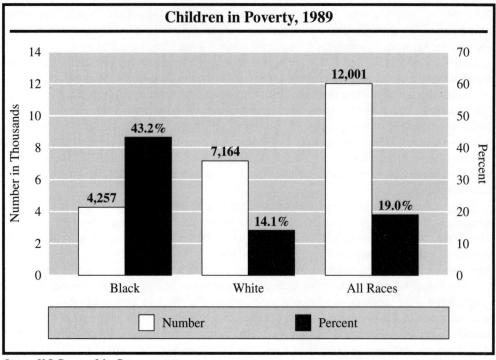

Children in Poverty, 1989

Source: U.S. Bureau of the Census.
Note: "All Races" includes other races not shown separately. Data covers only related children under 18 years of age living in families.

Americans' oral tradition helped to preserve the cultural memory of slaves. Folktales, myths, and songs could be passed on from generation to generation. The oral tradition was instrumental in conserving the double consciousness of African American writers, enabling them to freely borrow from European and African traditions. Folk literature became a source of solidarity amid the diversity of heritage, which included a wide range of African languages and traditions. The spirituals of African Americans blend folk music with religious fervor. The spirituals signify more than a spiritual yearning; they also depict the nostalgia for the lost state of freedom. Slaves made use of spirituals as sophisticated texts; appearing innocent, the lyrics could, for example, guide runaways.

Paul Laurence Dunbar   Paul Laurence Dunbar's poetry captures the African American voice in American literature. Dunbar's mixed use of oral and written conventions was also practiced by realists such as Mark Twain. It is not surprising that a renowned realist writer, William Dean Howells, praised Dunbar for integrating the African American voice into literature.

The 1920's marked the beginning of the Harlem Renaissance, when African American writers transcended the constraints of the European tradition to infuse an independent perspective into American literature. The Harlem Renaissance produced powerful works of poetry by, among others, Langston Hughes, who cites his African heritage to claim ties to the grandeur of ancient civilizations. At the same time, he depicts the ravages of social and economic disparity. The liberating influence of the Harlem Renaissance invigorated African American literature.

The African American interest in fiction can be traced back to the nineteenth century. A recurrent theme to appear in the fiction of African American writers is the identity of the mulatto in relation to an environment of rejection. African American fiction treats such rejection as a lingering social phenomenon. Toward the end of the nineteenth century novelist Pauline E. Hopkins addressed racism in her serial novels, exposing the hypocrisy within race relationships. Hopkins' fiction is prophetic in the sense that, as did Du Bois, she saw that the problem of the color line would be the great problem of the twentieth century. Later, Jean Toomer's collection of short fiction, *Cane* (1923), embraced the tensions of segregation and victimization of the mulatto from the male perspective. He makes powerful use of folk sound, imagery, and symbol to portray racial barriers that signal that a claim to an interracial heritage is a social taboo.

The Harlem Renaissance allowed for novels that captured the reality of African American experience. Richard Wright's novel *Native Son* (1940) remains a masterpiece that portrays the fate of a black man who is overpowered by economic oppression. The protagonist accidentally kills the liberal daughter of his employer. Wright pursues the prevailing conventions of naturalism to depict the helpless condition of African Americans. His novel resembles Theodore Dreiser's *An American Tragedy* (1925): Both writers were inspired by real trials. In response to Wright's fiction, there were some black writers who were not interested in depicting merely the helpless condition of the black man; they were also interested in probing the challenges and complexities of African American experience to understand their own cultural identity in America. Among the leading male novelists who focus on the quest for identity is Ralph Ellison, who wrote *Invisible Man* (1952). This novel combines realism with surrealism and draws upon black folklore and myth. James Baldwin was another African American novelist who investigated the archetypal theme of initiation and discovery of self in his novel *Go Tell It on the Mountain* (1953). This novel draws heavily upon the author's childhood experiences.

A contemporary leading black male novelist is Ishmael Reed. In his novel *Mumbo Jumbo* (1972), Reed experiments with the conventions of fiction to capture the complexity of African American identity as he integrates multiple layers of meaning in his prose. He parodies Western tradition and African American conventions. Reed decries any idealism that imposes unrealistic restrictions on the artist.

Among those African American writers whose style Reed parodies is the female black writer, Zora Neale Hurston, who grew up in the black community of Eatontown. Her work marks a major breakthrough for feminist literature. For example, in her novel *Their Eyes Were Watching God* (1937), she combines the voice of self-expression with the social challenges encountered by African American women. The Hurston legacy matures in Alice Walker's fiction. Walker uses a self-reflective voice in her epistolary novel *The Color Purple* (1982).

Probably the most memorable female African American voice in the twentieth century is that of Toni Morrison. In *Beloved* (1987) she takes an innovative approach to a ghost story. She traces the historical context of slavery and exposes the hazards of allowing the past to override the present.

SUGGESTED READINGS

Baker, Houston. *Modernism and Harlem Renaissance*. Chicago: University of Chicago Press, 1987. Claims that, for African American writers, the Harlem Renaissance brought liberation from traditional literary constraints.

Gates, Henry Louis. *The Signifying Monkey: A Theory of Afro-American Literary Criticism*. New York: Oxford University Press, 1988. Examines the influence of African folk tradition and the revisionist trends in African American literature.

Morrison, Toni. *Playing in the Dark*. New York: Vintage Books, 1990. Criticizes the perspective of critical theory that treats African American presence in literature from a fixed viewpoint and disregards the symbiotic interracial relationships.

Tate, Claudia. *Black Women Writers at Work*. New York: Continuum, 1983. Surveys feminist African American scholarship and provides fifteen interviews with leading black women writers.

—Mabel Khawaja

See also Alienation; *Autobiography of Malcolm X*; Baldwin, James; *Color Purple, The*; Douglass, Frederick; Du Bois, W. E. B.; Dunbar, Paul Laurence; Ellison, Ralph; Hughes, Langston; Hurston, Zora Neale; *Invisible Man*; Malcolm X; Morrison, Toni; Racism and ethnocentrism; Reed, Ishmael; Slave narratives; Slavery; *Their Eyes Were Watching God*; *Up from Slavery*; Walker, Alice; Washington, Booker T.; Wheatley, Phillis, poetry of; Wright, Richard

Against Interpretation and Other Essays

AUTHOR: Susan Sontag (1933-   )

FIRST PUBLISHED: 1966

IDENTITIES: European American; women

   Susan Sontag created a sensation in the mid-1960's with her essay "Against Interpretation." Although she made it clear that she was not against all interpretation of works of art, her position quickly became associated with the idea of art for art's sake—that is, with a concern only with form and style, not with morality and content. She later conceded that her approach was too polemical; she was attacking message-mongering critics but left herself open to the charge of being amoral. She later corrected her position in *Under the Sign of Saturn* (1980), a collection of essays in which she explicitly argues that a work's style or aesthetic properties cannot be viewed in isolation from its creator's moral sensibility.

   "Sensibility" is a key term in Sontag's vocabulary. As she points out in the paperback edition of *Against Interpretation and Other Essays*, her work is actually the revelation of her evolving sensibility, of her way of looking at the world. She is not a critic who is especially interested in explicating works of art; rather, she explores art for what it says about the sensibility—the mindset—of its author. For example, her essay "Spiritual Style in the Films of Robert Bresson" is less concerned with his individual films than with his way of imagining the world.

   Sontag has been lauded and attacked for her catholic tastes. *Against Interpretation and Other Essays* contains essays on pornography and science fiction, and on psychoanalysis, literary criticism, and the contemporary French novel. Her range of interests not only breaks down the distinction between art and entertainment but also reflects her personal taste. She invites readers to ponder the development of her own sensibility rather than submitting her critical power only to the canon of recognized masterpieces.

   Against Interpretation and Other Essays, then, is a record of Sontag's intellectual development. As she remarks in her preface to the paperback edition, the book is to be regarded as a work-in-progress in which she explores and embraces positions, some of which she has later rejected, modified, or returned to with a new perspective. She is less concerned with specific judgments than with the theoretical positions that underlie those judgments. She writes as an enthusiast and partisan—rarely attacking work she does not like. What makes *Against Interpretation and Other Essays* so exhilarating is that it shows a critic in the midst of forming her opinions, realizing that everything she writes is subject to revision and that she remakes her identity through confronting new and old works of art.

SUGGESTED READINGS

Bruss, Elizabeth. *Beautiful Theories: The Spectacle of Discourse in Contemporary Criticism.* Baltimore: The Johns Hopkins University Press, 1982.

Kennedy, Liam. *Susan Sontag: Mind as Passion.* Manchester, England: Manchester University Press, 1995.

Sayres, Sohnya. *Susan Sontag: The Elegiac Modernist.* New York: Routledge & Kegan Paul, 1990.

Vidal, Gore. "Miss Sontag's New Novel." In *United States: Essays, 1952-1992.* New York: Random House, 1993.

—Carl Rollyson

See also Canon; Existentialism; Literary standards; Popular culture

Age of Innocence, The

AUTHOR: Edith Wharton (1862-1937)

FIRST PUBLISHED: 1920

IDENTITIES: European American; Northeast; women

   Set in the last decades of the nineteenth century, *The Age of Innocence* narrates the love story of Newland Archer and Ellen Olenska. When the novel opens, Archer is engaged to May Welland, a young woman from one of New York's oldest society families, and Ellen Olenska is married to a Polish count, who has abused her in unspoken ways. Ellen, May's cousin, returns to New York from Europe because she wants to obtain a divorce in the United States. Her family welcomes her back into the fold, but they want to make it clear that divorce is not accepted in their world.

As a respected attorney who is soon to be a family member, Newland is elected to broach this topic with Ellen. Attempting to discourage the divorce, he explains that the customs of their New York society are based on loyalty to one's actual family and to one's social "family." Over the course of several meetings, during which Ellen and Newland are compelled to discuss matters of deep and delicate feeling, they fall in love. Each grows to admire the other's rarity and virtuous sincerity.

Realizing that their union would socially ostracize them and hurt others, Ellen and Newland decide to give up each other and walk away from the most genuine love evident in all of Edith Wharton's writing. In doing so, they adhere to social conventions that may be destructive of the most precious aspect of self—the capacity to love. Wharton makes the reader see, however, that Ellen Olenska and Newland Archer love each other for who they are, which is defined largely by the moral vision that they share, a vision forged by their society. To violate that vision would not only harm the others that they cherish, but also would undermine a key part of what each loves in the other.

Their choice of renunciation is a difficult one, and Wharton, who allows her readers to cry out against Newland and Ellen's decision, understands that although lovers may want to consider society irrelevant, they cannot. Lovers carry their society within them. Social values are a significant part of Ellen and Newland and are a significant reason why each grows to love the other.

Wharton attains her greatest philosophical clarity in *The Age of Innocence*, the novel for which she was awarded the Pulitzer Prize in fiction in 1921. *The Age of Innocence* is the work that most clearly articulates her major philosophical conclusions, namely, that individual character is inextricably bound to the society that nourishes, forms, and reforms that character. Another version of this conclusion is that life places individual longings and needs in direct conflict with the needs and desires of others. Which side should have ascendancy is not always clear.

SUGGESTED READINGS

McDowell, Margaret B. *Edith Wharton*. Boston: Twayne, 1976.

Wershoven, Carol. *The Female Intruder in the Novels of Edith Wharton*. Madison, N.J.: Fairleigh Dickinson University Press, 1982.

Wolff, Cynthia Griffin. "*The Age of Innocence*: Wharton's 'Portrait of a Gentleman.'" *Southern Review* 12, no. 2 (1976): 640-658.

—*Linda Costanzo Cahir*

See also Class and identity; *Ethan Frome*; Wharton, Edith

Agee, James

BORN: Knoxville, Tennessee; November 27, 1909

DIED: New York, New York; May 16, 1955

PRINCIPAL WORKS: *Permit Me Voyage*, 1934; *Let Us Now Praise Famous Men*, 1941; *The Morning Watch*, 1951; *A Death in the Family*, 1957; *Agee on Film*, 1958, 1960 (2 vols.); *Letters of James Agee to Father Flye*, 1962; *The Collected Short Prose of James Agee*, 1968; *The Collected Poems of James Agee*, 1968; *James Agee: Selected Journalism*, 1985

IDENTITIES: European American; family; South; religion

SIGNIFICANT ACHIEVEMENT: A strong sense of place, the search for identity, and the tension between the romantic and modern viewpoints permeates James Agee's diverse and complex work.

James Agee's writing is influenced by two boyhood experiences in Tennessee: the death of his father, killed in an automobile accident in 1916 (and fictionalized in *A Death in the Family*), and the Anglican religious training he received at St. Andrew's, a boarding school run by a monastic order of the Episcopal church (explored in *The Morning Watch*). At St. Andrew's Agee met Father

James Harold Flye, with whom he traveled to France and England in 1925. Agee and Flye were lifelong friends and correspondents.

As a young man Agee expressed an interest in writing poetry and fiction and in film. As president of Phillips Exeter Academy's Lantern Club, he was responsible for the screening of a variety of classic silent films. Agee was fascinated with the documentary potential of movies and their ability to create immediate felt emotion. These concerns are expressed in his later screenplays and film reviews for *The Nation* and *Time*, among other journals. Experimentation with cinematic technique—panorama, flashback, montage, and closeup—is evident in much of Agee's writing.

At Harvard, Agee became known as a poet and was editor of the Harvard *Advocate*, a notable literary magazine. Eager for the more rural experiences of his childhood, he spent the summer of 1929 as a migrant farmworker in Nebraska and Kansas. This experience put Agee in touch with the struggle of the rural poor during the early days of the Depression.

As a result of the *Advocate*'s parody issue of *Time* magazine, Agee was hired as a staff writer for *Fortune* magazine in 1932. A concern for social responsibility coupled with a skepticism regarding the role of journalism are expressed in his famous documentary report on the sharecropping system in the South. The work was found inappropriate for publication in *Fortune*, and was published in book form as *Let Us Now Praise Famous Men*, a remarkable blend of narrative, autobiography, social history, and philosophy. The book was issued with photographs by Walker Evans.

SUGGESTED READINGS

Barson, Alfred T. *A Way of Seeing: A Critical Study of James Agee*. Amherst: University of Massachusetts Press, 1972.

Lofaro, Michael, ed. *James Agee: Reconsiderations*. Knoxville: University of Tennessee Press, 1992.

Madden, David. *Remembering James Agee*. Baton Rouge: Louisiana State University Press, 1974.

Moreau, Genevieve. *The Restless Journey of James Agee*. New York: William Morrow, 1977.

—*Michelle A. Balée*

See also American identity: South; *Death in the Family, A*; *Let Us Now Praise Famous Men*; Migratory workers; Poverty

Ageism

IDENTITIES: Aging

DEFINITION: Ageism, a term coined by Robert Butler, is the stereotyping of old people.

At issue Like all forms of prejudice, ageism influences the popular image of a group of people in a negative way that allows them to be categorized as less than human. Discriminatory cartoons, films, and television shows categorizing old people as lonely, confused, and unattractive perpetuate the myth that growing old is something to dread. Such myths, according to psychiatrist Robert Butler, reflect a profound prejudice against the elderly that goes beyond a classic fear of old age to "unreasonable fear and/or hatred of old people."

Negative images in literature In most instances elderly characters are depicted as physically unattractive or infirm, with wrinkled skin, failing eyesight, and poor hearing. In the Robert Inman novel *Old Dogs and Children* (1991), a girl attends a party with her mother, where she observes some "frightfully old" women—one of them with dark liver spots on her arms, who is hard of hearing, cups her hand behind her ear, and speaks in a loud voice. Another woman, who has dark facial hair on her upper lip, is constantly out of breath. An elderly servant is described as "a gnarled old prune." Such characterizations are all too common.

With so many negative images, the dread of old age has become ingrained to the point that literature often seeks to avoid it by resorting to a fountain of youth theme. In such stories, old people relive their youth. This technique, depicted in the film *Cocoon* (1985), was also used by Nathaniel Hawthorne in the story "Dr. Heidegger's Experiment," first published in 1837. A group of characters described as "three old, withered grandshires . . . contending for the skinny ugliness of a shriveled grandam" suffer the illusion that they are returned to youthful vigor after they drink water provided by the mysterious doctor.

In addition, elderly characters are often described as confused and disoriented. Twentieth century author Katherine Anne Porter, in her short story "The Jilting of Granny Weatherall," describes Granny Weatherall as unclear about the present and the past as she faces the last day of her life. When she remembers her daughter Hapsy holding a child, she mistakes her for herself holding Hapsy. She is incoherent about events, selective in memory, and mistaken about identities. In "A Good Man Is Hard to Find," a short story by Flannery O'Connor, a grandmother's confused memory and lack of restraint lead to disaster for the family when she misdirects them on a journey and then thoughtlessly identifies a criminal to his face. Even old characters who are depicted in a sympathetic light are often presented as old and funny, or old but cute, perhaps possessing a childlike wisdom not understood by others.

When older characters reminisce about past experiences, more often than not their failures are reviewed. In Ernest Hemingway's "The Snows of Kilimanjaro," a writer on the point of death thinks of his wasted life and regrets the stories he did not write. Regrets also come to an old man—nearsighted and hard of hearing—in Samuel Beckett's play *Krapp's Last Tape* (1958), when the old man listens to events recorded on his thirty-ninth birthday, thirty years before. "Perhaps my best years are gone. When there was a chance of happiness," he says. Above all, old people are categorized as lonely and isolated. The lonely, elderly woman in "Miss Brill," by Katherine Mansfield, observes other people on a park bench as looking as "though they'd just come from dark little rooms or even closets." Ironically the description fits Miss Brill herself, but she is unaware of her condition until she is called a "stupid old thing" by a young person—with company—nearby. Stung by the realization of her image, she returns to her own dark little room.

Ageism not only influences the popular image of the elderly, but also affects the self-view of older people, who may adopt the negative definitions of themselves based on the perceptions of others. In one survey, half the people over sixty-five questioned accepted negative images of the elderly, shown on television, as accurate.

Implications for identity

SUGGESTED READINGS

Butler, Robert N. *Why Survive: Being Old in America.* New York: Harper & Row, 1975.
Friedan, Betty. *The Fountain of Age.* New York: Simon & Schuster, 1993.

—Joyce Chandler Davis

See also Aging; Demographics of identity

Aging

IDENTITIES: Aging

DEFINITION: Literature about growing old may have themes of unresolved conflicts, stereotypical attitudes, family relationships, and physical limitations.

The unfolding of one's identity through time is often expressed in old age in the form of autobiography. May Sarton's poetry and extensive journals exemplify the qualities of introspection, creativity, and self-awareness available in old age. In her poem "Gestalt at Sixty," she charts the patterns of her existence that have contributed to her development. In "On a Winter Night," she meditates on the aging process and finds images of clarity, growth, seasoning, and regeneration to overcome the anxieties and tensions of old age. Sarton's journals are a record of her aging and her struggle to resolve tensions between her need for solitude and her obligations to society as a writer. Representative works include *Journal of a Solitude* (1973), *At Seventy* (1984), and *After the Stroke* (1988). *Endgame: A Journal of the Seventy-ninth Year* (1992) summarizes the indignities of chronic illness, frailty, loneliness, loss, and recurring bouts of depression that dominate her old age. She feels a loss of identity—she feels that the Sarton people have known has become a stranger, someone who is ill and frail. Her next journal, *Encore* (1993), shows her rejuvenated and restored to her former strength as she engages life.

Autobiography

Aging has presented a variety of experiences—not all of domestic contentment—to different authors. (National Archives)

Other significant autobiographical works include Alan Olmstead's *Threshold: The First Days of Retirement* (1975), Elizabeth Gray Vining's *Being Seventy: The Measure of a Year* (1978), and Florida Scott-Maxwell's *The Measure of My Days* (1968). The former texts emphasize the pitfalls, pleasures, and eventual fulfillment experienced in retirement. Scott-Maxwell explores issues of aging and identity with subtlety and depth. She maintains that the task of old age is to add to and clarify one's sense of self, whatever the cost.

Life in review   Older adults find meaning in their lives and gain insights into their identities through the processes of reminiscence and life review. Identity in old age is forged through self-reflection, memory, and integration. Such concerns may be addressed by older adults in autobiographical works, as noted above. Similar concerns may be addressed as well in fictional works. In some cases elderly characters fail to complete a life review that provides a sense of perspective. For example, the old woman in Katherine Anne Porter's story "The Jilting of Granny Weatherall" rehashes on her deathbed the awful events that led to her life of isolation and loneliness. She dies with the effects of her early loss unresolved in her memory. Willy Loman's life review, in Arthur Miller's play *Death of a Salesman* (1949), leads to a stripping-away of the lies that have been the basis of his character and identity. He is exposed as lonely, vulnerable, and a dreamer. He dies without resolving important personal and family conflicts.

Other characters in fiction use life review to gain insights into their identities. The retired literary agent in Wallace Stegner's novel *The Spectator Bird* (1976) faces feelings of guilt over the death of his adult son and uncertainties over an unresolved relationship with a woman he met on a trip twenty years earlier. He exorcises these demons from the past only by confronting his memories and remaining receptive to his supportive and loving wife. Similar ghosts from the past haunt Hagar Shipley, in Margaret Laurence's *The Stone Angel* (1964). At ninety, Hagar maintains a grudge against God because her favorite son died in a tragic accident. By confronting her past, Hagar begins to learn that her unforgiving character, and her inability to acknowledge the love of key people in her life, have kept her alienated and isolated. A similar movement toward integration through life review is experienced by Eva, the main character in Tillie Olsen's novella *Tell Me a Riddle* (1976). Eva has lived for others her entire married life. When her husband wishes to move to an old folks' home, she rebels. As the conflict between husband and wife emerges in the story, Eva begins to reminisce and relive her turbulent childhood in Russia and her mentoring by a woman who was a political activist.

Old people often are portrayed as mentors in literary works. The basis of their identity is their capacity to pass on truths and inspire the young. Examples include the novels *Set for Life* (1991), by Judith Freeman, and *Balancing Acts* (1981), by Lynn Sharon Schwartz. In Lisa Koger's story "Ollie's Gate," a young woman finds love and wisdom in a neighbor woman once disgraced for having an illegitimate child. **Mentors**

The tensions inherent in intergenerational relationships are vividly re-created in many works. Two examples are Daniel Menaker's collection of stories, *Old Left* (1987) and Ernest Thompson's play *On Golden Pond* (1979). In the first example a young man spends years resisting the influence of his uncle, an irascible old man who has never lost his appetite for radicalism. After years of caregiving the nephew begins to yield to the old man's influence over his life. In Thompson's play an old man works out a lifelong tension with his adult daughter when she arrives for a visit to her parents' New Hampshire cabin.

The identity of African American elders is often based on relationships within the family. Commitment to family and to traditions is a recurring role in fictional portrayals. For example, Peter Taylor's story "What You Hear from 'Em?" is about an illiterate old woman, Aunt Munsie, who lives in a small Tennessee town and raises two white children after their mother dies. Aunt Munsie lives in hope that the boys she has raised, successful businessmen in Nashville, will return to live in the small town. Her loss of a well-defined role represents the tragedy of being cast aside for the sake of progress and social conformity.

Alice Walker's story "To Hell with Dying" portrays a town's response to a similar character, a man named Mr. Sweet, who relies on neighbor children to rejuvenate him when he seems near death. The narrator recalls the importance of this man to her personal development. The central role of spiritual life to the identity of African American elders is expressed in the Allan Gurganus novella, *Blessed Assurance* (1990). In this story an African American woman becomes an unlikely mentor to a white teenager, who sells funeral insurance one summer to poor black people in rural North Carolina. The old woman is ninety-four, nearly blind, and a devoted Christian. Her goodness and spirituality overwhelm the young man and provide him with new perspectives on wisdom and old age.

Ernest Gaines's novel *The Autobiography of Miss Jane Pittman* (1971) is structured as an oral history of a former slave who has lived more than one hundred years and has witnessed the beginnings of the Civil Rights movement in the South. Miss Jane's tenacity of character, her faith in the land, and her dedication to her loved ones are the essential traits of her identity. Her story offers painful testimony to the injustices inflicted upon African American people throughout American history. This story illustrates the importance of African American family life and reveals the quality of perseverance that is essential to Miss Jane's character.

African American culture and Jewish ethnicity collide in the play *Driving Miss Daisy* (1988) by Alfred Uhry. In this play Daisy Werthan, in her seventies, gradually mellows under the firm and loving hand of Hoke Coleburn, twenty years her junior, an itinerant laborer hired as a chauffeur. The two grow old together and become the closest of friends, despite the differences in race and class. A devout Jew is the focus of Max Apple's novel *Roommates: My Grandfather's Story* (1994). In his memoir, *Patrimony: A True Story* (1991), Philip Roth gains insights into his inheritance of the familial, cultural, and religious qualities that characterized his father. In doing so, he realizes how much his father's Jewish heritage means to his own identity and values.

Sometimes old people are stereotyped as always being frail, ill, or disabled. These physical conditions do have a serious impact on how the elderly regard themselves. They are not, however, the final determinant of one's identity in old age. For instance, Tracy Kidder's *Old Friends* (1993) **Frailty** is a study of life in a nursing home. The two men Kidder profiles continue to sustain meaningful lives despite the limitations of blindness and the effects of a stroke. Mark Van Doren's poem "The First Snow of the Year" tells of an elderly couple maintaining their affection for each other, and recovering memories of their youthful love, despite the husband's increasing frailty.

Sometimes the effects of a particular disease seem to overwhelm one's identity and hope for a normal life in old age. Memoirs are often the chosen medium for depicting the ravaging effects of Alzheimer's disease on the victim as well as on the family. Rosalie Walsh Honel's *Journey with Grandpa: Our Family's Struggle with Alzheimer's Disease* (1988) and Carol Wolfe Konek's *Daddyboy* (1991) are two examples. Richard Stern's story "Dr. Cahn's Visit" illustrates a son's dedication to affirm the identities of his parents despite his mother's wasting away from cancer and his father's dementia.

Loss, grief, death   Understanding the complexity of identity in old age requires an examination of literary works about the end of life. Key works include Linda Pastan's poems in *The Five Stages of Grief* (1978) and Mary Jane Moffat's anthology of stories and poems, *In the Midst of Winter: Selections from the Literature of Mourning* (1982).

Robert Anderson's play *I Never Sang for My Father* (1968) portrays a middle-aged son's fruitless attempts to find the perfect image or ideal of father. Eventually he acknowledges his father's identity as a bitter, unforgiving old man. Two poems, William Carlos Williams' "The Last Words of My English Grandmother," and Robert Frost's "An Old Man's Winter Night," portray contrasting responses to the end of life. In the first poem an irascible old woman ends life raging against what she considers to be life's inequities. In the second poem an old man, living alone in a remote farmhouse, acknowledges the uneasy balance that must be struck so that the old can sustain themselves in their own homes.

Summary   Identities of aging in literature reflect the delicate balancing acts faced in old age. Older adults strive to remain active, healthy, and engaged in life. At the same time they draw upon a rich storehouse of memories, continue to face unresolved conflicts relating to families and other relationships, and are constantly challenged by loss, grief, and death.

SUGGESTED READINGS

Cole, Tom. *The Journey of Life: A Cultural History of Aging in America*. Cambridge, England: Cambridge University Press, 1992. An important contribution to social history, literature, and religious life as they apply to aging.

Rubin, Rhea Joyce. *Of a Certain Age: A Guide to Contemporary Fiction Featuring Older Adults*. Santa Barbara, Calif.: ABC-Clio, 1990. More than three hundred novels and stories written after 1980 are annotated and indexed according to a variety of subjects.

Shenk, Dena, and W. Andrew Achenbaum. *Changing Perceptions of Aging and the Aged*. New York: Springer-Verlag, 1994. Essays reflecting upon personal impressions of aging, aging in various cultures, images of women, and images of aging in literary works.

Yahnke, Robert E., and Richard M. Eastman. *Literature and Gerontology: A Research Guide*. Westport, Conn.: Greenwood Press, 1995. More than 340 annotated entries on novels, plays, poems, stories, and autobiographical works. Each entry is cross-referenced to one of forty-four topics in gerontology.

—*Robert E. Yahnke*

See also Ageism; Psychological theories of identity; Stereotypes and identity

Ai (Florence Anthony)

BORN: Albany, Texas; October 21, 1947

PRINCIPAL WORKS: *Cruelty*, 1973; *Killing Floor*, 1979; *Sin*, 1986; *Fate*, 1991; *Greed*, 1993
IDENTITIES: African American; European American; Japanese American; multiracial; Native American; women

Significant achievement: Ai has renewed the poetic dramatic monologue in poems that record moments of public and private history.

Ai is a multiracial American woman. Her mother's immediate ancestors were African American, Native American (Choctaw), and European American (Irish and Dutch). Her father's ancestors were Japanese. Ai has said that the history of her family is the history of America. She does not find her identity in any racial group. She insists on the uniqueness of personal identity. One of the aims of her work is to destroy stereotypes. She has said that she is "irrevocably tied to the lives of all people, both in and out of time." Consequently, whoever "wants to speak" in her poems "is allowed to speak regardless of sex, race, creed, or color."

Ai grew up in Tucson, Arizona. When she was seven, her family moved to Las Vegas, Nevada, for a year, then spent two years in San Francisco, California, before returning to Tucson. They moved again when Ai was twelve, this time to Los Angeles, California, returning again to Tucson three years later, when Ai was fifteen. Ai attended Catholic schools until the seventh grade. Her first poem, written when she was twelve, was a response to an assignment by the nuns to write a letter from the point of view of a Christian martyr who was going to die the next day. When she was fourteen, intending to enter a contest for poems about a historical figure, Ai began writing poems regularly.

History was Ai's best subject in high school, which she attended in Tucson. At the University of Arizona, also in Tucson, Ai found her identity in the "aesthetic atmosphere" of intellectual life. She was graduated from the university in 1969 with a degree in Oriental studies. She earned an M.F.A. degree in creative writing from the University of California at Irvine in 1971. When Ai published her first book of poetry, *Cruelty*, in 1973, she became a nationally known figure, so striking were her grimly realistic and violent poems. Ai married the poet Lawrence Kearney in 1976. In 1979, her second book, *Killing Floor*, won the Lamont Poetry Prize. She separated from Kearney in 1981, and the couple divorced in 1984. In 1986, her third book, *Sin*, won an American Book Award from the Before Columbus Foundation. She has since published *Fate* in 1991 and *Greed* in 1993.

Suggested reading

Ai. "On Being One-Half Japanese, One-Eighth Choctaw, One-Fourth Black, and One-Sixteenth Irish." *Ms.* 6, no. 11 (May, 1978): 58.

—James Green

See also *Cruelty*; *Greed*; Mixed race and identity

AIDS

Identities: Disease

Definition: Acquired immunodeficiency syndrome is a fatal disease that causes the breakdown and eventual failure of the immune system.

AIDS has quickly reached North America's consciousness and culture since its beginning manifestations there in the early 1980's. At that time, before AIDS was even recognized as a viral disease, it had a frightening and powerful impact on the identities of those infected, and on the imaginations of everyone. Discrete periods of AIDS consciousness have been identified by AIDS theorists, and there are definable attributes of comprehension as evidenced in the media and general populace. Little was known about AIDS at first, but the medical and technological knowledge base continues to grow. AIDS education is offered to elementary schoolchildren and an actor has received an Oscar award for portraying an AIDS-afflicted individual. AIDS has reached, at a minimum, the consciousness of people around the world; as a result of the variety of perceptions—including moral perceptions—of the disease, being marked by AIDS creates a complex identity distinct from that brought about by having any other fatal illness.

History

AIDS originally was considered, in North America, to be an illness of marginalized individuals: gay men, IV drug users, and Haitians. Early case studies suggested that AIDS is a disease that is sexually transmitted. This created a stigma attached to any individual with the AIDS virus because of cultural discomfort with issues of sexuality in general and homosexuality in particular. Persons with AIDS were evicted from housing and were refused admission to school programs as an effect of panic and hatred rather than as an effect of medical understanding. To provide general knowledge about AIDS, and thus lessen fear, the United States Department of Health and Human Services released a brochure, sent to all households in 1988, that delineated risk factors in AIDS transmission. This mass mailing and other such information campaigns broadened the scope of public knowledge. AIDS was seen as a gay problem, however, and not that of the general population, until such cases as that of Ryan White, a young hemophiliac, were publicized. AIDS devastated the gay community early on, with Larry Kramer being one of the first to sound the alarm about the AIDS crisis in his essay "1,112 and Counting." Kramer, founder of the Gay Men's Health Crisis in New York, wrote numerous essays to espouse sexual self-protection among gay men.

AIDS has continued to kill primarily gay men, but in 1995 the Centers for Disease Control released statistics that show AIDS to be the number-one killer of men and women in the United States aged twenty-five to forty-four. Much has been written about this catastrophic disease and its impact on the identity of afflicted individuals and on the community. The presence of AIDS does not foster attitudes of neutrality, and this condition is evident in the literature of AIDS. To have AIDS creates an identity. Considerable literature has been written about living with AIDS.

Early AIDS literature, 1981-1988

The earliest AIDS literature is often testimonial. The earliest gay AIDS novel is Paul Reed's *Facing It* (1984). This novel describes the beginning of the AIDS panic in 1981-1982. Reed uses simple medical terminology and the AIDS-afflicted gay male character rapidly deteriorates, which was common in that time. Barbara Peabody's *The Screaming Room: A Mother's Journal of Her Son's Struggle with AIDS* (1986) offers a testimonial tribute to her son. She cared for him in the final stages of his illness and her loving description testifies to her son's fine qualities as a man and a son. Paul Monette's *Love Alone: Eighteen Elegies for Rog* (1988) uses poetry to highlight Monette's relationship with his lover, who died of AIDS in 1986. This poetry serves as a testament to their bond throughout the trials of maintaining a relationship over an extended period of time and during a terminal illness. Monette also produced *Borrowed Time: An AIDS Memoir* (1988), which chronicles his own struggle with AIDS while his lover dies of AIDS. This autobiographical work received critical acclaim and was widely read.

Additional works of fiction include Alice Hoffman's best-selling novel *At Risk* (1988), which provided a first exposure to the specter of AIDS for many middle-class suburban readers. This novel has a child protagonist who is infected through a blood transfusion. Young adult author M. E. Kerr published *Night Kites* in 1986, which has the protagonist trying to come to terms with his gay older brother's HIV-positive status. Another young adult novel is *Good-Bye Tomorrow* (1987) by Gloria Miklowitz. Again, the protagonist has AIDS as a result of a transfusion and Miklowitz portrays the reaction of the immediate community. These young adult novels demonstrate that much was misunderstood about AIDS transmission, and that widespread fear and rejection of the afflicted occurred. There was often an attempt made by friends and family to maintain secrecy about AIDS infection, to protect the afflicted from societal censure.

Gay authors also produced novels in this era. Robert Ferro wrote *Second Son* in 1988, which mixes the real symptoms of AIDS with the desire for a utopian society. Armistead Maupin uses comic realism in his Tales of the City series for *The San Francisco Chronicle*. His novel *Babycakes* (1984) has a central character lose his lover to AIDS. The final volume in his series, *Sure of You* (1989), features AIDS much more peripherally but illustrates the devastation felt by the entire San Francisco community. Christopher Davis produced a novel in which the protagonists, both gay men, perish from AIDS. This novel, *Valley of the Shadow* (1988), features a New York setting. Gay authors of this era showed that people with aids were often rejected by their biological families and cared for by lovers and friends.

Plays were being produced Off-Broadway, and one of the most recognized of them was Larry Kramer's *The Normal Heart* (1985). His play demanded more governmental involvement for funding and researching the AIDS virus. William Hoffman's *As Is* (1985) is a more personal play

AIDS
Milestones

1977	A Danish woman surgeon dies in Zaire of complications of AIDS.
1981	Playwright Larry Kramer and writer Edmund White gather approximately eighty men together to discuss the strange new disease affecting their community. The group becomes the Gay Men's Health Crisis.
1984	Isolation of the HIV virus.
1984	Paul Reed's *Facing It*.
1985	Larry Kramer's *The Normal Heart*.
1986	Barbara Peabody's *The Screaming Room: A Mother's Journal of Her Son's Struggle with AIDS*.
1987	Editor Michael Callen's anthology *Surviving and Thriving with AIDS: Hints for the Newly Diagnosed*.
1988	Cindy Ruskin's *The Quilt: Stories from the NAMES Project*, about the AIDS quilt.
1988	Editors Ines Reider and Patricia Ruppelt's anthology *AIDS: The Women*.
1988	Paul Monette's *Love Alone: Eighteen Elegies for Rog*.
1988	Alice Hoffman's best-selling novel *At Risk*.
1989	The final volume in Armistead Maupin's Tales of the City series, *Sure of You*, illustrates the devastation felt by the entire San Francisco community.
1991	Dominique LaPierre's *Beyond Love*.
1993	Christopher Coe's *Such Times*.
1995	The Centers for Disease Control release statistics that show AIDS to be the number-one killer of men and women in the United States age twenty-five to forty-four.

in that the focus is on the relationship of two men, one having been diagnosed with the AIDS virus. Hoffman's play illustrates that AIDS can renew the love between two individuals, rather than create a chasm.

Nonfiction works of literature, such as autobiographies and personal essays, were prevalent in the gay press, in magazines such as *The Advocate* and *Christopher Street*, and in mainstream magazines and newspapers. Numerous essays and articles were written about living with AIDS, and some of these have been collected into anthologies. Michael Callen edited *Surviving and Thriving with AIDS: Hints for the Newly Diagnosed* (1987). This anthology has essays of gay individuals struggling with AIDS. A second anthology, *Surviving and Thriving with AIDS: Collected Wisdom* (1990), covers a broad spectrum of individuals living with AIDS, including a chapter on pediatric AIDS. J. W. Money wrote *To All the Girls I've Loved Before: An AIDS Diary* in 1987. This book's self-reflective essays are lightly humorous. Ines Reider and Patricia Ruppelt edited an anthology about women and AIDS titled *AIDS: The Women* (1988). This text has first-person accounts by women who are HIV-positive, people with aids, prostitutes, health care professionals, and educators. The nature of these essays is frequently testimonial.

AIDS literature was being produced in small amounts during the first era of AIDS awareness, from 1981 to 1988. At that time, many of the texts were elegiac in tone, but by late 1988 there was a change in the tone. Some of the literature was more openly angry and critical of slow governmental response to the outbreak. Some authors broadened their perspective and, rather than tell a first-person story of their immediate experience with AIDS, made powerful suggestions about what was to be done. The literature of the first period concerns itself with the experience of the problem; the literature of the second period also concerns itself with the realization that the problem is not going to go away. AIDS became part of a continuing landscape; the first AIDS pieces with a historical perspective were written. By 1991, AIDS had been evident in North American culture for approximately a decade. AIDS literature became increasingly knowledgeable about AIDS symptoms and treatments. The focus shifted from tales of those dying to tales of those living with the virus. The names of those living with the AIDS virus more often became public knowledge; the stigma diminished somewhat. The cultural response to the virus became, to an extent, less one of fear and more one of compassion.

AIDS literature after 1988

There is no stronger visual representation of the impact of AIDS upon the individual than the NAMES Project, or the AIDS quilt. These quilt blocks, each one lovingly created in the memory of an AIDS-deceased person, have been presented in many communities. Cindy Ruskin's book, *The Quilt: Stories from the NAMES Project* (1988), depicts the colorful quilt blocks and the beginnings of the project.

More testimonials and personal essays were published by diverse authors as more of the population became HIV-positive and openly wrote about it. Elizabeth Glaser and Laura Palmer produced *In the Absence of Angels: A Hollywood Family's Courageous Story* (1991). This is Glaser's tale of her transfusion infection and her bravery in caring for her two infected children. Another woman author, Fran Peavey, wrote *A Shallow Pool of Time* (1989), which chronicles her struggle with AIDS and her grassroots political activism. The American public had heard of the trials that Ryan White had suffered as a result of attempting to continue at public school; his autobiography became a best-seller. There was public interest in learning more about the lives of people with AIDS.

In another sign of growing acknowledgment of the AIDS epidemic, television programs and screenplays were produced. The film *Longtime Companion* (1990) focused on the lives of gay men over the course of the epidemic. The screenplay by Craig Lucas was released in paperback form. Many plays that remain unpublished were performed.

Poets were releasing their impressions of AIDS and identity in a variety of texts. Michael Klein edited the volume *Poets for Life: Seventy-Six Poets Respond to AIDS* (1989). These poets capture perfectly the issue of AIDS and identity in poems such as "Turtle, Swan" by Mark Doty and "Heartbeats" by Melvin Dixon. Michael Lassell's collection, *Decade Dance*, chronicles gay life in the 1980's before and after AIDS. Lassell's work won the Lambda Literary Award for best poetry collection. The poet May Sarton captured the essence of the epidemic in her poem "AIDS."

The fiction after 1988 strongly identified people as being as unique, quirky, and lovable or unlovable after acquiring the virus as they had been before acquisition. Many gay authors contributed novels that had a long historical tracing of the protagonist's life, such as Christopher Coe's *Such Times* (1993), Christopher Bram's *In Memory of Angel Clare* (1988), and David Feinberg's *Eighty-Sixed* (1989). Gay authors richly detailed the changes the AIDS crisis wrought on beloved individuals. Holly Uyemoto, in her novel *Rebel Without a Clue* (1989), portrays an AIDS-infected character who continues to participate in unprotected sex. Other authors highlighted the characteristics of the afflicted individual rather than the characteristics of the disease, which suggests a greater understanding of the parameters of living with the AIDS virus. AIDS even reaches the romance novel in Dominique LaPierre's *Beyond Love* (1991). AIDS literature continues to grow and evolve as the culture grows more familiar with AIDS and its complete ramifications.

SUGGESTED READINGS

Aggleton, Peter, and Hilary Homans, eds. *Social Aspects of AIDS*. New York: The Falmer Press, 1988. Essays on the presence of AIDS internationally and on the language of AIDS.

Murphy, Timothy F., and Suzanne Poirier, eds. *Writing AIDS: Gay Literature, Language, and Analysis*. New York: Columbia University Press, 1993. Critiques AIDS fiction, the depiction of AIDS on television, and AIDS testimonials.

Nelson, Emmanuel S., ed. *AIDS: The Literary Response*. New York: Twayne, 1992. Analyzes American and other works of AIDS fiction, drama, and cinema.

Pastore, Judith Laurence, ed. *Confronting AIDS Through Literature: The Responsibilities of Representation*. Champaign: University of Illinois Press, 1993. Provides samples of AIDS literature and AIDS curriculum.

Shilts, Randy. *And the Band Played On: Politics, People, and the AIDS Epidemic*. New York: St. Martin's Press, 1987. Unravels the development of AIDS in the United States, the governmental and medical community response, and the political activism created by the outbreak.

Sontag, Susan. *AIDS and Its Metaphors*. New York: Farrar, Straus & Giroux, 1989. A companion text to *Illness as Metaphor*. Examines the presence of AIDS in American culture and the meaning attached to AIDS as an illness.

—*Cherelyn Bush*

See also *Babycakes*; Coe, Christopher; Coming out; Gay identity; *Illness as Metaphor*; Kramer, Larry; Kushner, Tony; Maupin, Armistead; Monette, Paul

Aiiieeeee! An Anthology of Asian-American Writers

EDITORS: Jeffery Paul Chan (1942-   ), Frank Chin (1940-   ), Lawson Fusao Inada (1938-   ), and Shawn Wong (1949-   )
FIRST PUBLISHED: 1974, rev. ed. 1983
IDENTITIES: Asian American

Many literary anthologies have the straightforward purpose of preserving the work of a particular historical period or artistic movement; others are much more polemical and focused on political issues. *Aiiieeeee! An Anthology of Asian-American Writers* fits the latter category. Originally published in 1974 and significantly revised in 1983, this anthology was adopted as a textbook and used in many college multicultural literature classes. In an important introductory essay the editors denounce well-known works such as Pardee Lowe's *Father and Glorious Descendant* (1943), Jade Snow Wong's *Fifth Chinese Daughter* (1945), and C. Y. Lee's *Flower Drum Song* (1957) as examples of a literature that merely reinforced mainstream American stereotypes of Asians similar to the demeaning caricatures in Earl Derr Biggers' popular Charlie Chan mysteries of the 1920's. Such literature, write the editors, is "not only offensive to Chinese and Japanese America but was *actively inoffensive* to white sensibilities" and actively supported notions of white supremacy and Asian exoticism.

To counter this tradition the editors offer Toshio Mori, John Okada, and Louis Chan as precursors of a more realistic and militant literature, as well as other works primarily addressed to Asian American readers. Mori, a Japanese American Nisei (born in the United States of Japanese immigrant parents), wrote short stories that highlight the ability of the immigrant community to assimilate American mainstream values while retaining important elements of Japanese culture. Okada's novel *No-No Boy* (1957) recounts the experiences of Japanese Americans in the internment camps of World War II; and Louis Chu's *Eat a Bowl of Tea* (1961) depicts a realistic version of urban neighborhoods that hardly resemble the picturesque Chinatown of *Flower Drum Song*. Frank Chin's play *The Chickencoop Chinaman*, first produced in 1972, follows Louis Chu's realistic approach, focusing on the difficulties of cultural assimilation and the generation gap that develops between immigrants and their more Americanized children. This theme also appears in stories such as Shawn Hsu Wong's "Each Year Grain" and Hisaye Yamamoto's acclaimed "Yoneko's Earthquake." The anthology allowed these works to reach a wide audience.

Aiiieeeee! An Anthology of Asian-American Writers established a precedent for Asian American writers to explore the experience of their communities and families in a self-defining way while protesting the damaging effects of ethnic stereotypes. The anthology provides inspiration and direction for Asian American fiction writers, playwrights, and poets.

SUGGESTED READINGS

Baker, Houston A., Jr., ed. *Three American Literatures*. New York: Modern Language Association, 1982.
Berson, Misha, ed. *Between Worlds: Contemporary Asian-American Plays*. New York: Theatre Communications Group, 1990.
Bruchac, Joseph, ed. *Breaking Silence: An Anthology of Contemporary Asian American Poets*. Greenfield Center, N.Y.: Greenfield Review Press, 1983.
Chan, Jeffery Paul, et al., eds. *The Big Aiiieeeee! An Anthology of Chinese American and Japanese American Literature*. New York: Meridian, 1991.

Kim, Elaine H. *Asian American Literature: An Introduction to the Writings and Their Social Context*. Philadelphia: Temple University Press, 1982.

—*Lorenzo Thomas*

See also Acculturation; Asian American identity: China, Japan, and Korea; Asian American identity: Pacific Islands; Chin, Frank; *Eat a Bowl of Tea*; *Fifth Chinese Daughter*; Identity crisis; Japanese American internment; Mass media stereotyping; Okada, John; World War II

Albany Cycle, The

AUTHOR: William Kennedy (1928-   )

FIRST PUBLISHED: *Legs*, 1975; *Billy Phelan's Greatest Game*, 1978; *Ironweed*, 1983; *Quinn's Book*, 1988; *Very Old Bones*, 1992; *The Flaming Corsage*, 1996

IDENTITIES: European American; family; Northeast

William Kennedy's Albany novels tell the saga of the Irish American Phelan, Quinn, and Daugherty families, and a sixth, *Legs*, deals with the Depression-era gangster Jack "Legs" Diamond. All share the upstate New York region, the city of Albany in particular, as their principal location and involve historical and fictional figures and events. The Albany cycle portrays events and characters during many decades, and the most influential characters and events are interwoven through several novels.

Legs, the first novel of the cycle to be published, stands outside the family saga and is the fictionalized story of Legs Diamond, a complex antihero who achieved mythic status among the urban working classes during the politically corrupt years of Prohibition. Its narrator, Marcus Gorman, is a decadent Albany lawyer who is fascinated with Diamond. Gorman befriends and legally defends Diamond, acting as the intelligent observer of societal norms and corrupt deviance from them. He appears as a minor character in the second novel, *Billy Phelan's Greatest Game*, which also involves the seamier side of Albany political life. Billy Phelan, the central character, is the abandoned son of the man who is the central character of Kennedy's breakthrough work, the Pulitzer Prize-winning *Ironweed*, which properly begins the saga of individual, family, and ethnic identity.

Francis Phelan is the guilt-ridden father who has abandoned his family in self-imposed isolation after having killed a scab worker in a labor fight and after having accidentally killed his infant son. Francis' twenty-two-year exile leads him through the nightmarish world of derelict alcoholics, where his suffering bespeaks the essential humanity of a man who recognizes and cannot forgive his transgressions. Francis' moral introspection extends to his Irish American youth, during which strained relations with his mother and sister led to his separation from his family. These troubles augur the tormented history of the entire Phelan clan.

Quinn's Book, set between 1849 and 1864, chronicles Irish emigration (resulting from famine) to post-Civil War Albany and the complex social milieu that evolves into the twentieth century setting for the Phelans, Quinns, and Daughertys. *Very Old Bones* traces the destructive matriarchal influence exerted on the Phelan family in response to a brutal murder committed out of sexual frustration. *The Flaming Corsage* weaves together motifs from the earlier novels in its depiction of the marital travails of a Phelan neighbor, Edward Daugherty, and his seductive wife Katrina, whose brief liaison with the youthful Francis resulted in the first of his exiles from his family.

SUGGESTED READINGS

Kennedy, William. *O Albany! Improbable City of Political Wizards, Fearless Ethnics, Spectacular Aristocrats, Splendid Nobodies and Underrated Scoundrels*. New York: Viking Press, 1983.

Reilly, Edward C. *William Kennedy*. Boston: Twayne, 1991.

Van Dover, J. K. *Understanding William Kennedy*. Columbia: University of South Carolina Press, 1991.

—*Robert J. Lysiak*

See also Alcoholism; American identity: Northeast; Catholicism; Erotic identity; Patriarchy and matriarchy; Urban life

Alcoholism

IDENTITIES: Disease

DEFINITION: Alcoholism is the psychological and physiological addiction to alcohol that eventually leads to dementia and death if left untreated.

Study of alcohol-related literary works may be enriched by an understanding of how alcohol dependence affects the creative process. In reading the work of an alcoholic writer, a perceptive reader will not only discover some of the more common truths about the human condition (which are implicit in the work of any good writer), but also learn about the pathology, the compulsions, and the fears that are such a part of the alcoholic perspective.

Psychological foundations of alcoholic writing

Most alcoholics are compulsive in protecting their delusions of power and in nurturing the fallacious image that they are emotionally stable. This may be the critical reason why so many writers are alcohol-dependent. For an addicted writer, the frustrations manifested in striving to overcome social barriers and behavioral limits are frequently projected and defused through the written word. Much of the poetry written by Allen Ginsberg, for example, has focused on the effects of self-mutilation, frustration, alcoholism, addiction, nonconformity, and poverty, and has done so in the interest of presenting a new image and a new medium of expression. A contemporary of Ginsberg, John Berryman, was deeply concerned with describing the texture and focus of alcoholic rebellion, denial, and social protest, most especially as they related to his own problems with alcohol and his difficulties staying in recovery. That same concern can also be found in certain poems written by Edwin Arlington Robinson. In "Mr. Flood's Party," Robinson describes the struggle and grandiosity of an intoxicated, lonely old man who fantasizes that he has been somehow endowed with tragic nobility. Another poem, "Miniver Cheevy," tells how the commonplace deflated Miniver's comforting illusion of history, with its facade of heroism, its pretentious nobility, and its art. Cheevy concludes that he was born in the wrong time, and so he relapses into self-pity, destroys his sensibilities with liquor, and allows himself the illusion that he might have been something other than a drunken failure. In the realm of fiction, John Cheever wrote a number of fascinating short stories on the effects of drunkenness, especially as it relates to the violation of social norms and relationships. Similarly, in *The Sun Also Rises* (1926), Ernest Hemingway presents an excellent and timely portrait of the drunkenness, aimlessness, and dissipation of his Parisian compatriots after World War I.

Alcoholic fantasies

For many writers, fantasy often includes what ought to happen rather than what does. Writing is an act of fantasy; a writer creates a perfectly compliant set of fictional actors and circumstances, a luxury in the world of fact. As the alcoholic writer tries to rewrite perceptions to suit prescriptions, the writer's vision of the human condition may become inflated far out of proportion. This act of transposition allows the writer to become a self-involved orchestrator of an extraordinary menagerie of fictional events. An occupational hazard of writing, then, is experience of one's fear of life's unmanageability. A writer may attempt to internalize that unmanageability by creating fictional contexts that comply with a writer's escapist perceptions. This trait is often pronounced in works by or about alcoholics. Ginsberg, Theodore Roethke, Hart Crane, Edna St. Vincent Millay, Robert Lowell, Delmore Schwartz, and a host of others have referred repeatedly to events in their own lives with a revisionist impulse that suggests an alcoholic perspective.

Sometimes the revision of an author's life in fiction takes the form of a qualified inventory or oblique confession, as is often the case with Crane and Millay. On the other hand, the alcoholic interest in control and re-creation takes quite a different and more inclusive turn in the case of Robinson, who fashioned an entire fictional community of misplaced and forgotten souls in his Tilbury Town. Berryman chose a somewhat more limited field of interest, but he also rearranged his psychological and poetic landscape by creating an alcoholic alter ego by the name of Henry.

Alcoholism
Twenty Key Works

1903	Samuel Butler's *The Way of All Flesh*.
1913	Jack London's *John Barleycorn*.
1925	F. Scott Fitzgerald's *The Great Gatsby*.
1929	Dorothy Parker's "Big Blonde."
1944	Charles Jackson's *The Lost Weekend*.
1945	Richard Wright's *Black Boy: A Record of Childhood and Youth*
1947	Tennessee Williams' *A Streetcar Named Desire*
1947	Malcolm Lowry's *Under the Volcano*.
1949	Nelson Algren's *The Man with the Golden Arm*.
1950	William Inge's *Come Back, Little Sheba*.
1956	Eugene O'Neill's *Long Day's Journey into Night*.

1962	*The Days of Wine and Roses*, a feature film with a screenplay by J. P. Miller.
1964	John Cheever's *The Wapshot Scandal*.
1974	Tillie Olsen's *Yonnondio: From the Thirties*.
1975	William Kennedy's *Legs*.
1976	John Berryman's *Recovery*.
1981	Raymond Carver's *What We Talk About When We Talk About Love*.
1983	*Ironweed*, by William Kennedy.
1983	W. P. Kinsella's *The Moccasin Telegraph and Other Indian Tales*.
1994	Alma Luz Villanueva's *Naked Ladies*.
1996	David Foster Wallace's *Infinite Jest*.

In fiction, almost all of Ernest Hemingway's novels and short stories are thinly veiled autobiographies. As the character Frederic Henry, he makes a connection with his boyhood sweetheart, Agnes Kurowsky, who served as the model for Catherine Barkley in *A Farewell to Arms* (1929), and his Parisian relationship to Lady Duff Twysden is revised and enhanced through the character of Lady Brett Ashley in *The Sun Also Rises* (1926). Hemingway's good friend F. Scott Fitzgerald was also a revisionist of sorts. Fitzgerald, who ultimately died of alcoholism, writes of fabulous drinking parties in mansions populated by beautiful people in novels such as *The Great Gatsby* (1925) and *Tender Is the Night* (1934). These beautiful people included a number of characters who were modeled after his wife, Zelda.

Alcoholic aggression and alcoholic spirituality

Many writers who have been concerned about alcoholism and alcohol abuse have created fictional demons of the darkest complexion imaginable to satisfy whatever addictions or appetites they wish to exorcise or nurture. Fear is the mainspring of the alcoholic's perception, and it is predicated on a deep sense of insecurity, unsatisfied needs and appetites, and an addiction to certain forms of overachievement. Thus, a writer may seek refuge from his fear of life's unmanageability through violence, melodrama, bathos, anger, social disorientation, and a remarkable—although paradoxical—fatalism. Malcolm Lowry, who was an alcoholic, writes of alcoholic fatalism and insanity and ritual exorcism in *Under the Volcano* (1947). The film *The Days of Wine and Roses* (1962, screenplay by J. P. Miller) is remarkably effective in portraying the utter devastation and despair that come with the final, terrible stages of the disease of alcoholism. In *John Barleycorn* (1913), a classic novel of alcoholic self-destruction, Jack London presents a terrifying autobiographical fiction of unrelenting pessimism, addiction, and morbidity. Finally, readers are reminded of the morbidity, the alcoholic and narcotic obsession, and the near insanity of Edgar Allan Poe, one of the most gifted of America's nineteenth century writers, and, apparently, an alcoholic.

In the dramatic realm, Tennessee Williams created an extraordinary menagerie of oddities and drunks in a number of his plays, although his most memorable creation may be the terrified and desperate Blanche DuBois of *A Streetcar Named Desire* (1947). Williams' contemporary Eugene O'Neill crowded his plays with a number of arrogant, controlling alcoholics. Much of O'Neill's work is intensely personal and derived from the scarring effects of his childhood. In any case, the more willful of his characters sometimes appear bent on alcoholic self-destruction. This is especially notable in the case of the Tyrone family in *Long Day's Journey into Night* (1956) and in the case of the bar patrons and the salesman, Hickey, in *The Iceman Cometh* (1946).

In considering the nature of alcoholic aggression, it should be noted that most alcoholic writers focus on a select group of destructive elements, which may serve as a catalyst for their spiritual frustration. As a rule, practicing alcoholics are likely to feel that they are invested with an extraordinary perspective on the connection between creativity and spirituality. In "Ave Maria," Crane writes of the utter loneliness of the spiritual pilgrim. Lowell has written a number of poems about melancholy Christian souls with a taste for alcohol. Concerned with drinking and drunkenness, Robinson frequently elevates each man who is alone to a tragic posture of titanic proportions. Berryman often describes his drinking problems in terms of catastrophic opposites and irreconcilable patterns that may only be resolved through some kind of grace.

Alcoholic intimacy

Regardless of whether they are writers, alcoholics are likely to remain alienated in their intimate relationships. Alcoholics are likely to devise a complicated host of strategies to reconcile their insatiable need for human companionship and for remaining social outcasts. The poet Alan Dugan has provided some hilarious perspectives on the alcoholic tendency to equate self-obsession and masochism with intimacy. On the other hand, for Ginsberg, Lowell, Dugan, Berryman, and e. e. cummings, one's connection to the physical, intimate, and procreative is, when the element of liquor is present, viewed as a stultifying and unrestrained compulsion to fulfill selfish needs.

From the perspective of an alcoholic writer, the power of romantic love lies in the tragic equation that love manifests. Love is a sedative for deep-seated fears, although it also amplifies them. Attraction leads to dependence and addiction; loving leads to the terrible possibility of betrayal and a loss of identity. The perverse nature of such a perspective is readily apparent. It discloses the distorted perspective of the alcoholic temperament, which confuses fear and dependence with love. Thus, Millay may insist that she will substitute kisses for thoughts, but her poetry suggests a fear of commitment; on the other hand, self-pity, loneliness, sexual betrayal, and withdrawal are integral to the definition of love forwarded by Berryman, cummings, Dugan, Lowell, and Roethke.

The creative impulse

Much alcoholic thinking and writing is fanciful and self-destructive in the extreme. Most writers hope for some measure of control exceeding the merely concrete and substantive. In pursuing that hope, however, they are likely to focus on a menagerie of lonely, self-involved characters who seem blithely unaware of the full extent of their own humanity. The very nature of these fictional creations suggests that the writers are likely to confuse alcoholic addiction, self-infatuation, and power-centeredness with personal fulfillment.

For many writers, then, life without alcohol is unnatural, flat, boring, and insipid. As Berryman writes in "Henry's Confession," nothing much happens in sobriety. In fact, this is the core and substance of the alcoholic viewpoint and perhaps the basic fuel of alcoholic creativity. An addicted writer may thus invest his art with a strenuous aesthetic that insists on meanings and actions that border on the extreme. As Lowell writes: "Is there no way to cast my hook/ Out of this dynamited brook?" ("The Drunken Fisherman"). For the controlling spiritual perfectionist, fishing in the stream of life is a rotten prospect because it is impossible to catch anything through will power or by trying harder—as he puts it, by dynamiting the brook. In fact, some writers are so pessimistic, so estranged from their emotions, and so deeply addicted to chemically induced feelings that they are incapable of sustained intimate and respectful relationships of any kind.

SUGGESTED READINGS

Alcoholics Anonymous. *Alcoholics Anonymous: The Story of How Many Thousands of Men and Women Have Recovered from Alcoholism.* 3d ed. New York: Alcoholics Anonymous World Services, 1976. Referred to as the Big Book, the basic text for recovery group Alcoholics Anonymous. Outlines the twelve steps to recovery, discusses methods for dealing with the recovering alcoholic, and provides testimonials of recovering alcoholics.

_____. *Twelve Steps and Twelve Traditions.* New York: Alcoholics Anonymous World Services, 1953. Companion work to the Big Book. Provides a detailed discussion of the twelve-step program and the twelve traditions.

Dardis, Tom. *The Thirsty Muse: Alcohol and the American Writer.* New York: Ticknor & Fields,

1989. Provides a psychological and a critical analysis of the relationship between alcoholism and creativity.

Gilmore, Thomas B. *Equivocal Spirits: Alcoholism and Drinking in Twentieth Century Literature*. Chapel Hill: University of North Carolina Press, 1987. A detailed examination of the work and alcoholic personality of a number of major authors.

Goodwin, Donald W. *Alcohol and the Writer*. Kansas City: Andrews and McMeel, 1988. Provides an excellent psychological foundation and general overview of the connection between alcoholism and creativity.

—*Matts G. Djos*

See also Addiction; Drugs; Identity crisis; Mental disorders; Twelve-step programs

Alegría, Ciro

Born: Sartimbamba, Peru; November 4, 1909
Died: Lima, Peru; February 17, 1967
Principal work: *El mundo es ancho y ajeno*, 1941 (*Broad and Alien Is the World*, 1941)
Identities: Latino; Native American
Significant achievement: Alegría's work supports human rights for the Peruvian indigenous population, using a realistic literary style known as *indigenismo*.

The son of wealthy landowners with strong ties to the national literary scene, Ciro Alegría received a classical education, emphasizing Peruvian history. He started writing for a student newspaper, but he left the university after his strong interest in local politics brought him fame as an activist. Although he continued to write newspaper articles, he soon became known as a novelist. His early novels won literary prizes in Chile. After the appearance in English of *Broad and Alien Is the World*, Alegría received recognition that led to his coming to the United States as a professor of literature.

Alegría is famous for being a fine observer of Latin American nature, the Peruvian landscape in particular, and for being a committed political writer and defender of the Latin American indigenous populations. He creates detailed descriptions of the mighty Peruvian Andes, which become a living background for ancient Inca customs. Alegría is not, however, a naturalist. His presentation of nature bears a political connotation. For him, life in the Andes illustrates the complex social structures among the native Peruvians and the Indians' political and economic plight. As their ancestors suffered repression during the Spanish Conquest, the indigenous people of Alegría's writing suffer at the hands of national political forces.

Alegría's nation's exclusion of indigenous life and thinking led him to help to organize a political party: the Acción Popular Revolucionaria Americana (American popular revolutionary action). This party's political platform called for guerrilla warfare, so Alegría was imprisoned in 1934. He suffered torture and was exiled to Chile. Further commitment to political causes is evident in his *La revolución cubana: Un testimonio personal* (1973; *The Cuban Revolution: A Personal Testimony*, 1973), written as an autobiographical journal based on his experiences in Cuba from 1953 to 1957.

Despite his activism, however, Alegría was foremost a novelist. Critics have associated his style with the Latin American trend of *indigenismo*, a realistic approach to indigenous characters and their plights as marginalized social groups. Unlike other *indigenista* writers, Alegría avoids the tendency to produce one-dimensional characters who exist to demonstrate a didactic point. Without heavy-handed symbolism, Alegría presents indigenous characters faced with crises. Alegría sees the rural native Peruvian as an Indian with a rich and ancient Incan identity and as a Peruvian citizen who struggles to survive in a world of rapid economic and technological changes.

Alegría's knowledge of ancient Peruvian philosophy is the center of his works. Alegría's main contribution to the *indigenista* movement is his offer of Incan religious views as a possible means for the country to overcome the existential malaise of modern life.

SUGGESTED READINGS

Early, Eileen. *Joy in Exile: Ciro Alegría's Narrative Art*. Washington, D.C.: University Press of America, 1980.

Gonzalez-Pérez, Armando. "Social Protest and Literary Merit in *Huasipungo* and *El mundo es ancho y ajeno*." *Revista Interamericana de Bibliografía/Inter American Review of Bibliography* 38 (1988): 329-338.

—Rafael Ocasio

See also Allende, Isabel; Caribbean American literature; Colonialism; Economics of identity; *One Hundred Years of Solitude*; Rural life

Alexander, Meena

BORN: Allahabad, India; February 17, 1951

PRINCIPAL WORKS: *Stone Roots*, 1980; *House of a Thousand Doors: Poems and Prose Pieces*, 1988; *Women in Romanticism: Mary Wollstonecraft, Dorothy Wordsworth, and Mary Shelley*, 1989; *Fault Lines: A Memoir*, 1993

IDENTITIES: South Asian; women

SIGNIFICANT ACHIEVEMENT: Alexander's work examines women in society from the perspective of an expatriate feminist.

Meena Alexander spent her early life in Kerala, a state at the southwestern tip of India. She received her English education in the Sudan, traveling between her parents' home in Africa and her grandparents' home in India. She received her bachelor's degree in 1969 from the University of Khartoum and a Ph.D. from the University of Nottingham in 1973. After teaching at universities in Delhi and Hyderabad, she moved to New York City in 1979. By the age of forty-four, she had published six volumes of poetry, a novel, a play, two volumes of literary criticism, and an autobiography.

Alexander describes herself as a "woman cracked by multiple migrations," acted on by the disparate and powerful influences of the languages and customs of the four continents on which she has lived. Although her works are written in English, she grew up speaking Malayalam, a Dravidian language of southwest India, and Arabic, the language of her Syrian Christian heritage, spoken in North Africa. Her writing reflects the tension created by the interplay of these influences and serves as a way to derive meaning from her wide range of experience.

The most prominent theme of Alexander's work is the difficulty inherent in being a woman, of having a woman's body and coping with the societal, physiological, and personal pressures on and responses to that body as it develops through childhood into maturity and middle age. Her grandmothers serve as mythical figures with whom Alexander closely identifies. Her perspective is further complicated by her alienation from the language and culture of her childhood, and by her need to recover something of that past. The images of fecundity and beauty with which Alexander's work is suffused derive from her youth in Kerala; these images may be juxtaposed with images of infirmity, sterility, or brutality, underscoring the writer's need to integrate the fragmented components of her life as an expatriate woman.

The imagination provides a synthesis of the elements of history and personality in Alexander's work. Her poems "begin as a disturbance, a jostling in the soul" which prompts her to write, seeking "that fortuitous, fleeting meaning, so precious, so scanty."

SUGGESTED READINGS

Dave, Shilpa. "The Doors to Home and History: Post-Colonial Identities in Meena Alexander and Bharati Mukherjee." *Amerasia Journal* 19 (Fall, 1993): 103.

Perry, John Oliver. Review of *Nampally Road*, by Meena Alexander. *World Literature Today* 65 (Spring, 1991): 364.

—Andrew B. Preslar

See also Asian American identity: India; Expatriate identity; Feminism

Alexie, Sherman

BORN: Spokane, Washington; October 7, 1966

PRINCIPAL WORKS: *The Business of Fancydancing: Stories and Poems*, 1992; *First Indian on the Moon*, 1993; *The Lone Ranger and Tonto Fistfight in Heaven*, 1993; *Old Shirts and New Skins*, 1993; *Reservation Blues*, 1995

IDENTITIES: Native American; Northwest

SIGNIFICANT ACHIEVEMENT: Alexie, an accomplished writer of poetry and fiction, is a spokesman for the realities of reservation life.

Sherman Alexie is a Spokane-Coeur d'Alene Indian who grew up in Wellpinit, Washington, on a reservation. He acknowledges that his origin and upbringing affect everything that he does in his writing and otherwise.

Alexie's father retired from the Bureau of Indian Affairs and his mother worked as a youth drug and alcohol counselor. The first of their five children to leave the reservation, Alexie attended Gonzaga University in Spokane for two years before entering Washington State University, where he studied creative writing with Alex Kuo. He was graduated in 1991.

Among the five books Alexie produced between 1992 and 1995, the seventy-seven-line free verse poem "Horses," from *Old Shirts and New Skins*, typifies the passion, anger, and pain in some of his most effective poems. Focused on the slaughter of a thousand Spokane horses by General George Wright in 1858, the long lines echo obsessively: "1,000 ponies, the United States Cavalry stole 1,000 ponies/ from the Spokane Indians, shot 1,000 ponies & only 1 survived." The poem is one of Alexie's favorites at readings, where it acquires the incantatory power of the best oral poetry.

Although Alexie's poems often have narrative and dramatic qualities, he is also adept at the short lyric, and his published work includes examples of the sestina and the villanelle. "Reservation Love Song," from *The Business of Fancydancing*, reflecting on the poverty of reservation life, with its government-built housing and low-quality food, begins:

> I can meet you
> in Springdale buy you beer
> & take you home
> in my one-eyed Ford.

First Indian on the Moon is largely composed of prose poems. "Collect Calls" opens with an allusion to Crazy Horse, who appears often as a mythic figure in Alexie's writing: "My name is *Crazy Horse*, maybe it's *Neil Armstrong* or *Lee Harvey Oswald*. I am guilty of every crime; I was the first man on the moon." As in his fiction, Alexie tempers the anger and pain of his poems with satiric wit, as in "The Marlon Brando Memorial Swimming Pool," from *Old Shirts and New Skins*, in which activist Dennis Banks is imagined as "the first/ Native American real estate agent, selling a 5,000 gallon capacity dream/ in the middle of a desert." Not surprisingly, there is no water in the pool.

SUGGESTED READINGS

Bellante, John, and Carl Bellante. "Sherman Alexie, Literary Rebel." *Bloomsbury Review* 14 (May-June, 1994): 14-15, 26.

Kincaid, James R. "Who Gets to Tell Their Stories?" *The New York Times Book Review*, May 3, 1992, 1, 24-29.

Price, Reynolds. "One Indian Doesn't Tell Another." *The New York Times Book Review*, October 17, 1993, 15-16.

Silko, Leslie Marmon. "Big Bingo." *Nation* 260 (June 12, 1995): 856-858, 860.

—*Ron McFarland*

See also *Lone Ranger and Tonto Fistfight in Heaven, The*; Native American identity; *Reservation Blues*

Algren, Nelson

BORN: Detroit, Michigan; March 28, 1909

DIED: Sag Harbor, New York; May 9, 1981

PRINCIPAL WORKS: *Somebody in Boots*, 1935; *Never Come Morning*, 1942; *The Neon Wilderness*, 1947; *The Man with the Golden Arm*, 1949; *A Walk on the Wild Side*, 1956; *The Last Carousel*, 1973; *The Devil's Stocking*, 1983

IDENTITIES: European American; Jewish; Midwest

SIGNIFICANT ACHIEVEMENT: Algren's novels and short stories depict the bitter consequences of poverty.

Nelson Algren (Nelson Ahlgren Abraham), of Swedish and German Jewish extraction, grew up in Chicago. Many of his writings, such as *The Man with the Golden Arm*, reflect the Polish neighborhoods of his childhood. Other works, however, such as his first novel, *Somebody in Boots*, and the later reworking, *A Walk on the Wild Side*, are based on his travels in the South and Southwest during the Depression years of the 1930's.

Algren's characters, whether in New Orleans, Chicago, or Calcutta, are marginal types living in subcultures that seem to be apart from the mainstream society. Carnival workers and migrant workers, pimps and prostitutes, drug pushers and addicts, gamblers and con men survive harsh environments only by exploiting one another. Algren met many of these people during his life. After being graduated from college in 1931 with a bachelor's in journalism, he hitchhiked and rode freight trains throughout the South and Southwest. Later, during World War II, Algren served as a private in the United States Army Field Artillery and toured Wales, Germany, and France. Algren also traveled extensively throughout the world during the 1960's.

Married in the summer of 1936, Algren worked as an editor for the Works Progress Administration's Illinois Writers' Project and during this time wrote short stories and poetry about the grueling

Nelson Algren put Chicago's mean streets at the center of his fiction.
(Library of Congress)

dance marathons of the 1930's and about prostitutes and brothels. Algren went into seclusion in 1940, possibly as a result of divorce and the death of his father. It was at this time that he wrote his first novel, *Somebody in Boots*.

During the 1940's, Algren received grants and published *The Man with the Golden Arm*. The novel was made into a film, one of the first to deal with drug addiction in a serious way. Algren, however, was unhappy with changes in plot and theme. Algren also became bitter over several critics' comments that his works were overwritten descriptions about colorful but flat characters. Other critics, however, have pointed out that Algren's style is lyrical prose based on jazz and that his characters represent victims in the quest for survival. Algren is said to have influenced the works of Hubert Selby, Jr., and John Rechy, who also have written about the harsh life of those who live at street level.

SUGGESTED READINGS

Cox, Martha Heasley, and Wayne Chatterton. *Nelson Algren*. Boston: Twayne, 1975.

Frohock, W. M. *The Novel of Violence in America*. Dallas: Southern Methodist University Press, 1957.

Giles, James R. *Confronting the Horror: The Novels of Nelson Algren*. Kent, Ohio: Kent State University Press, 1989.

—Helen O'Hara Connell

See also Poverty; Prostitution; Urban life

Alienation

DEFINITION: Alienation in literature expresses itself as a rejection of established social values and a consequent search for self-definition.

Thematic significance

As Alfred Kazin points out in *On Native Grounds* (1956), much twentieth century American literature "rests upon a tradition of enmity to the established order, more significantly a profound alienation from it." In its celebration of democracy and individualism, post-World War II American literature has consistently demonstrated its suspicion of and antagonism toward the established order. The theme of alienation is objectified in characters' emotional conflict as well as in their detestation of social establishments, which are not only oppressive in nature but also ethically ambiguous. Such experiences result from characters' having to deal with a reality that belies their true identity.

Alienation and identity

In contemporary American literature, there is a large group of characters whose attempt to define their relationship with society leads them to alienation from their true identity. From Arthur Miller's Willy Loman to the protagonist in Ralph Ellison's *Invisible Man* (1952), tragedy becomes ineluctable when characters believe that they do not have any other identity than the one that is imposed on them by society. The invisibility of the main character in *Invisible Man*, for example, is occasioned by society's prejudice, or in the narrator's words: a "matter of the construction of" people's inner "eyes, those eyes with which they look through their physical eyes upon reality," and by the character's lack of self-awareness. It takes the narrator almost twenty years to realize that he cannot expect other people to treat him as who he really is if he himself does not know who he really is.

Alienation and culture

The celebration of multiculturalism has brought the importance of reconnecting people with their ethnic and cultural roots to the fore. Many contemporary American writers, especially writers of color, have taken it as their responsibility to celebrate their ethnic cultural heritage and to reclaim their sense of history and identity by giving voice to where silence used to reign. In their works, characters' lack of self-awareness is frequently associated with their alienation from their culture. In Maxine Hong Kingston's *The Woman Warrior: Memoirs of a Girlhood Among Ghosts* the author portrays a group of characters who, in their attempts to assimilate into the mainstream of American society, have rendered their relationships with their own culture dubious. Woodrow, Roosevelt, Worldster, and Ed are first-generation Chinese immigrants who can barely speak English. Worldster has "a thick mustache" and tries "to look like Clark Gable"; Ed dresses "like Fred Astaire"; Ed and Woodrow once catch "sight of themselves in windows and hubcaps" on Fifth Avenue in New York City and think that they look "all the same American." Not accidentally, Woodrow, Roosevelt, and Worldster start their cultural transformation by trying to change their physical appearance; they complete the metamorphosis by closing Ed out of a Laundromat deal. In doing so, Woodrow, Roosevelt, and Worldster have betrayed a traditional Chinese ethical code, which has been repeatedly chanted by Ed, the dupe in the money game: Friends are "fairer than brothers."

Because of the restrictive and sometimes oppressive role society often plays in relation to individuals, many contemporary American writers believe that society works against democracy and individualism. Ellison once posited that "all literature is about minority; the individual is a minority." In T. S. Eliot's narrative poem, "The Love Song of J. Alfred Prufrock," the poet creates a very complicated character. Prufrock is very perceptive; he is aware of what his problems are but refuses to face them. His ambivalent relationship with society reveals his vulnerability as a human being. Prufrock, a white, well-educated man, is still a minority of one.

Alienation and society

Alienation has demonstrated its recurrent power in literature. Whether alienation results from characters' estrangement from their true selves, or from their cultural heritage, or from society, the thematic concern has been used successfully by many contemporary American writers to study the relationship between an individual's true and false identities, between assimilation and cultural heritage, and between the individual and society. For some characters, the feeling of alienation is brief. For others, tragedy becomes ineluctable when they fail to reconcile who they are with who they are meant to be.

SUGGESTED READINGS

Chase, Richard. *The American Novel and Its Tradition*. Garden City, N.Y.: Doubleday, 1957.

Cowley, Malcolm. *A Second Flowering*. New York: Viking, 1973.

Fiedler, Leslie A. *Love and Death in the American Novel*. New York: Delta, 1966.

Graff, Gerald. *Literature Against Itself*. Chicago: The University of Chicago Press, 1979.

Hoffman, Frederick J. *The Modern Novel in America*. Chicago: Henry Regnery, 1951.

Kazin, Alfred. *On Native Grounds*. Garden City, N.Y.: Doubleday, 1956.

Leary, Lewis. *Criticism*. New York: Holt, Rinehart and Winston, 1971.

Ruland, Richard. *The Rediscovery of American Literature*. Cambridge, Mass.: Harvard University Press, 1967.

—*Qun Wang*

See also Acculturation; American Dream; Identity crisis; *Invisible Man*; *Woman Warrior, The*

All God's Children Need Traveling Shoes

AUTHOR: Maya Angelou (Marguerite Johnson, 1928-   )
FIRST PUBLISHED: 1986
IDENTITIES: African American; women

All God's Children Need Traveling Shoes belongs to a series of autobiographical narratives tracing Maya Angelou's personal search for identity as an African American woman. In this powerful tale, Angelou describes her emotional journey to find identity and ancestral roots in West Africa. Angelou reveals her excitement as she emigrates to Ghana in 1962 and attempts to redefine herself as African, not American. Her loyalty to Ghana's founding president, Kwame Nkrumah, reflects hope in Africa's and her own independence. She learns the Fanti language, toys with thoughts of marrying a prosperous Malian Muslim, communes with Ghanaians in small towns and rural areas, and identifies with her enslaved forebears. Monuments such as Cape Coast Castle, where captured slaves were imprisoned before sailing to America, stand on African soil as vivid reminders of an African American slave past.

In Ghana Angelou hopes to escape the lingering pains of American slavery and racism. Gradually, however, she feels displaced and uncomfortable in her African environment. Cultural differences and competition for employment result in unpleasant encounters between Ghanians and African Americans. Despite such frustrations, Angelou's network of fellow African American emigrants offers mutual support and continuing hope in the African experience. A visit by Malcolm X provides much needed encouragement, but his presence is also a reminder of ties with the United States. Angelou and her African American friends express their solidarity with the American Civil Rights movement by demonstrating at the United States embassy in Ghana.

As she sorts through her ambivalent feelings about Africa, Angelou also rethinks her role as mother. At the beginning of *All God's Children Need Traveling Shoes*, Angelou's son Guy almost dies in an automobile accident. Later in the narrative he develops a relationship with an older woman and struggles to gain admittance to the University of Ghana. In dealing with all these events, Angelou learns to balance her maternal feelings with her son's need for independence and self-expression. Finally recognizing the powerful ties binding her to American soil, Angelou concludes her narrative with a joyful journey home from Ghana and a renewed sense of identity as an African American.

SUGGESTED READINGS

Kallen, Stuart A. *Maya Angelou: Woman of Words, Deeds, and Dreams*. Edina, Minn.: Abdo and Daughters, 1993.

McPherson, Dolly A. *Order Out of Chaos*. London: Virago, 1990.

Shapiro, Miles. *Maya Angelou*. New York: Chelsea House, 1994.

Shuker, Nancy. *Maya Angelou*. Morristown, N.J.: Silver Burdett, 1990.

—Thomas J. Sienkewicz

See also African American identity; Angelou, Maya; Angelou, Maya, poetry of; Civil Rights movement; Emigration and immigration; Expatriate identity; *I Know Why the Caged Bird Sings*; Identity crisis; Racism and ethnocentrism

All Rivers Run to the Sea: Memoir

AUTHOR: Elie Wiesel (1928-   )
FIRST PUBLISHED: *Tous les fleuves vont à la mer: Mémoires*, 1994 (English translation, 1995)
IDENTITIES: Family; Jewish

Taking the title of his autobiography from Ecclesiastes, Elie Wiesel presents the important people and events of his life, beginning with his childhood in Sighet, Romania, and culminating in his 1969 marriage in Jerusalem. Wiesel, through stories and remembrances, tells of a family full of piety, moral courage, and selfless devotion to Judaism. From his mother and grandmother, Elie learned goodness and love; from his grandfather, the Jewish legends he would later use in fiction and essays; from his father, rectitude and altruism. His teachers, at various times of his life, inculcated in him a reverence for learning, an exactness in biblical or philosophical discourse, and above all the joy, sadness, and truth of the old masters.

World War II and the persecution of the Jews destroyed Wiesel's idyllic world forever. He and his family were taken to Auschwitz. He later was transferred to Buchenwald. Unable to understand German cruelty, angry at those who did not intervene on the victims' behalf, angry too at God for letting it happen, Wiesel emerged alive after terrible trials. At age seventeen he was endowed with a special knowledge of life and death.

Shortly after his liberation from Buchenwald he went to France, where he eventually enrolled at the university, enduring hardship and contemplating suicide. Saved by Zionist fervor, he worked as a journalist for an Israeli newspaper in Paris. A crucial meeting with novelist François Mauriac in 1955 was to decide his literary career: Mauriac encouraged him to break his self-imposed silence about his experience in concentration camps and found a publisher for Wiesel's first novel, *La Nuit* (1958; *Night*, 1960), to which he contributed the foreword.

After Wiesel moved to New York to become his newspaper's American correspondent, he soon applied for U.S. citizenship. In a series of amusing anecdotes he describes his life in a Jewish

American milieu. He also tells of his relations with his French publishers and of his meeting with Marion, his future wife and translator. More moving and bittersweet are his return to his native town, where relatives and friends have disappeared and only the ghosts of his youth remain; his personal and literary campaign for Russian Jewry; the fear caused by the Six-Day War of 1967, since it could have meant the end of Israel and the Jewish dream; and his prayer of thanksgiving at the newly liberated Wailing Wall.

Throughout, a celebration of life and of the great Hasidic teachers and thinkers as well as a moral and ethical strength permeates Wiesel's conduct and writings over his first forty years. In memorializing his relatives and friends and in bearing witness to their passing, he leaves his own mark behind.

SUGGESTED READINGS

Berenbaum, Michael. *The Vision of the Void: Theological Reflections on the Works of Elie Wiesel.* Middletown, Conn.: Wesleyan University Press, 1979.

Roth, John K. *A Consuming Fire: Encounters with Elie Wiesel and the Holocaust.* Atlanta: John Knox Press, 1979.

Stern, Ellen N. *Elie Wiesel: Witness for Life.* New York: Ktav Publishing House, 1982.

—Pierre L. Horn

See also Anti-Semitism; Holocaust; *Night*; Religion and identity; Wiesel, Elie

All the King's Men

AUTHOR: Robert Penn Warren (1905-1989)

FIRST PUBLISHED: 1946

IDENTITIES: European American; South

All the King's Men charts the rise of Willie Stark, a populist political boss based on Huey Long, the Louisiana governor and U.S. senator who was assassinated in 1935. The novel's real subject, however, is not politics, but the influence of history on personal identity. For Robert Penn Warren, history is the burden of guilt and responsibility that all must bear. The acceptance of guilt and responsibility allows Warren's characters to know themselves and to take their places in society, while their attempts to assert their innocence and freedom lead only to isolation and a sense that the universe is meaningless.

The real focus of *All the King's Men* is not on Stark, but on the narrator, Jack Burden. When the novel opens, Burden is estranged from everyone who has been important to him and uncertain of his role in the world. Having abandoned graduate study in history and a career as a journalist, he works as one of Stark's henchmen. When ordered to look into the past of Judge Irwin, a longtime friend of Burden's family, and find something with which Stark can blackmail him, Jack begins an exploration of his own past.

As Burden searches for the flaw in Irwin, he becomes freshly involved in the lives of his childhood friends—Adam Stanton, now a surgeon, and his sister Anne, who was Jack's first love—and brings them in contact with Stark. Burden is appalled when Anne becomes Stark's mistress, for he has cherished the memory of Anne's youthful innocence, which he now feels he has helped destroy. He drives off alone, trying to free himself from the past, and comes to think of himself as alone in a meaningless world, much like the one described by the existentialists. He returns, however, to face responsibilities deeper than those of self-examination. When Irwin, refusing to be blackmailed, kills himself, Burden's mother reveals that the judge was Jack's true father. Adam, enraged that Stark may have put him in charge of a hospital as a kind of pimp's fee, kills Stark and is shot down himself. In response to his part in these disasters, Burden does not try to escape responsibility. Rather, he embraces it, marrying Anne, caring for the man he has thought of as his father, and returning to finish the biography of an ancestor. Accepting his part of the guilt for all that has happened, Burden finds his place in the world, as well as his own identity.

SUGGESTED READINGS

Casper, Leonard. *Robert Penn Warren: The Dark and Bloody Ground.* Seattle: University of Washington Press, 1960.

Feldman, Robert. "Responsibility in Crisis: Jack Burden's Struggle in *All the King's Men.*" In *"To Love So Well the World": A Festschrift in Honor of Robert Penn Warren*, compiled by Dennis L. Weeks. New York: Peter Lang, 1992.

Mizener, Arthur. "Robert Penn Warren: *All the King's Men.*" *The Southern Review* 3, no. 4 (Autumn, 1967): 874-894.

—*Brian Abel Ragen*

See also American identity: South; Existentialism; Religion and identity

Allen, Paula Gunn

BORN: Cubero, New Mexico; October 24, 1939

PRINCIPAL WORKS: *The Blind Lion*, 1974; *Coyote's Daylight Trip*, 1978; *A Cannon Between My Knees*, 1981; *Star Child*, 1981; *Shadow Country*, 1982; *The Woman Who Owned the Shadows*, 1983; *Studies in American Indian Literature*, 1983; *The Sacred Hoop: Recovering the Feminine in American Indian Traditions*, 1986; *Wyrds*, 1987; *Skin and Bones: Poems 1979-87*, 1988; *Spider Woman's Granddaughters: Traditional Tales and Contemporary Writing by Native American Women*, 1989 (editor)

IDENTITIES: Family; gay, lesbian, and bisexual; Native American; women

SIGNIFICANT ACHIEVEMENT: As a novelist, poet, literary critic, and scholar, Allen preserves and creates Native American literature.

Paula Gunn Allen, as an American Indian woman, sees her identity in relation to a larger community. She is proud to be part of an old and honored tradition that appreciates the beautiful, the harmonious, and the spiritual. She also recognizes that since in the United States there are more than a million non-Indians to every Indian, she must work to stay connected to her Native American heritage.

Allen frequently refers to herself as "a multicultural event"; people of many ethnicities are related to her. Her mother was a Laguna Indian whose grandfather was Scottish American. Allen says that she was raised Roman Catholic, but living next door were her grandmother, who was Presbyterian and Indian and her grandfather, who was a German Jew. Her father's family came from Lebanon; he was born in a Mexican land-grant village north of Laguna Pueblo. She grew up with relatives who spoke Arabic, English, Laguna, German, and Spanish. Her relatives shared legends from around the world.

Even with such cultural diversity in her family, as a teenager Allen could find no Native American models for her writing. Consequently, she read Charlotte Brontë's *Jane Eyre: An Autobiography* (1847) about twenty times; her other literary favorites were Louisa May Alcott, Gertrude Stein, and the Romantic poets John Keats and Percy Bysshe Shelley. When she went to the University of New Mexico and wanted to focus on Native American literature in her Ph.D. program in English, it was impossible. The scholarship was not there to study. She came to write the books that she wanted to read and teach the courses that she wanted to take.

Allen has taught at San Francisco State University, at the University of New Mexico, in the Native American Studies Program at the University of California at Berkeley, and at the University of California, Los Angeles.

In enumerating the influences that have made her who she is, Allen first honors her mother, who taught her to think like a strong Indian woman and that animals, insects, and plants are to be treated with the deep respect one customarily reserves for high-status humans. She honors her father for teaching her how to weave magic, memory, and observation into the tales she tells. Finally, the Indian collective unconscious remains the source of her vision of spiritual reality.

SUGGESTED READINGS

Chapman, Abraham. *Literature of the American Indians: Views and Interpretations*. New York: New American Library, 1975.

Coltelli, Laura. *Winged Words: American Indian Writers Speak*. Lincoln: University of Nebraska Press, 1990.

Fisher, Dexter, ed. *The Third Woman: Minority Women Writers of the United States*. Boston: Houghton Mifflin, 1980.

Hanson, Elizabeth I. *Paula Gunn Allen*. Boise State University Western Writers Series 96. Boise, Idaho: Boise State University Press, 1990.

—*Constance M. Fulmer*

See also Erdrich, Louise; Lesbian identity; Native American identity; *Sacred Hoop, The*; *Spider Woman's Granddaughters*

Allende, Isabel

BORN: Lima, Peru; August 2, 1942

PRINCIPAL WORKS: *La casa de los espíritus*, 1982 (*The House of the Spirits*, 1985); *De amor y de sombra*, 1984 (*Of Love and Shadows*, 1987); *Eva Luna*, 1987 (English translation, 1988); *El plan infinito*, 1991 (*The Infinite Plan*, 1993); *Paula*, 1995

IDENTITIES: Latino; women; world

SIGNIFICANT ACHIEVEMENT: Allende brings a feminist perspective to the traditions of Latin American literature.

The daughter of a Chilean diplomat, Isabel Allende was born in Lima, Peru. Following her parents' divorce, she lived first with her grandparents in Santiago and later with her mother and stepfather in Europe and the Middle East. She returned to Chile as a young woman and began her career as a television and newsreel journalist and as a writer for a feminist journal.

In 1973, Allende found herself at the center of Chile's turbulent political life when her uncle and godfather, the country's Marxist president Salvador Allende, was assassinated during a military coup. In the months that followed, Allende worked to oppose the new dictatorship headed by General Pinochet until fears for her safety led Allende to move to Venezuela with her husband and two children.

Allende's first novel, *The House of the Spirits*, was published to international acclaim. It is a family saga set against a backdrop of political upheaval in an unnamed South American country. Her second book, *Of Love and Shadows*, followed two years later and also drew on her country's troubled history. Both works placed Allende firmly within the Latin American tradition of novels that take a strong stand in their fictionalized portrayals of political events. Allende's third novel, *Eva Luna*, traces the extraordinary life of its title character and the Austrian journalist who becomes her lover. All three novels are examples of the literary style known as Magical Realism, in which strange, supernatural occurrences are intermingled with everyday events. Allende's work, however, brings a distinctly feminist perspective to a literary style that is predominantly male.

Following her divorce from her husband of twenty years, Allende moved to the United States in the 1980's, where she remarried and settled in California. Her next novel, *The Infinite Plan*, draws on her American experience in its story of a man's life from his childhood in the barrios of Los Angeles to his adult search for meaning and happiness. In 1995, Allende published one of her most personal works, *Paula*, a chronicle of her daughter's death following a long illness. Allende examines her experience as a woman and a mother in her portrayal of love, pain, and loss.

Allende's position as a woman working within the traditions of Latin American literature has led her to create strikingly original stories and characters, and she remains a consistently intriguing and rewarding writer.

SUGGESTED READINGS

Allende, Isabel. "Writing As an Act of Hope." In *The Art and Craft of the Political Novel*, edited by William Zinsser. Boston: Houghton Mifflin, 1989.

Foster, David William, ed. *Handbook of Latin American Literature*. New York: Garland, 1987.

Meyer, Doris, and Margarite Fernandez Olmos, eds. *Contemporary Women Authors of Latin America*. New York: Brooklyn College Press, 1983.

—Janet E. Lorenz

See also Feminism; *House of the Spirits, The*; *Infinite Plan, The*; Latino American identity

Along This Way

AUTHOR: James Weldon Johnson (1871-1938)
FIRST PUBLISHED: 1933
IDENTITIES: African American

James Weldon Johnson claimed that one of the reasons for publishing his autobiography, *Along This Way*, was to finally make clear that his novel *The Autobiography of an Ex-Coloured Man* (1912) was not a record of his life. A public figure as important as Johnson hardly needed, however, a justification for adding another book to the growing shelf of autobiographies of distinguished African Americans, such as Frederick Douglass, Booker T. Washington, and W. E. B. Du Bois. In a controlled and often ironic narrative tone, Johnson not only provides insights into his life and times but also focuses on African American accomplishments in the hostile social climate that he battled against all his life.

Despite a middle-class upbringing, a university degree, and immediate success first as a school principal, in passing the Florida bar examination—the first African American to do so—and then as songwriter, writer, consul, and civil rights activist, Johnson always committed himself to the cause of African Americans. When on university vacation, he spent three months teaching African American farmers' children in rural Georgia, realizing "that they were me, and I was they; that a force stronger than blood made us one." Accordingly, all his artistic work was committed to improving the social situation of African Americans and to exploring African American art forms. When embarking on his composing and songwriting career, he "began to grope toward a realization of the American Negro's cultural background and his creative folk-art." In much of his poetry, too, Johnson built on African American folk traditions. He did so because he believed in the uniqueness of the African American heritage, based as it was on a deep spirituality. Thus, he implies that African Americans are a main resource for the United States in matters of artistry and spirituality, and that, in turn, the United States will be measured by how it treats African Americans. He pithily summarizes this belief in saying "that in large measure the race question involves the saving of black America's body and white America's soul."

A considerable part of the book is devoted to Johnson's fight for racial justice and his time in the leadership of the National Association for the Advancement of Colored People. Johnson reveals explicitly that his program for improving the social status of African Americans, despite his own artistic, legal, and political efforts, is really a moral one: "The only kind of revolution that would have an immediately significant effect on the American Negro's status would be a moral revolution." As *Along This Way* makes clear, Johnson did his best on all fronts.

SUGGESTED READINGS

Butterfield, Stephen. *Black Autobiography in America*. Amherst: University of Massachusetts Press, 1974.

Fleming, Robert E. *James Weldon Johnson*. Boston: Twayne, 1987.

Levy, Eugene. *James Weldon Johnson: Black Leader, Black Voice*. Chicago: University of Chicago Press, 1973.

—Martin Japtok

See also American identity: South; Harlem Renaissance; Johnson, James Weldon

Alther, Lisa

BORN: Kingsport, Tennessee; July 23, 1944

PRINCIPAL WORKS: *Kinflicks*, 1975; *Original Sins*, 1981; *Other Women*, 1984; *Bedrock*, 1990; *Five Minutes in Heaven*, 1995

IDENTITIES: European American; family; gay, lesbian, and bisexual

SIGNIFICANT ACHIEVEMENT: Alther's novels depict the efforts of contemporary women to find sexual identities and to escape dysfunctional families.

The female characters at the center of Lisa Alther's fictions have similar experiences. They come from families that are nonsupportive and are dominated by parents with unrealistic expectations for their children. The heroines grow up with the assumption that heterosexuality is the only kind of sex. At some point in the protagonists' lives they find fulfillment with other women and realize that they are either lesbian or bisexual.

Several of these characters are married and have children. The marriages of these characters break up. At some point in their lives, the characters have what can be called an identity crisis. This may be the result of a conscious or subconscious recognition that they seem to bring death to those close to them, or it may be a result of a perception that they would be more secure in a marital relationship. The characters may try suicide before deciding that life is better than the alternative. The characters may try psychotherapy, with positive results.

The theme of Alther's fiction is the difficulty of finding permanent satisfaction in a lesbian relationship. This is to some extent the result of societal disapproval of such relationships, but it often seems to result from an inherent failing within the relationships. Only in *Bedrock*, in which two women who have been friends for many years embark on an affair in their forties, is there a novel with a lesbian pairing that does not end badly.

Alther's handling of what could be depressing material is, in most of these novels, delicate and humorous. Especially in *Kinflicks* and *Bedrock* the problems of the characters are lightened by humor. Such matters as adolescence and mishandled suicide attempts become, in Alther's prose, funny. Even in the darker world of *Other Women* there are flashes of amusement. The novels deal realistically with serious problems, but the telling of the stories of these characters is less grim than it could be.

SUGGESTED READINGS

Ferguson, Mary Anne. "Lisa Alther." In *Contemporary Fiction Writers of the South: A Bio-Bibliographical Sourcebook*, edited by Joseph W. Flora and Robert Bain. Westport, Conn.: Greenwood Press, 1993.

_____. "Lisa Alther: The Irony of Return." *The Southern Quarterly* 20 (Summer, 1983): 103-115.

Kawada, Louise. "Liberating Laughter: Comedic Form in Some Lesbian Novels." In *Sexual Practice, Textual Theory*, edited by Susan J. Wolfe. New York: Basil Blackwell, 1993.

Peel, Ellen. "Subject, Object, and the Alternation of First- and Third-Person Narration in Novels by Alther, Atwood, and Drabble." *Critique* 16 (Spring, 1989): 107-122.

—*John M. Muste*

See also American identity: South; Bisexual identity; Feminism; *Kinflicks*; Lesbian identity; *Other Women*

Alvarez, Julia

BORN: New York, New York; March 27, 1950

PRINCIPAL WORKS: *Homecoming: Poems*, 1984; *How the García Girls Lost Their Accents*, 1991; *In the Time of the Butterflies*, 1994; *The Other Side-El Otro Lado*, 1995

IDENTITIES: Latino; women

Julia Alvarez's works make funny and poignant examination of the acculturation issue.

SIGNIFICANT ACHIEVEMENT: Alvarez expresses the complexities of being cross cultural and an immigrant to the United States.

Although she was born in New York City, Julia Alvarez spent much of her childhood in the Dominican Republic. Her parents were from the island. Her mother came from a well-positioned and wealthy family, but her father was rather poor. The family's divided economic position was tied to political problems within the Dominican Republic. Her father's family, which once was wealthy, supported the wrong side during the revolution and her mother's family benefited by supporting those who gained power. Julia's family, although poorer than most of their relatives, enjoyed a privileged position in the Dominican Republic.

Although she was raised in the Dominican Republic, Alvarez describes her childhood as "an American childhood." Her extended family's power, influence, American connections, and wealth led to Alvarez's enjoying many of the luxuries of America, including American food, clothes, and friends. When Alvarez's father became involved with the forces attempting to oust the dictator of the Dominican Republic, Rafaél Leonidas Trujillo Molina, the secret police began monitoring his activity. Immediately before he was to be arrested in 1960, the family escaped to America with the help of an American agent. In an article appearing in *American Scholar* ("Growing Up American in the Dominican Republic") published in 1987, Alvarez notes that all her life she had wanted to be a true American girl. She thought, in 1960, that she was going to live in her homeland, America.

Living in America was not quite what Alvarez expected. As her fictional but partly autobiographical novel *How the García Girls Lost Their Accents* (Alvarez) hints, Alvarez was faced with many adjustments in America. She experienced homesickness, alienation, and prejudice. Going from living on a large family compound to living in a small New York apartment was, in itself, quite an adjustment. Alvarez's feeling of loss when moving to America caused a change in her. She became introverted, began to read avidly, and eventually began writing.

Alvarez attended college, earning degrees in literature and writing. She took a position as an English professor at Middlebury College in Vermont. She has published several collections of poetry, but her best-known work is her semiautobiographical novel *How the García Girls Lost Their Accents*. Alvarez can be praised for her portrayal of bicultural experiences, particularly for her focusing on the women's issues that arise out of such an experience.

SUGGESTED READING

Garcia-Johnson, Ronie-Richele. "Julía Alvarez." In *Notable Hispanic American Women*, edited by Diane Telgen and Jim Kamp. Detroit: Gale Research, 1993.

—Angela Athy

See also Acculturation; Bilingualism; Emigration and immigration; Feminism; *How the García Girls Lost Their Accents*; Latino American identity

Always Running: La Vida Loca, Gang Days in L.A.

AUTHOR: Luis J. Rodríguez (1954-   )
FIRST PUBLISHED: 1993
IDENTITIES: Adolescence and coming-of-age; family; Latino

Luis J. Rodríguez began writing *Always Running* as a sixteen-year-old gang member in East

Los Angeles, but he did not complete it until his own son, Ramiro, joined a similar street gang in Chicago at age fifteen. Rodríguez's description of *la vida loca* (the crazy life) is a testament to his difficult adolescence in a poor barrio, a memorial to friends of days and times long dead or lost, and an attempt to communicate with his son and save him from a fate that Rodríguez himself narrowly escaped.

As have many children of Spanish-speaking background, Rodríguez began school at a disadvantage, unable to speak English. "In those days there was no way to integrate the non-English-speaking children. So they just made it a crime to speak anything but English. If a Spanish word sneaked out . . . kids were often sent to the office to get swatted or to get detention. Teachers complained that maybe the children were saying bad things about them." Rodríguez thus entered mainstream culture as a social outcast, uncomfortable in the English of the dominant culture, and made uncomfortable in his native language.

Rodríguez had his first skirmish with the police at ten, after climbing a school fence to play basketball after hours. "We were constant prey," writes Rodríguez. He and his friends were pursued by the police, known to be racist and violent toward minorities, pursued by gangs, by junkies, by older white adolescents, even by teachers who seemed to hate Mexicans. "We were always afraid. Always running."

Rodríguez dropped out of school and became deeply involved with gangs and drugs, seeking his identity in relationships with cronies who shared his poverty. Thrown out of the house, he lived in the garage, edging closer and closer to the destruction by drugs or violence that claimed the lives of his friends. Then, in 1970, Luis meets Chente Ramírez at one of the community centers created in response to the escalation of violence. A university-educated Chicano, Chente introduced Luis to political activism and Chicano pride. Luis returned to high school, where he too led political actions. He became the first non-Anglo to serve as mascot to the school football team, the Aztecs. He was graduated and briefly attended college. It was only by leaving his hometown, however, that he escaped the nefarious influence of gangs.

Rodríguez closes his memoir with a reflection on the Los Angeles riots of 1992 and the place of gangs, which thrive in the absence of solid education, "social recreation," and jobs. A former gang member, Rodríguez redefines himself as a journalist, poet, and peacemaker. *Always Running* is his attempt to save his son Ramiro and all the other Ramiros.

SUGGESTED READINGS

Publishers Weekly. Review of *Always Running: La Vida Loca, Gang Days in L.A.*, by Luis J. Rodríguez. 240, no. 5 (February 1, 1993): 86.

Soto, Gary. Review of *Always Running: La Vida Loca, Gang Days in L.A.*, by Luis J. Rodríguez. *The New York Times Book Review*, February 14, 1993, 26.

—Linda Ledford-Miller

See also Chicano identity

Ambassadors, The

AUTHOR: Henry James (1843-1916)
FIRST PUBLISHED: 1903
IDENTITIES: European American; family; world

Chad Newsome of Woolett, Massachusetts, is in Europe, where he has gone for an extended stay. He has become entangled romantically with a Parisian woman. Chad views himself as a freewheeling man-about-town. His mother views his identity in another way. She thinks he should come home, marry well, enter the family business, and become responsible.

To achieve this end, Mrs. Newsome dispatches her ambassador, Lambert Strether, a fifty-five-year-old widower, a writer who is her protégé and fiancé, to Paris to rescue Chad. Strether never liked Chad, but on meeting him in Paris, he is struck by Chad's improvement. Mme de Vionnet captivates Strether, who assumes that Chad's interest is in her daughter, who is approximately Chad's age.

This illusion is shattered when the daughter marries. When Strether meets Chad and Mme de Vionnet, who is separated but not divorced from her husband, in the south of France, it becomes clear that the older woman is Chad's mistress. Strether begins to feel sympathy for the two, believing that Chad has a moral responsibility to Mme de Vionnet.

Meanwhile, Mrs. Newsome, growing impatient, has dispatched four additional ambassadors to Paris with a mandate to bring Chad home. Among them is Mamie Pocock, whom the Newsomes presume Chad will marry. The arrival of this quartet from Woolett throws into striking contrast the manners and morals of Paris against those of Massachusetts. To Strether, continental identity is far more appealing than Woolett's. He has been enticed into Chad's camp simply by observing how living in Paris and having Mme de Vionnet in his life have enhanced Chad's personality. Chad's married sister, Sarah, who is among the newly arrived ambassadors, shuns Mme de Vionnet's attempts to establish a relationship. Sarah considers the changes that have taken place in Chad outrageous.

Under pressure to return home, Chad, still infatuated by Mme de Vionnet, is weak and indecisive, thereby humiliating his mistress. She offers her affection to Strether, who summarily but gently rejects it.

It appears that Chad will do his mother's bidding and return to the deadening routine of helping run the family business. It is Strether, finally successful as an ambassador, who is forever changed by his ambassadorship. He has experienced two national identities, much as Henry James did early in his life, and is destined to hover between them for the rest of his days.

The Ambassadors is about identity, comparing that of the innocent American and the worldly European. It is also about the identity of the solid family member and the freewheeling individual. Strether, Chad, and Mme de Vionnet suffer and learn as a result of the conflicts that arise between these two groups of identities.

SUGGESTED READINGS

Griffin, Susan M. "The Selfish Eye: Strether's Principles of Psychology." In *On Henry James: The Best from American Literature*, edited by Louis J. Budd and Edwin H. Cady. Durham, N.C.: Duke University Press, 1990.

Hocks, Richard A. *Henry James and Pragmatistic Thought*. Chapel Hill: University of North Carolina Press, 1974.

McElderry, Bruce R., Jr. *Henry James*. New York: Twayne, 1965.

Yeazell, Ruth Bernard. *Language and Knowledge in the Late Novels of Henry James*. Chicago: University of Chicago Press, 1976.

—*R. Baird Shuman*

See also American identity: Northeast; *Bostonians, The*; Expatriate identity; James, Henry

American Dream

DEFINITION: The American Dream—belief in the ideal of freedom, individualism, and equal opportunity for all, as well as its nightmarish dark side—has pervaded American literature from its inception.

It has been said that the United States is the only nation that prides itself on having a national dream and that gives its name to one. Initial dreams about America were imports from Europe, where Renaissance writers dreamed of a utopia in the New World. Perhaps, as some have insisted, there is no such thing as the American Dream, only a diversity of dreams about America and dreams in America. Whether one calls it extravagant expectation, faith in entrepreneurial success, or confidence in the American cornucopia, the American Dream is an inherent part of social, cultural, political, and literary America.

Background   Perhaps the first and clearest verbalization of the American Dream, written long before the phrase was coined, is Thomas Jefferson's statement from the Declaration of Independence: "We hold these truths to be self-evident, that all men are created equal, that they are endowed by their

Creator with certain unalienable rights, that among these are Life, Liberty, and the pursuit of Happiness." This statement, and the American Dream itself, are highly romantic, implying belief in the goodness of nature and rejecting belief in human nature's being tainted. Because of this seemingly anti-Calvinistic, even anti-Christian, strain, it has been argued that the American Dream is a product of the frontier and the West (or of Rousseauian romanticism) rather than of Puritan New England.

Some trace the American Dream to the early settlement of the country, often to 1630, the date of John Winthrop's *A Model of Christian Charity*, best known for its description of the colony as "a City upon a Hill" with the eyes of all people upon it. Part of the American Dream is America being a shining example to the rest of the world. The American Dream, to the Puritans, was divine election, freedom to worship God as they chose, and the blessings of the sovereign God upon their errand into the wilderness.

The essence of the American Dream in the colonial period was "the Blessings of Liberty to ourselves and our Posterity," a phrase from the Preamble to the U.S. Constitution (1787). A Frenchman who became a naturalized American citizen, Michel-Guillaume-Jean de Crèvecœur offered a generally optimistic answer to the question "What is an American?" and first wrote of America as a melting pot in his *Letters from an American Farmer* (1782). In the nineteenth century, another Frenchman, Alexis de Tocqueville, wrote glowingly of American individualism and democracy in his two-volume *De la démocratie en Amérique* (1835, 1840; *Democracy in America*, 1835, 1840). Perhaps it was Benjamin Franklin who gave the definitive formulation of the American Dream in his *Autobiography* (begun in 1771, published in 1818). At least five characteristics of the American Dream have been noted in Franklin's work: the rise from rags to riches through industry and thrift; the rise from insignificance to importance, from helplessness to power; a philosophy of individualism; the efficacy of free will and action; and a spirit of hope, even of optimism.

Manifestations of the American Dream in the works of many nineteenth century writers take the form of the primal myth of the American as Adam before the Fall, a theme discussed in a seminal study by R. W. B. Lewis entitled *The American Adam: Innocence, Tragedy, and Tradition in the Nineteenth Century* (1955). The Adamic myth became the driving force of much of the work of nineteenth century writers including James Fenimore Cooper, Oliver Wendell Holmes, Henry Wadsworth Longfellow, Ralph Waldo Emerson, Henry David Thoreau, and especially Walt Whitman. For example, in the poem "Pioneers! O Pioneers!" Whitman sings of the frontier spirit of the emerging U.S. democracy, urging "the tan-faced children," "the youthful sinewy races," to follow with pistols and sharp-edged axes and settle the new land. Similarly, in "Song of the Redwood-Tree," a mighty dying tree willingly sacrifices itself to clear the ground "for broad humanity, the true America." In "Mannahatta," anticipating Carl Sandburg's "Chicago," Whitman expresses his deep affection for New York City, with its towering buildings, active harbors, and busy people. Aspiring to be a poet of progress and quest, Whitman identified himself with Columbus, addressing the explorer in "Passage to India" and affirming the explorer's dream: "Ah Genoese thy dream! thy dream!/ Centuries after thou art laid in thy grave,/ The shore thou foundest verifies the dream."

For other American writers, from the mid-nineteenth century onward, the shore and the disenchanting life thereon did not verify the dream. Nathaniel Hawthorne, Herman Melville, Edgar Allan Poe, Henry James, and Mark Twain probed the dark side of the dream. Twain, writing during the rise of nineteenth century finance capitalism and industrialism, became increasingly disillusioned with social corruption in the Gilded Age. In *The Tragedy of Pudd'nhead Wilson* (1894), he addresses the dehumanizing, brutal aspects of slavery, and in "The Man That Corrupted Hadleyburg" he depicts the greed and self-serving hypocrisy of an allegedly honest and upright town. In his classic novel *Adventures of Huckleberry Finn* (1884), before Huck "lights out for the territory" to escape being civilized, he struggles with a corrupt world of frauds, desperadoes, and money-grubbing confidence men. Perhaps most disturbing of all is that Huck's friend, Tom Sawyer, whom

Huck admires, subjects Jim to numerous indignities to "rescue" him according to romantic books while knowing all along that he is a free man. Such preoccupation with Southern honor, carried further, leads to the cold-blooded murder of Boggs by Colonel Sherburn, the senseless feuding of the Shepherdsons and Grangerfords, and ultimately to the Civil War. It is significant that the wrecked boat on the Mississippi is the *Walter Scott*, named after the writer of romantic novels about chivalry and defense of honor. Twain's comment elsewhere that Sir Walter Scott was the cause of the American Civil War was not completely facetious. Twin suggests that perhaps the American Dream is flawed at the core.

The twentieth century nightmare

Twain set the tone for twentieth century versions of the American Dream, most of which have depicted the American Dream turned nightmare. Twain's legacy is certainly discernible in such a writer as F. Scott Fitzgerald, whose short story "The Diamond as Big as the Ritz" is an attack on the American nightmare. The protagonist, Braddock Washington, a descendant of George Washington and of Lord Baltimore, has kept his colossal diamond mountain hidden from the world by manipulating and sacrificing innocent people who have stumbled upon it. Wealth and material possessions are shown as the constituents of the American Dream, a theme Fitzgerald further develops in *The Great Gatsby* (1925). In the novel, James Gatz of North Dakota has, five years before the story begins, lost the wealthy young woman he loves, Daisy, because he lacks wealth and social class. He changes his name to Jay Gatsby, amasses wealth by dealing with tycoons and gangsters, and buys a mansion across the bay from Daisy's green-lighted dock. He is at "the service of a vast, vulgar, and meretricious beauty, as Fitzgerald sees the American Dream, a dream for which Gatsby loses his life. The novel ends with an elegy for the lapsed American Dream of innocent success. Nick Carraway, the narrator, contemplates the "fresh, green breast" of the New World that "flowered once for Dutch sailors' eyes."

In American fiction the dream has often been personified in the form of a beautiful young woman such as Fitzgerald's Daisy. Realtor George F. Babbitt's fairy girl in Sinclair Lewis' *Babbitt* (1922) is beautiful but vacuous. Faye Greener in Nathanael West's *The Day of the Locust* (1939) is another example. The nude dancer with a small American flag tattooed on her belly says to the black men in Ralph Ellison's *Invisible Man* (1952) what the American Dream has often said to minorities: "Look and long, but don't dare to touch!" Later when the nameless protagonist gets a job at Liberty Paints on Long Island, American flags flutter in the breeze, the company's logo is a screaming eagle, the Optic White paint is said to be "as white as George Washington's Sunday-go-to-meetin' wig," and the motto is "If It's Optic White, It's the Right White." The major lesson Invisible Man learns is that for all the patriotic fluff, the message is always the same: "Keep this nigger-boy running."

Theodore Dreiser, John Dos Passos, Upton Sinclair, Thomas Wolfe, Henry Miller, William Faulkner, and John Steinbeck are other modern American novelists who wrote of the dream's hollowness. When young Clyde Griffiths, in Dreiser's *An American Tragedy* (1925), longs for the American Dream (money and the beauty it buys), seeking to escape from his family's drab life, he kills and is destroyed, enacting what Dreiser considered a peculiarly American tragedy.

The tragedy of dreams deferred is treated as well in twentieth century American drama. Perhaps prototypical of the movement from idealist dream to realist nightmare is the career of Eugene O'Neill. Early plays, such as *Bound East for Cardiff* (1916) and *The Moon of the Caribbees* (1918), seem to affirm the dream, whereas most of the later work, such as *The Hairy Ape* (1922), *Desire Under the Elms* (1924), and *Long Day's Journey into Night* (1956), reveal the nightmare side.

More recent playwrights such as Arthur Miller, Tennessee Williams, and Edward Albee have written of the dream's falsity. At the end of Miller's *Death of a Salesman* (1949), Willy Loman's son, Biff, says of his father, "He had the wrong dreams. All, all, wrong." Continuing the satire of American society, Edward Albee's *The American Dream* (1961), a seriocomic play in the absurdist vein, attacks the substitution of artificial for real values in American society. Even more caustically satirical is Norman Mailer's novel *An American Dream* (1965), which demonstrates the corruption of power and the power of the corrupt.

Modernist and postmodernist poets have also depicted "the lost America of love," as Allen Ginsberg puts it in "A Supermarket in California." Whitman's "barbaric yawp" has become Ginsberg's *Howl* (1956). Similarly, Louis Simpson has written in "Walt Whitman at Bear Mountain," "Where are you, Walt?/ The Open Road goes to the used-car lot." In Simpson's poem "American Dreams," people speak a language strange to the speaker and strange even to themselves. Perhaps language of the American Dream is becoming increasingly more alien to Americans themselves.

SUGGESTED READINGS

Allen, Walter. *The Urgent West: The American Dream and Modern Man*. New York: E. P. Dutton, 1969. Traces the dream motif in American literature chronologically, concluding that the dream has become the property of the Western world.

Benne, Robert, and Philip Hefner. *Defining America: A Christian Critique of the American Dream*. Philadelphia: Fortress Press, 1974. A thoughtful overview and assessment of the dream from a Christian perspective.

Bewley, Marius. "Scott Fitzgerald and the Collapse of the American Dream." In *The Eccentric Design: Form in the Classic American Novel*. New York: Columbia University Press, 1963. A perceptive discussion of the jaundiced view of the American Dream.

Boorstin, Daniel J. *The Image: Or, What Happened to the American Dream*. New York: Atheneum, 1962. An illuminating sociological examination of how the American Dream has become a disenchanting illusion, the problem having arisen less from American weaknesses than from strengths such as wealth, optimism, and progress.

Carpenter, Frederick I. *American Literature and the Dream*. New York: Philosophical Library, 1955. An excellent beginning source, although dated. Presents an overview of major literature relating to the dream.

Ericson, Edward L. *The American Dream Renewed: The Making of a World People*. New York: Continuum, 1991. A sociological study of American pluralism, concluding that the dream never died but only needs to be renewed.

Long, Elizabeth. *The American Dream and the Popular Novel*. London: Routledge & Kegan Paul, 1985. A helpful overview of the success theme in best-selling novels.

Madden, David, ed. *American Dreams, American Nightmares*. Carbondale: Southern Illinois University Press, 1970. A collection of nineteen scholarly articles discussing individual authors, with a helpful introduction.

—D. G. Kehl

See also Columbus, Christopher, literature about; Emigration and immigration; Melting pot

American Dream, An

AUTHOR: Norman Mailer (1923-   )
FIRST PUBLISHED: 1965
IDENTITIES: African American; men; women

In *An American Dream*, Stephen Rojack, World War II veteran, former congressman, psychiatrist, and television personality, murders his wife Deborah. He tries to make the murder look like a suicide by throwing her lifeless body out of her apartment window. Much of the novel then details Rojack's effort to escape from police suspicion and begin a new life with a new woman, Cherry, a nightclub singer he meets shortly after the murder. Rojack is not a cold-blooded killer. He strangled Deborah in a fit of passion after she taunted him and belittled his manhood. Norman Mailer makes no particular apologies for his antihero. Rojack is battling to recover a heroic sense of himself that has slowly attenuated since his service in World War II.

The novel is structured as a series of confrontations with warring identities. After murdering Deborah, he attacks and sodomizes her German maid, Ruta, simultaneously reliving his World War II encounter with a German soldier and the sense of violation that the war provoked in him.

To secure his love for Cherry, Rojack must do battle with her former boyfriend, an African American, whom Rojack ends up kicking down the steps of Cherry's apartment building. Then there is his confrontation with Barney Oswald Kelly, Deborah's father and a powerful, sinister, rich man, whom Rojack fears but resists. Ironically, the police interrogation of Rojack seems to relieve him of any sense of guilt, forcing him to concentrate on his own survival.

The gruesome details of Mailer's plot, especially when baldly stated, do not do justice to the novel's style and mood, which convey the intensity of Rojack's search for self-definition in a violent, conspiratorial world in which independent people rarely survive. It seems in the nature of things that Rojack should lose Cherry—she is murdered before he can return to her apartment to defend her.

Certain critics have made moral objections to *An American Dream*, treating the novel as they would an event in life. The novel, a work of fiction, uses violence and sexual exploitation as metaphors for the male's quest for integrity, a quest that is inescapably brutal, in Mailer's view, even if it is capable of being redeemed in the nobler love Rojack feels for Cherry. The dark side of the American Dream, Mailer's novel implies, is the awareness of the self's isolation and the potential for antisocial behavior. If the American Dream holds out the promise of self-fulfillment, that same dream seems inescapably linked to self-indulgence and corruption as well.

SUGGESTED READINGS

Gordon, Andrew. *An American Dreamer: A Psychoanalytic Study of the Fiction of Norman Mailer*. Rutherford, N.J.: Fairleigh Dickinson University Press, 1980.

Lennon, J. Michael, ed. *Conversations with Norman Mailer*. Jackson: University Press of Mississippi, 1988.

Millett, Kate. *Sexual Politics*. Garden City, N.Y.: Doubleday, 1970.

Rollyson, Carl. *The Lives of Norman Mailer: A Biography*. New York: Paragon House, 1991.

—*Carl Rollyson*

See also American Dream; Erotic identity; Women and identity; World War II

American Hunger

AUTHOR: Richard Wright (1908-1960)
FIRST PUBLISHED: 1977
IDENTITIES: African American

American Hunger, the second part of Richard Wright's autobiography, focuses on his life in Chicago, Illinois, from 1927 to 1937. The book was written in 1944. The Northern experience recurs as a new slave narrative. It demonstrates how modern African Americans were deceived. Wright opens the text in 1927, when nineteen-year-old Richard, his alter ego, arrives in Chicago with his Aunt Maggie. Wright juxtaposes the terms "strange" and "familiar" to express Richard's dismay at seeing African Americans openly consort with whites in public facilities. He learns quickly that appearances are deceptive.

Wright employs literary naturalism to illustrate racial and environmental barriers erected by whites to imprison African Americans in modern slavery. Richard discovers that migrants have traded Southern plantations for urban ghettos. They live in the black belt of Chicago and remain racially and economically disfranchised. Richard's economic status soon imitates that of his impoverished Southern experience. Richard earns low wages at menial jobs during the following six years. The intermittent checks from his postal service job or the relief agency barely sustain Richard's family.

Consistent with *Black Boy*, Richard becomes the outsider, in conflict with his family, community, and professional affiliations. A major source of conflict is his independent thinking. His attempts at writing cause alarm to his Aunt Maggie, who believes that fiction writing and book reading serve no value unless Richard is studying law. Richard's white employer cannot understand why an African American dishwasher would read newspapers. Once Richard joins professional writing groups, between 1933 and 1935, he discovers that his intelligence poses a threat to members of the John Reed Club of the Communist Party, the Southside Writers' Group, and the Federal Theatre Project. They attack him for being an "intellectual" just as Southerners attacked the "smart Negro." The Communists even label Richard a Trotskyite or traitor, and physically assault him at the May Day parade of 1936.

His freedom from slavery culminates with Richard's resignation from the Communist Party. He takes physical flight to New York in 1937. In his ongoing quest for freedom, his psychological emancipation is the real moral to his narrative. It coincides with the successful publication of fiction, which frees Richard to write "art for art's sake," not propaganda, and to accelerate his "war with words."

SUGGESTED READINGS

Fabre, Michel. *The Unfinished Quest of Richard Wright*. New York: William Morrow, 1973.

Hakutani, Yoshinobu. *Critical Essays on Richard Wright*. Boston: G. K. Hall, 1982.

Rampersad, Arnold. *Richard Wright: A Collection of Essays*. Englewood Cliffs, N.J.: Prentice-Hall, 1995.

—*Virginia Whatley Smith*

See also African American identity; *Black Boy*; Slave narratives; Urban life; Wright, Richard

American identity: life on the sea

DEFINITION: Life at sea is a metaphor for the search for identity in much of American literature.

American identity begins with the sea: For the Europeans, crossing the ocean was a defining moment, marking a decisive break with European identity. The American Revolution solidified that break, and Americans looked to the sea for sustenance and national definition. With *The Pilot* (1823), James Fenimore Cooper established the sea novel as part of the American national identity. Long Tom Coffin, the coxswain of the *Ariel*, is a representative American seaman; he establishes a national identity on the sea. Cooper's subsequent sea novels, *The Red Rover* (1827), *The Two Admirals* (1842), *The Wing-and-Wing* (1842), and *Afloat and Ashore* (1844), portray and create an

The dangers, ethical problems, and adventures of life on the sea have inspired many works of literature. (Library of Congress)

identity wrested from the sea. Richard Henry Dana's autobiographical *Two Years Before the Mast* (1840) portrays the sea as a place where Americans define themselves, and by implication, define their country. In his nonfiction narration, he tells the story of how he created an active, aggressive identity out of sickly, upper-class Boston boy.

Romanticism and identity

The rise of Romanticism and its concern with individual identity brought with it the world's greatest sea novelist. Herman Melville was, like Cooper and Dana, a sailor, and he made his career writing about the sea. Melville's early works, *Typee* (1846) and *Omoo: A Narrative of Adventures in the South Seas* (1847), for example, are fact-based accounts of his experiences as a sailor. His masterpiece, *Moby Dick: Or, The Whale* (1851), however, has, in addition to its factual and realistic descriptions of life on the sea, a highly symbolic structure. The sea for the character Ishmael represents the possibilities for self-definition. The book can be interpreted as a search for God; it is also certainly a quest for individual identity in an age of national uncertainty. The sailors on board the *Pequod* come from all races and form an alternative society; this pluralistic society serves as an implicit comment on American social identity. Melville's short fiction also uses shipboard society to question the national identity: "Benito Cereno," for example, tells the story of a revolt on a slave ship and is a scathing indictment of American identity. Melville's short, posthumous sea novel, *Billy Budd, Foretopman* (1924), also serves as a critique of American society. Stephen Crane's "The Open Boat" discusses the brotherhood the immense sea fosters. As does Melville, Crane imagines individual identity as related to a community. For these writers, the sea serves not as an escape from American society but as a means of apprehending what lies at the bottom of social identity: the physical and emotional need of one person for another.

The twentieth century

Jack London's *The Sea-Wolf* (1904), on the other hand, portrays society as interfering with the development of individual identity. The sea in this novel is a place where an integral self can be forged. Ernest Hemingway develops these ideas in the sea novels *To Have and Have Not* (1937), *Islands in the Stream* (1970), and *The Old Man and the Sea* (1952). In the first two works, Hemingway uses the sea to mirror the conflict between individual and social identities. For Santiago, in *The Old Man and the Sea*, the sea offers self-definition apart from society and affords a livelihood and an identity as a fisherman. *The Old Man and the Sea* marks a turning point in American literature about the sea. In earlier works, life on the sea has implications for the life of the nation. *The Old Man and the Sea*, on the other hand, detaches itself from a concern with national or social identities in favor of individual identity apart from society.

American Identity: Life on the Sea
Milestones

1823	*The Pilot*, by James Fenimore Cooper.	1860's-1890's	Sea novels widely read; writers include Bill Adams, Archie Binns, Thorton Jenkins Hains, Richard Matthews Hallet, Arthur Mason, Felix Riesenberg, and Morgan Robertson.
1827	James Fenimore Cooper's *The Red Rover*.		
1840	Richard Henry Dana's autobiographical *Two Years Before the Mast*.	1897	Stephen Crane's "The Open Boat," a short story.
1842	James Fenimore Cooper's *The Two Admirals*.	1904	Jack London's *The Sea-Wolf*.
1842	James Fenimore Cooper's *The Wing-and-Wing*.	1924	Melville's short, posthumous sea novel, *Billy Budd, Foretopman*.
1844	James Fenimore Cooper's *Afloat and Ashore*.		
1846	Herman Melville's *Typee*.	1952	Ernest Hemingway's *The Old Man and the Sea*.
1847	Herman Melville's *Omoo: A Narrative of Adventures in the South Seas*.	1963	There are satiric descriptions of late-twentieth century naval life in Thomas Pynchon's *V.*
1851	*Moby Dick: Or, The Whale*, the masterpiece of the world's greatest sea novelist, Herman Melville.	1970	Ernest Hemingway's *Islands in the Stream*.
		1975	Peter Matthiessen's *Far Tortuga*.

The sea also figures prominently in the works of playwright Eugene O'Neill, who spent time as a seaman. For O'Neill, the sea often represents beauty, mystery, and escape from society. There are satiric descriptions of late-twentieth century naval life in Thomas Pynchon's *V.* (1963).

SUGGESTED READINGS

Baker, Carlos. *Hemingway: The Writer as Artist.* 4th ed. Princeton, N.J.: Princeton University Press, 1972.

Bender, Bert. *Sea-Brothers: The Tradition of American Sea Fiction from "Moby-Dick" to the Present.* Philadelphia: University of Pennsylvania Press, 1988.

Lewis, Charles Lee. *Books of the Sea: An Introduction to Nautical Literature.* Annapolis: Naval Institute Press, 1943.

Martin, Robert K. *Hero, Captain, and Stranger: Male Friendship, Social Critique, and Literary Form in the Sea Novels of Herman Melville.* Chapel Hill: University of North Carolina Press, 1986.

Philbrick, Thomas. *James Fenimore Cooper and the Development of American Sea Fiction.* Cambridge, Mass.: Harvard University Press, 1961.

—Joe Boyd Fulton

See also *Bildungsroman* and *Künstlerroman*; Emigration and immigration; Hemingway, Ernest; London, Jack; Pynchon, Thomas

American identity: Midwest

IDENTITIES: Midwest

An understanding of the midwestern identity as it is expressed in the literature of the region first requires a working definition of the region itself. Most often the Midwest is simply defined as twelve states: Illinois, Indiana, Iowa, Kansas, Michigan, Minnesota, Missouri, Nebraska, North and South Dakota, Ohio, and Wisconsin. The Midwest also is often referred to as the heartland, but what area is meant by this name is subject to interpretation. Some scholars include portions of other states, including eastern Colorado or eastern Montana. Others include all of West Virginia and Oklahoma, while still others limit the Midwest to a far smaller area that includes only wheat states or corn states. Many critics use geographical rather than state boundaries to define the Midwest. A western boundary commonly used to define the Midwest is the Missouri River. Some argue for a southern boundary that divides corn and cotton country. No matter which definition one chooses to accept, however, the Midwest encompasses topographical variety and human diversity, and although the region includes many metropolitan areas, it has been the literature of the rural experience that has gained acceptance as the writing that most appropriately characterizes life in the Midwest.

The central characteristic that defines a work as midwestern, aside from the setting, is an illustration of the relationships between the land and people and the changes that have occurred in those relationships since European settlement. More specifically, these relationships are seen in two key themes: farm life and small-town life.

Farm life

The family farm has been the dominant cultural enterprise in the Midwest until the later decades of the twentieth century, when large agribusiness corporations turned farming from a social foundation into a cog in the corporate machine. This dramatic change, driven by economics and technology, is not remarkable in the history of midwestern farming. Change has been the one consistent fact of farm life in the Midwest.

Farm fiction began with Hamlin Garland's *Main-Travelled Roads* (1891). Garland wanted to tell the truth about farming, and to Garland that truth meant avoiding the romanticized vision of farming as a happy pastoral existence lived in harmony with nature. Opposite Garland are perhaps two of the most beautiful novels ever written about farming, Willa Cather's *O Pioneers!* (1913) and *My Ántonia* (1918). In both, Cather depicts strong female protagonists who struggle with the Nebraska prairie sod until it gives in to their will and produces food. Cather's ability to capture the beauty of life on the prairie and its extraordinary effects on her characters is rivaled by few.

American Identity: Midwest
Milestones

1673	French explorers explore the Mississippi and Illinois Rivers.
1779	Jean Baptiste Point Sable settles in Chicago.
1803	The Louisiana Purchase.
1809	Congress decrees Illinois a territory.
1816	Indiana is granted statehood.
1818	Illinois achieves statehood.
1837	Michigan is granted statehood.
1871	October 8-10, the Chicago fire causes more than $200,000,000 in property damage.
1883	Edgar Watson Howe's *The Story of a Country Town*.
1891	Hamlin Garland's *Main-Travelled Roads*, a realistic characterization of farm life in the Middle West.
1906	Chicago's South Side becomes notorious with publication of Upton Sinclair's *The Jungle*.
1912-1925	Chicago Renaissance. Some prominent writers of this period include Sherwood Anderson, Edgar Lee Masters, Carl Sandburg, and Vachel Lindsay.
1913	Vachel Lindsay's *General William Booth Enters into Heaven and Other Poems*.
1913	*O Pioneers!*, a novel by Willa Cather.
1915	Edgar Lee Masters' *Spoon River Anthology*. From their graveyard more than two hundred of the dead citizens of Spoon River (probably Lewiston, Illinois) tell the truth about themselves.
1916	Carl Sandburg's *Chicago Poems*.
1917	Hamlin Garland's *A Son of the Middle Border*.
1918	Zona Gale's *Birth*, a novel.
1918	Willa Cather's *My Ántonia*, a celebration of life on the plains.
1919	Sherwood Anderson's *Winesburg, Ohio*, about a small town and its lonely, frustrated inhabitants.
1920	Sinclair Lewis' *Main Street*, one of the most significant novels of midwestern small-town life.
1920	Zona Gale's *Miss Lulu Bett* details the bleak life of a Midwestern woman.
1922	Herbert Quick's *Vandemark's Folly*.
1924-1925	Ole Rölvaag's *Giants in the Earth*.
1928	Vachel Lindsay's *Johnny Appleseed and Other Poems*.
1930	The first American to be awarded a Nobel Prize in Literature is Sinclair Lewis, critic of the small midwestern town.
1932	Phil Stong's *State Fair*.
1933	Phil Stong's *Stranger's Return*, about a woman from New York who visits the Iowa farm of her grandfather.
1937	In *Buckskin Breeches*, Phil Stong recounts pioneer life from 1830 to 1840.
1944	Frederick Manfred's *The Golden Bowl* depicts a generational conflict between two midwestern farmers.
1946	Herbert Krause, in his novel *The Thresher*, portrays the hard life of a wheat farmer.
1954	Herbert Krause's *The Oxcart Trail* depicts life in a frontier town.
1962	Lois Phillips Hudson's *The Bones of Plenty*.
1968	Frederick Manfred's *Eden Prairie*.
1973	Curtis Harnack's *We Have All Gone Away*.
1975	Larry Woiwode's *Beyond the Bedroom Wall: A Family Album*, an account of several generations of a family from North Dakota.
1977	Frederick Manfred's *Green Earth*.
1979	Douglas Bauer's *Prairie City, Iowa*.
1984	Douglas Unger's *Leaving the Land*.
1985	Garrison Keillor's *Lake Wobegon Days*. His radio show, *A Prairie Home Companion*, is a nationwide hit.
1986	Verlyn Klinkenborg's *Making Hay* takes the single farm practice of raising alfalfa and describes the roles of three communities in the production of this crop.
1987	Linda Hasselstrom's *Windbreak*.
1991	William Least Heat-Moon's *PrairyErth (a deep map)*
1991	Jane Smiley's *A Thousand Acres*.
1995	*South of the Big Four*, by Don Kurtz.

Herbert Quick's *Vandemark's Folly* (1922), while suffering from a melodramatic plot, compares with Cather's work in its ability to describe the native Iowa prairie in several inspiring passages. In Cather's and Quick's novels a key theme is the immigrant experience, and this is also true in Ole Rölvaag's *Giants in the Earth* (1924-1925), which is considered by some to be the best farm novel ever written. Rölvaag's central couple, Per and Beret Hansa, find that the founding of a farm in America is as much a question of learning to farm as it is learning to become or not to become like other Americans. Per and Beret find they must decide what to keep of their Norwegian roots. Unlike Rölvaag's serious and tragic *Giants in the Earth*, Phil Stong's *State Fair* (1932) is a more lighthearted look at midwestern farm life. *State Fair* describes a family's trip to the fair with their prize hog as a decent, clean, and enjoyable experience. Stong's view, however, is in the minority. Like Garland before him, Herbert Krause, in his long novel *The Thresher* (1946), presents a view of farm life as brutal and tough, compounded by the rigors of the German Lutheran ancestry of his characters. Another of the most significant of farm novelists is Frederick Manfred. His two early novels, *The Golden Bowl* (1944) and *This Is the Year* (1947), began the farming and family themes set in Siouxland (a word of his own coinage that names the area where Iowa, Minnesota, South Dakota, and Nebraska meet) that he would continue to write about for decades. His later works included *Eden Prairie* (1968), *Green Earth* (1977), and *Of Lizards and Angels* (1992). In all his farm novels Manfred attempts to detail the struggles of immigrant farmers in a rambling lyrical style that earned him wide praise and recognition. Lois Phillips Hudson's *The Bones of Plenty* (1962) is perhaps the least appreciated of quality farm fiction. Set in a fifteen-month period during the 1930's, the novel is extraordinary in its ability to dramatize the complicated web of economic and social forces facing a North Dakota family.

Since the 1960's the production of farm novels has dropped off considerably, but the crisis in farming of the 1970's and 1980's, in which agribusiness has taken control of farming, seems to have spurred a new generation of farm novels with some provocative new themes. Douglas Unger's *Leaving the Land* (1984) is a two-part novel that dramatizes the life of a South Dakota farmer's daughter whose freedom and growth as a girl are countered by her disillusionment in later years. Wendell Berry's *Remembering* (1988) is a nostalgic look back to the years of the small family farm in an age of industrial farming that destroys families and land. Jane Smiley's *A Thousand Acres* (1991) is a startling account of the darker side of an Iowa family farm. Told from the point of view of a farmer's daughter, this novel is unique in its challenge to the family structure that underlies family farming in the Midwest. Don Kurtz's *South of the Big Four* (1995) is an account of a son's return home to the family farm and of his process of accepting what he finds there.

Along with farm life, an essential part of the midwestern cultural identity is found in the small town. The myths about farms are rivaled by those about small towns. The small town was to be the ideal democratic community—safe, decent, and educated—which would serve the farmers with goods, services, and culture. It is no surprise then, that the success of the novels of the small town lay in their ability to expose these false assumptions. It is telling that the first American to be awarded a Nobel Prize in Literature was Sinclair Lewis, who made a stronger case against the small town than nearly any other writer.

Small-town life

Edgar Watson Howe's *The Story of a Country Town* (1883) is the first significant novel to attack the sentimental portraits of small towns. Life in Howe's town, Twin Mounds, is characterized by monotonous trivial activities that are made bearable only by mean gossip. Creativity and happiness are stifled by a constricting puritanical code that Howe felt to be the central damaging force in midwestern life. The poetry of Edgar Lee Masters' *Spoon River Anthology* (1915) was very similar to Howe's fiction. Masters' 242 residents of Spoon River speak from their graves of loneliness, isolation, and spiritual longing. Although many of Zona Gale's eighty-three stories celebrate life in the small town, and although her Friendship Village is the locale of many happy and loving folks, she eventually turned more toward a rejection of the small-town point of view, and in her novel *Birth* (1918) her picture of the town of Boarger is bleak and repulsive. Sherwood Anderson's *Winesburg, Ohio* (1919) and Sinclair Lewis' *Main Street* (1920) are two of the most significant novels of midwestern small-town life. Anderson's stories are linked by the narrator, George Willard, whose knowledge and insight gained from his honest interactions with the townspeople leave him no alternative but to get on a train for the city and leave Winesburg. It is a beautiful and tragic book filled with stunted, frustrated lives of sadness and loss. Lewis, in turn, is devastating in his portrayal of Gopher Prairie, Minnesota. Unlike Anderson, he shows no beauty in the small town's sadness, and one has few feelings of loss for his characters.

Larry Woiwode's *Beyond the Bedroom Wall: A Family Album* (1975) is an enormous family chronicle that covers several small towns in North Dakota and in Illinois. The opening chapter describes the narrator's dream of his boyhood main street of Hyatt, North Dakota, a dream that the narrator cannot escape or completely understand until years later. This novel, more effectively perhaps than any other, dramatizes the positive and the negative realities of living in a small town and their impact on the emotional lives of the characters. Completely different in approach but equal in its balance of positive and negative qualities is Garrison Keillor's *Lake Wobegon Days* (1985). Keillor's novel sold very well because of his high profile as a radio performer, and the book is a series of interwoven tales that have been read—over the last twenty years, in different forms—on his radio show, *A Prairie Home Companion*. Keillor's view of the small town is satiric and nostalgic, often at the same time. Some critics who do not approve of his popularity call his work kitsch, but others find his work an essentially ambiguous and subtly thoughtful portrayal of Lake Wobegon, Minnesota.

Nonfiction   In the later decades of the twentieth century the genre of personal nonfiction has blossomed in midwestern letters, and, as in the literary works, the most characteristic of these nonfictional accounts describe the relationships between people and the land. Curtis Harnack's *We Have All Gone Away* (1973) and Douglas Bauer's *Prairie City, Iowa* (1979) are stories about childhoods spent on the farm and the impact of such a background on adult life. Unlike most writers of such stories, Harnack and Bauer manage to avoid the typical sentimentalized nostalgia associated with describing a childhood growing up on the farm. Verlyn Klinkenborg's *Making Hay* (1986) takes the single farm practice of raising alfalfa and describes the roles of three communities in the production of this crop. Linda Hasselstrom's *Windbreak* (1987) is the journal of a year in the life of a South Dakota rancher. Her keen observations of the competing responsibilities of raising cattle and writing cut to the heart of the midwestern character. Finally, William Least Heat-Moon's *PrairyErth (a deep map)* (1991) attempts to understand a place first by looking with exhaustive detail at the landscape and history, and then by seeing more deeply into the spiritual aspects of place.

SUGGESTED READINGS

Martone, Michael, ed. *A Place of Sense: Essays in Search of the Midwest*. Iowa City: University of Iowa Press, 1988. Eight essays that attempt to define the Midwest in all its contradictions. Includes photographs by David Plowden.

Nemanic, Gerald, ed. *A Bibliographical Guide to Midwestern Literature*. Iowa City: University of Iowa Press, 1981. Provides dozens of subject bibliographies and more than one hundred author introductions and bibliographies.

Shortridge, James R. *The Middle West: Its Meaning in American Culture*. Lawrence: University Press of Kansas, 1989. Investigates the subjective aspects of place, including the contradictory images, the origins of the name, and the Middle West as metaphor.

Stryk, Lucien, ed. *Heartland: Poets of the Midwest*. DeKalb: Northern Illinois University Press, 1967. An anthology of some thirty contemporary midwestern poets linked by themes common to the region's writing.

_____, ed. *Heartland II: Poets of the Midwest*. DeKalb: Northern Illinois University Press, 1975. A second volume containing more than twice the number of contributors.

Vinz, Mark, and Thom Tammaro, eds. *Imagining Home: Writing from the Midwest*. Minneapolis: University of Minnesota Press, 1995. A collection of essays by upper midwestern writers that attempt to describe the influence of place on their work.

_____, eds. *Inheriting the Land: Contemporary Voices from the Midwest*. Minneapolis: University of Minnesota Press, 1993. An anthology of poetry, fiction, and nonfiction organized around characteristic themes of midwestern life: climate, the presence of the past, town and country, and gains and losses.

Weber, Ronald. *The Midwestern Ascendancy in American Writing*. Bloomington: Indiana University Press, 1992. Describes the achievement of midwestern literature from the late nineteenth century into the 1920's.

—Keith Fynaardt

See also Anderson, Sherwood; Berry, Wendell; Cather, Willa; *Dakota: A Spiritual Geography*; Erdrich, Louise; *Growing Up in Minnesota*; Lewis, Sinclair; Rural life

American identity: Northeast

IDENTITIES: Northeast

Many critics contend that early Northeast literature might more aptly be called English literature in America. There is truth in that contention, but even at the nation's beginning there were differences between British and American writing. Religion, specifically Calvinist doctrine, was an important factor in the nation's founding and has thus been reflected in American writing from colonial times onward. When the eighteenth century began, however, the native European Americans had become more secularized than their Puritan predecessors, and concepts of individual self-reliance, idealism, and the natural beauty of the land had taken firm hold in life and literature. The spirit of that period is best recognized in the writing of Benjamin Franklin, Philip Freneau, and Charles Brockden Brown.

Background

THE DESTRUCTION OF TEA AT BOSTON HARBOR.

Colonists, disguised as Indians, participate in one of the most-written-about events of the American Revolution. (Library of Congress)

Benjamin Franklin	Franklin came not from Puritan New England, but from the Quaker colony of Pennsylvania. Franklin's *Poor Richard's Almanack* (1732-1757) combines a rustic presentation of miscellaneous data and his famous proverbs, which are summations culled from expressions of past wisdom. *The Autobiography of Benjamin Franklin* (1791) is considered an American classic. *The Power of Sympathy* (1789), often called the first American novel, was written by "a lady of Boston," who was later found to be not Sarah Wentworth Morton but rather William Hill Brown. The novel marks the American beginning of a long line of luridly sensational best-selling books written for women. These novels were frowned upon by religious and educational leaders. Under the guise of moral instruction, this British-derived genre tells of seduction, suicide, and betrayal, and is rife with sad revelations of the consequences of unwise love. Another widely read romance of the type, Hannah Webster Foster's *The Coquette* (1797), testifies to the popularity of these formulaic books. An 1805 issue of the *Boston Monthly Anthology* voiced indignation at the infection of ladies by such "vermin." The magazine's editors then rushed to review each new novel as it came off the presses.

American Identity: Northeast
Milestones

1607 — First colonization of North America by English settlers, at Jamestown.

1620 — First Pilgrims arrive at Plymouth.

1620-1647 — Period covered in William Bradford's *History of Plymouth Plantation, 1620-1647*.

1630 — Founding of the Massachusetts Bay Colony.

1630 — John Winthrop's address to the Pilgrims of the Massachusetts Bay Colony, *A Model of Christian Charity* (first published in full in 1838), describes the American settlement as a city set upon a hill; the community would serve as an example to the rest of the world of Christian living.

1645? — Edward Taylor, cleric and poet, born (d. 1729). Came to America in 1668; minister at Westfield, Massachusetts. *The Poetical Works of Edward Taylor*, 1939.

1650 — *The Tenth Muse Lately Sprung Up in America*, by Anne Bradstreet.

1678 — *Several Poems Compiled of Great Wit and Learning*, by Anne Bradstreet.

1692 — Accusations of witchcraft among the colonists of Salem begin a terror that continues for about a year. The secular authorities, not the clergy, are the most zealous prosecutors. Resentments, mostly economic, among two groups of colonists fuel the accusations. Two families, the Porters and the Palmers, and two areas, Salem Village and Salem Town, are the principal demarcations. The symptoms of the first accusers suggest that, rather than suffering from Satanic possession, they ate bad rye bread, resulting in convulsions. Hawthorne's "Young Goodman Brown" (1835), Arthur Miller's *The Crucible* (1953), and Ann Petry's *Tituba of Salem Village* (1964) are based on these events.

1732-1757 — *Poor Richard's Almanak*, published serially by Benjamin Franklin. Its proverbs on industry, clean living, and thrift become staples of the language and thought of the United States.

1773 — Boston Tea Party.

1773 — *Poems on Various Subjects, Religious and Moral*, by Phillis Wheatley, who was taken in childhood as a slave to Boston, began writing poetry in English at age thirteen, was freed in 1778, became famous, and traveled to England.

1775-1781 — Revolutionary War. Much of the literature of the period was propagandistic; among the enduring works are Francis Hopkinson's *The Battle of the Kegs* (1777), a satiric, patriotic story in verse. Benjamin Franklin's *Edict by the King of Prussia* (1773) is a satiric denunciation of Britain's policies toward the colonies. Philip Freneau wrote many patriotic pieces, the best of which are in verse; most are in the vein of satiric attacks on British rule or celebrations of revolutionary triumphs. *The British Prison-Ship* (1781) describes his experience as a prisoner. John Dickinson's *Letters from a Pennsylvania Farmer* (1768) describes many common grievances of the colonists. Thomas Paine's *Common Sense* (1776) and the review *The Crisis* (1776-1783) served to incite overthrow of the British government. Herman Melville's *Israel Potter: Or, Fifty Years of Exile* (1855) describes the captivity of an American sailor; it is based on *A Narrative of Colonel Ethan Allan's Captivity* (1779), by Ethan Allan.

The sentimental novel captured the imagination of American women in the first years of independence and continued to be widely read well into the nineteenth century.

Hartford Wits

Aside from the sentimental novel, popular writing in the period surrounding independence was dominated by didactic, revolutionary pamphleteers seeking to separate themselves from Europe and define their place in the New World. The desire to break with European literature and create an indigenous writing style motivated the eighteenth century Hartford Wits, whose efforts represent the first focused attempt to establish formal American literary standards for aesthetic production. The Hartford Wits included such authors as Timothy Dwight, David Humphreys, and Joel Barlow. Barlow's "The Hasty Pudding" (1793) and *The Columbiad* (1807) are two examples of literary works intended to glorify America.

In the odes of Freneau, specifically *The Wild Honeysuckle* (1786), which is a lyric expression of emotional feeling for nature, and the novels of Brown, specifically *Edgar Huntley: Or, Memoirs of a Sleep-Walker* (1799), with its impressionist descriptions of natural settings, readers encounter

---

American Identity: Northeast Milestones — CONTINUED

1783	Britain recognizes independence of the United States.
1800-1850	Era of the Knickerbocker School, a group of writers who made New York an important literary center. The school included Washington Irving, James Fenimore Cooper, William Cullen Bryant, and Lydia M. Child.
1819-1820	*The Sketch Book of Geoffrey Crayon, Gent.*, by Washington Irving, published serially.
1821	*The Spy: A Tale of Neutral Ground*, by James Fenimore Cooper. His second novel; about the Revolutionary War.
1823-1841	The Leatherstocking Tales, by James Fenimore Cooper: *The Pioneers: Or, The Sources of the Susquehana* (1823), *The Last of the Mohicans: A Narrative of 1757* (1826), *The Prairie: A Tale* (1827), *The Pathfinder: Or, The Inland Sea* (1840), *The Deerslayer: Or, The First Warpath* (1841).
1830	Emily Dickinson born (d. 1886). She began to write seriously about 1850, with a peak in the early 1860's; only a handful of her poems were published in her lifetime.
1837	"The American Scholar," address by Ralph Waldo Emerson, celebrates the cultural independence of New World from the Old.
1837	*Twice-Told Tales*, by Nathaniel Hawthorne.
1841	*Ballads and Other Poems*, by Henry Wadsworth Longfellow.
1841	*Essays, First Series*, by Ralph Waldo Emerson.
1847	*Evangeline*, by Henry Wadsworth Longfellow. The widely read story of the displacement of the Acadian people by the English.
1847	*Poems*, by Ralph Waldo Emerson.
1849	*A Week on the Concord and Merrimack Rivers*, by Henry David Thoreau.
1850	*The Scarlet Letter*, by Nathaniel Hawthorne. The famous story of crime and punishment in Puritan New England.
1850	Approximate beginning of productive period of Emily Dickinson.
1851	*The House of the Seven Gables*, by Nathaniel Hawthorne.
1851	*Moby Dick: Or, The Whale*, by Herman Melville. About the last voyage of a Yankee whaleboat.
1854	*Walden*, by Henry David Thoreau. Describes Thoreau's experience living in a cabin near Concord, Massachusetts.
1855	*Leaves of Grass*, by Walt Whitman. Printed for the first time in Brooklyn.
1857-1858	Serial publication of *The Autocrat of the Breakfast-Table*, essays by Oliver Wendell Holmes.
1859	*The Minister's Wooing*, by Harriet Beecher Stowe.
1861-1865	The Civil War is probably the war about which the most books have been written. Some works about the war by writers from the Northeast include Walt Whitman's *Drum Taps* (1865) and *Sequel to Drum-Taps* (1865-1866; and included in the 1867 edition of *Leaves of Grass*); the sequel contains "When Lilacs Last in the Dooryard Bloom'd," an elegy for Lincoln. James Russell Lowell wrote against slavery, against the Mexican War, and on behalf of the Northern cause in the Biglow papers, which were first published in periodicals and then collected and published as *(continued)*

the stirrings of a literary appreciation of the American landscape that is revolutionary.

Knickerbocker School

In the first quarter of the nineteenth century New York City surpassed Boston as the country's leading literary center. New York was home to the Knickerbocker School of writers. This loosely defined group was associated simply with being from New York. Among them were Washington Irving, James Fenimore Cooper, and William Cullen Bryant. The Knickerbocker School took its name from the region, rather than from any shared style. Irving, perhaps the country's first great literary talent, was influenced by the Hudson River Valley and by Dutch legends about the region. These influences are felt in his impressionistic *A History of New York* (1809), while the pleasures of the region's pathless woods incited Cooper's imagination; he wrote the adventure novels known collectively as the Leatherstocking Tales, which are set in the country's earliest frontier. Bryant, a newspaper editor most of his life, is remembered for exploring humankind's relation to nature in such works as *Poems* (1821).

In Boston, the literary scene of the nineteenth century included Henry Wadsworth Longfellow,

---

American Identity: Northeast Milestones — CONTINUED

books. The first book was *The Biglow Papers, First Series* (1848); more Biglow papers, serialized during the war, were published as *The Biglow Papers, Second Series* in 1867. The poet William Cullen Bryant was politically active for the Republican Party. Henry David Thoreau's *Civil Disobedience* (1849) recounts his night in jail that resulted from his refusal to pay a poll tax. Thoreau did not want to give monetary support to the Mexican War, which he saw as an attempt to extend slavery into new territories. He was freed from jail when the tax was paid by someone else. Harriet Beecher Stowe's *Uncle Tom's Cabin: Or, Life Among the Lowly* (1852) was greatly influential in raising antislavery sentiment. Herman Melville's *Battle-Pieces and Aspects of the War* (1866) is a collection of poems about the war. Stephen Crane's 1895 novel *The Red Badge of Courage: An Episode of the American Civil War* is perhaps the most read novel about the war. Robert Lowell's *For the Union Dead* (1964) contains the elegy of the same title.

1861	*Elsie Venner: A Romance of Destiny*, by Oliver Wendell Holmes.
1863	*Tales of a Wayside Inn*, by Henry Wadsworth Longfellow. Includes "Paul Revere's Ride."
1868	*Little Women*, by Louisa May Alcott.
1877	*Deephaven*, by Sarah Orne Jewett. Describes life in Maine.
1881	*Washington Square*, by Henry James. About Catherine Sloper, a resident of Washington Square in New York City.
1885	*The Rise of Silas Lapham*, by William Dean Howells.
1886	*The Bostonians*, by Henry James.

1896	*The Country of the Pointed Firs*, by Sarah Orne Jewett.
1901	*The Great White Way*, a play by Albert Bigelow Paine, gives Broadway, the capital of live theater in the United States, its nickname.
1907	*The Education of Henry Adams*, by Henry Adams, an autobiography of a Boston Brahmin.
1911	*Ethan Frome*, by Edith Wharton. The title character, a laconic, repressed New Englander, fails in an attempt at happiness.
1914	*North of Boston*, by Robert Frost. Poems about the Northeast.
1914-1918	World War I. Much of the American literature about World War I would be written by expatriates, including Ernest Hemingway and John Dos Passos, both of whom were born in the Midwest. In 1915, Edith Wharton published, on behalf of the war relief effort, *The Book of the Homeless*, a literary collection that she had edited. Wharton lived in Paris during World War I. In 1922, e. e. cummings published *The Enormous Room*, which is about his experience as a prisoner during World War I.
1917	*The Rise of David Levinsky*, a drama by Abraham Cahan.
1920's	The Harlem Renaissance. A group of black artists, including the writers Claude McKay, Jean Toomer, Zora Neale Hurston, Nella Larsen, and Langston Hughes, make a deeply influential cultural contribution to the United States. Works include Larsen's *Quicksand* (1928), Toomer's *Cane* (1923), and McKay's *Home to Harlem* (1928) and *Banana Bottom* (1933).
1920	*The Age of Innocence*, by Edith Wharton.

best known for three narrative poems, *Evangeline* (1847), *The Song of Hiawatha* (1855), and *The Courtship of Miles Standish* (1858); the critic and poet James Russell Lowell, best known for *The Biglow Papers* (1848, 1867), a series of essays attacking slavery, opposing the war with Mexico, and opposing the annexation of Texas; and Oliver Wendell Holmes, Sr., the first major humorist in American literature, best known for "The Deacon's Masterpiece," a satire on Calvinism.

By the second and third decades of the nineteenth century, the religious and intellectual environment conducive to a free exchange of ideas is most strongly evident in New England, where Unitarians engaged in active cultural rebellion against the Calvinist church. Unitarian ministers interpreted the gospel for their congregations in accordance with their own conscience and intelligence, and thereby undermined Puritan prohibitions against individual imaginative inspiration. Such creativity cleared the way for the development of American literature. The Transcendentalists, the intellectual counterparts of the Unitarian churchmen, were led by Ralph Waldo Emerson, whose *Nature* (1836) and essays defined the new school of thought as one rejecting

American Identity: Northeast Milestones — CONTINUED

1925	*An American Tragedy*, by Theodore Dreiser. Takes place in upstate New York.
1925	*The Great Gatsby*, by F. Scott Fitzgerald. A classic novel of American ambition, set in the New York City area.
1929	The stock market crash.
1929	*Street Scene*, a drama by Elmer Rice. Takes place in 1929 in New York. The forerunner of the social drama of the 1930's.
1931	*Axel's Castle*, by Edmund Wilson. A study of symbolism by an influential writer and critic.
1931	*Mourning Becomes Electra*, by Eugene O'Neill. A trilogy of plays about the destruction of a New England family after the Civil War.
1936	*The Last Puritan*, by George Santayana.
1937	*The Late George Apley*, by J. P. Marquand.
1938	*Tales of a Wayward Inn*, by Frank Case, telling of the famous Algonquin Round Table.
1939	*Tropic of Capricorn*, by Henry Miller. One of his many writings about the fourteenth ward of Brooklyn.
1939-1945	World War II. Works about World War II by writers from the Northeast include H. D.'s *Trilogy* (1942-1944; Hilda Doolittle was in London during the Blitz), Norman Mailer's *The Naked and the Dead* (1948), Joseph Heller's *Catch-22* (1961), and Thomas Pynchon's *Gravity's Rainbow* (1973).
1946	*Lord Weary's Castle*, by Robert Lowell. A denunciation of the spiritual decay of Protestant New England.
1946	*Paterson*, book 1 (book 2, 1948; book 3, 1949; book 4, 1951), by William Carlos Williams. About Paterson, New Jersey.
1947	The writing career of Louis Auchincloss, a chronicler of New York City's upper crust, begins with the publication of *The Indifferent Children*.
1947	*On These I Stand*, collected poems by Countée Cullen, New Yorker and participant in the Harlem Renaissance.
1949	*Complete Poems* of Robert Frost.
1951	*The Catcher in the Rye*, by J. D. Salinger. A classic novel about an adolescent in New York.
1952	*Invisible Man*, by Ralph Ellison. Set in a city resembling New York.
1954	*The Collected Poems of Wallace Stevens*, by Wallace Stevens. A summary of his career.
1954-1973	The Vietnam War. Mary McCarthy and Norman Mailer were the two most prominent writers from the Northeast to write about this war, which has a vast literature. Mailer's *Why Are We in Vietnam?* (1967) and McCarthy's *Vietnam* (1967), a nonfiction protest of the United States' involvement in Vietnam, are two of their works about the war.
1955	*Ten North Frederick*, by John O'Hara. Describes the Chapin family of Gibbsville, Pennsylvania, the name O'Hara used in his fiction for his native Pottsville.
1956	*Long Day's Journey into Night*, by Eugene O'Neill. Based on O'Neill's family story, this drama recounts a day in the life of a family spending its summer on Cape Cod.
1957	*The Wapshot Chronicle*, by John Cheever. Introduces St. Botolphs, a once-thriving Yankee seaport, and the Wapshot family.
1959	*Brown Girl, Brownstones*, by Paule Marshall. About growing up in Brooklyn.

(continued)

scientific rationalism and adhering to the sufficiency of the individual. This talented literary circle formed the core of a robust Romantic protest against the doctrines of damnation, doubt, and pessimism preached by the Puritans. Aside from Emerson, Henry David Thoreau was the most famous of the Transcendentalists. Thoreau wrote a great number of antislavery articles and some poetry, but *Walden* (1854), with its clear narrative of Thoreau's two-year solitary sojourn in nature, recording the development of his theories and beliefs, sets him apart as one of the nation's finest prose stylists.

Whitman and Melville

Walt Whitman, America's poet of optimistic individualism, and Herman Melville were New Yorkers whose writing was essential in forging an American literature. Both writers had sympathy for ordinary life and common occupations. Whitman's *Leaves of Grass* (1855) speaks to the hopeful side of American freedom; Melville's *Moby Dick: Or, The Whale* (1851) gives readers the thunderous dark. Nathaniel Hawthorne was a descendant of the Puritans of Massachusetts. His early work was influenced by Irving. Hawthorne's first book, laden with allegory and parables, is

American Identity: Northeast Milestones — CONTINUED

1959	*Life Studies*, by Robert Lowell. Poems about historical figures, including New Englanders, and personal poems that mark the beginning of what is called the confessional school of poetry. Boston is home for many poets of this group.
1960	*Apologies to the Iroquois*, by Edmund Wilson.
1960	*Rabbit, Run*, by John Updike. The first of the four novels about Harry Angstrom, nicknamed "Rabbit." The novels follow Harry's life, which is in part a summary of the cultural developments of his time (from his young adulthood in the late 1950's to the late 1980's). The other novels are *Rabbit Redux* (1971), *Rabbit Is Rich* (1981), and *Rabbit at Rest* (1990).
1961	*Last Exit to Brooklyn*, by Hubert Selby, Jr.
1961	*Obra poética*, by Julia de Burgos, a Puerto Rican Spanish-language journalist who lived in New York.
1963	*The Bell Jar*, by Sylvia Plath.
1963	*The Group*, by Mary McCarthy. Follows the lives of eight promising graduates of Vassar from 1933, the year of their graduation, to 1940.
1963	*V.*, by Thomas Pynchon. Much of the novel is set in New York City in 1958.
1964	*Dutchman*, by Amiri Baraka.
1964	*Tituba of Salem Village*, by Ann Petry.
1965	*The Autobiography of Malcolm X*, by Malcolm X, with Alex Haley. Recounts Malcolm X's coming-of-age in Boston.
1965	*Manchild in the Promised Land*, by Claude Brown. Autobiography about growing up in Harlem.
1966	*Against Interpretation*, by Susan Sontag.
1969	*The Poems of Robert Frost*, published posthumously.
1974	*Enormous Changes at the Last Minute*, by Grace Paley. It and *Later the Same Day* (1985) are set in New York City.
1975	*Self-Portrait in a Convex Mirror*, by John Ashbery.
1975	*El Bronx Remembered: A Novella and Short Stories*, by Nicholassa Mohr.
1976	*for colored girls who have considered suicide/when the rainbow is enuf: a choreopoem*, by Ntozake Shange.
1978	*The Stories of John Cheever*, by John Cheever.
1980	*Bellefleur*, by Joyce Carol Oates. A gothic novel set in upstate New York.
1981	*The Hotel New Hampshire*, by John Irving.
1981	*Rhode Island: Eight Poems*, by Michael S. Harper.
1982	*The Changing Light at Sandover*, by James Merrill.
1983	*Ironweed*, by William Kennedy. Part of The Albany Cycle about Albany, New York, and the fortunes of the Phelan family.
1986	*The Beans of Egypt, Maine*, by Carolyn Chute.
1987	*Slaves of New York*, by Tama Janowitz.
1988	*The Heidi Chronicles*, by Wendy Wasserstein.
1990	*Lucy*, by Jamaica Kincaid. A woman comes to New York from Antigua to be an au pair.

Twice-Told Tales (1837), a collection. His masterpiece, *The Scarlet Letter* (1850), with its dark picture of the Puritan past, is recognized as a skillful blending of character development, mood, and poetic prose.

New Englander Harriet Beecher Stowe, the daughter and wife of clergymen, wrote *Uncle Tom's Cabin: Or, Life Among the Lowly* (1852), an antislavery book. The book sold extremely well and was better known than any other American nineteenth century novel. The book stirred strong feeling against the fugitive slave laws. Stowe's novel is about slavery in the South; Harriet E. Wilson of New Hampshire wrote *Our Nig* (1859), an autobiographical novel about the pitiful life of an indentured black woman servant in the North. Her novel is the first by an African American to be published in the United States. Sarah Orne Jewett is a local colorist; *The Country of the Pointed Firs* (1896) masterfully displays Jewett's familiarity with her native Maine, and the work is considered a minor classic.

Poetry

Unknown in her lifetime, Emily Dickinson never sought, with any diligence, publication for her poetry. Her verse is unique, having nothing in common with poetic schools or any regional theme. Dickinson relied entirely on her personal experiences and considered no theme too intimate or too trivial to record. She contributed to American literature a freedom in verse that was unsurpassed.

Poet Amy Lowell, with her collection *Sword Blades and Poppy Seed* (1914), became a leader in poetic circles by advocating what Dickinson had practiced—that the language of verse resemble common speech and that freedom of choice and subject be absolute. Lowell's poetry helped to bring a focus not only to her brilliant work but also to the great contribution of her intellectual antecedents, Whitman and Dickinson. These poets contributed greatly toward a distinctly American poetry. Robert Frost, perhaps the twentieth century's greatest regional poet, also was of the opinion that poetry should be precise and concentrated. His verse portraits of the rural northeast are direct, unaffected, and beautifully sensitive to realistic detail. Frost's famous poetry is recognized for its profound sense of the American spirit. He, more than Whitman or Dickinson, is identified with the Northeast because he wrote specifically about it.

Drama

Poetry, short stories, and novels fared far better than drama in the Northeast. In Puritan-controlled areas any tendency to represent ideas through pantomime or physical representation was viewed harshly—theater was immoral; dancing was of the devil. Eugene O'Neill, the first American dramatist to command worldwide praise, was born in New York City. O'Neill, strongly influenced by Sigmund Freud's theories and Swedish playwright August Strindberg's techniques, brought a new degree of sophistication to American theater. *Anna Christie* (1921), a study of frustrated lives, is noted for its dramatic intensity and atmosphere of realism. O'Neill's plays won the Pulitzer Prize for drama four times, and he won the Nobel Prize in Literature in 1936. The Puritan influence has a long legacy in literature of the Northeast; while more pronounced in the novels and short stories of, for example, Hawthorne, it also, arguably, has a presence in the plays of O'Neill. New York playwright Arthur Miller used the haunting history of the Salem witch trials in *The Crucible* (1953), in which the issue of freedom of conscience and the witchcraft trials of 1692 are employed to invoke a parallel to America, suffering from delusions of widespread communist infiltration, during the 1950's.

SUGGESTED READINGS

Brooks, Van Wyck. *The Flowering of New England*. New York: E. P. Dutton, 1936. A widely reprinted classic.

Buell, Lawrence. *New England Literary Culture: From Revolution Through Renaissance*. Cambridge, England: Cambridge University Press, 1986. Covers early Northeastern literature.

Canby, Henry Seidel. *Classic Americans: A Study of Eminent American Writers from Irving to Whitman, with an Introductory Survey of the Colonial Background of Our National Literature*. New York: Harcourt Brace Jovanovich, 1931. Traces the influence of the Northeast on American literature.

Murdock, Kenneth B. *Literature and Theology in Colonial New England*. Cambridge, Mass.: Harvard University Press, 1949. Describes religious influences on the literature of the Northeast.

Ziff, Larzer. *The Literature of the Colonial Period.* New York: McGraw-Hill, 1970. Surveys the formative years of Northeastern literature.

—*Barbara Day*

See also African American identity; Colonialism; Jewett, Sarah Orne; Melting pot; O'Neill, Eugene; *Poetry of Robert Frost, The*; Puritan and Protestant tradition; Racism and ethnocentrism; *Uncle Tom's Cabin*; Urban life

American identity: South

IDENTITIES: South

The literature of the American South has never been one of arbitrary and convenient geographic classification. Residents of what now constitutes the states south from Virginia and Maryland to Florida and west to Louisiana—despite diversity in peoples and terrain—have long identified themselves as a distinct civic and cultural group. The literature of this region possesses unique qualities and a full consciousness of its own uniqueness. Not surprisingly, whatever else may be the subject, a governing concern of Southern literature is with identity, the identity of the individual as a Southerner and the identity of Southerners—black and white, rich and poor, urban and rural—as a group and as a culture. Even stylistically, Southern literature has a distinct identity. It

American Identity: South
Milestones

1776	The Declaration of Independence is written by Virginian Thomas Jefferson; the drama of its prose is a feature of the rhetoric of Southern writers and orators.	1886	Henry W. Grady delivers his famous speech "The New South."
1834-1864	*The Southern Literary Messenger*, one of the most important publications to come out of the South. Early in his career, Edgar Allan Poe served as an assistant editor and then as editor.	1901	*Up from Slavery*, Booker T. Washington's autobiography.
		1927	Roark Bradford's *Ol' Man Adam an' His Chillun* adapted as the play *Green Pastures* (1930) by Marc Connelly, which is awarded the Pulitzer Prize in drama in 1930.
1843	Edgar Allan Poe's *The Tell-Tale Heart*.	1927-1930	Vernon Parrington's *Main Currents in American Thought*.
1845	Edgar Allan Poe's *The Raven and Other Poems*. Poe is a key figure in the development of the Southern gothic style, which profoundly affects the writers who follow him, including William Faulkner, Carson McCullers, Flannery O'Connor, Truman Capote, Anne Rice, and Tennessee Williams. The gothic style may include such features as grotesquerie, fright, curses, mystery, creepy mansions, unusual situations, and extreme or strange emotional states.	1929	Thomas Wolfe's acerbic *Look Homeward, Angel*.
		1929	William Faulkner's *The Sound and the Fury*.
		1930	*I'll Take My Stand*, essays from a group of twelve Southern writers and intellectuals. The group is known as the Agrarians and includes John Crowe Ransom and Robert Penn Warren.
		1931	William Faulkner's *Sanctuary*.
1861-1865	The Civil War.	1932	Erskine Caldwell's *Tobacco Road*.
1877	Sidney Lanier's *Poems*. After Edgar Allan Poe, Lanier is considered the most important nineteenth century poet of the Southern United States.	1936	Margaret Mitchell's popular novel, *Gone with the Wind*.
		1938	Allen Tate's *The Fathers*, set during the Civil War.
1880-1955	Joel Chandler Harris' *Tales of Uncle Remus*; anthologized as *The Complete Tales of Uncle Remus* in 1955. A collection of African American folktales.	1938	Faulkner's *The Unvanquished*, about the Civil War and the Reconstruction era.
		1939	Lillian Hellman's *The Little Foxes*.

is typically romantic and frequently grotesque, a quality which has come to be called Southern gothic. The gothic quality is distributed across genres, including the folktale, the romance, the history, the drama, and the agrarian fable.

With the onset of European migration into Virginia there emerged a literature of the responsibility of the gentlemen of the oligarchy. These men, who rather self-consciously comprised the intellectual elite, were to provide political leadership. Although there is a strong sense of democracy in Thomas Jefferson's Declaration of Independence (1776), there is no question that it was written by a Southern gentleman, not a Northern egalitarian. The document's pledge at its end of "our Lives, our Fortunes and our Sacred Honor" is undeniably romantic. Nothing about the self-consciously elegant writings of George Washington or of Jefferson smacks of the plain style, for example, of the Northern Benjamin Franklin.

In another variation of the gentleman's prose style, Joel Chandler Harris of Georgia wrote folktales in carefully presented, stereotypical dialect of the black slave; one may argue that Chandler Harris' intention is that readers understand that the writer is a gentleman observer and is creating a romance about African Americans. The black folktale tradition was carried forward by Roark Bradford in *Ol' Man Adam an' His Chillun* (1927), which was adapted into the play *Green Pastures* (1930) by Marc Connelly, which won the Pulitzer Prize in drama in 1930.

While Harris, Bradford, and other white writers such as Paul Green were fashioning an image

Genres

American Identity: South Milestones — CONTINUED

1940	*The Heart Is a Lonely Hunter*, by Carson McCullers. The intolerance, poverty, and isolation of the South are depicted in this novel.	1963	Martin Luther King, Jr., delivers his "I Have a Dream" speech.
1941	Joseph Wilbur Cash's *The Mind of the South*.	1964	Anne Tyler's *If Morning Ever Comes*.
1941	John Crowe Ransom's *The New Criticism* highlights the literary movement of the same name.	1966	Walker Percy's *The Last Gentleman*.
		1967	William Styron's *Confessions of Nat Turner*.
1941	Carson McCullers' *Reflections in a Golden Eye*, a novel set on a Southern military base.	1970	Anne Tyler's *A Slipping-Down Life* is set in North Carolina.
1946	Robert Penn Warren's novel *All the King's Men*, which is awarded the Pulitzer Prize in fiction in 1947.	1976	Anne Rice's *Interview with the Vampire*.
		1979	Beth Henley's *Crimes of the Heart*, a play.
1946	Eudora Welty's *Delta Wedding*.	1980	John Kennedy Toole's *A Confederacy of Dunces*, a hilarious novel set in New Orleans that is awarded the Pulitzer Prize in fiction in 1981.
1947	Tennessee Williams' *A Streetcar Named Desire*.		
1949	Faulkner becomes the first Southern writer to receive the Nobel Prize in Literature.	1981	Beth Henley's *The Debutante Ball*.
1949	Eudora Welty's *The Golden Apples*, a collection of short stories set in Morgana, Mississippi.	1982	Alice Walker's *The Color Purple* wins the Pulitzer Prize for fiction in 1983.
		1982	Marsha Norman's *'night Mother* wins the Pulitzer Prize in drama in 1983.
1952	*Wise Blood*, by Flannery O'Connor, a novel.	1985	Robert Penn Warren is appointed the first poet laureate of the United States.
1954	Eudora Welty's *The Ponder Heart*.		
1957	*A Death in the Family*, a novel, by James Agee.	1988	Alfred Uhry's play, *Driving Miss Daisy*.
1957	William Faulkner's *The Town*.	1988	August Wilson's *Piano Lesson*. Although not a Southerner by birth, Wilson writes of the South of his family's past.
1960	Flannery O'Connor's *The Violent Bear It Away*.	1990	August Wilson's *Two Trains Running*.

of Southern blacks, a parallel effort by African American authors to give identity to blacks begins with the writings of Booker T. Washington and develops into the clearly Southern gothic novels of Richard Wright and Alice Walker. In *The Color Purple* (1982), for example, Walker depicts the lives of poor black farmers and sharecroppers. The rural poor among white Southerners had been portrayed earlier by Erskine Caldwell, Flannery O'Connor, and James Agee with sympathy, humor, and unflinching naturalism. Even the more realistic presentations (such as Agee's) of these authors are cast in what can be called a Southern gothic mode. The gothic is unmistakable in O'Connor's twisted and horrific short stories or in Caldwell's *Tobacco Road* (1932). One may also label such works, as well as those of Carson McCullers and Eudora Welty, as agrarian fables. Intense religious experience, especially that of Fundamentalist Protestantism, is also a familiar motif in the literature dealing with the rural poor, whether black or white.

The exporting of Southern gothic to Europe, in the works of Edgar Allan Poe, was greatly influential upon the French Symbolist movement of the early twentieth century, which in turn had a profound effect on the literature and art of the rest of the century. Poe's works are dark, morbid pictures of torment, as in the poem "The Raven," or of the criminal mind, as in the short story "The Tell-Tale Heart," both from the early 1840's.

In the twentieth century, William Faulkner combined the Southern gothic, the narrative of the gentleman, and the historical in a series of novels about the inhabitants of a mythological Mississippi county, Yoknapatawpha. One greatly admired work, *The Sound and the Fury* (1929), experiments with retelling the same events from the viewpoints of four distinct participants, each searching for an identity within the South: an idiot, two very different white men, and a black servant. In 1949, Faulkner became the first Southern writer to receive the Nobel Prize in Literature.

In l930, twelve Southern writers and intellectuals came together for a symposium at Vanderbilt University. The result was a volume of essays, *I'll Take My Stand* (1930), which reaffirmed the Southern faith in its cultural identity and called for the return to an ideal life based on agriculture. Henceforth the group was known as the Agrarians and included important literary theorists, notably John Crowe Ransom and Robert Penn Warren.

With Cleanth Brooks, Warren headed an influential group that practiced what became known as New Criticism. He won the Pulitzer Prize in fiction with his novel, *All the King's Men* (1946), a study of a poor Southern man who seeks his identity in the manipulation of political power, only to yield to corruption and violence.

Literary forms   Southern writing is found in a variety of literary forms. Poe and Sidney Lanier are two early poets who began a tradition enlarged upon by Ransom, Allen Tate, Elizabeth Maddox Roberts, and Warren, who in 1985 was appointed the first poet laureate of the United States. Washington and Jefferson are the progenitors of a strong group of Southern essayists who include many of the New Critics as well as the sensible voice of the journalist Ralph Magill and the irascible wit of H. L. Mencken. In oratory the eloquence of the South is reflected in a range of fiery speeches from Patrick Henry to Huey Long and to Martin Luther King, Jr., most having to do with race, freedom, and political issues. Southern fiction abounds in novels and short stories. Considering the intense contrasts—hence conflict—embodied in Southern culture, it is not surprising that quite a large number of Southern writers have turned to drama.

Tennessee Williams is perhaps the best-known Southern dramatist. His powerful and pungent play, *A Streetcar Named Desire* (1947), is a study of the destruction of the personality of Blanche Dubois, who is an embodiment of the genteel, hypocritical, and impossible ideals of the Old South. Her destroyer is her brother-in-law, Stanley, an uncouth representative of a new urban industrial culture. Lillian Hellman, in *The Little Foxes* (1939), also examines the identity of the Southern belle in all her vixenish complexity. The Southern belle stereotype is thoroughly exploited by Margaret Mitchell in a popular novel, *Gone with the Wind* (1936), which was adapted into one of the world's most famous films. Southern women writers wrestling with the definition of women in the South have been especially successful in the theater, with both Beth Henley (*Crimes of the Heart*, 1979) and Marsha Norman (*'night Mother*, 1982) winning the Pulitzer Prize in drama.

That there is an identifiable Southern culture and a group of people who are Southerners is rarely denied. The nature and quality of Southern culture, however, is the subject of a seemingly endless debate. Prior to the Civil War, there was an Old South whose identity as an ideal of ancient Greek democracy was widely proclaimed by Southerners and seriously analyzed by such intellectuals as Edward Parrington (*Main Currents in American Thought*, 1927-1930). After the Civil War, there emerged, in the words of Henry W. Grady, a new South, but this South still retained a powerful group identity, so powerful that much of Southern literature since the Civil War is centered on the individual's struggle to fit into the South or to escape from the South, or somehow to accomplish both ends simultaneously without complete destruction of personality. This conflicted desire is the burden of works such as William Styron's *Confessions of Nat Turner* (1967) and Walker Percy's *The Last Gentleman* (1966).

Fixed and long established cultures tend to foster stereotypes, and much of the torment over personal identity in the South is brought on by the need to accept or reject the group ideal or stereotype. Such a struggle can be seen in Thomas Wolfe's acerbic *Look Homeward, Angel* (1929). Even a writer such as August Wilson, not a Southerner by birth, senses the South of his family's past always intruding on the present. The historical informs two of his most powerful dramas: *Two Trains Running* (1990) and *The Piano Lesson* (1988). African Americans, poor whites, and Southern women in general find interfacing with forceful stereotypes both amusing and maddening. In Alfred Uhry's play, *Driving Miss Daisy* (1988), both the black chauffeur and the Jewish lady from Atlanta finally accept and enjoy living up to their stereotypes. Ignatius J. Reilly, in turn, clearly fulfills his identity as a peculiar, grotesque parody of the stereotype of urban poor white trash in John Kennedy Toole's brilliant comic piece, *A Confederacy of Dunces* (1980), but Henley's women in *The Debutante Ball* (1981) both rage against and retreat to their identity as Southern ladies. Those Southern women who do find their personal realization in the cultural stereotype are, in Robert Harling's words, steel magnolias.

Just exactly what is Southern identity has produced a number of studies, the most famous of which is Joseph Wilbur Cash's work, *The Mind of the South* (1941). Similar studies, some critical of Cash, followed, including *The Mind of the Old South* (1961), *The Americanization of Dixie, the Southernization of America* (1974), and *The Idea of the American South* (1979). The Southern gothic has continued to impose its identity in the late twentieth century in such works as the vampire sagas of Anne Rice or the urban middle-class stories of Anne Tyler. In many works of literature, Southerners are often committed to struggling for personal identity both within and separate from the traditions of the South.

SUGGESTED READINGS

Bartley, Numan V. *The New South 1945-1980: The Story of the South's Modernization*. Baton Rouge: Louisiana State University Press, 1996. Argues that the South was forced to embrace moderation, without entirely losing its culture, by the growth of cities in the region.

_____, ed. *The Evolution of Southern Culture*. Athens: University of Georgia Press, 1988. Eight essays on crucial aspects of Southern culture, ranging from religion to agrarianism, from politics to the hero in literature.

Gray, Robert. *Writing the South: Ideas of an American Region*. Cambridge, England: Cambridge University Press, 1986. Essays on Southern writers who specifically write about the region, including the Agrarians, Welty, Faulkner, and Percy.

Griffin, Larry J., and H. Doyle. *The South as an American Problem*. Athens: University of Georgia Press, 1996. Twelve essays by important historians and observers of the South. Argues that much of American culture has been fashioned by attitudes about the South.

Hall, B. C., and C. T. Wood. *The South*. New York: Charles Scribner's Sons, 1995. A tour of the South and the cultural identities and icons of each subregion, from the swamps of Louisiana to the mountains of Tennessee.

Ransom, John Crowe, ed. *I'll Take My Stand: The South and the Agrarian Tradition*. New York: Harper & Row, 1930. Twelve essays by leading Southern writers espousing agrarian over industrial life.

Singhal, Daniel Joseph. *The War Within: From Victorian to Modernist Thought in the South*. Chapel Hill: University of North Carolina Press, 1982. A thoughtful and illuminating study of the evolution of Southern culture and its literature in the nineteenth and twentieth centuries.

Young, Stark. *A Southern Treasury of Life and Literature*. New York: Charles Scribner's Sons, 1937. A well-rounded collection of samples of the writing of important literary figures from colonial days to the mid-twentieth century.

—*August W. Staub*

See also African American identity; Christianity and Christian Fundamentalism; Class and identity; Poverty; Rural life; Slavery; Stereotypes and identity

American identity: West and the frontier

IDENTITIES: West and Southwest

For Americans, the frontier will always be a literal and mythic place. Even as early settlers struggled against a harsh landscape to create new homes for themselves, a variety of thinkers sought to present the frontier as a figurative place where pioneers could make themselves into whatever they wanted to be. Certain ideas closely associated with the frontier—self-reliance, individualism, Manifest Destiny, regeneration, even democracy—were designed to portray a young America as a place where one's future was absolutely a matter of what one was willing to make it.

Although from a twentieth century standpoint the West and the frontier have often been identified as the same, the frontier actually changed over time as the United States expanded. When the first colonists arrived, the frontier was the Atlantic coast. Once these colonists established settlements, the frontier became the land immediately beyond the Appalachians; later the Ohio Valley; later still the Mississippi Valley; and so forth, until the nation was completely settled. Despite changes in the frontier's location, however, American attitudes toward expansion and settlement have remained remarkably consistent over time, with the New England Puritans establishing the basic ideological tenets of the frontier myth shortly after their arrival.

The frontier to 1890

Though they came to the New World seeking the right to worship, the Puritans hardly believed in religious freedom as it would later be defined. Rather, they felt that God had destined them to convert America into a theocracy in which people would live according to Puritan doctrine. This plan caused so much strife with Native Americans, who often refused to abide by white beliefs, that many Europeans in America (including the prominent ministers, Increase Mather and Cotton Mather) soon came to see extermination of Indians as tantamount to religious duty. Thus the essential frontier contest of civilization versus savagery was born in the seventeenth century, with civilization loosely defined as anything white, European, and Christian, and savagery loosely defined as anything nonwhite, non-European, and pagan. Even later Americans who were sympathetic to certain Native American causes held a European American view of the nation's future. Thomas Jefferson, for example, who wrote in 1803 that "our system is to live in perpetual peace with the Indians," declared in the same essay that "we presume that our strength and their weakness is now so visible that they must see we have only to shut our hand to crush them."

These confrontational attitudes carried over into early American literature about the frontier. Novels such as Robert Montgomery Bird's *Nick of the Woods* (1837) and William Simms's *The Yemassee* (1835), though somewhat different in tone and racial outlook, both ultimately endorsed hearty, sadistic white heroes who reveled in killing Indians. In fiction, however, the frontier was truly immortalized by James Fenimore Cooper—especially in the Leatherstocking Tales (1823-1841), a collection of five novels unified by their focus on Cooper's archetypal frontiersman, Natty Bumppo. Unlike Bird and Simms, Cooper had mixed feelings about the contest between "civilization" and "savagery." On one hand, he was attracted to the idea of the noble savage, which held in part that industrialized society deprived humans of their innate virtue and sense of self-worth. To that end, he romanticized many of his native characters and Bumppo, making them "natural"

THE FAR WEST.—SHOOTING BUFFALO ON THE LINE OF THE KANSAS-PACIFIC RAILROAD.

To many writers of the twentieth century, the much-hailed grandeur of Westward expansion had violence, ecological destruction, and the encroachment of technology at its center. (Library of Congress)

moralists who acted with integrity despite their wild surroundings. Cooper also believed, however, that just as the wilderness allowed for the full development of virtue, it failed to restrict humanity's most evil impulses (a fact substantiated by the abundance of bad Indians in his novels). Therefore, Cooper acknowledged the necessity of white expansion and the correspondent rule of law and morality, no matter how artificial, that civilization entailed.

Cooper's writing sparked many later novels that feature white heroes settling the West, often by killing villains and Indians. In 1858, Erasmus Beadle, an editor and businessman, began to market dime novels—inexpensive paperback volumes filled with action-packed frontier plots, most of them based on formulas developed by Beadle and his writers (hence the phrase "formula Western"). These volumes were wildly popular with audiences through the 1890's and accentuated the other kinds of rampant frontier marketing occurring at the time, such as Buffalo Bill's Wild West Show or even George Armstrong Custer's ostensibly true accounts of battles with the Indians. In short, by the late nineteenth century, frontier literature was part of a larger entertainment industry geared to romanticize the West for a mostly Eastern audience, exhorting bands of people to try their luck in settling along the frontier and driving anti-Native American sentiment to a fever pitch.

Despite the success of people such as Cooper and Beadle, however, it would be a mistake to believe that their version of the West went unchallenged. Women writers especially took exception both with Cooper's view of the frontier as a male-dominated space and with his depiction of Indians as largely savage and ignorant. Lydia Maria Child's *Hobomok* (1824) and Catherine Maria Sedgwick's *Hope Leslie: Or, Early Times in Massachusetts* (1827), for example, question the spurious representations and severe treatment of Native Americans by white Americans, directly inverting the ideology of the Leatherstocking Tales. This trend continued with later works such as

Helen Hunt Jackson's *Ramona* (1884), which sympathetically depicted the mixed-race relationship of a half-white protagonist and a full-blooded Indian. More canonical writers, as well, undermined the overtly mythological version of the frontier espoused by Cooper and his descendants. Mark Twain's *Roughing It* (1872), for example, debunked the claims of economic opportunity and social equality along the frontier that Eastern ideologues used to persuade people to settle there. And Bret Harte's *The Luck of Roaring Camp* (1868) presented a sentimental version of the West, where citizens rarely took up guns to solve their problems. Even in the nineteenth century, then, writers and public figures disagreed drastically on what the frontier and the West were like and on how the two places affected the development of a distinctively American culture.

The frontier after 1890

In 1893, however, American views on the frontier were forever changed by the writings of Frederick Jackson Turner. Turner, a historian responding to critics who saw American history as a product of friction between North and South, argued instead that the frontier had been the central factor in national development. Land at the frontier was free, Turner maintained, so citizens could always fulfill the American Dream of self-determination simply by moving West onto "vacant" farmland. Like their forebears, these people would continue to carve civilization out of wilderness and, subsequently, would infuse the rest of the nation with a new democratic spirit. In this way, America would be regenerated, both economically and politically, as frontier settlers continued to remind other citizens of the individual freedoms and accomplishments that had made the country great. Ironically, Turner's ideas were occasioned by the 1890 census, which announced that an

---

American Identity: West and the Frontier
Milestones

1823-1841	James Fenimore Cooper invents the Western in the Leatherstocking Tales, a collection of five novels unified by their focus on Cooper's archetypal frontiersman, Natty Bumppo.	1869	Two railroads—one heading east from the West and one heading west from the East—are linked, providing the first link between the Mississippi Valley and the West Coast.
1824	Lydia Maria Child's *Hobomok*.	1872	Mark Twain's *Roughing It*.
1827	Catherine Maria Sedgwick's *Hope Leslie: Or, Early Times in Massachusetts*.	1874	*My Life on the Plains*, by George Armstrong Custer. A detailed account of Custer's days on the battlefield.
1835	William Simms's *The Yemassee*.		
1837	Robert Montgomery Bird's *Nick of the Woods*, a novel in the frontier genre.	1883	William Cody, or Buffalo Bill, begins his Wild West show.
1848-1849	The California gold rush. People from all around the world flock to California to find their fortunes, establishing California's multiethnic heritage. When the gold rush begins, California has a population of fourteen thousand; by 1849 there are an estimated one hundred thousand people in the state.	1884	Helen Hunt Jackson's *Ramona*.
		1894	Frederick Jackson Turner's *The Significance of the Frontier in American History*. Turner, a historian, contends that the frontier has been the central factor in national development.
1850-1900	Era of a genre of novels and short stories that are set in the West. Notable authors include James Fenimore Cooper, Owen Wister, Zane Grey, and Louis L'Amour.	1902	Frederic Remington's *John Ermine of the Yellowstone*.
		1902	Owen Wister's *The Virginian*. Famous for the phrase "when you say that, smile."
1860	Erastus Beadle, an editor and businessman, begins marketing dime novels—inexpensive paperback volumes filled with action-packed frontier plots, most of them based on formulas developed by Beadle and his writers (hence the phrase "formula Western").	1903	Andy Adams' *The Log of a Cowboy*.
		1912	Zane Grey's *Riders of the Purple Sage*, perhaps the most famous Western.
		1919	*The Untamed*, by Frederick Schiller Faust, a novel.
		1926	Zane Grey's *Under the Tonto Rim*.

actual frontier in America no longer existed. Turner's writing was important, then, not only because it placed the frontier at the center of historical debate, but also because it suggested that in the absence of a literal frontier Americans would have to rely on a figurative frontier.

Since the frontier had always been a mixture of fact and fiction, writers had no problem answering Turner's call to elegize its passing. Particularly important was Turner's focus on regeneration, his belief that the frontier embodied the concept of freedom more completely than any other place in America. Other writers, however, did not see the frontier as a symbol to bolster democratic ideals; rather, many used the mythic West to call for "racial revitalization" and sometimes racial supremacy. The beginning of the twentieth century marked a period of staunch racism in which certain whites attempted to "regain" the glories of America, which they believed had been taken from them by immoral whites and non-whites generally. For heroes, these men turned to the West, arguing that the landscape had been "tamed" through the efforts of archetypal white figures—the hunter, the soldier, and the cowboy. Such figures were immortalized in books like Owen Wister's *The Virginian* (1902), Zane Grey's *Riders of the Purple Sage* (1912), and later in Louis L'Amour's *Hondo* (1953) as well as in films such as *Red River* (1948) and *High Noon* (1952). Some novels, such as Frederic Remington's *John Ermine of the Yellowstone* (1902), continued to present Native Americans as largely savage—even after the last tribes were placed on reservations—to justify the push for predominantly white, male, and violent control of the nation.

American Identity: West and the Frontier Milestones — CONTINUED

1929	Oliver La Farge's *Laughing Boy*.	1961	Larry McMurtry's *Horseman, Pass By*, set on a Texas ranch. In 1963, the novel is made into the feature film, *Hud*.
1936	D'Arcy McNickle's *The Surrounded*.		
1937	*Of Mice and Men*, by John Steinbeck. A novel about the land and the people of Salinas Valley, California.	1962	John Steinbeck is awarded the Nobel Prize in Literature.
1939	*The Day of the Locust*, by Nathanael West. A novel set in Hollywood.	1964	*Sometimes a Great Notion*, by Ken Kesey.
		1966	Louis L'Amour's *The Broken Gun*.
1939	John Steinbeck's *The Grapes of Wrath*, about the preciousness of the land in California.	1966	Larry McMurtry's *The Last Picture Show* deals with small-town life in a North Texas town. Made into a film in 1971.
1939	*Stagecoach*, a classic Western film directed by John Ford.	1968	N. Scott Momaday's *House Made of Dawn*, awarded the Pulitzer Prize in fiction.
1940	Walter van Tilburg Clark's *The Ox-Bow Incident*.	1977	Leslie Marmon Silko's *Ceremony*.
1942	Frank Waters' *The Man Who Killed the Deer*.	1979	Louis L'Amour's *Bendigo Shafter*.
1947	A. B. Guthrie, Jr.'s *The Big Sky*, noted for its realism and sharp insight into the psychology of the American Western pioneer.	1980	Sam Shepard's *True West*.
		1981	Leslie Marmon Silko's *Storyteller*.
1949	A. B. Guthrie's *The Way West*.	1983	Sam Shepard's *Fool for Love* wins four Obie Awards and is made into a movie in 1985.
1952	John Steinbeck's *East of Eden* traces two families in California.	1985	Cormac McCarthy's *Blood Meridian: Or, The Evening Redness in the West*.
1952	*High Noon*, a classic Western film starring Gary Cooper.	1985	Larry McMurtry's *Lonesome Dove*, a novel of the frontier past.
1953	*Hondo*, by Louis L'Amour, one of the most prolific writers of the Western genre.	1993	Larry McMurtry's *Streets of Laredo*.

Certain writers used the Western for racial and political ends (or simply to create a mythical version of the frontier only tenuously related to historical reality), but other twentieth century writers did their best to offer more realistic or evenhanded depictions. Andy Adams' *The Log of a Cowboy* (1903) presents cowboy life as it often actually is—tedious, mundane, and exhausting—while novels like Walter van Tilburg Clark's *The Ox-Bow Incident* (1940) and A. B. Guthrie, Jr.'s *The Big Sky* (1947) portrayed the mythic West as an overly violent place where characters' ready willingness to draw guns often resulted in tragedy. Also, white writers such as Oliver La Farge (*Laughing Boy*, 1929) and Frank Waters (*The Man Who Killed the Deer*, 1942) began to explore the complexities of Native American culture, viewing Indians as more than a nemesis of American pioneers. Additionally, Indian writers began to produce fictions that told their own story, offering an incisive counterpoint to mostly white versions of the West. The finest of these works include D'Arcy McNickle's *The Surrounded* (1936), N. Scott Momaday's *House Made of Dawn* (1968), and Leslie Marmon Silko's *Ceremony* (1977), along with many others.

Recently, the West has experienced a resurgence in American letters. Writers such as Sherman Alexie, Cormac McCarthy, Ken Kesey, Thomas King, and Larry McMurtry have consciously invoked Western settings and sometimes formula devices in their fiction. Literary critics, unsatisfied with the mythic version of the frontier left to them by several decades of popular films, television, and radio, have begun to interrogate the formula Western aspects of canonical writers such as Willa Cather, Nathanael West, and John Steinbeck. Even the film industry, despite its reputation of being among the most shameless purveyors of the frontier formula, began to produce such films as *Unforgiven* (1992), an explicit debunking of the dime-novel perception of the West. The West continues to supply Americans with a wealth of material for artistic and critical discourse more than a century after the close of the literal frontier.

SUGGESTED READINGS

Cawelti, John G. *The Six-Gun Mystique*. 2d ed. Bowling Green, Ohio: Bowling Green State University Popular Press, 1977. Analyzes the twentieth century formula Western in terms of literary antecedents and in terms of psychological and cultural function.

Milton, John. *The Novel of the American West*. Lincoln: University of Nebraska Press, 1980. Analyzes several Western texts that supposedly defy the conventions of frontier writing.

Slotkin, Richard. *The Fatal Environment: The Myth of the Frontier in the Age of Industrialization 1800-1890*. New York: Atheneum, 1985. Historical extension of arguments made in *Regeneration Through Violence*, listed below.

_____. *Regeneration Through Violence: The Mythology of the American Frontier, 1600-1860*. Middletown, Conn.: Wesleyan University Press, 1973. A seminal text in addressing the role that the frontier has played in defining American culture.

Smith, Henry Nash. *Virgin Land*. Cambridge, Mass.: Harvard University Press, 1950. The pre-eminent work on American frontier writing. Looks closely at several basic myths that underscore the larger frontier myth.

Tompkins, Jane. *West of Everything: The Inner Life of Westerns*. New York: Oxford University Press, 1992. A reader-response analysis of several Western texts, including film, which focuses on sexual dynamics of frontier literature.

Turner, Frederick Jackson. *The Frontier in American History*. New York: Holt, Rinehart and Winston, 1962. Brought the frontier, as myth and as reality, into the center of American historical and cultural debate in the twentieth century.

—*David Stevens*

See also Abbey, Edward; Canadian identity; Cather, Willa; Colonialism; Jackson, Helen Hunt; Latino American identity; McMurtry, Larry; Native American identity; Stegner, Wallace

American Indians. *See* Native American identity

American Tragedy, An

AUTHOR: Theodore Dreiser (1871-1945)

FIRST PUBLISHED: 1925

IDENTITIES: European American

While a newspaper reporter in the 1890's, Theodore Dreiser noticed a particular type of crime: A young man who was successful would murder his pregnant fiancée so that he might free himself from her and marry another woman who had more money and higher social standing. For years Dreiser collected these stories from the newspapers, planning someday to write a novel based on one of these crimes, because he felt that such a crime was typically American. This crime represented what was wrong with U. S. society. *An American Tragedy* is based on one such murder.

In 1906, Chester Gillette, a worker in his uncle's skirt factory, drowned Grace Brown, a coworker. The crime was prompted by Grace Brown's pregnancy, which restricted Gillette's pursuit of a local socialite whose family was wealthy. Dreiser based Clyde Griffiths, the main character in *An American Tragedy*, on Chester Gillette. Clyde is born to a poor religious family, as were Dreiser and Gillette. Clyde longs for fine clothes, material goods, friends, and women. As a bellboy in various hotels, he improves his clothing and his financial status, but he always longs for more. Eventually he, like Chester, meets a wealthy uncle who offers him a position in the uncle's factory—this position leads to further social and career opportunities. During Clyde's advancement he develops a relationship with Roberta Alden, who becomes pregnant. While Clyde at one time promises Roberta that he will marry her, his success changes his plans. He wishes to marry Sandra Finchley, the daughter of a wealthy factory owner. When Clyde fails to find a doctor who will perform an abortion, he drowns Roberta, but he is caught, tried, and executed.

As in all of his works Dreiser realistically explores the motives of people in America. This long novel is considered Dreiser's masterpiece. It weaves numerous perspectives and social issues into its fabric, never offering easy answers or solutions, always questioning the motives and values of characters who mean well. *An American Tragedy* represents the first time in American literature that a murderer is depicted with a degree of sympathy. This novel exposes the tragedies that occur when people seek wealth by quick, easy means. Dreiser's complex and multifaceted representation of this crime moves beyond simple realism or journalism, revealing an elaborate portrait of an America that Dreiser saw as tragic.

SUGGESTED READINGS

Bloom, Harold, ed. *Theodore Dreiser's "An American Tragedy."* New York: Chelsea House, 1988.

Gerber, Philip L. *Theodore Dreiser Revisited.* New York: Twayne, 1992.

Lingeman, Richard. *Theodore Dreiser: An American Journey, 1908-1945.* New York: G. P. Putnam's Sons, 1990.

Michaels, Benn Walter. "*An American Tragedy*: Or, The Promise of American Life." *Representations* 25 (Winter, 1989): 71-98.

Pizer, Donald. *The Novels of Theodore Dreiser: A Critical Study.* Minneapolis: University of Minnesota Press, 1976.

—*Roark Mulligan*

See also Dreiser, Theodore; *Sister Carrie*; Urban life

Amish. *See* Religious minorities

Anarchism

DEFINITION: Anarchism is a social and political philosophy that rejects all forms of authority and coercive control.

Anarchism in the literature of North America is rooted in the tradition of anarchist social and political writings. In their influence upon literature, anarchist writers fall roughly into two groups:

collectivists and individualists. While collectivists emphasize the importance of systematic cooperation among members of society, individualists emphasize the importance of individual freedom above all else. Both groups reject authority and coercive control. Among collectivist anarchists, the ideas of writers such as Mikhail Bakunin and Pyotr Kropotkin have been most influential. Among individualists the ideas of writers such as William Godwin, Pierre-Joseph Proudhon, and Benjamin Tucker have had the most influence.

Autobiographies

Historically, autobiography occupies an important place in anarchist literature. Many classic anarchist thinkers wrote autobiographies, the best known being Kropotkin's *Paroles d'un Révolté* (1885; *Memoirs of a Revolutionist*, 1899). In North American literature an important autobiographical work by an anarchist is Emma Goldman's *Living My Life* (1931).

In *Living My Life* Goldman describes the formation of her identity as an anarchist and a feminist. She points to the prejudice that she experienced growing up as a Jew in Russia, to the brutality against women and peasants that she witnessed there, and to her exposure to the revolutionary doctrines circulating in Russia during her youth as important factors in shaping her mature values and beliefs. As an adult Goldman identifies herself with all who are oppressed and in particular with oppressed women. Goldman embraces elements of collectivist as well as individualist anarchism.

Poetry and fiction

In poetry and fiction, collectivist anarchism is primarily represented in the works of George Woodcock, Lawrence Ferlinghetti, and Ursula K. Le Guin, while individualist anarchism is primarily represented in the works of Paul Goodman and Karl Shapiro. In considering the identities embodied in the works of these authors, it is important to keep in mind that identities embraced by collectivist anarchists commonly differ significantly from those embraced by individualist anarchists. Collectivist anarchists generally conceive of their identity in social and political terms, as individuals who are part of a social group or movement. Individualist anarchists, on the other hand, especially those who are artists, often desire absolute freedom from authority in order to express and explore their own personal identities.

Collectivist anarchism

The authors whose works depict collectivist anarchism emphasize social issues over personal issues. In his travel memoirs Woodcock described his impressions of diverse societies with an eye to the political and communal potentials of these societies. Out of Woodcock's numerous travel memoirs the most notable for the libertarian perspectives contained in them are *Ravens and Prophets: Travels in Western Canada* (1952) and *Kerala: A Portrait of the Malabar Coast* (1967). Ferlinghetti expresses his pacifist anarchism in works such as *A Political Pamphlet* (1976) and *Populist Manifestos* (1981). These works focus on the threats that capitalist society poses to human well-being and to the natural world. In her science-fiction novel *The Dispossessed* (1974), Le Guin explores the internal politics of an anarchist society existing on a barren moon. By comparing this anarchist society to the capitalist and socialist societies of the moon's mother planet, Le Guin brings the political and social issues involved in collectivist anarchism more sharply into focus. Additional depictions of collectivist anarchist societies occur in the works of ecological feminists, such as *The Fifth Sacred Thing* (1993) by Starhawk.

Individualist anarchism

Goodman's work contrasts sharply with that of collectivist anarchists. Emphasizing the value of tradition and advocating a version of individualist anarchism drawn from classic texts, Goodman sees the principles of anarchism at work in the everyday interactions of individuals. In his *Collected of Poems* (1973), he does not identify himself with a movement or political aim, but instead freely explores his identity as a Jewish gay man and as an inheritor of the Western tradition. Like Goodman's poetry, Shapiro's poetry is also confessional, and it also deals with issues concerning his identity as a Jewish American. In contrast to Goodman's love of tradition, however, Shapiro's individualist anarchism takes the form of a rejection of the Western tradition, as evidenced in *The Bourgeois Poet* (1964).

The works of Henry David Thoreau, John Dos Passos, Henry Miller, and Edward Abbey have also been associated with anarchism. Although works by these authors do not exhibit the direct influence of classical anarchist thought, they do contain strong currents of antiauthoritarianism and individualism and thus are relevant to the study of anarchism in literature.

The identities involved in a work of anarchist literature derive from the types of anarchism represented. While anarchist literature encompasses a broad spectrum of identities, all of these identities share the belief that external authority is harmful and that human beings benefit from the freedom to organize their lives as they see best.

SUGGESTED READINGS

Cummins, Elizabeth. *Understanding Ursula K. Le Guin*. Columbia: University of South Carolina Press, 1990.

Guerin, Daniel. *Anarchism: From Theory to Practice*. Translated by Mary Klopper. New York: Monthly Review Press, 1970.

Heider, Ulrike. *Anarchism: Left, Right, and Green*. Translated by Danny Lewis and Ulrike Bode. San Francisco: City Lights Books, 1994.

Hughes, Peter. *George Woodcock*. Toronto: McClelland and Stewart, 1974.

Kropotkin, Pyotr Alekseyevich. *The Essential Kropotkin*. Edited by Emile Capouya and Keitha Tompkins. New York: Liveright, 1975.

Parisi, Peter, ed. *Artist of the Actual: Essays on Paul Goodman*. Metuchen, N.J.: Scarecrow Press, 1986.

Runkle, Gerald. *Anarchism, Old and New*. New York: Delacorte Press, 1972.

Solomon, Martha. *Emma Goldman*. Boston: Twayne, 1987.

Woodcock, George. *Anarchism: A History of Libertarian Ideas and Movements*. Cleveland: Meridian Books, 1962.

—*Michael L. Bazemore*

See also Abbey, Edward; *Civil Disobedience*; Countercultures; Ferlinghetti, Lawrence; Miller, Henry

Anaya, Rudolfo A.

BORN: Pastura, New Mexico; October 30, 1937

PRINCIPAL WORKS: *Bless Me, Ultima*, 1972; *Heart of Aztlán*, 1976; *Tortuga*, 1979; *The Silence of the Llano*, 1982; *Alburquerque*, 1992; *Zia Summer*, 1995; *Jalamanta*, 1996; *Rio Grande Fall*, 1996

IDENTITIES: Latino; West and Southwest

SIGNIFICANT ACHIEVEMENT: Anaya is the foremost Chicano novelist of the twentieth century.

Rudolfo Anaya began writing during his days as a student at the University of New Mexico. His poetry and early novels dealt with major questions about his existence, beliefs, and identity. Anaya ended that phase of his life by burning all of the manuscripts of his work.

After college he took a teaching job and got married. He found his wife to be a great source of encouragement and an excellent editor and companion. Anaya began writing *Bless Me, Ultima* in the 1960's. He struggled with the work until in one of his creative moments Ultima appeared to him. She became the strongest character of the novel as well as the spiritual mentor for the novelist and the protagonist. Ultima led the way to a successful work. Anaya's next task was to get his novel published. After dozens of rejection letters from major publishers, Anaya turned to Quinto Sol Publications, a Chicano small press in Berkeley, California. The publishers not only accepted the work for publication but also recognized Anaya with the Quinto Sol Award for writing the best Chicano novel of 1972.

Bless Me, Ultima represents the first novel of a trilogy. The other two are *Heart of Aztlán* and *Tortuga*. *Heart of Aztlán* came as a result of Anaya's travels in Mexico during the 1960's, which raised the question of the relationship between the pre-Columbian Aztec world, called Aztlán, and Chicano destiny. *Tortuga* was inspired by an diving accident at an irrigation ditch during Anaya's high school days. The accident left Anaya disabled; the protagonist in the novel also experiences such events. The quality of the first three works enshrined Anaya as the foremost Chicano novelist of his time. His numerous other excellent works have confirmed this high regard. The essence of his literary production reflects the search for the meaning of existence as it is expressed in Chicano community life.

Anaya's works blend realistic description of daily life with the hidden magic of humanity; his work may be categorized as having the qualities of Magical Realism, which mingles in a straightforward narrative tone the mystical and magical with the everyday. Most of his developed characters reflect this duality.

SUGGESTED READINGS

González-T, César A, ed. *Rudolfo A. Anaya: Focus on Criticism.* La Jolla, Calif.: Lalo Press, 1990.
Tatum, Charles M. *Chicano Literature.* Boston: Twayne, 1982.
Vasallo, Paul, ed. *The Magic of Words: Rudolfo Anaya and His Writings.* Albuquerque: University of New Mexico Press, 1982.

—David Conde

See also American identity: West and the frontier; *Bless Me, Ultima*; Chicano identity; Chicano Renaissance; *Heart of Aztlán*; *Tortuga*

Ancient Child, The

AUTHOR: N. Scott Momaday (1934-   )
FIRST PUBLISHED: 1989
IDENTITIES: Native American; West and Southwest

A complex and richly evocative work, N. Scott Momaday's *The Ancient Child* is the story of two Native Americans—a middle-aged painter and a young woman—who come to a fuller understanding of themselves. Native American folklore and mythology are woven into their story, lending cultural and psychological depth to the two's quests for, essentially, rebirth.

Locke Setman, called "Set" throughout the novel, is in many ways a representative Momaday protagonist because he is cut off from his past and therefore lives an unexamined life. Brought up in an orphanage by an embittered academic, Set's connection to the Kiowa culture of his ancestors is tenuous. Because Set does not know his past "it was in Set's nature to wonder, until the wonder became pain, who he was." His quest to achieve a more profound sense of self begins when he receives a telegram begging him to attend the funeral of one Kope' mah. Mystified by a past he has never known, Set goes to the funeral and meets Grey, who is training to become a medicine woman because she "never had . . . to quest after visions."

Like Set, Grey has not achieved her true identity, largely because she rejects the modern world. After being raped by a white farmer, she goes to live in an abandoned sod house in a ghost town. She literally dwells in the past. She speaks Kiowan fluently, so she is befriended by Kope' mah, and becomes the link between Set's past and his future. When the two meet, Grey gives Set a medicine bag containing "the spirit of the bear." The bear, Set's unacknowledged totem animal, is as much a curse as a blessing, however, since the life that Set has lived must be stripped away before his true identity can be recognized. Set suffers a mental breakdown and his nightmares are dominated by "a dark, impending shape" that draws him into itself, into "the hot contamination of the beast."

Eventually, when he is completely stripped of illusions, Set is drawn back to Kiowan tribal lands, and back to Grey. Set is healed and the two forge a relationship, one tied to an awareness of themselves and their culture. Grey teaches Set to speak the language of her people, and by the novel's end, Set is profoundly aware of his place in their culture: "he knew . . . its definition in his mind's eye, its awful silence in the current of his blood." He belongs.

SUGGESTED READINGS

Coltelli, Laura. *Winged Words.* Lincoln: University of Nebraska Press, 1990.
Vizenor, Gerald. *Manifest Manners.* Middletown, Conn.: Wesleyan University Press, 1994.

—Michael R. Meyers

See also American identity: West and the frontier; *House Made of Dawn*; Momaday, N. Scott; Native American identity

And the Earth Did Not Part

AUTHOR: Tomás Rivera (1935-1984)

FIRST PUBLISHED: . . . *y no se lo tragó la tierra/And the Earth Did Not Part*, 1971 (rev. ed. 1977; also translated as *And the Earth Did Not Devour Him*)

IDENTITIES: Adolescence and coming-of-age; Latino; West and Southwest

And the Earth Did Not Part, Tomás Rivera's only published novel, exerted a great influence on the blossoming of Chicano literature. The book explores the psychological and external circumstances of a boy who is coming of age in a Mexican American migrant family. The novel is a collection of disjointed narratives, including twelve stories and thirteen vignettes, told with various voices. This unusual structure evokes impressions of a lifestyle in which the continuity of existence is repeatedly broken by forced migration, in which conflicting values tug at the emerging self, and in which poverty creates a deadening sameness that erases time.

The story begins with "The Lost Year," which indicates the boy has lost touch with his identity and with the reality of events. Several sections portray the dismal, oppressed condition of migrant farmworkers. "Hand in His Pocket" tells of a wicked couple—immigrants who prey on their own people. In "A Silvery Night," the boy first calls the devil, then decides that the devil does not exist. Religious awakening continues in the title chapter, in which the boy curses God and is not punished—the earth remains solid.

The nature of sin, the mystery of sex, and the injustices and tragedies visited upon his people are all confusing to the boy. Brief moments of beauty are eclipsed by injuries and horrible deaths. A mother struggles to buy a few Christmas presents for her children and is thwarted by the disturbing confusion and noise of the town. In a swindle, a family loses their only photograph of a son killed in the Korean War. Bouncing from place to place in rickety trucks, the workers lose all sense of continuity. The boy becomes a man, hiding under his house. The final scene offers a glimmer of hope, as he climbs a tree and imagines that someone in another tree can see him.

The simple language and humble settings make the book accessible, but the novel's unique structure and symbolism present challenges to the reader. *And the Earth Did Not Part* has been reprinted several times, and a retelling in English (*This Migrant Earth*, 1985) was published by Rolando Hinojosa. A film version, *And the Earth Did Not Swallow Him*, was released in 1994.

SUGGESTED READINGS

Olivares, Julian, ed. *International Studies of Tomás Rivera*. Houston, Tex.: Arte Público Press, 1986.

_____, ed. *Tomás Rivera: The Complete Works*. Houston, Tex.: Arte Público Press, 1991.

Rivera, Tomás. *The Man and His Work*. Edited by Vernon E. Lattin, Rolando Hinojosa, and Gary D. Keller. Tempe, Ariz.: Bilingual Review Press, 1988.

—Laura L. Klure

See also Adolescent identity; American identity: West and the frontier; Bilingualism; Chicano identity; Chicano Renaissance; Latino American identity; Migratory workers; Poverty

Anderson, Sherwood

BORN: Camden, Ohio; September 13, 1876

DIED: Colón, Panama Canal Zone; March 8, 1941

PRINCIPAL WORKS: *Winesburg, Ohio*, 1919; *Poor White*, 1920; *The Triumph of the Egg*, 1921; *Dark Laughter*, 1925; *Death in the Woods and Other Stories*, 1933

IDENTITIES: European American; Midwest

SIGNIFICANT ACHIEVEMENT: Anderson's short stories and novels about life in the agrarian Midwest are among the best in American regionalist fiction.

Sherwood Anderson began writing during the period from 1907 to 1912, when he was manager of a paint business in Elyria, Ohio. He had settled there in 1907 with his wife and growing family, apparently eager for success. The child of an impoverished harness maker whose skills had been made obsolete by advancing technology, Anderson had lived a life of hardship, meager education, and tireless moving about in search of employment. After a few years of writing advertising in Chicago and then marriage to Cornelia Lane, who was from a solid, middle-class family in Toledo, Anderson decided to go into business for himself. Soon, however, his attitude toward business changed, and he began to spend increasing amounts of time at night in an attic writing novels. In 1912, his business and personal affairs in a precarious condition, Anderson was strained to the breaking point by the contrary claims of business and writing. In November, he abruptly ceased dictation to his secretary in midsentence and walked out the door. Several days later, he was discovered wandering in Cleveland. Dazed and incoherent, he had suffered a breakdown.

Anderson's rejection of middle-class life, which eventually led to his abandoning business and personal ties and becoming part of a literary group in Chicago, provided the fundamental experience in most of his writings. Anderson turned to characters in the agrarian Midwest, who are faced with confusion brought on by a world grown complex. Anderson saw himself as a spokesman for these repressed characters. George Willard, in *Winesburg, Ohio*, would become a voice for all the inarticulate people of Anderson's early life who looked to him to write what was in their hearts and reestablish their connection with humanity.

Frustration and loneliness continued to plague Anderson, taking their toll on relationships and consuming three marriages. In later years, he realized that his yearning to live communally with his fellows was an impossible dream, to be found only in the past, but cherished in the process of living. His encouragement of other struggling writers was as notable as their gratitude, evident in William Faulkner's praise and Ernest Hemingway's imitation. As did Mark Twain, Anderson found significance in the seemingly unliterary people of the rural Midwest and in the intense revelation of life beneath the surface. A recorder of buried lives, Anderson transformed the story of his own life into experience as a circumstance of America's growth into the industrial era.

SUGGESTED READINGS

Anderson, David D. *Sherwood Anderson: An Introduction and Interpretation*. New York: Holt, Rinehart and Winston, 1967.

Burbank, Rex. *Sherwood Anderson*. New York: Twayne, 1964.

Howe, Irving. *Sherwood Anderson*. New York: William Sloane, 1951.

Schevill, James. *Sherwood Anderson: His Life and Work*. Denver, Colo: Denver University Press, 1951.

—*Mary Hurd*

See also American identity: Midwest; European American identity

Angela Davis: An Autobiography

AUTHOR: Angela Yvonne Davis (1944-   )
FIRST PUBLISHED: 1974
IDENTITIES: African American; women

Angela Davis: An Autobiography, Angela Davis' most notable literary work, is the personal narrative of her development as an African American and feminist political activist. The autobiography explores how the forces of institutionalized racism shaped her consciousness as an African American and compelled her to seek political solutions. Her personal account also explores how her experiences as a woman in a movement dominated by males affected her awareness of the special challenges African American women face in overcoming sexism and racism.

The autobiography opens not with Davis' birth but with her flight from California legal authorities. She was charged with murder and kidnapping in relation to a failed escape attempt at a California courthouse. Her constant self-awareness as an African American woman attempting to evade discovery within an overwhelmingly white society underscores the problems African Americans have in establishing their identity. From the writer's perspective, the charges against her stemmed not from a legal system that seeks justice but from a legal system that works to destroy those who fight to change the system.

As a child in racially segregated Birmingham, Alabama, Davis' fight to establish such an identity began at an early age. Growing up on "Dynamite Hill," a racially mixed neighborhood that acquired its name from the frequent bombings of African American residences, she was, as a child, aware of the danger of simply being black and of fighting for the right to have an equal voice in society. In detailing her experiences within the Black Liberation movement, Davis expresses her growing awareness of attempts to stifle the voices of African American women in particular within the movement. Communism, she contends, would eradicate all such oppression.

Davis is further convinced of the oppressive nature of the American legal system after she is captured and incarcerated to await trial. She describes continual attempts by the prison authorities to control the minds of her fellow prisoners through humiliating and nonsensical rules. She also gives an account of attempts to deprive her of her basic rights as a prisoner. When she is finally acquitted, Davis sees the verdict not as a vindication of the legal system but as a vindication of the political efforts to fight racial oppression. Many critics contend that Davis' constant focus on political ideology prevents her from giving an honest and insightful account of her experiences in her autobiography. Most agree, however, that, in spite of such perceived flaws, the autobiography presents a powerful portrait of an African American woman passionately devoted to her battle against oppression.

SUGGESTED READINGS

Ashman, Charles R. *The People vs. Angela Davis*. New York: Pinnacle Books, 1972.

Jackson, George. *Soledad Brother*. New York: Coward, McCann, 1970.

Smith, Nelda J. *From Where I Sat*. New York: Vantage, 1973.

—*Lisa R. Aunkst*

See also African American identity; Feminism

Angelou, Maya (Marguerite Johnson)

BORN: St. Louis, Missouri; April 4, 1928

PRINCIPAL WORKS: *I Know Why the Caged Bird Sings*, 1970; *Just Give Me a Cool Drink of Water 'fore I Diiie*, 1971; *Gather Together in My Name*, 1974; *Oh Pray My Wings Are Gonna Fit Me Well*, 1975; *Singin' and Swingin' and Gettin' Merry Like Christmas*, 1976; *And Still I Rise*, 1978; *The Heart of a Woman*, 1981; *Shaker, Why Don't You Sing?*, 1983; *All God's Children Need Traveling Shoes*, 1986; *Wouldn't Take Nothing for My Journey Now*, 1993

IDENTITIES: African American; South; women

SIGNIFICANT ACHIEVEMENT: Through poems and autobiographical narratives, Angelou describes her life as an African American, single mother, professional, and feminist.

Before her first autobiographical work, *I Know Why the Caged Bird Sings*, was published, Maya Angelou had a richly varied, difficult life. Her work has made her one of the most important African American female voices in the twentieth century. All of her writing is steeped in recollection of African American slavery and oppression. It also includes frank discussion of the physical and psychological pain of child abuse, the sexual anxieties of adolescence, unmarried motherhood, drug abuse, unhappy marriage, and divorce.

In *Gather Together in My Name*, Angelou struggles as a single mother to raise her son, while earning a living as Creole cook, army enlistee, madam, and prostitute. In *Singin' and Swingin' and Gettin' Merry Like Christmas*, she becomes a singer and an exotic dancer in San Francisco before joining the traveling cast of a George Gershwin musical on a twenty-two-nation tour. In *The Heart of a Woman*, she describes her later work as northern coordinator of Martin Luther King, Jr.'s

Southern Christian Leadership Conference. In *All God's Children Need Traveling Shoes*, her frustrations with American racism and yearnings for her African roots lead her to a four-year stay in Ghana.

In her writings Angelou describes racism, prejudice, oppression, and other social ills. She comes to know males as pimps, drug pushers, occasional lovers, traditional and untraditional husbands, and Muslim polygamists. Angelou responds to these experiences with an increasing sense of what it means to be an African American woman in the twentieth century. In *Wouldn't Take Nothing for My Journey Now*, Angelou offers her philosophy of life based upon tolerance and respect for diversity.

SUGGESTED READINGS

Kallen, Stuart A. *Maya Angelou: Woman of Words, Deeds, and Dreams*. Edina, Minn.: Abdo and Daughters, 1993.

McPherson, Dolly A. *Order Out of Chaos*. London: Virago, 1990.

Shapiro, Miles. *Maya Angelou*. New York: Chelsea House, 1994.

Shuker, Nancy. *Maya Angelou*. Morristown, N.J.: Silver Burdett, 1990.

Spain, Valerie. *Meet Maya Angelou*. New York: Random House, 1994.

—Thomas J. Sienkewicz

See also African American identity; *All God's Children Need Traveling Shoes*; American identity: South; Feminism; *I Know Why the Caged Bird Sings*; Identity crisis; Racism and ethnocentrism; Rape

Angelou, Maya, poetry of

AUTHOR: Maya Angelou (Marguerite Johnson, 1928-   )

IDENTITIES: African American; South; women

PRINCIPAL WORKS: *Just Give Me a Cool Drink of Water 'fore I Diiie*, 1971; *Oh Pray My Wings Are Gonna Fit Me Well*, 1975; *And Still I Rise*, 1978; *Shaker, Why Don't You Sing?*, 1983; *The Complete Collected Poems of Maya Angelou*, 1994

Maya Angelou's poetry complements the search for self-identity as an African American woman described in her series of autobiographical narratives beginning with *I Know Why the Caged Bird Sings*. The caged bird image, which she borrows from a poem by African American poet Paul Laurence Dunbar, recurs in her work and expresses the collective yearning of African Americans for freedom as well as Angelou's search for individuality and independence.

In her poetry Angelou often focuses on the oppression of African Americans, including some that the media love to demonize: welfare mothers, prostitutes, and drug pushers. She describes the female African American experience with particular power in "Our Grandmothers," which begins with a slave mother dreading the approaching sale of her children. Angelou also proudly celebrates the accomplishments of African Americans such as Martin Luther King, Jr., and Malcolm X.

Angelou's childhood in Stamps, Arkansas, merges with the Southern slave experience of her African American ancestors in poems about Arkansas, Georgia, Virginia, and the Southern slave plantation. Frequently, Angelou uses the vocabulary and slang of African American English. She also broadens her focus and speaks of urban African Americans and comfortable working white liberals.

Some of these themes are found in "On the Pulse of Morning," written for the inauguration of Bill Clinton as president of the United States in 1993. Using geographic references to Arkansas, to the Mississippi and Potomac rivers, and to the many peoples of the United States, Angelou affirms the diversity and brotherhood of humanity and a dawn of equality in American history.

Another important theme for Angelou is Africa. Angelou lived in Ghana for the four years described in *All God's Children Need Traveling Shoes*. For Angelou, Africa's pyramids and history are a source of pride; its black inhabitants are a criterion of beauty.

Finally, in her poems Angelou reflects on love and her own erotic feelings. Her search for physical and emotional satisfaction in her relationships is sometimes satisfying and sometimes frustrating. Always, however, the poet Angelou defines herself as a woman and an African American.

SUGGESTED READINGS

Kallen, Stuart A. *Maya Angelou: Woman of Words, Deeds, and Dreams*. Edina, Minn.: Abdo and Daughters, 1993.

King, Sarah E. *Maya Angelou: Greeting the Morning*. Brookfield, Conn.: Millbrook, 1994.

Lisandrelli, Elaine Slivinski. *Maya Angelou: More Than a Poet*. Springfield, N.J.: Enslow, 1996.

Pettit, Jayne. *Maya Angelou: Journey of the Heart*. New York: Lodestar Books, 1996.

Shapiro, Miles. *Maya Angelou*. New York: Chelsea House, 1994.

—Thomas J. Sienkewicz

See also African American identity; *All God's Children Need Traveling Shoes*; American identity: South; Feminism; *I Know Why the Caged Bird Sings*; Identity crisis; Racism and ethnocentrism; Women and identity

Angels in America: A Gay Fantasia on National Themes

AUTHOR: Tony Kushner (1956-   )

FIRST PUBLISHED: *Millennium Approaches*, pr. 1990, pb. 1993 (part 1); *Perestroika*, pr. 1991, pb. 1994 (part 2)

IDENTITIES: Disease; European American; gay, lesbian, and bisexual; Jewish

A two-part, seven-hour play, *Angels in America: A Gay Fantasia on National Themes* is an epic of life in America in the mid-1980's. In the play, self-interest has overtaken love and compassion, acquired immune deficiency syndrome (AIDS) is decimating the gay male population, and victory in the ideological battle between liberals and conservatives seems to be going to the conservatives. Tony Kushner's leftist politics are unmistakably present in his play, but *Angels in America* is not a polemic. Instead, it is a fantastic journey through the lives of two couples. One couple is Louis, a Jewish word processor, and Prior Walter, a former drag queen who has AIDS. The other is Joe Pitt, a Mormon republican and lawyer, and his wife, Harper. Another key player is the ethically questionable lawyer Roy Cohn, a dramatized version of the real person. (Cohn was counsel to Senator Joseph McCarthy during the "Communist witch-hunts" of the 1950's.) Cohn is dying of AIDS and is in the process of being disbarred.

Angels in America uses AIDS as a metaphor for an investigation of life in the 1980's. Kushner views the greed of that era as having frightening implications for personal relations. Louis spouts grand ideas in bombastic speeches but flees when faced with a lover who has AIDS. Louis is unable to face the responsibilities associated with caring for a person with AIDS. Joe, who becomes Louis' lover, abandons his wife, deciding that he can no longer repress his homosexuality. Cohn tries to enlist Joe's help in stopping the disbarment process by getting Joe a job in the Reagan Administration, but Joe refuses.

Prior, the protagonist, is the character who suffers most. As AIDS-related complications jeopardize his health, he becomes more panicked. He also becomes a prophet after being visited by an angel at the end of part 1, *Millennium Approaches*. With the help of Hannah Pitt, Joe's mother, he learns how to resist the Angel and how to make the Angel bless him. In spite of his failing health, Prior tells the Angel: "We live past hope. If I can find hope anywhere, that's it, that's the best I can do. It's so much not enough, so inadequate. . . . Bless me anyway. I want more life."

This message of hope, near the end of part 2, *Perestroika*, affirms the movement of the play toward the interconnectedness of people across boundaries of race, religion, sexuality, or ideology. Julius Rosenberg and Ethel Rosenberg say kaddish over the dead body of Cohn. Hannah, a devout Mormon, nurses Prior, a stranger to her. Belize, a black, gay nurse, advises Cohn on his medical treatment. Louis and Prior get back together, as the epilogue reveals.

SUGGESTED READINGS
Clum, John. *Acting Gay: Male Homosexuality in Modern Drama.* New York: Columbia University Press, 1994.
Felman, Jyl Lynn. "Lost Jewish (Male) Souls: A Midrash on *Angels in America.*" *Tikkun* 10, no. 3 (May, 1995): 27-30.
Savran, David. "Ambivalence, Utopia, and a Queer Sort of Materialism: How *Angels in America* Reconstructs the Nation." *Theater Journal* 47 (1995): 207-227.

—Chris Freeman

See also AIDS; Gay identity; Jewish American identity; Kushner, Tony

Angle of Repose

AUTHOR: Wallace Stegner (1909-1993)
FIRST PUBLISHED: 1971
IDENTITIES: Disability; family; West and Southwest

Angle of Repose, which won, in 1972, the Pulitzer Prize for Wallace Stegner, unites past and present in telling two stories: Lyman Ward's history of his grandparents and his need to keep his identity and independence as he copes with his disability. Lyman, a historian forced to retire because of a debilitating disease, wants to write about the marriage of his grandparents, Oliver Ward and Susan Burling Ward, an author, artist, and illustrator. Oliver was an engineer and manager of mines, and Lyman's history chronicles the couple's settlement of the West in the late 1800's. The title is taken from the geological term meaning the angle at which dirt, pebbles, and sand no longer roll.

Through Susan's letters to her friend Augusta, Lyman sketches out his grandparents' life, filling in the areas with what he assumes must have happened. Susan, a young woman who is on the brink of entering New York society, shocks everyone when she marries Oliver Ward. Oliver moves to New Almaden, California, and Susan goes out to him later. Susan's belief that her move to the West is temporary and her wish to be back in New York society make adjusting to her new life difficult. She finds the West vulgar and disappointing. In her isolation, Susan turns to drawing the unusual sights around her and writing short sketches, which she sells to help support the family.

During Oliver's attempts to mine and irrigate the West, he and Susan live in New Almaden and Santa Cruz, California; Leadville, Colorado; Michoacán, Mexico; Idaho; and Grass Valley, California, where Oliver finally finds his place as the manager of the Zodiac mine. Oliver and Susan have difficult times, including a two-year separation following the drowning of their five-year-old daughter, Agnes. Oliver blames Susan for their daughter's death because he believes Susan had been secretly meeting his assistant, Frank Sargent, when Agnes drowned.

For Lyman, who had sought refuge in the past of his grandparents in order to escape his wife's infidelity and desertion of him and his son's attempts to take away his independence, the past is as relevant and painful as the present. Although Lyman thought his grandparents lived at the angle of repose, he discovers they were emotionally separated by Agnes' death. In exploring his grandparents' past, Lyman learns about himself and at the end of the novel begins to think it is possible for him to forgive his wife and reconcile with his son.

SUGGESTED READINGS
Etulain, Richard W. *Conversations with Wallace Stegner on Western History and Literature.* Rev. ed. Salt Lake City: University of Utah Press, 1990.
Lewis, Merrill, and Lorene Merrill. *Wallace Stegner.* Boise, Idaho: Boise State College, 1972.
Robinson, Forrest G., and Margaret G. Robinson. *Wallace Stegner.* Boston: Twayne, 1977.
Stegner, Wallace. *Where the Bluebird Sings to the Lemonade Springs: Living and Writing in the West.* New York: Random House, 1992.

—Charmayne Richardson Mulligan

See also American identity: West and the frontier; Physical disabilities and identity; Stegner, Wallace

Annie John

AUTHOR: Jamaica Kincaid (Elaine Potter Richardson, 1949-   )

FIRST PUBLISHED: 1985

IDENTITIES: Adolescence and coming-of-age; Caribbean; family; women

Annie John, Jamaica Kincaid's first novel, is a story of a girl's coming-of-age. On a conscious level the protagonist is contemplating death, friendship, sexual desire, and the developments in her body; she is also experiencing a deeper need to cut herself off from her mother, even if in the process she must hurt them both. The novel is set on the Caribbean island of Antigua. As a young child, Annie John clings to her beautiful and loving mother. She likes to caress her, smell her perfume, take baths with her, and wear dresses made of the same fabric as hers. At school, Annie shows that she has a mind of her own, but at home she takes note of everything her mother says or does.

Soon, however, Annie begins to realize that human relationships are fragile. They can be dissolved by death, by infidelity, or by changes in one's feelings. At a new school, Annie finds herself abandoning her best friend, Gwyneth Joseph, for a dirty, defiant red-haired girl. At home, Annie betrays her mother's trust and love. She lies to her about unimportant matters, such as whether or not she has any marbles, and she even insults her. To some degree Annie is acting out her feelings about her parents' lovemaking and about her own sexual development. Annie is also reacting to her mother's evident embarrassment when Annie assumes a woman's identity. On a deeper level, Annie's love for her mother is so strong that only by rejecting her can she establish a space for herself and a personality of her own.

At school, Annie gets into trouble by writing under the picture of Christopher Columbus the same words that her mother had said in mockery of her father, Pa Chess. Clearly, Annie senses that there is a similarity between the colonial system, which guaranteed that blacks would remain low in the economic system, and the patriarchal family, which ensures the subordination of females. By the time she is fifteen, Annie is thoroughly miserable, loathing her mother, herself, and her existence. She becomes ill, and for almost four months she is bedridden, nursed by her mother, her father, and finally, by her grandmother, Ma Chess, who appears mysteriously and evidently effects a cure. At last, when she is seventeen, Annie is sent to England. As the ship prepares to sail, Annie and her mother weep, and Annie relents enough to wave good-bye. Now free to find her own identity, she is free to love her mother, if only at a distance.

SUGGESTED READINGS

Bemrose, John. "Growing Pains of Girlhood." *Maclean's*, May 20, 1985, 61.

Kenney, Susan. "Paradise with Snake." *The New York Times Book Review*, April 7, 1985, 6.

Kreilkamp, Ivan. "Jamaica Kincaid: Daring to Discomfort." *Publishers Weekly* 243 (January 1, 1996): 54-55.

Van Wyngarden, Bruce. "First Novel." *Saturday Review* 11 (May-June, 1985): 68.

—*Rosemary M. Canfield Reisman*

See also *At the Bottom of the River*; Caribbean American literature; Feminism; Kincaid, Jamaica; Women and identity

Another Life

AUTHOR: Derek Walcott (1930-   )

FIRST PUBLISHED: 1973

IDENTITIES: Caribbean

Another Life describes, celebrates, and reevaluates Derek Walcott's life, art, love, landscape, language, history, Caribbean, and spiritual resilience. Walcott examines the standard view of Caribbean history and sees that colonization has left a distorted history, one filled with numerous gaps. In Caribbean history as Walcott finds it, the absence of facts renders the history as hollow as a coconut shell. Walcott's intention is to provide autobiography, which he decorates with art, as an alternative to history, to the accumulation of dead facts or to the writing of a grocery list. Through autobiography, Walcott aims at the whole truth, which is multifaceted. In the work, he changes his personal experience into art, providing an artistic vision and form through a synthesis of writing and painting.

Another Life focuses on three recurring names, Harry (Harold Simmons, who is Walcott's painting mentor), Gregorias or Dunstan (Dustin St. Omer, who is his superior painting friend), and Anna (his teenage romance, the embodiment of art and the representative of the transcendence of art over history). The circumstances surrounding the struggles and triumphs of Harry, Dunstan, and Anna depict growth in Walcott, St. Lucia, and the Caribbean.

Another Life uses contrast to advance the journey of the young poet and postcolonial Caribbean (Walcott) from adolescence to adulthood. The painter, whose talents wane, grows into the writer whose talents wax as a result of the prophetic insight of his dying mentor, Harry. The poet's valuable friendship with Gregorias, who is a better painter, is also instrumental in Walcott's growth. Death is juxtaposed to life and resurrection, the sea to fire, the poor to the rich. Other contrasts, and resolutions, include the fatherless poet in book 1 and Gregorias and his parents at home in book 2; art and life; old and new; light and dark; and fulfillment and disillusionment. At its end, the book reaches toward a linguistic, cultural, artistic, religious, and historical resolution.

Walcott nostalgically re-creates the Caribbean landscape, particularly St. Lucia, with a rich congruence of painting imageries, figures, and theories. *Another Life* opens with the young artist striving to sketch the landscape at sunset and ends with the maturing writer. The journey motif becomes a vehicle for the poet's exploration of the beauty and fire of St. Lucia. Merging these with his references to heroic classical and contemporary figures, the poet produces a rich montage of intertextuality and multiculturalism.

SUGGESTED READINGS

Baugh, Edward. *Derek Walcott—Memory as Vision: Another Life*. New York: Longman, 1978.

_____. "Painters and Painting in *Another Life*." *Caribbean Quarterly* 26 (March-June, 1980): 83-93.

Brown, Stewart, ed. *The Art of Derek Walcott*. Mid-Glamorgan, Wales, England: Dufour, 1991.

Hamner, Robert D., ed. *Critical Perspectives on Derek Walcott*. Washington, D.C.: Three Continents, 1993.

Ismond, Patricia. "*Another Life*: Autobiography as Alternative History." *Journal of West Indian Literature* 4, no. 1 (January, 1990): 41-49.

Olaogun, Modupe. "Sensuous Imagery in Derek Walcott's *Another Life*." *World Literature Written in English* 27, no. 1 (Spring, 1987): 106-118.

Terada, Rei. *Derek Walcott's Poetry*. Boston: Northeastern University Press, 1992.

—*Seodial Deena*

See also Caribbean American literature; *Collected Poems*; Walcott, Derek

Antin, Mary

BORN: Polotzk, Russia; June 13, 1881
DIED: Suffern, New York; May 17, 1949
PRINCIPAL WORKS: *From Plotzk to Boston*, 1899; *The Promised Land*, 1912; *They Who Knock at the Gates: A Complete Gospel of Immigration*, 1914
IDENTITIES: European American; Jewish; women
SIGNIFICANT ACHIEVEMENT: Antin's *The Promised Land* is the classic Jewish American immigrant autobiography.

Mary Antin was born in Polotzk in what was then czarist Russia. Antin's place of birth and her Jewishness determined what her identity would have been had her family stayed in Polotzk. Had they stayed, she would have been an Orthodox Jewish wife of a Jewish man, the mother of Jewish children, and a woman with only enough education to enable her to read the Psalms in Hebrew.

As a Jew, she could not live beyond the pale of settlement in Russia and could never become assimilated into Russian society. As a young child, she felt stifled by this identity.

In *The Promised Land* she compares her moving at age thirteen to America, where she felt she had freedom to choose her own identity, to the Hebrews' escape from bondage in Egypt. In America, she received a free education in Boston public schools. She had access to public libraries. She had access to settlement houses, like Hale House (in which she later worked), where she experienced American culture. She had a freedom of which she could hardly dream in Europe. The woman who in Polotzk would never have become more than barely literate chose for herself in the New World the identity of a writer and social worker. At fifteen, she published her first poem in the *Boston Herald*. At eighteen, she published her first autobiographical volume, *From Plotzk to Boston*, which resulted in her being hailed as a child prodigy. Eventually, she reworked the material from this book into her masterpiece, *The Promised Land*.

After being graduated from Girls Latin School in Boston, Antin went to the Teachers College of Columbia University in New York City and then to Barnard College, where she met and married Amadeus W. Grabau, a geologist, Columbia professor, and gentile. She felt that her marriage cemented her chosen identity as a fully assimilated American. Although her husband eventually left her and settled in China, she never lost her faith in the possibilities of total assimilation into American society. She felt that since she had become fully assimilated, so could all other Jewish immigrants to the country she spoke of without irony as the promised land.

SUGGESTED READINGS

Guttmann, Allen. *The Jewish Writer in America: Assimilation and the Crisis of Identity*. New York: Oxford University Press, 1971.

Liptzin, Sol. *The Jew in American Literature*. New York: Bloch, 1966.

Tuerk, Richard. "Jewish-American Literature." In *Ethnic Perspectives in American Literature: Selected Essays on the European Contribution*, edited by Robert J. DiPietro and Edward Ifkovic. New York: Modern Language Association of America, 1983.

—Richard Tuerk

See also Acculturation; American Dream; American identity: Northeast; Emigration and immigration; Jewish American identity; Melting pot; *Promised Land, The*; Religion and identity

Anti-Semitism

IDENTITIES: Jewish

DEFINITION: Anti-Semitism is prejudice against Jews.

When, as a child, Charles Dickens worked in a factory, he received kindness and instruction from the Jewish orphan Bob Fagin. Dickens later wrote that he felt contaminated by such companionship. In *Oliver Twist* (1838), he named a villainous corrupter of children Fagin, and, in the first edition, repeatedly calls him "the Jew." After Jewish complaints, as if in compensation, Dickens eventually placed the virtuous but vapid Jewish character Mr. Riah in *Our Mutual Friend* (1865).

These incidents encapsulate two phases of anti-Semitism that alternate through literary history. First, anti-Semites experience an anxiety, often from indebtedness to or envy of Jewish influence. Thus, the Jew (and the one Jew, in anti-Semitic literature, stands for a diverse group) is pictured as evil, such as Shylock in William Shakespeare's *The Merchant of Venice* (c. 1596-1597) or Fagin, helping children into a life of crime. Second, a reaction against anti-Semitism comes, occasioning token redress. Jews have served as scapegoats for millennia; long before Christianity settled the blame for Christ's crucifixion more on the Jews than on the Romans, Jews were envied, hated, excluded, and subject to mob violence.

The United States and Canada inherited a tradition of vile and virtuous Jewish characters, largely from British literature. For example, *The Jew* (1794), by British playwright Richard Cumberland, was written to expiate for its author's many Jewish villains. The play's character Sheva is virtuous. By the end of 1795, the play had been performed in Philadelphia, Charleston, Hartford, Providence,

North America

Anti-Semitism
Eleven Key Works

c. 1596-1597	The Jewish character Shylock in William Shakespeare's *The Merchant of Venice* is portrayed unsympathetically; Shakespeare's portrayal is nevertheless more tolerant than those of many other playwrights who add to the villainy of their villains by making them Jewish.
1794	British playwright Richard Cumberland makes amends for his many portrayals of Jewish villains with the upstanding Sheva in *The Jew*.
1838	Charles Dickens' *Oliver Twist* depicts a Jewish character as an unscrupulous corrupter of children.
1865	After many Jewish protests to Dickens' treatment of Jews in his work, his Jewish character in *Our Mutual Friend* is portrayed as a man of virtue.
1898	"Concerning the Jews," an article by Mark Twain, condemns anti-Semitism.
1920	*The Jewish Peril*, a new title for an old forgery, *The Protocols of the Elders of Zion*, which alleges a worldwide Jewish conspiracy, is widely read in the United States after it is promulgated by auto magnate Henry Ford, who is convicted of libel in 1927.
1930's	Father Charles Coughlin's national radio program promotes anti-Semitism.
1934	T. S. Eliot's *After Strange Gods* argues for a Christian society and against a Jewish one.
1935	Thomas Wolfe's "Death and Proud Brother" shows contempt for the Jews.
1962	Kurt Vonnegut's novel *Mother Night* tells of a writer who sentences himself to death for anti-Semitism.
1969	*Portnoy's Complaint*, by Jewish author Philip Roth, is criticized for its negative characterization of Jews.

New York, and Boston. The play ran through five editions before 1797. Throughout the nineteenth century, some American works imitated its portrait of a saintly Jewish benefactor who never collected debts. These compositions acquired their novelty because they were so few compared to the flood of defamatory portraits. For example, what may be the first American play with a Jewish character is Susanna Haswell Rowson's vicious *Slaves in Algiers* (1794).

Henry Wadsworth Longfellow's poem "The Jewish Cemetery at Newport" (1858) and Mark Twain's article "Concerning the Jews" (1898) denounce anti-Semitism. Such fair treatment of Judaism, however, was in the extreme minority among gentile authors. Jewish writers, writing for Jewish audiences, treated Jewish themes with honesty, however, in such literary arenas as Yiddish drama, which began during the 1890's.

The twentieth century

The twentieth century brought not an end to anti-Semitism but acceleration of it in reaction against the rise of Jews to positions of affluence and power. Thomas Wolfe, for example, owed to his Jewish mistress his access to wealthy society. He expressed his contempt for her race in such stories as "Death and Proud Brother" (1935). The economic and social ills of the Depression years particularly inspired the search for scapegoats, with the Jews often chosen. Two conspicuous voices of anti-Semitism were the Nobel laureate T. S. Eliot and the influential poet and critic Ezra Pound. In *After Strange Gods* (1934), Eliot argues for a Christian society that would largely exclude Jews; his early poetry strangely mixes anti-Semitism with his disgust at sexuality. World War II, however, caused him to distance himself from the racism of his friend Pound, and he never allowed *After Strange Gods* to be reprinted.

Pound had a phobic reaction to Jews, as if their presence were a taboo or contagion. In Italy during World War II, Pound made radio broadcasts for fascism and for Italy's fascist government; Italy and the United States were at war at the time, and Pound did not renounce his U.S. citizenship. In the broadcasts, he obsessively likened Jewish power to a disease. Captured and tried for treason at the end of World War II, Pound was judged insane and was sentenced to a long confinement in a mental hospital. He finally recanted his anti-Semitism in the 1960's. In Canada, anti-Semitism was spread by such popular figures as the Presbyterian minister and novelist Charles Gordon and the historians John Murray Gibbon and Frederick Philip Grove, but lost fashion after 1945.

Jewish Gamblers Corrupt American Baseball

"The Cleanest Sport" Near Its Doom From "Too Much Jew." Baseball Has Passed Under Control of "the Sport Spoilers." Can It Be Saved?

THERE are men in the United States who say that baseball has received its death wound and is slowly dying out of the list of respectable sports. There are other men who say that American baseball can be saved if a clean sweep is made of the Jewish influence which has just dragged it through a period of bitter shame and demoralization.

Whether baseball as a first-class sport is killed and will survive only as a cheap-jack entertainment; or whether baseball possesses sufficient intrinsic character to rise in righteous wrath and cast out the danger that menaces it, will remain a matter of various opinion. But there is one certainty, namely, that the last and most dangerous blow dealt baseball was curiously notable for its Jewish character.

Yet only lesser Jews were indicted. Inevitably the names of other Jews appeared in the press accounts, and people wondered who they were. A Jewish judge presided. Jewish lawyers were prominent on both sides of the cases. Numerous strange things occurred.

But strangest of all is the fact that although American fans felt that something epochal had happened in baseball, few really know what it is.

There has been time enough for others to tell the truth if they were so disposed. Many sport editors have come as near telling it as their newspapers would permit them. But it becomes daily more evident that if the whole matter is to be laid bare, so that Americans may know where to look for danger, THE DEARBORN INDEPENDENT will have to do it.

Jews Are Not Good Sportsmen

AND this is not of our own choosing. Baseball is a trivial matter compared with some of the facts that are awaiting publication. Yet it is possible to see the operation of the Jewish Idea in baseball as clearly as in any other field. The process is the same, whether in war or politics, in finance or in sports.

To begin with, Jews are not sportsmen. This is not set down in complaint against them, but merely as analysis. It may be a defect in their character, or it may not; it is nevertheless a fact which discriminating Jews unhesitatingly acknowledge. Whether this is due to their physical lethargy, their dislike of unnecessary physical action, or their serious cast of mind, others may decide; the Jew is not naturally an out-of-door sportsman; if he takes up golf it is because his station in society calls for it, not that he really likes it; and if he goes in for collegiate athletics, as some of the younger Jews are doing, it is because so much attention has been called to their neglect of the sports that the younger generation thinks it necessary to remove that occasion of remark.

And yet, the bane of American sports today is the presence of a certain type of Jew, not as a participant but as an exploiter and corrupter. If he had been a sportsman for the love of sport he might have been saved from becoming an exploiter and corrupter, for there is no mind to which the corrupting of a sport is more illogical and even unexplainable than the mind of the man who participates in it.

Exploiting and Corrupting Clean Sports

THERE will be a very full case made out in justification of the use of the above terms "exploiter" and "corrupter" with regard to baseball. But it would be just as easy to make out the same sort of case with regard to wrestling and horse-racing. Wrestling is so completely ruled by Jews as to have become an outlawed sport. The story of wrestling is not only the story of the demoralization of a sport, but also the story of the wholesale bunkoing of the public.

The same is true of horse-racing. The whole atmosphere of this sport has been tinged with dishonesty. The horses remain almost the only well-bred creatures connected with it. Yet why should the art of breeding and training and testing fine horses be debasing? Only because a certain class saw in it a chance to play upon the weaknesses of men for the sake of gain.

That, indeed, explains the presence of the Jew in modern sports and it also explains why the Jewish Idea in sport, instead of being preservative, is corruptive. The Jew saw money where the sportsman saw fun and skill. The Jew set out to capitalize rivalry and to commercialize contestant zeal.

This is not necessarily the only course the Jew could have taken with regard to sports, but it is the course that he most notably has taken, and as scandal follows scandal it would seem to be high time that organized Jewry should undertake to control or repudiate those Jews who have been most instrumental in corrupting and nearly destroying our cleanest, most manly public sports.

VOLUME two of this series of Jewish Studies is now off the press. It is entitled "Jewish Activities in the United States," being the second volume of "The International Jew," twenty-two articles, 256 pages. Sent to any address at the cost of printing and mailing, which is 25 cents.

It is worth noting that in Chicago, where the Jewish Anti-Defamation League has its headquarters, there was not a word of reproof sent out from Jews to the Jewish culprits, chiding them for their activities. Not a word. But at the same time the pressure of the Anti-Defamation League was heavy on the whole American newspaper press to prevent the public statement that the whole baseball scandal was a Jewish performance from end to end.

Baseball had a close call for its life back in 1875. Rowdyism, gambling, drinking and general disorderliness on the baseball fields brought the sport very low in public estimation, so low that attendance at the games fell heavily.

In this year 1921 there is another public rebuke being administered baseball by the same means—a very heavy reduction of public support in attendance at the games.

The storm began to be heard as far back as 1919. The Cincinnati Nationals had defeated the Chicago Americans in the World Series of that year, and immediately thereafter the country became a whispering gallery wherein were heard mysterious rumors of crooked dealing. The names of Jews were heard then, but it meant nothing to the average man. The rumors dealt with shady financial gains for a number of Jew gamblers of decidedly shady reputation.

But "they got away with it," in the parlance of the field. There was not enough public indignation to force a show-down, and too many interests were involved to prevent baseball being given a black eye in full view of an adoring public.

Some Strange Occurrences Favor Jews

HOWEVER, not everyone forgot the incident. Some who had the interest of honest sport at heart, and a regard for facts as well, kept on the trail—long after the trail grew cold, long after the principal wrongdoers forgot their early caution. Where money had once been taken successfully, the gang would be sure to return.

Time went on until the 1920 season began to wane. One day when the Chicago and Philadelphia National League teams were engaged in a series at Chicago, strange messages began to reach the office of the Chicago club. The messages were dated from Detroit and informed the Chicago club and management that several "well-known" Jews were betting heavily on Philadelphia. The bets involved large sums of money, and as the contest was only the ordinary run of daily game, not an important contest at all, the unusual interest of Jewish plungers attracted attention. At the same time it was observed that money began rolling into the pool rooms on Philadelphia.

Chicago club officials called a hasty conference on receipt of the messages. They called in Grover Cleveland Alexander, explained the situation to him, and told him it was up to him to save the game. It was not Alexander's turn to pitch, Claude R. Hendryx having been chosen for that day; neither was Alexander in training to pitch that day. However, he did go to the box, and although he hurled his heart out to beat Philadelphia and thwart the Jew gamblers, he failed.

Then came the big scandal. A Cook County grand jury was called into session at Chicago and asked to investigate. When this grand jury had completed its labors, eight members of the Chicago American League team were under indictment for throwing the World Series of 1919, the previous year, to the Cincinnati Reds. And all along the line of the investigation the names of Jews were plentifully sprinkled.

It was discovered that the indictments brought by the first grand jury were faulty; a second one was called and it was under the second group of indictments that the famous trial at Chicago was held.

One difference in the work of the two grand juries was that the second indicted five Jews who had escaped the first one. Two of these men were Carl Zork and Benny Franklin who were just as much implicated at the time of the first grand jury as at the second, but the prosecutor's office did not try to secure their indictment. Why? Because Replogle, the attorney representing the prosecution, said there were enough men indicted without Zork and Franklin. These two St. Louis Jews were represented by Alfred S. Austrian, a Jewish lawyer, of Chicago.

This second grand jury also indicted Ben and Louis Levi and their brother-in-law, D. A. Zelser, gamblers from Des Moines. Their indictment was not secured at the first grand jury investigation directed by Replogle, assistant to Hoyne who was then acting for the state of Illinois. Between the first and second grand juries a political change had occurred, and the public interests in the second grand jury were in the care of a new prosecuting attorney, Robert Crowe, a former judge.

"Who's Who" of Jews in Baseball

IT BECOMES necessary at this point in the narrative to give a brief "Who's Who" of the baseball scandal, omitting from the list the names of the baseball players who are sufficiently known to the public. This list will comprise only those who have been in the background of baseball and whom it is necessary to know in order to understand what has been happening behind the scenes in recent years.

For the first name let us take Albert D. Lasker. He is a member of the American Jewish Committee, was recently appointed by President Harding to be chairman of the United States Shipping Board, and is known as the author of the "Lasker Plan," a widely heralded plan for the reorganization of baseball, which practically took the sport out of non-Jewish control. He is reputed to be the second richest Jew in Chicago and was head of the advertising agency which became famous under the Gentile names of Lord & Thomas. Moreover he is a heavy stockholder in the Chicago Cubs—the Chicago Nationals.

The so-called "Lasker Plan" has been attributed to Mr. Lasker, although it is not here intimated that he has specifically claimed to be its originator. The intimation is not made for the reason that to do so might be putting Mr. Lasker in the position of claiming what is not true. Until he makes the claim, the term "Lasker Plan" must remain merely a designation, and not a description of its origin.

This matter brings us to the name of Alfred S. Austrian, a Jewish lawyer of Chicago, who is a warm friend both of Mr. Lasker and of the Replogle aforementioned. It is said that Mr. Austrian was really the originator of the "Lasker Plan" which for certain reasons was handed to Mr. Lasker who was not averse to publicity and who knew the art of self-advertising. Now, it appears that Austrian was also the legal representative of Charles A. Comiskey, owner of the Chicago Americans, and that he was also, if he is not now, the legal adviser of William Veeck, president of the Chicago National League Club, in which it has just been said that Lasker is a heavy stockholder. It was this club which was touched by the questionable game of August, 1920, and which afterward released Hendryx, the pitcher chosen for and withdrawn from that game. The Chicago National League Club has never explained why it released Hendryx and he has never demanded redress.

Meet Mr. Rothstein—"Real Estate Man"

MR. AUSTRIAN'S further activities will appear when the narrative of the investigation and trial is resumed.

Then there is Arnold Rothstein, a Jew, who describes himself as being in the real estate business but who is known to be a wealthy gambler, owner of a notorious gambling house at Saratoga, a race track owner, and is reputed to be financially interested in the New York National League Club.

Rothstein was usually referred to during the baseball scandal as "the man higher up." It is stated that in some manner unknown he received the secret testimony given before the grand jury and offered it to a New York newspaper. However, the fact is this: the grand jury testimony disappeared from the prosecuting attorney's safe-keeping. It is stated that when Rothstein found out it did not incriminate him, he then offered it for publicity purposes. The price which it is said to have cost is also stated. It is further stated that the New York paper to whom the secret stolen testimony was offered, in turn offered its use for a larger sum to a Chicago newspaper, and that the Chicago newspaper, to protect itself, called up Robert

A page from Henry Ford's Dearborn Independent. (Library of Congress)

During World War II, Adolf Hitler's Nazis exterminated six million Jews in their zeal to create an ethnically "pure" Aryan state. This genocide, which came to be known as the Holocaust, provoked some of the richest literature of identity in the twentieth century. Among post-Holocaust reactions against anti-Semitism have been Richard Maibaum's play *Birthright* (1933), based on some of the first reports of Nazi persecution; John Hersey's *The Wall* (1950), a retelling of the Warsaw Ghetto uprising; and Kurt Vonnegut's novel *Mother Night* (1962), about a writer who condemns himself to death for anti-Semitism. Since the Holocaust, unflattering portraits of Jews bring criticism, as when the Judaic scholar Gershom Scholem described *Portnoy's Complaint* (1969, by the Jewish author Philip Roth) as the book anti-Semites had been trying to write for a century.

Implications for identity
Anti-Semitism spawns Jewish self-hatred. Such bigotry is also deleterious to American identity, warping it into an exclusive club that some can never join and that others can enter only by conforming to fashionable prejudices. As people who have often been reluctant or unable to assimilate, Jews easily become the other against whom a nation or racial group unites. Anti-Semitism at its most virulent leads the anti-Semite to interpret everything from economic woes to Israeli policies as part of a vast Hebraic conspiracy. Anti-Semitic writings are usually studied as cases of individual and collective pathology.

SUGGESTED READINGS

Casillo, Robert. *The Genealogy of Demons: Anti-Semitism, Fascism, and the Myths of Ezra Pound.* Evanston, Ill.: Northwestern University Press, 1988.

Cheyette, Bryan. *Between "Race" and Culture: Representations of "the Jew" in English and American Literature.* Stanford, Calif.: Stanford University Press, 1996.

Craig, Terrence. *Racial Attitudes in English-Canadian Fiction, 1905-1980.* Waterloo, Ontario, Canada: Wilfrid Laurier University Press, 1987.

Julius, Anthony. *T. S. Eliot, Anti-Semitism and Literary Form.* Cambridge, England: Cambridge University Press, 1995.

Mayo, Louise A. *The Ambivalent Image: Nineteenth-Century America's Perception of the Jew.* Rutherford, N.J.: Fairleigh Dickinson University Press, 1988.

Poliakov, Léon. *The History of Anti-Semitism.* Translated by George Klim. 4 vols. New York: Vanguard, 1965-1985.

—*James S. Whitlark*

See also Jewish American identity; Racism and ethnocentrism

Antiwar literature

IDENTITIES: Men

Rather than glorifying the romance of combat, antiwar works demythologize war by illustrating the debilitating effects of warfare on the individual combatant, typically a young man whose wartime experience leaves him psychologically or physically shattered. Antiwar literature aims at debunking popular myths about war: The soldier as romantic hero, war as a proving ground for manhood, and death in combat as the patriotic ideal. Antiwar literature subverts these illusions about war through realistic, frequently first-person portrayals of the horrors of combat and its destructive aftermath. Although some writers have a discernible political perspective, most antiwar texts share a broader concern for exposing the horror and brutality of all war. Thus, there is a timeless, universal quality to antiwar literature that aims to provoke a rejection of, rather than a fascination for, war and warfare.

History
Among the most powerful antiwar statements to emerge from the American Civil War are the short stories of Ambrose Bierce, collected in *Tales of Soldiers and Civilians* (1891). In "Chickamauga," the inarticulate horror of the story's protagonist, a deaf-mute child surveying the carnage of the battlefield, bears poignant witness to the war's human toll. Stephen Crane's *The Red Badge of Courage: An Episode of the American Civil War* (1895) similarly evokes the wasting

effects of the war. Henry Fleming enlists in the Union Army dreaming of heroism, but the terror of the battlefield transforms his quest for personal identity into a cynical rebellion against war and, ultimately, into cowardice. Henry's identity is shaped by his painful struggle for personal integrity after he deserts his regiment.

The horrors of World War I are captured in William March's *Company K* (1933) and in Dalton Trumbo's *Johnny Got His Gun* (1939), which is widely regarded as the quintessential antiwar novel. Narrated by a young soldier who has returned from battle hideously disfigured, Trumbo's work delivers a stark and profoundly pacifistic message about the dehumanizing effects of combat.

Antiwar Literature Milestones

Revolutionary War (1775-1781)

Herman Melville *Israel Potter: Or, Fifty Years of Exile* (1855)

Civil War (1861-1865)

Ambrose Bierce *Tales of Soldiers and Civilians* (1891)
Stephen Crane *The Red Badge of Courage: An Episode of the American Civil War* (1895)
Edmund Wilson *Patriotic Gore: Studies in the Literature of the American Civil War* (1962)

Spanish American War (1898-1899)

Stephen Crane *Wounds in the Rain* (1900)
Mark Twain *A Pen Warmed-up in Hell* (1972)

World War I (1914-1918)

Edna St. Vincent Millay *Aria da Capo* (1919)
John Dos Passos *Three Soldiers* (1921)
Maxwell Anderson *What Price Glory* (1924)
Ford Madox Ford *No More Parades* (1925)
John Dos Passos *U.S.A.* (1937)
William March *Company K* (1933)
Dalton Trumbo *Johnny Got His Gun* (1939)
Eric J. Leed *No Man's Land: Combat and Identity in World War I* (1979)

Spanish Civil War (1936-1939)

Sinclair Lewis *It Can't Happen Here* (1935)
Stephen Vincent Benét *Burning City* (1936)
Edna St. Vincent Millay *Huntsman, What Quarry?* (1939)
Upton Sinclair *A World to Win* (1946)

World War II (1939-1945)

Thomas Heggen *Mister Roberts* (1946)
Norman Mailer *The Naked and the Dead* (1948)
Joseph Heller *Catch-22* (1961)

Kurt Vonnegut *Slaughterhouse-Five* (1969)
Thomas Pynchon *Gravity's Rainbow* (1973)
Marge Piercy *Gone to Soldiers* (1987)

Korean War (1950-1953)

Martin Russ *Last Parallel: A Marine's War Journal* (1957)
A. M. Harris *Tall Man* (1958)
Quentin Reynolds *Known But to God* (1960)
Richard Kim *The Martyred* (1964)

Vietnam War (1954-1975)

Norman Mailer *Why Are We In Vietnam?* (1967)
Norman Mailer *The Armies of the Night* (1968)
David Rabe *The Basic Training of Pavlo Hummel* (1973)
David Rabe *Sticks and Bones* (1973)
John Balaban *After Our War* (1974)
Ron Kovic *Born on the Fourth of July* (1976)
David Rabe *Streamers* (1976)
Philip Caputo *A Rumor of War* (1977)
Michael Herr *Dispatches* (1977)
Tim O'Brien *Going After Cacciato* (1978)
Gustav Hasford *The Short-Timers* (1979)
Wallace Terry *Bloods: An Oral History of the Vietnam War by Black Veterans* (1982)
John Del Vecchio *The Thirteenth Valley* (1982)
W. D. Ehrhart *To Those Who Have Gone Home Tired* (1984)
Bruce Weigl *Song of Napalm* (1988)

General Nonfiction

Jeffrey Walsh *American War Literature: 1914 to Vietnam* (1982)
Michael True *An Energy Field More Intense than War: The Nonviolent Tradition and American Literature* (1996)

The dislocating effects of America's entry into World Wars I and II are explored in fiction and drama. John Dos Passos provided three decades of sustained literary protest against the social upheaval of war. In *Three Soldiers* (1921), his acclaimed trilogy *U.S.A.* (1937), and such later works as *Mr. Wilson's War* (1962), Dos Passos exposes the political corruption and profiteering spawned by America's war industry. Using techniques of documentary realism, he captures the breakdown of the nation's social and moral order in wartime. On the stage, Edna St. Vincent Millay's *Aria da Capo* (1919) and Maxwell Anderson's *What Price Glory?* (1924) dramatized the human costs of America's involvement in World War I.

The rise of dictatorships in Europe and sympathy for the Loyalist resistance in the Spanish Civil War of 1936-1939 produced an array of antiwar literature by a number of America's most distinguished writers. Among those who published protest works during these years were novelists Sinclair Lewis, who wrote *It Can't Happen Here* (1935), and Upton Sinclair, who wrote *A World to Win* (1946). Poet Stephen Vincent Benét wrote *Burning City* (1936), and Millay, *Huntsman, What Quarry?* (1939). Playwright Clifford Odets wrote the antiwar *Till the Day I Die* (1935). Paradoxically, ardent opposition to fascism propelled many left-wing writers to advocate the use of force to end tyranny.

The dropping of the atomic bomb that ended World War II in 1945 and the United States' entry into the Korean War prompted a number of critiques of American militarism, among them Joseph Heller's *Catch-22* (1961) and Kurt Vonnegut's *Slaughterhouse-Five: Or, The Children's Crusade, a Duty-Dance with Death* (1969), darkly comic novels exposing the absurdity of the American military bureaucracy and the destructive power of the air war in Europe. Norman Mailer provided an increasingly cynical perspective on American Cold War politics. *The Naked and the Dead* (1948), his romanticized novel of the war in the Pacific, was followed by two dissident works, *Why Are We in Vietnam?* (1967) and *The Armies of the Night* (1968), potent statements against the war in Vietnam.

No previous war in which the United States was involved produced so large a body of antiwar literature as the war in Vietnam. Written mainly by veterans, these works angrily indict U.S. military policy and the nation's failure to support its soldiers. Novels such as Tim O'Brien's *Going After Cacciato* (1978), Gustav Hasford's *The Short-Timers* (1979), and John Del Vecchio's *The Thirteenth Valley* (1982) capture the grim reality of the combat experience, while memoirs such as Philip Caputo's *A Rumor of War* (1977), Ron Kovic's *Born on the Fourth of July* (1976), and Michael Herr's journalistic exposé *Dispatches* (1977) detail the loss of innocence and identity experienced by the war's combatants. Similar themes dominate the poetry collections of John Balaban, *After Our War* (1974), W. D. Ehrhart, *To Those Who Have Gone Home Tired* (1984), and Bruce Weigl, *Song of Napalm* (1988). David Rabe's trilogy of plays, *The Basic Training of Pavlo Hummel* (1973), *Sticks and Bones* (1973), and *Streamers* (1976), produced between 1969 and 1976, voice the anguish and bitterness of America's returning soldiers. Collectively, these works chronicle the tragic history of the United States' longest war and represent the culmination of over a century of American literary protest against war.

SUGGESTED READINGS

Gilman, Owen W., Jr., and Lorrie Smith, eds. *America Rediscovered: Critical Essays on Literature and Film of the Vietnam War*. New York: Garland, 1990.

Leed, Eric J. *No Man's Land: Combat and Identity in World War I*. New York: Cambridge University Press, 1979.

Rideout, Walter B. *The Radical Novel in the United States, 1900-1954*. New York: Hill & Wang, 1956.

Salzman, Jack, ed. *Years of Protest: A Collection of American Writings of the 1930's*. New York: Pegasus, 1967.

True, Michael. *An Energy Field More Intense than War: The Nonviolent Tradition and American Literature*. Syracuse, N.Y.: Syracuse University Press, 1996.

Walsh, Jeffrey. *American War Literature: 1914 to Vietnam*. New York: St. Martin's Press, 1982.

Wilson, Edmund. *Patriotic Gore: Studies in the Literature of the American Civil War.* New York: Oxford University Press, 1962.

—Jacqueline Lawson

See also Korean War; Spanish Civil War; Vietnam War; Violence; World War I; World War II

Appearance and identity

DEFINITION: Appearance—how one looks—influences identity according to what a society values and the stereotypes it holds.

One thing is undebatable: Physical appearance does matter, in consistent and measurable ways, despite whatever platitudes may be spoken about looks not being important. Some religions (for example Christianity, which distrusts worldly things) view personal physical beauty as unrelated or even contrary to spiritual virtue. A culture's emphasis on ethics, intellect, or accomplishments can reduce the emphasis on appearances. Beginning in ancient Greece, however, if not longer ago, the attractive body has been seen as proof of an attractive and even moral personality.

Social and psychological studies show that the kinds of appearance that are valued vary from society to society and within the same society over time. Charles Darwin, in 1874, looked for a basic standard of human beauty, but failed to find it. There is much debate over whether these standards of beauty are natural or learned—a debate that will probably never be solved. The answer may be some combination, with biological differences emphasized within a culture and given symbolic meaning. For example, the fact that women tend to more body fat than men may be seen positively as evidence of female strength or nurturing, or negatively as evidence of female weakness or lack of self-control. People within a culture may try to reduce or exaggerate that characteristic: Most women in contemporary Western culture try to lose weight, but Hawaiian royalty were deliberately fattened.

Preferring some appearances above others, however, seems as universal as the specific preferences are various. Three kinds of appeal interact in a complex manner: what is familiar, what is outstanding, and what is seen as symbolic of other good things. Individuals tend to pick friends and romantic partners who resemble them in height, weight, and general attractiveness. In one study, people saw the face with the most average proportions as the most beautiful. On the other hand, what is rare is often valued, such as blond or red hair when brown is most common. This is especially true if this rare characteristic is considered desirable, such as the extreme height and slenderness of contemporary female fashion models.

Appearance may also be valued or devalued based on symbolism alone, especially economic. For example, pale skin was fashionable when only the wealthy could rest indoors, and a suntan became attractive when work became, for most, an indoor activity and wealth meant leisure outdoors. Traits linked to the ability to accomplish important work may also be preferred, in contradiction to the preference for those traits that indicate sufficient wealth to allow idleness. Wide hips in women, for example, representing fertility, or muscles in men, indicating strength, are often valued.

More problematically, physical beauty is often seen as a sign of overall worth. This can become a self-fulfilling cycle in two ways. First, many studies show that people who view themselves as less attractive have lower overall self-confidence; even in specific situations, how attractive others think one is can change how they act toward one and how one acts toward them. Second, cultural ideas of beauty can be shaped by and reinforce other kinds of prejudice, such as ageism, racism, and sexism. If small noses, smooth skin, and slender hips are rewarded in a society, then African Americans, old people, and women will always be at a disadvantage, apart from other progress toward equality.

Unfortunately, ideas of how people should look, and discrimination against those who are seen as unattractive, start early. Girls as young as five, for example, draw themselves smaller than they

Appearances count

Appearances and discrimination

draw male peers, although at that age they are the same size. Schoolchildren viewing photos of strangers their age have described the less physically attractive strangers as less intelligent, more dishonest, and less enjoyable to be with. People may accept stereotypes or fight against them, but the stereotypes are powerful in either case.

These ideas are so strong, and generally unacknowledged, that they actually change what people perceive. Not only are people who are more attractive often considered more worthwhile, but people who are judged to be more worthwhile are often seen as more attractive. For example, people overestimate the height of men in authority, while someone who values thinness may think of an obese friend as not fat. In such cases, how people are judged by others and how people judge themselves is much more important to personality and identity than actual height, weight, facial features, or bodily proportions.

The mass media   Films, television, print, and advertising broadcast one ideal to a diverse audience and show it as the only path to romance and success. Feminists from Simone de Beauvoir to Susan Faludi also connect society's emphasis on women's appearance with society's seeing women as powerless except in their ability to attract men. Exactly what kinds of appearance are valued in what ways is a complicated question; still, some patterns are clear. The strongest prejudice may be against fat people, who not only are rejected as unattractive and discriminated against in jobs, but also are seen as lazy and out of control. A movement against antifat prejudice began in the 1970's and has gained strength. Studies have shown how difficult permanent weight loss is, thus diminishing the validity of the common perception that fat is the result of the moral weakness of overeating. Yet overall fear of fat seems to be increasing, with a rise in eating disorders such as bulimia and anorexia nervosa, children dieting at early ages, and the ideal body (as defined by psychological studies) growing smaller and smaller.

Tallness is also valued in Western culture; shortness is condemned, although not as much as fatness, and it is much easier to be considered too tall than to be too thin. When tallness is associated with authority and shortness with cuteness, either can be positive or negative. Still, almost as many people are unhappy with their height as with their weight, and the cultural stereotypes about height can be as strong, and as untrue, as those about weight. Economic discrimination against shortness is proven: In one study, male graduates of the University of Pittsburgh earned an average $1,000 per year less for every inch they were under six feet tall.

Almost every aspect of human appearance is judged: facial features, bodily parts and proportions, skin color and texture, hair or baldness. The look of youth is highly valued by most cultures, but only in some is there also an extreme distaste for the looks of old age. Makeup and clothing can be a way to try to fit cultural standards for appearance, and hence can themselves be areas in which people can be judged, and judge themselves, lacking.

Undoubtedly, people are preoccupied with appearances. In a 1986 survey, 82 percent of men and 93 percent of women said they often thought about their looks and cared greatly about their attractiveness; they were less concerned about health. Unhappiness with some aspect of appearance—from weight to specific features—ran from 17 percent to 57 percent. This preoccupation is not unrealistic, when studies show that people who are considered unattractive have less self-confidence, are treated less well from infancy on, and receive less social reward for the same behavior.

Appearances and gender   Appearance is often seen as a woman's issue, and much of the best research and writing is being done from a feminist approach. The importance of appearance to women, however, does not mean that appearance is not important to men. In the 1986 study, men's concerns about appearance were only slightly less than women's, still highly significant.

More important than gross percentages of people who say they are concerned or dissatisfied with their appearance may be the nature of these issues for each sex. In one study, women cared more about weight, while men cared more about baldness and height; in another, men and women were equally bothered about weight, but the men worried about being too fat or too thin, while almost all the women worried about fatness. Moreover, specific concerns about attractiveness damage overall self-confidence and self-image much more often in women than in men. Women also are more likely to try to change their appearance, with diet, makeup, or dress.

Gender and appearance issues also connect in other ways. Sexism may influence values: Men tend to be tall, and tallness is valued, while women tend to have more fat, and fatness is condemned. Conversely, some writers argue that tallness is biologically linked to respect, a problem for 25 percent of men but 90 percent of women. When men and women are seen as very different (and that is seen as good), characteristics that exaggerate the difference will be valued, while those that undermine it—from facial hair in women to shortness or a feminine distribution of fat in men—will be seen as problems.

Conclusions

It is undesirable and probably impossible to eliminate personal preferences in appearance; even societal ideas of beauty seem to fill a human need and help create a richer life. Rather, many writers on this issue encourage an appreciation of a broader variety of appearances, with many different standards of beauty. Also, they argue that appearances should not form the only measure of worth, stressing the importance of also considering a person's intelligence, actions, and virtues, rather than assuming those from stereotypes based on looks. When stereotypes about appearance lead to discrimination on the job, or to teasing or social exclusion, that can and must be taken as seriously as other kinds of prejudiced actions.

SUGGESTED READINGS

Banner, Lois W. *American Beauty*. Chicago: University of Chicago Press, 1983. Readable, well documented history of standards of woman's beauty since the nineteenth century, related to social trends and values.

Barthel, Diane. *Putting on Appearances: Gender and Advertising*. Philadelphia: Temple University Press, 1988. Sophisticated yet clear critique of the business of beauty, in terms of both gender roles and capitalist values.

Brownmiller, Susan. *Femininity*. New York: Fawcett Columbine, 1984. Important discussion of society's standards of appearance and action for women and—despite the title—men.

Cash, Thomas F., and Thomas Pruzinsky. *Body Images: Development, Deviance, and Change*. New York: Guilford Press, 1990. Demanding but rewarding psychological approach.

Chernin, Kim. *The Obsession: Reflections on the Tyranny of Slenderness*. New York: Harper & Row, 1981. Discussion of demands on women to be thin, viewed as the cause and the effect of prejudice against women.

Freedman, Rita. *Beauty Bound: Why We Pursue the Myth in the Mirror*. Lexington, Mass.: Lexington Books, 1986. Based on research and the social and psychological problems of a psychologist's clients.

Hatfield, Elaine, and Susan Sprecher. *Mirror, Mirror . . . : The Importance of Looks in Everyday Life*. Albany: State University of New York Press, 1986. Studies the importance of looks and analyzes why they are important.

Keyes, Ralph. *The Height of Your Life*. Boston: Little, Brown, 1980. A clear, well-documented examination of height's role in love, work, and society, concerning men and women.

Schwartz, Hillel. *Never Satisfied: A Cultural History of Diets, Fantasies, and Fat*. New York: Free Press, 1986. Highly researched history of American attitudes toward food and weight control, including social values and the symbolism of fat and of eating.

Wolf, Naomi. *The Beauty Myth*. New York: William Morrow, 1991. Strikingly written examination of how standards of beauty continue discrimination against women when more obvious sexism is not allowed.

—*Bernadette Lynn Bosky*

See also Ageism; Brownmiller, Susan; *Feminine Mystique, The*; Food and identity; Friedan, Betty; Mass media stereotyping

Arab Americans. *See* Islamic literature

Arenas, Reinaldo

BORN: Holguín, Oriente, Cuba; July 16, 1943

DIED: New York, New York; December 7, 1990

PRINCIPAL WORKS: *Celestino antes del alba*, 1967 (revised as *Cantando en el pozo*, 1982; *Singing from the Well*, 1987); *El mundo alucinante*, 1969 (*Hallucinations: Being an Account of the Life and Adventures of Friar Servando Teresa de Mier*, 1971); *El palacio de las blanquísimas mofetas*, 1975 (*The Palace of the White Skunks*, 1990); *El portero*, 1989 (*The Doorman*, 1991)

IDENTITIES: Gay, lesbian, and bisexual; Latino

SIGNIFICANT ACHIEVEMENT: Arenas' novels reflect his rural upbringing and his fight against Cuban revolutionary institutions that condemned him because of his homosexuality.

Reinaldo Arenas overcame a poor rural upbringing to become a renowned novelist and short-story writer. He belongs to a generation of young writers who received literary training in official programs to promote literacy among the Cuban poor. Such training, however, also involved heavy indoctrination by political organizations that promoted only revolutionary readings. Although his career depended upon his incorporation into such political agenda, Arenas refused to take an ideological stand. His decision caused him prosecution by legal authorities, imprisonment, and exile.

A superb storyteller, Arenas, in his first novel, *Singing from the Well*, presents young peasant characters who find themselves in an existentialist quest. Surrounded by a bleak rural environment, these protagonists fight the absolute poverty that keeps them from achieving their dreams. They also must confront their homosexual feelings, which force them to become outcasts. Although the subject of homosexuality is not an essential theme of the novel—the subject is merely hinted—Arenas' novel received a cold reception from Cuban critics.

Hallucinations brought Arenas' first confrontations with revolutionary critics and political authorities. Dissatisfied with the Castro regime, Arenas in the novel equates the Cuban Revolution to the oppressive forces of the Spanish Inquisition by drawing parallels between the persecutory practices of the two institutions. He also published the novel abroad without governmental consent, a crime punishable by law. That violation caused him to lose job opportunities and made him the target of multiple attempts at indoctrination, which included his imprisonment in a forced labor camp in 1970.

In spite of constant threats, Arenas continued writing antirevolutionary works that were smuggled out of the country by friends and published abroad in French translations. The theme of these works is constant: denunciation of Castro's oppressive political practices, most significantly the forced labor camps. The novels also decry the systematic persecution of homosexuals by military police and the relocation of homosexuals in labor camps.

After an incarceration of almost three years (1973-1976), Arenas made several attempts to escape from Cuba illegally. He finally succeeded in 1980, when he entered the United States by means of the Mariel boat lift. In the United States he continued his strong opposition to the Castro regime and re-edited the literary work he had written in Cuba. In addition, he intensified his interest in homosexual characters who, like his early young characters, find themselves in confrontation with the oppressive societies that punish them because of their sexual orientation. His open treatment of homosexuality makes him a forerunner of writers on that subject in Latin American literature.

SUGGESTED READING

Soto, Francisco. *Reinaldo Arenas: "The Pentagonía."* Gainesville: University Press of Florida, 1994.

—Rafael Ocasio

See also *Arturo, the Most Brilliant Star*; Caribbean American literature; Censorship of literature; Erotic identity; Gay identity; Latino American identity; *Pentagonía, The*; Poverty; Rural life

Arturo, the Most Brilliant Star

AUTHOR: Reinaldo Arenas (1943-1990)

FIRST PUBLISHED: *Arturo, la estrella más brillante*, 1984 (English translation, 1989)

IDENTITIES: Gay, lesbian, and bisexual; Latino

Reinaldo Arenas' commitment to resist and denounce Cuba's indoctrination practices is evident in his short novel *Arturo, the Most Brilliant Star*. This work is also significant in that Arenas links his political views on the Cuban Revolution with his increasing interest in gay characters. The plot was inspired by a series of police raids against homosexuals in Havana in the early 1960's. The process was simple: The police picked up thousands of men, usually young men, and denounced them as homosexuals on the grounds of their wearing certain pieces of clothing commonly considered to be the garb of gay men. Those arrested had to work and undergo ideological training in labor camps.

Arturo is one of the thousands of gay men forced into a work camp. He becomes a fictional eyewitness of the rampant use of violence as a form of punishment. The novel's descriptions of the violence coincide with eyewitness accounts by gay men who have made similar declarations after their exile from Cuba.

Arturo faces the fact that a labor camp foments homosexual activity between the prisoners and the guards. A dreary and claustrophobic existence prompts some men to do female impersonations. If caught, those impersonators become a target of police brutality. Arturo, a social outcast, suffers rejection by his fellow prisoners because initially he does not take part in the female impersonations. Partly as the result of verbal and physical abuse, he joins the group at large and becomes the camp's best female impersonator. His transformation, especially his fast control of the female impersonator's jargon, reminds the reader of the revolutionary jargon forced upon the prisoners, which at first they resist learning and later mimic to ironic perfection.

Arturo's imagination forces him to understand his loneliness in the camp. In order to escape from the camp, he strives to create his own world, one that is truly fantastic and one of which he is king. The mental process is draining, and he has to work under sordid conditions that threaten his concentration, but he is successful in his attempt and his world grows and extends outside the camp. The final touch is the construction of his own castle, in which he discovers a handsome man waiting for him on the other side of the walls. In his pursuit of his admirer Arturo does not recognize that his imaginary walls are the off-limits fences of the camp. When he is ordered to stop, he continues to walk out of the camp, and he is shot dead by a military officer.

Arenas' novel represents the beginning of a literary trend in Latin America that presents homosexuals as significant characters. It also focuses on the sexual practices of homosexual men, something that was a literary taboo.

SUGGESTED READING

Schwartz, Kessel. "Homosexuality and the Fiction of Reinaldo Arenas." *Journal of Evolutionary Psychology* 5, nos. 1-2 (1984): 12-20.

—*Rafael Ocasio*

See also Arenas, Reinaldo; Caribbean American literature; Erotic identity; Gay identity; Latino American identity; *Pentagonía, The*; Violence

Asian American identity: China, Japan, and Korea

IDENTITIES: Asian American

Although East Asia has been subjected to the challenges and influences of Western civilization, including pressures of modernization and of capitalism, it did not succumb, as did other regions of Asia, to the colonization efforts of the West. Contacts between East Asia and the West resulted, however, in political, economic, military, and ideological conditions that have contributed to mass emigration, through displacement and recruitment, from China, Japan, and Korea.

The United States of America, emerging as a world power in the late nineteenth century and as an increasingly dominant world power in the twentieth, became one of the main destinations of East Asian emigrants. This historical pattern has resulted in an impressive literature. Asian immigration has followed a pattern of labor shortages followed by legal restrictions. Recruited as laborers during different periods (the Chinese, 1850-1882; the Japanese, 1885-1924; the Koreans,

Many Asian immigrants first came to North America as agricultural workers. (Library of Congress)

1903-1905), East Asians often came first to work in the fields of Hawaii or in the western areas of the United States mainland. Many of the Hawaiian Asians later moved to the mainland, but as a result of Asian immigration, Hawaii in the 1990 census was the only state of the union where Asian Americans constituted the majority of the population. Until after World War II, Asian Americans were subjected to many discriminatory practices and laws. Their property rights and civil rights were often limited or violated, and citizenship was often no protection. Dramatic increases in the Asian American population resulted from the Immigration and Nationality Act of 1965 and subsequent legislation, which eased certain restrictions on immigration. Late twentieth century Asian immigrants to the United States also found their settlement ameliorated by the improved social climate that resulted from the Civil Rights movement. Asian American identity has always featured great diversity of geographic origins, linguistic and economic backgrounds, and perceptions. There have long been interethnic tensions and alliances among Asian Americans and other groups.

The experience of East Asian immigrants has often been distorted in the literature and mass media of North America. The stereotypes that abound in European American portrayals of Asians dominated the literary world until late in the twentieth century. Stereotypes served the purpose of exclusion and discrimination. In the late 1980's, many Asians found that even an apparently positive image could create trouble for them. The portrayal of Asians, especially East Asians, as a model minority placed a divisive wedge among different ethnic groups of America.

The points of view of East Asians themselves, rather than those of others, have become available thanks to the writings of Asian American authors. During much of the history of East Asians in North America, their writings and testimonies have been ignored or selectively endorsed and exploited. The success of writers such as Maxine Hong Kingston, Amy Tan, Cynthia Lynn Kadohata, and David Henry Hwang, however, has done much to change this situation. The success of such writers, however, does not mean that many East Asian Americans do not have to continue to struggle to define themselves.

Some common themes of literature by Americans of East Asian descent are the hardships of immigrant life, the negative treatments that East Asian immigrants and their descendants have received, struggles to find a place in a country dominated by whites, connections to and conflicts with the past, the problem of coming to terms with being both American and Asian, and critiques and appreciations of American society and culture. There are rich nuances in the many variations on such themes in East Asian American literature, which began to be written in the mid-nineteenth century and came of age in the Asian American renaissance of the 1980's.

Anthologies

Anthologies of Asian American literature, which feature a wide perspective on the Asian American experience, include *Aiiieeeee! An Anthology of Asian-American Writers* (1974), *Asian-American Authors* (1976), *Breaking Silence: An Anthology of Contemporary Asian American Poets* (1983), *Making Waves: An Anthology of Writings by and About Asian American Women* (1989), and *Home to Stay: Asian-American Women's Fiction* (1990).

Chinese American literature

The Chinese began to immigrate to the United States in 1820, but their numbers remained small until the late 1840's, when the decaying empire of China was defeated in 1848 by Britain in the First Opium War. The California gold rush (1849) started shortly after the United States acquired California as a result of the Mexican-American War (1848). These events coincided to produce a wave of Chinese immigration. When the Chinese Exclusion Act (1882) put a halt to Chinese immigration, more than 100,000 Chinese had settled in the United States. As a result of the exclusion, and because males far outnumbered females, the American Chinese population remained stable until the 1950's. The Chinese participated in a broad range of economic activities, including railroad building, mining, farming, fishing, industry, and family businesses. The influx of Americans into the West and the fierce economic competition that it brought about, compounded by the decline of China's international standing, led to pervasive anti-Chinese sentiments and violence. Legislation such as the Chinese Exclusion Act, Alien Land Laws, the Cable Act, and the National Origins Act aggravated rather than alleviated discrimination against the Chinese.

Chinese American experience, 1850-1942

The first phase (roughly 1850-1942) of the Chinese American experience is recorded primarily in three types of literature. The first type is the largely negative, or at least stereotypical, representation of the Chinese in European American writings. In popular literature, caricatures, stereotypes, and racist portrayals of the Chinese abounded. Examples include Sax Rohmer's Fu Manchu and Earl Derr Biggers' Charlie Chan. A variety of objectionable Chinese characters also populate Jack London's stories. Mark Twain, Bret Harte, and Ambrose Bierce, despite their sympathies for the Chinese, largely failed to recognize and assert their humanity.

The second type provides counterpoints to the stereotypes. This type of literature is the work of Chinese diplomats, travelers, and immigrants. Such writing is crucial to the formation of the identity of the Chinese American. A notable example is *Island: Poetry and History of Chinese Immigrants on Angel Island, 1910-1940* (1980), which contains a collection of Chinese poems found inscribed on the barrack walls of the Angel Island Detention Center. The common fate of a displaced people in distress looms large in the collective voice of these poems. Another collection, *Songs of Gold Mountain: Cantonese Rhymes from San Francisco Chinatown* (1987), also provides glimpses into the psyches of Chinese immigrants in the early 1900's. Sui Sin Far's (pseudonym of Edith Eaton) representation of the Chinese and the Chinese American experience in *Mrs. Spring Fragrance* (1912) is informed by an intimate knowledge of her subjects and enhanced by her mastery of the English language's literary idioms. Far, who was Amerasian, chose allegiance to her Chinese heritage at a time when it was demeaned. Such courage in the struggle to establish an ethnic identity has been required of many Asian Americans.

The third type of literature dealing with the first phase of the Chinese American experience involves the more-or-less-historical re-creation, by later writers, of the lives of their forebears. One example is Kingston's *China Men* (1980), in which the narrator attempts to reconstruct the tribulations and struggles of her male forebears who labored in the Hawaiian plantations, built the transcontinental railroad, and survived as Americans. Another example is Ruthanne Lum McGunn's *Thousand Pieces of Gold* (1981), which chronicles the immigration, destitution, survival, and independence of a Chinese woman pioneer in the late nineteenth century. McGunn's second historical novel, *Wooden Fish Songs* (1995), covers the period from 1842 to 1915 and the life story of Lue Gim Gong, whose contribution to citrus-growing technology was instrumental to the industry. In this type of literature, historical research and creative imagination are employed to open a window on the past, describe the beginnings of Chinese American identity, and affirm the connectedness between the past and the present. A significant instance of the historical imagination is Tan's *The Hundred Secret Senses* (1995), in which the author traces the protagonist's ancestry to the Hakkas, the ethnic Chinese group that started the Taiping Rebellion (1850-1864), one of the most cataclysmic events in Chinese history.

Chinese American experience, 1942-1965

The image of Chinese Americans improved during the second phase of the Chinese American experience. This period consists of the years 1942, the first full year of U.S. war against Japan, to 1965, the year of the Immigration and Nationality Act. This improvement was in part the result of China's being an important ally of the United States in World War II. A public awareness of the difference between Chinese Americans and Japanese Americans began to develop, at the expense of the latter. Accordingly, the literature of this period is dominated by two sentiments. The first is what may be called the diplomatic sentiment, which seeks to explain the values and virtues of the Chinese heritage to the general (that is, white) reader. Implicit in such literature is an attempt to cement the sense of alliance between the Chinese and the American. The tone may range from apology to celebration. A good example is Jade Snow Wong's *Fifth Chinese Daughter* (1945). Lin Yutang's extensive writings about China and Chinese culture, which have been well received by Western readers but often criticized by Chinese readers, also may be placed in this diplomatic context. The second sentiment is of belonging, of claiming America as home. This sentiment emerged as a dominant theme. A good example of this sentiment is Louis Chu's *Eat a Bowl of Tea* (1961), a novel about the precarious attempts of a Chinese American veteran and his Chinese wife to start a family in New York's Chinatown. The novel marks the transition from the bachelor society of the older generation to the next generation of Chinese Americans, who were in the United States not only to stay but also to multiply. The sentiment of belonging entails dealing with the issue of assimilation and Americanization. This issue is crucial to Chinese American literature. Some critics argue that certain writers (such as Pardee Lowe, *Father and Glorious Descendant*, 1943; C. Y. Lee, *Flower Drum Song*, 1957; Virginia Lee, *The House That Tai Ming Built*, 1963) deny, repress, or trivialize their Chinese heritage in order to gain acceptance. The theme of claiming America does lend itself to the construction of a distinct sense of Chinese American identity.

Another generation of Chinese American writers, those who came of age during the second phase of Chinese American experience, continue to be informed by the diplomatic sentiment, in some cases decrying it, in others, accepting it. Shawn Wong's lyrical novel *Homebase* (1979) locates the home in the United States and not in China. Ironically, the distinctive American identity of many Chinese has been challenged (and thereby strengthened, one may argue) by the continuing arrival of Chinese immigrants from Taiwan, Hong Kong, Southeast Asia, and mainland China.

Chinese American experience, since 1965

During the third phase (after 1965) of the Chinese American experience, the Chinese population of the United States rose from 250,000 in 1966 to 1.6 million in 1990. An important debate arises from continuing immigration: What, if any, distinction should be drawn between the native-born and the foreign-born? Frank Chin and the other editors of *Aiiieeeee! An Anthology of Asian-American Writers* (1974) and *The Big Aiiieeeee! An Anthology of Chinese American and Japanese American Literature* (1991) attempt to differentiate between the native-born and the foreign-born, implying that Chinese American identity should be determined on the basis of an American, rather than Chinese, mindset. Newcomers (sometimes derided as "fresh off the boat," source of the title of Hwang's *FOB*, 1979) and more recent arrivals have brought with them significant resources and skills. These conditions render moot the American-centered definition of Chinese American identity. The increased diversity of the Chinese American community has made the issue of identity complex. A case in point is the background of Chinese Indonesian American writer Li-Young Lee, the author of two acclaimed volumes of poetry (*Rose*, 1986; *The City in Which I Love You*, 1990) and *The Winged Seed: A Remembrance* (1995). A further complexity arises when writers (for example, feminist poet Nellie Wong and polemicist Chin) disagree regarding what, how, and for whom to write about their experience. To complicate things further, interracial families, marriages, and relationships (as in Lisa See's *On Gold Mountain*, 1995, and Shawn Wong's *American Knees*, 1995) can so entangle ethnic identity that it can amount to a Gordian knot. In sharp contrast to entanglement is the position of avant-garde poets such as John Yau, who appears to eschew considerations of ethnicity. Somewhere between is the case of Chinese Hawaiian authors such as Eric Chock and Wing-Tek Lum. The complex issues of ethnic identity will continue to unfold, but three discernible patterns in twentieth century Chinese American literature can be emphasized.

One pattern is the continuation of the positive literary trends started in the first two historical phases of Chinese American identity. Three such trends may be described. The first trend is the reclaiming of the past by reconstructing history. Examples of works of literature that attempt this reclamation or re-creation are Kingston's *The Woman Warrior* (1976) and *China Men*, McGunn's *Wooden Fish Songs*, Denise Chong's *The Concubine's Children* (1994) and Chin's *Donald Duk* (1991). The second trend is challenging stereotypes by asserting the Americanness of Chinese American identity. Chin's *The Chickencoop Chinaman* (1972) and *The Year of the Dragon* (1981) are examples. Another way to assert the Americanness of Chinese American identity is to place the home in America, as in Wong's *Homebase*. The third trend is to celebrate the Americanization of the Chinese. Gus Lee's *China Boy* (1991) and *Honor and Duty* (1994) and Ben Fong-Torres' *The Rice Room: Growing Up Chinese-American from Number Two Son to Rock 'n' Roll* (1994) are examples.

The second pattern in Chinese American literature is the exploration of specifically Chinese aspects of Chinese American culture. Chinatowns, the home of many Chinese American families, acquire vital reinterpretations in much Chinese American literature, for example in Chin's *Donald*

Several popular books by Asian authors. (Dawn Dawson)

Duk and his plays, Fae Myenne Ng's *Bone* (1993), Aimee E. Liu's *Face* (1994), and Fong-Torres' *The Rice Room*. China receives extensive treatment, especially in the autobiographical writings of immigrants such as Nien Cheng (*Life and Death in Shanghai*, 1986), Anchee Min (*Red Azalea*, 1994), and human rights activist Harry Wu (*Bitter Winds: A Memoir of My Years in China's Gulag*, 1994). There is also a body of literature inspired by the search for ancestral roots in China or the reconstruction of family histories. Examples include Frank Ching's *Ancestors: Nine Hundred Years in the Life of a Chinese Family* (1988), Leslie Li's *Bittersweet* (1992), and Belle Yang's *Baba: A Return to China upon My Father's Shoulders* (1994). The reclaiming of China as a cultural fountainhead holds true in the writings of the native-born, for example Tan's *The Joy Luck Club* (1989), *The Kitchen God's Wife* (1991), and *The Hundred Secret Senses*. Japanese-Chinese American author Gail Tsukiyama's *Women of the Silk* (1991) portrays China as a cultural and historical framework for the creative impulse. This body of literature often contains explicit or implicit critiques of the communist ideology of Red China or the inadequacies of the patriarchal Chinese tradition. Presenting North America as the new, better home country and presenting China as the symbolic or "other" homeland, some Chinese American literature tends to tilt the definition of identity toward the American side of the balance.

The third and most important pattern in twentieth century Chinese American literature is the critical representation of social issues. Cultural conflicts, generation gaps, and gender troubles are common to the experiences of many Chinese Americans from diverse backgrounds. Written in the context of the Civil Rights movement, feminism, multiculturalism, and deconstruction, this literature (Kingston's *The Woman Warrior* and *Tripmaster Monkey: His Fake Book*, 1989, are examples) is essential to Chinese American identity, and tends to problematize rather than resolve its dualities. This exploration of social issues has given rise to critiques of the American Dream (for example, Gish Jen's *Typical American*, 1991), of Western ideology regarding Asia (Hwang's *M. Butterfly*, 1988), and of the intricate complicities between American and Chinese ideologies, which work together to warp the minds of the modern Chinese in such works as Edna Wu's *Clouds and Rain: A China-to-America Memoir* (1994). These thoughtful works epitomize the complex maturity of the Chinese American identity.

Japanese American literature

In the second half of the nineteenth century, Japan, unlike China, responded to the challenges of the West by joining its ranks. When Emperor Mutsuhito, who reigned from 1868 to 1912, came to the throne, he inaugurated the Meiji era of political reform and technological modernization. The feudal system was eliminated and peasants were given land to farm. Also during Mutsuhito's reign, Japan defeated China (1894-1895) and Russia (1904-1905) in two wars and became the major regional power of East Asia, moving rapidly toward colonialism and global domination. This historical context has led some historians to speculate that the emigration of the Japanese was part of Japan's imperialist project, but a more likely interpretation is simply that Japanese peasants were so heavily taxed that many soon found life in Japan impossible. In either case, many Japanese made the Pacific crossing to the United States (see Milton Murayama's *Five Years on a Rock*, 1994). Haru Matsukata Reischauer's family saga, *Samurai and Silk: A Japanese and American Heritage* (1986), offers a century-long overview of the relationship between the United States and Japan.

The Japanese were first brought to Hawaii in 1869, but apart from these few immigrants and the several hundred students studying at American universities during the 1870's, the Japanese did not leave for Hawaii and the United States mainland in large numbers until the exclusion of the Chinese in 1882 resulted in a short supply of cheap labor. In 1885, the Japanese government began to allow its nationals to emigrate. By the end of the nineteenth century some 160,000 were working in the United States and Hawaii, mainly as migrant farmers and plantation laborers. In 1908, the United States and Japan negotiated the Gentlemen's Agreement, which restricted the immigration of the Japanese laborers. The family reunion provisions of this agreement, however, led to the introduction of picture brides. Yoshiko Uchida's *Picture Bride* (1987) and Murayama's *Five Years on a Rock* tell of this circumstance. Hence, in contrast to the Chinese, who were the object of legal restrictions intended to prevent their forming families, the Japanese Americans rose steadily in population, from about 150,000 around 1910 to about 300,000 at the outbreak of World War II. More than half of the Japanese in America when World War II started were Nisei (American-born children of Japanese immigrants). They were subjected to the same kind of discrimination that the Chinese suffered, but because of the relatively normal family life that the Japanese Americans could have, they settled down and concentrated on agriculture. Prohibited from owning land, they nevertheless became successful in farming cash crops and distributing produce. An activist group called the Japanese American Citizens League was founded by the Nisei in 1939 to combat racism and to promote Americanism.

Japanese American experience, 1869-1942

Apart from materials in Japanese such as haikus published in Japanese-language newspapers, the literature documenting the first phase of the Japanese American experience (1869-1942) may be placed, for convenience, in three thematic groups. The first group may be called the cosmopolitan group, as expressed in the prolific writings of Sadakichi Hartmann (1867-1944), born in Japan of a Japanese mother and a German father, and Yone Noguchi (1875-1947). They participated in the international literary scene, knew Ezra Pound and W. B. Yeats, and played an important role in the cultural exchange between East and West. Examples are Hartmann's *Tanka and Haiku: Fourteen Japanese Rhythms* (1915) and Noguchi's *Japanese Hokkus*, 1920. The second group is characterized by a sense of aristocratic nostalgia for the culture and tradition left behind. Typifying this impulse is the fiction of Etsu Inaki Sugimoto, whose *A Daughter of the Samurai* (1925) is filled with descriptions of fairy tales, legends, customs, and festivals that define the traditional culture of Japan, which the author regrets being lost to modernization. The book, followed by *A Daughter of the Narikin* (1932), *A Daughter of the Nohfu* (1935), and *Grandmother O Kyo* (1940), served a diplomatic function in explaining Japan and appreciating America. The third group, which overlaps with the first two to a certain degree, is the sociohistorical (whether biographical, autobiographical, or fictional) representation of Japanese American life. Examples include Noguchi's *The American Diary of a Japanese Girl* (1901), *The American Letters of a Japanese Parlor-Maid* (1905), and *The Story of Yone Noguchi, Told by Himself* (1915); Shidzue Ishimoto's *Facing Two Ways: The Story of My Life* (1935); Chiyono Sugimoto Kiyooka's two autobiographies, *Chiyo's Return* (1935) and *But the Ships Are Sailing—Sailing—* (1959); and Haru Matsui's *Restless Wave: An Autobiography* (1940). As suggested in Nisei author Toshio Mori's collection of short stories, *Yokohama, California* (1949; the volume was prepared for publication in 1941), an important trend in this material is the attempt to identify America rather than Japan as the homeland. Mori's Japanese American characters have totally acclimatized to California and feel perfectly at home there. Hisaye Yamamoto's short-story collection *Seventeen Syllables* (1988) captures the same sense of identification. *Seventeen Syllables* further enriches the definition of Japanese American identity by introducing generational, gender, and ethnic tensions. Contemporary writers continue to add to this sociohistorical archive by reconstructing, through reminiscences or research, the lives of their forebears. One example is Kazuo Miyamoto's *Hawaii: End of the Rainbow* (1964), a historical novel about Japanese immigrants in Hawaii. Another example is the ambitious family saga by Milton Murayama, *Five Years on a Rock* and *All I Asking for Is My Body* (1975). This broad range of materials suggests an impressively well-defined sense of ethnic identity in the first phase of the Japanese American experience.

Japanese American experience, since 1942

The second phase (1942 onward) began with the dispossession, relocation, and internment of 120,000 Japanese Americans residing on the West Coast in the wake of the attack on Pearl Harbor. The internment was the most revealing moment of Japanese American identity because it not only deprived Japanese Americans of their livelihood and civil rights but also shattered their assumptions about themselves, their nationalities, and their loyalties. The ordeal spawned a whole range of literary responses and expressions that haunt the memories of the Japanese American community and challenge the conscience of America as a democracy. Japanese Canadians went through a similar persecution; the most well-known literary recounting is Joy Kogawa's *Obasan* (1981). The literature of the internment experience expresses three types of sentiment. The first is defiance and anger, which is typified by World War II veteran John Okada's *No-No Boy* (1957), in which some Nisei characters refuse to prove their loyalty by serving in the United States military. *No-No Boy* was the first of a stream of protest literature among younger Japanese American writers. Examples include Edward T. Miyakawa's *Tule Lake* (1974), and Janice Mirikitani's *Shedding Silence* (1987) and *We the Dangerous* (1995). The second sentiment is more complex in that although outrage is present, it is subdued and sometimes diluted with humor or stoicism (and even shame and self-abnegation), with implications that justice can be entrusted to the good will and good judgment of the American public. Examples of this approach include Monica Sone's *Nisei Daughter* (1953), and *Farewell to Manzanar* (1973) by Jeanne Wakatsuki Houston and James Houston. The third sentiment overlaps with the first two but is distinguished from the protest of the first and the resignation of the second by a realism that concentrates on the factual aspects of the lives of the internees. Examples of this sentiment include Mitsuye Yamada's *Camp Notes and Other Poems* (1976) and Lawson Fusao Inada's *Legends from Camp* (1993). The significance of this approach lies in the fact that the internment is used as a framework for the meditation on and exploration of Japanese American identity. In the process of such meditation, the generational, cultural, and national differences between the Issei and Nisei are also bridged, thus reaching a cohesive sense of community.

At the end of World War II, by which time the valor of Japanese American veterans, who suffered extremely high casualty rates in missions intended to demonstrate their loyalty, had laid to rest the question of the loyalty and allegiance of Japanese Americans, an assimilationist sentiment began to emerge in the literature, even to the extent that the internment experience was enveloped by a veil of shame and silence. Sone's *Nisei Daughter*, although it does not evade issues of racism and oppression encountered in her life (part of which was spent in the internment camp), focuses on the humorous dimensions and cultural conflicts in the dualities of her almost innocent existence. Gene Oishi, in *In Search of Hiroshi* (1988), also eschews bitterness in documenting his camp experience and in chronicling his career as a journalist. Further examples of this approach include Daniel Inouye's *Journey to Washington* (1967), Daniel I. Okimoto's *American in Disguise* (1971), and *The Two Worlds of Jim Yoshida* (1972) by Jim Yoshida and Bill Hosokawa. Some critics have disparaged these books on the ground that their assimilationist approach grants that Americanness needs to be emphasized and that the Japanese part of one's heritage needs to be diminished, lest it arouse suspicion. The assimilationist success story, which tends to exact the price of repression and self-denial, finds its counterpoint in the works of authors who believe in breaking the silence. One such author is Janice Mirikitani. Kogawa's poignant *Obasan* offers a unique approach to the tension between repression and breaking silence by demonstrating that neither speaking out nor keeping silent about the wartime injustices is easy.

In 1989, the United States government closed the case of wartime internment with an apology and a cash payment to some 60,000 Japanese American victims who were still alive. The closure of the case appears to have encouraged Japanese American authors to look beyond the internment and assimilation for additional themes. Japanese American literature has diversified as a result. Many writings have been inspired by the history and memory of immigration and settlement. These include Wakako Yamauchi's *Songs My Mother Taught Me* (1994) and Jessica K. Saiki's *From the Lanai and Other Hawaii Stories* (1991). A variety of works testify to the high level of maturity and confidence in Japanese American literature. Cynthia Kadohata's *In the Heart of the Valley of Love* (1992) is a futuristic novel about a young woman's struggle to survive and love in an absurd and destitute world. Karen Tei Yamashita's *Through the Arc of the Rain Forest* (1990) is a satirical allegory about the monstrous operations of multinational corporations. Garrett Hongo's *Volcano* (1995) is a lyrical memoir of Hawaii that interweaves personal memories and appreciations of poetry and the environment. Gail Tsukiyama's *Women of the Silk* (1991) is a novel with strong feminist implications in its portrayal of an autonomous women's community in early twentieth century China. David Mura's roots-searching memoir *Turning Japanese* (1991) and Lydia Mina-toya's travelogue *Talking to High Monks in the Snow* (1992) indicate that the issue of ethnic identity continues to visit Japanese Americans, who, despite their survival and triumph, often find themselves surprised by the persistence of the identity issue. This persistence is clear in the case of recent Japanese immigrants such as Kyoko Mori, who fitfully interrogates her Japanese identity and diffidently assumes her American identity in *Shizuko's Daughter: The Dream of Water* (1995). Native Japanese writers such as Yoshimi Ishikawa, who has written about the United States, add international insights to the issue of Japanese American identity.

The Western powers attempted to wrest Korea from Chinese influence, but it was Japan, following its victories in the Sino-Japanese War (1894-1895) and the Russo-Japanese War (1904-1905), that finally annexed Korea and subjected it to colonial rule from 1905 to 1945. To suppress Korean resistance, the Japanese purged nationalists, controlled the land system, and imposed rigid rules. The oppression led to the March First Movement of 1919, in which millions of Koreans demonstrated for independence. The Japanese crushed the revolt, and introduced drastic measures such as banning Korean language and even family names to erase their national identity (see Richard E. Kim's *Lost Names: Scenes from a Korean Boyhood*, 1970). After Japan was defeated in World War II, Korea split into South Korea and North Korea.

Korean American literature

The first hundred Koreans arrived at Hawaiian plantations in 1903, and about eight thousand more departed before Japan took over Korea and stopped Korean emigration in 1905. Thereafter only limited numbers of students, political refugees, and picture brides managed to leave for the United States, where discriminatory practices also applied to Korean immigrants. As a result of their small numbers, the first phase (1903-1945) of the Korean American experience is characterized by the sense of uprootedness and invisibility. The small body of Korean American literature written in this period deals mainly with life in Korea. Examples are New Il-Han's *When I Was a Boy in Korea* (1928) and Younghill Kang's *The Grass Roof* (1931). Other themes include displacement and exile (No-Yong Park's *Chinaman's Chance: An Autobiography*, 1940) and immigrant life (Kang's *East Goes West: The Making of an Oriental Yankee*, 1937). Kang's *East Goes West* describes the life of Korean students as exiles, migrants, and immigrants in New York and in Canada. The book is also a passionate, soul-searching meditation on the relative strengths and weaknesses of Asian and American civilizations. In presenting the tragedies of American Koreans as exiles caught up in the enchantment of American life, thereby losing their cultural bearings (and sometimes even their lives through suicide), Kang attempts to negotiate a new identity by amalgamating the legacies of the two cultures. His intimation that in order to survive as a Korean American he had to re-create himself as an "Oriental Yankee" continues to be relevant.

In the second phase of Korean American experience (since 1945), Korean Americans gained increasing visibility in the wake of the Korean War (1950-1953). The United States sided with South Korea. As a result of this military connection, after the Korean War South Koreans began to come to the United States in increasing numbers. Among the first to come were war brides, Amerasian children, orphans, and refugees. Immigration after 1965 increased at such a rate that Korean Americans numbered more than 800,000 in 1990. A large proportion of them are Christians, the legacy of missionaries. Many Korean Americans are urban professionals and owners of grocery stores and small enterprises.

Post-Korean War literary developments

Two developments can be identified in Korean American literature written during the post-Korean War period of immigration. The first development is the continuing reconstruction, whether autobiographical or fictional, of the experience of exile, immigration, and settlement. One example is Peter Hyun's autobiography, *Man Sei! The Making of a Korean American* (1986), which describes the author's childhood in Korea under Japanese occupation, his exile to Shanghai, and his arrival in Hawaii. Kim Ronyoung's novel *Clay Walls* (1986) covers the period from 1920 to 1945. In it, the author describes a Korean couple's immigration to Los Angeles and their attempt to put down roots. Told from the perspectives of characters from different generations, the novel negotiates a tentative Korean American identity by interweaving themes of Korean culture, American racism, Korean nationalism, and Japanese colonialism. Including episodes about espionage (a conscience-stricken Korean captain spies unwillingly for the Japanese), the novel raises many questions about nationality and identity. Mary Paik Lee's *Quiet Odyssey: A Pioneer Korean Woman in America* (1990), which details her family's day-to-day struggles to make a living in various parts of California in the years 1905 to 1990, is a particularly valuable account because Paik Lee's life coincides with Korean American history generally. The author was born in 1900 and emigrated to the United States in 1905.

The second development in contemporary Korean American literature shares a historical theme with the first, but is further complicated by the diversity of sensibilities that the postwar generations bring. An early example of this trend is Richard E. Kim's mystery novel, *The Martyred* (1965). The book, which describes the deaths of fourteen Christian ministers captured by communists during the Korean War, also attempts to capture existential insights from the tragedy. In Korean Chinese Hawaiian poet Song's imaginative explorations of her grandparents' lives in *Picture Bride*

Asian American Identity Milestones

1800's	Many white authors of the West of the nineteenth century originate or contribute to Asian stereotypes, including Jack London, Bret Harte, and a host of dime novelists.
1820	The Chinese begin to immigrate to the United States in numbers. Immigration increases when the empire of China is defeated in 1848 by Britain in the First Opium War.
1848	United States acquires California as a result of the Mexican-American War.
1850-1864	The Taiping Rebellion. The gold rush, the Opium War, and the Taiping Rebellion are the carrot and the two sticks, respectively, that motivate many Chinese to emigrate to California.
1868	China and the United States sign the Burlingame Treaty, which allows unrestricted voluntary migration between the two countries.
1868	Emperor Mutsuhito, who reigns from 1868 to 1912, comes to the throne and inaugurates the Meiji era of political reform and technological modernization.
1869	First Japanese arrive at Hawaii as laborers.
1875	The beginnings of Chinese literature can be traced to the publication of Wong Sam's *An English-Chinese Phrase Book*.
1882	Chinese Exclusion Act bans Chinese immigration; those present in the United States—mostly men—cannot send for their wives in China.
1885	The Japanese government begins to allow its nationals to emigrate. By the end of the nineteenth century some 160,000 are working in the United States and Hawaii, mainly as migrant farmers and plantation laborers.
1887	Lee Yan Phou's *When I Was a Boy in China*.
1891	*Chinese World*, the first bilingual daily newspaper, begins publication in San Francisco.
1894	The Western powers attempt to wrest Korea from Chinese influence, but Japan is the nation that annexes Korea and subjects it to colonial rule from 1905 to 1945.
1895-1905	Japan defeats China (1894-1895) and Russia (1904-1905) in two wars and becomes the major regional power of East Asia.
1901	Yone Noguchi's *The American Diary of a Japanese Girl*.
1903	The first hundred Koreans arrive at Hawaii plantations.
1905	Yone Noguchi's *The American Letters of a Japanese Parlor-Maid*.
1907-1908	The United States and Japan negotiate the Gentlemen's Agreement, which restricts the immigration of the Japanese laborers. The agreement allows for brides to come to the U.S. Thus many Japanese form families while many Chinese are prevented from doing so.
1909	Yung Wing's *My Life in China and America*.
1910-1940	Immigrants entering the United States are sent to the Angel Island detention center where they are detained to determine whether or not they meet the eligibility requirements for entry into the country. Most of these immigrants are of Chinese descent.
1912	Sui Sin Far (pseudonym of Edith Eaton) represents the Chinese and the Chinese American experience in *Mrs. Spring Fragrance*.

(1983), history is filtered through the personal, artistic lenses of an Americanized, yet ethnically conscientious, generation. In contrast to Song's lyrical approach is Theresa Hak Kyung Cha's modernist and political *Dictée* (1982), an intentionally jarring collage of multilingual fragments that conjure the tragic inscriptions of family history, Korean politics, and Western civilization. Another example of the mutual illumination of the historical and the personal is journalist Connie Kang's *Home Was the Land of Morning Calm* (1995), which focuses on her family's tortuous journey in the wake of the Korean War from North Korea to the United States by way of South Korea and Japan. The book fills an important gap in the history of Korean immigration and the relations among Korea, Japan, and the United States. Kang also explores with critical acumen the paradoxical dimensions of her life and wonders how she can reconcile her different cultures. In fiction, the conspiracy novel *Native Speaker* (1995) by Chang-Rae Lee pursues a related paradox. In the novel, a fully assimilated Korean American finds he must come to terms with his conscience

Asian American Identity Milestones — CONTINUED

1913	Alien Land Law is passed in California to prevent aliens ineligible for U.S. citizenship from buying or leasing land.	1935	Chiyono Sugimoto Kiyooka's autobiography *Chiyo's Return*.
1913	*Dr. Fu Manchu*, first of the many novels featuring arch-villain Fu Manchu, by Sax Rohmer, pen name of Englishman Arthur Sarsfield Ward.	1935	Shidzue Ishimoto's *Facing Two Ways: The Story of My Life*.
		1935	*My Country and My People*, by Lin Yutang, a noted Chinese author and scholar.
1915	Yone Noguchi's *The Story of Yone Noguchi, Told by Himself*.	1937	Younghill Kang's *East Goes West: The Making of an Oriental Yankee*.
1915	Sadakichi Hartmann's (born in Japan of a Japanese mother and a German father) *Tanka and Haiku: Fourteen Japanese Rhythms*.	1940	The Korean No-Yong Park's *Chinaman's Chance: An Autobiography*.
		1940	Etsu Inaki Sugimoto's *Grandmother O Kyo*.
1919	March First movement, a nationwide uprising in which millions of Koreans demonstrate for independence.	1940	Haru Matsui's *Restless Wave: An Autobiography*.
1920	"In the Camp," a story about farm labor by James Chun.	1941	Japan attacks Pearl Harbor and the United States declares war on Japan.
1920	Yone Noguchi's *Japanese Hokkus*.	1941	Toshio Mori's collection of short stories, *Yokohama, California*, prepared for publication (published 1949).
1922	The Cable Act is passed, a law that discourages Chinese Americans from marrying immigrants.	1942	The internment of the Japanese on the West Coast begins after the signing of Executive Order 9066.
1925	Etsu Inaki Sugimoto's *A Daughter of the Samurai*.	1943	Carlos Bulosan's *America Is in the Heart*.
1925	Earl Derr Biggers' Charlie Chan is featured in *House Without a Key*. The stereotype proves enduring.	1943	*Father and Glorious Descendant*, by Pardee Lowe, details the writers' struggle with intercultural and intracultural conflict.
1928	New Il-Han's *When I Was a Boy in Korea*.	1945	World War II ends as Japan surrenders.
1931	*The Grass Roof* by Younghill Kang, the first Korean-born comparative literature professor at New York University.	1945	Jade Snow Wong's *Fifth Chinese Daughter* deals with cultural conflicts.
1932	Etsu Inaki Sugimoto's *A Daughter of the Narikin*.	1948	Lin Yutang's *A Chinatown Family*.
		1948	Florence Frisbe's *Miss Ulysses of Puka*.
1934	Tydings-McDuffie Act restricts Filipino immigration.	1950-1953	The Korean War.
		1953	*Nisei Daughter* is the account of the Japanese

(continued)

upon realizing that his success is built on the destruction of his community. The novel raises the issue of ethnic identity to a new level by questioning the political processes by which ethnic identity is turned into a weapon.

SUGGESTED READINGS

Chan, Sucheng. *Asian Americans: An Interpretive History*. Boston: Twayne, 1991.

Cheung, King-Kok, and Stan Yogi. *Asian American Literature: An Annotated Bibliography*. New York: Modern Language Association, 1988.

Chin, Frank, et al., eds. *Aiiieeeee! An Anthology of Asian-American Writers*. Washington, D.C.: Howard University Press, 1974.

_____. *The Big Aiiieeeee! An Anthology of Chinese American and Japanese American Literature*. New York: Meridian, 1991.

Kim, Elaine H. "Asian American Literature." In *Columbia Literary History of the United States*,

---

Asian American Identity Milestones — CONTINUED

	American search for identity and the World War II internment experience, by Monica Sone, a second-generation Japanese American.
1956	Diana Chang's *Frontiers of Love* describes life in Shanghai from the point of view of a Eurasian from the United States.
1957	C. Y. Lee's *Flower Drum Song* examines the conflict between the old and young and the Asian and Western ways of life in a comical fashion.
1957	John Okada's *No-No Boy*.
1959	Chiyono Sugimoto Kiyooka's second autobiography, *But the Ships Are Sailing—Sailing—*.
1961	*Eat a Bowl of Tea*, a novel by Louis Chu.
1963	Virginia Lee's *The House That Tai Ming Built*.
1964	Kazuo Miyamoto's *Hawaii: End of the Rainbow*.
1965	Immigration and Nationality Act allows for increased Asian immigration. The act and the Vietnam War lead to a surge in Asian immigration. Among the immigrants are writers, some with books published in their native countries. Asian American writing begins to assume greater stature and readership.
1965	Jon Shirota's *Lucky Come Hawaii*.
1965	Richard E. Kim's mystery novel, *The Martyred*.
1967	Daniel Inouye's *Journey to Washington*. Inouye is the first Japanese American elected to the House of Representatives.
1968	Albert Masori Kiki's autobiography *Kiki: Ten Thousand Years in a Lifetime*.
1970	Vincent Eri's *The Crocodile*.
1970	Richard E. Kim's *Lost Names: Scenes from a Korean Boyhood*.
1971	Daniel I. Okimoto's *American in Disguise*.
1971	Lawson Fusao Inada's *Before the War*.
1972	Frank Chin's *The Chickencoop Chinaman*. The works of Chin and others address issues of Asian American anger at discrimination, previously a topic more notable for its absence than for its presence in Asian American literature.
1972	*The Two Worlds of Jim Yoshida,* by Jim Yoshida and Bill Hosokawa, the autobiography of a second-generation Japanese American.
1973	*Farewell to Manzanar*, by Jeanne Wakatsuki Houston and James Houston, depicts the wartime injustices suffered by Japanese Americans.
1974	Edward T. Miyakawa's *Tule Lake*.
1975	The war in Vietnam comes to an end; Vietnamese refugees begin to come to the United States in large numbers.
1975	Milton Murayama, *All I Asking for Is My Body*. His material suggests an impressively well-defined sense of ethnic identity.
1975	Jessica Hagedorn's *Dangerous Music*.
1975	Vo Phien, a winner of the Vietnamese National Literary Prize, arrives in United States and founds *Van Hoc Nh Thuat*, a literary journal in Vietnamese.
1976	Bessie Lai's *Ah Ya, I Still Remember*.
1976	Mitsuye Yamada's *Camp Notes and Other Poems*, a book of poetry based on her internment at Minidoka.

edited by Emory Elliott et al. New York: Columbia University Press, 1988.

_____. *Asian American Literature: An Introduction to the Writings and Their Social Context.* Philadelphia: Temple University Press, 1982.

Kim, Elaine H., and Yu Eui-Young, eds. *East to America: Korean American Life Stories.* New York: The Free Press, 1996.

Lim, Shirley Geok-lin. "Twelve Asian American Writers: In Search of Self-Definition." In *Redefining American Literary History*, edited by A. LaVonne Brown Ruoff and Jerry W. Ward, Jr. New York: Modern Language Association, 1990.

Lim, Shirley Geok-lin, and Amy Ling, eds. *Reading the Literatures of Asian America.* Philadelphia: Temple University Press, 1992.

Takaki, Ronald. *Strangers from a Different Shore: A History of Asian Americans.* New York: Penguin Books, 1989.

Asian American Identity Milestones — CONTINUED

Year	Event	Year	Event
1976	Nora Vagi Brash's *The High Cost of Living Differently*.	1983	Wendy Law-Yone's *The Coffin Tree*.
1976	Maxine Hong Kingston's *The Woman Warrior*, a best-seller addressing feminist anger.	1983	Korean Chinese Hawaiian poet Cathy Song's imaginative explorations of her grandparents' lives in *Picture Bride*.
1978	Janice Mirikitani's *Awake in the River*.	1985	*The Bone People*, by Keri Hulme.
1978	Monica Clare's *Karobran: The Story of an Aboriginal Girl*.	1985	Minh Duc Hoai Trinh's novel *This Side, the Other Side*.
1978	Eric Chock's *Ten Thousand Wishes*.	1986	Kim Ronyoung's novel *Clay Walls*.
1979	David Henry Hwang's *FOB*.	1986	Nien Cheng's *Life and Death in Shanghai*.
1979	Shawn Wong's lyrical novel *Homebase*.	1986	Peter Hyun's autobiography, *Man Sei! The Making of a Korean American*.
1980	Maxine Hong Kingston's *China Men*.	1986	Li-Young Lee's *Rose*.
1980	Editors Him Mark Lai, Genny Lim, and Judy Young's *Island: Poetry and History of Chinese Immigrants on Angel Island, 1910-1940*.	1986	Haru Matsukata Reischauer's family saga, *Samurai and Silk: A Japanese and American Heritage*.
1980	Editor Albert Wendt's *Lali: A Pacific Anthology*.	1987	Jessica Saiki's *Once, a Lotus Garden* is an account of what many Japanese Americans went through before and during World War II.
1981	Jully Sipolo's *Civilized Call Girl*.	1987	Yoshiko Uchida's *Picture Bride*.
1981	Joy Kogawa's *Obasan* recounts the suffering of a Japanese Canadian family forced from their home on the Canadian west coast during World War II.	1987	*Songs of Gold Mountain: Cantonese Rhymes from San Francisco Chinatown* provides glimpses into the psyches of Chinese immigrants in the early 1900's.
1981	Ruthanne Lum McGunn's *Thousand Pieces of Gold*.	1988	Gene Oishi, *In Search of Hiroshi*.
1981	Frank Chin's *The Year of the Dragon*.	1988	David Henry Hwang's *M. Butterfly* opens in Washington, D.C., at the National Theater.
1982	Theresa Hak Kyung Cha's modernist and political *Dictée*.	1988	Hisaye Yamamoto's short-story collection *Seventeen Syllables*.
1982	Nguyen Ngok Ngan's *The Will of Heaven* explores the end of tradition as characters survive the Vietnam War, only to become exiles.	1989	The United States government closes the case of Japanese American internment during World War II with an apology and a cash payment to some 60,000 victims who are still alive.
1983	Tran Van Dinh's novels and short stories, notably *Blue Dragon, White Tiger: A Tet Story*.		

(continued)

White-Parks, Annette, et al., eds. *A Gathering of Voices on the Asian American Experience*. Fort Atkinson, Wis.: Highsmith Press, 1994.

Wong, Sau-ling Cynthia. *Reading Asian American Literature from Necessity to Extravagance*. Princeton, N.J.: Princeton University Press, 1993.

—*Balance Chow*

See also Acculturation; *Aiiieeeee!*; American Dream; American identity: West and the frontier; Chin, Frank; Chu, Louis; Civil Rights movement; *Concubine's Children, The*; Demographics of identity; Hongo, Garrett Kaoru; Hwang, David Henry; Identity crisis; Inada, Lawson Fusao; Japanese American internment; Kadohata, Cynthia Lynn; Kingston, Maxine Hong; Korean War; Lee, Li-Young; Multiculturalism; *Native Speaker*; Okada, John; Racism and ethnocentrism; Song, Cathy; Stereotypes and identity; Tan, Amy; Vietnam War; Wong, Jade Snow; World War II; Yamada, Mitsuye Yasutake; Yamamoto, Hisaye

---

Asian American Identity Milestones — CONTINUED

1989	Nguyen Thi Thu-Lam's *Fallen Leaves*.
1989	Cynthia Lynn Kadohata's *The Floating World*.
1989	Amy Tan's *The Joy Luck Club*.
1989	Le Ly Hayslip's *When Heaven and Earth Changed Places*.
1990	In the 1990 census, Hawaii has a majority of Asian Americans.
1990	Li-Young Lee's *The City in Which I Love You*.
1990	Wing Tek Lum's *Matrices, Paradoxes and Personal Passions*.
1990	Mary Paik Lee's *Quiet Odyssey: A Pioneer Korean Woman in America*.
1990	Karen Tei Yamashita's *Through the Arc of the Rain Forest*.
1991	Gus Lee's *China Boy*.
1991	Jessica K. Saiki's *From the Lanai and Other Hawaii Stories*.
1991	Amy Tan's *The Kitchen God's Wife*.
1991	David Mura's roots-searching memoir, *Turning Japanese*.
1991	Gish Jen's *Typical American*.
1991	Japanese-Chinese American author Gail Tsukiyama's *Women of the Silk*.
1992	Leslie Li's *Bittersweet*.
1992	Cynthia Kadohata's *In the Heart of the Valley of Love*.
1992	Lydia Minatoya's travelogue *Talking to High Monks in the Snow*.
1993	Fae Myenne Ng's *Bone*.
1993	Lawson Fusao Inada's *Legends from Camp*.
1994	Belle Yang's *Baba: A Return to China upon My Father's Shoulders*.
1994	Chinese dissident Harry Wu's *Bitter Winds: A Memoir of My Years in China's Gulag*.
1994	Edna Wu's *Clouds and Rain: A China-to-America Memoir*.
1994	Denise Chong's *The Concubine's Children: The Story of a Chinese Family Living on Two Sides of the Globe*.
1994	Aimee E. Liu's *Face*.
1994	Milton Murayama's *Five Years on a Rock*.
1994	Editor Sucheng Chan's *Hmong Means Free: Life in Laos and America*.
1994	Gus Lee's *Honor and Duty*.
1994	Anchee Min's *Red Azalea*.
1994	Ben Fong-Torres' *The Rice Room: Growing Up Chinese-American from Number Two Son to Rock 'n' Roll*.
1994	Wakako Yamauchi's *Songs My Mother Taught Me*.
1995	Shawn Wong's *American Knees*.
1995	Lisa See's *On Gold Mountain*.
1995	Connie Kang's *Home Was the Land of Morning Calm*.
1995	*Native Speaker*, by Chang-Rae Lee.
1995	Kyoko Mori's *Shizuko's Daughter: The Dream of Water*.
1995	Garrett Hongo's *Volcano*, a memoir of Hawaii.
1995	Li-Young Lee's *The Winged Seed: A Remembrance*.
1995	McGunn's second historical novel, *Wooden Fish Songs*.

Asian American identity: Hmong

IDENTITIES: Hmong American

Most of the Hmong peoples of Asia live in what is now the northern part of Vietnam. Indigenous to the area for centuries, the Hmong helped to fight their Japanese conquerors and the French when they attempted to colonize Vietnam. When the Americans engaged in their lengthy and disastrous war of the 1960's and 1970's, many Hmong farmers were recruited by agents of the Central Intelligence Agency (CIA) and the American Ranger Army forces to fight for the Americans. The Hmong were so situated that their allegiance was seen to be strategic in importance, although the Hmong people were all farmers and fairly primitive in their standard of living. The Hmong were largely known for their unorthodox but successful cultivation processes, usually farming in rows on steep, hilly land that was not particularly fertile. By strapping their plows around their necks, they were able through agility and strength to develop crops in areas that seemed nonfarmable.

Americans recognized that many, perhaps all, Hmong would be treated badly by the North Vietnamese, the enemy, who was winning. American troops and others helped Hmong move to South Vietnam and ultimately to ships and airplanes headed for the United States. Many Hmong did not make the trip for diverse reasons, and although many died under the new rule in Vietnam, the Hmong still exist as a people in Southeast Asia.

Once in the United States (the largest populations settled in California, Colorado, and the upper Midwest), the Hmong faced most of the problems that immigrants have faced. The primary issues facing the Hmong in acculturation were the language and being able to make a living. Their form of agriculture simply does not work in the United States, and, as typically happens, the children were immersed in American culture and thinking, along with the English language.

As the Hmong began to acculturate, some of the people fell prey to what social scientists have described as lucid dreaming, a process by which a member of the Hmong who remembered Vietnam would lapse into destructive dreams. Many Hmong believe that dreaming is parallel to living, that there is really no difference, so many believe that what they dream will actually happen. Bad dreams of memories of war and of culture shock have resulted in difficulties for Hmong Americans.

There is almost no literature by the Hmong in the United States. Lucid dreaming seems to be a substitute for almost all forms of art, including the transmission of indigenous cultural material through writing. The Hmong do have a culture of stories that are passed down by generation, but thus far this process has been strictly oral. The Hmong believe that important messages are passed down through the process of dreaming. As is common with many immigrant groups, however, the children and grandchildren of those who arrived in the mid-1970's may write someday their stories into the literatures of America.

SUGGESTED READINGS

Quincy, Keith. *Hmong: History of a People*. Cheney, Wash: EWUP, 1995.
Smalley, William Allen. *Mother of Writing: The Origin and Development of a Hmong Messianic Script*. Chicago: University of Chicago Press, 1990.

—John Jacob

See also Acculturation; Asian American identity: Vietnam; *Hmong Means Free*

Asian American identity: India

IDENTITIES: South Asian

American writers of Asian Indian origin bring a distinct style and subject matter to the literature of the Americas. Issues emerging in their writings include the struggle to break free of imperialism, cultural assimilation, expatriation, and racial prejudice. In the literature of Asian Indians living in North America, two distinct styles have evolved. One concerns itself with the need to integrate into mainstream American culture; this literature is declarative in tone and has as its locale the broad landscapes of America. Literature of this first type often presents situations that give rise to

Asian American Identity: India
Milestones

1940	Ahmed Ali, a Pakistani who taught in American Universities, publishes *Twilight in Delhi*, a novel about Muslim life in India before the Partition.		1984	Shiva Naipaul's *Beyond the Dragon's Mouth: Stories and Pieces*.
1958	Ruth Prawer Jhabvala, of English citizenship and a New York resident after 1975, publishes *Esmond in India*.		1985	Bharati Mukherjee's *Darkness*.
			1985	*Sound-Shadows of the New World* recounts Ved Mehta's years at the Arkansas School for the Blind.
1968	Ruth Prawer Jhabvala's *A Stronger Climate: Nine Stories*.		1986	Vikram Seth's *The Golden Gate*, a novel in verse about a group of friends and lovers in San Francisco.
1970	Shiva Naipaul's *Fireflies*.			
1971	*The Tiger's Daughter*, by Bharati Mukherjee, a Canadian Indian.		1986	Ruth Prawer Jhabvala's *Out of India*.
1972	Ved Mehta's autobiographical series *Continents of Exile* begins with *Daddyji*, a biography of Mehta's father.		1987	Ruth Prawer Jhabvala's *Three Continents*.
			1987	Uma Parameswaran's *Trishanku*, poetry.
1972	Ruth Prawer Jhabvala's *An Experience of India*.		1988	*House of a Thousand Doors*, by Meena Alexander.
1973	Shiva Naipaul's *The Chip-Chip*.		1988	Boman Desai's *The Memory of Elephants*.
1975	Ruth Prawer Jhabvala's *Heat and Dust*.		1988	Bharati Mukherjee's *The Middleman and Other Stories*.
1975	Bharati Mukherjee's *Wife*.			
1976	Ruth Prawer Jhabvala's *How I Became a Holy Mother and Other Stories*.		1989	Sara Suleri's *Meatless Days*.
1977	*Fire on the Mountain*, by Anita Desai, an Indian of Indo-German parentage who writes in English, receives worldwide acclaim.		1989	*The Stolen Light* recounts Ved Mehta's study at Pomona College in California.
			1990	Chitra Ban Divkakaruni's *The Reason for Nasturtiums*.
1978	Zulfikar Ghose's *A Different World*.		1991	Meena Alexander's *Nampally Road: A Novel*.
1979	Ved Mehta's *Mamaji*, about his mother.		1992	Meena Alexander's *Fault Lines*.
1982	Ved Mehta's *Vedi*.		1993	Bapsi Sidhwa's *An American Brat*.
1983	Shiva Naipaul's *A Hot Country*.		1993	Bharati Mukherjee's *The Holder of the World*.
1983	Ruth Prawer Jhabvala's *In Search of Love and Beauty*.		1993	Ruth Prawer Jhabvala's *Poet and Dancer*.
			1995	Ruth Prawer Jhabvala's *Shards of Memory*.

violent cultural collisions. The second type has as its focus the necessity of maintaining the customs and communities of origin. This literature questions the pull to assimilation, giving rise to an interrogative quality. The two orientations mingle with each other. Asian Indian literature gives voice to the interweave of a life of an Asian in America by often combining the literary canons of the West and East. The Greek poet Homer, the English poet John Milton, and the American poet Walt Whitman are evoked as comfortably as the ancient Sanskrit poems of Kālidāsa.

Categorization   Categorizing Asian American literature into tidy ethnic groups is problematic. The breadth, variety, and complexity of Asian cultures defy easy categorization. India is a country two-thirds the size of the United States. It is divided into twenty-three states and several federal territories. Each state has cultural, social, linguistic, historical, geographical, and culinary characteristics that are unique. It is almost impossible to talk about an Asian Indian experience because such a discussion lends itself to generalities that are not applicable to the entire nation. Similarly, organizing the multicultural nations of Asia into neat compartments for the convenience of Western audiences has given rise to severe criticism from Asian scholars and thinkers. They argue that pigeonholing vastly different people into patterns that are convenient for the West is another way of dominating and controlling other peoples.

For example, those belonging to the South Asian American category include peoples of different religious, linguistic, and ethnic backgrounds from India, Pakistan, Bangladesh, Sri Lanka, and the Maldive Islands. Individuals of Asian Indian origin living in America are generally referred to as South Asian Americans. The term "Indian Americans" tends to be avoided because it gives rise to confusion with Native Americans, who are referred to as American Indians.

History

Immigration from India to North America began in numbers in the 1880's. In 1923, the U.S. Supreme Court ruled that Indians could not become American citizens because they are not Caucasian. In 1924, the Immigration Act was passed, denying entry into the United States to those who were ineligible for citizenship. It was not until 1965, when immigration laws changed, that another wave of immigration occurred. Immigration reform removed the European bias in immigration laws.

South Asians emigrated to North America with hopes of a better life. Lacking strong ties with traditional America, they found themselves being treated as outsiders. Their dark skin made them suspect. Their history was previously marked by the oppressive British colonizers. South Asians in America looked for ways to escape this imperialist history by becoming accepted and appreciated for their differences in the free world. South Asian Americans found themselves the victims of racism in a predominantly white society. To give voice to their fears and anxieties, South Asian American writers have become active participants in writing their own stories, creating different ways of looking at the world in a literature that is rich and complex.

South Asian American literature

The forging of new identities and the creation of a society that stretches its paradigms to include new Americans are the subjects of various South Asian works. A list of noted twentieth century South Asian writers includes Ved Mehta, Santha Rama Rau, Meena Alexander, Agha Shahid Ali, G. S. Sharat Chandra, Anita Desai, Chitra Banerjee Divakaruni, Zulfikar Ghose, Amitava Ghosh, Gita Mehta, Bharati Mukherjee, Raja Rao, and Sara Suleri.

Mukherjee, one of the most famous of the group, has exhorted immigrant writers to abandon the Third World material they sentimentalize as exiles and to take up, or continue, writing about "the messiness of rebirth as an immigrant." She has also pointed out that as new patterns of immigration alter the American cultural fabric, the necessity of participation in literature is twofold. Immigrants must speak for themselves, and, in doing so, a new America speaks for itself.

Wanting to be known as an American rather than as a South Asian American writer, Mukherjee calls for a need to assimilate, to view life from within America rather than from its periphery. Her writing uses cinematic techniques, showing the dominant culture surrounding, all-pervasive, immigrant society. She argues that assimilation must occur. In most of Mukherjee's works, this melding happens in violent, dramatic ways in which a resolution of issues comes with a forced break from the old culture in favor of the new.

Her first novel, *The Tiger's Daughter* (1971), captures the experiences of Tara Banerjee Cart-

This Sikh American private asked for permission to keep his long hair, as required by his religion, from the president of the United States. (National Archives)

wright, an Indian woman from the state of Bengal. Her Indian values collide with those of her American husband. In *Wife* (1975), her second novel, an Indian woman is trapped in the loneliness of a New York apartment and confused by a world created by television. Bereft of any meaningful interaction with a community (as she enjoyed in her own culture), she kills her husband while he eats a bowl of cereal and waits for him to come back to life as people do in the movies. In *Darkness* (1985) and *The Middleman and Other Stories* (1988), Mukherjee focuses on stories of expatriation, many of which stem from the author's personal experiences. Mukherjee has been the recipient of racial slurs, has been made to feel invisible, and for a while remained unacknowledged for her contributions.

Poet, novelist, and educator Meena Alexander lived in Asia, Africa, and Europe before moving to America. Her work is situated at the confluence of many cultures, a space of maddening ambiguity and irresolution, a place where there are no right or wrong answers. Alexander has said that for years she has been haunted by the sense that the act of writing creates a shelter. For Alexander, writing allows space to that which otherwise would be hidden, covered over, crossed out, or mutilated. Alexander's novel *Nampally Road* (1991) and memoir *Fault Lines* (1992) give voice to her various selves. Her writing describes the split image, the memory that is restored to present a self that sustains itself in all locales, to present a geography that spans many continents. For example, Mira Kanadical, the protagonist of *Nampally Road*, returns to India after receiving her Western education and attempts to negotiate a safe space for herself, a place where she may belong. This struggle for belonging, coupled with India's political instability, makes for a protracted search for meaning and identity.

In the hands of South Asian American writers such as Mukherjee, Alexander, and others, internal and external geographies are explored. The South Asian American experiences a complex relationship with the Western world. The literature of South Asian Americans serves to expand the Western canon in literature.

SUGGESTED READINGS

Mohanty, Chandra Talpade, ed. *Third World Women and the Politics of Feminism*. Bloomington: Indiana University Press, 1991.

Rustomji-Kerns, Roshni, ed. *Living in America: Poetry and Fiction by South Asian American Writers*. Boulder, Colo.: Westview Press, 1995.

—Anuradha M. Mitra

See also Acculturation; Alexander, Meena; Asian American identity: China, Japan, and Korea; Asian American identity: Hmong; Asian American identity: Pacific Islands; Asian American identity: Vietnam; Colonialism; Eastern religion and philosophy; Emigration and immigration; Fatwā; Mehta, Ved; Melting pot; Mukherjee, Bharati; Racism and ethnocentrism

Asian American identity: Pacific Islands

IDENTITIES: Pacific Islander

Background

A web of themes, shaped by the angst of acculturation or assimilation, or by intergenerational conflict, or by a legacy of colonialism, or by continuing resistance to economic and cultural oppression, threads its way through the tapestry of much English-language literature written by Pacific Islanders.

Creative writing in English by Pacific Island writers, immigrants, and children of immigrants has been around since the islands had substantial contact with English-speaking people of the West. Evolution of themes over time in English-language Pacific Island writing points to significant development of attitudes and perspectives; fundamental themes, however, are remarkably similar.

Assimilation into Western ways and intergenerational conflict, for example, are old themes in literature of the Pacific Islands. James Chun's short story "In the Camp" (1920) is one of the few accounts available concerning plantation life for early Chinese immigrants. Bessie Lai's *Ah Ya, I*

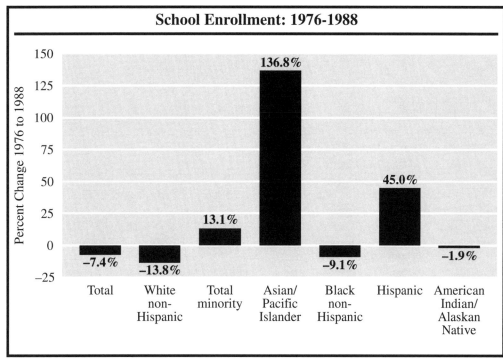

School Enrollment: 1976-1988

Percent Change 1976 to 1988

- Total: −7.4%
- White non-Hispanic: −13.8%
- Total minority: 13.1%
- Asian/Pacific Islander: 136.8%
- Black non-Hispanic: −9.1%
- Hispanic: 45.0%
- American Indian/Alaskan Native: −1.9%

Source: U.S. Department of Education.

Still Remember (1976), recounts the experiences of Chinese immigrants after their arrival in Hawaii in 1859.

Much literature about Polynesia, Melanesia, and Micronesia was written by outsiders. Among the seminal literary works published by Pacific Islanders, however, is Florence Frisbe's *Miss Ulysses of Puka* (1948), an autobiographical story of a girl and her life with her grandfather on the island of Pukapuka. The first novel may be *Makutu* (1960), by Tom Davis and Lydia Davis. For the most part, however, poetry, fiction, and drama written in English by indigenous writers did not start to emerge until the 1960's and 1970's. This literature is part of the process of decolonization and the cultural revival taking place in the region. It was inspired by anticolonial struggles in Ireland, Africa, the Caribbean, and India, the Civil Rights movement in the United States, the international student protest movement, and the opposition to the Vietnam War.

In Hawaii, there is a literary history in English. Hawaiian literature is lively and vibrant and concerns itself with making a contemporary Asian American life in Hawaii. There are tales of settlers, generations, and languages. Western and Eastern traditions have blended in Hawaii, as have peoples of different ethnic provenance. A significant number of works, written since the 1920's, is readily accessible in various literary journals and collections.

Pacific writing's coming into its own was signaled by three events: the appearance of Albert Wendt's anthology *Lali: A Pacific Anthology* (1980), a representative selection of prose and poetry in English from the Cook Islands, Fiji, Kiribati, Niue, Papua New Guinea, Vanuatu, the Solomon Islands, Tonga and Samoa; the critical study *South Pacific Literature: From Myth to Fabulation* (1985), and the award-winning novel *The Bone People* (1985), by Keri Hulme. Works usually identified as marking the beginnings of an authentic Pacific literature also include Albert Masori Kiki's autobiography, *Kiki: Ten Thousand Years in a Lifetime* (1968); Vincent Eri's novel *The Crocodile* (1970); Witi Ihimaera's and Patricia Grace's short story collections *Pounamu, Pounamu* (1972) and *Waiariki* (1975); and Wendt's novel *Sons for the Return Home* (1973).

Themes of assimilation may be found in Fijian Jo Nicola's collection of plays, *I Native No More* (1976); Papua New Guinean Nora Vagi Brash's radio dramas *The High Cost of Living Differently*

(1976) and *Which Way, Big Man?* (1977); Solomon Islander Jully Sipolo's poetry book *Civilized Call Girl* (1981); and Aborigine Monica Clare's prose *Karobran: The Story of an Aboriginal Girl* (1978); Sally Morgan's autobiography, *My Place* (1987); and Faith Bandler's historical study, *Turning the Tide* (1989). Black women writers of these and other works are participants in a conscious drive by Pacific Islanders to develop written literatures.

SUGGESTED READINGS

Braxton, Joanne, and Andree Nicola McLauglin. *Wild Women in the Whirlwind: Afra-American Culture and the Contemporary Literary Renaissance*. New Brunswick, N.J.: Rutgers University Press, 1989. A landmark work, concentrating on the writing of black-identified women engaged in the process of transforming their societies.

Lum, Darrell H. Y. *Pake: Writing by Chinese in Hawaii*. Honolulu, Hawaii: Bamboo Ridge Press, 1989. Double issue of Bamboo Ridge, the Hawaii writers' quarterly. An introduction to Chinese American writing in the Pacific Islands.

Sharrad, Paul. *Readings in Pacific Literature*. Wollongong, Australia: New Literature Research Centre, University of Wollongong, 1993. A history and criticism of Pacific Island English literature. Includes bibliographical references.

Wendt, Alfred. *Nuanua: Pacific Writing in English Since 1980*. Honolulu: University of Hawaii Press, 1995. "Nuanua" means rainbow, and so is an appropriate description for the diversity of cultures contained in this volume.

—Barbara Day

See also Asian American identity: China, Japan, and Korea; Asian American identity: Vietnam

Asian American identity: Vietnam

IDENTITIES: Vietnamese American

Background

Asian American groups saw the emphasis on civil rights and ethnic awareness that developed in the 1970's as an opportunity to explore their identities. This opportunity continued into the years after 1975, when Vietnamese refugees began expressing issues as exiles from their homeland. The war in Vietnam had changed much. Not only was it a civil war; it was also a conflict of two imported philosophies (Western liberal capitalism and communism) that crushed much of traditional Vietnamese culture and identity. Issues varied between the generation who fled Vietnam and the subsequent generations born in the United States, but common themes appear in English and in Vietnamese-language literature. Issues include struggles with Marxist ideology, traditional beliefs in fate, different views on cultural survival in isolation, the loss of roots, and the conflict between assimilation and maintaining traditions. There are differing perspectives from men and women writers as well.

Since 1953, two distinct traditions influenced later refugee writers. Writers with a background from North Vietnam tended to carry a Communist emphasis on realism and political themes; the majority of Southern refugees, influenced by French and Chinese literatures, tended to have more romantic, individual voices of a personal bent, reflecting struggles with alienation and isolation.

Images typical of postwar literature reflect resettlement and symbols of success in America, changes in status and language, and themes of justification for voluntary exile. Stories recount being refugees, boat people troubled by piracy, rape, starvation, and the difficulties of becoming Americans. American culture is often perceived as mechanical and hectic.

The growth of the Vietnamese American population after the fall of Saigon led to a boom of publications in the 1980's and 1990's that exhibit a wealth of Vietnamese experience. These works are addressed to a wide readership. Important works include Tran Van Dinh's novels and short stories, notably *Blue Dragon, White Tiger: A Tet Story* (1983), considered a significant exploration of bicultural identity, of white culture's penetration into Vietnam, and of the conflict between tradition and Communist demands. Nguyen Ngok Ngan's *The Will of Heaven* (1982) also explores the end of tradition as characters survive war to become exiles.

The theme of bringing Vietnamese culture to America also is evident in Le Ly Hayslip's *When Heaven and Earth Changed Places* (1989) and Nguyen Thi Thu-Lam's *Fallen Leaves* (1989) which focus more on life in Vietnam than the assimilation process. Minh Duc Hoai Trinh's novel *This Side, the Other Side* (1985) overlays familial conflicts with the political conflicts of the war.

Writers who choose to work in Vietnamese include Vo Phien, a winner of the Vietnamese National Literary Prize, who came to the United States in 1975 and founded *Van Hoc Nh Thuat*, a literary journal in Vietnamese. Translated into English, his short stories use the alien landscape of America to represent the difficulty of preserving or adapting traditions in a new land. Like the Vietnamese exile writers publishing in English, Phien attempts to educate Western audiences about his homeland. Elizabeth Gordon, whose first work appeared in *Home to Stay: Asian American Women's Fiction* (1990), exemplifies younger writers exploring the issues of racial identity and biculturalism.

SUGGESTED READINGS

Karlin, Wayne, Le Minh Khue, and Truong Vu, eds. *The Other Side of Heaven: Postwar Fiction by Vietnamese and American Writers*. Willimantic, Conn.: Curbstone, 1995.

Lim, Shirley Geok-lin, and Amy Ling, eds. *Reading the Literatures of Asian America*. Philadelphia: Temple University Press, 1992.

Pratt, John Clark. *Vietnam Voices: Perspectives on the War Years, 1941-1982*. New York: Viking Press, 1984.

Rottman, Larry. *Voices from the Ho Chi Minh Trail: Poetry of America and Vietnam, 1965-1993*. Desert Hot Springs, Calif.: Horizon Press, 1993.

Tran, Qui-Phiet. "Vietnamese Artists and Writers in America: 1975 to the Present." *Journal of the American Studies Association of Texas* 20 (1989): 101-110.

—*Wesley Britton*

See also Acculturation; Asian American identity: China, Japan, and Korea; Asian American identity: Hmong; Asian American identity: India; Asian American identity: Pacific Islands; Vietnam War; *When Heaven and Earth Changed Places*

Assimilation. *See* Acculturation

Assistant, The

AUTHOR: Bernard Malamud (1914-1986)
FIRST PUBLISHED: 1957
IDENTITIES: Family; Jewish

In *The Assistant*, Bernard Malamud carefully structures his realistic second novel so that the story of the intertwined fates of Frank Alpine and the Bobers grows to symbolize self-discipline and suffering. The hero, Frank Alpine, unlike the hero of Malamud's *The Natural* (1952), achieves self-integration and the subsequent identification with a group.

Frank enters the life of the Bobers when he comes with Ward Minoque, who represents his worst self, to the struggling neighborhood store of Morris Bober to steal. Unlike Ward, Frank immediately recognizes Morris as a suffering human being. Indeed, Morris is the suffering Jew, an Everyman. Now old, he has achieved none of his dreams and must deprive his daughter, Helen, of her dream of attending college.

To expiate his crime and to change his life, Frank returns to the store and, promising to work for nothing, persuades Morris to use him as an assistant. Unaware that Frank is the one who stole from him, Morris helps the hungry and homeless Frank with room and board and a small salary. Morris then becomes the moral guide Frank never had.

Frank begins to change, but his progress is fitful, and he steals small sums from the register. His moral growth is accelerated by his falling in love with Helen, an idealistic young woman who will give Frank her love if he earns it. Motivated by this hope and a memory of the beauty of the selfless life of Saint Francis of Assisi, Frank tries to discipline himself. When Frank has nearly won the love of Helen, his hopes slip away when Morris, who suspects that Frank has been stealing, catches him with his hand in the register. Sent away from the store on the day he expects Helen to proclaim her love, Frank gives in to despair and frustration. First saving her from rape by Ward, he then forces himself on her against her will.

Alienated from the Bobers, Frank's redemption comes when he moves beyond himself. The opportunity arises when Morris is hospitalized and then dies. Frank takes over the store when Helen and her mother are too overwhelmed by their misfortunes to protest. To support them all, he works two jobs. Though he sometimes questions the dreary life to which he has submitted himself, he patiently endures, replacing Morris, whose example he has internalized. After a year, Frank even sends Helen to college. He then reflects his new attitudes by having himself circumcised, a symbolic act of his transformation.

SUGGESTED READINGS

Astro, Richard, and Jackson J. Benson, eds. *The Fiction of Bernard Malamud*. Corvallis: Oregon State University Press, 1977.

Field, Leslie, and Joyce Field, eds. *Bernard Malamud: A Collection of Critical Essays*. Englewood Cliffs, N.J.: Prentice-Hall, 1975.

Richman, Sydney. *Bernard Malamud*. New York: Twayne, 1966.

—*Bernadette Flynn Low*

See also American Dream; *Fixer, The*; Malamud, Bernard; *Natural, The*

At the Bottom of the River

AUTHOR: Jamaica Kincaid (Elaine Potter Richardson, 1949-   )
FIRST PUBLISHED: 1983
IDENTITIES: Caribbean; family; women

Some critics call *At the Bottom of the River* a novel; others call it a collection of stories. Certainly the stories' interconnections lend a sense of continuity to this thin volume. Much of *At the Bottom of the River* is a recollection of Jamaica Kincaid's childhood on the Caribbean island of Antigua. The author captures the identity of this region and its people with remarkable accuracy in her sketches. By telling her stories largely from a child's point of view, Kincaid gracefully intermixes the outside world with her protagonist's mental world of dreams, images, fantasy, and mysticism.

The book's ten stories dwell upon racial and mother-daughter relationships. The daughter is obsessed by her mother, an overpowering love object for her. Her attempts to break from her maternal dependence are central to many of the sketches. The sketch "My Mother" recounts with great poignancy a girl's emotional odyssey from early childhood to the point of needing to loose herself from a reliance upon the mother she dearly loves. The narrative is disarmingly simple and direct. The child's dreamworld intrudes constantly upon the outside world, with which she must necessarily merge. She cries a "pond of tears" at separating from her mother. The girl's exile, expressed in the words "she [the mother] shook me out and stood me under a tree," is connected to her memory of the childhood punishment of being banished, when she had misbehaved, from her house to take her dinner under the breadloaf trees. This story is about lost innocence and the attempt to recapture it.

The sketch "At Last" considers the essence of things. The child asks what becomes of the hen whose feathers are scattered, whose flesh is stripped away, whose bones disappear. Kincaid broaches similar universal questions in "Blackness," in which she deals with the mystery of the generations, with the child who grows up to become a mother to the succeeding generation. The questions posed in this story are questions that puzzled the ancient Greek philosophers and that still puzzle thinking people everywhere.

SUGGESTED READINGS

Natov, Roni. "Mother and Daughters: Jamaica Kincaid's Pre-Oedipal Narrative." In *Children's*

Literature: Annual of the Modern Language Association Seminar on Children's Literature and the Children's Literature Association. New York: Modern Language Association, 1990.

Perry, Donna. "Initiation in Jamaica Kincaid's *Annie John*." In *Caribbean Women Writers: Essays from the First International Conference*, edited by Selwyn R. Cudjoe. Wellesley, Mass.: Calaloux, 1990.

Timothy, Helen Pyne. "Adolescent Rebellion and Gender Relations in *At the Bottom of the River* and *Annie John*." In *Caribbean Women Writers: Essays from the First International Conference*, edited by Selwyn R. Cudjoe. Wellesley, Mass.: Calaloux, 1990.

—R. Baird Shuman

See also *Annie John*; Caribbean American literature; Feminism; Identity crisis; Kincaid, Jamaica

Atwood, Margaret

BORN: Ottawa, Ontario, Canada; November 18, 1939

PRINCIPAL WORKS: *The Animals in That Country*, 1968; *The Edible Woman*, 1969; *Surfacing*, 1972; *Survival: A Thematic Guide to Canadian Literature*, 1972; *Lady Oracle*, 1976; *Life Before Man*, 1979; *Bodily Harm*, 1981; *Second Words*, 1982; *Bluebeard's Egg*, 1983; *The Handmaid's Tale*, 1985; *The Robber Bride*, 1993

IDENTITIES: Canada; women

SIGNIFICANT ACHIEVEMENT: Atwood has given voice to the women's movement and affirmed the uniqueness of Canadian culture; her sensitivity to environmental and animal rights issues is devoid of sentimental clichés.

Margaret Atwood achieved fame with provocative novels and challenging poems while still a young woman. By age fifty she was acclaimed worldwide for her poetry, fiction, criticism, and essays. Quotable and frequently abrasive, she became a media celebrity as well. Two concerns remained foremost in her work: the self-realization of women and the cultural independence of Canada. To celebrate Canada was also to venerate its environment and respect the habitat of wild animals.

Atwood's early years provided broad experience of North American life. The daughter of a University of Toronto scientist, she accompanied her father on field trips into the Quebec bush. After undergraduate work in Ontario, she attended Radcliffe on a Woodrow Wilson Fellowship. Since matrimony was expected of her generation and class, she dutifully married a Harvard student, whom she later divorced. Returning to Canada, she taught at several major universities.

In 1970, Atwood met the Canadian novelist Graeme Gibson, who was to be her permanent companion. Their daughter Jess was born in 1976, and a farm near Alliston, Ontario, became their home. Atwood and Gibson emerged as major figures in the lively Canadian literary scene. They were also untiring advocates of freedom for writers everywhere and spoke for Amnesty International.

Atwood's critical survey of Canadian literature, *Survival*, was acknowledged as a major study. She described Canada, despite its richness of ethnic diversity, as a threatened cultural entity, intimidated by its giant neighbor. The one literary genre developed by Canadians had been, predictably, she believed, the realistic animal story. Canadians identified with animal prey, stalked through the bush by the heavily armed hunter from the south, the American.

Despite an anti-Americanism which even some of her compatriots labeled xenophobic, Atwood claimed her largest readership in the United States. Even before the North American women's movement had identified its chief symbols and themes, *The Edible Woman* provided a definitive portrait of the female who sees herself as merely another consumer product. Sixteen years later, with *The Handmaid's Tale*, Atwood published a novel about a horrifying society built on female oppression. Readers valued Atwood for her ability to articulate their deepest apprehensions and entertain them with wittily crafted novels.

SUGGESTED READINGS

Davidson, Arnold E., and Cathy N. Davidson, eds. *The Art of Margaret Atwood: Essays in Criticism*. Toronto: Anansi, 1981.

Rosenberg, Jerome H. *Margaret Atwood*. Boston: Twayne, 1984.

Wilson, Sharon Rose. *Margaret Atwood's Fairy-Tale Sexual Politics*. Jackson: University Press of Mississippi, 1993.

—Allene Phy-Olsen

See also Canadian identity; Feminism

Autobiographies of Chester Himes

AUTHOR: Chester Himes (1909-1984)

FIRST PUBLISHED: *The Quality of Hurt*, 1972; *My Life of Absurdity*, 1976

IDENTITIES: African American

"I grew to manhood in the Ohio State Penitentiary," writes Chester Himes in *The Quality of Hurt*, a book that is less an organized autobiography than a series of poignant sketches, in which he writes about the many hurts that poisoned his life in the United States. Himes is one of the least known, most prolific African American writers of the twentieth century. Over a fifty-year career, Himes wrote scores of novels, short stories, articles, and poems, all marked by a naked sincerity and raging anger at racism.

Himes began writing, drawing on his experiences as a young man in prison. He gained critical attention first with a short story, "To What Red Hell," a fictionalized account of the 1930 fire that killed more than three hundred inmates at the Ohio State Penitentiary.

Released during the Depression, Himes became involved with the Federal Writers' Project, the labor movement, and the Communist Party. He also worked as a journalist in Cleveland. In 1941, Himes moved to California, where he began writing novels of rage and frustration, including *If He Hollers, Let Him Go* (1945), *Lonely Crusade* (1947), and *Cast the First Stone* (1952). By 1953, disgusted with the racism he encountered and the lukewarm, when not hostile, reception his work received, Himes left for Europe.

My Life of Absurdity is not a deep examination of his life so much as a commentary on the meaning of being a black expatriate writer. "No American," he writes, "has lived a life more absurd than mine." In Europe, Himes published the series of detective stories that brought him fame in later years. Among them are *The Crazy Kill* (1959), *The Heat's On* (1966), and *Cotton Comes to Harlem* (1965). Himes also wrote stories that are sometimes painfully funny and often bitterly desolate. In them, cops, robbers, and all-around losers—the people Himes knew well in his youth—trade in the debased currency of lies and secrets.

Himes's work resounds with wit and indignation but is too often incorrectly identified simply as social protest. His novels made the best-seller lists in foreign countries as well as in the United States.

SUGGESTED READINGS

Milliken, Stephen. *Chester Himes: A Critical Appraisal*. Columbia: University of Missouri Press, 1976.

Skinner, Robert. *Two Guns from Harlem: The Detective Fiction of Chester Himes*. Bowling Green, Ohio: Bowling Green State University Popular Press, 1989.

—Barbara Day

See also African American identity; Expatriate identity; Himes, Chester; Racism and ethnocentrism

Autobiographies of Langston Hughes

AUTHOR: Langston Hughes (1902-1967)

FIRST PUBLISHED: *The Big Sea*, 1940; *I Wonder as I Wander*, 1956

IDENTITIES: Adolescence and coming-of-age; African American

In the opening of Langston Hughes's first autobiography, *The Big Sea*, the author recalls how he heaved his books overboard at the start of his first journey to Africa in 1923. The gesture may be seen as adolescent and anti-intellectual, but it suggests the commencement of Hughes's role as a Renaissance man in Black American letters. The book chronicles the first twenty-seven years of Hughes's life, from the 1920's, when he explored the idiom and jazz rhythms of African Americans in his poetry, to the shift to his bitter prose of the 1930's.

The autobiography is written typically as a confession, but it remains comparatively impersonal. Only three guarded personal accounts appear in the text of *The Big Sea*. The first concerns a religious revival Hughes attended at age thirteen at which he waited in vain for Jesus. The second describes the morning in Mexico when he realized that he hated his father. The third, at the book's end, details the break with his patron and mentor, Charlotte Mason. He ties the latter experience to the other two: "The light went out with a sudden crash in the dark, and everything became like that night in Kansas when I had failed to see Jesus and had lied about it afterwards. Or that morning in Mexico when I suddenly hated my father."

Other than these specific episodes, controversy rarely enters the book. Instead, Hughes presents himself as a man who loves his race and is optimistic about his people. He nevertheless carries doubts and fears within himself. The book, furthermore, is peopled by Hughes' many friends, including Jean Toomer, Zora Neale Hurston, and others involved with the Harlem Renaissance. Hughes's publisher, Blanche Knopf, thought that the references were excessive, but Hughes convinced her to retain them. Consequently, *The Big Sea* is perhaps the best chronicle of the Harlem Renaissance.

The second autobiography, *I Wonder as I Wander*, received less favor than its predecessor, although Hughes thought that his second autobiography was more important to his future as a writer. Knopf rejected the book, claiming it was "pretty weighted . . . and not a book." Covering his life from 1929 to 1950, it includes his travels to Haiti, Spain, and Russia. More than half of the collection explores his 1932 trip to the Soviet Union, and a second long section covers his excursion to Spain during its civil war. The book seems less a literary life than a political commentary on his travels.

One of the criticisms directed at *I Wonder as I Wander* was its detachment from the personal and reflective. *The Big Sea* contains few enough personal reflections, but those that it contains are balanced between pain and joy. *I Wonder as I Wander* shows a Hughes who is more secure in his world and who is suffering less, despite his poverty (which fame did little to diminish). *I Wonder as I Wander* is a mature recollection, written without radicalism or prejudice.

SUGGESTED READINGS

Bloom, Harold, ed. *Langston Hughes*. New York: Chelsea House, 1989.

Miller, R. Baxter. *The Art and Imagination of Langston Hughes*. Lexington: University of Kentucky Press, 1989.

Rampersad, Arnold. *The Life of Langston Hughes: 1902-1941*. Vol. 1. New York: Oxford University Press, 1986.

_____. *The Life of Langston Hughes: 1941-1967*. Vol. 2. New York: Oxford University Press, 1988.

—*Mark Sanders*

See also African American identity; Harlem Renaissance; Hughes, Langston; Hurston, Zora Neale; *Selected Poems of Langston Hughes*; Spanish Civil War; *Ways of White Folks, The*

Autobiography of a Brown Buffalo, The

AUTHOR: Oscar "Zeta" Acosta (1936-1974?)

FIRST PUBLISHED: 1972

IDENTITIES: Latino; West and Southwest

Oscar "Zeta" Acosta's first novel, *The Autobiography of a Brown Buffalo*, is a fictional journey through many facts of his life. His tale is vulgar, gross, obscene, frankly carnal, truly pained, wildly raucous, and funny in turns. Acosta's anti-intellectual stance and his rejection of literary convention express the shock and chaos he invokes to undo his own assimilation, re-create his life, and construct for himself a new and revitalizing identity. Acosta declares his novel an autobiography to dramatize the powers of artistic transformation and re-creation that Chicanos can apply to their lives. One's identity, like a novel, is a work of art.

On Monday morning, July 1, 1967, Acosta is a lawyer with one year's experience in an antipoverty agency in Oakland, California. Born in El Paso, Texas, and long a resident of California, Acosta feels increasing tensions between his Mexican ancestry and his personal and professional assimilation into mainstream American culture. He bursts with self-loathing; he sees himself as a little brown Mexican boy in a barrel-bellied, sweating, tormented wild Indian adult body. Crazed with tranquilizers, alcohol, and the bad food he uses to appease his ulcer, Acosta snaps when he discovers his secretary Pauline has died. He walks away from his work and his life.

His quest takes him from California through the Southwest to his birthplace in El Paso, Texas. Then he goes to Mexico, where he recounts his life. All the while he is manufacturing and assuming new fictional identities and reliving old ones. Six months of exploring his past and present lead to his reclaiming his Mexican self and reaffirming his American identity. Both, however, are quickly rejected in the novel's close with the assertion of his new being as a Brown Buffalo. He and his people are like the buffalo, slaughtered by everyone, and like their Aztec ancestors, brown. He discovers true identity is something one constructs for oneself. He calls his new self Zeta and takes up a new life in East Los Angeles as an activist.

Acosta mysteriously disappeared in 1974, and his fate has never been determined. With only two novels and few stories he nevertheless remains one of the first and most original voices of Chicano literature.

SUGGESTED READINGS

Rivera, Tomás. "Into the Labyrinth: The Chicano in Literature." *Southwest American Literature* 2, no. 2 (1972): 90-97.

Rodriguez, Joe D. "The Chicano Novel and the North American Narrative of Survival." *Denver Quarterly* 16 (Fall, 1981): 229-235.

_____. "God's Silence and the Shrill of Ethnicity in the Chicano Novel." *Explorations in Ethnic Studies* 4 (July, 1981): 14-21.

Simmen, Edward. *The Chicano: From Caricature to Self Portrait*. New York: Mentor, 1971.

Smith, Norman D. "Buffalos and Cockroaches: Acosta's Siege at Aztlan." *Latin American Literary Review* 5 (Spring-Summer, 1977): 85-97.

—Virginia M. Crane

See also American identity: West and the frontier; Chicano identity; Chicano Renaissance; Identity crisis

Autobiography of an Ex-Coloured Man, The

AUTHOR: James Weldon Johnson (1871-1938)

FIRST PUBLISHED: 1912

IDENTITIES: Adolescence and coming-of-age; African American; South

The Autobiography of an Ex-Coloured Man was first published anonymously in 1912, but only became a success when republished in 1927 at the height of the Harlem Renaissance. The novel chronicles the coming-of-age of its unnamed protagonist, who switches back and forth between ethnic identities until he finally decides to pass as a European American. Its most striking feature might well be that it calls the notion of ethnic identity into question.

In order to explore ethnic identity, James Weldon Johnson has his protagonist experience both sides of the "color line," to use the famous phrase by W. E. B. Du Bois. Growing up believing himself European American, as the white-looking child of a light-skinned African American mother and a European American father, the protagonist finds out in school that he is African American. Having harbored prejudice against African Americans, he now becomes an object of prejudice. Once over this initial shock, he resolves to become famous in the service of African Americans. In order to learn about his mother's heritage, he leaves for the South, where he often finds himself an outsider to African American society. He knows little of African American folk customs, so at first he reacts to African Americans ambiguously. In this way, Johnson shows that the culture of one's upbringing is a more important factor in determining one's outlook on other cultures than ethnic bloodlines are.

After losing his money in the South, the protagonist eventually embarks on a musical career, which takes him to New York. He discovers ragtime there and is fascinated by it, renewing his resolve to become famous, and intending to do so through African American music. After a sojourn in Europe, he returns to the South in order to learn more about the roots of African American music, which he calls "a mine of material" when visiting a religious meeting at which spirituals are sung. The reader discovers that the protagonist's interest in African American culture is mainly commercial. He nevertheless often comments enthusiastically on African American contributions to American culture. The protagonist gives up his idea of becoming famous through African American music, however, after witnessing a lynching. He returns North, marries a European American woman, and becomes a white businessman. In the end, he wishes he had followed his musical inclinations, which are connected to his African American heritage, instead of achieving material success. Thus, the novel shows that a hostile social climate can bring people to forsake their heritage, but also that ethnic identity is partly a matter of choice.

SUGGESTED READINGS

Fleming, Robert E. *James Weldon Johnson*. Boston: Twayne, 1987.

Stepto, Robert B. *From Behind the Veil: A Study of Afro-American Narrative*. Champaign: University of Illinois Press, 1979.

Sundquist, Eric J. *The Hammers of Creation: Folk Culture in Modern African-American Fiction*. Athens: University of Georgia Press, 1992.

—Martin Japtok

See also *Along This Way*; Appearance and identity; Mixed race and identity

Autobiography of Malcolm X, The

AUTHOR: Malcolm X (1925-1965), with the assistance of Alex Haley

FIRST PUBLISHED: 1965

IDENTITIES: Adolescence and coming-of-age; African American

The Autobiography of Malcolm X was hailed as a literary classic shortly after it appeared. Its description of Malcolm X's discovery of an African American identity continues to inspire its readers. The two most memorable phases of Malcolm X's life described in his autobiography, and quite possibly the two phases most formative of his identity, are his self-education and religious conversion while in prison and his last year of life, in which he set out to organize a multiracial coalition to end racism. The first of these phases followed a difficult childhood and life as a criminal. In prison, Malcolm X felt inspired by fellow inmates to improve his knowledge. He started on a rigorous program of reading books on history and philosophy. He also worked on his penmanship and vocabulary by copying an entire dictionary. His readings revealed to him that school had taught him nothing about African and African American history. School had also been silent on the crimes that Europeans and European Americans had committed against people of color. In prison, members of the Nation of Islam urged Malcolm X to reject the negative self-image he had unconsciously adopted and to replace it with black pride.

Malcolm X taught the Nation's doctrine of black self-reliance after his release from prison, and he married Betty Shabazz, eventually becoming the father of six children. Disappointed by the divergence between the practices of some of the leaders of the Nation of Islam and the rules of self-discipline and honor that the Nation taught, he left the Nation and, after traveling to Mecca, became an orthodox Muslim. Islam and his experiences in the Middle East and Africa also changed his outlook on racial relations. Before, he had seen an unbridgeable gulf between African Americans and European Americans. His positive experiences with white Muslims, white students, and white reporters caused him to reevaluate that position. Deciding that cooperation between whites and blacks was possible, he remained devoted to the liberation of people of African descent to the end of his life.

The Autobiography of Malcolm X is important as an account of the life of a charismatic American intellectual. The book is also an important literary work in the African American tradition of the autobiographies of Frederick Douglass and W. E. B. Du Bois and in the American tradition of Benjamin Franklin. Like Douglass and Franklin, Malcolm X can be described as a self-made man.

SUGGESTED READINGS

Breitman, George. *The Last Year of Malcolm X: The Evolution of a Revolutionary*. New York: Pathfinder Press, 1984.

Clarke, John Henrik, ed. *Malcolm X: The Man and His Times*. New York: Collier Books, 1969.

Dudley, David L. *Intergenerational Conflict in African American Men's Autobiography*. Philadelphia: University of Pennsylvania Press, 1991.

—*Martin Japtok*

See also African American identity; Malcolm X; Nation of Islam

Autobiography of Miss Jane Pittman, The

AUTHOR: Ernest J. Gaines (1933-)
FIRST PUBLISHED: 1971
IDENTITIES: African American; South

In *The Autobiography of Miss Jane Pittman* the heroine and many African Americans in south Louisiana move from passivity to heroic assertion and achieve a new identity. Gaines's best-known novel is not an autobiography but a first-person reminiscence of a fictional 110-year-old former slave whose memories extend from the Emancipation Proclamation to Martin Luther King, Jr. *The Autobiography of Miss Jane Pittman* tells her unschooled but adept version of state and national occurrences and personalities (Huey Long, the flood of 1927, the rise of black athletes such as Jackie Robinson and Joe Louis). Her version of history is given to a tape-recording young schoolteacher who wants historical facts; Jane helps him to understand the dynamics of living history, the way she remembers it. Her accounts are loving, sane, and responsible. Her language—speech patterns and pronunciations—is authentic, since Gaines read interviews with former slaves.

Renamed Jane Brown by a Union soldier because Ticey (her original name) is "a slave name," Jane wears her new designation proudly, as a badge of her identity as a free woman, when she and other former slaves attempt to escape from Louisiana. Many of them are brutally murdered by Klansmen. Jane, who is about ten at the time, escapes along with a small orphan, Ned. Jane becomes Ned's mother and during Reconstruction she raises him when they settle on another plantation as fieldhands. Ned receives some schooling and as a teenager is involved in civil rights struggles. His life in danger, Ned escapes to Kansas. Jane chooses to remain in Louisiana.

Ned represents the first of three African American males in Jane's life who struggle to define their racial and personal identities. The second is Joe Pittman, with whom Jane lives after Ned leaves. Joe loves Jane and wants her with him even though she is barren as a result of childhood beatings. He finds personal fulfillment in breaking wild horses on a Texas ranch; he accepts danger and the risk of death unflinchingly. Like Ned, who is murdered after he returns to Louisiana and sets up a school for black children, Joe is also killed fulfilling his destiny. Ned describes his identity as that of a black American who cares, and will always struggle. With these men, Jane finds a personal identity as a woman and demonstrates her desire to work with her black men but not to control them.

When Jimmy, a young civil rights worker much loved by Jane and others, is murdered, Jane—age 110—goes into the nearby town to drink from the segregated water fountain at the courthouse. She moves from the safety of silence and obscurity to join the ranks of African Americans who assert themselves and who risk losing their homes and lives but gain courage, dignity, and a heroic identity.

SUGGESTED READINGS

Babb, Valerie. *Ernest Gaines*. Boston: Twayne, 1991.

Rowell, Charles H. "The Quarters: Ernest Gaines and the Sense of Place." *Southern Review* 21 (1985): 733-750.

Simpson, Anne K. *A Gathering of Gaines*. Lafayette: University of Southwestern Louisiana, 1991.

—*Philip A. Tapley*

See also African American identity; Gaines, Ernest J.

Autobiography of W. E. B. DuBois: A Soliloquy on Viewing My Life from the Last Decade of Its First Century, The

AUTHOR: W. E. B. Du Bois (1868-1963)

FIRST PUBLISHED: *Vospominaniia*, 1962 (English edition, 1968)

IDENTITIES: African American

The Autobiography of W. E. B. DuBois is the inspiring story of a foremost African American intellectual and civil rights leader of the twentieth century. He discusses his individual struggles and accomplishments, as well as his major ideas dedicated to promoting racial equality for Africans and African Americans. Moving from the reconstruction era after the U.S. Civil War, through World Wars I and II, to the height of the Cold War and the atomic age, Du Bois' personal reflections provide a critical, panoramic sweep of American social history. Du Bois did not simply observe the American scene; he altered it as a leader of African Americans in the American Civil Rights movement.

The chronological structure of *The Autobiography of W. E. B. DuBois* begins with five chapters on his travels to Europe, the Soviet Union, and China. After these travels, Du Bois announces the crowning ideological decision of his life: his conversion to communism. The remainder of *The Autobiography of W. E. B. DuBois* answers the question: How did Du Bois arrive at this crucial decision in the last years of his life? Du Bois chronicles his life patterns of childhood, education, work for civil rights, travel, friendships, and writings. This information is written in such a way that it explains his decision to adopt communism as his political worldview.

Perhaps the most fascinating section of the book is Du Bois' account of his trial and subsequent acquittal in 1950 and 1951 for alleged failure to register as an agent of a foreign government, a sobering story of public corruption. His fundamental faith in American institutions, already strained by racism, was destroyed. He moved to Ghana and threw his tremendous energies into that nation as it shed its colonial experience.

The autobiography is subtitled as a soliloquy, but this categorization reflects the political realities of 1960 more than the specific literary form of speaking to oneself. At the time, the Cold War between the United States and the Soviet Union made communism an abhorrent choice to many Americans. The autobiography finally appeared in English in 1968, at a publishing house known for its communist writings. The autobiography is the least read of Du Bois' autobiographies, although it is an engaging exposition in which Du Bois shows his continuing growth and faith in human nature during his tenth decade.

SUGGESTED READINGS

Baber, Willie L. "Capitalism and Racism." *Critique of Anthropology* 12, no. 3 (1992): 339-363.

Du Bois, W. E. B. *W. E. B. Du Bois: A Reader*, edited by David Levering Lewis. New York: Henry Holt, 1995.

—Mary Jo Deegan

See also African American identity; Civil Rights movement; Du Bois, W. E. B.; *Souls of Black Folk*

Awakening, The

AUTHOR: Kate Chopin (1851-1904)

FIRST PUBLISHED: 1899

IDENTITIES: European American; South; women

The Awakening, Kate Chopin's masterpiece, is a psychologically realistic portrait of a *fin de siècle* woman's search for her identity. The novel, which chronicles Louisiana society woman Edna Pontellier's quiet rebellion against the strictures of a male-dominated society, shocked contemporary readers with its theme and its frank presentation of women's sexuality, but its compelling presentation of the quest for self-fulfillment has earned it classic status.

On Grand Isle, a Gulf of Mexico resort where she is vacationing with her somewhat dull husband and their two children, Edna becomes aware of "her position in the universe," and she begins to yearn for an escape from the cage of bourgeois matrimony. She realizes that she wishes to be more than merely one of the "mother-women" who "idolized their children, worshipped their husbands, and esteemed it a holy privilege to efface themselves as individuals and grow wings as ministering angels."

Edna falls in love with handsome young Robert Lebrun, who reciprocates her feelings but who dares not overstep the bounds of convention with a married woman. After Lebrun leaves for Mexico and her husband leaves on an extended business trip, Edna begins an affair with a young roué, Alcée Arobin, who completes the sexual "awakening" that Lebrun had begun; she also moves out of her husband's house into a smaller one, where she revels in her newly found independence.

Oceanic imagery suffuses the novel, the shore marking the boundary of the patriarchal mainland. Edna learns to swim, and her education in swimming is also a larger lesson in staying afloat. Her swimming is about survival after getting in over one's head; it is also a spiritual baptism into a new life. As Edna swims away from the beach while her husband watches, she swims away from the shore of her old life to a female fantasy of paradise—freedom and fulfillment.

At the novel's end, Edna is overcome by a desire to swim away from the shore, "on and on," until exhaustion overcomes her and she drowns. Her swim away from the empty summer colony is equated with a retreat from the empty fictions of marriage and maternity, back into her own life and vision. Ultimately, whether or not Edna intentionally commits suicide is a moot point because the ambiguity makes *The Awakening* a daring vision of a woman's sexual and spiritual development. Chopin's contemporaries, however, received the novel with derision, feeling no compassion for Edna's torment. Not until the feminist movement of the 1970's revived interest in Chopin's work was *The Awakening* appreciated as a masterful exploration of the search for personal fulfillment.

SUGGESTED READINGS

Gilbert, Sandra M., and Susan Gubar. *The Madwoman in the Attic: The Woman Writer and the Nineteenth-Century Literary Imagination*. New Haven, Conn.: Yale University Press, 1981.

Platizky, Roger. "Chopin's *The Awakening*." *The Explicator* 53, no. 2 (Winter, 1995): 99-103.

Seyersted, Per. *Kate Chopin: A Critical Biography*. Baton Rouge: Louisiana State University Press, 1969.

Toth, Emily. *Kate Chopin*. New York: William Morrow, 1990.

—Thomas D. Petitjean, Jr.

See also American identity: South; Chopin, Kate; Creole and Acadian literature; Erotic identity; Feminism

Awful Rowing Toward God, The

AUTHOR: Anne Sexton (1928-1974)

FIRST PUBLISHED: 1975

IDENTITIES: European American; religion; women

When Anne Sexton committed suicide in October, 1974, she had planned very carefully how her poetry would be published after her death. She considered much of her poetry miscellany or unworthy of publication; these poems have been collected in the *Complete Poems*. Prior to her demise she put together three collections of poetry with explicit instructions to her publisher regarding her wishes about publication dates. The first of these three volumes was *The Awful Rowing Toward God*, which represents several significant departures from her earlier poetry.

As early as Sexton's first book, published in 1960, there are references to God and the Bible. The role of Christ in one's life is also given reference in a few poems, and such would be the case throughout most of her poetic career, with the exception of her book *Transformations* (1971). Still, the core of the earlier books was the presentation and investigation of Sexton's place in the world. Many of her poems tell stories in a lyrical manner, stories that she hopes to decode as the poems accumulate.

The poems in *The Awful Rowing Toward God* are much more speculative. They ask questions about the individual's position in the world in terms of the Christian religion. Was Christ intended to provide humanity with mercy? When one dies, is it likely that one will find the paradise promised in the concept of Heaven? Some of these poems sound almost panic-stricken in their questioning. The reader should remember that these poems were written, in all likelihood, in the last year of Sexton's life. When Sexton decided to commit suicide this last time, she abandoned the mechanism of all of her previous attempts: overdosing on pills. She chose carbon monoxide gas, which succeeded.

Undoubtedly she knew that her death was assured. The poems take on a more definite attitude than previous poems about her suicide attempts or instincts. Sexton also raises the issue of whether one's actions while alive will affect one's disposition when one dies. She must have known that she was no saint during her life. Would God forgive her transgressions? This book presents far more questions than it does conclusions, and in that respect the book is unique among Sexton's works.

SUGGESTED READINGS

George, Diana Hume. *Oedpius Anne: The Poetry of Anne Sexton*. Champaign: University of Illinois Press, 1988.

_____. *Sexton: Selected Criticism*. Champaign: University of Illinois Press, 1988.

McClatchy, J. D. *Anne Sexton: The Artist and Her Critics*. Bloomington: Indiana University Press, 1978.

Morton, Richard Everett. *Anne Sexton's Poetry of Redemption: The Chronology of a Pilgrimage*. Lewiston, N.Y.: E. Mellen Press, 1988.

—John Jacob

See also American identities: Northeast; *Complete Poems*; *Searching for Mercy Street*; *To Bedlam and Part Way Back*

B

Babbitt

AUTHOR: Sinclair Lewis (1885-1951)
FIRST PUBLISHED: 1922
IDENTITIES: European American; Midwest

Babbitt deploys a series of detailed episodes that critique a whole way of life in a typical American city of its day. The main character, George Babbitt, is depicted as an average middle-aged American, living the good life in the bustling commercial city of Zenith, Ohio. Equipped with a house, car, two children, modern conveniences, modern gadgets, and a healthy bank account, Babbitt finds that the meaning of life has somehow eluded him. Although he is proud of his home and fond of family, he is undergoing a midlife crisis. A successful real estate salesman, he secretly hates himself for using bullying and dishonest tactics in order to make a profit and is stifled by a homogenous group of equally chubby, boisterous businessmen with similar homes and families. The lack of joy and freedom in his life is obvious from the moment he wakes up in his comfortable but somehow soulless household. To all appearances, Babbitt is on top of the world, soon to consolidate his rising business and social status with a speech before the prestigious Real Estate Board. This speech, delivered with bumptious energy and peppered with the folksy slang of the day, is a model of mindless self-congratulation and narrow, know-nothing bigotry. The speech is a resounding success.

Beneath Babbitt's buoyant, optimistic surface is an emptiness and desolation that is registered at first through the character of his best friend Paul Reisling. Paul, a disaffected roofing salesman, is unhappily married to a woman who personifies the most venal and self-serving aspects of Zenith. When Paul finally attempts to murder the exasperating Zilla, Babbitt loses heart, seeing in Paul's gesture some of his own sense of despair and entrapment. Babbitt begins to understand more clearly the falsity of his life and tries to change by launching an affair with Tanis Judique, a free spirit who introduces him to a bohemian set of friends. This new life, however, brings Babbitt little pleasure; he is still restless and discontented and begins to suspect his rebellion is a typical, empty middle-class gesture that does little to change the status quo. When his wife Myra becomes ill, he returns to the security of his home with some relief and joins The Good Citizens League, an intolerant group of white Protestant businessmen devoted to a narrow "Americanism."

Babbitt's cultural identity has lent his name to the language; a Babbitt is a smug, middle-class conformist. Babbitt returns meekly to the fold but has enough spirit left at the end of the novel to urge his son to resist the social pressures and codes of his day and to be true to himself.

SUGGESTED READINGS

Bucco, Martin, ed. *Critical Essays on Sinclair Lewis* Boston: G. K. Hall, 1986.
Grebstein, Sheldon Norman. *Sinclair Lewis*. New York: Twayne, 1962.
Love, Glen A. *Babbitt: An American Life*. New York: Twayne, 1993.
O'Connor, Richard. *Sinclair Lewis*. New York, McGraw-Hill, 1971.

—Margaret Boe Birns

See also American identity: Midwest; Lewis, Sinclair; *Main Street*

Babycakes

AUTHOR: Armistead Maupin (1944-   )
FIRST PUBLISHED: 1984

IDENTITIES: Disease; European American; family; gay, lesbian, and bisexual

Armistead Maupin's *Babycakes*, the fourth volume in his Tales of the City series about life in San Francisco, is about the acquired immune deficiency syndrome (AIDS) crisis. *Babycakes* provides a psychological study of how individuals and families suffer and recover from the loss of loved ones. In this case, the family is one of choice rather than one of origin.

As the novel opens, the reader discovers that Michael Tolliver has recently lost his lover, Dr. Jon Fielding, to AIDS. One of the first thousand people in the United States to succumb to the disease, Jon withered to ninety pounds. He died, however, surrounded by his loving chosen family, including not only Michael but also his landlady Anna Madrigal and his friends Mona Ramsey, Brian Baxter, and Mary Ann Singleton.

Before Michael can begin his recovery, he is forced to face painful memories and emotions. That he and Jon were never sexually faithful to each other weighs heavily on Michael's conscience. Worse, he feels that he never clearly communicated to Jon how much he loved him. Too often, they fought and turned to others for solace. These haunting thoughts make Michael feel helpless and despondent. In an effort to assuage the pain, he chooses to do volunteer work for an AIDS organization. His chosen family members even encourage Michael to start dating again, but emotionally he is far from ready to take this step.

In his recovery process, Michael finds help from the same family of choice who saw Jon through his final illness. The family's matriarch is the nonjudgmental, unconditionally loving Anna Madrigal, a pot-smoking, transsexual landlady in her sixties. In her presence Michael feels protected and mothered: "He sat there in the musty embrace of Mrs. Madrigal's sofa and counted his blessings while she puttered about in the kitchen." Anna also gives Michael $1,000 toward a therapeutic trip to England.

On his vacation, Michael is helped by another family member, Mona Ramsey. Actually Anna Madrigal's blood-related child, Mona is a lesbian who lives in a castle in England. Mona welcomes Michael and a friend of his, offering unconditional love similar to Mrs. Madrigal's.

Anna, Mona, and the other members of Michael's chosen family continue to encourage Michael in his recovery. They also function as a group that must take concrete steps of its own to recover from the loss of Jon. Thus, the family absorbs two new members during the novel. One is a black, gay, teenaged orphan whom Michael meets in England. Mona shelters, mothers, and eventually adopts the teenager. The second is the newborn daughter of an acquaintance who dies in childbirth. Brian and Mary Ann adopt Shawna, the newborn, and name Michael her godparent.

By the novel's end, the rest of the chosen family has made clear progress in recovering from Jon's death. Michael, although less emotionally hollow than in the beginning of the novel, remains fearful of resuming life.

SUGGESTED READINGS

Block, Adam. "Out on the Town." *Mother Jones*, November, 1989, 54.

O'Connor, John. "Back to Free-Spirited San Francisco of the 70's." *The New York Times*, January 10, 1994, p. C11.

Spain, Tom. "A Talk with Armistead Maupin." *Publishers Weekly*, March, 1987, 53-54.

—Steven A. Katz

See also AIDS; *Back to Barbary Lane*; Gay identity; Lesbian identity; Maupin, Armistead; Women and identity

Baca, Jimmy Santiago

BORN: Sante Fe, New Mexico; January 2, 1952

PRINCIPAL WORKS: *Immigrants in Our Own Land*, 1979; *Swords of Darkness*, 1981; *What's Happening*, 1982; *Poems Taken from My Yard*, 1986; *Martín; &, Meditations on the South Valley*, 1986; *Black Mesa Poems*, 1989; *Working in the Dark: Reflections of a Poet of Barrio*, 1992

Jimmy Santiago Baca began to write poetry as an almost illiterate vato loco. (Lawrence Benton)

IDENTITIES: Latino; Native American; West and Southwest

SIGNIFICANT ACHIEVEMENT: Baca's poetry expresses the experience of a "detribalized Apache," reared in a Chicano barrio, who finds his values in family, the land, and a complex cultural heritage.

Jimmy Santiago Baca began to write poetry as an almost illiterate *vato loco* (crazy guy, gangster) serving a five-year term in a federal prison. He was twenty years old, the son of Damacio Baca, of Apache and Yaqui lineage, and Cecilia Padilla, a Latino woman, who left him with his grandparents when he was two. Baca stayed with them for three years, then went into a boys' home, then into detention centers and the streets of Albuquerque's barrio at thirteen. Although he "confirmed" his identity as a Chicano by leafing through a stolen picture book of Chicano history at seventeen, he felt himself "disintegrating" in prison. Speaking of his father, but alluding to his own situation when he was incarcerated, Baca observed: "He was everything that was bad in America. He was brown, he spoke Spanish, was from a Native American background, had no education."

As a gesture of rebellion, Baca took a guard's textbook and found that "sounds created music in me and happiness" as he slowly enunciated the lines of a poem by William Wordsworth. This led to a zealous effort at self-education, encouraged by the recollection of older men in detention centers who "made barrio life come alive . . . with their own Chicano language." Progressing to the point where he was writing letters for fellow prisoners, he placed a few poems in a local magazine, *New Kauri*, and achieved his first major publication with *Immigrants in Our Own Land*, a book whose title refers to the condition of inmates in a dehumanizing system and to his own feelings of estrangement in American society. This was a turning point for Baca, who realized that he could reclaim the community he was separated from and sing "the freedom song of our Chicano dream" now that poetry "had lifted me to my feet."

With this foundation to build on, Baca started a family in the early 1980's, restored an adobe dwelling in Albuquerque's South Valley, and wrote *Martín; &, Meditations on the South Valley* because "the entire Southwest needed a long poem that could describe what has happened here in the last twenty years." Continuing to combine personal history and communal life, Baca followed this book with *Black Mesa Poems*, which links the landscape of the South Valley to people he knows and admires. Writing with confidence and an easy facility in Spanish and English, Baca uses vernacular speech, poetic form, ancient Mexican lore, and contemporary popular culture.

SUGGESTED READINGS

Coppola, Vincent. "The Moon in Jimmy Baca." *Esquire* (June, 1993): 48-56.

Levertov, Denise. Introduction to *Martín; &, Meditations on the South Valley*, by Jimmy Santiago Baca. New York: New Directions, 1987.

Olivares, Julian. "Two Contemporary Chicano Verse Chronicles." *American Review* 16 (Fall-Winter, 1988): 214-231.

—*Leon Lewis*

See also American identity: West and the frontier; Chicano identity; *Martín*; *Working in the Dark*

Back to Barbary Lane: The Final Tales of the City Omnibus

AUTHOR: Armistead Maupin (1944-   )

FIRST PUBLISHED: 1991

IDENTITIES: Disease; European American; family; gay, lesbian, and bisexual

In 1991, Armistead Maupin released a collection of the final three works in his Tales of the City series, grouping them under the title *Back to Barbary Lane: The Final Tales of the City Omnibus*. The naturalistic novels *Babycakes* (1984), *Significant Others* (1987), and *Sure of You* (1989) deal with Michael Tolliver's continuing recovery from the loss of his lover to acquired immune deficiency syndrome (AIDS). They reflect Maupin's main theme—acceptance of and compassion for all people.

Babycakes is a psychological study of the effects of death from AIDS on those who survive. Michael's progress in overcoming the emptiness in his heart is painfully slow. He is encouraged, however, through the love of his compassionate chosen family to begin to recover from his loss.

In *Significant Others* Michael's recovery progresses. As his pain lessens, his interest in the world around him increases. He interacts with a larger number of friends, straight and gay. He swims a dangerous river at night to help a loving but demanding woman solve the mystery of the disappearance of her weekend lover. Michael has tested positive for the human immunodeficiency virus (HIV), but he reaches the point that he gives rather than receives help. When his old friend Brian is exposed to AIDS and must anxiously await the results of an HIV test, Michael takes him on a soothing trip to the country. More important, Michael's capacity to love reawakens. He meets a handsome visitor to San Francisco, Thack Sweeney, and begins to feel stirrings of the heart.

Michael and Thack display maturity and compassion. Realizing that he is ready to open himself to a new lover, Michael nevertheless delays his own gratification to help his friend Brian. Thack refuses to be dissuaded from a possible relationship by Michael's HIV-positive status. Thack sees Michael as a human being worthy of love, not as a person with HIV.

The final novel, *Sure of You*, continues to follow the development of Michael and Thack as loving and compassionate men. Two years have passed since the events of *Significant Others*, and Michael and Thack are now partners living together. Thack realizes the preciousness of Michael's love, for Michael's advancing HIV indicates a short future together. Yet the couple's emotional chemistry is clear, and the reader feels certain of the solidity of their relationship. When Brian and his daughter are abandoned by Brian's wife, Brian once again turns to Michael and Thack for friendship and solace.

Michael and Thack speak Maupin's themes eloquently. It is true that Thack occasionally voices darker ideas—anger over the AIDS crisis, a militantly gay political agenda, and little tolerance for those in the closet. Michael and Thack, however, consistently demonstrate Maupin's more positive theme—the importance of loving and accepting all humanity. In espousing these values, Michael and Thack ultimately find fulfillment in life and in each other.

SUGGESTED READINGS

O'Connor, John. "Armistead Maupin, Not Dreamt Up but Inspired." *The New York Times*, June 24, 1993, p. C20.

Spain, Tom. "A Talk with Armistead Maupin." *Publishers Weekly*, March, 1987, 53-54.

—*Steven A. Katz*

See also AIDS; *Babycakes*; Gay identity; Lesbian identity; Maupin, Armistead

Backlash: The Undeclared War Against American Women

AUTHOR: Susan Faludi (1959-   )

FIRST PUBLISHED: 1991

IDENTITIES: Women

The thesis of *Backlash* is that in the 1980's North American society reacted vigorously to take back the gains made by the women's movement during the previous decades. According to Susan

Faludi's meticulously documented work, the backlash phenomenon has followed each era of women's advances throughout history. The 1980's reaction followed the perception that women had made giant strides toward equality during the 1960's and 1970's, but that this equality had created two generations of miserable women. Faludi holds that these perceived gains were much inflated. She indicates that 75 percent of women workers made less than $20,000 a year, that the average female college graduate earned less than her male same-age counterpart with a high school diploma and that most women still worked in traditionally female jobs.

The author refutes a number of "statistical" studies widely publicized during the 1980's. These include the much-touted "man shortage," which documented the meager-to-nil chance of older college-educated women for marriage. Less publicized than the fallacious man shortage was the work of other scholars whose scrutiny of the original study revealed flaws in its methods and models. The book further demonstrates the error of other studies: the "infertility epidemic" and the depression and increased suicide rates attributed to intense career pursuit.

In the 1960's and 1970's, the media downplayed the women's movement, with some few exceptions. The media settled comfortably, however, into the backlash in the 1980's, reinforcing the tenets of the antifeminists. The book points out films' portrayal of strong women primarily as wives and mothers, while single career women are sadistic destroyers of the family, a full turnabout from the films of the 1970's.

Faludi indicts television also for its move away from portrayal of strong independent women to the happy homemaker. The trend on TV shows in the 1980's was toward patriarchal families and stay-at-home mothers. Working mothers, Faludi says, were portrayed as miserable neurotics, negligent of their children.

The fashion world took a similar path toward "feminizing" its models with little girl and baby doll looks that featured flounces and petticoats. In addition, the beauty industry bombarded women with products and cosmetic surgery techniques that focused on the appearance of women. Despite claims that these trends in the media and fashion were what women wanted, the facts, according to the author, indicate that women rejected them.

One chapter of *Backlash* focuses on those the author sees as perpetrating the backlash: the New Right, George Gilder, Robert Bly, Sylvia Ann Hewlett, and Michael Levin. The effects of the backlash on women, according to Faludi, are domestic violence, ambivalence about identity, job discrimination, and denial of reproductive rights.

SUGGESTED READINGS

Friedan, Betty. *The Feminine Mystique*. New York: W. W. Norton, 1973.

_____. *The Second Stage*. New York: Summit Books, 1981.

Steinem, Gloria. *Outrageous Acts and Everyday Rebellions*. New York: Holt, Rinehart and Winston, 1983.

—Patricia J. Huhn

See also Appearance and identity; Faludi, Susan; Mass media stereotyping; Television and identity

Bailey's Cafe

AUTHOR: Gloria Naylor (1950-   )
FIRST PUBLISHED: 1992
IDENTITIES: African American; women

Set in 1948, *Bailey's Cafe*, Gloria Naylor's fourth novel, is her self-described "sexual novel." Similar to *The Women of Brewster Place*, it tells the tragic histories of female characters who suffer simply because they are sexual. The underlying structure of blues music recasts these feminist rewritings of biblical stories. The characters' own blues-influenced narrations provide the equivalent of melody, and the male narrator supplies the connecting texts linking one story to another.

The proprietor of Bailey's Cafe, who is the narrator, sets the pattern by telling how he was saved by Bailey's Cafe, a magical place. It is a cafe that does not serve customers, and its magic is not the redemptive kind. The cafe provides "some space, some place, to take a breather for a while" by suspending time. Not fixed in any one city, it is "real real mobile," so that anyone can get there. It features a back door that opens onto a void where patrons re-create scenes to help them sustain life, or, alternatively, to end it. The street on which Bailey's Cafe may be found contains three refuges that form a "relay for broken dreams": Bailey's Cafe, Gabe's Pawnshop, and Eve's Boardinghouse and Garden.

Eve transforms her suffering into a haven. She aids only those women who know what it means to "walk a thousand years." Her boarders include Esther, who hates men because of the sexual abuse she suffered as a child bride; Peaches, a woman so beautiful she disfigures herself; Jesse, a spunky heroin addict; and Mariam, a fourteen-year-old Ethiopian Jew who is pregnant but still a virgin. The community also includes men. The unforgettable Miss Maple is a man who forges a strong identity despite the racism that threatens his manhood. The novel explores positive models of masculinity and steadily subverts the idea that sexual women are whores. Such a characterization oppresses all women, who must transcend the personal consequences of this destructive label.

The arrival of the outcast and pregnant Mariam threatens to disrupt the characters' safety because the birth could destroy their world: "For all we knew, when that baby gave its first cry, this whole street could have just faded away." The women on the street fear they will find themselves back in "those same hopeless crossroads in our lives." Instead, the baby is born in Mariam's homeland, magically re-created in the void. All the characters gather to celebrate its arrival. Their participation in the Jewish birth ceremony brings hope for the future and shows the healing power of a diverse community.

SUGGESTED READINGS

Gates, Henry Louis, and K. A. Appiah, eds. *Gloria Naylor: Critical Perspectives Past and Present.* New York: Amistad, 1993.

Montgomery, M. L. "Authority, Multivocality, and the New World Order in Gloria Naylor's *Bailey's Cafe*." *African American Review* 29, no. 1 (1995): 27-33.

Wilentz, Gay. "Healing the Wounds of Time." *The Women's Review of Books* 10, no. 5 (1993): 15-16.

—*Christine H. King*

See also African American identity; Erotic identity; Naylor, Gloria; *Women of Brewster Place, The*

Bajan Americans. *See* Caribbean American literature

Baldwin, James

BORN: New York, New York; August 2, 1924
DIED: St. Paul de Vence, France; November 30, 1987
PRINCIPAL WORKS: *Go Tell It on the Mountain*, 1953; *Notes of a Native Son*, 1955; *Giovanni's Room*, 1956; *The Fire Next Time*, 1963; *Going to Meet the Man*, 1965
IDENTITIES: African American; gay, lesbian, and bisexual
SIGNIFICANT ACHIEVEMENT: Baldwin's experiences as an African American gay man became the source for essays and fiction that were often angry but always honest.

At nineteen, James Baldwin left Harlem, the black section of New York City. He traveled across Europe and the United States, living for years in France, where he died at age sixty-three. More than any other place, Harlem shaped Baldwin's identity. He never completely left the ghetto behind.

Baldwin returned often to Harlem to visit family. Much of his writing features the stores and streets of Harlem, in such essays as "The Harlem Ghetto" and "Notes of a Native Son," in stories such as "Sonny's Blues" and "The Rockpile," and in such novels as *Go Tell It on the Mountain*.

Baldwin claimed to love and hate Harlem, a place of old buildings, empty lots, fire escapes, and tired grass. Harlem was also rich with churches and corner stores, with railroad tracks and the Harlem River. Such scenes molded Baldwin's worldview. Baldwin's identity was also shaped by his sexuality. He was admittedly gay, though he never embraced that term or what he called the gay world. He considered it limiting to separate gay and straight worlds. People were people, according to him. Baldwin's second novel, *Giovanni's Room*, deals with gay themes; writing and publishing such a work in the 1950's was a considerable act of courage. Baldwin explores similar themes in *Another Country* (1962). Baldwin said that he wrote *Giovanni's Room* to understand his own sexuality, that the book was something he had to finish before he could write anything else.

Baldwin's thoughts and writings were shaped most powerfully, however, by his identity as an African American. He experienced racism early, yet still excelled in school and at writing for school newspapers. As a young adult he endured segregation. Only by moving to France in his twenties did Baldwin gain the emotional distance to understand what being black in America meant. He participated in the Civil Rights movement, taking part in demonstrations and writing about that struggle. Baldwin uses his gay and African American identities to explore universal themes of loneliness, alienation, and affection.

SUGGESTED READINGS

Campbell, James. *Talking at the Gates: A Life of James Baldwin*. New York: Viking Press, 1991.
Leeming, David. *James Baldwin*. New York: Alfred A. Knopf, 1994.
Rosset, Lisa. *James Baldwin*. New York: Chelsea House, 1989.
Weatherby, W. J. *James Baldwin: Artist on Fire*. New York: Donald I. Fine, 1989.

—*Charles A. Gramlich*

See also African American identity; Gay identity; *Giovanni's Room*; *Notes of a Native Son*

Ballad of the Sad Café, The

AUTHOR: Carson McCullers (1917-1967)

FIRST PUBLISHED: 1943

IDENTITIES: European American; gay, lesbian, and bisexual; South

The Ballad of the Sad Café depicts a triangular romance similar to the complicated relationship involving Carson McCullers and Reeves McCullers, David Diamond, and Annemarie Clarac-Schwarzenbach. Diamond loved Carson and Reeves; Reeves loved Carson and Diamond; and Carson loved Diamond and Annemarie and felt ambivalent toward Reeves, whom she was divorcing. In the novel Miss Amelia Evans owns a café in a Southern mill town. When Cousin Lymon, a dwarf and hunchback, appears and claims kinship with her, she invites him to live with her. She falls in love with Lymon, and the café becomes a lively place where isolated townspeople gather and form a community. When Amelia's former husband, Marvin Macy, gets out of prison, he returns to the café to seek revenge upon Amelia for humiliating him.

In *The Ballad of the Sad Café* McCullers portrays bisexuality and androgyny. Although living with Amelia, Lymon longs for a male lover, and Macy seeks Lymon's affection to spite Amelia. Lymon becomes obsessively in love with Macy, and Amelia allows Macy to stay with her for Lymon's sake. Justifying her actions, Amelia says, "It is better to take in your mortal enemy than face the terror of living alone." A loner with masculine qualities, Amelia denies her feminine identity. Her masculine characteristics are expressed in her attire, her attitudes, and her unconsummated marriage to Macy.

Mythic qualities combined with folktale elements create a surreal atmosphere that explores the complications of romantic love and the search for communal identity. The climax occurs when Amelia and Macy physically battle for the love of Lymon. Amelia is winning the fight, when Lymon leaps onto her back and helps Macy. Macy and Lymon defeat Amelia, rob her of her possessions, and leave town. Deeply depressed, Amelia awaits Lymon's return for three years, then closes the café.

The story of Amelia, Lymon, and Macy is told through the use of flashbacks, repeatedly interrupted by narrative comment. Narrative commentary blends with the plot, demonstrating the paradox of romantic love and human isolation. McCullers suggests that love is both a powerful and destructive form of identity that enigmatically attracts and repels: "The lover and the beloved . . . come from different countries. . . . The beloved fears and hates the lover. . . . The lover is forever trying to strip bare his beloved."

In the opening and closing descriptions of the town, references to a chain gang are made. The novel ends with an epilogue describing twelve men working on a chain gang. The chain gang represents the human condition, implying that escape from solitude is only possible through chained connections with others. Connecting with others paradoxically provides freedom from loneliness and personal bondage.

SUGGESTED READINGS

McDowell, Margaret B. *Carson McCullers*. Boston: Twayne, 1980.

Phillips, Robert S. "Painful Love: Carson McCullers' Parable." *Southwest Review* 51 (Winter, 1966): 80-86.

Stebbins, Todd. "McCullers' *The Ballad of the Sad Café*." *The Explicator* 46, no. 2 (Winter, 1988): 36-38.

—Laurie Champion

See also American identity: South; Bisexual identity; Erotic identity; McCullers, Carson; *Reflections in a Golden Eye*

Bambara, Toni Cade

BORN: New York, New York; March 25, 1939
DIED: Wallingford, Pennsylvania; December 9, 1995
PRINCIPAL WORKS: *Gorilla, My Love*, 1972; *The Sea Birds Are Still Alive: Collected Stories*, 1977; *The Salt Eaters*, 1980
IDENTITIES: African American; women
SIGNIFICANT ACHIEVEMENT: Bambara saw herself as a literary combatant who wrote to affirm the selfhood of blacks.

Given the name Miltona Mirkin Cade at birth, Toni Cade acquired the name Bambara in 1970 after she discovered it as part of a signature on a sketchbook she found in her great-grandmother's trunk. Bambara spent her formative years in New York and Jersey City, New Jersey, attending public and private schools in the areas. Although she maintained that her early short stories are not autobiographical, the protagonists in many of these pieces are young women who recall Bambara's inquisitiveness as a youngster.

Bambara attended Queens College, New York, and received a bachelor of arts degree in 1959. Earlier that year she had published her first short story, and she also received the John Golden award for fiction from Queens College. Bambara then entered the City College of New York, where she studied modern American fiction, but before completing her studies for the master's degree, she traveled to Italy and studied in Milan, eventually returning to her studies and earning the master's in 1963.

From 1959 to 1973, Bambara saw herself as an activist. She held positions as social worker, teacher, and counselor. In her various roles, Bambara saw herself as working for the betterment of the community. During the 1960's, Rutgers State University developed a strong fine arts undergraduate program. Many talented black artists joined the faculty to practice their craft and to teach. Bambara was one of those talented faculty members. She taught, wrote, and participated in a program for raising the consciousness of minority women.

Like many artists during the 1960's, Bambara became involved in the black liberation struggle. She realized that all blacks needed to be liberated, but she felt that black women were forgotten in the struggle. She was of the opinion that neither the white nor the black male was capable of understanding what it means to be a black female. White and black males created images of women, she argued, that "are still derived from their needs." Bambara saw a kinship with white women, but admitted: "I don't know that our priorities are the same." Believing that only the black woman is capable of explaining herself, Bambara edited *The Black Woman: An Anthology* (1970).

In 1973, Bambara visited Cuba, and in 1975 she traveled to Vietnam. Her travels led her to believe that globally, women were oppressed. Her experiences found expression in *The Sea Birds Are Still Alive*. In the late 1970's, Bambara moved to the South to teach at Spellman College. During this period she wrote *The Salt Eaters*, which focuses on mental and physical well-being. With her daughter, Bambara moved to Pennsylvania in the 1980's, where she continued her activism and her writing until her death.

SUGGESTED READING

Tate, Claudia. *Black Women Writers at Work*. New York: Continuum, 1983.

—Ralph Reckley, Sr.

See also African American identity; Black English; Feminism; *Gorilla, My Love*; *Salt Eaters, The*

Baraka, Amiri (LeRoi Jones)

BORN: Newark, New Jersey; October 7, 1934

PRINCIPAL WORKS: *Blues People: Negro Music in White America*, 1963; *Dutchman*, pr., pb. 1964; *The Slave*, pr., pb. 1964; *The System of Dante's Hell*, 1965; *Home: Social Essays*, 1966; *Selected Poetry of Amiri Baraka/LeRoi Jones*, 1979; *Daggers and Javelins: Essays 1974-1979*, 1984; *The LeRoi Jones/Amiri Baraka Reader*, 1991 (edited by William J. Harris); *Transbluesency: Selected Poems of Amiri Baraka/LeRoi Jones (1961-1995)*, 1995

IDENTITIES: African American

SIGNIFICANT ACHIEVEMENT: Baraka's poetry, drama, and music criticism make him one of the most influential African American writers of his generation.

Introspective yet concerned with public, political issues, Amiri Baraka's works frequently focus on his personal attempt to define an African American identity. Born into a close-knit family that had migrated from the South, Baraka was a bright student. In adolescence Baraka became aware of differences between African American middle-class and working-class lives and viewpoints. He recalls the identity crisis that grew out of his developing class awareness in such works as "Letter to E. Franklin Frazier," his novel *The System of Dante's Hell*, and short stories collected in *Tales* (1967). His interest in jazz and blues also began in adolescence and was reinforced by the mentorship of poet Sterling A. Brown, one of Baraka's professors at Howard University.

After an enlistment in the Air Force, Baraka settled in New York's Greenwich Village in 1957 and began publishing *Yugen*, a poetry magazine that became one of the important journals of the Beat generation. After the success of his play *Dutchman* and his recognition as an important critic for his study *Blues People: Negro Music in White America*, the assassination of Malcolm X was a shocking event that caused Baraka to reject his previous faith in the possibilities of a racially integrated society. In 1965, he embraced a Black Nationalist political viewpoint and helped establish the Black Arts Repertory Theatre/School in Harlem, which became the center of a nationwide Black Arts movement. This movement attempted to produce literature, music, and visual art addressed to the masses of African Americans. The Black Arts movement aimed at expressing a unique ethnic worldview and what Baraka called "a Black value system." His works of this period often depict a hostile white society and question whether middle-class aspirations and individualism endangered the progress of African Americans as a group. He saw the collective improvisation of jazz as a model for the arts and for political activism.

Turning to Marxism in 1974, Baraka extended these ideas. Dedicating his work to revolutionary action, Baraka suggested that the situation of African Americans paralleled that of colonized Third World peoples in Africa and Asia. Teaching at the State University of New York and other colleges, Baraka produced highly original poems, plays, and essays that continued to address controversial issues and to reach a wide international readership. His experiments with literary form—particularly the use of African American vernacular speech—also has influenced many younger American writers.

SUGGESTED READINGS

Baraka, Amiri. *The Autobiography of LeRoi Jones*. New York: Freundlich Books, 1984.

Brown, Lloyd W. *Amiri Baraka*. Boston: Twayne, 1980.

Harris, William J. *The Poetry and Poetics of Amiri Baraka: The Jazz Aesthetic*. Columbia: University of Missouri Press, 1985.

Reilly, Charlie, ed. *Conversations with Amiri Baraka*. Jackson: University Press of Mississippi, 1994.

Sollors, Werner. *Amiri Baraka/LeRoi Jones: The Quest for a "Populist Modernism."* New York: Columbia University Press, 1978.

—Lorenzo Thomas

See also Adolescent identity; African American identity; Black English; *Blues People*; Class and identity; *Daggers and Javelins*; *Dutchman*; *Selected Poetry of Amiri Baraka/LeRoi Jones*

Barbadian Americans. *See* Caribbean American literature

Barthelme, Donald

BORN: Philadelphia, Pennsylvania; April 7, 1931

DIED: Houston, Texas; July 23, 1989

PRINCIPAL WORKS: *Come Back, Dr. Caligari*, 1964; *Snow White*, 1967; *Unspeakable Practices, Unnatural Acts*, 1968; *City Life*, 1970; *Sadness*, 1972; *Guilty Pleasures*, 1974; *The Dead Father*, 1975; *Amateurs*, 1976; *Great Days*, 1979; *Sixty Stories*, 1981; *Overnight to Many Distant Cities*, 1983; *Paradise*, 1986; *Forty Stories*, 1987; *The King*, 1990; *The Teachings of Don B.*, 1992

IDENTITIES: European American

SIGNIFICANT ACHIEVEMENT: Barthelme's fiction, especially his short fiction, is an example of what has been termed "metafiction" because of its self-consciousness and its use of irony as an inherent tone.

The son of an avant-garde Houston architect, Donald Barthelme inherited his father's sense of irony, humor, and iconoclasm and applied it to his writing. After serving as a reporter in the Army and for the *Houston Post*, he first became director for Houston's Contemporary Arts Museum, then moved to New York City to edit *Location*, an arts magazine. The formal techniques of painting, sculpture, graphics, and other fine arts influenced his writing.

Barthelme published his first short piece, "L'Lapse," in *The New Yorker*, in 1963. Soon, he was publishing regularly in the magazine. A lapsed Catholic, Barthelme is skeptical about received systems of knowledge. The individual in Barthelme's work is bombarded with a kind of information overload. Consciousness, he seems to say, is made up of dozens of influences; many of them are texts that come in expected, many times hackneyed, forms: newspapers, magazines, advertisements, television news programs, sitcoms, and so on. Some of the most powerful influences with which people are confronted come through the structures of the narratives (novels,

Donald Barthelme's surreal short stories helped to define the fractured sensibilities of a generation. (Bill Wittliff)

plays, films, fairy stories) to which they are exposed. According to Barthelme, many, if not all, of these structures have lost the authentic meaning that was contained in their original contexts. This he calls "the Trash Phenomenon" in *Snow White*. By focusing on not only the what (the information) of what is carried by these texts, but also their how (their structures), Barthelme frees himself and the reader from a ready-made reality, full of worn-out expectations and limitations. Through the use of the collage technique, Barthelme playfully recombines clichéd ideas using irony and parody, forcing the reader into a new relationship with the texts to which he or she is exposed.

SUGGESTED READINGS

Gordon, Lois. *Donald Barthelme*. Boston: Twayne, 1981.

Klinkowitz, Jerome. *Literary Disruptions: The Making of a Post-Contemporary American Fiction*. Champaign: University of Illinois Press, 1975.

Molesworth, Charles. *Donald Barthelme's Fiction: The Ironist Saved from Drowning*. Columbia: University of Missouri Press, 1982.

Stengel, Wayne B. *The Shape of Art in the Short Stories of Donald Barthelme*. Baton Rouge: Louisiana State University Press, 1985.

—*Gary P. Walton*

See also Countercultures; Popular culture; Television and identity

Barthelme, Donald, short stories of

AUTHOR: Donald Barthelme (1931-1989)

PRINCIPAL WORKS: *Come Back, Dr. Caligari*, 1964; *Unspeakable Practices, Unnatural Acts*, 1968; *City Life*, 1970; *Sadness*, 1972; *Guilty Pleasures*, 1974; *Amateurs*, 1976; *Great Days*, 1979; *Sixty Stories*, 1981; *Overnight to Many Distant Cities*, 1983; *Forty Stories*, 1987; *The Teachings of Don B.*, 1992

IDENTITIES: European American

Donald Barthelme is best known for his short fiction. Unlike traditional stories that concentrate on creating characters in a fictive world with which the reader can readily identify, Barthelme creates language objects that are self-conscious of themselves as language. Barthelme's stories are full of parody, irony, and an infectious playfulness. The critic Wayne Stengel groups Barthelme's stories into four major categories: identity stories, such as "Me and Miss Mandible," communication stories, such as "On the Steps of the Conservatory," society stories, such as "Report," and art objects such as "At the Tolstoy Museum." Another critic, Charles Molesworth, places Barthelme's stories into five different categories: total incoherency, such as "Bone Bubbles," the surreal place, such as "Paraguay," the counterpointed plot, such as "Daumier," the extended conceit, such as "Sentence," and parodies of narrative structure, such as "The Glass Mountain."

Barthelme's early collections introduce the reader to the basic collage technique that becomes the mainstay of his fiction construction. He refines his strategies in his later collections, but he never abandons them. *Guilty Pleasures* and his posthumous *The Teachings of Don B.* contain pieces that come as close as Barthleme ever gets to traditional parody and satire. Barthelme's playful, sophisticated technique attempts to reinvent fiction as a relevant art form. He starts with the assumption that contemporary life is made up of a flood of received ideas that come in the form of clichéd images and texts. The writer must take these ideas out of their original contexts and put them back together in innovative, usually ironic, ways so the reader can consider them anew.

"Robert Kennedy Saved from Drowning," for example, shows how the personality of a famous man is created by what is said about him. This identity contrasts sharply to the real man himself. The abundance of information about "K" only clutters the reader's attempt to get at the real character, thus "K" becomes form without substance. A similar problem arises for the son in "Views of My Father Weeping."

Barthelme also likes to bring to the foreground the manner in which fiction is created. By doing this, he forces readers to reevaluate their relationship to the ideas contained in the language and not innocently accept them as reality or truth. For example, "The Glass Mountain," a story built out of numbered sentences, allows the reader to see the fairy tale as a constructed thing that may or may not be relevant to the reader's life. The parody delivered in the structure leads the reader to reexamine the ideas inherent in the story.

SUGGESTED READINGS

Molesworth, Charles. *Donald Barthelme's Fiction: The Ironist Saved from Drowning*. Columbia: University of Missouri Press, 1982.

Roe, Barbara. *Donald Barthelme*. Boston: Twayne, 1992.

Stengel, Wayne B. *The Shape of Art in the Short Stories of Donald Barthelme*. Baton Rouge: Louisiana State University Press, 1985.

—*Gary P. Walton*

See also Barthelme, Donald; Metafiction

Bean Trees, The

AUTHOR: Barbara Kingsolver (1955-   )
FIRST PUBLISHED: 1988
IDENTITIES: Native American; South; West and Southwest; women

The Bean Trees, Barbara Kingsolver's first novel, is the initiation story of twenty-three-year-old Marietta (Taylor) Greer, who drives west from Kentucky, finding a new name and a child and ultimately making a life in Tucson, Arizona. In a plot structured on the hero's journey of separation, initiation, and reintegration, Taylor Greer achieves her adult identity by accepting and making a home for the three-year-old child, Turtle, who was given to her by a frightened Cherokee woman.

Taylor answers a newspaper ad for a housemate and meets Lou Ann Ruiz. Lou Ann and Taylor are both from Kentucky, and their similar accents and diction spark a friendship. Lou Ann—a single parent whose husband has abandoned her and their infant son, Dwayne Ray—and Taylor portray fearful and confident motherhood. Lou Ann represents fearful motherhood and self-conscious, self-critical femininity. She sees the world as fraught with sharp objects threatening her infant and small round objects that could block his windpipe. She also bewails her bad appearance: "I look like I've been drug through hell backwards." The truth of Lou Ann's portrait is borne out in Kingsolver's recollection of a hometown book signing where "more than one of my old schoolmates had sidled up and whispered: 'That Lou Ann character, the insecure one? I know you based her on me.'" Taylor realizes she and Lou Ann "were like some family on a TV commercial, with names like Myrtle and Fred," stereotypes of husband and wife. The two talk through their situation over beer, tortilla chips, pimento-cheese slices, and sardines in mustard, sharing secrets, becoming friends, and eventually working out a schedule to share housework.

Taylor finds work at Jesus Is Lord Used Tires, a business with an upstairs apartment that also serves as a sanctuary for Central American refugees. Despite its incongruous name, the tire store is a place where Taylor faces her fear: She has a strong childhood memory of seeing an exploding tractor tire throw a man high into the air. All the characters in this novel face fears, as represented most dramatically by Turtle and the refugee couple Esperanza and Estevan. Taylor volunteers to drive the couple to another hiding place in Oklahoma, and seek legal adoption of Turtle. The couple helps Taylor by pretending to be Turtle's biological parents, signing adoption papers in a lawyer's office.

Naming is a significant motif in the novel. Taylor's given name, Marietta, is the name of the Georgia town in which she was born. When Taylor drives away from Pittman County Kentucky, she decides that her name will be determined by wherever her car runs out of gas: "I kept my fingers crossed through Sidney, Sadorus, Cerro Gordo, Decatur, and Blue Mound, and coasted into Taylorville on the fumes." Taylor names Turtle to match the strength of her grip: Turtle holds on like a snapping turtle. The naming process combines choice and circumstance, power and powerlessness in an apt reflection of Kingsolver's themes.

Suggested readings

Freitag, Michael. "Writing to Pay the Rent." *The New York Times Book Review*, April 10, 1988, 15.

Mossman, Robert. Review of *The Bean Trees*. *English Journal* 79 (October, 1990): 85.

Perry, Donna. *Backtalk: Women Writers Speak Out*. New Brunswick, N.J.: Rutgers University Press, 1993.

—*Janet Taylor Palmer*

See also Kingsolver, Barbara; *Pigs in Heaven*

Beattie, Ann

Born: Washington, D.C.; September 8, 1947

Principal works: *Secrets and Surprises*, 1978; *Falling in Place*, 1980; *The Burning House*, 1982; *Picturing Will*, 1989

Identities: European American; family; women

Significant achievement: Beattie articulates the values and anxieties of those in the baby-boomer generation whose early idealism gave way to cynicism and self-involvement.

Born Charlotte Ann Beattie, the only child of a housewife and a government official, Ann Beattie has said that she developed an identity as an "adult-child" who, although dependable and mature, continued to surround herself with toys and called her writing a playtime activity. She has also suggested that as a teenager she suffered from an undiagnosed clinical depression. Her insightful depiction of too-mature children and of depressive personalities can be traced back to her own formative years. Beattie came into her own at American University, where she discovered literature, and went on to graduate work at the University of Connecticut. Finding the graduate program uninspiring, she turned to writing about her own peer group, who grew up in the shadow of the Vietnam War and whose experiments with sexual freedom and drug use produced a flourishing

Ann Beattie's short stories have captured the rootlessness of late-twentieth century American life. (Benjamin Ford)

counterculture. Her marriage to the writer and musician David Gates followed a nontraditional route, with no plans for children and with a circle of friends replacing a network of family relations. Beattie's life and work were peopled at this time by well-educated men and women in their late twenties or early thirties, living in comfortable country houses not too far from Manhattan and possessing the freedom and the funds to fly to Europe or to the West Coast, to break off marriages, blend new families, change jobs, partners, and sexual orientation at the prompting of their own desires, all the while listening to the latest, best music and catching the best new films.

Beattie does not celebrate this life in a vanguard ruled by a new morality. The theme of Beattie's fiction is that the expectation of a happier life promised by the discoveries and acts of the Woodstock generation did not come to pass. Many of her bleak early stories anticipated the end of her marriage to Gates, whom she divorced in 1980. Beattie moved to Charlottesville, Virginia, where she settled with her second husband, the painter Lincoln Perry. While her early stories explored love and loss in a disturbingly unemotional and ironic way, her later work is warmer, more generous, and more optimistic. It is her early fiction, however, with its sense of disappointment and despair, that has supplied her with an identity as the voice of another lost generation.

SUGGESTED READINGS

Aldridge, John. "Less Is a Lot Less (Raymond Carver, Ann Beattie, Amy Hempel, Frederick Barthelme)." In *Talents and Technicians*. New York: Charles Scribner's Sons, 1992.

Montresor, Jaye Berman, ed. *The Critical Response to Ann Beattie*. Westport, Conn.: Greenwood Press, 1993.

Murphy, Christine. *Anne Beattie*. New York: Twayne, 1986.

—*Margaret Boe Birns*

See also Alienation; American identity: Northeast; *Burning House, The*; Divorce; Erotic identity

Becoming a Man: Half a Life Story

AUTHOR: Paul Monette (1945-1995)

FIRST PUBLISHED: 1992

IDENTITIES: Disease; European American; gay, lesbian, and bisexual

It took the loss of his life partner Roger Horwitz, who died of acquired immune deficiency syndrome (AIDS) in 1987, to turn Paul Monette from the poetry and fiction with which he began his career to the powerful autobiographical writing that will perhaps be seen as his chief contribution as a gay author. To memorialize the suffering and bravery of Horwitz's battle with AIDS, Monette wrote *Borrowed Time: An AIDS Memoir* (1988), which was much praised for its urgent, unflinching look at the disease and the ignorance and hatred surrounding it during the early years of the epidemic. In *Becoming a Man: Half a Life Story* Monette tells the rest of his story, narrating the history of his childhood and youth and focusing on his tortuous journey toward the acceptance of his gay identity. Part morality tale and part manifesto, the personal narrative goes beyond the account of Monette's emergence from self-loathing to self-affirmation and becomes a denunciation of the closet to which society consigns its gay and lesbian citizens.

The book's candor and insight won it the National Book Award for nonfiction in 1992. It not only anatomizes the closet with uncanny precision and passion but also provides a searing critique of the harrowing process by which all boys become men in an American culture that prizes violent games and denies male intimacy. Certainly Monette's history of growing up in the 1950's and 1960's reveals the casualties produced by a culture that insists on demonizing certain kinds of diversity.

Born into a New England family, Monette grew up puritanically denying his physical body and hoping that his well-mannered, self-effacing demeanor would disguise his secret sexual life. At Philips Academy, Andover, he buried himself in literature and art to avoid the golden athletes whose blithe sense of heterosexual entitlement he outwardly envied but secretly despised and resisted. An outsider, he was made to feel that his sexual difference was unspeakable, criminal, pathological. Later at Yale, where he recognized his true vocation as a writer, editing poetry magazines and administering arts festivals, he could still not admit his true gay nature. He remained in a cramped closet, forced to more and more contorted acts of ventriloquism in order to appear normal. He broke through these walls when he met Horwitz in 1974, and the two men began their twelve-year relationship.

Becoming a Man is intended as an account of Monette's difficult personal struggle to embrace, explore, and celebrate his sexual nature. It is also, as the author suggested in numerous interviews, intended as a road map for future generations of gays and lesbians. It was Monette's hope that through reading his story they might resist the oppression of the closet, reject the lies and distortions that lead to despair and self-hatred, and thereby create for their life stories a radically different plot.

SUGGESTED READINGS

Martin, Wendy. Review of *Becoming a Man: Half a Life Story*, by Paul Monette. *The New York Times Book Review*, July 26, 1992, 5.

See, Lisa. "Paul Monette." *Publishers Weekly*, June 29, 1992, 42-43.

—*Thomas J. Campbell*

See also Gay identity; Monette, Paul

Beet Queen, The

AUTHOR: Louise Erdrich (1954-   )
FIRST PUBLISHED: 1986
IDENTITIES: Family; Midwest; Native American

Louise Erdrich's second novel, *The Beet Queen*, is centered in the fictional little town of Argus, somewhere in North Dakota. Unlike her other novels of people living on reservations, the characters in this story are mostly European Americans, and those Native Americans who exist have very tenuous ties to their roots and to the reservation that lies just outside the town. Racism, poverty, and cultural conflict are not in the foreground in this novel, which makes it different from most novels by Native American authors. Instead, European Americans, Native Americans, and mixed bloods are all in the same economic and cultural situation, and each of them is involved in a search for identity.

The prose in *The Beet Queen* is lyrical and finely crafted, as is evident in the description of Mary Adare, the novel's central character. Abandoned by a mother who literally vanishes in the air, she builds her identity by developing a solid grounding. She is described as heavy and immovable, and she makes a home for herself in a butcher shop that is described as having thick walls and green, watery light coming through glass block windows. She has found an earthy den, which attaches her to the one thing that will never abandon her—the earth. Her brother, Karl, is her opposite. Thin, flighty, always moving, he is a European American who fits perfectly the archetype of the Native American trickster figure. He is the destroyer, lover of men and women, game-player, and cocreator of the character who ties the main characters of the novel together, his daughter, Dot.

Dot is a strong, willful girl who is adored by her mother, a strong, mixed blood Chippewa woman named Celestine, her Aunt Mary, and Walter Pfef, a town leader and her father's former lover. It is Dot, the Beet Queen in a contest fixed by Pfef, who brings together the web of characters who are otherwise loosely joined in fragile relationships. During the Beet Celebration in which she is to be crowned, her father returns. Pfef, Celestine, and Mary are also there, and Russell, Celestine's paralyzed war-hero brother, is the centerpiece of a float honoring veterans. Mary's vain cousin, Sita, is also there, although she is dead. When the day is over, the circle of family is complete. Poetic and graceful, *The Beet Queen* is widely recognized as one of Erdrich's finest accomplishments.

SUGGESTED READINGS

Owens, Louis. *Other Destinies: Understanding the American Indian Novel*. Norman: Oklahoma University Press, 1992.

Rainwater, Catherine. "Reading Between Worlds: Narrativity in the Fiction of Louise Erdrich." *American Literature* 62, no. 4 (1990): 405-422.

White, Sharon, and Glenda Burnside. "On Native Ground: An Interview with Louise Erdrich and Michael Dorris." *Bloomsbury Review* 8, no. 4 (1988): 16-18.

—*Jacquelyn Kilpatrick*

See also Class and identity; Mixed race and identity; Native American identity

Beggar in Jerusalem, A

AUTHOR: Elie Wiesel (1928-   )
FIRST PUBLISHED: *Le Mendiant de Jérusalem*, 1968 (English translation, 1970)
IDENTITIES: Jewish; world

A Beggar in Jerusalem is told in the first person by David, heir to a bloody history of anti-Semitic persecutions. It is a novel in which Jewish survivors of destruction must confront their miraculous escape. In the process, although they suffer from guilt and anger, they ultimately forge an identity based on hope.

In June, 1967, the forty-year-old David goes to fight against the united Arab armies. He wishes to die in order to finally overcome the despair caused by God's abandonment of the Jews during World War II and by his own pointless survival. At the front, he meets Katriel, and both soon agree that whoever comes back will tell the other's story. Israel wins a resounding victory in what comes to be called the Six-Day War, and as the narrative opens, there are celebrations all over the land, especially in Jerusalem. Katriel, however, does not come back.

David not only tells his comrade's story—much as King David told of Absalom—but also wonders whether he ought to live it as well. This he does, at the end, by marrying Katriel's widow, not out of love, which would imply a total gift of self and of which he does not feel himself capable, but rather out of affection and sympathy, perhaps out of friendship. The hero has realized that, beyond suffering and bitterness, he can arrive at self-discovery.

Whereas Albert Camus favored revolt in the face of the absurd, Wiesel advocates laughter. By laughing one succeeds in conquering oneself, and by dominating one's fear one learns to laugh: "Let our laughter drown all the noises of the earth, all the regrets of mankind." There is no longer a need to search for an antidote against distress, but simply to abandon oneself to the joy of an event without precedent—the reunion of Israel with Jerusalem, uniting those absent and present, the fighters and mad beggars, in similar euphoria and similar ecstasy: "I want to laugh and it is my laughter I wish to offer to Jerusalem, my laughter and not my tears."

In his tireless attempt to understand the awesome and terrifying mystery of Jewish suffering, the once-tormented David is resolutely optimistic, for the recaptured Jerusalem means the end of despair for Jews in Israel and abroad. The victory celebrations are a memorial to the dead, a song to and of life, and an appeal in behalf of history's wandering outcasts—the allegorical beggars who, after the annihilation of European Jewry, have come to Jerusalem to give God the last chance to save his people.

SUGGESTED READINGS

Estess, Ted L. *Elie Wiesel*. New York: Frederick Ungar, 1980.
Patterson, David. *In Dialogue with Elie Wiesel*. Wakefield, N.H.: Longwood Academic, 1991.
Sibelman, Simon P. "The Mystical Union: A Re-Examination of Elie Wiesel's *Le Mendiant de Jérusalem*." *Literature and Theology* 7, no. 2 (June, 1993): 186-197.

—*Pierre L. Horn*

See also *All Rivers Run to the Sea*; Anti-Semitism; Holocaust; *Night*; Wiesel, Elie

Bell Jar, The

AUTHOR: Sylvia Plath (1932-1963)
FIRST PUBLISHED: 1963
IDENTITIES: Adolescence and coming-of-age; European American; family; women

Sylvia Plath published *The Bell Jar* under the pseudonym Victoria Lucas a month prior to her death by suicide. *The Bell Jar*, her novel, and *The Colossus* (1960), a book of her poetry, came to life before she ended hers. Plath's successive publications were posthumous. Plath portends her suicide in *The Bell Jar*, which recounts an earlier suicide attempt. The novel is an autobiographical account of Plath's early life as a college student who is elected to spend the summer in New York as a guest writer for a women's magazine. Her encounters in the city highlight her naïveté and initiate her rebellion against the conventional roles into which women were pressed.

Sylvia Plath's father's death when she was eight years old significantly altered her perception of life. His early departure from her life lead to a one-sided, love-hate relationship with death and her father. In her poem "Daddy," Plath curses her father and blames him for her cynicism regarding men. *The Bell Jar* and Plath's extremely intense poetry, much of which was published posthumously, earned Plath great stature as a feminist literary figure.

Plath suffered significant challenges during the two and one-half years she spent writing *The Bell Jar*: a miscarriage, an appendectomy, pregnancy with her second child, separation from her husband (the poet Ted Hughes), depression, and thoughts of suicide. During her third college year, Plath attempted suicide with an overdose of sleeping pills; this is recounted in the novel. She chronicles this event as well as her relationships with men in *The Bell Jar*. The novel's title is a reference to a central theme of alienation that is so extreme as to be a form of disembodiment. The narrator relates at one point that she feels that she is inside a bell jar (a bell-shaped jar with no bottom that is placed over objects to contain or isolate them). This theme is augmented with descriptions of hospital autopsy rooms, of hideous specimens preserved in jars, and of encounters with grotesque men in New York. Continuing the theme of defamiliarization, Plath writes with witticisms about disturbing events and images. Plath's style in *The Bell Jar* is honest and strongly emotional. The reader may experience difficulty, however, in engaging in Plath's view of death, which is held to be enchantingly desirous and overwhelmingly dreadful.

SUGGESTED READINGS

Aird, Eileen. *Sylvia Plath: Her Life and Works*. New York: Harper & Row, 1973.
Allen, Mary. "Sylvia Plath's Defiance: *The Bell Jar*." In *The Necessary Blankness: Women in Major American Fiction of the Sixties*. Champaign: University of Illinois Press, 1976.
Alvarez, Alfred. *The Savage God*. New York: Random House, 1971.
Butscher, Edward. *Sylvia Plath: Method and Madness*. New York: Seabury Press, 1975.
Newman, Charles, ed. *The Art of Sylvia Plath*. Bloomington: Indiana University Press, 1970.

—*Craig Gilbert*

See also Feminism; Mental disorders; Plath, Sylvia; Women and identity

Bellow, Saul

BORN: Lachine, Quebec, Canada; June 10, 1915

PRINCIPAL WORKS: *Dangling Man*, 1944; *The Victim*, 1947; *The Adventures of Augie March*, 1953; *Seize the Day*, 1956; *Henderson the Rain King*, 1959; *Herzog*, 1964; *Mr. Sammler's Planet*, 1970; *Humboldt's Gift*, 1975; *The Dean's December*, 1982; *More Die of Heartbreak*, 1987

IDENTITIES: Jewish

SIGNIFICANT ACHIEVEMENT: Bellow was perhaps the first Jewish writer in America to reject the categorization of his work as being Jewish American literature; he became a major American novelist.

Saul Bellow grew up in the polyglot slums of Montreal and Chicago. He was saved from a bleak existence by his love of learning. He acquired a knowledge of Yiddish, Hebrew, and French, in addition to Russian and English. His Russian immigrant parents were orthodox Jews; Bellow's exposure to other cultures led him to reject a purely Jewish identity. He discovered the work of Mark Twain, Edgar Allan Poe, Theodore Dreiser, and Sherwood Anderson, all leaders in shaping Americans' consciousness of their national identity.

After being graduated from Northwestern University, Bellow obtained a scholarship to pursue graduate study in anthropology at the University of Wisconsin but found his real interest lay in creative writing. He considered his first two novels, *Dangling Man* and *The Victim*, "apprentice work." Not until the publication of *The Adventures of Augie March* did he achieve recognition as a major new voice in American fiction. He had forged a spontaneous, exuberant personal style which was a poetic synthesis of lower-class vernacular, Yiddishisms, profuse neologisms, the language of polite society, and the jargon of academia.

Bellow thought too much had been made of persecution and exclusion. He pointed to the exciting opportunities for growth available to all Americans. He insisted on being not a Jew addressing other Jews, but an American addressing other Americans. Creative writing for him was an adventure in self-discovery. He called his breakthrough novel *The Adventures of Augie March* because he considered life an adventure in spite of hardships, disappointments, and failure.

Among his numerous honors, Bellow received National Book Awards for *The Adventures of Augie March* in 1954, *Herzog* in 1964, and *Mr. Sammler's Planet* in 1970. His crowning achievement was the Nobel Prize in Literature in 1976. Most of his fiction concerns a search for self-realization in a confusing, often hostile world. Bellow's heroes rarely know what they want but know what they do not want: they are chronically dissatisfied with the complacency, inertia, and materialism around them.

Bellow was also inspirational as a teacher. He is most closely identified with the University of Chicago. The fact that Bellow was married and divorced four times reflects the quixotic spirit seen in Augie March, Eugene Henderson, and other autobiographical creations.

Saul Bellow, author of Herzog *(1964), was awarded the Nobel Prize in Literature in 1976.* (The Nobel Foundation)

Bellow will be best remembered for his example to writers attempting to discover and declare their identities, often as members of disadvantaged minorities. Bellow expressed—and was shaped by—the adventurous, iconoclastic, and fiercely democratic spirit of twentieth century America.

SUGGESTED READINGS

Hyland, Peter. *Saul Bellow*. New York: St. Martin's Press, 1992.
Kiernan, Robert F. *Saul Bellow*. New York: Continuum, 1989.
Miller, Ruth. *Saul Bellow: A Biography of the Imagination*. New York: St. Martin's Press, 1991.

—Bill Delaney

See also *Adventures of Augie March, The*; Jewish American identity

Beloved

AUTHOR: Toni Morrison (1931-   )
FIRST PUBLISHED: 1987
IDENTITIES: African American; family; women

Beloved's dedication, "Sixty Million and more," commemorates the number of slaves who died in the middle passage—from Africa to the New World. Toni Morrison's protagonist, Sethe, is modeled upon the historical figure of a fugitive Kentucky slave, who in 1851 murdered her baby rather than return it to slavery.

A pregnant Sethe flees on foot to Cincinnati, Ohio, sending her children ahead by way of the Underground Railroad. Her overwhelming concern is to join her baby daughter, who needs her milk. On the bank of the Ohio River she goes into labor, her delivery aided by a white girl who is herself fleeing mistreatment. The new baby is named Denver. Although Sethe reaches her destination, slave-catchers soon follow to return her to Kentucky. Frantic, she tries to kill her children rather than submit them to slavery, but she succeeds only with the older baby. "Beloved" is carved on the child's tombstone.

Sethe accepts her identity of black woman, escaped slave, wife, mother. Her antagonist is life, which has taken so much from her. She and Paul D, the man who becomes her lover, are the last survivors of Sweet Home, the Kentucky farm that was neither sweet nor home to them. Their charge is to endure memory and accept the unforgivable past.

A vengeful spirit, that of the dead baby, invades Sethe's house. After Paul D drives it away, a strange young woman appears in the yard, and they take her in. Her name is Beloved. She is the ghost of Sethe's dead child. She is also, less clearly, a ghost from the slave ships and an African river spirit. She alters relationships in the household, exerting control over the two adults and Denver. Denver hovers over Beloved; Beloved dotes on Sethe. Once Sethe recognizes Beloved as her daughter, she struggles to make amends while Beloved grows plump and cruel.

Denver develops a new identity. At eighteen, she is self-centered, jealous, and lonely. Beloved becomes her dear companion. Gradually, Denver grows aware that Beloved's presence is destroying Sethe, who loses her job along with her meager income and begins to waste away. Denver, who has rarely ventured past her own yard because of the neighbors' hostility, realizes that only she can save her mother. Terrified, she walks down the road to seek work from strangers and, by accepting this responsibility, becomes a woman.

Morrison expected this painful, fiercely beautiful novel to be controversial. Instead, it was widely praised, receiving the Pulitzer Prize for fiction in 1988.

SUGGESTED READINGS

Carmean, Karen. "Trilogy in Progress: *Beloved* and *Jazz*." In *Toni Morrison's World of Fiction*. Troy, N.Y.: Whitston, 1993.

Rushdy, Ashraf H. A. "Daughters Signifyin(g) History: The Example of Toni Morrison's *Beloved*." *American Literature* 64, no. 3 (September, 1992): 567-597.

Schmudde, Carol E. "Knowing When to Stop: A Reading of Toni Morrison's *Beloved*." *College Language Association Journal* 37, no. 2 (December, 1993): 121-135.

—*Joanne McCarthy*

See also African American identity; Morrison, Toni; Slavery; *Song of Solomon*

Berry, Wendell

BORN: Henry County, Kentucky; August 5, 1934

PRINCIPAL WORKS: *Nathan Coulter*, 1960 (rev. ed. 1985); *A Place on Earth*, 1967 (rev. ed. 1983); *The Hidden Wound*, 1970; *A Continuous Harmony*, 1972; *The Memory of Old Jack*, 1974; *The Unsettling of America: Culture and Agriculture*, 1977; *The Gift of Good Land*, 1981; *Recollected Essays, 1965-1980*, 1981; *Standing by Words*, 1983; *Collected Poems: 1957-1982*, 1985; *The Wild Birds: Six Stories*, 1986; *Home Economics*, 1987; *Sabbaths: Poems*, 1987; *Remembering*, 1988; *What Are People For?*, 1990; *Fidelity: Five Stories*, 1992; *Sex, Economy, Freedom, and Community*, 1993; *Entries: Poems*, 1994; *Watch with Me: And Six Other Stories*, 1994; *Another Turn of the Crank*, 1995; *A World Lost*, 1996

IDENTITIES: European American; family; South

SIGNIFICANT ACHIEVEMENT: Berry's novels, short stories, poems, and essays are among America's best expressions of community and the connection between humanity and the earth.

Wendell Berry grew up in the 1930's and 1940's in a world of rural farming communities where people were wedded to place. This world was in jeopardy by the middle of the twentieth century. Berry's life and writing are attempts to preserve and promote the best traditions of that world: fidelity to home, family, and place; memory as an abiding and sustaining part of community; local nature as teacher and judge; rural work as art.

Having left his native home to study, teach, and write for a time in New York, California, and abroad, Berry in the early 1960's went home for good to live and work in his ancestral community of Port Royal, Kentucky. Beginning his literary career with a novel in 1960 and afterward periodically teaching English at the University of Kentucky and elsewhere, and while continually working his farm, Berry had amassed by the late 1990's a canon of over forty books of fiction, nonfiction, and poetry.

His work as a whole is a thorough and well-grounded exploration of the connections between people and land. Much of it examines the ecological and cultural damage caused by the escalating divorce between humans and the natural world. In *The Unsettling of America*, for example, perhaps his most widely known and influential book, Berry argues convincingly that many of the maladies of modern American culture are linked to the industrialization of agriculture.

Central to all of his work is the conflict between the cyclic and linear views of humankind's role in the world. The industrial worldview, governed by the doctrines of a linear vision, sees the earth as commodity. The worldview that Berry espouses, however, is governed by natural cyclic principles, which he delineates in an early and

Wendell Berry's writings reflect on the positive values of living close to the land. (Dan Carraco)

seminal essay, "Discipline and Hope." Among these principles are "atonement with the creation" rather than "the conquest of nature"; usufruct and relinquishment rather than possession; quality rather than quantity; renewal rather than newness; education as cultural process rather than training or programming. Many of the characters in Berry's fiction and narrative poetry are avatars of these principles.

SUGGESTED READINGS

Angyal, Andrew J. *Wendell Berry*. New York: Twayne, 1995.

Merchant, Paul, ed. *Wendell Berry*. Lewiston, Idaho: Confluence Press, 1991.

—*Morris Allen Grubbs*

See also *Collected Poems: 1957-1982*; Environment and identity; Rural life

Betsey Brown

AUTHOR: Ntozake Shange (Paulette Williams, 1948-   )

FIRST PUBLISHED: 1985

IDENTITIES: Adolescence and coming-of-age; African American; women

Betsey Brown tells the story of its thirteen-year-old title character's struggles with adolescence, with discovering who she is and who she might become. Ntozake Shange wrote the novel specifically to provide reading matter for adolescent African American girls. In her own youth, Shange could find no books to help her sort out her life: Books about young women were written by whites for whites, and most books by blacks were by and about men.

Betsey Brown is the oldest of five unruly children in a middle-class family. Like most adolescent girls, she feels separated from the rest of her family: They do not understand her; they do not appreciate her. Betsey's father wants her to grow up to lead her people to freedom. He wakes the children every morning with a conga drum and chanting and then leads them through a quiz on black history. All of the children can recite poetry by Paul Laurence Dunbar and Countée Cullen; they know the music of Dizzy Gillespie, Chuck Berry, and Duke Ellington. Betsey herself was once rocked to sleep by W. E. B. Du Bois. Betsey's mother fears that this exposure will limit her children instead of expanding them. She would like the children to grow up with nice middle-class manners and tastes. In many ways, she has denied her own heritage, her own identity. Eventually, she leaves the family for a time.

The story is firmly rooted in its specific time and place. In 1959, St. Louis took its first steps toward integrating its public schools, and the Brown children are among the first black children bussed to formerly all-white schools. The father has tried to prepare the children by giving them a firm sense of self and heritage. He is eager for them to enter the struggle for civil rights, even as the mother fears that they will be in danger if they become too involved.

A central issue of the novel is the importance of passing down one's cultural heritage. It is not until the mother decisively embraces her heritage that she can again join the family. While she is absent, the housekeeper assumes her role as mother and guide and teaches Betsey and the other children how to follow the dreams of both parents. They learn to stand up for themselves and honor their culture and history and also to be well-mannered and self-sufficient. When Jane returns, it is to a new Betsey, one who has taken the first steps in forging her adult identity.

SUGGESTED READINGS

Shange, Ntozake. "At the Heart of Shange's Feminism: An Interview." Interview by Neal A. Lester. *Black American Literature Forum* 24 (Winter, 1990): 717-730.

_____. "An Interview with Ntozake Shange." Interview by Neal A. Lester. *Studies in American Drama, 1945-Present* 5, no. 1 (1990): 42-66.

_____. *See No Evil: Prefaces, Essays, and Accounts 1976-1983*. San Francisco: Momo Press, 1984.

Tate, Claudia, ed. *Black Women Writers at Work*. New York: Continuum, 1983.

—Cynthia A. Bily

See also Adolescent identity; African American identity; Civil Rights movement; Shange, Ntozake

Biculturalism. *See* Multiculturalism

Big Blonde

AUTHOR: Dorothy Parker (1893-1967)
FIRST PUBLISHED: 1929
IDENTITIES: European American; women

"Big Blonde," a story of illusion and reality, avoidance and consequence, tells the tale of an aging party girl who makes a failed attempt at evading the truths of her life. Dorothy Parker's incisive characterization and witty narration explore the social facades that mask loneliness and desperation. The story won the O. Henry Memorial Prize for best short story of 1929.

Hazel Morse is a big blonde. Like the other big blondes in her company, her life is an unremarkable stream of parties and men. Accepting unquestioningly that popularity is important, she strives to endear herself to many men. Hazel builds her external identity around an image—that of the good sport. At first it is easy, but gradually it becomes a matter of practice, for her to be cheerful and bubbly, carefree and gay. She begins to tire of the game and decides to marry, believing that this will enable her to discard the facade she had so carefully constructed. She soon learns, however, that the Hazel she presented at parties is the Hazel her husband wants her to be. When she ceases to be that Hazel, her husband grows disenchanted and leaves. Alone and without financial support, she falls into relationships with a variety of men, each expecting the jolly, compliant Hazel in exchange for their patronage.

Hazel cannot escape the consequences of the life she has chosen, nor can she escape recognizing the mistakes upon which those consequences are built. Her understanding of her circumstances is at first subverted by her own confusion: "Her days were a blurred and flickering sequence, an imperfect film, dealing with the actions of strangers. . . . She never pondered if she might be better occupied doing something else." She falls deeper into the trap of posturings and pretensions, but certain realities nevertheless grow harder to deny; she wearies of always being accommodating and cheerful and begins to dwell on the things she must say and do to maintain her appeal. She hurries to banish these worries with alcohol. After a while, even the alcohol cannot blur the face of truth; she begins "to feel toward alcohol a little puzzled distrust, as toward an old friend who has refused a simple favor." Hazel turns to suicide. When she is unsuccessful at permanently blotting out her painful existence, and can no longer retreat into a blissful alcoholic stupor, she realizes that truth is immutable and is compelled to face the dismal future wrought by her own hands.

Parker's presentation of the conflict is drawn with bold strokes. Her economy with words brings a depth of understated emotion to the work and her trenchant commentary on Hazel's world is sardonic and tragic.

SUGGESTED READINGS
Calhoun, Randall. *Dorothy Parker: A Bio-Bibliography*. Westport, Conn.: Greenwood Press, 1993.
Gill, Brendan. Introduction to *The Portable Dorothy Parker*, by Dorothy Parker. New York: Viking Press, 1973.
Kinney, Arthur. *Dorothy Parker*. Boston: Twayne, 1978.
Meade, Marion. *Dorothy Parker: What Fresh Hell Is This?* New York: Villard Books, 1988.

—H. C. Aubrey

See also Appearance and identity; Parker, Dorothy

Bildungsroman and Künstlerroman

IDENTITIES: Adolescence and coming-of-age
DEFINITION: *Bildungsroman* and *Künstlerroman* are terms, German in origin, for novels of personal development.

The *Bildungsroman* is often called the novel of formation, the novel of education (in the broad sense of the word), or the apprenticeship novel. It shows the development of the protagonist's mind and character through a number of stages and a variety of experiences, often from childhood to early adulthood. He or she encounters conflicts and challenges, often including a spiritual crisis, which enable the protagonist to achieve a mature identity and eventually play his or her proper role in the world.

The *Künstlerroman*, also called the artist novel, is an important subtype of the *Bildungsroman*. It represents the growth of a writer or other artist into a condition of maturity that is marked by a recognition of art as the protagonist's calling and by a mastery of an artistic craft. A related subtype is the *Erziehungsroman* (educational novel), which also presents the development of a hero from childhood to maturity, and has one or more teachers directly guiding the protagonist. Another subtype that occasionally overlaps with the *Bildungsroman* is the picaresque novel, which narrates the escapades of a rascal who lives by his wits in a sordid environment. The picaresque novel, however, has its origins in Spain; the *Bildungsroman*, as one might expect, has its roots in German literature.

The concept of the *Bildungsroman* as an arduous journey from inwardness into social integration is central to German fiction. Johann Wolfgang von Goethe, Germany's greatest writer, is the composer of its most influential apprenticeship novel, *Wilhelm Meisters Lehrjahre* (1795-1796; *Wilhelm Meister's Apprenticeship*, 1812). Wilhelm Meister is the son of a prosperous merchant; from childhood on, he is fascinated by the theater. A business trip taken for his father brings him into contact with a group of actors, whom he then accompanies and finances. After many difficulties, Wilhelm and his fellow actors join a famous theatrical company, which then puts on a production of William Shakespeare's *Hamlet, Prince of Denmark* (c. 1600-1601). After the public has grown weary of Shakespeare, however, the troupe stages more trivial plays and Wilhelm becomes estranged from them, finding other ways to explore his personality. He learns to become practical and to make the choices appropriate to his temperament and talents. He decides to study to become a surgeon, seeking his true self by obtaining a solid place in the community. Through Wilhelm, Goethe advocates the satisfactions of a stable social existence, of inner harmony and self-certainty. Goethe also indicates that Wilhelm will continue to doubt, seek, and err, to have

The *Bildungsroman* in German literature

great difficulty achieving mastery of his life. Critics have often been divided in their appraisals of this novel, disparaging its vague descriptions and long digressions from the central theme, but also admiring its subtleties and profundity.

Thomas Mann   Thomas Mann, the foremost German fiction writer of the twentieth century, wrote several full-length novels as well as novellas that belong to the *Bildungsroman* and *Künstlerroman* genres. His greatest novel, *Der Zauberberg* (1924; *The Magic Mountain*, 1927), is a deliberate renewal of the Goethean form of the novel of education and maturation. Its central character, Hans Castorp, an apparently mediocre young Hamburg engineer, visits his cousin, who is a patient in a Swiss mountain sanatorium. Hans's visit turns into a seven-year stay when a doctor there diagnoses a tubercular infection in one of Hans's lungs. At the end of the book he returns to the plains to enlist—it is 1914, and World War I has begun. Mann makes Castorp the representative of a generation of European middle-class persons. He is a young man in search of an education and becomes exposed to a rich variety of people and ideas. The "magic" mountain where the sanatorium is located has a dual aspect: as a realm of death, and as a possibility of rebirth. Its hermetic isolation removes it from the normal concerns of the land below, and makes it a place for enlightenment. Castorp turns out to be intellectually and morally adventurous. Mann makes the mountain a microcosm of European society, with the Voltairian rationalist Settembrini, apostle of humanism and liberalism, outnumbered by the forces of darkness and dissolution. They are represented most dangerously by Claudia Chauchat and Leo Naphta. She is a Lilith figure, a sinister temptress, while the Jesuit Naphta is the dialectical opponent of Settembrini: an advocate of absolutism, terror, warfare, and sadism. In a late chapter, "Snow," Hans frees himself from his mentors and attains his own vision: He will understand life through his knowledge of death, health through his knowledge of disease, love through his knowledge of hatred.

In *Doktor Faustus: Das Leben des deutschen Tonsetzers Adrian Leverkühn, erzählt von einem Freunde* (1947; *Doctor Faustus: The Life of the German Composer Adrian Leverkühn as Told by a Friend*, 1948), Mann wrote a *Künstlerroman* which represents in symbolic form the decline and ruin of Germany before and during the Hitler era. The composer, Adrian Leverkühn, is the Faust figure who makes his pact with the devil by having sex with a prostitute he knows to be venereally infected. By contracting syphilis and separating himself from the world of the healthy, Leverkühn becomes a great composer, gaining twenty-four years of heightened genius. He cannot love or marry, however, without disastrous consequences, and the deliberate rebarbarization of German society by the Nazi regime is paralleled in Adrian's demoniac art and life. He holds bourgeois values in cold contempt. He ends his life after having fallen into total madness. The novel is an ambitious, complex tapestry that has awed many readers but also has discouraged a large number because of the novel's extreme slowness in its narrative pace, its pedantic tone, and its flatness of characterization.

Far livelier is Mann's comic masterpiece, *Bekenntnisse des Hochstaplers Felix Krull: Der Memoiren erster Teil* (1954; *Confessions of Felix Krull, Confidence Man: The Early Years*, 1955). In this novel, Mann stands the *Bildungsroman* on its head by linking it not only with the *Künstlerroman* but also with the picaresque novel. Like Wilhelm Meister, Felix is the son of a merchant who leaves his middle-class environment to roam the road, and sometimes speaks in Goethean aphoristic fashion. He is a criminal and an artist—a paradox that Mann never tired of illustrating. His thefts, masquerades, and other escapades are motivated less by greed or hunger than by the sheer joy of demonstrating his virtuosity. Mann's parodistic approach is both deflating, showing the maculate individual behind the immaculate charm of art, and exalting, emphasizing the inspired talents of an artist behind Felix Krull's roguery and narcissism.

The   Honoré de Balzac created about ninety interlocking novels to which he gave the comprehensive
***Bildungsroman* in**   title *La Comédie humaine* (1829-1848; *The Comedy of Human Life*, 1885-1893, 1896; also *The*
French literature   *Human Comedy*, 1895-1896, 1911). One of the most ambitious of these novels was a novel in three closely connected tales, *Illusions perdues* (1837-1843; *Lost Illusions*, 1893), which is a *Bildungsro-man* and a *Künstlerroman* of epic proportions and encyclopedic content. It features an intelligent,

The *Bildungsroman* and *Künstlerroman*
Twelve Key Works

1795-1796	Johann Wolfgang von Goethe's premier apprenticeship novel, *Wilhelm Meisters Lehrjahre*.
1837-1843	Honoré de Balzac's *Illusions perdues*.
1849-1850	Charles Dickens' *David Copperfield*, both a *Bildungsroman* and a *Künstlerroman*.
1903	Samuel Butler's *The Way of All Flesh*.
1913	D. H. Lawrence's *Sons and Lovers*.
1913-1927	Marcel Proust's *À la recherche du temps perdu*, perhaps the greatest single portrait of the artist in fiction.
1914-1915	James Joyce's *A Portrait of the Artist as a Young Man*, a *Künstlerroman*.
1915	*The Song of the Lark*, a *Künstlerroman* by Willa Cather.
1924	Thomas Mann's *Der Zauberberg*.
1929	Thomas Wolfe's *Look Homeward, Angel: A Story of the Buried Life*.
1947	Mann's *Doktor Faustus: Das Leben des deutschen Tonsetzers Adrian Leverkühn, erzählt von einem Freunde*.
1953	Saul Bellow's *The Adventures of Augie March*.

ambitious, but morally weak young poet, Lucien Chardon, who changes his last name to that of his noble maternal ancestors, de Rubempré. Lucien seeks shortcuts to fame and fortune in Paris by consorting with corrupt aristocratic women and entering a sordid literary and journalistic world where success depends on bribery, flattery, forgery, and character assassination. After he has brought ruin to his family, Lucien falls under the sway of a brilliant criminal, Vautrin, who paraphrases the discourses of Satan to Christ, yet becomes the head of the Paris police.

Marcel Proust wrote one of the world's greatest novels, *À la recherche du temps perdu* (1913-1927; *Remembrance of Things Past*, 1922-1931, 1981). It is a *Bildungsroman* and perhaps the greatest single portrait of the artist in fiction. The narrative is related in the first person by Marcel, whose life resembles but does not wholly duplicate that of the author. The book describes how Marcel's mind, by a progressive extension in breadth and depth, finally acquires that perception of life which distinguishes the vision of the artist from that of other people. The reader follows Marcel's life from childhood to middle age as he awakens to his literary vocation. Proust stresses the disparity between what an artist appears to be in person and what he is in his art. Thus a prudish music master turns out to be the great musician Vinteuil, and the writer Bergotte, whose books delight the young Marcel, proves to be an awkward, ridiculous-looking man. In the novel's course Marcel despairs of his literary talent and frequents the social world, mingling both with the bourgeoisie and high society. Yet society, friendship, love, and travel all prove disappointing. In the long novel's last section, Marcel, after several years of solitude and poor health, decides to spend an evening in the salon of his old friend, the Princesse de Guermantes. There he experiences a series of involuntary recollections that restore to him significant events of his life. He determines to create a work of art that will unite the essences of his disparate experiences and reflect the special world of the artist's consciousness. He decides, therefore, to write the novel that the reader has just read.

Charles Dickens' *David Copperfield* (1849-1850) is highly autobiographical. It is both a *Bildungsroman* and a *Künstlerroman*. As in *Wilhelm Meister's Apprenticeship*, the plot is frequently burdened with incidents that have no direct relation to David's story. Yet the work succeeds as a journey toward maturation, with David surviving loneliness and cruel exploitation in childhood, misplaced loyalties in some of his friendships, the early deaths of his parents, and marriage to Dora, a childish, shallow woman. After Dora's death, he has the good sense and luck to marry a suitably understanding woman and prepares to become, like his creator, a novelist. While David's placidity and calm make him an unlikely candidate for the role of artist, Dickens does stress his love of reading and storytelling, his gift for close observation, and his ability to withdraw into the shelter of his strong imagination.

The *Bildungsroman* in English literature

Samuel Butler wrote, in *The Way of All Flesh* (1903), a hymn of hatred for Victorian Christianity and for the Victorian bourgeois family, bitterly attacking their shams and false sanctities. The book is so overtly autobiographical that it employs letters written by Butler's relatives, and establishes the pattern of parent-son conflicts that was to be followed in such *Bildungsromane* as D. H. Lawrence's *Sons and Lovers* (1913) and James Joyce's *A Portrait of the Artist as a Young Man* (1914-1915). Butler's novel covers four generations of the Pontifex family. In the first three, overbearing fathers beat and bully their children and force them to become clergymen or be disinherited. Ernest Pontifex, Butler's hero and alter ego, is a pathetic failure much of his life. He does poorly at school and then as a minister, being physically weak and mentally morose. Extremely naïve, he entrusts his grandfatherly inheritance to a false friend who cheats him of it, becomes innocently entangled in legal snares, is disowned by his father, and marries out of mistaken kindness a former family maid who is an alcoholic. At last Ernest's luck changes: His wife is exposed as a bigamist, a wealthy aunt leaves him her fortune, and he is then content to lead a bachelor life, writing, painting, and reflecting upon the world's follies. Butler's work is a brilliant, embittered attack on the cant and cruelty of conventional bourgeois life.

Lawrence wrote *Sons and Lovers* as a highly autobiographical *Bildungsroman*. Paul Morel, the protagonist, is the youngest son of a mother, Gertrude, who has married beneath her station as a schoolteacher. She is married to a miner who declines into alcoholism and brutality. In her disillusionment, Gertrude turns to her children, particularly Paul, who is shy and sensitive and loves to read and paint. Their mutual devotion becomes intensely Oedipal, with Gertrude seeking to plan Paul's life and fulfill her fantasies through him. As a young man Paul tries to escape his mother's domination through two relationships with women. One is with the possessive Miriam, whose intellectual interests he shares, but whom he cannot enjoy physically; and another is with independent Clara, separated from her husband, who is emancipated and sensual. While Miriam trespasses on his mother's ground by demanding a wholly committed love, Clara offers Paul sexual bliss but remains emotionally unreachable. Paul reunites Clara with her husband, helps his cancer-stricken mother end her pain with an overdose of morphine, and says farewell to Miriam. He has freed himself for an autonomous new life.

Joyce composed what may be the most influential of English *Künstlerromane*, his *A Portrait of the Artist as a Young Man*. The book traces the education into young manhood and recognition of his calling as an artist of sensitive, brilliant, proud, and shy Stephen Dedalus, whose life is close to a literal transcript of Joyce's first twenty-two years. The work's early chapters relate Stephen's unrelievedly sad childhood, with the first few pages superbly presenting a continuum of the infant's tastes, smells, sights, and sounds. Soon Stephen begins to associate his feelings with phrases and show other literary interests. At Clongowes Wood College, then at University College in Dublin, Stephen is subjected to public humiliations by bullying teachers, only to assert his contempt for received authority and demand justice for himself. For a while he is tempted to join the Jesuit order, but then dedicates himself to a wholly different priesthood—that of literature. Eventually he frees himself from his declining family, Catholicism, and even his native country, using the strategies of silence, exile, and cunning. Stephen's last name refers to Daedalus, a mythical Athenian craftsman who made wings for himself and his son in order to escape a prison. The name symbolizes the artist with his aloofness from society, total absorption with his craft, and escape. These traits are Stephen's, and Joyce's. With this novel, the archetype of the artist figure became firmly established for modern literature in English.

The *Bildungsroman* in American literature

In 1899, Kate Chopin published *The Awakening*, which was largely neglected until the 1970's, when feminist critics began to reevaluate it as a *Bildungsroman* about a courageous woman's rebellion against a tedious, self-important, and selfish husband. The novel has gained a prominent place on the syllabi of many American fiction courses. The heroine, Edna Pontellier, awakens to her identity during a summer vacation spent with her two children and a stockbroker husband who joins the family on weekends. Tired of his cold self-centeredness after eight years of matrimony, she spends time with her landlady's handsome son, Robert, and turns seriously to what used to be only a hobby, painting. When her husband leaves on a long business trip, Edna sends the children away to their grandmother, moves into a cottage by herself, works hard at her painting, and takes Robert as her lover. When he leaves after a few weeks, she revisits the site of their first meeting and from there swims to her death in the sea. It is no wonder that the book's contemporary reviewers were shocked, charging the author with immorality, even though most of them admitted that the novel was engrossingly written in an intense, vivid style. Chopin's heroine, who was ahead of her time, has been welcomed by many readers as a bold, sensual, and imaginative nonconformist.

Willa Cather reviewed *The Awakening* disparagingly, declaring that the failure of romantic love had already been definitively explored by Gustave Flaubert. In a reference to Flaubert's masterpiece *Madame Bovary* (1857; English translation, 1886) Cather wrote that the world could do without a "Creole *Bovary*." In *The Song of the Lark* (1915) Cather wrote a *Künstlerroman*, creating a protagonist who, unlike Chopin's, is not caught in a conflict between her feminine and artistic needs. Cather's Thea Kronborg is as single-minded in her devotion to singing as Cather was to her writing. Born in a Colorado small town, Thea ends up as a Metropolitan Opera star. On her way a number of men become her mentors and benefactors. The family doctor encourages her; a piano teacher, symbolically named Wunsch (German for "desire"), assures her that she can achieve her fervent ambition; in Chicago, her voice teacher tells her she is, should she work hard enough, destined for greatness; and a rich St. Louis beer brewer, Fred, helps her financially and by betraying her. He entices her to Mexico for an affair, only to have Thea discover that he cannot marry her because he already has a wife. Thereafter she never again commits herself to a man, emphatically rejecting bourgeois benedictions for her art. In Cather's preface to a later edition of this novel she notes that she regretted having allowed her publisher to use "lark" in the book's title: Thea was more aptly to be called an eagle—willful, wild, powerful, and soaring to great heights. In the work's last section Thea triumphs as a singer, but at the cost of having become cold, hard, and unapproachably self-sufficient. Like Stephen Dedalus, she has sacrificed friends, family, and love on the altar of Almighty Art.

Thomas Wolfe drew virtually no distinction between his life and his art, so that his four enormous novels can be considered a single autobiographic *Bildungsroman* or *Künstlerroman*. The first, *Look Homeward, Angel: A Story of the Buried Life* (1929), deals with the childhood, youth, and early manhood of Eugene Gant, the name Wolfe gave his fictive self. Eugene is born in a small town in North Carolina and is descended from hill people. His parents are cruelly mismatched: The mother, Eliza, lusts for property and acquires land until she is wealthy, meanwhile nursing every penny. The father, Oliver, a stonecutter who cannot abide his wife's stinginess, is alcoholic and promiscuous but also wildly generous and lyrical; his cancerous condition forces him to return to Eliza after they have lived in separate houses for years. Eugene resembles his father in his strong imagination and appetite for life. At home he is taunted by siblings envious of his brilliance. His older brother Ben, the noblest of the Gants, is the only one who does not tease Eugene. Ben succumbs to pneumonia, probably because his mother fails to seek out a competent physician in time. Eugene's prospects brighten when he is permitted to attend a private school, where the principal's wife encourages his love of literature. At fifteen, he enrolls in the state university (Wolfe was a precocious student at Chapel Hill). After graduation, Eugene prepares to move north to attend graduate school, but first he is forced by his brothers and sister to sign a document forswearing his family inheritance, since they insist he has received its equivalent in school and college costs. Relieved to put his largely unhappy Southern upbringing behind him, Eugene sets out for northern adventures, to be chronicled in *Of Time and the River: A Legend of Man's Hunger in His Youth* (1935). Wolfe's last two, posthumously published novels, *The Web and the Rock* (1939) and *You Can't Go Home Again* (1940), revisit the terrain of his first two, with the hero's name changed to George Webber.

William Faulkner wrote the great novelette "The Bear" as part of a collection of tales published under the title *Go Down, Moses* (1942). Its protagonist is Isaac "Ike" McCaslin, and his age in the work varies from ten to young adulthood. Ike is taught a love for the wilderness, humility, patience, and self-reliance by Sam Fathers, son of an Indian chief. He acquires other qualities on his own. The quarry of the hunters is an immense, seemingly immortal bear, Big Ben, who has become legendary. The annual hunt for him is a near-sacred ritual presided over by Sam as priest of the wilderness. Sam traps and tames an initially wild great mongrel dog, Lion. When the bear appears to the hunters, neither Sam nor Ike are eager to kill it. One year Lion manages to stop Old Ben for a few seconds, but the bear escapes. The next year Lion jumps and clings to Old Ben's throat while one of the hunters plunges a knife into the bear's heart. With Old Ben's death, Sam collapses. The next day he and Lion die.

In the fourth part of "The Bear," Ike is twenty-one, the last living descendent of his male line and expected to take possession of his family's plantation. Instead, he renounces his inheritance. He gives two reasons: Nature belongs to all humanity, so no individual can own it. Second, he feels guilty for having descended from a line of slaveholders. In a long talk with his cousin Cass, Ike insists that white men settling America brought with them the curse of slavery, thereby repeating Adam's Original Sin. Moreover, Ike has discovered a shameful heritage: His grandfather not only begot a daughter with one of his slaves, that grandfather had also committed incest with that daughter. He seeks to expiate this ancestral sin by leading a simple life, even buying carpenter's tools to emulate Jesus. His marriage breaks up when his wife cannot persuade him to accept his inheritance. Sadly, Ike comes to realize that, with lumber companies felling timber, an irreparable divorce has occurred between humankind and nature.

Saul Bellow wrote a *Bildungsroman* that is also a picaresque novel in *The Adventures of Augie March* (1953). Augie is a Chicago-born Jewish youth who calls himself self-taught and free-styled. Bellow bounces the episodic, haphazard action of the book from Chicago to Mexico to Manhattan to an Atlantic voyage to France, as Augie quests for his true vocation and love. He finds neither, but he does make devoted friends and maintains a continued enthusiasm for existence. Augie is complex: He has the driving energy of a Ulysses but also the passive enervation of an Orpheus. His family, girlfriends, and employers often succeed in manipulating him but never in confining him. Above all he is Proteus, sliding away from full commitments, assuming varying guises, never sure of what he really wants and who he really is. In a revealing episode, Augie and his lover Thea travel to Mexico to train their captive American bald eagle to capture gigantic iguanas. The bird proves reluctant: Bitten by a small iguana, it pulls back; attacked by a large one, it retreats altogether. Augie applauds the eagle's cowardice; Thea is furious. Their relationship sunders, and Augie moves on, headlong and restless, insisting on a life untrammeled by theories.

In a pluralistic and fragmented world, a stable reality is often impossible to secure; a rootless spirit such as Augie March seems far more representative. The protagonists of many twentieth century novels often find themselves compelled to question and to reject the beliefs they inherit or experience. Even in a world that is often absurd and disordered, however, writers still compose *Bildungsromane* that show an individual's self-discovery and maturation.

SUGGESTED READINGS

Alden, Patricia. *Social Mobility in the English Bildungsroman*. Ann Arbor: University of Michigan Press, 1986. Treats the social and political views expressed in the fiction of George Gissing, Thomas Hardy, Arnold Bennett, and D. H. Lawrence. A solid, scholarly account.

Beebe, Maurice. *Ivory Towers and Sacred Faunts: The Artist as Hero in Fiction from Goethe to Joyce*. New York: New York University Press, 1964. Concentrates on *Künstlerromane* as well as short stories dealing with the artist by Goethe, Mann, Balzac, Flaubert, James, Lawrence, Joyce and a number of others.

Buckley, Jerome Hamilton. *Season of Youth: The Bildungsroman from Dickens to Golding*. Cambridge, Mass.: Harvard University Press, 1974. A leading authority on Victorian literature, Buckley writes with learning and grace.

Harper, Margaret Mills. *The Aristocracy of Art in Joyce and Wolfe*. Baton Rouge: Louisiana State University Press, 1990. Compares the autobiographical fiction of Joyce and Wolfe to each other's work and to each other's lives.

Lemon, Lee T. *Portraits of the Artist in Contemporary Fiction*. Lincoln: University of Nebraska Press, 1985. Lemon's governing thesis is that, between the generation of Joyce and that of John Fowles, the fictional portrait of the artist changed from that of an isolated hero contemptuous of the ordinary world to that of an ordinary human being trying to connect with nonartists who are equally important. The writers Lemon studies are Lawrence Durrell, Doris Lessing, and John Fowles, all British, the Australian Patrick White, and the American John Barth.

—Gerhard Brand

See also Adams, Henry; Bellow, Saul; Cather, Willa; Chopin, Kate; Conversion, religious; Environment and identity; Faulkner, William; Identity crisis; James, Henry; School; Wolfe, Thomas

Bilingualism

IDENTITIES: Latino; Native American
DEFINITION: Bilingualism is the use of two languages; such use may represent a cultural heritage.

At issue

Bilingualism in literature is a means by which writers may clarify, interpret, and communicate a community's cultural identity. The technique produces a synthesis of cultural attitudes, values, beliefs, and perspectives. One may argue that bilingualism in literature is a powerful way of maintaining a community's identity within a larger culture. For example, switching from English to Spanish and then back again is one way Chicanos can reflect the norms of their community. In addition, the use of two languages in one literary work produces compelling images.

Code switching

In Chicano literature, bilingualism, especially in poetry, may take two different forms. One form is to have one language on the even-numbered pages of a book and the other language on the odd-numbered pages; readers see more or less the same literary piece in two separate languages. This form lends itself most readily to poetry. A reader who is able to read only one of the two languages may, in a sense, read the work. Another form is to mix the two languages together in one piece of writing. This mixing is called code switching, after the linguistic term for the practice of switching languages while speaking. The advantage of code switching is that it may capture accurately the speech and experience of a bilingual person; the clear disadvantage, from a publishing standpoint, is that the audience for a code-switching bilingual work is limited to those who speak both languages.

Mexican American poetry

For Mexican Americans and others who are reared in an environment in which two languages are in constant use, bilingualism in literature may be seen as a means of establishing a distinctive sense of community identification. Further, many contemporary Mexican American poets have found that, by code switching, they may discover the most apt phrase or image. For those who are bilingual, bilingualism in literature enhances and accurately reflects their artistic powers. Mexican American literature is in its origins a hybrid of Spanish, Mexican, Indian, and Anglo elements, and it is a result of intense historical cultural conflict. Bilingualism in literature is a natural response to this cultural situation and is a technique for the clarification of a community's cultural identity.

The use of two languages within a single work of literature is not the exclusive domain of Mexican American writers. The technique, however, does hold political significance for this group. Chicano author Rudolfo A. Anaya, in his essay "Take the Tortilla out of Your Poetry" (in *Censored Books: Critical Viewpoints*, 1993), writes that the use of bilingualism in literature is one way to preserve cultural identity. He also states that bilingualism may often prevent certain writers from getting an unbiased reading from editors. Anaya's novel *Bless Me, Ultima* (1972) uses bilingualism as well as elements of religion and mysticism that are specific to Mexican American culture. Ironically, the book, which is set in New Mexico, was banned from high school classes in New Mexico.

Bilingualism has also been utilized in literary works by such groups as Puerto Ricans, Native Americans, and others. For example, while writing primarily in English, Native American poet Simon Ortiz incorporates words and speech patterns from his culture. Cormac McCarthy, winner of numerous fiction awards, also uses elements of bilingualism in his work. This device creates a heightened sense of contrasting cultural identities, which mirrors the philosophical and emotional conflicts within the characters. Other works, including Ernest Hemingway's *For Whom the Bell Tolls* (1940) and José Antonio Villarreal's *Pocho* (1959), are in one language (English) but that language is influenced in grammar and syntax by a second (Spanish). *Pocho* also uses bilingualism to chart its Chicano protagonist's assimilation. The beginning of the book includes a few Spanish words. As the character moves toward assimilation, the book no longer uses Spanish and its English is less affected by Spanish.

Alurista (Alberto Urista) is credited with being one of the pioneers of bilingualism in contemporary poetry. Using combinations of Spanish, English, and popular idiom, his work reveals the heritage of his community. Alurista's collections of poetry include *Floricanto en Aztlán* (1971), *Nationchild Plumaroja* (1972), and *Timespace Huracán* (1976). Other notable bilingual poets include Tino Villanueva and Jose Montoya. Some Chicana writers intermingle words that reflect issues of cultural identity and of gender.

A prime example of the cultural resonance of bilingualism among Mexican Americans is la Malinche, who figures in the history of the conquest of Mexico by the Spaniards in the early sixteenth century. Traditionally she has been thought of as one who betrayed her people by helping Hernán Cortés conquer the Aztecs, but she has been rehabilitated by some Chicana writers. La Malinche spoke Aztec, learned Spanish, and acted as Cortés' interpreter. She has been recast as the first Mexican bilingual, the first of a new breed of people who bridged cultures and adapted to a reality that was not of their making. La Malinche, many Chicana writers point out, found an important role in a world in which men were powerful, and male historians were responsible for her vilification. By rehabilitating la Malinche and by acknowledging their bilingualism, many Chicana writers endeavor to present the reality of the cultural identity of Mexican American women.

Another character often seen in Mexican American literature is the pachuco. This figure is drawn from twentieth century urban life and can be briefly described as a hero and a hoodlum. Luis Valdez's *Zoot Suit* (1978), the first Mexican American play to be produced on Broadway, has a narrator-chorus figure named El Pachuco. Valdez uses this spiritlike, bilingual character to symbolize the consciousness of urbanized Mexican Americans. In a similar way, Alfredo Vea, Jr.'s *La Maravilla* (1993) intermingles Spanish words, sounds, and phrases with English and even some Yaqui words to illustrate the confluence of cultures that helped to produce his character's distinctly Mexican American identity. Thus folklore, myth, and legend combine with bilingual elements to emphasize the hybrid cultural heritage of Mexican Americans.

SUGGESTED READINGS

De Dwyer, Carlota Cardenas, ed. *Chicano Voices*. Boston: Houghton Mifflin, 1985.

Gutierrez, Ramon, and Genaro Padilla, eds. *Recovering the U.S. Hispanic Literary Heritage: Chicano Literature*. Houston, Tex.: Arte Público Press, 1993.

Lattin, Vernon, ed. *Contemporary Chicano Fiction*. New York: Bilingual Press, 1986.

Simmen, Edward, ed. *North of the Rio Grande*. New York: Penguin Books, 1992.

Sommers, Joseph, and Tomás Ybarra-Frausto, eds. *Modern Chicano Writers: A Collection of Critical Essays*. Englewood Cliffs, N.J.: Prentice Hall, 1979.

—Lois Roma-Deeley

See also Acculturation; Anaya, Rudolfo A.; *Bless Me, Ultima*; Chicano identity; Latino American identity; *Pocho*; Villarreal, José Antonio

Biracial identity. *See* Mixed race and identity

Birth control. *See* Abortion and birth control

Bisexual identity

IDENTITIES: Gay, lesbian, and bisexual

Background

Writers have always sought to portray all aspects of life, including the myriad varieties of human sexuality. Traditional proscriptions against homosexuality have relegated depictions of non-heterosexual relationships to the periphery, or have cast them as evil, unhealthy, or dangerous to society.

It is nevertheless known that many men in ancient Greece had wives and male lovers, as vividly portrayed in the historical novels of Mary Renault. William Shakespeare's sonnets allude to the poet's attraction for the Dark Lady and for the beloved male friend. The work of nineteenth century poet Walt Whitman is filled with a generally inclusive eroticism. The novels of Virginia Woolf reflect her own bisexuality. The bisexual marriage of Vita Sackville-West, Woolf's lover, and Harold Nicolson is chronicled by their son, Nigel Nicholson, in *Portrait of a Marriage* (1973).

Transition

After the advent of the Gay Pride movement in the 1960's and 1970's, lesbians and gay men became more common in literature. Bisexuals remain relatively scarce in literature. In many cases, bisexuality is regarded, in literature as in life, as a transitional phase in the life of an essentially monosexual (exclusively homo- or heterosexual) character. James Baldwin's *Giovanni's Room* (1956), a celebrated novel of homosexual angst, offers a protagonist with male and female lovers who is clearly journeying toward homosexuality. Such works as Marge Piercy's *Small Changes* (1972), Albert Innaurato's *Gemini* (1977), and Tony Kushner's *Angels in America: A Gay Fantasia on National Themes* (1990) include characters passing through a bisexual stage. In Paul Monette's 1992 memoir *Becoming a Man*, he describes, after coming out as a gay man, a period of sexual activity with both genders; he delights in this capricious phase, but the underlying homosexual preference is never at issue.

Bisexuality is often presented amid clouds of confusion. Such works as Carson McCullers' *Reflections in a Golden Eye* (1941) and *The Ballad of the Sad Café* (1951) and Robert Anderson's *Tea and Sympathy* (1953) offer versions of this confusion. In these works, characters are attracted to both genders but are limited by societal assumptions or personal idiosyncrasy. A striking example of confusion is in David Henry Hwang's *M. Butterfly* (1988), in which cultural assumptions bring an unsuspecting heterosexual man into a long-term sexual affair with a male transvestite.

Exploration

Rather than be confused, some characters are unconcerned with labeling their sexuality. The sexual liberality of the late twentieth century led to many forms of sexual exploration, and a de

---

Bisexual Identity
Eleven Key Works

1936 In Djuna Barnes's *Nightwood*, the lead female character has affairs with males and females.	1977 Albert Innaurato's *Gemini* presents characters who have experimented with bisexuality.
1941 *Reflections in a Golden Eye*, by Carson McCullers, depicts a character's frustrated bisexuality.	1988 *M. Butterfly*, by David Henry Hwang, depicts how cultural assumptions can be misleading, as in the case of the heterosexual character who becomes involved with a male transvestite.
1953 In Robert Anderson's *Tea and Sympathy*, the main character is attracted to someone of the same gender, but does not act on her attraction.	1990 Tony Kushner's *Angels in America: A Gay Fantasia on National Themes* portrays characters going through a bisexual phase.
1956 In *Giovanni's Room*, by James Baldwin, the main character has male and female lovers.	1992 *Becoming a Man,* by Paul Monette, details the author's experience with bisexuality.
1967 The men in John Herbert's *Fortune and Men's Eyes* explore bisexuality not out of curiosity, but because they are in jail.	1994 E. Lynn Harris' *Just as I Am* characterizes bisexuals in a positive light.
1972 *Small Changes*, by Marge Piercy, includes characters who engage in bisexuality.	

---

facto bisexuality has been part of a larger identity of openness and freedom. Ernest Hemingway's unfinished *The Garden of Eden* (1986) follows a newlywed couple who welcome another woman into their relationship. In Djuna Barnes's *Nightwood* (1936), a woman takes a series of male and female lovers amidst the decadence of American expatriate life in Paris. Canadian dramatist Brad Fraser, in *Unidentified Human Remains and the True Nature of Love* (1991), offers a group of variously self-identified characters searching for love and identity in a fluid sexual landscape. In *Can Can* (1991), a one-act play by Romulus Linney, a young housewife takes a female lover. In these works, questions of sexuality and fidelity never enter the equation; the gay-or-straight dichotomy and the bisexual label become irrelevant.

Particular situations foster other forms of bisexual exploration. John Herbert's *Fortune and Men's Eyes* (1967) and, more affirmatively, John Cheever's *Falconer* (1977) depict situational bisexuality among incarcerated males. In a different vein, Isaac Bashevis Singer's fantastical Yiddish tales occasionally include spiritually motivated sexual exploration: In "Teibele and Her Demon," the heroine invites her best friend to bed in order to please her demon lover.

Affirmative bisexual identity

Exploration may translate into an affirmative bisexual identity. In the genre of science fiction, writers have created worlds in which bisexuality is the cultural norm. Ursula K. Le Guin, in *The Left Hand of Darkness* (1969), and Robert A. Heinlein, in *Friday* (1982), depict openly bisexual characters. In *Woman on the Edge of Time* (1976), Marge Piercy offers a future in which women, freed from childbearing, explore lesbian relationships while maintaining their connections with men. Leaving behind contemporary societal baggage, writers imagine bisexuality to be a normative identity.

Positive depictions of bisexuals are, however, rare. In Harvey Fierstein's *Torch Song Trilogy* (1979), the bisexual man is a threat to the gay identity of his lover. In Armistead Maupin's *Tales of the City* (1980), he is the image of sleaze and marital deceit. *Beyond Therapy*, Christopher Durang's 1982 satire, includes a vapid bisexual in a world of equally quirky monosexuals. Thus, bisexuals are portrayed most often either as menaces to straight and gay societies or as careless clowns in the circus of sexual liberty.

As awareness of human sexuality expands, however, and as gay culture embraces bisexuals and transgendered persons, affirmative portrayals emerge. A classic work is James Baldwin's *Another Country* (1960), in which an array of ethnically diverse characters seek love and sexual fulfillment. Baldwin, himself primarily homosexual, infused the work with respect, compassion, and complexity. Baldwin's seeming heir is E. Lynn Harris, whose first three novels—*Invisible Life* (1994), *Just as I Am* (1994), and *And This Too Shall Pass* (1996)—explore bisexuality in an African American milieu, including positively self-identified bisexuals and supportive gays and straights. Marge Piercy's *Summer People* (1989) offers an affirmative portrait of a married couple and their shared female lover. Like the experience of other oppressed or unconventional groups, the emergence of bisexuals in literature validates the life choices of all who sense that they belong somewhere between exclusive homosexuality and exclusive heterosexuality.

SUGGESTED READINGS

DeCecco, John P., and Michael G. Shively, eds. *Bisexual and Homosexual Identities*. Binghamton, N.Y.: Haworth Press, 1994.

Garber, Marjorie. *Vice Versa: Bisexuality and the Eroticism of Everyday Life*. New York: Simon & Schuster, 1995.

Geller, Thomas, ed. *Bisexuality: A Reader and Sourcebook*. Ojai, Calif.: Times Change, 1990.

Hutchins, Loraine, and Lani Kaahumanu, eds. *Bi Any Other Name*. Boston: Alyson Publications, 1991.

Klein, Fritz. *The Bisexual Option*. Binghamton, N.Y.: Haworth Press, 1978.

—Barry Mann

See also AIDS; Alther, Lisa; Baldwin, James; Coming out; Erotic identity; Gay identity; Lesbian identity; Piercy, Marge; Women and identity

Bishop, Elizabeth

BORN: Worcester, Massachusetts; February 8, 1911

DIED: Boston, Massachusetts; October 6, 1979

PRINCIPAL WORKS: *North & South*, 1946; *Poems: North & South—A Cold Spring*, 1955; *Questions of Travel*, 1965; *The Complete Poems*, 1969; *Geography III*, 1976; *The Complete Poems 1927-1979*, 1983

IDENTITIES: European American; gay, lesbian, and bisexual; women

SIGNIFICANT ACHIEVEMENT: Often referred to as a "poet's poet," Bishop is regarded as one of America's finest postwar poets, a master of the poetic craft.

Much of Elizabeth Bishop's work is informed by a childhood of dislocation and loneliness. Fatherless at eight months of age, Bishop and her widowed mother moved from Massachusetts to Nova Scotia. When Bishop was four, her mother was permanently institutionalized after several nervous breakdowns, and Bishop never saw her again. After a brief, unhappy stay with her father's family, she was placed in her aunt's care in Boston. Thus travel and identity as a guest are two of Bishop's most persistent metaphors.

After graduation from Vassar College, Bishop traveled extensively in Europe, finally settling in Key West, Florida, for nine years. In 1946, she received an award for her first book of poetry, *North & South*. Using simple, everyday occurrences of tropical life as subject matter, she established her reputation as a master of poetic craft, exploring themes of isolation, loneliness, and self-discovery through allegory, myth, and exquisite observation of detail.

On a visit to South America, Bishop fell in love with a wealthy acquaintance, Lota Soares. Bishop remained in Brazil with Lota for fifteen years, where she completed the Pulitzer Prize-winning *Poems: North & South—A Cold Spring*. These poems revisit Nova Scotia, her travel themes. Images of Brazil with its lush tropics, and political unrest and race and class distinctions would figure prominently in her later books.

Elizabeth Bishop has been widely hailed as one of the finest poets of her time. (J. L. Castel)

When her relationship with Lota fell apart, Bishop returned to the United States in 1965, first teaching at the University of Washington in Seattle and, in 1970, at Harvard. Until the 1980's, literary critics tended to focus on her stylistic precision in form and imagery. Her work was viewed as sensitive to social problems but not overtly political; rather, her poems were seen as objective and impersonal inquiries into unanswered metaphysical questions. Intimacy is established through conversational tone and language, pulling the reader into a shared quest to discover the nature of reality. Recent scholarship, however, suggests a feminist rereading of her work. Although Bishop resisted the classification of "woman writer," many critics believe that Bishop's poems are informed by issues of race, class, and gender and allude to her homosexuality, alcoholism, and depression. They point to poems such as the four "Songs for a Colored Singer," in which Bishop explores the limitations placed by men on women. From this perspective, Bishop can be viewed not only as a major literary force but also as an important feminist voice.

SUGGESTED READINGS

Lombardi, Marilyn May, ed. *Elizabeth Bishop: The Geography of Gender*. Charlottesville: University Press of Virginia, 1993.

Miller, Brett Candish. *Elizabeth Bishop: Life and the Memory of It*. Berkeley: University of California Press, 1993.

Travisano, Thomas J. *Elizabeth Bishop: Her Artistic Development*. Charlottesville: University Press of Virginia, 1988.

—Susan Chainey

See also Erotic identity; Feminism; *Geography III*; Lesbian identity; Women and identity

Black Boy: A Record of Childhood and Youth

AUTHOR: Richard Wright (1908-1960)
FIRST PUBLISHED: 1945
IDENTITIES: Adolescence and coming-of-age; African American; South

Black Boy: A Record of Childhood and Youth stands as a classic African American autobiography. It tells of Richard Wright's escape from figurative slavery in the South to freedom in the North. The text opens in 1912 on Wright's earliest memory at age four. Richard is living in Jackson, Mississippi, in the crowded home of his grandparents. The household includes Richard, his mother, father, brother, and his uncle, and it replicates the subhuman living conditions of slaves.

Richard's father is illiterate and an unskilled laborer; in search of work, he moves his family to another state, which initiates Richard's life of emotional and physical instability. These disruptions occur in three cycles. From age four to age twelve, Richard moves frequently from Mississippi to Tennessee to Arkansas and back again. From age twelve to age seventeen, he remains in Jackson. From age seventeen to age nineteen, he escapes, first to Tennessee and then to Illinois. Before age twelve, Richard suffers abandonment by his father, life in an orphanage, street life, heavy drinking, and the illness of his mother.

Wright employs the literary technique of naturalism to portray the racial and environmental factors that create a hostile world for Richard. Whites consider African Americans to be inferior because of their skin color, and Richard hears of violent acts against African Americans in the form of murders, lynchings, and beatings. He personally experiences verbal threats, physical assaults, and animal attacks. Whites pay African Americans low wages to keep them economically enslaved and unable to escape the mandated segregated housing, which is substandard. Richard consistently suffers from hunger, poor housing, insufficient clothing, and erratic schooling.

Richard grows up an isolated figure because he does not fit the servile demeanor required of African Americans to live in the South. He rejects religion since he cannot understand how a white God allows his mother, family, and community to suffer. In turn, they assail his reading and writing of fiction, which his grandmother charges is "Devil's work." The school principal even denounces Richard when he refuses to deliver the stock valedictory speech of humility at his graduation ceremony from ninth grade. Whites, too, attack Richard for being a "smart Negro" when he undertakes menial jobs in private homes or at businesses during his stay in the South.

Richard resists these oppressive forces in his quest for knowledge and for freedom. At nineteen, he discovers the writer H. L. Mencken, and decides that he, too, wants to become a writer to "wage war with words." *Black Boy* concludes in 1927, with Richard's flight to the North in the tradition of former slaves before him.

SUGGESTED READINGS

Fabre, Michel. *The Unfinished Quest of Richard Wright*. New York: William Morrow, 1973.

Stepto, Robert T. *Behind the Veil: A Study of Afro-American Narrative*. 2d ed. Champaign: University of Illinois Press, 1979.

Wright, Richard. *Conversations with Richard Wright*. Edited by Keneth Kinnamon and Michel Fabre. Jackson: University Press of Mississippi, 1993.

—Virginia Whatley Smith

See also African American identity; American identity: South; Wright, Richard

Black church

IDENTITIES: African American; religion

At issue

The black church has been described as the single greatest institution in the black community. It has traditionally served the spiritual, social, cultural, educational, and political needs of its clientele. The black church is distinctive in a number of ways, owing to the early intermixing of African religious beliefs and practices with Christian influences. Although Christianity has historically been the form of religion most frequently practiced in African American communities, it was not successful in eradicating traditional thoughts and practices of the slave societies into which it was introduced. From the rhetorical style of ministers to its music, the black church has influenced the cultural life of America in general, and the black church has shaped the content and form of African American literature in specific ways.

History

The black church evolved out of the contradiction of white slave owners' treating Africans and African Americans as soulless and nonhuman while encouraging them to seek Christian salvation. During the time of the American Revolution white church officials suspended their attention to the religious education of blacks. Blacks in turn responded to their incomplete indoctrination by turning white religious ideas in the direction of surviving African traditions, thereby conceiving their own vision of Christianity. Free blacks began to establish their own churches as early as 1776.

Representation in literature

African Americans have traditionally written from a religious perspective. Jupiter Hammon's poem "An Evening Thought: Salvation by Christ with Penitential Cries" (1761) is reported to be the first poem published by a black man in America. It reflects a strong influence of Methodism and the Wesleyan Revival present in America during the mid-eighteenth century. Phillis Wheatley's volume *Poems on Various Subjects, Religious and Moral* (1773) treats, among other things, recognition of the African's possession of a soul. Similarly, spiritual and secular narratives written during the eighteenth and nineteenth centuries reflect a strong religious influence. The spiritual narratives of Julia Foote, Jarena Lee, Zelpha Elaw, and Amanda Barry Smith, among others, suggest a spiritual authority that overtly challenges traditional female roles.

As the black church gained in prominence, writers turned to it as a feature of black life to complement historical and sociological accounts. W. E. B. Du Bois' *The Souls of Black Folk* (1903) outlines the characteristics of the black church with observations on preachers, music, and spiritual, social, and political concerns. Carter G. Woodson's *History of the Negro Church* (1921) posits the church as central to all enterprises—economic, education, and political—in the black community. Benjamin E. Mays' *The Negro's God as Reflected in His Literature* (1938) challenges stereotypes, asserting that "the Negro's ideas of God grow out of the social situation in which he finds himself."

Creative works depicting the black church are numerous and varied. In such works, the church may be used as central organizing feature or as backdrop to black community life. Charles W.

Chesnutt's *Marrow of Tradition* (1901) features the character Sandy, who is censured by the Methodist church for having participated in a cakewalk. James Weldon Johnson's *God's Trombones: Seven Negro Sermons in Verse* (1927) provides a tribute to the rhetorical skills and poetic impulses of the preacher's sermon. Zora Neale Hurston's first novel, *Jonah's Gourd Vine* (1934), depicts the religious life of a small Southern community. Its central character, John Buddy, is a preacher who is something of a heroic figure in the black community. Later, in her award-winning autobiography *Dust Tracks on a Road* (1942), Hurston depicts a rivalry between Methodist and Baptist members of the famed community of Eatonville, Florida.

James Baldwin's *Go Tell It on the Mountain* (1953) is the story of a black religious tradition. The novel explores the religious conversion of John Grimes, a youth who, on his fourteenth birthday, accepts his family's faith in a Harlem storefront church. Maya Angelou's comic treatment of the visiting preacher at the dinner table in her *I Know Why the Caged Bird Sings* (1969) also enhances the black church's representation in African American literature.

Implications for identity

As Woodson asserts in his 1939 article "The Negro Church, an All-Comprehending Institution":

> The Negro church touches almost every ramification of the life of the Negro. . . . All efforts of the Negro in things economic, educational and political have branched out of or connected in some way with the rise and development of the Negro church.

Woodson's observation extends to the creative enterprise of literature. The presence of the black preacher, the rivalry between Methodists and Baptists, the struggle of women to hold leadership positions in the church, the spirituality engendered by Fundamentalist sects, and the church as social stabilizing force or social outlet are all accounted for in the literature from the eighteenth century to the twentieth.

In addition to full-blown treatments of religious life, central to fiction and histories, such works as Jean Toomer's *Cane* (1923), James Baldwin's *The Fire Next Time* (1963), and Toni Morrison's *Song of Solomon* (1977) evoke the spiritual power derived from Scripture.

SUGGESTED READINGS

Du Bois, W. E. B. *The Souls of Black Folk: Essays and Sketches*. 1903. Reprint. New York: Dodd, Mead, 1961.

Mays, Benjamin E. *The Negro's God as Reflected in His Literature*. Boston: Chapman & Grimes, 1938.

Simpson, George Eaton. *Black Religions in the New World*. New York: Columbia University Press, 1978.

Spiritual Narratives. New York: Oxford University Press, 1988.

—*Adele S. Newson*

See also Baldwin, James; Christianity and Christian Fundamentalism; Religion and identity

Black English

IDENTITIES: African American

DEFINITION: Black English or "ebonics," African American vernacular, has often been used in literary works.

Background

The term "black English" was coined during the 1960's to identify African American language styles. Beginning in the 1940's with seminal studies by Lorenzo Turner of the Gullah dialect, the investigation of black English was continued by such scholars as J. L. Dillard, Geneva Smitherman, Molefi Kete Asante, and Joseph Holloway.

Generally, Africans brought to North America during slavery were denied formal education. Having their own languages, they adapted linguistic patterns of their mother tongues, creating dialects that blended African and English expressions. The syntactical and grammatical structures of African languages merged with English forms. Black English has been primarily associated with the Southern states, although Africans were also transported to the North. Furthermore, internal migration resulted in the transfer of Southern black dialects to Northern urban areas.

Recognized by its alteration of standard English verbs and pronouns, suggesting the influence of grammatical structures of African languages, black English is also identified by a lexicon. The study of English spoken by African Americans can also be linked to black folklore in which altered spelling has been used to approximate the sound of black dialect.

Black English can be found in folktales, narratives, short stories, novels, poems, and dramas. Although slave narratives were primarily written in standard English, black language styles are often elements of those texts. In Frederick Douglass' *Narrative of the Life of Frederick Douglass: An American Slave* (1845), there is an allusion to a plantation song that contains vernacular. One of the characters in Harriet Jacobs' *Incidents in the Life of a Slave Girl* (1861) uses such words as "nebber" (never) and "chile" (child).

Black English is also present in the first novels written by African Americans, many of which portray plantation life. William Wells Brown's *Clotel: Or, The President's Daughter* (1853), perhaps the first novel written by an African American, and his play, *The Escape: Or, A Leap for Freedom* (1856), contain passages of vernacular. To a limited degree, Frank J. Webb's *The Garies and Their Friends* (1857) characterizes enslaved Africans through dialect that includes such words as "gwine" (going). Harriet E. Wilson's *Our Nig* (1859), the first novel published by an African American in the United States (*Clotel* was first published in England), uses black English in its treatment of the North. Martin Delany in *Blake: Or, The Huts of America* (1859), set in Mississippi, uses the slave experience as a vehicle for black dialect.

Black English was primarily used to give authenticity to dialogue voiced by folk characters, whose speech patterns differ from those of the mulatto elites. In the post-Reconstruction period, black English was used to portray folk characters in Frances E. W. Harper's novel, *Iola Leroy: Or, Shadows Uplifted* (1892). Charles Chesnutt's *The Conjure Woman* (1899) furthered the plantation tale, which was a popular form in American literature. One story in the collection, "The Goophered Grapevine," offers an extensive use of black English in the characterization of Julius McAdoo, who uses such words as "truf" (truth) and "vimya'd" (vineyard).

Certain European American writers also fashioned literary works that used black English. George Washington Cable depicts creole culture in New Orleans in *Old Creole Days* (1879), and Joel Chandler Harris popularized plantation folklore with his Uncle Remus books, which began with *Uncle Remus, His Songs and His Sayings* (1880). Mark Twain also uses elements of black speech in *Adventures of Huckleberry Finn* (1884), in which Jim uses such expressions as "sich" (such) and "sumfn" (something). These and other examples of writings by European Americans who use black English have sometimes been considered to foster racial stereotypes.

By the end of the nineteenth century, black English had become a standard in African American dialect poetry. The authors James Edwin Campbell and Paul Laurence Dunbar are the most celebrated practitioners of the form. Campbell's *Echoes from the Cabin and Elsewhere* (1895) represents the height of his poetic achievement, and Dunbar's third collection of poetry, *Lyrics of Lowly Life* (1896), which contains an introduction by William Dean Howells, helped launch Dunbar to national prominence. "When de Co'n Pone's Hot" is typical of his dialect poetry; however, Dunbar also wrote poems and fictional works in standard English.

In the twentieth century, black and white American writers have used black English. Eugene O'Neill's *All God's Chillun Got Wings* (1924), whose title uses vernacular, was followed by Garland Anderson's *Appearances* (1925), one of many dramas by black playwrights during the 1920's. A series of plays by black women writers show the varied uses of black English. Eulalie Spence's *Undertow* (1929), set in Harlem, exemplifies the transfer of vernacular to the urban North. In the play, Hattie, a Harlem resident, uses such expressions as " 'cept" (accept) and "sence" (since). Georgia Douglas Johnson's *A Sunday Morning in the South* (1925) also contains vernacular, as did most folk plays, which were particularly suited to black dialect. Jean Toomer's *Balo* (1924), John Matheus' *'Cruiter* (1926), and Randolph Edmonds' *Bad Man* (1934) are examples of folk plays that employ black English.

Nineteenth century

The modern era

Certain Southern white writers continued to use black language styles, most notably William Faulkner, whose novels and short stories often depict black characters. In *The Sound and the Fury* (1929), Dilsey and Luster speak in black English; short stories such as "That Evening Sun" also show this trait in Faulkner's writing. Another popular Southern writer, Julia Mood Peterkin, re-creates the patterns of Gullah in *Scarlet Sister Mary* (1928).

However, the most pronounced use of black English in the modern era has come from African American writers. During the Harlem Renaissance of the 1920's, Langston Hughes and Sterling Brown were advocates of black vernacular in an era that viewed the dialect poetry of Dunbar as anachronistic, a remnant of plantation identity. The younger generation of writers faced a dilemma in their use of black English. They wanted to avoid the association with plantation stereotypes, but they also sought a genuine treatment of folk sources. Brown, who extended the tradition of Dunbar, valorized folk expression in such poems as "Odyssey of Big Boy," in which there are references to folkloric figures, Casey Jones, Stagolee, John Henry, and Jazzbo. The vernacular voice in Hughes's "Mother to Son" (1922) is evoked in such lines as "I'se been a-climbin' on." Hughes's blues and jazz poems in *The Weary Blues* (1926) contain expressions of the rural and urban folk. Certain post-Harlem Renaissance poems by Hughes, such as "Motto," use urban black expressions, such as "dig," "cool," and "jive."

In fiction, Rudolph Fisher and Zora Neale Hurston were among the Harlem Renaissance writers who presented the authentic voice of black English, a sign of their attention to cultural identity. Fisher's Harlem short stories portraying Southern black characters who have migrated to the North reflect the transfer of vernacular from rural to urban settings, as in "The South Lingers On." Hurston, who considered folk culture a source for anthropological research, was the most prominent advocate of black vernacular during this period. Her short stories, such as "Spunk," and her most celebrated work, *Their Eyes Were Watching God* (1937), use the black speech patterns of Eatonville, Florida, the first black town in the United States to be incorporated. Hurston's characters use the metaphorical expressions of rural speech influenced by local references and folk humor. Her works replicate the unique identity of Eatonville society.

Black English is also a feature of post-Harlem Renaissance African American literature about the urban North. Richard Wright's *Native Son* (1940), Ann Petry's *The Street* (1946), and Ralph Ellison's *Invisible Man* (1952) use black English as a natural rather than overstated characteristic of dialogue. In the 1950's, James Baldwin and playwright Lorraine Hansberry used black expressions to define particular characters. In Hansberry's *A Raisin in the Sun* (1959), Mama's black English is especially memorable. Baldwin's *Go Tell It on the Mountain* (1953), set in Harlem, suggests the black church as a source of language styles. Chester Himes, a writer of black detective fiction, gives a black voice to his Harlem characters in *For Love of Imabelle* (1957) and his other novels in the series. Baldwin's plays of the 1960's, such as *The Amen Corner* (1957) and *Blues for Mister Charlie* (1964), exemplify the way black drama is sustained by authentic black vernacular, which is part of the verbal identity of Northern life.

The black arts era and beyond

In poetry, African American writers of the 1960's and 1970's continued to avoid the servility associated with dialect. Gwendolyn Brooks, Don Lee, Amiri Baraka, Jayne Cortez, and Sonia Sanchez are among the numerous black poets who updated black English during the protest era in which folk dialect suggested oppression. Black poets used the rhythmic patterns of black speech closely related to the phrasing of jazz melodies. However, varied spelling, similar to alterations in nineteenth century dialect, were sometimes employed along with black expressions of the day. For example, in "blues," Sonia Sanchez uses "u/shd" (you should), suggesting protest through the modification of standard forms.

Prominent African American novelists have also used black phrasing. Toni Morrison's novels, including *Sula* (1973), *Beloved* (1987), and *Jazz* (1992), are known for their replication of African American voices. Alice Walker's *The Third Life of Grange Copeland* (1970) and *The Color Purple* (1982) reproduce black Southern vernacular. Considered a Southern black novelist, Ernest J. Gaines maintains the rural voice by re-creating the syntactical flow of black speech. Gaines's *The*

Autobiography of Miss Jane Pittman (1971) and *A Gathering of Old Men* (1983) reproduce the black dialect of Louisiana.

African American playwrights have continued to use black English as an authenticating characteristic of the black literary identity. Douglass Turner Ward's *Day of Absence* (1966), set in a Southern town, Ntozake Shange's *for colored girls who have considered suicide/when the rainbow is enuf: a choreopoem* (1976), portraying young urban black women, and August Wilson's dramatic project, which includes a series of plays set in various decades of the twentieth century, all rely on dialogue based on black speech patterns. Wilson's *Ma Rainey's Black Bottom* (1985), *The Piano Lesson* (1990), and *Seven Guitars* (1996) show a sustained interest in black language styles.

African American literature has been maintained by writers who have recognized that the sound of black English gives validity and cultural identity to their literary works.

SUGGESTED READINGS

Asante, Molefi K. "African Elements in African-American English." In *Africanisms in American Culture*, edited by Joseph E. Holloway. Bloomington: Indiana University Press, 1990. A very informative study of the African sources influencing African American vocal patterns.

Baker, Houston A., Jr. *Blues, Ideology and Afro-American Literature: A Vernacular Theory*. Chicago: University of Chicago Press, 1984. A theoretical study of African American discourse using the blues as conceptual framework.

Dillard, J. L. *Black English: Its History and Usage in the United States*. New York: Random House, 1972. One of the major statements emerging from the linguistic analysis of black language patterns.

Gates, Henry Louis, Jr. *The Signifying Monkey: A Theory of African-American Literary Criticism*. New York: Oxford University Press, 1988. Uses the trickster figure as a basis for analyzing texts by such authors as Hurston and Walker.

Holloway, Karla F. C. *The Character of the Word: The Texts of Zora Neale Hurston*. Westport, Conn.: Greenwood Press, 1987. Focuses on the sources of Hurston's complex uses of black language styles.

North, Michael. *The Dialect of Modernism: Race, Language, and Twentieth-Century Literature*. New York: Oxford University Press, 1994. A study of modernist writing and its connection to standard language patterns.

Smitherman, Geneva. *Talkin and Testifyin: The Language of Black America*. Detroit: Wayne State University Press, 1986. A highly informed study of black language patterns and modes of discourse from African origins to popular urban variations.

Turner, Lorenzo D. *Africanisms in the Gullah Dialect*. Chicago: University of Chicago Press, 1949. A pioneer study of African linguistic elements in the Gullah dialect.

—*Joseph McLaren*

See also African American identity; Black church; Dunbar, Paul Laurence; Harlem Renaissance; Hurston, Zora Neale; Slavery; Wilson, August

Black Feeling, Black Talk

AUTHOR: Nikki Giovanni (1943-   )
FIRST PUBLISHED: 1968
IDENTITIES: African American

Although Nikki Giovanni's reputation as a revolutionary poet is based upon this work, fewer than half of its poems address the theme of revolution. Critics point to often quoted incendiary poems in this collection to indicate Giovanni's revolutionary stance. They also note the poems about political figures and poems addressing black identity to illustrate Giovanni's militancy. These poems are important in this volume, but they are not Giovanni's sole concern.

What has been overlooked are the highly personal poems. In tallying the themes that appear in this work, it becomes apparent that love, loss, and loneliness are important to Giovanni. She also writes personal tributes and reminiscences to those who helped shape her life and ideology. Then there are Giovanni's personal responses to political events. She mourns the deaths of John F. Kennedy, Martin Luther King, Jr., and Robert Kennedy. She states that the 1960's were one long funeral day. She also notes atrocities in Germany, Vietnam, and Israel and compares them to 1960's America.

Black Feeling, Black Talk, then, is a compilation of political and personal poetry. Amid calls for revolution and affirmations of blackness are an insistence on maintaining one's individuality in the face of the political. There is also the importance of acknowledging the contributions of others in one's development. Thus, what is central to Giovanni's revolution is helping people to think about new ways of viewing and understanding their lives, personally and politically. *Black Feeling, Black Talk* is not a call for revolution that will destroy the world. The book is about how people, in the words of its final poem, may "build what we can become when we dream."

SUGGESTED READINGS

Fabio, Sarah Webster. "Black Feeling, Black Talk, Black Judgment." *Black World*, December, 1970, 102-104.

Fowler, Virginia. *Nikki Giovanni*. New York: Twayne, 1992.

Lee, Don L. *Dynamite Voices I: Black Poets of the 1960's*. Detroit: Broadside Press, 1971.

—Paula C. Barnes

See also African American identity; Civil Rights movement; *Gemini*; Giovanni, Nikki

Black Ice

AUTHOR: Lorene Cary (1956-   )
FIRST PUBLISHED: 1991
IDENTITIES: African American; family; Northeast; women

Black Ice, Lorene Cary's autobiographical novel, chronicles her teen years during the 1970's. At the age of fourteen, she was transplanted from her home in West Philadelphia into the white, male terrain of St. Paul's, an exclusive boarding school in Concord, New Hampshire. Cary recalls her struggle and determination to succeed as an ambitious scholarship student under disquieting circumstances. The book records her efforts to secure and define her identity as a young black woman.

Cary's resolve is born from a sense of duty to her family, ancestors, and community. She carries her mother's proud defiance and her father's fortitude with her as she encounters pain and triumph at St. Paul's. She meets and befriends students and adults from many diverse backgrounds and learns that alienation, ignorance, love, and devotion are not bound by racial or cultural boundaries.

Cary discloses a realm of cathartic and celebratory firsts with poignant sensibility and perception. A seemingly innocent rendezvous results in her first sexual encounter. It is, technically, date rape. A tacit, selfish betrayal turns affection and trust into bitterness and loathing. Cary has her first experiences with the dark, manic behaviors surrounding finals: cramming, sleeplessness, agitation, and neglect. She encounters the specters of drugs and alcohol and wrestles the psychological demons that threaten to compromise her mentally and physically. She faces her first academic failure, with calculus, in spite of her best efforts and the support of others. Cary learns tenacity and forgiveness for herself and others. She receives her first honors and is elected vice president of her class. She later sits on the Disciplinary Committee. She is also the first black graduate to receive the coveted Rector's award. Cary understands that she will be irrevocably changed as she emerges from her experiences, but what she does not know is who or what she will be as a consequence. Ultimately, Cary is able to free herself of many delusions and fears by coming to terms with her cultural identity and its imperatives. She is able to look honestly at herself and her life in America not as an aberration or flaw in the social fabric but as an integral and pertinent thread.

Cary returns to the school fifteen years later for a reunion. A wife and mother, she is also a St. Paul's trustee and member of the Board of Directors. She searches the faces of incoming black and Latino students and understands as she welcomes them that she is standing on the shoulders of those who ushered in and welcomed her. For Cary their faces recall the same hunger and fears that were transformed into a purposeful identity.

SUGGESTED READINGS
Cary, Lorene. "Making Peace with Her Girlhood: An Interview with Lorene Cary." Interview by Rosemary L. Bray. *The New York Times Book Review*, March 31, 1991, 7.
Lopate, Phillip. Review of *Black Ice*, by Lorene Cary. *The New York Times Book Review*, March 31, 1991, 7.

—Nefretete S. Rasheed

See also American identity: Northeast; Caribbean American literature; Melting pot; Racism and ethnocentrism; School; Women and identity

Black Mesa Poems

AUTHOR: Jimmy Santiago Baca (1952-   )
FIRST PUBLISHED: 1989
IDENTITIES: Latino; Native American; West and Southwest

Set in the desert of New Mexico, Jimmy Santiago Baca's *Black Mesa Poems* explores the poet's continuing search for connections with his family, home, and cultural heritage. In vivid detail and striking imagery, the loosely connected poems catalog the poet's complex relationships with his past and the home he makes of Black Mesa.

Baca's intricate relationship to the land includes his knowledge of its history. He is keenly aware of the changes the land has gone through and the changes the people of that land have experienced. He writes of his personal sense of connection with arroyos and cottonwoods and of the conflicts between the earlier inhabitants of Black Mesa and the changes brought by progress. Dispossessed migrant workers are portrayed as the price of Anglo progress, and the arid land that once nourished strong cattle now offers only "sluggish pampered globs" from feedlots. Even the once sacred places have been unceremoniously "crusted with housing tracts." His people have been separated from their ancestral land, yet Baca celebrates his identification with the old adobe buildings and Aztec warriors in the face of modern Anglo society.

Despite nostalgia, Baca eludes naïve sentimentality by attaching himself to the land. His sense of self and identity with his race is rooted in the physical landscape of Black Mesa. He evokes a strong connection with the history of his people through rituals, including drum ceremonies that "mate heart with earth." Sketches evoke a rich sense of community life in the barrio. The poet presents himself in terms of his own troubled history, but he knows that the conflict between the "peaceful" man and the "destructive" one of his past is linked to the modern smothering of noisy jet fighters and invading pampered artists looking to his land for a "primitive place."

Memories and images of snapshotlike detail combine in these poems to create a portrait of a man defining himself in relation to his personal and cultural history. The poet knows he is "the end result of Conquistadores, Black Moors, American Indians, and Europeans," and he also notes the continuing invasion of land development. Poems about his children combine memories of his troubled past with Olmec kings and tribal ancestors. The history of his ancestors' relationship with the land informs his complex and evolving sense of identity. Throughout the *Black Mesa Poems*, Baca's personal history becomes rooted in Black Mesa.

SUGGESTED READINGS
Levertov, Denise. Introduction to *Martin and Meditations on the South Valley*, by Jimmy Santiago Baca. New York: New Directions, 1987.
Olivares, Julian. "Two Contemporary Chicano Verse Chronicles." *Americas Review* 16 (Fall-Winter, 1988): 214-231.
Rector, Liam. "The Documentary of What Is." *Hudson Review* 41 (Summer, 1989): 393-400.

—William Vaughn

See also American identity: West and the frontier; Baca, Jimmy Santiago; Chicano identity; Homelessness

Black militancy. *See* **African American identity; Civil Rights movement; Nation of Islam**

Black Muslims. *See* **Nation of Islam**

Black nationalism. *See* **Nation of Islam**

Black No More: Being an Account of the Strange and Wonderful Workings of Science in the Land of the Free

AUTHOR: George S. Schuyler (1895-1977)

FIRST PUBLISHED: 1931

IDENTITIES: African American

George S. Schuyler's *Black No More* offers a bitingly satirical attack upon America's color phobia. His targets included bigoted whites who see the perpetuation of racism as a matter of economic and political interest, black leaders who waffle between appealing to white financial backers and appeasing their black constituents, and all who cloak their ignorance and hatred with racial rhetoric.

The plot of *Black No More* centers upon Schuyler's speculation of what might happen if America were to find a means to rid itself of the "Negro problem." In an effort to uplift his race, Dr. Junius Crookman, a respected black physician, invents a process by which black people can inexpensively turn themselves permanently white. The success of his process leads him to open up numerous Black No More clinics across America to handle the throngs of hopeful clients.

His first and most eager customer is Max Disher, who sees "chromatic enhancement" initially as a chance to get a white woman and eventually to run various fund-raising shams under the auspices of the Knights of Nordica, led by the Imperial Grand Wizard, Reverend Givens. As a white man, Max takes a new name, Matthew Fisher. He soon is proving his talents as a brilliant organizer, political manipulator, and white supremacist working for "the cause." Ironically, the woman of his Harlem dreams and eventual wife, Helen, turns out to be the daughter of Reverend Givens.

Matthew's schemes initially are simply quick-money ploys that amusingly take advantage of the Knights of Nordica's ignorance and obsession for racial supremacy. As the plot moves along, however, Matthew begins to sound too sincere in his racist rhetoric and becomes obsessed with earning money and political power. An old friend, Bunny Brown, arrives to keep Matthew in line. With the numbers of blacks steadily dwindling, thanks to Crookman's clinics, Matthew and Bunny plot to expose and destroy the institution of racism in America, along with its vested leaders.

The novel concludes in a calamity as the national presidential race becomes a matter of reciprocated political tricks. The former blacks are whiter than whites, the two most notorious bigots in the book go up in flames, and Matthew's wife gives birth to a mulatto child.

Schuyler, through frequent barbs and sarcastic commentaries, exposes the hypocrisy of both white and black leaders. There are numerous thinly disguised caricatures of the black leaders of the time of the novel: W. E. B. Du Bois, Marcus Garvey, C. J. Walker, James Weldon Johnson, and many others. Schuyler's satire contends that blacks are motivated by the same economic and political interests as whites, and once given the opportunity, will resort to the same means to preserve those interests.

SUGGESTED READINGS

Davis, Arthur P. "George Schuyler." In *From the Dark Tower*. Washington, D.C.: Howard University Press, 1974.

Gayle, Addison, Jr. *The Way of the World: The Black Novel in America*. Garden City, N.J.: Anchor Press, 1975.

Schuyler, George. *Black and Conservative: The Autobiography of George S. Schuyler.* New
Rochelle, N.Y.: Arlington House, 1966.
                                                                    —Betty L. Hart
See also African American identity; Harlem Renaissance; Mixed race and identity; Schuyler,
George S.

Black Thunder
AUTHOR: Arna Bontemps (1902-1973)
FIRST PUBLISHED: 1936
IDENTITIES: African American

   Black Thunder, Arna Bontemps' defining novel, is a fictionalized account of the early nineteenth century Gabriel Insurrection, in Virginia. The novel, which chronicles the Gabriel Prosser-
led rebellion against the slave owners of Henrico County, was generally lauded by critics as
one of the most significant black American works of fiction. Richard Wright praised the work
for dealing forthrightly with the historical and revolutionary traditions of African Americans.

   Gabriel, a slave convinced that anything "equal to a grey squirrel wants to be free," urges other
slaves to revolt against their owners. The rebellion is hastened when a tyrannical slave owner whips
another slave, Bundy, to death. Although the insurrection ultimately fails, Prosser nonetheless
emerges a hero. The "power of black folk" credo is important to this novel. Bontemps' treatment
of Bundy's funeral is faithful in detail to the customs of the time. Bontemps' use of signs and
portents pushes the story to its heroic ending. Stunning characterizations of Pharaoh, Drucilla,
Ben, and Gabriel become multileveled, believably universal personalities through Bontemps'
skillful use of folk material. Elements of magic appear in *Black Thunder* just as they appear in
folktales and beliefs as recorded by collectors.

   Bundy's spirit returns to haunt Pharaoh, the slave who betrays the rebellion and whose death is
foreshadowed. Use of charms and countercharms is rampant, conjure-poisoning looms at all times,
and rebellious slaves debate omens in the stars. The tapestry that Bontemps weaves shows the
intricate beliefs of slaves to be colorful and compelling. Bontemps' narrative techniques have
origins in black folklore about death, ghosts, and spirits.

   Black Thunder's strength, largely, is in its depiction of an alternate worldview, which, while
retaining the power to sanctify or punish, is painfully adapting to a new land and people. Critics
note that Bontemps situates his story in the politics of the times: Readers see blame for slave unrest
placed at the feet of Thomas Jefferson during John Quincy Adams' bitter reelection campaign.
Bontemps depicts the Virginia legislature debate considering sectional segregation of blacks, slaves
and free, and chronicles the press. *Black Thunder* was written during the 1930's; some critics
believe it reflects the mood of the Depression.

SUGGESTED READINGS
Bontemps, Arna. Introduction to *Black Thunder*. Beacon Press: Boston, 1968.
Davis, Arthur P. *From the Dark Tower: Afro-American Writers, 1900-1960.* Washington, D.C.:
Howard University Press, 1974.
Jones, Kirkland C. *Renaissance Man from Louisiana: A Biography of Arna Wendell Bontemps.*
Westport, Conn.: Greenwood Press, 1992.
Sundquist, Eric J. *The Hammers of Creation: Folk Culture in Modern African-American Fiction.*
Athens: University of Georgia Press, 1992.
Weil, Dorothy. "Folklore Motifs in Arna Bontemps' *Black Thunder*." *Southern Folklore Quarterly*
35 (March, 1971): 1-14.
                                                                    —Barbara Day

See also African American identity; Bontemps, Arna; *Great Slave Narratives*; Harlem Renaissance; Hurston, Zora Neale

Blacker the Berry: A Novel of Negro Life, The

AUTHOR: Wallace Thurman (1902-1934)

FIRST PUBLISHED: 1929

IDENTITIES: African American; women

The Blacker the Berry: A Novel of Negro Life is Wallace Thurman's first novel and perhaps his most well-known work. The title is part of an African American folk saying: "The blacker the berry, the sweeter the juice." *The Blacker the Berry* was written during the Harlem Renaissance. Thurman's novel was among the first to explore prejudice within the African American community and was consequently controversial.

The identity of the novel's protagonist, Emma Lou, as well as that of the other characters, is directly related to the color of their skin. Emma Lou bears the "burden of blackness" in a family that has been striving to become lighter with every generation. During the course of the novel, Emma Lou acquires several identities. These identities are placed upon her by her family in Idaho, her college peers in Southern California, the community in Harlem, and herself.

As a teen Emma Lou's attitude reflects her family's rejection of her very dark coloring. Like her blue-veined grandmother, Emma identifies herself as the only black student in an all-white student body. Because of her jet-black skin, it seems inevitable that Emma Lou will never amount to anything.

Entering college on a campus hosting other African Americans, Emma Lou soon discovers that her black skin makes her unpopular. Men on campus identify Emma Lou as "Hottentot." A very derogatory term, popular during the 1920's, "Hottentot" was applied to young women who had pronounced African features. Likewise, she is rejected from the black women's society because she is not "high brown."

Relocating after college, Emma Lou seeks a new identity in Harlem as a teacher. In trying to make herself lighter, Emma Lou only succeeds in acquiring a clownlike identity. The arsenic wafers and excessive makeup result in an "ugly purple tinge" on her face. Emma Lou becomes involved in an abusive relationship with a Filipino mulatto.

Emma Lou triumphs in the end, as she finally accepts who she is and what she looks like. *The Blacker the Berry* was a landmark in its subject matter.

SUGGESTED READINGS

Lewis, David Levering. *When Harlem Was in Vogue*. New York: Oxford University Press, 1979.

Locke, Alain, ed. *The New Negro: Voices of the Harlem Renaissance*. Introduction by Arnold Ramperstad. New York: Antheneum, 1992.

—Susan R. Dominguez

See also African American identity; Harlem Renaissance; Mixed race and identity; School

Bless Me, Ultima

AUTHOR: Rudolfo A. Anaya (1937-   )

FIRST PUBLISHED: 1972

IDENTITIES: Adolescence and coming-of-age; Latino; West and Southwest

Bless Me, Ultima is Rudolfo Anaya's first novel of a trilogy that also includes *Heart of Aztlán* (1976) and *Tortuga* (1979). It is a psychological and magical portrait of a quest for identity by a child. In this classic work, Antonio, the protagonist, is subjected to contradicting influences that he must master in order to mature. These influences include symbolic characters and places, the most powerful of which are Ultima, a *curandera* who evokes the timeless past of a pre-Columbian world, and a golden carp, which swims the river waters of the supernatural and offers a redeeming future.

Antonio is born in Pasturas, a very small village on the Eastern New Mexican plain. Later, the family moves across the river to the small town of Guadalupe, where Antonio spends his childhood. His father belongs to the Márez family and is a cattleman; Antonio's mother is of the Luna family, whose background is farming. They represent the initial manifestation of the divided world into which Antonio is born. Division is a challenge he must resolve in order to find himself. Antonio's father wants him to become a horseman of the plain. Antonio's mother wants him to become a priest to a farming community, which is in the highest tradition of the Luna family.

The parents' wishes are symptoms of a deeper spiritual challenge facing Antonio involving his Catholic beliefs and those associated with the magical world of a pre-Columbian past. Ultima, the *curandera* and a creature of both worlds, helps guide Antonio through the ordeal of understanding and dealing with these challenges.

Ultima is a magical character who touches the core of Antonio's being. She supervised his birth. Later she comes to stay with the family in Guadalupe when Antonio is seven. On several occasions, Antonio is a witness to her power.

Antonio's adventure takes him beyond the divided world of the farmer and the horseman and beyond the Catholic ritual and its depictions of good and evil. With Ultima's help, he is able to bridge these opposites and channel them into a new cosmic vision of nature, represented by the river, which stands in the middle of his two worlds, and by the golden carp, which points to a new spiritual covenant.

The novel ends with the killing of Ultima's owl by one of her enemies. He discovered that the owl carried her spiritual presence. This killing also causes Ultima's death, but her work is done. Antonio can choose his destiny.

SUGGESTED READINGS

González-T., César A., ed. *Rudolfo A. Anaya: Focus on Criticism.* La Jolla, Calif.: Lalo Press, 1990.

Trejo, Arnulfo D. "*Bless Me, Ultima*: A Novel." *Arizona Quarterly* 29 (1973): 95-96.

—David Conde

See also Anaya, Rudolfo A.; Chicano identity; Chicano Renaissance; *Heart of Aztlán*; *Tortuga*

Blood Red Sunset: A Memoir of the Cultural Revolution

AUTHOR: Ma Bo (Lao Gui, 1948-   )
FIRST PUBLISHED: *Xuese huanghun*, 1988 (English translation, 1995)
IDENTITIES: Chinese American

Blood Red Sunset: A Memoir of the Cultural Revolution is a candid account of the author's experience as an educated youth in Inner Mongolia from 1968 to 1976. Filled with ideological fervor, Ma Bo and three other youngsters wrote in their own blood a petition to make a revolution in Genghis Khan's birthplace. In Mongolia, Ma Bo joined his comrades in the often brutal effort to reeducate herd owners and "capitalist Chinese" according to the Maoist principle of class struggle. Ironically, he learned about being humane from those so-called class enemies and went through a painful disillusionment with revolutionary ideals. After casually criticizing a Chinese leader, Ma Bo was denounced as an active counterrevolutionary and imprisoned. He left Mongolia in 1976 with memories of a regretful eight years of ignorance, fanaticism, and brutality. Mao Zedong's rule had brought nothing but an ecological disaster to the grasslands.

Ma Bo's memoir was first published under his pen name, Lao Gui (Old Ghost), as a nonfiction novel. Besides the political uproar aroused by its publication, the work was hailed as the first masculine novel of twentieth century China. Its language is deliberately coarse. Its thematic loss of faith and unadorned narrative style reveal the influence of Ernest Hemingway, who is noted for his masculine style. It also reflects the influences of Chinese classical novels. Ma Bo's fantasy of brotherhood was repeatedly dispelled by unexpected betrayals. His story becomes a caricature of human victimizing and victimization, an acid denunciation of the Cultural Revolution.

Ma Bo's memoir fully reveals the realities experienced by young intellectuals during the Cultural Revolution. Unlike Nien Cheng's *Life and Death in Shanghai* (1986) and Anchee Min's *Red Azalea* (1994), which were first written in English for Western readers, *Blood Red Sunset* was first published in Chinese in 1988 and sold 400,000 copies. The book started a reappraisal of the Cultural Revolution in China. As did Nien Cheng and Anchee Min, Ma Bo emigrated to North America. The English version of *Blood Red Sunset* has joined the nightmarish literature of recent immigrants from mainland China.

The Cultural Revolution used to be held as a utopian model by some Western intellectuals. Ma Bo's life story warns against fanatic idealism.

SUGGESTED READINGS

Liang, Heng, and Judith Shapiro. *Son of the Revolution.* New York: Alfred A. Knopf, 1983.
Yang Mo. *The Song of Youth.* Peking: Foreign Languages Press, 1964.

—Qingyun Wu

See also Asian American identity: China, Japan, and Korea; *China Men*; Min, Anchee

Blues People: Negro Music in White America

AUTHOR: Amiri Baraka (LeRoi Jones, 1934-   )
FIRST PUBLISHED: 1963
IDENTITIES: African American

The first full-length analytical and historical study of jazz and blues written by an African American, *Blues People: Negro Music in White America* presents a highly original thesis suggesting that music can be used as a gauge to measure the cultural assimilation of Africans in North America from the early eighteenth century to the twentieth century. Broad in scope and insightfully opinionated, *Blues People* caused controversy among musicologists and other critics. Intending his remarks as negative criticism, Ralph Ellison was accurate in noting that Amiri Baraka is "attracted to the blues for what he believes they tell us of the sociology of Negro American identity and attitude."

Baraka contends that although slavery destroyed many formal artistic traditions, African American music represents certain African survivals. Most important, African American music represents an African approach to culture. As such, the music sustains the African worldview and records the historical experience of an oppressed people.

Baraka also argues that while Africans adapted their culture to the English language and to European musical instruments and song forms, they also maintained an ethnic viewpoint that is preserved and transmitted by their music. Stylistic changes in the music mirror historical changes in the attitudes and social conditions of African Americans. The chapter "Swing— From Verb to Noun" compares the contributions of African American and white jazz musicians in the 1920's and 1930's, demonstrating how some artists developed and extended an ethnic folk music tradition while others added what they learned from that tradition to the vocabulary of a more commercialized American popular music. Baraka's view that music is capable of expressing and maintaining a group identity leads to his assertion that even in later decades, increasingly dominated by the recording and broadcasting industry, African American artists continued to be the primary contributors and innovators. A classic work of its kind, *Blues People* offers an interesting view of how cultural products reflect and perhaps determine other social developments.

SUGGESTED READINGS

Ellison, Ralph. *Shadow and Act.* New York: Vintage Books, 1972.
Harris, William J., ed. *The LeRoi Jones/Amiri Baraka Reader.* New York: Thunder's Mouth Press, 1991.
Kofsky, Frank. *Black Nationalism and the Revolution in Music.* New York: Pathfinder Press, 1970.
Sollors, Werner. *Amiri Baraka/LeRoi Jones: The Quest for a "Populist Modernism."* New York: Columbia University Press, 1978.

—Lorenzo Thomas

See also Acculturation; Baraka, Amiri; Popular culture

Bondage

AUTHOR: David Henry Hwang (1957-   )
FIRST PRODUCED: 1992; first published, 1993
IDENTITIES: Chinese American; men; women

Bondage, a one-act play set in a fantasy bondage parlor, is an exploration of racial, cultural, and sexual stereotypes. It is presented as an allegory depicting their overwhelming influence in society and offering one alternative for society's progressing beyond them. The play demonstrates Chinese American playwright David Henry Hwang's development beyond exclusively Asian American themes to encompass the destructiveness of all stereotyping, be it racial, cultural, or sexual.

Mark, identifiable only as a male, is the client of dominatrix Terri, identifiable only as a female, in a fantasy bondage parlor. Both characters' identities are fully disguised. They are merely a man and a woman who assume the characteristics required for whatever fantasy is suggested. During this encounter, however, both Mark and Terri refuse to accept the stereotypes associated with their fantasy roles.

Terri informs Mark that today he will be a Chinese man and she will be a blonde woman. She immediately characterizes Mark as a horn-rimmed-glasses-wearing engineer afraid of her because she is popular with cowboys and jocks. Mark rejects her Asian stereotypes and, in turn, uses blonde stereotypes to describe her. A personal confrontation ensues because Mark will not accept her ridicule.

This leads to male-female stereotyping, and on to progressive levels of racial stereotyping. As they are unable to resolve this confrontation, they move on to become a white man and a black woman, with underlying stereotyped images of the white liberal. Terri charges that he may try to "play" all races, but she has already "become" all races. Next they assume the roles of Chinese American man and an Asian American woman, exploring intercultural stereotypes. Finally they explore Mark's need for penitence as a stereotypical businessman, which drives him to the bondage parlor to be dominated and humiliated in a fantasy world as he dominates and humiliates in the real one. The plight of both men and women, and the roles society forces upon them, dominate the final confrontation. Her resistance having been worn down by Mark's arguing, Terri begins to remove her disguise. She offers Mark his moment of victory, but instead he, too, removes his mask. When he confesses his real love for Terri, she reveals herself—they are as the original fantasy, an Asian man and a blonde woman. Their confrontation has put the stereotypes of their disparate groups behind them. They see each other as individuals and are ready to move beyond their fantasies.

Hwang's optimism that society can move beyond oppressing societal stereotypes pervades *Bondage*. He presents a balanced attack on all stereotyping, showing that regardless of cultural, political, or sexual identity, society will only move forward when all stereotypes are destroyed and people are regarded as individuals.

SUGGESTED READINGS

Hwang, David Henry. Introduction to *FOB and Other Plays*, by David Henry Hwang. New York: Plume, 1990.

Skloot, Robert. "Breaking the Butterfly: The Politics of David Henry Hwang." *Modern Drama* 33, no. 1 (March, 1990): 59-66.

Street, Douglas. *David Henry Hwang*. Boise, Idaho: Boise State University Press, 1989.

—Gerald S. Argetsinger

See also Asian American identity; *Dance and the Railroad*; *Family Devotions*; Hwang, David Henry; *M. Butterfly*

Bone

AUTHOR: Fae Myenne Ng (1956-   )
FIRST PUBLISHED: 1993
IDENTITIES: Chinese American; family; women

Fae Myenne Ng's *Bone* continues in a tradition of Asian American novels by women that mediate between the demands of addressing issues of gender and of ethnicity. As a woman writing from a strongly patriarchal cultural heritage, Ng has had to create new strategies in order to express the paradox of resistance to and affirmation of her cultural heritage.

Bone relates the story of the Leong family, which has recently suffered the death by suicide of the Middle Girl, Ona. Ona committed suicide by jumping from one of Chinatown's housing projects. She left no note, and although the police reported she was "on downers," or depressants, there was no apparent cause for the suicide. The novel is narrated by the First Girl, Leila Fu Louie, Ona's half-sister and the eldest daughter in the Leong family. Leila's attempts to come to terms with her sister's death, and thereby her own life, lead her to muse about incidents from their childhood and the everyday circumstances of the present. The novel unfolds in a series of stories that move from the present into the past.

The children of immigrants have often been called upon to translate for their parents. Their ability to switch from the language of their parents to the English of their birthplace makes them the bridge between the customs of the Old World and the expectations and demands of the New. This enormous responsibility can become an overwhelming burden. Although Leila must continually face the chasm between her parents' expectations and her own reality, her ability to build a bridge of translation is grounded in her strong need and appreciation for the family.

Her youngest sister, Nina, the End Girl, refuses to shoulder this burden of translation. Her rebellion has caused her to move to New York, far away from her parents in San Francisco's Chinatown. She declares her independence by refusing to lie about her life in order to appease her parents. It is the self-imposed silence of Ona, however, that is at the center of the novel. Ona, the middle child, is caught in the middle; she learned too well how to keep secrets.

Ng does not seek to solve the mystery of Ona's death in this novel. It is a mystery that is unsolvable; rather, through the narrative voice of Leila, Ng explores the languages and silences of love, grief, assimilation, avoidance, anger, guilt, and, finally, acceptance. Ng, who grew up in San Francisco, is the daughter of Chinese immigrants and in an interview explained the title of her novel: "Bone is what lasts. And I wanted to honor the quality of endurance in the immigrant spirit."

Bone is a journey into a territory that is the common heritage of all second-generation immigrant Americans and the particular traditions of Chinese immigrants. The path to assimilation into American society is fraught with contradictions and ambivalence. Ng provides few answers; she simply reveals one family's experience.

SUGGESTED READINGS

Lim, Shirley Geok-Lin. "Feminist and Ethnic Literary Theories in Asian American Literature." *Feminist Studies* 19, no. 3 (Fall, 1993): 571-589.

Miller, Heather Ross. "America the Big Lie, the Quintessential." *Southern Review* 29, no. 2 (April, 1993): 420-430.

Ng, Fae Myenne. "False Gold: My Father's American Journey." *New Republic*, July 19-26, 1993, 12-13.

—Jane Anderson Jones

See also Acculturation; Asian American identity: China, Japan, and Korea; Ng, Faye Myenne

Bontemps, Arna Wendell

BORN: Alexandria, Louisiana; October 13, 1902

DIED: Nashville, Tennessee; June 4, 1973

PRINCIPAL WORKS: *God Send Sundays*, 1931; *Black Thunder*, 1936; *Great Slave Narratives* (editor), 1969

IDENTITIES: African American

SIGNIFICANT ACHIEVEMENT: Bontemps, recognized as a scholar and historian of the Harlem Renaissance, is considered one of the most significant African American writers.

Arna Bontemps, at age twenty-one, accepted a teaching position in New York City at the beginning of the Harlem Renaissance. Through his poetry, novels, short stories, and essays, he became one of that movement's defining writers. Bontemps, whose father was a bricklayer and whose mother, a schoolteacher, instilled in him a love of books, was born in Louisiana, but, because of white threats against his family, was reared and educated in California, where he was graduated from Pacific Union College in 1923.

The Bontemps family settled in the Watts section of Los Angeles in 1905. At the time they were the only African American family in the neighborhood. When Bontemps was twelve years old, his mother died, and he was sent to live with relatives in the California countryside. There, by becoming his Uncle Buddy's "companion and confidant in the corn rows," Bontemps gained access to a living embodiment of Southern black folk culture. According to Bontemps, Uncle Buddy was an "old derelict" who drank alcohol and loved "dialect stories, preacher stories, ghost stories, slave and master stories. He half-believed in signs and charms and mumbo-jumbo, and he believed whole-heartedly in ghosts." Concerned at Uncle Buddy's influence, Bontemps' father sent his son to a white boarding school, admonishing him, "Now don't go up there acting colored." Fifty years later, the rebuke still rankled: Recalling his father's advice in 1965, Bontemps exclaimed, "How dare anyone, parent, schoolteacher, or merely literary critic, tell me not to act colored?" Pride in color and heritage stamps all Bontemps' works.

The African American experience is at the heart of all Bontemps' work. His novel *God Send Sundays*, which he and Countée Cullen adapted for Broadway in 1946, is based loosely on the life of Uncle Buddy. The work offers a glimpse of the Southern racing circuit through the eyes of a black jockey in the late 1800's. Another novel, *Black Thunder*, is based on Gabriel Prosser's slave rebellion. Bontemps edited an anthology, *Great Slave Narratives*, and *The Book of Negro Folklore* in 1958. With Langston Hughes, Bontemps edited *The Poetry of the Negro 1746-1949* (1963). Bontemps was a central figure in the rediscovery and dissemination of African American literature.

Bontemps was a librarian at Fisk University from 1943 to 1965. Although he left to teach at the University of Illinois and then at Yale during the late 1960's, he returned to Fisk in 1971 and remained there until his death in 1973.

SUGGESTED READINGS
Baker, Houston A., Jr. *Black Literature in America*. New York: McGraw-Hill, 1971.
Bontemps, Arna. *Arna Bontemps-Langston Hughes Letters, 1925-1967*. Selected and edited by Charles H. Nichols. New York: Paragon House, 1990.
Davis, Arthur P. *From the Dark Tower: Afro-American Writers, 1900-1960*. Washington, D.C.: Howard University Press, 1974.

—*Barbara Day*

See also African American identity; *Black Thunder*; Cullen, Countée; *Great Slave Narratives*; Harlem Renaissance; Hughes, Langston

Bostonians, The

AUTHOR: Henry James (1843-1916)
FIRST PUBLISHED: 1885-1886
IDENTITIES: European American; gay, lesbian, and bisexual; Northeast; women

Unlike many of Henry James's novels, *The Bostonians* is set in the United States. Its female characters are involved in the reform movement that swept New England during the latter half of the nineteenth century. In the novel, James presents compelling but not sympathetic characters. A central figure in the reform movement is Olive Chancellor, a proponent of women's rights, a movement upon which her identity is based. Presumably, American educator Elizabeth Peabody was James's prototype for Olive. Olive is inspired by Miss Birdseye, an abolitionist in her eighties, and seeks to become a force in the women's reform movement.

Lacking the articulateness required to be a successful spokesperson, Olive latches onto Verena

Tarrant, an attractive but docile young woman who has received some public notice on account of her association with her mesmerist father's public performances. Olive liberates Verena from her squalid surroundings, bringing her to the Beacon Street house in which she lives.

Verena, never encouraged to find her own identity in a world dominated by men, becomes the mouthpiece through which Olive can communicate her ideas of reform to audiences. Verena tries to remain loyal to Olive, who tyrannizes her. The two live together, travel together, and move toward sharing a single identity, one constructed wholly by Olive. Olive, if viewed in the light of modern psychoanalytical theory, has a lesbian attraction to the submissive Verena.

All runs smoothly, however, until Basil Ransom, Olive's cousin, a Confederate veteran from Mississippi, arrives to stay with Olive. He totally opposes his cousin's ideas. His presence allows James to create two philosophical polarities that produce the novel's dramatic tension. James exaggerates both sides for dramatic effect.

Ransom, predictably, proposes to rescue Verena by marrying her, although Olive made Verena promise long before Ransom's arrival that she would never marry. Verena, however, has few firm convictions. Her compliant nature makes her malleable, adapting to the pressures closest to her at any given time.

Finally, Ransom essentially abducts Verena in what appears to be the rescue of a distressed maiden who does not really want to be rescued. Verena leaves the scene in tears, fated to be Ransom's wife. James does not write this ending as a happy one. The final sentence reads, "It is to be feared that with the union, so far from brilliant, into which she was about to enter, these were not the last [tears] she was destined to shed."

SUGGESTED READINGS

Anderson, Charles R. "James's Portrait of the Southerner." In *On Henry James: The Best from American Literature*, edited by Louis J. Budd and Edwin H. Cady. Durham, N.C.: Duke University Press, 1990.

Davis, Sara de Saussure. "Feminist Sources in *The Bostonians*." In *On Henry James: The Best from American Literature*, edited by Louis J. Budd and Edwin H. Cady. Durham, N.C.: Duke University Press, 1990.

Howe, Irving. Introduction to *The Bostonians*, by Henry James. New York: Modern Library, 1956.

Samuels, Charles. *The Ambiguity of Henry James*. Champaign: University of Illinois Press, 1971.

—*R. Baird Shuman*

See also *Ambassadors, The*; American identity: Northeast; Feminism; James, Henry; Lesbian identity

Boyle, T. Coraghessan (Thomas John Boyle)

BORN: Peekskill, New York; December 2, 1948

PRINCIPAL WORKS: *The Descent of Man*, 1979; *Water Music*, 1981; *Budding Prospects: A Pastoral*, 1984; *Greasy Lake and Other Stories*, 1985; *World's End*, 1987; *If the River Was Whiskey*, 1989; *East Is East*, 1990; *The Road to Wellville*, 1993; *Without a Hero and Other Stories*, 1994; *The Tortilla Curtain*, 1995

IDENTITIES: European American

SIGNIFICANT ACHIEVEMENT: Boyle's fiction about cultures in collision uses humor and irony to illuminate the differences that separate cultures and the commonalities that unite them.

The biographical facts of T. Coraghessan Boyle's life abound with the incongruous juxtapositions that one finds in his fiction. Born and reared in Peekskill, a town in New York's historic Hudson Valley, he has moved to teach in Southern California. A troubled son of alcoholic parents who himself indulged in a weekend heroin habit, he achieved early distinction for his fiction and has become that rare writer who earns critical respect and a wide audience.

Boyle was born Thomas John Boyle in 1948, but officially changed his middle name to

Coraghessan when he was seventeen. He entered the State University of New York at Potsdam as a music major, but switched to English literature and writing. He enrolled at the University of Iowa Writers' Workshop, where he studied under John Irving and John Cheever, and was graduated in 1977 with a doctorate in nineteenth century British literature. That same year, he and his wife Karen, with whom he has three children, moved to California, where Boyle became head of the creative writing program at the University of Southern California.

Boyle distinguished himself as a writer capable of assuming a wide variety of personalities in his highly regarded first collection, *The Descent of Man*, among them a rapist ("Drowning"), a female scientist ("Descent of Man"), an African dictator ("Dada"), and even a dog ("Heart of a Champion"). Subsequent collections garnered his stories comparisons to those of Robert Coover and Donald Barthelme for their audaciousness.

Boyle's novel-length works expand the vivid scenarios of his short fiction. *Water Music* chronicles the adventures of nineteenth century British colonials exploring the Niger River, and *World's End* describes the parallels among Dutch, Native American, and European American experience in the Hudson River Valley during three centuries. *East Is East* and *The Tortilla Curtain* focus on the plight of illegal aliens in America from, respectively, Japan and Mexico.

Invariably, Boyle's novels show that people's hopes and dreams are the same across all cultures and times, but that the different means of achieving them within a specific society lead to problems with comic and tragic dimensions. Boyle's interest in the universality of human aspirations has allowed him to use themes as different as marijuana farming (*Budding Prospects*), physical fitness (*The Road to Wellville*), apartment clutter ("Filthy with Things"), and pop kitsch ("The Miracle at Ballinspittle") as springboards for his inquiries into the human condition.

SUGGESTED READINGS

Adams, Elizabeth. "An Interview with T. Coraghessan Boyle." *Chicago Review* 37, nos. 2-3 (1991): 51-63.

Boyle, T. Coraghessan. "T. Coraghessan Boyle." Interview by David Stanton. *Poets and Writers* 18 (January-February, 1990): 29-34.

Friend, Tad. "Rolling Boyle." *The New York Times Magazine*, December 9, 1990, 50, 64-68.

Neubauer, Alexander. *Conversations on Writing Fiction: Interviews with Thirteen Distinguished Teachers of Fiction Writing in America*. New York: HarperCollins, 1994.

Pope, Dan. "A Different Kind of Post-Modernism." *The Gettysburg Review* 3 (Autumn, 1990): 658-669.

—*Stefan Dziemianowicz*

See also American identity: West and the frontier; Asian American identity: China, Japan, and Korea; Colonialism; *East Is East*; Emigration and immigration; *Hector Quesadilla Story, The*; Melting pot; Popular culture; *Road to Wellville, The*; *Tortilla Curtain, The*

Boy's Own Story, A

AUTHOR: Edmund White (1940-   )

FIRST PUBLISHED: 1982

IDENTITIES: Adolescence and coming-of-age; European American; gay, lesbian, and bisexual

Part fiction and part autobiography, *A Boy's Own Story* is the tale of a youth discovering his homosexuality in the 1940's and 1950's in America. The work is remarkable for its lyrical celebration of physical beauty and for its sharp criticism of a homophobic society.

In his teens, the boy Edmund enjoys a brief sexual relationship with Kevin, a slightly younger friend. Their intimacy is represented as natural and idyllic, undisturbed by the guilt and self-hatred that society will later impose upon Edmund because he is homosexual. The joyous experience with Kevin is something that Edmund will never be able to recapture, for society's prejudice and Edmund's internalized homophobia will make it very difficult for him to achieve a positive homosexual identity.

When he is an older teen, Edmund feels physically attracted to Tom, another male friend, but he dares not act on his desires for fear of being labeled a homosexual. Instead, Edmund tries to convince himself that he is in love with Linda, a popular young woman, and he indulges in escapist fantasies of a heterosexual marriage that will gain him society's approval. Edmund also turns to Buddhism in the belief that it will help him to escape all desire. Finally, Christianity and psychoanalysis fail to affirm his identity as a young gay man: Father Burke tells him that homosexuality is a sin, and Dr. O'Reilly tries to cure him, as if being gay were a disease.

Unfortunately, Edmund's father does not serve as a positive role model either. A chronic adulterer, the father eventually abandons Edmund's mother for another woman, leaving the family bereft of affection and money. The father considers his athletic daughter to be more like the son he had wanted, rejecting the bookish Edmund as a sissy. In the end, Edmund acts on his gay desires: He has sex with an older teacher, Mr. Beattie. Society has made Edmund feel guilty about his homosexuality, however, so he turns Mr. Beattie in to the school authorities. In this way, Edmund attempts to deny his sexual identity. Furthermore, he is unconsciously repeating his father's pattern of behavior, abandoning the people he loves.

A Boy's Own Story ends on a pessimistic note, with Edmund still unable to achieve a positive gay identity. His struggle to affirm his homosexuality is not over; a sequel, *The Beautiful Room Is Empty* (1988), follows Edmund into the 1960's and the beginnings of the gay liberation movement.

SUGGESTED READINGS

Bergman, David. *Gaiety Transfigured: Gay Self-Representation in American Literature*. Madison: University of Wisconsin Press, 1991.

Bonetti, Kay. "An Interview with Edmund White." *Missouri Review* 13 (Spring, 1990): 89-110.

—Douglas Keesey

See also Coming out; Gay identity; White, Edmund

Bradstreet, Anne

BORN: Northampton, Northamptonshire, England; 1612?

DIED: Andover, Massachusetts Bay Colony; September 16, 1672

PRINCIPAL WORKS: *The Tenth Muse Lately Sprung Up in America*, 1650; *Several Poems Compiled with Great Variety of Wit and Learning*, 1678

IDENTITIES: European American; family; Northeast; religion; women

SIGNIFICANT ACHIEVEMENT: Bradstreet was the first New England poet to publish a volume of poetry in England, and her work is among the best produced in colonial America.

In 1630, Anne Bradstreet, about eighteen years old, sailed to America aboard the *Arbella*, the flagship of the great Puritan migration to the New World. Bradstreet's father, Thomas Dudley, and her husband, Simon Bradstreet, had decided to trade a comfortable life in England for a difficult one in the New England colonies—and religious freedom. As a dutiful Puritan daughter and wife, Bradstreet submitted to their wishes, although she later confessed that her "heart rose" in despair after seeing the desolate Salem settlement in the Massachusetts Bay Colony. The tension generated by her conflicting identities as a Puritan, as a loving wife, mother, and grandmother, and as a woman poet in a decidedly patriarchal culture informs much of Bradstreet's poetry.

Bradstreet's life in New England, as expected, was difficult. The family moved several times as her husband and her father sought land and political power (both would serve as governor of Massachusetts Bay Colony) before settling in Andover. Puritan women were responsible for domestic affairs, and Bradstreet presumably dismantled and reassembled the household for each move, in addition to caring for the eight children she bore between 1634 and 1652. It is amazing that Bradstreet found time to write at all, but in 1650 *The Tenth Muse Lately Sprung Up in America*, her first volume of poetry, was published in London after her brother-in-law, John Woodbridge, took the manuscript to England without her permission. Bradstreet confronts her culture's resistance to female poets when she acknowledges in the volume's prologue, itself a poem, that she is vulnerable "to each carping tongue/ Who says my hand a needle better fits."

Bradstreet continued to write after the publication of *The Tenth Muse Lately Sprung Up in America*, and the later poems were published posthumously in 1678. More personal than the predominantly philosophical poetry of *The Tenth Muse Lately Sprung Up in America*, they document crises in Bradstreet's life as a woman on the New England frontier and reflect the Puritan struggle to submit absolutely to God's will. In "Here Follows Some Verses upon the Burning of Our House, July 10th, 1666," Bradstreet mourns the loss of material objects and lingers on the pleasant memories associated with her home before concluding that the things of this world are "mold'ring dust" and anticipating eternal life in a permanent "house on high erect/ Fram'd by that mighty Architect." In several elegies for her grandchildren, Bradstreet's submission to God's plan comes grudgingly. Note the ambiguous wording in a 1669 elegy for her grandson Simon: "Such was His will, but why, let's not dispute/ With humble hearts and mouths put in the dust,/ Let's say He's merciful as well as just."

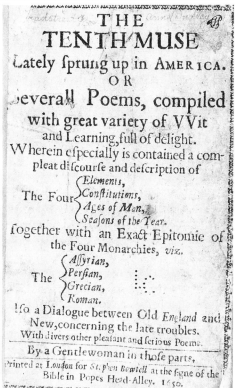

The title page from the English edition of Anne Bradstreet's famous work. (Library of Congress)

Bradstreet's later poems undermine stereotypes of Puritans as grim, joyless people. Bradstreet's "Letters" to her husband Simon, often absent on colonial business, are surprisingly passionate. One depicts Bradstreet as a cold, dormant Earth awaiting the return of Simon, her sun, to burn "Within . . . my glowing breast." "In Reference to Her Children, 23 June, 1659" voices Bradstreet's strong maternal feelings, presenting her children as baby chicks raised by an anxious mother who is happy only when all is well with her brood. While these poems may have violated the Puritan doctrine not to become attached to the pleasures of this world, they serve to humanize Bradstreet for twentieth century readers. Anne Bradstreet died in 1672 in Andover, but her work would live to influence a variety of American poets, from fellow seventeenth century Puritan Edward Taylor to twentieth century poets John Berryman and Adrienne Rich.

SUGGESTED READINGS

Dolle, Raymond. *Anne Bradstreet: A Reference Guide*. Boston: G. K. Hall, 1990.

Stanford, Ann. *Anne Bradstreet: The Worldly Puritan*. New York: Franklin, 1974.

White, Elizabeth Wade. *Anne Bradstreet: "The Tenth Muse."* New York: Oxford University Press, 1971.

—*Peter J. Higgins*

See also American identity: Northeast; Puritan and Protestant tradition; Religion and identity; Rich, Adrienne

Brainard, Cecilia Manguerra

BORN: Cebu, Philippines; November 21, 1947

PRINCIPAL WORKS: *Woman with Horns and Other Stories*, 1987; *Philippine Woman in America*, 1991; *Song of Yvonne*, 1991 (published in the United States as *When the Rainbow Goddess Wept*, 1994); *Fiction by Filipinos in America*, 1993; *Acapulco at Sunset and Other Stories*, 1995

IDENTITIES: Asian American; women

SIGNIFICANT ACHIEVEMENT: Brainard has reminded American readers of how Filipinos earned their independence.

Born one year after the Philippines gained its independence, Cecilia Manguerra Brainard was surrounded from the start with a sense of her country's having been born at almost the same time as herself. After centuries of Spanish colonialism, more than four decades of American control, and four years of Japanese occupation, finally, in 1946, Filipinos were free to determine their own future. The Americans had helped prepare for this moment through elective models and had fought side by side with Filipinos during the war, and the Americans were vital to the difficult postwar reconstruction, but Brainard grew up well aware of her fellow Filipinos' own proud contributions toward establishment of an independent Philippines. The street on which she lived in Cebu was called Guerrillero Street in honor of her father, a guerrilla and then a civil engineer involved in rebuilding shattered Philippine cities. Many of the anecdotes in her first novel, *Song of Yvonne*, came from tales of war remembered by her family.

As a result, even when Brainard left home for graduate studies at the University of California at Los Angeles in the late 1960's, she brought with her an identity as a Filipina. She married a former member of the Peace Corps, Lauren Brainard, who had served on Leyte, an island close to Cebu. In California, she worked on documentary film scripts and public relations from 1969 to 1981. Then she began the newspaper columns later collected in *Philippine Woman in America*, which describe the enrichment and frustration felt by Philippine Americans who are straddling two cultures. Conscious of her own Americanization and anxious to provide her three sons with cultural choices, she formed Philippine American Women Writers and Artists, an organization intent on publishing remembered legends and scenes from the contributors' childhoods. Brainard's organization was intended to provide a continuum of presence from varied pasts to a shared future. Such dedication to the "memory of a people" is in the ancient Philippine tradition of the female *babaylan*, or priestess.

SUGGESTED READINGS

Casper, Leonard. *Sunsurfers Seen from Afar: Critical Essays 1991-1996*. Metro Manila, Philippines: Anvil, 1996.

Zapanta Manlapaz, Edna. *Songs of Ourselves*. Metro Manila, Philippines: Anvil, 1994.

—*Leonard Casper*

See also Antiwar literature; Asian American identity: Pacific Islands; Colonialism; Hagedorn, Jessica Tarahata; Rosca, Ninotchka; World War II

Brautigan, Richard

BORN: Tacoma, Washington; January 30, 1935

DIED: Bolinas, California; September, 1984

PRINCIPAL WORKS: *A Confederate General from Big Sur*, 1964; *Trout Fishing in America*, 1967; *In Watermelon Sugar*, 1968; *The Abortion: An Historical Romance*, 1971; *Revenge of the Lawn: Stories 1962-1970*, 1971

IDENTITIES: European American

SIGNIFICANT ACHIEVEMENT: A spokesman for youthful disillusionment with American society in the 1960's, Brautigan is remembered for his contributions to literary style.

From 1967 to 1971, Richard Brautigan's popularity was based on his association with West Coast youth movements. His books, particularly his short, fanciful novels, were viewed as expressions of a generation disillusioned with the American myth. His gentle, comic books mourned the apparent loss of the American Eden, and his stories often focus on the search for a new American pastoral utopia. Such a search, his works point out, ultimately results in despair and disillusionment. Brautigan's works comment upon social and personal values in America, linking life and nature. An implicit belief in Brautigan's work is that one cannot find personal happiness in a contaminated, polluted environment.

Critical views differ widely on Brautigan's vision, some emphasizing his apocalyptic, melancholy America, others pointing to his gentle, sweet, optimistic imagery that transcends the hard, workaday world. His use of nature is often compared to that of Henry David Thoreau's *Walden* (1854), especially *Trout Fishing in America*, regarded as Brautigan's best novel. Like Thoreau, Brautigan is considered to be an advocate of the individual conscience rather than the dictates of social laws, a theme explored in all of his early works, perhaps best demonstrated in his *The Abortion: An Historical Romance*, in which a couple live in a library of unpublished books and in which the woman has, without much guilt or any medical complication, an abortion.

Critics generally agree that Brautigan's prose is more important than his verse, and that earlier,

Richard Brautigan's often-whimsical fiction and poetry describe the loss of open space and personal freedom brought by the closing of the frontier. (Erik Weber)

more stylistically innovative writings present his themes more concisely than his later work. Brautigan's canon is widely discussed for his use of metaphorical, whimsical language rather than for any depth of philosophy or meaning. His use of America's past as being both bankrupt of ideas and a necessity for understanding the present, his concern for the fluidity and stability of nature, and his quirky, surreal examinations of social disintegration remain of interest despite his reputation for merely being a spokesman for the revolutionary attitudes of the 1960's.

While continuing to publish after 1971, Brautigan found both his critical and popular support eroding with each successive book. Brautigan apparently committed suicide in September, 1984, but his body was not discovered until October 25 of that year.

SUGGESTED READINGS

Abbott, Keith. *Downstream from Troutfishing in America: A Memoir of Richard Brautigan.* Santa Barbara, Calif.: Capra Press, 1989.

Barber, John F., comp. *Richard Brautigan: An Annotated Bibliography.* Jefferson, N.C.: McFarland, 1990.

Malley, Terence. *Richard Brautigan: Writers for the Seventies.* New York: Warner Books, 1972.

Tanner, Tony. *City of Words: American Fiction, 1950-1970.* New York: HarperCollins, 1971

—Wesley Britton

See also Abortion and birth control; American Dream; American identity: West and the frontier; Countercultures; Popular culture

Broad and Alien Is the World

AUTHOR: Ciro Alegría (1909-1967)
FIRST PUBLISHED: *El mundo es ancho y ajeno*, 1941 (English translation, 1941)
IDENTITIES: Latino

Broad and Alien Is the World reveals Ciro Alegría's commitment to the ideological platform of Acción Popular Revolucionaria Americana (American popular revolutionary action), a socialist-oriented political party that he cofounded in 1930. As a result of his political engagement, which included involvement with guerrilla groups, Alegría was forced into exile. The novel openly attacks the violations of the human rights of the indigenous Peruvian population by national corporations and governmental institutions. The novel's publication caused Peru to become the target of international outcry.

In its open treatment of life among native groups, Alegría's novel moves away from traditional treatment of the Inca. Peru's indigenous people were portrayed in previous works as living in the perfect state of natural existence, in the Romantic tradition of the noble savage. Alegría's realistic descriptions of indigenous rural life are connected to a social movement known as *indigenismo*. This proindigenous movement encouraged a fuller, more honest understanding of the Peruvian national identity. For them, nature and people are interdependent. The city's vicious exploitation of nature, the novel implies, may account for various economic and social crises.

Alegría's novel presents a major character, Rosendo Maquis, mayor of a community of Indians, as a representative of the Incas. Rosendo is wise and hardworking. He is aware of his physical and intellectual limitations but is working toward personal improvement. Considered the intellectual leader of his village, Maquis takes upon himself the task of fighting legally against the local landowner, who has decided to sell to foreign investors the land that is worked by the villagers. The confrontation brings upon Maquis a jail sentence and death resulting from ill treatment during his incarceration.

At a point of desperation, when even natural causes seem to oppose the villagers, Benito Castro, Maquis' adopted son, who has abandoned the village for city life, returns and takes over his father's fight. Benito's youth and socialist ideals oppose the traditional views of the town's elders, who fear his radical politics. Benito's preaching to the youth, however, succeeds in promoting an armed rebellion, a political agenda of the Acción Popular Revolucionaria Americana. Although the movement does not resolve the village's needs, it raises the people's understanding of the importance of political grouping.

Alegría's ideological position in his novel is to promote formation of coalitions among various indigenous groups and urban and rural proletariat factions. Alegría sought to produce an anti-imperialist democracy. Such unity among destitute and marginal social classes, he reasoned, was not possible without a historical analysis of the reasons for their differences. As a novel of thesis, *Broad and Alien Is the World* attempts to provide that analysis by presenting multiple characters who are representative of the Peruvian social structure.

Suggested readings

Early, Eileen. *Joy in Exile: Ciro Alegría's Narrative Art*. Washington, D.C.: University Press of America, 1980.

González Pérez, Armando. *Social Protest and Literary Merit in "Huasipungo" and "El mundo es ancho y ajeno."* Milwaukee: University of Milwaukee, Center for Latin America, 1988.

—*Rafael Ocasio*

See also Alegría, Ciro; Class and identity; Colonialism; Environment and identity; Latino American identity; Poverty

Bronx Remembered, El

Author: Nicholasa Mohr (1935-   )
First published: 1975
Identities: Latino; Northeast; women

Nicholasa Mohr's *El Bronx Remembered* is a collection of short stories depicting life in a Puerto Rican barrio in New York City during the 1960's and 1970's. Well known for her treatment of child, adolescent, and young adult characters, Mohr's depiction of Puerto Rican urban life concentrates on subjects of particular importance to those age groups. Mohr's narratives do not offer a denunciation of the troubled lives of these immigrants and children of immigrants. Instead, her stories bring forward voices that were often, in literature, considered unimportant. Female characters of several age groups and social backgrounds stand out for analysis.

Mohr writes from autobiographical memories; she grew up in a barrio much like the one in her stories. In her hands, the barrio is a strong presence that affects the lives of her characters in myriad ways. City life and traditional Puerto Rican family values are set against each other, producing the so-called Nuyorican culture, or Puerto-Rican-in-New-York culture. The clashes within that hybrid culture are the thematic center of Mohr's short stories.

The introduction to the collection sets a strong historical context for the stories. The 1940's saw an increase in Puerto Rican migration to New York. The arrival of thousands of immigrants changed the ethnic constitution of the city, especially of Manhattan's Lower East Side and the South Bronx. El Bronx, as it is called by the Puerto Ricans, became home to new generations of Puerto Rican immigrants. The center of Nuyorican culture, El Bronx challenges the Nuyorican characters in their struggle to survive in a world of rapid economic and technological changes.

The short stories in *El Bronx Remembered* speak openly about the struggles of the first immigrants with linguistic and other cultural barriers and with racist attitudes within institutions. Mohr's stories, however, attempt to go beyond social criticism. Puerto Rican characters challenge such obstacles. Some succeed in their attempts. Others are overwhelmed by city life, facing the barrio's multiple problems, including drug abuse and gang-related troubles. The message, however, is not pessimistic. Although some characters succumb to tragedy because they are ill prepared to face adversity, others around them survive by learning from the plight of the weak.

Mohr's contribution to ethnic American literature is significant. She has made an important contribution to Latino literature by describing Puerto Rican life in New York City. Her writing has a twofold significance. One, it links the Puerto Rican experience to that of other groups, emphasizing women's issues and those of other marginal characters, such as gays, within the Puerto Rican community. Two, Mohr's work provides a link between the literature written in English about Puerto Rican life in the United States and the literature in Spanish on Puerto Rican issues.

SUGGESTED READINGS

Barbato, Joseph. "Latino Writers in the American Market." *Publishers Weekly* 238, no. 6 (February 1, 1991): 17-21.

Mohr, Eugene V. *The Nuyorican Experience: Literature of the Puerto Rican Minority*. Westport, Conn.: Greenwood Press, 1982.

Reed, Ishmael. *Hispanic American Literature*. New York: HarperCollins, 1995.

Zarnowski, Nyra. "An Interview with Author Nicholasa Mohr." *The Reading Teacher* 45, no. 2 (October, 1991): 106.

—*Rafael Ocasio*

See also Chicano identity; Emigration and immigration; Feminism; Gay identity; Latino American identity; Mohr, Nicholasa; Urban life

Brooks, Gwendolyn

BORN: Topeka, Kansas; June 7, 1917

PRINCIPAL WORKS: *A Street in Bronzeville*, 1945; *Annie Allen*, 1949; *Maud Martha*, 1953; *The Bean Eaters*, 1960; *In the Mecca*, 1968; *Riot*, 1969; *Family Pictures*, 1970; *Report from Part One: An Autobiography*, 1972; *Beckonings*, 1975; *To Disembark*, 1981; *The Near-Johannesburg Boy and Other Poems*, 1986; *Blacks*, 1987; *Gottschalk and the Grand Tarantelle*, 1988; *Winnie*, 1988; *Children Coming Home*, 1991

IDENTITIES: African American; women

SIGNIFICANT ACHIEVEMENT: The first black author to win the Pulitzer Prize in poetry, Brooks affirms the power of ordinary people.

Gwendolyn Brooks, the child of loving parents who valued learning, was encouraged to write. Her father provided a desk and bookshelves; her mother took her to meet the writers Langston Hughes and James Weldon Johnson. After being graduated from Wilson Junior College, she was married to Henry Lowington Blakely, also a writer, in 1939.

From Langston Hughes she received encouragement to write about the everyday aspects of black life. She wrote about relatives she knew or stories she heard growing up. Her early poetry also reflects her dreams for romance. The Pulitzer Prize-winning *Annie Allen* traces the growth of a young woman from childhood to maturity. Brooks is not, however, a romantic poet. Her work exhibits a realistic and unsentimental understanding of what it means to be a black woman in twentieth century America. The strength of her poetry lies in its illumination and criticism of a society that does not respect and reward those who are good. The forms of her work often contain a similar criticism of the literary world: *Annie Allen*, for example, is a parody of a traditional epic poem.

Brooks's novel *Maud Martha* compassionately explores a woman's search for identity and her resulting spiritual growth. Many African American themes are illumined: The light skin versus dark skin motif is one. Much in the novel is taken from Brooks's life. Her autobiography, *Report from Part One*, is a creative composite of experiences, memories, photographs, and interviews. It is less a literary chronology than it is a storytelling experience in the oral tradition.

In the late 1960's, Brooks began working closely with young black writers whose concerns for the poor and oppressed mirrored her own. Her poetry of this period, *Riot* and *Family Pictures*, exhibits a strong voice, an increased use of black speech patterns, and a larger focus on black consciousness. She celebrated her achievement of selfhood with a decision to publish her work with African American publishers. Throughout her career Brooks has looked to the men, women, and children in her black community for inspiration. Through them and for them she has made a difference.

SUGGESTED READINGS

Brooks, Gwendolyn. *Report from Part One*. Detroit: Broadside Press, 1972.

Evans, Mari. *Black Women Writers*. Garden City, N.Y.: Doubleday, 1984.

Kent, George E. *A Life of Gwendolyn Brooks*. Lexington: University Press of Kentucky, 1990.

Melhem, D. H. *Gwendolyn Brooks: Poetry and the Heroic Voice*. Lexington: University Press of Kentucky, 1987.

—Carol F. Bender

See also African American identity; *Street in Bronzeville, A*

Brooks, Gwendolyn, poetry of

AUTHOR: Gwendolyn Brooks (1917-   )

PRINCIPAL WORKS: *A Street in Bronzeville*, 1945; *Annie Allen*, 1949; *The Bean Eaters*, 1960; *Selected Poems*, 1963; *In the Mecca*, 1968; *Riot*, 1969; *Family Pictures*, 1970; *Aloneness*, 1971; *Beckonings*, 1975; *Primer for Blacks*, 1980; *To Disembark*, 1981; *The Near-Johannesburg Boy*, 1986; *Blacks*, 1987; *Gottschalk and the Grand Tarantelle*, 1988; *Winnie*, 1988

IDENTITIES: African American; women

Gwendolyn Brooks, who began her career in 1945 with the publication of her first book, *A Street in Bronzeville*, was first inspired by encouraging parents, her own wisdom, and a personal dedication to words. The Civil Rights movement of the late 1960's, which fostered cultural renewal in black America, expanded her consciousness, nourished her continued growth, and sustained her lifelong love and appreciation for blackness. It is not unusual to hear Brooks speak of the period before 1967 as a time when she had "sturdy" artistic ideas, and the period after 1967 as a time when she felt "sure."

The sturdy years   Her first two books of poetry, *A Street in Bronzeville* and *Annie Allen*, and others written in the 1950's and 1960's appear to conform to tradition in their use of the sonnet form and of slant rhyme. There is, however, nothing traditional about one 1945 sonnet's subject: abortion. In many ways, *A Street in Bronzeville* is untraditional, innovative, and courageous, although written with a sturdy respect for tradition. *Annie Allen*, for which Brooks was awarded a Pulitzer Prize in poetry—the first awarded to an African American—uses narrative verse to trace the growth of a semiautobiographical character from girlhood to womanhood. Brooks drew upon personal experiences and social issues as subjects for many early poems. In 1960, she published *The Bean Eaters*, a collection containing two well-known poems: "We Real Cool," about seven pool players at the Golden Shovel, and "The Chicago *Defender* Sends a Man to Little Rock," written after the 1957 murder of Emmett Till. Her early career also includes publication of *Bronzeville Girls and Boys* (1956), a children's book, and *Selected Poems*.

Although her poetry remained grounded in the joy, frustration, injustice, and reality of black life, Brooks's involvement with young writers in the late 1960's and her poetry workshops for the Blackstone Rangers, a Chicago gang, produced a new voice. Earlier structured forms gave way to free verse. Vocabulary flowed more freely into black vernacular. In *In the Mecca*, a book-length poem about Chicago's old Mecca Building, a mother's search for her child ultimately becomes a metaphor for the individual search for self in an inhumane society: "The Lord was their shepherd./ Yet did they want." **The sure years**

Her sure years produced another identity-affirming change in Brooks's career: the decision to publish with black publishers. *Riot*, *Family Pictures*, and *Beckonings* chronicle social unrest and anger. Although discouraged by the lack of societal change, Brooks continually praises the indefatigable black spirit. Little Lincoln West in "The Life of Lincoln West" finds comfort in knowing he is "the real thing" in spite of society's abuse. In "To Black Women" from *To Disembark*, she calls upon her black sisters in the diaspora to create flowers, to prevail despite "tramplings of monarchs and other men." Later books, such as *The Near-Johannesburg Boy* and *Winnie*, reflect the wider black community. Whether writing about leaders in Africa or children in Chicago, Brooks is conscious of the fact that her people are black people. To them she appeals for understanding.

SUGGESTED READINGS

Evans, Mari. *Black Women Writers*. Garden City, N.Y.: Doubleday, 1984.

Kent, George E. *A Life of Gwendolyn Brooks*. Lexington: University Press of Kentucky, 1990.

Melhem, D. H. *Gwendolyn Brooks: Poetry and the Heroic Voice*. Lexington: University Press of Kentucky, 1987.

Mootry, Maria K., and Gary Smith. *A Life Distilled: Gwendolyn Brooks, Her Poetry and Fiction*. Chicago: University of Illinois Press, 1987.

—Carol F. Bender

See also African American identity; Brooks, Gwendolyn; *Street in Bronzeville, A*

Brothers and Keepers

AUTHOR: John Edgar Wideman (1941-   )
FIRST PUBLISHED: 1984
IDENTITIES: African American

Brothers and Keepers, John Edgar Wideman's most popular novel, is a psychologically realistic portrait of two brothers. Although they grow up in the same environment, Homewood, these brothers travel diverse paths. Wideman is a black star pulsing brilliantly in a white universe; his brother, Robby, sinks into a life of crime and drug addiction. Robby's path leads to his serving a life sentence without parole for taking part in a robbery in which a man was killed. *Brothers and Keepers* is a novel of tragic dimensions, grave despair, and spiritual survival.

This novel had to be written as much for Wideman as for Robby. It is a homecoming for Wideman—a return to the community of brotherhood, concern, and understanding. In part 1, "Visits," readers learn that although Wideman never sees his color as an obstacle to his own success, he views Robby as a black victim of society's ills: "A brother behind bars, my own flesh and blood, raised in the same house by the same mother and father; a brother confined in prison has to be a mistake, a malfunctioning of the system."

In the second part of the novel, "Our Time," Wideman describes his growth and maturation while he spends time with his brother on visits to the prison. Wideman is seen as searching for his own identity while he searches for reasons for Robby's fall from grace. Learning that he needs as much help as Robby does, Wideman gains respect for Robby's intelligence. Wideman also learns the truth about the foiled robbery attempt.

In the final section, "Doing Time," a spirituality operates to bring harmony to the two brothers. Especially moving is Robby's graduation speech as he receives his associate degree, and his promise to Wideman that he will "forever pray." From a sociological point of view, it is interesting that prison can rehabilitate someone like Robby and motivate him to work on his education. It is an equally moving experience to see Wideman connect with his own identity and return to his roots. Wideman learns that he cannot escape genetics or the ghetto. Until Robby is free, Wideman is not free.

SUGGESTED READINGS

Bennetts, Leslie. "Seeds of Violence." *Vanity Fair*, March, 1989, 156-161, 210-214.

Bertley, Christopher. "Brothers and Keepers." Review of *Brothers and Keepers*, by John Edgar Wideman. *Black Enterprise* 15 (May, 1985): 15.

Coleman, J. W. "Going Back Home: The Literary Development of John Edgar Wideman." *College Language Association* 28 (March, 1985): 326-343.

Fraser, C. Gerald. "Brothers and Keepers." Review of *Brothers and Keepers*, by John Edgar Wideman. *The New York Times Book Review*, November 10, 1985, 56.

—*Barbara Cecelia Rhodes*

See also African American identity; Class and identity; Demographics of identity; Drugs

Brown, Claude

BORN: New York, New York; February 23, 1937

PRINCIPAL WORKS: *Manchild in the Promised Land*, 1965; *The Children of Ham*, 1976

IDENTITIES: African American; Northeast

SIGNIFICANT ACHIEVEMENT: Brown's autobiography, *Manchild in the Promised Land*, is considered one of the best and most realistic descriptions of coming of age in a black urban ghetto.

By the time he was thirteen years old, Claude Brown had been hit by a bus, whipped with chains, thrown into a river, and shot in the stomach. Spending more time on the streets of Harlem than in school, Brown was an accomplished thief by the age of ten, when he became a member of the Forty Thieves, a branch of the infamous Buccaneers gang. In a desperate attempt to save their son from his early downward spiral into the penal system, the Browns sent Claude to live with his grandparents for a year. The sojourn seemed to have little effect on him, because soon after his return to Harlem he was sent to the Wiltwyck School for emotionally disturbed boys.

Brown's early life was a seemingly endless series of events leading to one form or another of incarceration. All told, Brown was sent to reform school three times, and in between those times he ran con games and sold hard drugs. He avoided heroin addiction only because the one time he tried it he nearly died. Avoiding drug dependency may have been the key factor in his ability to escape the fate of early death or lengthy incarceration that met so many of his peers. Sensing that he would perish if he remained in Harlem, Brown moved to Greenwich Village at seventeen and began to attend night school.

As he began to understand that living in the ghetto did not mean a certain destiny of crime, misery, and poverty, he no longer believed that living in Harlem would inevitably ruin his life. While selling cosmetics he devoted many hours daily to playing the piano, and eventually enrolled in and was graduated from Howard University. During Brown's first year at Howard, he was urged to write about Harlem for a magazine by Ernest Papanek, who had been the school psychologist at Wiltwyck School. As Brown reflected on his life he began to understand what a difficult feat it is to survive the ghetto, and his writing describes the reasons for the general despair found there. The magazine article led to an offer from a publisher for Brown to write what eventually became *Manchild in the Promised Land*.

SUGGESTED READINGS
Brown, Claude. "Manchild in Harlem." *The New York Times Magazine*, September 16, 1984, 36-77.
Hartshorne, Thomas L. "Horatio Alger in Harlem: *Manchild in the Promised Land.*" *Journal of American Studies* 24, no. 2 (August, 1990): 243-251.

—*Christy Rishoi*

See also *Manchild in the Promised Land*

Brown, Rita Mae

BORN: Hanover, Pennsylvania; November 28, 1944

PRINCIPAL WORKS: *Rubyfruit Jungle*, 1973; *A Plain Brown Rapper*, 1976; *Six of One*, 1978; *Southern Discomfort*, 1982; *Sudden Death*, 1983; *High Hearts*, 1986; *Bingo*, 1988; *Wish You Were Here*, 1990; *Rest in Pieces*, 1993; *Venus Envy*, 1993; *Dolley*, 1994; *Murder at Monticello*, 1994; *Pay Dirt*, 1995; *Riding Shotgun*, 1996

IDENTITIES: European American; gay, lesbian, and bisexual; South; women

SIGNIFICANT ACHIEVEMENT: Brown's novels strive to present Southerners as individuals deserving of respect and consideration instead of caricature and ridicule.

Rita Mae Brown, born out of wedlock, was adopted by the working-class family of Ralph and Julia Ellen Buckingham Brown. Brown was not only a child of uncertain origin, but poor and female. This combination failed to impress the class-and gender-conscious students she trounced academically. Not surprisingly, Brown's works frequently involve a critical appraisal of the class system and the unfortunate tendency of some individuals to denigrate others in consequence of their wealth or gender.

When Brown was eleven, her parents moved to Florida. This change of scene allowed Brown to transcend the circumstance of her birth, but plunged her into an alien society on the verge of chaos. Brown survived the ensuing cultural shock, but her father's death shortly after proved a nearly insurmountable obstacle. Betrayed and abandoned at birth, she found herself again bereft of parental connection, one to death and another to extended grief, as she slipped into the turbulence of adolescence. Brown's father died before she observed any flaws, while her surviving parent daily stood revealed with human imperfections. In Brown's work, men are either paragons of virtue or feckless individuals devoid of redeeming features. As for the maternal portion of Brown's successive novels, although few attain the savagery of *Rubyfruit Jungle*, even the more affectionate assessment of *Six of One* is often delivered through clenched teeth.

The climate when Brown left for college in 1963 was unfavorable toward anyone committed to the equality of every human being without recourse to limitations imposed by birth or inclination. Convinced the South offered her no quarter, Brown headed north, where she found academic validation at New York University and the Institute for Policy Studies, where she was awarded a doctorate. Brown returned to the South; she was not the first Southern writer to seek refuge in the North but to return to the South in memory or in person. With a northern father and a mother of Southern sympathies, she appreciates both sides of the regional coin.

SUGGESTED READINGS
Chew, Martha. "Rita Mae Brown: Feminist Theorist and Southern Novelist." In *Women Writers of the Contemporary South*, edited by Peggy Whitman Prenshaw. Jackson: University Press of Mississippi, 1984.
Ward, Carol M. *Rita Mae Brown*. New York: Twayne, 1993.

—*J. K. Sweeney*

See also Class and identity; Feminism; Lesbian identity; *Rubyfruit Jungle*; *Southern Discomfort*

Brown, William Wells

BORN: Lexington, Kentucky; 1815
DIED: Chelsea, Massachusetts; November 6, 1884

PRINCIPAL WORKS: *Narrative of William W. Brown, a Fugitive Slave, Written by Himself*, 1847; *Clotel: Or, The President's Daughter, a Narrative of Slave Life in the United States*, 1853; *The Black Man: His Antecedents, His Genius, and His Achievements*, 1863

IDENTITIES: African American; South

SIGNIFICANT ACHIEVEMENT: A former slave and an outspoken critic of slavery, Brown wrote *Clotel*, which is the first known novel written by an African American.

The Southern laws that made slave literacy illegal were on the books for a reason. William Wells Brown, a former slave, employed his talents as a writer to argue for African American freedom. In the pre-Civil War years, his eloquence as an orator made him an important figure in the abolitionist crusade, and recognition of his literary activities led to appreciation of his pioneering uses of fiction to critique slavery.

Brown's speeches were often incisive and militant. He showed little admiration for those patriots (such as Thomas Jefferson) who, Brown pointed out, owned and fathered slaves even as they founded a new nation dedicated to liberty and equality. He questioned the respect that is generally accorded to the Declaration of Independence and to the Revolutionary War by revealing how these icons of American history failed to confront African enslavement. At an antislavery meeting in 1847 he said that if the United States "is the 'cradle of liberty,' they have rocked the child to death."

Opponents of abolition often founded their arguments on racist assumptions. Brown's detractors made much of the fact that Brown's father was a white man (probably his master's brother), and implied that his achievements stemmed from the "white blood" of his father. For example, when Brown traveled to Europe to gain overseas support for abolitionism, an English journalist sneered that Brown was "far removed from the black race . . . his distinct enunciation evidently showed that a white man 'spoke' within."

Brown never sought to deny his racial heritage. In later versions of *Clotel* published in 1860 and 1864, Brown recast his mulatto hero as a black rebel. As he makes clear in *Narrative of William W. Brown, a Fugitive Slave, Written by Himself*, his works were motivated by a deep commitment to the plight of the three million American slaves, a number that included his own family. Brown's literary efforts undertaken in behalf of his enslaved brethren were no doubt prepared by his earlier role in secreting fugitive slaves to Canada.

These fugitives, as Brown had himself, often fled slavery at the price of severing familial ties. He dramatized the strain that slavery places upon family connections in *Clotel*, the first known African American novel. Creating a historical fiction from the well-known fact that Jefferson had a slave mistress, Brown details the outrage of the auction block, the struggle for autonomy, and the tragic ends of slave women who could trace their bloodlines to the author of the Declaration of Independence. The mixed heritage of his heroines—white and black, free and enslaved—points to the contradictions of a nation that idealized liberty even as it practiced slavery.

SUGGESTED READINGS

Ernest, John. *Resistance and Reformation in Nineteenth-Century African-American Literature: Brown, Wilson, Jacobs, Delany, Douglass, and Harper*. Jackson: University Press of Mississippi, 1995.

Farrison, William Edward. *William Wells Brown: Author and Reformer*. Chicago: University of Chicago Press, 1969.

Yellin, Jean Fagan. *The Intricate Knot: Black Figures in American Literature, 1776-1863*. New York: New York University Press, 1972.

—*Russ Castronovo*

See also *Narrative of William W. Brown, a Fugitive Slave, Written by Himself*; Slave narratives; Slavery

Brown Girl, Brownstones

AUTHOR: Paule Marshall (1929-   )

FIRST PUBLISHED: 1959

IDENTITIES: Adolescence and coming-of-age; Caribbean; family; Northeast; women

Brown Girl, Brownstones, Paule Marshall's first novel, set in the Barbadian community of Brooklyn, focuses on the coming-of-age of Selina Boyce, whose parents emigrated from Barbados. Selina's initiation into adulthood is complicated by family strife and the racial prejudice she finds in Brooklyn in the 1940's. Her mother, mirroring the Barbadian community around her, strives for the American Dream of owning her own home, while her father refuses to be caught up in the pursuit of that dream, longing to return to the idyllic life he associates with Barbados. Selina is caught in the family tensions between her father's free spirit and her mother's power. Although most often drawn toward her father, she recognizes the pull of her mother. Selina discovers that she cannot find her own way by following either parent.

The first glimpse the reader gets of Selina highlights contradictions and conflicts: Although only ten, her eyes suggest an uncanny age; she springs forward while at the same time pulling herself backward with one arm; she imagines herself wearing a gown and belonging to the genteel white family that previously lived in the brownstone now rented by the Boyces, but she sees her lanky and ragged reflection in a mirror.

Several characters in the novel mark Selina's development from an awkward ten-year-old into a graceful dancer and successful college student. She quickly outgrows her childhood friend Beryl, who opts for conformity with the community; Selina's friendship with Miss Thompson, an African American, provides some solace from family strife and widens her knowledge about American society and prejudice; Selina leaves Clive, her lover, recognizing in him an inertia that also took hold of her father before his death.

By the novel's end, Selina decides to leave Brooklyn and travel to Barbados alone. Although often at odds with her mother and the Barbadian community, Selina, before leaving, makes peace with both; she leaves the brownstone and her community not with bitterness, but with determination to find her own way.

SUGGESTED READINGS

Byerman, Keith E. "Gender, Culture, and Identity in Paule Marshall's *Brown Girl, Brownstones*." In *Redefining Autobiography in Twentieth-Century Women's Fiction: An Essay Collection*, edited by Janice Morgan and Colette T. Hall. New York: Garland, 1991.

Christian, Barbara. "Sculpture and Space: The Interdependency of Character and Culture in the Novels of Paule Marshall." In *Black Women Novelists: The Development of a Tradition, 1892-1976*. Westport, Conn.: Greenwood Press, 1980.

Christol, Helene. "Paule Marshall's Bajan Women in *Brown Girl, Brownstones*." In *Women and War: The Changing Status of American Women from the 1930's to the 1950's*, edited by Maria Diedrich and Dorothea Fischer-Hornung. New York: St. Martin's Press, 1990.

—Marion Boyle Petrillo

See also Adolescent identity; American Dream; *Bildungsroman* and *Künstlerroman*; Caribbean American literature; Class and identity; Emigration and immigration; Women and identity

Brownmiller, Susan

BORN: Brooklyn, New York; February 15, 1935

PRINCIPAL WORKS: *Shirley Chisholm*, 1971; *Against Our Will: Men, Women and Rape*, 1975; *Femininity*, 1984; *Waverly Place*, 1989

IDENTITIES: European American; women

SIGNIFICANT ACHIEVEMENT: Brownmiller's work has called attention to important women's issues; in particular, Brownmiller framed the feminist discussion of rape as an act of domination.

Susan Brownmiller recalls, in her book *Femininity*, her early gender training, in which she was dressed in frilly clothing and told to stay clean, was given dolls and tea sets to play with, and learned from the stories, films, and advertisements with which she grew up that, as a girl, she was a fairy princess. She says she loved it. By the time she reached adolescence, however, Brownmiller was struggling with this feminine image, which required very strict behaviors and expectations, but which she knew, if lost, would have dire consequences.

As time went on she began to analyze not only the rigid codes of femininity but also other kinds of social codes imposed on women. In 1975, she published the work for which she is perhaps most well-known: *Against Our Will*. In her introduction to this book, Brownmiller describes her own growing awareness of the realities of rape over the preceding few years. During this time, she moved from a naïve denial that rape was anything more than a bizarre crime inflicted by deranged men on a certain type of woman, to an understanding that rape was not only something that could happen to any woman, and thus made every woman vulnerable, but also that rape was a method of enforcing and maintaining male dominance over women. This book has become a feminist classic and has defined the current understanding of rape as a crime not of sex but of domination and power, an act of violence that limits the freedom of all women. The book also documents the systematic way rape is used as an act of war, in which women are used as pawns in male struggles against each other. Brownmiller's first work of fiction, *Waverly Place*, addresses another feminist issue that has come to the forefront of her attention, that of domestic violence. The book was inspired by the widely publicized case of Hedda Nussbaum and Joel Steinberg. Brownmiller's fiction and nonfiction work has always been based in her feminist perspective and identity. Her works typically highlight feminist issues, including rape, the restrictions of feminine norms, and domestic violence.

SUGGESTED READINGS

Edwards, Alison. *Rape, Racism, and the White Women's Movement: An Answer to Susan Brownmiller*. 2d ed. Chicago: Sojourner Truth Organization, 1979.

Leo, John. "The Comeback of Feminine Wiles." *Time*, January 30, 1984, 82.

Sheffield, Carole J. "Sexual Terrorism." In *Women: A Feminist Perspective*, edited by Jo Freeman. 4th ed. Mountain View, Calif: Mayfield, 1989.

—*Eleanor B. Amico*

See also Feminism; Women and identity

Bulosan, Carlos

BORN: Binalonan, Pangasinan, Luzon, Philippines; November 2, 1911

DIED: Seattle, Washington; September 11, 1956

PRINCIPAL WORKS: *Letter from America*, 1942; *The Voice of Bataan*, 1943; *The Laughter of My Father*, 1944; *America Is in the Heart*, 1946

IDENTITIES: Pacific Islander

SIGNIFICANT ACHIEVEMENT: Bulosan provides the best introduction to the lives of Filipino immigrant workers in America.

Carlos Bulosan never forgot his background as a Filipino farmer's son. He expressed the pride he had in this background as well as the severe social situations which small farmers as well as other hired workers faced in their day-to-day attempts to earn a livelihood. A turning point in Bulosan's life, which fixed in his memory and conscience the small farmers' and hired workers' need for a voice, came when Bulosan's father lost the family's small farm and entered the world of serfdom—slavery—in his native Philippines.

Bulosan learned one important lesson from his father: By confronting his daily tasks and hardships with laughter and cunning, Bulosan saw his father retain his personal identity. Bulosan's father showed his son how one is able to speak as loudly against injustices through satire and laughter as through political diatribe. Bulosan recounts many stories of his father in the many pieces which appeared in leading American publications.

In search of a better life, Bulosan worked his way to America, landing in Seattle on July 22, 1930, and found himself on the streets with others looking for work during the Depression. The good life escaped Bulosan because jobs were few and because of the extreme jingoism rampant in America at the time. Although Bulosan never intended to lose his identity as a Filipino, those with whom he came into contact constantly berated him for being an outsider and a Filipino.

Bulosan began to take whatever job he could find, always being relegated to secondary positions because of his ethnicity. As hard as he tried to fit into the American Dream of a better life, he was denied entrance. Bulosan chronicles his father's difficult life in America as an unwanted outsider in his autobiographical novel, *America Is in the Heart.* Bulosan's dream of a life better than that of his father was never realized. He soon learned that he, too, was a slave to those controlling the jobs. This no doubt contributed to Bulosan's strong support and activity in the many workers' movements that arose during his life. Bulosan's hard life also, no doubt, contributed to his early death.

SUGGESTED READINGS

Evangelista, Susan, ed. *Carlos Bulosan and His Poetry: A Biography and Anthology.* Seattle: University of Washington Press, 1985.

San Juan, E., Jr. *Carlos Bulosan and the Imagination of the Class Struggle.* New York: Oriole Editions, 1976.

_____, ed. *Introduction to Modern Pilipino Literature.* New York: Twayne, 1974.

—*Tom Frazier*

See also Asian American identity: Pacific Islands; Class and identity; Racism and ethnocentrism

Burning House, The

AUTHOR: Ann Beattie (1947-   )
FIRST PUBLISHED: 1982
IDENTITIES: European American; family; Northeast; women

This collection of stories established Ann Beattie as one of the foremost voices of her generation and earned for her a reputation as a literary stylist. Her spare style suggests a sense of emptiness or absence that is also the subject of these stories, which deal with disintegrating relationships set within the context of the social changes and shifts in identity that came out of the 1960's. All her characters are white, middle-class people from the East Coast who are past their youth. They are rudderless, drifting in and out of relationships, marriages, families, and jobs with an alienation that holds little promise.

Many of her characters are having tremendous difficulty in giving up their youthful, counter-culture selves for a more adult identity. In the story "Winter: 1978," for example, two successful baby boomers are overwhelmed when death and loss enter their lives for the first time. The story "Jacklighting" also features a group of friends who are beginning to lose their youth without gaining much in the way of wisdom or maturity. In many of Beattie's stories, in fact, the principle of generation is subverted, with children assuming adult identities while their parents attempt to prolong their childhoods. In "Greenwich Time," a too-adult child reads existential psychiatrist R. D. Laing and eats French food while his disoriented father looks for mothering from the child's housekeeper. The title story concerns a weekend houseparty in which the all-male guests are portrayed as lost boys. The charmingly boyish husband in "The Cinderella Waltz" abandons his wife and his homosexual lover, and will eventually abandon his daughter. Abandonment is a strong theme in many of these stories. A story like "Playback" is typical in its portrayal of loneliness and loss. Often, high hopes for romance end in disillusionment, or, as in "Learning to Fall" and "Desire," a woman continues to live with a man she no longer loves. Sometimes, as in "Sunshine and Shadow," it is the man who can neither love nor leave. This theme of an emotional paralysis that freezes action and feeling is revisited in several other stories, such as "Waiting," in which a detached approach to sadness and loss blunts the pain but drains life of any vitality. This "minimal self" has sometimes been linked to the contemporary personality disorder known as narcissism, in which a cool, poised, detached persona cannot cope with love or intimacy.

SUGGESTED READINGS

Montresor, Jaye Berman. *The Critical Response to Ann Beattie*. Westport, Conn.: Greenwood Press, 1993.

Murphy, Christine. *Ann Beattie*. Boston: G. K. Hall, 1986.

Stillinger, Jack. *Multiple Authorship and the Myth of Solitary Genius*. New York: Oxford University Press, 1991.

—Margaret Boe Birns

See also Alienation; American identity: Northeast; Beattie, Ann; Divorce; Erotic identity

C

Cable, George Washington

BORN: New Orleans, Louisiana; October 12, 1844
DIED: St. Petersburg, Florida; January 31, 1925
PRINCIPAL WORKS: *Old Creole Days*, 1879; *The Grandissimes: A Story of Creole Life*, 1880; *Madame Delphine*, 1881; *Strong Hearts*, 1899; *The Cavalier*, 1901; *Kincaid's Battery*, 1908; *Gideon's Band: A Tale of the Mississippi*, 1914; *The Flower of the Chapdelaines*, 1918
IDENTITIES: African American; European American; South
SIGNIFICANT ACHIEVEMENT: Cable examined slavery and racial discrimination from a psychological base, refusing to be an apologist for whites.

The New Orleans into which George Washington Cable was born in 1844 was the most multiethnic city in the United States. The Creole majority was descended from early French and Spanish inhabitants. Acadians, also known as Cajuns, established themselves there after arriving from Canada's eastern provinces. Blacks, free and slave, did the work, and the Mississippi River, the nation's most traveled highway during the early 1800's, daily brought new arrivals from points north.

Cable's father died when George was fifteen, necessitating his taking a job. By 1861, Cable was in the grocery business. In 1863, with the Union occupation of New Orleans, the Cables relocated to Mississippi, where George joined the Confederate Army. He was wounded twice in battle. Returning to New Orleans after the war, Cable took various jobs and struggled against malaria. In 1869, he married Louise Stewart Bartlett, with whom he had six children.

Cable's literary career began as a writer for the New Orleans *Picayune*, in which his column, "Drop Shot," was popular. By 1872, he was writing a series of sketches about New Orleans history and life for the *Picayune*, basing his tales on materials from historical archives. These sketches capture Southern life with a verisimilitude similar to that of William Faulkner, Eudora Welty, and Reynolds Price.

In 1873, a journalist for *Scribner's* magazine met Cable and, intrigued by his sketches, took several of them to editors for *Scribner's* in New York, who earlier had rejected a book compiled from Cable's "Drop Shot" pieces. In October, 1873, Cable's "'Sieur George" appeared in *Scribner's*. Cable's writing career began to flourish. *Old Creole Days* was a resounding success, establishing Cable's reputation. Stories such as "Jean-ah Poquelin" expose authentically Southern loyalties, secrecy, deceptions, and decadence.

The publication of *Madame Delphine* and *The Grandissimes* placed Cable among America's leading writers. In 1884, he undertook a four-month reading tour with Mark Twain. He continued writing during the first two decades of the twentieth century, producing thirty volumes in all. Cable explores American identity from the viewpoint of a Southerner who is critical of the South's racism.

SUGGESTED READINGS
Butcher, Philip. *George W. Cable*. New York: Twayne, 1962.
Cleman, John. *George Washington Cable Revisited*. Boston: Twayne, 1996.
Turner, Arlin. *Critical Essays on George W. Cable*. Boston: G. K. Hall, 1980.
_____. *George W. Cable*. Durham, N. C.: Duke University Press, 1968.

—R. Baird Shuman

See also Creole and Acadian literature; Racism and ethnocentrism

Cahan, Abraham

BORN: Podberezy, Lithuania; July 6, 1860

DIED: New York, New York; August 31, 1951

PRINCIPAL WORKS: *Yekl: A Tale of the New York Ghetto*, 1896; *The Imported Bridegroom and Other Stories of the New York Ghetto*, 1898; *The White Terror and the Red: A Novel of Revolutionary Russia*, 1905; *The Rise of David Levinsky*, 1917

IDENTITIES: Jewish; Northeast

SIGNIFICANT ACHIEVEMENT: As a novelist and a journalist, Cahan was a voice for his fellow Jewish immigrants.

As a young man in Russia, Abraham Cahan experienced many different identities: pious Jew, Russian intellectual, Nihilist. By his early twenties, in response to prevalent anti-Semitism and recent pogroms, Cahan had become a full-fledged revolutionary socialist, dedicated to the overthrow of the czar and hunted by the Russian government. Hoping to create in America a prototype communist colony in which Jew and gentile were equal, Cahan immigrated to New York in 1882.

Upon his arrival, Cahan modulated his outspoken socialism and embarked on a distinguished career as a Yiddish-language journalist, English teacher, and novelist. As editor for the Yiddish-language *Jewish Daily Forward*, Cahan transformed the paper from a dry mouthpiece for socialist propaganda into a vital community voice, still socialist in its leanings but dedicated to improving the lives of its audience.

One of the early realists, Cahan is appreciated for his frank portrayals of immigrant life. *Yekl: A Tale of the New York Ghetto*, Cahan's first novel in English, follows the rocky road toward Americanization of Yekl Podkovnik, a Russian Jewish immigrant desperately trying to assimilate. Faced with two choices for a wife, Yekl chooses the more assimilated Mamie over his Old World spouse, Gitl, but for all his efforts to become "a Yankee," Yekl's tale ends on a melancholy note, demonstrating that he is unable to break out of his immigrant identity simply by changing his clothes, his language, and his wife.

Cahan's sense of the loss and confusion faced by immigrants to America is also evident in *The Rise of David Levinsky*. This masterful novel tells the rags-to-riches story of a clothier who, despite his wealth and success, is lonely and forlorn, distant from his Russian Jewish beginnings, and alienated from American culture. Following the publication of *Yekl*, Cahan was ushered into the national spotlight by William Dean Howells, who had encouraged many other regional and ethnic writers. Cahan's career in mainstream English-language publishing, however, was short-lived. After *The Rise of David Levinsky* Cahan wrote no more fiction in English, choosing instead to act as a mentor for other writers and to pour his energies into the *Jewish Daily Forward*.

SUGGESTED READINGS

Chametzky, Jules. *From the Ghetto: The Fiction of Abraham Cahan*. Amherst: University of Massachusetts Press, 1977.

Marovitz, Sanford E. "The Lonely New Americans of Abraham Cahan." *American Quarterly* 20 (Summer, 1968): 196-210.

Sanders, Ronald. *The Downtown Jews: Portraits of an Immigrant Generation*. New York: Harper & Row, 1969.

—*Anne Fleischmann*

See also Acculturation; Emigration and immigration; Jewish American identity; Melting pot

Cajuns. *See* Creole and Acadian literature

Calling Myself Home

AUTHOR: Linda Hogan (1947-   )

FIRST PUBLISHED: 1978

IDENTITIES: Native American; West and Southwest; women

The collection *Calling Myself Home* includes ten poems in the first section, "By the Dry Pond," dedicated to the author's sister. The second part has sixteen poems under the heading "Heritage." The first ten poems are reflective meditations that turn to an arid and materially impoverished landscape, yet the poems present memories full of wonder and reverent attention to details of landscape, as well as awareness of connectedness to a historic and prehistoric past. The frequent references to the ancient turtle inhabiting the now-dry pond, for instance, offer an image of patient endurance and survival and an allusion to the great tortoise that, in many Native American mythologies, supports the world on its back. The title poem, "calling myself home," weaves themes together in its imaginative depiction of old women dancing to the rattles they create from turtle shells and pebbles. The speaker goes on to express an identity of connection among herself, her people, and the ancient ones: All are compared to the turtle, a natural emblem of patience and ancient wisdom as well as a crucial figure in many American Indian myths. Such affinity between people—especially women—and their land creates great strength. The generations of women forebears the author celebrates become part of the strength of the earth. Paradoxically, the speaker ends the poem on a note of farewell, stating that she has come to say goodbye, yet the substance of the poem indicates that the speaker, like the turtle, will carry her "home" with her always.

The second section of *Calling Myself Home* includes more poems meditating on the author's personal and family experience and moves to larger themes of her heritage as a Chickasaw woman. The section's title poem, "Heritage," alludes specifically to events she has elsewhere described as happening to her great-grandparents and other relatives: a plague of grasshoppers that destroyed her great-grandfather's farm in Nebraska, her uncle who carved delicate wood and bone objects and passed on traditional Chickasaw lore, her silent grandfather, and the counsel and practice of her grandmother. She alludes to secret wisdom, suppressed knowledge, and the sense of "never having a home."

Other poems in *Calling Myself Home* celebrate metamorphosis and transformation, pervasive themes and modes of writing throughout the author's work. The natural transformation in the birth of a colt is acknowledged in "Celebration: Birth of a Colt," while "The River Calls Them" offers close observation of the metamorphosis of tadpoles into frogs. In "Man in the Moon" the speaker identifies with the mutating phases of the moon, now emaciated and nearly invisible, now fat with a house that will "fill up with silver." In "Rain" metamorphosis becomes method as well as theme, as rainfall is portrayed as fish falling from the sky, while the actual fish, revivified by the rain, feed the exuberant children. In "Vapor Cave" the theme of metamorphosis extends beyond cultural past to identification with the earth itself. The vapor cave is a womblike hollow, both erotically steamy and innocently purifying; the speaker enters to be cleansed and restored and finds herself transmuting as her limbs seem to be dissolving their boundaries. The poem echoes the meditation in "Calling Myself Home" on women's bones transmuted into the calcified, tortoise-like skeleton of the earth.

SUGGESTED READINGS

Ackerberg, Peggy Maddux. "Breaking Boundaries: Writing Past Gender, Genre, and Genocide in Linda Hogan." *Studies in American Indian Literatures* 6, no. 3 (1994): 7-14.

Hogan, Linda. " 'A heart made out of crickets': An Interview with Linda Hogan." Interview by B. Scholer. *The Journal of Ethnic Studies* 16, no. 1 (1988): 107-117.

_____. "An Interview with Linda Hogan." *The Missouri Review* 17, no. 2 (1994): 109-124.

_____. "Linda Hogan." Interview by Patricia Clark Smith. In *This Is About Vision: Interviews with Southwestern Writers*, edited by William Balassi, John F. Crawford, and Annie O. Esturoy. Albuquerque: University of New Mexico Press, 1990.

—*Helen Jaskoski*

See also *Daughters, I Love You*; Feminism; Native American identity

Calvinism. *See* Puritan and Protestant tradition; Religion and identity

Camp Notes and Other Poems

AUTHOR: Mitsuye Yamada (1923-   )
FIRST PUBLISHED: 1976
IDENTITIES: Japanese American; women

The poems in *Camp Notes and Other Poems* originated in the experience of a concentration camp. Mitsuye Yamada and her family were interned with other Japanese Americans from the West Coast during World War II. Yamada spent April, 1942, through September, 1943, at the internment camp near Minidoka, Idaho. Inmates could have few possessions; Yamada brought a tablet of paper on which she recorded her reflections on life in the camp. To the poems from this period she later added others concerning the time preceding and the time following the camp experience.

At the beginning of the book are poems about ancestors and parents: great-grandmother's box of treasured souvenirs, a young bride in a new and precarious environment, a folktale related by a sophisticated father. Following the poems about internment are poems related to the poet's later life. These poems frequently have themes that are a feature of the center section about the internment: justice, equity, and generosity. These themes are continuing threads in these poems, which occasionally have a feminist perspective.

The middle, or "Camp Notes," section contains the angriest poems. With irony, the speaker in the poems expresses and conquers the rage, humiliation, and despair of unjust captivity. A photographer's instruction to "smile" as internees are collected at staging points, the bus ride to the camps, a guard tower seen through the eyes of a child, makeshift furniture of packing crates and straw mattresses, stuffing rags into cracks in the shacklike barracks during a dust storm—each of these moments is crystallized. The poem titled "Curfew" ends in a particularly vivid commentary: After quoting the "block head" giving orders for lights out, the speaker simply remarks, "There must be no light." One of the briefest poems, "In the Outhouse," is also one of the most powerful. The stench of the outhouse becomes a metaphor for the entire camp and the mentality that created it; fear and racism relegate a whole group of people to the domain of "refuse" and "outsider." Many of the poems focus on the absurdity and duplicity of the language and thinking used to justify the camps. In "Desert Storm" the speaker notes the euphemisms that attempted to disguise injustice, noting how the reality of imprisonment was "sanitized" by the term "relocation." The speaker notes in "The Trick Was" that the "mind was not fooled."

Camp Notes and Other Poems is actually a cooperative and family project. Yamada's husband, Yoshikazu Yamada, contributed the calligraphs that translate titles and text for some of the poems. Her daughters, Jeni and Hedi, produced illustrations for some pages. Yamada also includes a translation of one of her father's poems, written while he was interned apart from his family in a different camp.

SUGGESTED READINGS

Schweik, Susan. "A Needle with Mama's Voice: Mitsuye Yamada's *Camp Notes* and the American Canon of War Poetry." In *Arms and the Woman: War, Gender, and Literary Representation*, edited by Helen M. Cooper, Susan Merrill Squier, and Adrienne Auslander Munich. Chapel Hill: University of North Carolina Press, 1989.

Yamada, Mitsuye. "A MELUS Interview: Mitsuye Yamada." Interview by Helen Jaskoski. *MELUS* 15, no. 1 (1988): 97-108.

—*Helen Jaskoski*

See also Asian American identity: China, Japan, and Korea; Japanese American internment

Campbell, Bebe Moore

BORN: Philadelphia, Pennsylvania; 1950

PRINCIPAL WORKS: *Sweet Summer: Growing Up with and Without My Dad*, 1989; *Your Blues Ain't Like Mine*, 1992; *Brothers and Sisters*, 1994

IDENTITIES: African American; women

SIGNIFICANT ACHIEVEMENT: Campbell offers telling portraits of people of many backgrounds.

As a child, Bebe Moore Campbell spent her school years in Philadelphia with her mother and her summers in North Carolina with her father. She writes of this divided life in *Sweet Summer: Growing Up with and Without My Dad*, drawing sharp contrasts between the two worlds. She credits both parents with shaping her into a writer.

Her mother, an avid storyteller, designated Sundays as church day and library day. Having learned the value of stories and writing, Campbell composed stories for her father, cliffhangers designed to elicit his immediate response. By the third grade, she knew that she wanted to be a writer; however, not until her mother gave her a book written by an African American did she feel affirmed in that ambition. The knowledge that African Americans wrote books gave her the permission she needed to pursue her dream.

Her first novel, *Your Blues Ain't Like Mine*, was inspired by the 1955 murder of Emmett Till, an African American teenager from Chicago who was killed in Mississippi after speaking to a white woman. Till's death was widely discussed in the African American community, and Campbell grew up feeling that she had known him. Since his murderers were never brought to justice, she sought in *Your Blues Ain't Like Mine* to create a fictional world in which the justice that society withheld exists. The novel showcases her ability to portray many diverse characters.

Her second novel, *Brothers and Sisters*, is set around another event affecting the African American community. Rodney King, an African American motorist, was beaten by police officers in Los Angeles in 1992. The beating was captured on videotape, but the policemen were found not guilty in their first trial, resulting in riots. Delving into the aftermath of this event, *Brothers and Sisters* explores the way in which race affects the relationship between an African American woman and a white woman.

Although Campbell's works reflect her experiences as a woman, she feels that she has been oppressed more for her color than for her gender. Her writings are primarily shaped by her identity as an African American, but her diverse characters reveal more of the commonalities that exist between people than the differences.

SUGGESTED READINGS

Campbell, Bebe Moore. "Bebe Moore Campbell: Her Memoir of 'A Special Childhood' Celebrates the Different Styles of Her Upbringing in a Divided Black Family." Interview by Lisa See. *Publishers Weekly*, June 30, 1989, 82-84.

Time. Review of *Your Blues Ain't Like Mine*, by Bebe Moore Campbell. November 9, 1992, 89.

—*Jacquelyn Benton*

See also African American identity; Civil Rights movement; Racism and ethnocentricism; *Your Blues Ain't Like Mine*

Canadian identity

IDENTITIES: Canada

Two cultures

Canada is a country in which two cultures, English and French, exist side by side. The French province of Quebec clings to French as its language, as do parts of Ontario. The Maritime Provinces, those in Canada's midwest, in the far west, and in the north are essentially British in their outlook and language. Canada's literature has also been influenced by its native and immigrant populations, including a strong Asian influence in British Columbia. Canadian literature has been written largely in two languages and has reflected two cultures that do not always coexist harmoniously. Added to this cultural split is the strong influence of the United States upon Canada.

Early Canadian literature

The first literature in English about Canada came from the pens of British explorers and military officers who were stationed in the sprawling country. Their writing largely took the form of diaries, journals, and letters. Frances Brooke, whose husband was a British army chaplain stationed in

Quebec, wrote an early epistolary novel in English, *The History of Emily Montague* (1769), that captures Quebec's milieu, both social and physical, remarkably well.

Among the earliest nonfiction writers, Samuel Hearne produced a stark narrative about his travels and explorations, *A Journey from Prince of Wales' Fort in Hudson's Bay to the Northern Ocean* (1795). This account emphasizes the wilderness landscapes and seascapes, the harshness of nature, and the sheer magnitude of all he saw. Six years later, Sir Alexander Mackenzie, a fur trader connected with the Hudson's Bay Company, produced *Voyages from Montreal* (1801), a

Canadian Literature in English
Milestones

1600's–1700's	Explorers, ship captains, and "writers" (literate people serving as accountants) for fur trading companies, most notably the Hudson's Bay Company, begin a new tradition in letters, the factual, unvarnished, first-person account, often the fruit of logs, journals, and company records-keeping. This rich lore is later mined by such authors and editors as Farley Mowat. Authors of exploration accounts include Daniel Harmon, Peter Fidler, and Matthew Cocking. Indian literature, especially the Indians' renowned and difficult-to-translate oratory, is notably recorded in written form in the 73 volumes of the *Jesuit Relations*, a series of reports from Québec to Paris covering the years 1610 to 1791 and published from 1896 to 1901.	1836	Catherine Parr Strickland Traill's *The Backwoods of Canada*.
		1836	Thomas Chandler Haliburton's *The Clockmaker*.
		1852	Susanna Strickland Moodie's *Roughing It in the Bush*.
		1874	Joseph Howe's *Poems and Essays*.
		1884	Isabella Valancy Crawford's *Old Spookses' Pass, Malcolm's Katie, and Other Poems*.
		1896	Sir Charles George Douglas Roberts' *Earth's Enigmas*. The realistic animal story genre, a Canadian invention, traces its origin to Roberts and to Ernest Thompson Seton.
1743	James Isham's *Observations on Hudson's Bay* compiled, published in 1949. Describes Indian life and customs.	1897	Poet Bliss Carman's *Ballads of Lost Haven: A Book of the Sea*.
1769	Frances Brooke's epistolary novel *The History of Emily Montague*.	1897	*The Habitant and Other French-Canadian Poems*, by William Henry Drummond.
1770	Approximate starting date of Andrew Graham's records of the flora, fauna, and peoples of Canada, published as *Observations on Hudson's Bay 1767-91* in 1969.	1898	Ernest Thompson Seton's *Wild Animals I Have Known*.
		1900	*The Poems of Archibald Lampman*, by Archibald Lampman.
1789	First publication of *Nova-Scotia Magazine*.	1902	*Glengarry School Days: A Story of Early Days in Glengarry*, by Ralph Connor, pen name of Charles William Gordon.
1795	Samuel Hearne's *A Journey from Prince of Wale's Fort in Hudson's Bay to the Northern Ocean*, which contains ample description of the environment.	1902	*Kindred of the Wild*, by Sir Charles George Douglas Roberts.
		1904	Sara Jeanette Duncan's *The Imperialist*.
1801	Sir Alexander Mackenzie's *Voyages from Montreal*, another account of exploration.	1907	Robert W. Service's *Songs of a Sourdough*.
1821–1823	Thomas McCullough's satirical *Letters of Mephibosheth Stepsure*.	1908	Lucy Maud Montgomery's *Anne of Green Gables*.
1825	Oliver Goldsmith's *The Rising Village*.	1912	Stephen Leacock's *Sunshine Sketches of a Little Town*.
1828	Joseph Howe purchases the magazine *Novascotian* and begins to turn it into an important cultural record.	1915	John McRae's "In Flanders' Fields," about World War I.
		1923	E. J. Pratt's *Newfoundland Verse*.
1832	John Richardson's *Wacousta: Or, The Prophecy, a Tale of the Canadas*.	1926	Duncan Campbell Scott's *The Poems of Duncan Campbell Scott*.

straightforward account of his perilous explorations into what was then designated on many maps as unknown territory, in pursuit of furbearing animals for whose pelts the Hudson's Bay Company and the North West Company had an insatiable appetite.

As early as 1789, an important literary publication, *Nova-Scotia Magazine*, appeared in Halifax. Before long several such journals existed in Nova Scotia, offering writers, particularly poets, a ready outlet for their writing. During the nineteenth century, poetry was the most significant form of literary expression in English-speaking Canada.

Literature in Nova Scotia

Canadian Literature in English Milestones — CONTINUED

1929	Bliss Carman's *Sanctuary*.
1932	*Signpost*, by Dorothy Livesay.
1933	Frederick Philip Grove's *Fruits of the Earth*.
1936	Sir Charles George Douglas Roberts' *Further Animal Stories*.
1937	Morley Callaghan's *More Joy in Heaven*.
1940	*Hath Not a Jew . . .* , by A. M. Klein.
1941	*As for Me and My House*, by Sinclair Ross.
1945	Hugh MacLennan's *Two Solitudes*.
1947	Paul Hiebert's satirical novel *Sarah Binks*.
1947	W. O. Mitchell's *Who Has Seen the Wind?*
1952	Ernest Buckler's *The Mountain and the Valley*.
1952	E. J. Pratt's *Towards the Last Spike*.
1954	Ethel Wilson's *Swamp Angel*.
1956	Adele Wiseman's *The Sacrifice*.
1957	*Anatomy of Criticism*, an influential work of criticism by Northrop Frye.
1957	*The Blasted Pine: An Anthology of Satire, Invective, and Disrespectful Verse, Chiefly by Canadian Writers*, edited by F. R. Scott and A. J. M. Smith.
1959	Mordecai Richler's *The Apprenticeship of Duddy Kravitz*.
1959	Hugh MacLennan's *The Watch That Ends the Night*.
1960	Farley Mowat publishes an edition of an exploration journal, *Ordeal By Ice*, the first of the Top of the World trilogy.
1960	Malcolm Ross publishes an influential anthology, *Poets of the Confederation*.
1962	Rudy Wiebe's *Peace Shall Destroy Many*.
1964	Margaret Laurence's *The Stone Angel*.
1964	Marshall McLuhan's *Understanding Media: The Extension of Man*.
1966	Leonard Cohen's *Beautiful Losers*.
1966	Francis Reginald Scott's *Selected Poems*.
1967	Editor Mowat's *The Polar Passion*, the second exploration journal of the Top of the World trilogy.
1969	*Crabdance*, an absurdist play by Beverly Simons.
1969	Margaret Atwood's *The Edible Woman*.
1970	*Fifth Business*, the first of the Deptford trilogy of novels by Robertson Davies.
1971	Alice Munro's *Lives of Girls and Women*.
1972	*The Manticore*, the second of the Deptford triology of novels by Davies.
1972	Atwood's *Surfacing*, about a woman's self-discovery in rural Canada.
1973	Editor Mowat's *Tundra*, the third exploration journal of the Top of the World trilogy.
1975	*World of Wonders*, the third of the Deptford trilogy of novels by Davies.
1976	Margaret Laurence's *Heart of a Stranger*.
1976	*Sticks and Stones*, a drama by James Reaney, the first of the Donnelly trilogy, which treats Ontario history as myth. The other two plays in the trilogy are *The St. Nicholas Hotel* (1976) and *Handcuffs* (1977).
1980	W. P. Kinsella's *Shoeless Joe Jackson Comes to Iowa*.
1980	Rudy Wiebe's *The Mad Trapper*.
1981	*Billy Bishop Goes to War*, a play by John Gray.
1981	*Home Truths: Selected Canadian Stories*, by Mavis Gallant.
1981	Joy Kogawa's *Obasan*.
1982	Sharon Pollock's drama *Generations*.
1983	W. P. Kinsella's *The Moccasin Telegraph*.
1985	Atwood's *The Handmaid's Tale*, a dystopic novel about life after a Christian theocratic revolution.

Nova Scotia became a center of cultural activity where writing flourished along with the other arts. This was partly because the province's first premier, Joseph Howe, was a poet and journalist who consistently encouraged the arts. Even before 1800, the province had several literary magazines. Nova Scotians had a strong sense of their region and helped, in their writing, to establish a solid Canadian literary identity.

Thomas McCullough satirized his fellow Nova Scotians, or Bluenoses, as they were called, in his serialized *Letters of Mephibosheth Stepsure* (1821-1823), while Thomas Chandler Haliburton, in *The Clockmaker* (1836), with its picaresque protagonist, Sam Slick, established the genre of folk humor in Canada.

Early poetry
Oliver Goldsmith, grandnephew of the British writer whose name he bore, celebrated the pioneering spirit and the development of Nova Scotia in *The Rising Village* (1825), a collection of heroic couplets that celebrates immigration and westward expansion. These poems are in direct response to his granduncle's "The Deserted Village," which decries the emigration of villagers from their homeland in search of opportunities elsewhere.

Among the early poets were two sisters, Susanna Strickland Moodie and Catherine Parr Strickland Traill. The former published *Roughing It in the Bush* (1852) in an effort to warn and dissuade future emigrants from England. Her sister's earlier collection, *The Backwoods of Canada* (1836), however, emphasizes the landscape and natural beauty of the new world.

After confederation in 1867, poets wrote mostly about Canada's landscape and its natural wonders, as Traill had done earlier. They were seeking and, indeed, establishing a poetic tradition that captured the identity of the new nation. Among these writers, Archibald Lampman and Duncan Campbell Scott were the most notable exemplars.

Isabella Valancy Crawford was perhaps the most innovative poet of this early period. She employed Indian folklore extensively in her work, which emphasized pioneer life. Her work was consciously imbued with the symbolic significance of the lively natural environment about which she wrote in her poems collected in *Old Spookses' Pass, Malcolm's Katie, and Other Poems* (1884).

Early fiction
During the nineteenth century, most writing came from the eastern provinces of Canada. The historical romance dominated Canadian fiction. In *Wacousta: Or, The Prophecy, a Tale of the Canadas* (1832), John Richardson tells the tale of Pontiac, Indian chief of the Ottawas, and of the uprising he led. William Kirby, in his gothic novel *The Golden Dog: A Legend of Quebec* (1877), focuses on the life of the ruling class in Quebec. James De Mille, in *A Strange Manuscript Found in a Copper Cylinder* (1888), presents a fantastic travel story, while Sir Charles George Douglas Roberts, originator of documentary animal stories, writes about the animal world and about Canada's identity with nature in *Earth's Enigmas* (1896) and *The Kindred of the Wild* (1902). By the time his *Further Animal Stories* (1936) appeared, he had published nineteen volumes.

Twentieth century poetry
Probably the best known Canadian poet, although he is far from the most gifted, is Robert W. Service, whose *Songs of a Sourdough* (1907) and other volumes contain rollicking poems about Canada's far north. Service captures the unique identity of that area, emphasizing its harshness, its independent spirit, its respect for individualism, and the romance associated with its remoteness from the more developed areas of the country.

William Henry Drummond wrote poetry in English about the French Canadian experience in *The Habitant and Other French-Canadian Poems* (1897). Pauline Johnson tells about the tribal rituals of the Mohawks in *Flint and Feather* (1911), but probably the most anthologized Canadian poem in English continues to be John McCrae's "In Flanders Fields" (1915), a paean about World War I, in which he died.

In *Newfoundland Verse* (1923), E. J. Pratt, a versatile poet who broke from the traditions of sentimentality and patriotism of the earlier twentieth century poets, writes lyrical poems about the isolated, seabound life of Newfoundland. In his monumental narratives, *The Titanic* (1935), *Brébeuf and His Brethren* (1940), and *Towards the Last Spike* (1952), Pratt proves himself master of the poetic and physical detail that transforms his verse into accurate documentary writing.

Such poets as A. M. Klein, Frank R. Scott, and A. J. M. Smith were part of the international movement of Imagism, which emphasized concrete images and details in a free verse. From this American- and British-influenced school they wrested a Canadian identity by depicting in pristine detail the Canadian landscape and the temper of its people. As the century progressed, Canadian poetry grew less formalistic. In *Signpost* (1932), Dorothy Livesay writes openly about sexual love, and in her later volume, *Day and Night* (1944), she broaches the exploitation of workers. Realism was the byword of the day, and poetry about Canada and Canadians was encouraged.

Local color fiction

By the turn of the century, local color novels had begun to gain an ascendancy over the romances that had characterized earlier Canadian fiction. Ralph Connor's *The Man from Glengarry* (1901) is set in Ontario, as is Sara Jeanette Duncan's *The Imperialist* (1904). Lucy Maud Montgomery's famed *Anne of Green Gables* (1908) and the other children's books in the series that followed are set on Prince Edward Island and clearly capture the unique character of the Maritime Provinces. Mazo de la Roche's *The Building of Jalna* (1927) and the books of the Jalna series that followed it until 1960 are set in western Ontario and are, in their social realism, sometimes compared to the prairie writings of Willa Cather.

The satirical stories of small-town Canadian life that Stephen Leacock captures in *Sunshine Sketches of a Little Town* (1912) offer penetrating insights into Canadian life in much the way that Sherwood Anderson's sketches in *Winesburg, Ohio* (1919) do, although Leacock lacks Anderson's psychological penetration.

Social realism

In the mid-1920's, a wave of fiction about the small, conservative farming communities of the Canadian prairie began to emerge. Frederick Philip Grove's *Settlers of the March* (1925) and *Fruits of the Earth* (1933) document the farmers' struggle to gain an existence in an unwelcoming environment.

The prairie novels continue into the 1940's and 1950's in such books as Sinclair Ross's *As for Me and My House* (1941), W. O. Mitchell's *Who Has Seen the Wind?* (1947), and Ernest Buckler's *The Mountain and the Valley* (1952), with its strong and authentic depictions of the unique Nova Scotian identity. Hugh MacLennan broaches questions of religious and social conflicts and of the breach between French and English Canadians in *Two Solitudes* (1945) and *The Watch That Ends the Night* (1959), both of which deal with divided national identities. The identity of British Columbia is explored and feminist questions are raised in Sheila Watson's *The Double Hook* (1959) and Ethel Wilson's *Swamp Angel* (1954).

In the 1970's, the internationally recognized Canadian novelist Robertson Davies produced his Deptford trilogy, consisting of *Fifth Business* (1970), *The Manticore* (1972), and *World of Wonders* (1975). In these books, Davies, who was nominated for a Nobel Prize in Literature, traces the development of his protagonists through their various stages of life.

The Canadian Jewish identity is found in such novels as Mordecai Richler's *The Apprenticeship of Duddy Kravitz* (1959) and *St. Urbain's Horseman* (1971). Feminist writing of the period includes such novels as Margaret Atwood's *The Edible Woman* (1969), *Surfacing* (1972), *Lady Oracle* (1976), and *The Handmaid's Tale* (1985), Audrey Thomas' *Real Mothers* (1981), and Alice Munro's *Lives of Girls and Women* (1971), all of which deal with identity questions of women in Canadian society.

SUGGESTED READINGS

MacMillan, Carrie. *Silenced Sextet: Six Nineteenth Century Canadian Women Novelists*. Montreal: McGill/Queen's University Press, 1992. A thorough, feminist approach to the writing of Canadian women in the nineteenth century.

New, William H., ed. *Canadian Writers, 1890-1920*. Detroit: Gale Research, 1990. An up-to-date coverage of an important era in Canadian literary development.

_____, ed. *Canadian Writers, 1920-1959*. Detroit: Gale Research, 1988. Perhaps the most usable book about a broad range of Canadian authors of the period covered. Accurate and readable.

_____, ed. *A History of Canadian Literature*. New York: New Amsterdam Press, 1989. A concise volume that covers the full span of Canadian writing.

Stouck, David. *Major Canadian Authors: A Critical Introduction to Canadian Literature in English*. Lincoln: University of Nebraska Press, 1988. A dependable resource.

—*R. Baird Shuman*

See also Canadian identity: Quebecois; Feminism; Language and identity

Canadian identity: Quebecois

IDENTITIES: Canada

DEFINITION: The Quebecois identity is based principally on the preservation of French language and culture in a predominantly English-speaking country.

Historical perspective

The area known as Quebec, one of Canada's ten provinces, was first explored by Jacques Cartier, who took possession of it in 1534 in the name of the King of France, Francis I. In 1608, the explorer Samuel de Champlain founded Quebec, the province's capital and the source of the term "Quebecois," which originally meant an inhabitant of the city of Quebec but which has come to designate a French-speaking citizen of the province. The seventeenth century saw extensive colonization of this area by approximately 10,000 French colonists. In 1759, the Battle of the Plains of Abraham resulted in a decisive defeat of French forces by the British. In 1763, the Treaty of Paris surrendered this territory to the British crown, and a royal proclamation gave the former French colony the name of Province of Quebec. When in 1867, the Dominion of Canada was created by the British North America Act, Quebec, at that time one of four Canadian provinces, was 85 percent francophone.

Canadian Literature in French
Milestones

1534	Jacques Cartier explores and claims for France the region of Québec.	1867	The Dominion of Canada is created by the British North America Act.
1608	Samuel de Champlain founds Québec.	1884	*Angéline de Montbrun*, by Québec's first woman novelist, Marie-Louise-Félicité Angers, whose pen name was Laure Conan.
1700's	French colonists arrive in numbers.		
1759	The Battle of the Plains of Abraham results in a decisive defeat of French forces by the British.	1887	Louis Fréchette publishes his long historical overview in verse of Québec's history, *La Légende d'un peuple*.
1763	The Treaty of Paris surrenders the territory to the British.	1895	Jules-Paul Tardivel's novel of the earth, *Pour la patrie*, promotes separatism.
1837	The first French Canadian novel, *L'Influence d'un livre*, is published by Philippe-Ignace-François Aubert de Gaspé, a young journalist.	1904	Pamphile Lemay's *Les Gouttelettes*.
		1904	*Marie Calumet*, by Rodolphe Girard, causes scandal because in it, a character reads the Song of Solomon in the Bible (the Bible was forbidden reading to Catholics at that time). The novel contains the offending biblical paean to love.
1846	*La Terre paternelle*, by Patrice Lacombe, marks the beginning of the Canadian novels of the earth, intended to be patriotic and to exemplify good morals.		
1854	*La Huronne de Lorette*, by the prolific adventure novelist Henri-Émile Chevalier.	1914	Louis Hémon's *Maria Chapdelaine: Récit du Canada français* published in serial form.
1859	Abbé Henri-Raymond Casgrain, one of Canada's most prolific authors, helps found *Le Mouvement littéraire de Québec*. This influential movement results from the itinerant Parliament's movement to Quebec City in the same year, which attracts a number of intellectuals.	1916	*La terre*, by Ernest Choquette, continues the tradition of the French Canadian novel celebrating rural life and condemning city life.
		1918	Albert Laberge's *La Scouine*, an early—perhaps the first—realistic novel in French Canadian literature, in opposition to the reigning novel of the earth.
1863	*Les Anciens Canadiens*, by Philippe-Joseph Aubert de Gaspé.	1934	*Les demi-civilisés*, by Jean-Charles Harvey.

During the twentieth century, there was pronounced political activity by those members of Quebec society who wished to secede from Canada, in the belief that the distinctness of the Quebec language and culture made it a country separate from the rest of Canada. Two referenda, held in 1982 and 1995, were unsuccessful in achieving a majority vote by those wishing to create their own country. The population of Quebec at the time of the 1995 referendum, approximately 6.9 million (compared to Canada's 26.2 million), was 82 percent francophone.

Throughout the history of modern Quebec, many francophone writers, artists, actors, and social activists endeavored to promote the Quebec identity through the protection of the francophone culture from assimilation into the majority anglophone culture and through the preservation of traditions that bear a distinctly Quebecois flavor. The political activism known as the independence movement was clearly strengthened by the participation of all levels of society.

Identity in modern Quebecois literature

The francophone literature of twentieth century Quebec evoked a rural, patriarchal society, steeped in Catholic tradition and conservative social and familial values. This evocation was a direct reflection of the dominant ideology, one that espoused the importance of preserving French social and religious customs. Fidelity to the beliefs of the Roman Catholic church, then an extremely powerful institution, was obligatory as was loyalty to family, the microcosm of Quebec society. The dominant agrarian ideology glorified country life, often ignoring, or portraying in a negative light, urban society.

An example of a work that extols the virtues of a conservative patriarchal society is Louis Hémon's *Maria Chapdelaine: Récit du Canada français* (1914, serial, 1916, book; *A Tale of the*

Canadian Literature in French Milestones — CONTINUED

1937	*Menaud: Maître-draveur*, by Félix-Antoine Savard.
1937	Hector de Saint-Denys Garneau publishes the influential book of poetry, *Regards et jeux dans l'espace*.
1937	Michel Beaulieu's *Variables*, a poetry collection.
1938	*Trente arpents*, by Philippe Panneton.
1944	Roger Lemelin's *Au pied du la pente douce*, about city life.
1945	*Bonheur d'occasion*, by Gabrielle Roy.
1948	*Les Plouffe*, by Roger Lemelin.
1948	Gratien Gélinas' play *Tit-Coq*, published 1950, opens in Montreal.
1951	*Testament de mon enfance*, by Robert Laroque de Roquebrune.
1953	André Langevin's *Poussière sur le ville*, a novel of a doctor who is unfaithful to his wife.
1953	*Le Tombeau des rois*, a book of poetry by Anne Hébert, uses symbolism to describe rebellion against the "dead kings" of the provincial Québec mentality.
1955	Marcel Dubé's *Zone*, a play about life in Montreal.
1958	Gérard Bessette's *La bagarre*, a study of three students dealing with French Canadian issues.
1958	Jacques Languirand's *Les Grands Départs*.
1958	Antonine Maillet's *Pointe-aux-Coques*, about Acadia.
1960	*Mystère de la parole*, an influential book of poetry by Anne Hébert.
1961	Anselme Chiasson's *Chéticamp: histoire et traditions acadiennes*.
1964	André Major's *Le Cabochon*.
1965	Gérard Bessette's *L'Incubation*.
1965	*Une Saison dans la vie d'Emmanuel*, by Marie-Claire Blais, decries the bleakness of rural Québec society.
1966	*L'Avalée des avalés*, by Réjean Ducharme.
1967	Jacques Godbout's *Salut Galarneau!*
1968	*Les Manuscrits de Pauline Archange*, by Marie-Claire Blais.
1969	Marcel Dubé's *Au retour des oies*.
1970	Roch Carrier's *La Guerre, Yes Sir!*, the play based on his novel of the same title, deals with misunderstandings between French-speaking and English-speaking Canadians.
1970	Anne Hébert's *Kamouraska*, a novel.
1972	Antonine Maillet's *La Sagouine*.
1974	*Don Quichotte de la démance*, by Victor-Lévy Beaulieu.
1979	Gérard Bessette's *Le Semestre*, an autobiographical novel.

Lake St. John Country, 1921). A classic in Quebec literature, this novel depicts the life of Samuel and Laura Chapdelaine, their four sons, and one daughter. The Chapdelaines are representative of the ideal Quebec family, for they are devout in the religious faith, and unflinching in their attachment to family values and the continuation of traditional ways of life.

Maria falls in love with one of her three suitors, the adventurer and lumberjack François Paradis. It is symbolic that she is named after the Virgin Mary, as are many daughters in Quebec fiction, and that she is associated throughout the work with the values of commitment to one's family and land as well as to the transmission to the next generation of the same value system. François Paradis dies tragically one winter in a snowstorm, and Maria, the following spring, marries Eutrope Gagnon, a solitary man who lives off the land. This final image of Maria as a young woman resigned to sacrificing her personal happiness in order to maintain the identity of the Quebec pioneers who live off the land, following the example of colonists of New France, appears frequently in Quebec literature as a symbol of the familial, social, and religious values that define Quebecois identity.

The influence of Hémon's novel was great in defining the identity of the Quebec pioneer as a conservative, religious individual who shows a very strong commitment to the preservation of an agrarian way of life. *Menaud: Maître-draveur* (1937; *Boss of the River*, 1947), by Félix-Antoine Savard, depicts the struggle of the widower Menaud, father of Marie and Joson, who exhorts his family, neighbors, and friends in an isolated area of Quebec to rebel against the presence of the English, identified in the novel as *étrangers* (foreigners, strangers), who are to take possession of the mountain and surrounding lands that Menaud and his ancestors consider their own. Marie, similar to Maria in *A Tale of the Lake St. John Country*, is a virginal figure, who reads to Menaud passages from *A Tale of the Lake St. John Country*. It is also Marie who, through her name, represents the importance of the Roman Catholic religion. She is the sole character in the novel to recite the evening prayer in her father's home for the benefit of Menaud, Joson, and, symbolically, the Quebec people. The territory depicted in the novel is considered by the characters as a *pays*, a country in itself. The use of this expression manifests the characters' ideal to protect and maintain this land, sovereign and distinctly their own. This work communicates an early example of the nationalist ideology that would become more pronounced.

Agrarianism and backlash

A Tale of the Lake St. John Country and *Boss of the River* undertake to paint a poetic picture of courageous and idealistic inhabitants of isolated regions in Quebec. The characters of the two novels wish to safeguard their francophone and Catholic identity. Social evolution, however, caused writers to reflect upon a modern Quebec society that became increasingly urban and less centered on agrarian activities. The publication of *Bonheur d'occasion* by Gabrielle Roy (1945; *The Tin Flute*, 1947) marked a turning point in the ways in which writers perceived the Quebecois identity. Set in St. Henri, a working-class district in Montreal, during the economic crisis of the late 1930's and during World War II, *The Tin Flute* casts a penetrating look at the reality of the time. The aesthetics of traditional Quebec novels, evoking an idyllic natural setting of countryside, forest, and mountain inhabited by simple, robust rural characters, gives way in *The Tin Flute* to a realistic portrayal of the struggle of the Lacasse family to overcome unemployment, sickness, and poverty. The francophone identity represented in this work is not the one-dimensional one that is often found in earlier *romans de la terre* (novels of the land) but rather one that is representative of an industrialized society undergoing profound change. The nationalist question, the conflict between francophone and anglophone, *étranger* and *québécois*, as evoked in *Boss of the River*, is absent from *The Tin Flute*. Roy's groundbreaking work speaks of compassion, understanding, and admiration for those who struggle to know themselves, overcome obstacles to happiness, improve their living conditions, and generally, survive in a dehumanizing industrialized world.

The 1960's were rich in literary production, and particularly in works that depict Quebec society in an authentic, nonidealized, and sometimes troubling manner. *Une Saison dans la vie d'Emmanuel* (1965; *A Season in the Life of Emmanuel*, 1966) by Marie-Claire Blais is an eloquent example of this type of aesthetics. Unlike *A Tale of the Lake St. John Country* or *Boss of the River*, *A Season in the Life of Emmanuel* offers glimpses of cruelty, sordidness, and abuse in a rural family.

Héloïse, one of the daughters of the family depicted in the novel, is expelled from a convent where she was unable to curb her sexual desires, and begins the life of a prostitute. Death, illiteracy, superstition, and poverty are counterbalanced by the quest for knowledge, symbolic of an escape from this narrow existence, represented by the young Jean Le Maigre, who ultimately dies of tuberculosis after having composed brooding and magnificent poetry. His death is, however, followed by the birth of a brother, and so the unrelenting cycle of misery continues.

An enigmatic novel, *L'Avalée des avalés* (1966; *The Swallower Swallowed*, 1968), by Réjean Ducharme exploded on Quebec's literary scene after it had been rejected by Quebec publishers. Its ultimate publication by a prestigious Paris firm can perhaps be explained by a somewhat fantastical plot whose main character, Bérénice Einberg, an adolescent with a distinctly more mature and sometimes diabolical single-mindedness makes her an intriguing figure. This novel is clearly an example of the work of a Quebec writer whose inspiration is not political in orientation but rather is one focusing on wordplay and stylistic innovation. Ducharme is, therefore, representative of Quebec writers who wish to open the limits of the imagination to areas not yet fully explored in Quebec society and not associated with political aspirations to create a separate country.

The aesthetics evident in Ducharme's work became more prevalent in subsequent decades. The idealization of Quebec society ceased to be the touchstone of its literature. Writers in the later part of the twentieth century strived to create innovation in style and content. They expressed the Quebecois identity in myriad forms, including those created by women writers, Italian expatriates, Jewish residents of Montreal, and Quebec's gay and lesbian community. Throughout the evolution of its identity, Quebec society has undergone profound changes. It has gone from being—or being depicted as—a rural and insular world, steeped in conservative values and dominated by the Roman Catholic church, to being one that is urban, cosmopolitan, and varied in its ethnic and religious mix. The Quebecois identity is still, however, represented to a large extent by the francophone population that wishes to achieve sovereignty within Canada.

SUGGESTED READINGS

Dionne, René. *Canadian Literature in French.* Ottawa: Canadian Studies Directorate, 1988. A study guide.

Kandiuk, Mary. *French-Canadian Authors: A Bibliography of Their Works and of English-Language Criticism.* Metuchen, N.J.: Scarecrow Press, 1990. Especially helpful for English speakers.

Shek, Ben-Zion. *French-Canadian and Quebecois Novels.* New York: Oxford University Press, 1991. Offers insights into Canadian culture.

_____. *Social Realism in the French-Canadian Novel.* Toronto: Harvest House, 1977. A study of modern Quebec society as it is portrayed in various novels.

Weiss, Jonathan M. *French-Canadian Theater.* Boston: Twayne, 1986. A general introduction.

—*Kenneth W. Meadwell*

See also Canadian identity; Colonialism; Identity crisis; Multiculturalism

Cancer Journals, The

AUTHOR: Audre Lorde (1934-1992)

FIRST PUBLISHED: 1980

IDENTITIES: African American; disease; gay, lesbian, and bisexual; women

The Cancer Journals, Audre Lorde's documentation and critique of her experience with breast cancer, is a painstaking examination of the journey Lorde takes to integrate this crisis into her identity. The book chronicles Lorde's anger, pain, and fear about cancer and is as frank in its themes of "the travesty of prosthesis, the pain of amputation, and the function of cancer in a profit society," as it is unflinching in its treatment of Lorde's confrontation with mortality.

Lorde speaks on her identity as a black, lesbian, feminist mother and poet with breast cancer. She illuminates the implications the disease has for her, recording the process of waking up in the recovery room after the biopsy that confirms her cancer, colder than she has ever been in her life. The following days, she prepares for the radical mastectomy through consultation with women friends, family, her lover, and her children. In the days that follow, Lorde attributes part of her healing process to "a ring of women like warm bubbles keeping me afloat" as she recovers from her mastectomy. She realizes that after facing death and having lived, she must accept the reality of dying as "a life process"; this hard-won realization baptizes Lorde into a new life.

The journal entries for 1979 and 1980, written while Lorde recovered from the radical mastectomy she chose to forestall spread of the disease, show Lorde's integration of this emergency into her life. She realizes that she must give the process a voice; she wants to be more than one of the "socially sanctioned prosthesis" women with breast cancer, who remain quiet and isolated. Instead, Lorde vows to teach, speak, and fight.

At the journal's end, Lorde chooses to turn down the prosthesis offered her, which she equates with an empty way to forestall a woman's acceptance of her new body, and thus, her new identity. If, Lorde realizes, a woman claims her full identity as a cancer survivor and then opts to use a prosthesis, she has made the journey toward claiming her altered body, and life. Postmastectomy women, however, have to find their own internal sense of power. *The Cancer Journals* demonstrates a black, feminist, lesbian poet's integration of cancer into her identity.

SUGGESTED READINGS

Bloom, Harold, ed. *Black Women Poets and Dramatists*. New York: Chelsea House, 1996.

Evans, Mari, ed. *Black Women Writers (1950-1980): A Critical Evaluation*. New York: Doubleday, 1984.

Tate, Claudia. *Black Women Writers at Work*. New York: Continuum Press, 1983.

—R.C.S.

See also African American identity; *Coal*; Lesbian identity; Lorde, Audre; *Zami*

Cannery Row

AUTHOR: John Steinbeck (1902-1968)
FIRST PUBLISHED: 1945
IDENTITIES: Asian American; European American; West and Southwest; women

In *Cannery Row*, John Steinbeck depicts the precarious survival of a heterogeneous human community in the cannery section of Monterey, California. In emphasizing alternative values to capitalistic greed as the basis for that survival, Steinbeck implies that the only means by which peaceful amalgamation of diverse economic, cultural, and gender groups can occur is through community.

The diversity of *Cannery Row* is represented by Lee Chong, the Chinese grocer; by the varied group of European American young men, led by Mack, who maintain the Palace Flophouse; by Dora and her girls, prostitutes at the Bear Flag Restaurant; and by Doc, the scientist owner of Western Biological Laboratory. The novel's rather simple plot concerns efforts to give a surprise birthday party for Doc, the cohesive force within this community. The problems but eventual success of these efforts clarify the alternative values allowing the peaceful transcendence of differences.

The characters in the novel constitute a genuine community because they defy the capitalistic greed and exploitation of Cannery Row. Mack and his friends refuse to work in the canneries except intermittently, and only when there is a specific, emotionally worthwhile objective. Thus, they get jobs in order to acquire enough money for Doc's party, but quit immediately afterward. Doc says of the group, "They could ruin their lives and get money. . . . They just know the nature of things too well to be caught in that wanting." Similarly, Doc limits his profitable animal harvesting, recognizing the inherent value of any life-form. This consciousness is symbolized by the floating dead girl Doc sees after his capture of twenty-two little octopi. He is haunted by the girl's beauty, "the face burned into his picture memory," representing Doc's awareness of the natural beauty he has destroyed.

Likewise, Lee Chong and Dora and her girls illustrate the primacy of noneconomic values in any real community. Lee Chong allows Mack and his friends to "rent" the Palace Flophouse (a former storehouse), knowing they will never actually pay him. Also, Lee Chong happily participates in Doc's successful party despite considerable monetary loss in the failed first attempt. Similarly, Dora and her girls are happiest at the party, presenting to Doc the beautiful quilt they made. Only their economic life causes problems, illustrated by tuna fishermen mistaking Doc's party for the Bear Flag Restaurant and barging in for service. The ensuing brawl nearly wrecks Western Biological, but affirms that the essence of this human community is beyond economic exploitation. Indeed, Steinbeck's narrator makes this point in writing that "Mack never visited the Bear Flag professionally. It would have seemed a little like incest to him." With characters who sublimate materialistic, capitalistic values to friendship, ecological concern, and giving to and celebration of life with others, Steinbeck postulates humanistic values as the solution to California's cultural, gender, and economic divisions.

SUGGESTED READINGS

Benton, Robert M. "The Ecological Nature of *Cannery Row*." In *Steinbeck: The Man and His Work*, edited by Richard Astro and Tetsumaro Hayashi. Corvallis: Oregon State University Press, 1971.

French, Warren. *John Steinbeck*. 2d rev. ed. Boston: Twayne, 1975.

Timmerman, John H. *John Steinbeck's Fiction*. Norman: University of Oklahoma Press, 1986.

—John L. Grigsby

See also *Grapes of Wrath, The*; Steinbeck, John; *Tortilla Flat*

Canon

DEFINITION: The canon is the body of texts that are central to a literary tradition.

Of making books, declares Ecclesiastes, there is no end. But, in a finite life, which books should one read? With almost 50,000 new titles published in the United States alone every year, even the most voracious reader cannot keep up with all of contemporary publishing, let alone the libraries of what has already been published. Readers are obliged to make choices, to set priorities among the vast supply of texts competing for attention. The canon is the body of writings endorsed as most worth reading. It is a weighty response to the question: Which ten (one hundred, one thousand) books would one take to an uninhabited island? More serious forms of this question include: Which books merit humanity's most immediate and enduring interest? Behind such a question lie two more questions: Who makes that decision? On what basis? **At issue**

The word "canon" derives from a Greek root meaning measuring rod. Canonical literary texts represent the standard against which any individual work is measured. Before the rise of modern secular literature, it was the Bible that provided the definitive canon for Western culture. The Bible (the words "the Bible" mean "the book") is itself a compilation of disparate sacred writings accumulated over centuries. At certain points in ecclesiastical history, religious leaders gathered to determine the precise composition of the Bible, to decide which texts would be included and which excluded. The premise of the canonical Bible is that if congregants have to make do with only one book, it ought to contain the central texts. The Bible's editorial history is an excellent example of how a canon is developed. Catholics, Jews, and Protestants disagree over entries; not every Bible includes Matthew or Revelations, and various canons arrange the order of entries differently. Believers are not prohibited from reading additional texts, but books such as Tobit, Judith, and Maccabees, which were not chosen to appear in the Bible and are designated as Apocrypha, are theologically marginal. The Bible is itself a canon—a collection of central works. More than any other books, the biblical canon, it has been assumed, offers the most direct access to human wisdom and divine revelation. **History**

During the Renaissance, when secular studies started to rival religious ones, a parallel canon began to be formed out of significant but non-Scriptural texts, works that came to be widely recognized as classics. Over the centuries in the West, a rough consensus developed that the writings of several authors (including classical Greek and Roman authors, Dante Alighieri, Miguel de Cervantes, William Shakespeare, Johann Wolfgang von Goethe, Gustave Flaubert, Leo Tolstoy, and John Milton) represent the summit of human literary achievement, that they articulate values crucial to Western culture, and that they are indispensable to any genuine education. Canons developed in other fields as well, including music and painting. While the literary canon was never as precisely formalized as the biblical one, its presence and authority have been manifest in high school and college curricula, in lectures and publishing programs, and in influential anthologies that purport to represent the most important authors throughout history. Some institutions, including the University of Chicago and St. John's College, have attempted to base their curriculum on an undergraduate's mastery of a set of great books. Elsewhere, classes in literary masterpieces attempt to cover the canon, and they are more likely to include Sophocles than Stephen King. While sometimes permitted to study Robert Heinlein, English majors are often required to read Geoffrey Chaucer.

The controversy   The canon, along with other institutions and practices in North America and Western Europe, has been subject to question and attack. Many argue that the canon is too narrow, that it is almost exclusively the product of dead white European males and needs to be opened up to authors from different backgrounds. Feminists fault anthologies and curricula for failing to include more than a few token women, and multiculturalists criticize the Eurocentric bias they find in the canon. The traditional canon seems almost entirely devoid of blacks, Asians, Latinos, and American Indians, for example. The existing canon is also charged with homophobic bias.

Liberal critics who attack the canon for being too narrow and who fight to reconfigure it to include previously excluded groups often nevertheless assume the basic validity and value of canonization. A more radical challenge to the canon comes from those who reject the concept of a canon, who argue that canons are inherently undemocratic and coercive. Instead of merely tinkering with the components of the canon, they call for a leveling of literary hierarchies, for a culture in which no text or reader is privileged over any other. There are no great books, they charge, because greatness is a political construction, one that gets in the way of analyzing all cultural activity. The remedy for Eurocentrism is elimination of all centers.

Conservatives respond to attacks by liberals on canonical choices and to attacks by radicals on the institution of canon by reaffirming the esthetic and moral value of those literary masterpieces that have managed to withstand the test of time. They insist that not all works merit an equal claim on humanity's limited attention, and they refuse to reduce assessments of artistic achievement to a political algebra. Regardless of Milton's race, gender, class, or sexual biases, *Paradise Lost* (1667), they maintain, is a masterpiece, and time spent studying it will enrich its readers. Because of the values that it embodies and its exemplary craft, the traditional canon, conservatives argue, ought to be the common heritage of every educated reader. For a student of literature, to be unversed in the canon is to be culturally illiterate.

Implications for identity   Canon formation is neither as conspiratorial as some fear nor as democratic as others wish. It is the product of collective preferences expressed over time by critics, teachers, editors, publishers, and general readers. Some people manage to exert more influence than others. The biblical canon was determined by an ecclesiastical elite at a particular place and time, but the literary canon develops more gradually and openly, and it is never entirely settled. Otherwise, masterpiece anthologies would not be revised with such startling frequency. Comparison of a compilation of major poets published in 1900, when Henry Wadsworth Longfellow was still in high repute, with one published in 1950, when John Donne provided the ambiguity and complexity then thought to be the defining qualities of great poetry, reveal as much change as continuity. Herman Melville, among others canonized in the 1930's and 1940's as geniuses, was unknown a few years earlier. In the last decade of the twentieth century, Kate Chopin's 1899 novella *The Awakening* became the most widely taught literary text in American universities; it was out of print a few years before. The vagaries of literary reputation ought to give pause to those who either champion or scorn the canon as a permanent body of timeless classics.

Within the United States, the controversy over canon has been part of a larger anxiety over cultural identity, which became particularly acute at the conclusion of the Cold War, when, with the end of a common public threat, consensus over national purpose and character eroded. A massive increase in immigration, especially from Asia and Latin America, challenged traditional assumptions about the European cultural heritage of the United States. Divisions over whether Americans could share a common set of values and even a common language multiplied. The canon was a casualty of increasing fragmentation and polarization; if Americans could no longer agree on their histories and principles, it became difficult to identify a body of texts that all could esteem.

Within high schools and colleges, the canon wars, often as militant as if waged with cannon, became a special case of disputes over the purpose and pattern of a liberal arts education. Advocates of a core curriculum, like champions of the canon, insisted that a central body of knowledge be required of every student. What constitutes that irreducible essence—mathematics and Latin but not microeconomics and music?—became as moot as the question of what are the great books. The position that, in a truly free society, all courses should be elective and none required echoes claims that any attempt at fixing a canon is oppressive. If a nation cannot agree on who its people are and what it wants to be, it is unlikely that it can agree on priorities for what to know and what to read. In such a lack of consensus, the idea of a core curriculum and a canon can be attractive as an antidote to anarchy. Choices of what to study and read can become almost arbitrary. So long as people agree to scrutinize anything together, whether Vergil or Michael Crichton, people counteract the entropy of pluralism.

The canon wars have been bitter not merely because of vested interests but also because of embattled ethnic and sexual identities. They have also occurred in an era in which serious reading by nonspecialists has dramatically diminished. In a society in which attention to books is ongoing and eclectic, the canon is suggestive but not decisive. An inquisitive adult will eventually get around to discovering Lady Murasaki and Frederick Douglass, whether or not they were assigned in class. When the bulk of one's reading, however, particularly of noncontemporary texts, concludes with graduation, lists of major authors bear a heavy burden. If one does not read the *Aeneid* (c. 29-19 B.C.) or *Candide: Ou, L'Optimisme* (1759; *Candide*, 1759) before one's senior year, one probably never will.

Readjustments of the canon are a constant sum operation. Absent any miraculous expansion in human capacity, addition of one text to the literary pantheon ordinarily necessitates subtraction of another. Time also continues to add books to the reading list. If the doors are pried open to admit Toni Morrison or Maxine Hong Kingston, which author must be evicted to make room? The question certainly vexes if reading is confined to formal education and formal education is confined to the first three decades of an American's life. When reading is reduced to a matter of classroom assignments, then it is crucial that the few books that one reads not be trite. Yet it is questionable whether any tidy pack of texts, however magnificent, can carry the burdens of an entire culture. Not even the *Odyssey* (c. 800 B.C.; English translation, 1616) and *À la recherche du temps perdu* (1913-1927; *Remembrance of Things Past*, 1922-1931, 1981) can compensate for a lifetime of lesser books left unread.

For current authors, the canon is inspirational, offering the impetus and standard for new classics. For the general reader, the canon provides a pot of social glue, the vocabulary of love and loss that constitutes a living culture. Conversations about the nature and value of any canon can serve the same function.

SUGGESTED READINGS

Arnold, Matthew. "The Study of Poetry." In *Culture and Anarchy and Other Writings*, edited by Stefan Collini. Cambridge, England: Cambridge University Press, 1993. An influential Victorian's attempt to develop criteria for greatness in poetry by using lines from earlier works as touchstones of excellence.

Berman, Paul, ed. *Debating P.C.: The Controversy over Political Correctness on College Cam-*

puses. New York: Dell, 1992. Reprints essays by Irving Howe, Edward W. Said, Henry Louis Gates, Jr., and Katha Pollitt that advance varied positions in the canon controversy.

Bloom, Harold. *The Western Canon: The Books and Schools of the Ages*. New York: Harcourt Brace Jovanovich, 1994. An ambitious attempt to define and review the canon question and to argue for the centrality of twenty-six authors to what Bloom calls the Aristocratic, Democratic, and Chaotic Ages.

Gates, Henry Louis, Jr. *Loose Canons: Notes on the Culture Wars*. New York: Oxford University Press, 1992. Discussions of literary canon, with particular reference to race, by a prominent African-American scholar.

Gilbert, Sandra M., and Susan Gubar, eds. *The Norton Anthology of Literature by Women: The Tradition in English*. New York: Norton, 1985. An influential argument for and demonstration of an alternative English literary canon, consisting exclusively of works written by women.

Hirsch, E. D., Jr. *Cultural Literacy: What Every American Needs to Know*. Boston: Houghton Mifflin, 1987. Argues the need for a canon of general knowledge for contemporary Americans and outlines what it might be like.

Leavis, F. R. *The Great Tradition*. Garden City, N.Y.: Doubleday, 1954. An opinionated attempt to define the tradition of the English novel.

Von Hallberg, Robert, ed. *Canons*. Chicago: University of Chicago Press, 1984. Essays, reprinted from the scholarly journal *Critical Inquiry*, that examine the concept and practice of canon formation.

—*Steven G. Kellman*

See also Ethnic composition of universities; Literary standards; Melting pot; Multiculturalism; Pluralism versus assimilation; Popular culture

Caribbean American literature

IDENTITIES: Caribbean

Background
Caribbean emigration to North America, out of which experience the literature of Caribbean Americans evolved, did not begin in earnest until the 1920's. The earliest Caribbean writers spoke with a Caribbean, rather than a Caribbean American, voice. Although these writers, such as Claude McKay, Nicholás Guillén, and Leon Damas, participated actively in the Harlem Renaissance, the most vibrant black consciousness movement of the era, they saw themselves as Caribbean visitors to mainland America. For the most part, therefore, their writing depicted life in the Caribbean and portrayed Caribbean characters.

The succeeding generation of writers (Paule Marshall, Michelle Cliff, Rosa Guy, Maryse Condé, Jamaica Kincaid, Carl Phillips, and Edwidge Danticat) either came to America as children or developed their adult careers in America. These writers tackle the issue of the Caribbean American experience directly. Also, while they are unequivocal about their African ancestry, and although they often empathize with African American concerns, they see the Caribbean American experience as distinct from that of Africans or of African Americans. The writings of many of these authors have a biographical undertone, and therefore focus on the experience of people from the island with which they are most familiar, depicting their culture, their expectations, and their own peculiar ways of navigating the challenges posed by their adopted country.

Life in America
Some of the characters in Caribbean American literature come to America desperate to escape an unbearable life in their island place. Others come to America reluctantly, and yet another group of characters are portrayed as not having much to say about the decision to travel abroad. In all cases, however, the common denominator is the American Dream. Whether characters are self-motivated in pursuing this dream or have the dream imposed upon them by a well-meaning relative, it is the potential of America to provide a better quality of life that leads the characters to undertake their journey to the mainland.

In Marshall's novel *Brown Girl, Brownstones* (1959), the great American Dream for Silla Boyce

---

Caribbean American Literature
Eight Key Works

1920   Claude McKay, who left his native Jamaica in 1912, details his homesickness in *Spring in New Hampshire and Other Poems*.

1937   *A Long Way from Home*, Claude McKay's autobiography, contemplates African American identity in the United States.

1959   Paule Marshall's *Brown Girl, Brownstones*, depicts Silla Boyce's pursuit of her American Dream—a brownstone—at the cost of her family's love.

1987   In *No Telephone to Heaven* by Michelle Cliff, the main character comes to America to further her education; however, she becomes disillusioned with America and travels to England.

1990   In Jamaica Kincaid's *Lucy*, the title character comes to the United States to study nursing.

1992   *I, Tituba, Black Witch of Salem*, by Maryse Condé, tells the story of a strong Caribbean woman who is a witch in Salem, Massachusetts.

1994   In Jamaica Kincaid's *The Autobiography of My Mother*, Kincaid comes to understand and sympathize with women who are limited to the roles that their culture has defined for them.

1994   Edwidge Danticat's *Breath, Eyes, Memory* depicts a woman who tries but fails to fulfill her Haitian mother's high expectations.

---

is the possession of a brownstone. This ownership of her own house becomes for Silla the singular pursuit of her life. Home ownership symbolizes fulfillment in America, and she is prepared to do anything to attain it. Marshall portrays Silla as a character whose obsession with American materialist values reduces her to a callous, egocentric, and evil person. This obsession renders Silla unable to express tenderness toward her children and her husband. Such is this character's obsession that whenever she identifies an obstacle or arrival to her goal, she becomes paranoid, and sets about destroying that obstacle, even if the barrier is a human being: family, friend, or foe.

A life-or-death pursuit of success in America as dramatized by Silla is unusual in Caribbean literature. The more common attitude is a routine pursuit: the acquisition of education or profession which will then lead to the attainment of a better life than that lived in the Caribbean. Such is the case with Clare Savage, who, in Cliff's *No Telephone to Heaven* (1987), comes to America to complete high school. In Kincaid's novel *Lucy* (1990), the main character, Lucy, is a nineteen-year-old au pair whose family has sent her away from the West Indies to work her way through college to become a nurse in America. Similarly, Sophie Caco, Danticat's Haitian heroine in *Breath, Eyes, Memory* (1994), is expected by her mother to become a doctor after her education in New York City. The American Dream of Deighton Boyce, Silla's husband in *Brown Girl, Brownstones*, is to become an accountant, or acquire any such professional skill that will enable him to set up a lucrative self-employed business upon his return to Barbados.

For the characters portrayed in these texts, the fulfillment of the dream does not come easily. In fact, they are compelled by circumstances of life in America to make compromises, which in some cases lead to disillusionment. After Silla buys her precious brownstone, she finds that her troubles are far from over. She had borrowed money for the transaction from loan sharks, and in order to service the exorbitant loan she has to keep two jobs, as well as sublet the building for extra income. At the end of the novel, Silla has won a pyrrhic victory. She does not enjoy the additional space which a new home should provide because tenants have taken over her space. She is estranged from her children and husband. It is because Silla has the brownstone that she is overworked and stressed. Silla's American Dream has become a major burden. Deighton, Silla's husband, does not fare much better. Deighton discovers to his surprise that studying through correspondence courses to become a motor mechanic or an accountant in America is not as easy as he had thought on leaving the Caribbean. Anticipating failure in these courses, and failure to secure employment due to what he believes to be racist employment practices in America, Deighton refuses to commit himself to a dream as aggressively as Silla. Eventually he becomes a full-time member of a religious cult and drops out of the work force completely.

In *Lucy*, the protagonist does not become a nurse as her parents had planned, and she fails to concentrate on her college work. Instead, she is employed as a photographer's assistant, a job that is more of a hobby than a profession. Lucy, Kincaid's protagonist, loses the power to dream after witnessing the disintegration of her employers' family. Lucy subconsciously rationalizes that if this white couple, who symbolize, to her, the realization of the American Dream, can fail, she should not try too hard for such a dream if she is to avoid disappointment. Far from becoming a doctor, Sophie, the main character in *Breath, Eyes, Memory*, does not even go to college. At eighteen, she marries Joseph, her American lover, and settles for the life of a housewife, moving to her new home in the suburbs of Providence. Sophie has a devoted husband and an adorable child, so it can be said she is successful. Her failure to acquire a college education and a profession nevertheless leaves her vulnerable in the education-driven American economy, especially as her husband is a freelance musician with an unstable income. Personally, Sophie is undaunted by these financial circumstances, and her failure to become a doctor is a greater disappointment for her mother and for the extended family in Haiti who hoped to enjoy the American Dream through the success of their Caribbean American relative. Unlike Danticat's heroine, Clare in Cliff's *No Telephone to Heaven* completes her college education. Like Danticat's heroine, however, Clare becomes a disappointment to her European Caribbean father. Contrary to her father's expectation, Clare is frustrated with life in America. She is frustrated with its rigid race classifications, its preoccupation with material success, and its race-inspired violence. After college, Clare leaves for England to explore that country, feeling no real connectedness to America.

The Caribbean reality

Despite depiction of the limitations of America and the difficulties which their characters experience in succeeding within the American system, many Caribbean American writers show that life in the Caribbean is worse. It is in order to escape the harsher realities of life in the Caribbean that these characters have come to take their chances with America.

Proponents of a return to the Caribbean, such as Deighton in *Brown Girl, Brownstones*, eventually find that their island is not a blissful alternative to America. Deighton enjoys a pampered life in Barbados, but as a young man there, success eludes him. He cannot fulfill the wish of his family to become a doctor or a teacher, and he is unemployed for most of his time there. America provides him another chance. Although he blames the racism of whites for his failure, Deighton's perception that he has failed in the land of opportunity, where anyone is expected to succeed, contributes to his suicide. As for Silla, Deighton's wife, a return to the Caribbean is not even a consideration. She remembers only bad things about her past. From the age of eight she is forced to work from dawn to dusk in the sugarcane fields of Barbados. Any complaint against this backbreaking slave labor is met with savage whippings. Silla has no recollections of love or tenderness, only that she was robbed of the innocence of childhood.

Occasionally, Lucy in Kincaid's novel is nostalgic for her Caribbean home, but most of the time Lucy feels that her past is "filled with confusion and dread." Behind this tension is Lucy's ambivalent feeling toward a mother whom she loves, and who she believes loves her, but who nevertheless named her Lucy, shortened from Lucifer, because she cursed the day she gave birth to her unwanted child. Lucy realizes that her mother was the victim of male-dominated Caribbean culture, which allows the woman no authority over her pregnancy. Ironically, the mother-and-daughter relationship is further complicated by the preferential treatment that Lucy sees her younger siblings receive from her parents simply because these siblings are male. This theme of a male-dominated Caribbean society as a motivating factor in the decision to come to America in search of freedom is explored more extensively in Danticat's novel *Breath, Eyes, Memory*.

Danticat's description of the Haitian landscape and flora attest to the natural beauty of the country. The uncompromising love and solidarity of the Caco family shows that there are things about Haiti to be cherished. Overwhelmingly, however, the sentiment expressed in the novel about Haiti is that it is a place "where in one instant, you can lose your father and all your other dreams." It is not a place where one makes a wish when stars fall because there, "each time a star fell out of the sky, it meant that somebody would die." Those responsible for this threat to life and property are men of the Tontons Macoutes, a law enforcement group whose propensity for brutality makes it more of a terrorist organization than a police force. It is a member of the Tontons Macoutes that the Caco family believes raped Sophie's mother, Martine, at the age of sixteen.

Danticat makes two issues of sexual violation: rape and the habit of testing the virginity of unmarried women by poking "fingers in their private part." Martine never recovers from her encounter with the rapist. It is in order to help her forget this traumatic experience in Haiti that she is sent to the United States. In New York, Martine is haunted by the memory and has constant violent nightmares. She is damaged emotionally and psychologically to the point that when she finds herself pregnant in New York, this time by a man she loves, she is unable to separate the new pregnancy from the old one which was the result of her rape. Traumatized by a feeling of being invaded by evil, Martine rips open her womb, killing herself and her unborn child. Like her mother, Sophie suffers from nightmares occasioned by thoughts of a mysterious and evil father. Additionally, the testing of her virginity, a Haitian practice done to please Haitian men, who insist on the virginity of newly wed women, reduces her to a sexual misfit whose notion of sex, even with a loving husband, is that it is a dirty, guilty, and evil act. For both women the life-denying problems they have to grapple with originate in Haiti, while the potential to solve the problems can be found in the United States. Through Sophie's successful marriage and her access to therapy, Danticat suggests that the cycle of abuse endured by the Caco family will be broken in America.

In Ana Lydia Vega's short story "Cloud Cover Caribbean," characters from the Dominican Republic and from Cuba all decide to take their chances on the dangerous sea using any means necessary to escape to Miami. What they are running away from is pain, poverty, deprivation, and exploitation. For them America represents opportunity, a new beginning, and a chance to succeed in life. Their first contact with America suggests that their dream will come true. As they are allowed on a rescue vessel by a white American, offered survival tips by a Hispanic American, and given dry clothes by an African American, the author suggests that these Caribbean characters have arrived at the refuge of immigrants. In their expectation of the Caribbean, other characters, such as Clare in *No Telephone to Heaven*, who are more disillusioned with America, do not differ much from those who embrace America. When Clare decides to leave the United States, she does not return to the Caribbean. Instead she heads for England. The implication is that after her youthful exploration, she will come back home to America. Another hint that Cliff provides to suggest that her character is not oblivious to problems in the Caribbean is that although Clare regards living in America as being raised in captivity, she does not equate her sister's experience in the Caribbean with freedom, but rather with being raised in the wild.

Identity

How other Americans view the Caribbean American characters, the manner in which the characters handle their individual past, and the evolving history of their island of origin, as well as the characters' aspirations in their adopted country, all feature in the portrayal of the West Indian American in literature. Language serves almost invariably as an identification factor. Whether Jamaican, Haitian, Dominican Republican, or Cuban, their English, French or Spanish patois is used to establish their country of origin and culture. Many authors insist that often this form of identification leads to misleading generalizations on the part of the non-Caribbean American because no patois is the monopoly of any particular island. This failure of others to see the uniqueness of the islands becomes a source of annoyance to Lucy in Kincaid's novel *Lucy*. Similarly, the larger American society's determination to impose a black racial classification on Clare's European Caribbean father, and on Clare, who is of mixed parentage, is troubling to Clare in *No Telephone to Heaven*.

Implicit in the generalizations about the Caribbean is the notion of the islands' inferiority. It is such prejudice that generates the negative stereotypes such as those described in Danticat's *Breath, Eyes, Memory*. Haitians are accused of carrying the AIDS virus and of having an especially offensive body odor. Bombarded by these types of negative images, Danticat's protagonist, Sophie, grows up feeling insecure in America. When she first meets her American husband-to-be, she is anxious to hide her identity. She "wanted to sound completely American."

Some authors use a visit to the islands as an effective therapy in the process of a character's search for self-awareness and self-acceptance. For example, Sophie's return to Haiti in *Breath, Eyes, Memory* helps her in the effort to exorcise her legacy of torment. In *Brown Girl, Brownstones*, even the new generation of the Caribbean Americans, represented by Selina, need a visit to the Caribbean to build up the cultural grounding necessary to withstand the prejudices of those who would treat them as oddities.

Collectively, Caribbean Americans in literature are portrayed as successful in meeting the challenge of balancing the pursuit of the American Dream and the maintenance of their cultural roots. They establish their own communities and form ethnic organizations. Through these agencies, Caribbean Americans are able to reinforce a sense of pride in their own language, food, music, history, and values, while networking for mutual survival within the larger American society. Contrary to the one-dimensional character portrait of the Caribbean in mainstream American literature (such as the Caribbean character Tituba in Arthur Miller's *The Crucible*, 1953), Caribbean American writers draw a more rounded portrayal of characters whose humanity is unquestionable. Some of the writers believe that the challenges that Caribbean Americans have overcome, coupled with their rich cultural background, make them stronger than either the purely Caribbean, or purely American, personality. It is within this mode of thinking that Condé's novel, *I, Tituba, Black Witch of Salem* (1992) is set. In this, her fictional reconstruction of the life of a Caribbean woman burnt as a witch in Salem, Massachusetts, in the eighteenth century, Tituba is no longer the blubbering victim portrayed in Miller's play. Instead, Tituba is portrayed as an assertive woman who uses her spiritual powers to control her environment. For Caribbean American writers, the ideal Caribbean American personality is one who refuses to be defined by stereotypes. Such a character is at peace with indigenous Caribbean culture but understands the benefits of life in America without becoming obsessed with its materialism.

SUGGESTED READINGS

Baugh, Edward, ed. *Critics on Caribbean Literature*. New York: St. Martin's Press, 1978. Excellent variety of critical commentary on diverse aspects of Caribbean literature.

Lamming, George. *The Pleasures of Exile*. London: Allison and Busby, 1984. An analysis of the experience of being an immigrant by one of the most accomplished writers from the Caribbean.

Philip, Marlene Nourbese. *Harriet's Daughter*. London: Heinemann, 1988. Set in Canada, this novel provides a broader dimension to the identity question of Caribbeans living on the North American mainland.

Phillips, Caryl. *Higher Ground: A Novel in Three Parts*. New York: Viking Press, 1989. Attempts to establish that the common experience of people of African descent globally is one of alienation.

Ramchand, Kenneth. *The West Indian Novel and Its Background*. Winchester, Mass.: Faber & Faber, 1972. One of the earliest commentaries on Caribbean writing. A valuable starting place in the study of the Caribbean experience in literature.

Sutton, C. R., and E. M. Chaney, eds. *Caribbean Life in New York City: Socio-Cultural Dimensions*. New York: Center for Migration Studies, 1987. Presents readers with factual information that reinforces the messages of many Caribbean fiction writers.

—G. A. Toks Pearse

See also African American identity; American Dream; Black English; Stereotypes and identity

Carver, Raymond

BORN: Clatskanie, Oregon; May 25, 1938
DIED: Port Angeles, Washington; August 2, 1988
PRINCIPAL WORKS: *Will You Please Be Quiet, Please?*, 1976; *Furious Seasons and Other Stories*, 1977; *What We Talk About When We Talk About Love*, 1981; *Fires: Essays, Poems, Stories*, 1983; *Cathedral*, 1983; *Where I'm Calling From: New and Selected Stories*, 1988

IDENTITIES: Disease; European American; family

SIGNIFICANT ACHIEVEMENT: Carver's portraits of America's working class are credited for igniting a revival of the short story in the 1970's and 1980's.

In style and subject matter, Raymond Carver's short-story collections reflect his life experiences. The son of working-class parents, he grew up knowing the financial and spiritual hardships of trying to earn a living in the logging districts of Yakima, Washington. The first in his family ever to graduate from high school, by the age of twenty he was married and the father of two children. Parenting, he later said, was a responsibility for which he was totally unprepared.

In 1958, Carver moved his family to Northern California, where he attended Chico State College and was encouraged by the novelist John Gardner. The next two decades were marred by a series of "crap jobs," marital turmoil, bankruptcy, and alcoholism. Carver had to steal time from other obligations in order to write and thus felt his best calling was being sacrificed to exigencies. During these years, however, he settled on his defining literary topics: the seemingly futile struggles of the working class and the relations between men and women. Delivered in a spare prose style that had been "cut to the marrow," his first two books are about people who inhabit the edges of the American Dream. Frustrated and deprived of opportunities, his characters do not recognize themselves in the lives they are living.

Raymond Carver's minimalist short stories gained wide influence in the 1980's and after. (Marion Ettlinger)

On June 2, 1977, Carver stopped drinking. Within a year, he met poet Tess Gallagher and began sharing with her a new "second life," for which he was always grateful. As if mirroring the positive changes in his personal life, *Cathedral* marked a dramatic shift in style and tone from his previous work. His stories became more generous, more hopeful. In the title piece, for example, a blind man entices the story's cynical narrator to close his eyes and draw with him a cathedral being described on a late night television documentary. The collaborative effort frees Robert to admit that "it's really something" to share one's imaginative vision with another person.

Cathedral and *Where I'm Calling From* secured Carver's literary reputation. Although he never expected to be famous, a few months before his death he said that he could not think of anything he would rather be called than a writer. His career marked by innovation, authenticity, and compassion for the disfranchised, Carver died of lung cancer at the age of fifty.

SUGGESTED READINGS

Gentry, Marshall Bruce, and William L. Stull, eds. *Conversations with Raymond Carver*. Jackson: University Press of Mississippi, 1990.

Saltzman, Arthur M. *Understanding Raymond Carver*. Columbia: University of South Carolina Press, 1988.

—Joe Nordgren

See also Alcoholism; Class and identity; *What We Talk About When We Talk About Love*

Catch-22

AUTHOR: Joseph Heller (1923-   )

FIRST PUBLISHED: 1961

IDENTITIES: Disease; Jewish

Joseph Heller's *Catch-22* details the physical and psychological struggles of a young airman named Yossarian, who feigns illness and madness in an attempt to avoid being killed over World War II Italy. Realizing that the war is putting him in personal danger, Yossarian mounts a series of protests against it. At first, his protests are passive, as when he feigns illness and seeks refuge in an army field hospital. Later, he refuses to fly bombing missions, goes AWOL, and attempts escape, by inflatable rubber lifeboat, from Italy to Sweden.

Catch-22 features a dizzying array of characters, each having a unique dysfunctional relationship with the military bureaucracy that Heller rails against. Yossarian fights against the system because it does not take him into account. Orr, one of Yossarian's peers, who shares Yossarian's distaste for the war, successfully turns the military's complete disregard for him into a tool that eventually enables him to escape. In contrast, Milo Minderbinder, one of the more insidious characters, harnesses the system for his own personal gain, counting on the self-interest of others to divert their attention from his ruthless profiteering.

One of the most haunting characters in the novel is the soldier in white. Completely wrapped, like a mummy, in strip bandages, the soldier in white first appears as a patient at the field hospital where Yossarian is hiding from the war. Yossarian observes that the soldier has no human characteristics whatsoever; even the soldier's life-sustaining processes (his catheter bag fills as his IV bag empties) are mechanized. When one bag is empty and the other full, the bags are simply switched. This absurd, darkly comical commentary on the suppression of human qualities during wartime permeates *Catch-22*.

Another theme found throughout the book is the difficulty of subverting military and bureaucratic controls, which are intended to undermine people's attempts at self-preservation. The book's title derives from a military rule stating that people who are mentally impaired cannot be required to fly bombing missions. The catch, or catch-22, is that in order to be relieved of duty, they must request not to fly. The request, should they make it, indicates that they are acting rationally, in their own self-interest. Once the request is made, the soldier is judged mentally healthy and fit to fly his missions. Thus, the system ensures that all soldiers fly missions, regardless of their mental state.

Heller has gone on record as being opposed to the Vietnam War, but describes *Catch-22* as a book about peacetime. Although the book was conceived and written prior to the involvement of the United States in the Vietnam War, *Catch-22* was embraced as the premier antiwar novel of the Vietnam War era. Its laugh-out-loud humor and strong antiestablishment message has contributed to its continued popularity, and the word "catch-22" has entered the language.

SUGGESTED READING

Nagel, James, ed. *Critical Essays on Joseph Heller*. Boston: G. K. Hall, 1984

—T. A. Fishman

See also Antiwar literature; Heller, Joseph

Catcher in the Rye, The

AUTHOR: J. D. Salinger (1919-   )
FIRST PUBLISHED: 1951
IDENTITIES: Adolescence and coming-of-age; European American

More than most modern novels, *The Catcher in the Rye* is about identity. It tells of the often frustrating and futile search for self by a young person wandering in an adult urban world. Holden Caulfield's emotional development has been arrested by the death of his younger brother Allie, and by a series of encounters that have shown him just what a "phony" world he is trying to grow up into. In the weekend in New York City that the novel chronicles, Holden searches for self, and, at the end, finds it.

The only good people in the novel are the innocent (his dead brother, his younger sister Phoebe, a pair of nuns he meets) and the misfits (former classmates Richard Kinsella and James Castle), who violate the rigid rules adults have set up for them. The adults Holden admires (his brother and his former teacher, Mr. Antolini) appear to have sold out. Holden is caught in mid-growth between the purity of childhood and the inevitable fall into adulthood. By the end of the novel, he realizes he has no sanctuary left (the Museum of Natural History he loved to visit has been contaminated), but he somehow feels happy sitting in the rain and watching Phoebe on the carousel in Central Park. It is a closing image of peace and acceptance: "The thing with kids is," Holden writes tellingly at the end, "if they want to grab for the gold ring, you have to let them do it, and not say anything." Holden is not through with his problems—he will soon suffer some kind of collapse and be institutionalized—but he has successfully let go of childhood and made the move toward adulthood.

The continuing popularity of *The Catcher in the Rye*—selling 250,000 copies in peak years— indicates that Holden's search for identity struck a responsive chord in many readers. Apparently, the difficulties of adolescence Salinger describes continue to be universal. The book's popularity also comes from Salinger's style and the way he has caught so perfectly the slangy vernacular of his young hero. Few characters in modern literature are so sharply defined by their language. All the readers who for generations have identified with Holden worldwide have seen in this character something of their own struggles for identity.

SUGGESTED READINGS

Bloom, Harold, ed. *Holden Caulfield*. New York: Chelsea House, 1990.

Marsden, Malcolm M. *If You Really Want to Know: A Catcher Casebook*. Boston: Scott, Foresman, 1963.

Pinsker, Sanford. *"The Catcher in the Rye": Innocence Under Pressure*. New York: Twayne, 1993.

Salzberg, Joel, ed. *Critical Essays on Salinger's "The Catcher in the Rye."* Boston: G. K. Hall, 1990.

Salzman, Jack. *New Essays on "The Catcher in the Rye."* New York: Cambridge University Press, 1991.

—*David Peck*

See also Adolescent identity; Identity crisis; Salinger, J. D.; Salinger, J. D., short stories of

Cather, Willa

BORN: Back Creek Valley, near Gore, Virginia; December 7, 1873
DIED: New York, New York; April 24, 1947
PRINCIPAL WORKS: *O Pioneers!*, 1913; *The Song of the Lark*, 1915; *My Ántonia*, 1918; *The Professor's House*, 1925; *Death Comes for the Archbishop*, 1927
IDENTITIES: European American; Midwest; women
SIGNIFICANT ACHIEVEMENT: Cather's novels of the Nebraska prairie portray women as the center of life, not merely as lovers and wives of men.

The single greatest trauma and most powerful positive influence on Willa Cather and her writing was her uprooting, at nine, from the farmlands of Virginia to the barren and lonely plains of Nebraska. The unfriendly landscape horrified her until she discovered the plains' underlying beauty—and then that landscape never left her. Her realization that such harshness could also yield splendor gave her a keen awareness of other dichotomies: of pain and pleasure, of love and hate, and of what one hopes to attain and what is actually attainable.

Her early intellectual development came from associations with the immigrants who settled in the wilderness of Red Cloud, Nebraska. A German piano teacher, the town drunk, spurred in her a lifelong appreciation of music; a Jewish couple, a love of French literature; an English clerk taught her Latin and Greek; two doctors, often taking her on rounds, whetted her interest in science, leading her to conclude that she abhorred needlework and would much prefer "amputating limbs." Cather was one of the first writers to portray strong female characters not defined solely by their relationship with men, but her own relationship with the feminist movement of her time was shaky. She was suspicious of the suffragists, thinking them too didactic, too fanatical, and too apt to idealize women. She once claimed that given the choice between a male and female novelist, she

Willa Cather has written masterpieces of investigation into the lives of women. (Library of Congress)

would always choose the former, thus aligning herself with George Eliot, who decried "silly lady novelists" and Nathaniel Hawthorne, who wrote of that "damned mob of scribbling women." She equated creativity with masculinity, saying that the "feminine mind has a hankering for hobbies and missions" and "the mind that can follow a 'mission' is not an artistic one." For a time during her adolescence, she took on the identity of a man, getting a crewcut, dressing in masculine garb, calling herself William Cather, Jr., and modeling her writing after that of Henry James.

In her 1915 novel, *The Song of the Lark*, the main character says: "Who marries who is a small matter," rather an astonishing concept considering that much literature up to that point had who married whom as its center. She abhorred the idealization of love. Although publicly acclaimed, Cather was sometimes patronized by critics. Many found her old-fashioned, not to mention old. Her first novel, *Alexander's Bridge*, appeared in 1912, her thirty-ninth year. She treasured the past, fearing modern materialism and its attendant loss of values.

Toward the end of her career, she became reclusive, burning old letters she had friends return and putting restrictions on the use of her published works. A 1947 obituary identified her as a secondary novelist, a notion that was common until a resurgence of interest in her work occurred in the early 1970's.

SUGGESTED READINGS

Acocella, Joan. "Cather and the Academy." *The New Yorker*, November 27, 1995, 56-71.

Brown, E. K. *Willa Cather*. New York: Alfred A. Knopf, 1953.

Gilbert, Sandra M., and Susan Gubar. *Sexchanges*. Vol. 2 in *No Man's Land: The Place of the Woman Writer in the Twentieth Century*. New Haven, Conn.: Yale University Press, 1989.

—*Gay Zieger*

See also *Death Comes for the Archbishop*; European American identity; Feminism; *My Ántonia*; "Paul's Case"

Catholicism

IDENTITIES: Religion

Background   The North American experience of Catholicism is tempered by the fact that English-speaking North America's major spiritual impulses were Northern European, Protestant, and anti-Catholic. By the time of the emergence of distinct American immigrant identities in the late nineteenth century, Roman Catholicism in North America had almost ceased to be regarded as a mainstream faith. Literature focusing on Catholicism tended to be as marginalized as the North American adherents of the Roman Catholic faith. Many works that treat Catholicism, then, also treat ethnicity and culture, including that of the immigrant. For example, James T. Farrell's *Studs Lonigan: A Trilogy* (1935), set in Depression-era Chicago, and Edwin O'Connor's *The Last Hurrah* (1956), detailing the rise and fall of an Irish Catholic Boston politician, are typical Roman Catholic ethnicity fictions, nearly a genre in their own right.

Often, an author whose works might be regarded as Catholic is categorized differently. For example, early twentieth century author Willa Cather, who utilizes Catholic themes and settings in works such as *Death Comes for the Archbishop* (1927) and *Shadows on the Rock* (1931), is more likely to be found categorized as a frontier novelist, because of her locales, or as a woman author.

Ernest Hemingway was a convert to Roman Catholicism for the sake of an early marriage, and many of his novels and stories are set in Catholic countries such as Italy and Spain. Hemingway may, if one wishes, be categorized as belonging to a survey of Catholicism in literature, but he seldom is. Jake Barnes, the protagonist of Hemingway's *The Sun Also Rises* (1926), openly professes his Roman Catholicism and clearly suggests that his faith informs his response to the world and others, even if he is not necessarily a churchgoer.

F. Scott Fitzgerald, who was Roman Catholic by birth, hardly touches upon religious matters of any sort in his fictions. His novels, such as *The Great Gatsby* (1925) and *Tender Is the Night* (1934), however, address topics of considerable moral weight. The playwright Eugene O'Neill makes no secret of his Irish Catholic background in the autobiographical work *Long Day's Journey into Night* (1956). The mother's Catholicism in the play is an aspect of her crippled spirituality. Ironically, the most Catholic of American authors, in the sense that he espouses a Catholic point of view in works of spiritual theme, is not always regarded as either American or Catholic. T. S. Eliot, an American who became a British citizen and an Anglican Catholic, beginning with *Ash Wednesday* (1930) and concluding with *Four Quartets* (1943), essays on an intensely personal level the universal qualities of spiritual yearning.

Two events in the 1960's brought changes in the general public's perception of the Catholic identity. First, Roman Catholic John F. Kennedy's successful campaign for the presidency in 1960 finally defused a long-standing tradition of anti-Catholicism in American life. Second, beginning in 1962, the Second Vatican Council initiated reforms in the Catholic church. These reforms had great influence on social and cultural aspects of the Catholic identity. The Church sought to make its teachings more in tune with the moral crises and social realities of the postindustrial, materialist cultures that dominated the twentieth century. These reforms resulted in alterations in the stereotype of Catholics as archaic, dogmatic individuals. One may cite James Farl Powers' *Morte d'Urban* (1962) as a turning point in North American Catholic literature. In its gentle, realistic satire of a Roman Catholic priest, the novel presents Catholic life in America as mainstream, not as part of ethnic literature only. Father Urban Roche, the main character, also helps defeat stereotypes of Catholics simply by not partaking of them. In the novels of Andrew Greeley, a Roman Catholic priest who writes about Roman Catholic priests, the issues of conflict between faith and worldliness take on, as they do in Powers' work, a wide cultural appeal. Greeley's novels, such as *The Cardinal Sins* (1981) and *The Brother's Wife* (1982) have been best-sellers.

The twentieth century

The general breakdown of religious faith seems to be a hallmark of twentieth century literature. In works such as Walker Percy's *Love Among the Ruins* (1971) and *The Thanatos Syndrome* (1987) and Brian Moore's *Catholics* (1972), a time is envisioned in which the sacramental nature of the Church has been forgotten.

Challenges to faith

Other writers, concerned with the secularism of the twentieth century, have made Catholicism a symbol for religious faith in general. In Andre Dubus' "A Father's Story," the protagonist's Catholicism becomes a metaphor for all faith. On the other hand, the sendup of Roman Catholicism in William Gaddis' *The Recognitions* (1955) stands as a satire of religious fraud in general. His characters often fail to find religious experience, even when it is right before their eyes. Faith in Christ, rather than Catholicism specifically, is often the concern in the works of Flannery O'Connor. A reader of her two novels *Wise Blood* (1952) and *The Violent Bear It Away* (1960), if unfamiliar with O'Connor's Catholic background, may imagine them an outgrowth of a Southern evangelical and Fundamentalist experience. Southern Fundamentalist culture shaped O'Connor's identity and her vision, but her works may be read from the perspective of her Roman Catholic beliefs in the sacramental presence of God. O'Connor's fictions are, ultimately, nothing but Catholic.

It is not very likely that Roman Catholicism will benefit much from emphasis on fostering a respect for multiculturalism in American society, since Catholicism has become perceived as Eurocentric and patriarchal. Catholicism is, perhaps, representative of the cultural status quo, which is undergoing challenge and revision. As cultural pluralism and inclusionary studies gain

Implications for identity

acceptance, however, the extensive body of literature defining American Catholic identity should become more widely recognized for having contributed to the American identity.

SUGGESTED READINGS

Franchot, Jenny. *Roads to Rome: The Antebellum Protestant Encounter with Catholicism.* Berkeley: University of California Press, 1994. Since Catholicism in literature also deals with religious bigotry and intolerance, readers would do well to start with this fascinating and extremely scholarly account of the forms and uses of anti-Catholicism in nineteenth century American fiction.

Friedman, Melvin J., ed. *The Vision Obscured: Perceptions of Some Twentieth Century Catholic Novelists.* New York: Fordham University Press, 1970. Articles on Powers and O'Connor do much toward defining the Catholic identity of what otherwise is intended as, and is critically received as, mainstream literature.

Gandolfo, Anita. *Testing the Faith: The New Catholic Fiction in America.* Westport, Conn.: Greenwood Press, 1992. Argues that the Second Vatican Council changed American Catholic fiction. Provides a comprehensive introduction to the American Catholic literary scene.

Kellogg, Jean. *The Vital Tradition: The Catholic Novel in a Period of Convergence.* Chicago: Loyola University Press, 1970. Limited to those writers who advance a Roman Catholic point of view. Focuses on Powers and O'Connor.

Messbarger, Paul R. *Fiction with a Parochial Purpose: Social Use of American Catholic Literature, 1884-1900.* Brookline: Boston University Press, 1971. Examines how American Catholics used fictions to define their emerging identity in a largely non-Catholic culture.

—Russell Elliott Murphy

See also Cather, Willa; Christianity and Christian Fundamentalism; Conversion, religious; Eliot, T. S.; Emigration and Immigration; Hemingway, Ernest; O'Connor, Flannery; O'Neill, Eugene; Religion and identity; Stereotypes and identity

Censorship of literature

DEFINITION: Suppression or destruction of the physical artifacts of literary production.

At issue

With literature comes censorship and attempts at constitutional guarantees; legal precedent and common sense have long had to contend with the ever-renewed desire to censor. For example, a bill introduced to the U.S. Congress on April 25, 1991, by a host of statesmen, the Pornography Victims' Compensation Act of 1991, was aimed at distributors of pornography. The bill caused great concern among educators and librarians because it could have been used against them, depending on how pornography was to be defined. Censorship of literature has included such works as folktales and Mother Goose rhymes. Claims may be made that such literature is pornographic.

At issue, then, are such basic values as the freedom to read, to exchange ideas, and to think for oneself. In the United States, such issues involve the First Amendment to the Constitution. Such freedoms require a continual vigilance in order to keep them vital. These freedoms, which may, at first glance, seem granted and long since established, are, in fact, undergoing a constant attack and redefinition. Censorship cases have risen dramatically since the mid-1970's.

History

Censorship is as old as speech. Censorship of literature is as old as literature. The sixteenth century, for example, witnessed battles between the papacy and Martin Luther, resulting in a split in the Christian church and the establishment of the Catholic *Index librorum prohibitorum* (1559), a list of prohibited books.

In the seventeenth century, censorship battles in England surrounded the Licensing Act of 1643, which forbade the printing or sale of any book without prior official approval. The following year, John Milton published *Areopagitica,* an eloquent and famous attack on censorship. Resistance to the law brought its end in 1695. Still, theatrical performance, for example, was not allowed in public without prior permission of the Lord Chamberlain. This law remained in effect until 1966.

In the nineteenth century, in England, Canada, and the United States, a repressive ideology, proclaiming the need for propriety, prudence, and sexual restraint, made itself felt among editors, publishers, librarians, and even writers, who felt a moral obligation to eliminate disagreeable or realistic portrayals of life. Novelists as scandalous as Jane Austen were censored in American editions. A federal statute was passed in 1842 in an attempt to limit the importation of "French" postcards. This law was broadened in 1865, when Congress passed a law to bar obscene materials from the mail. In 1857, Great Britain passed the Obscene Publications Act, which established official prohibition of purely sexual material, although it failed to define obscenity. In *Regina v. Hicklin*, 1857, obscenity was described as that which depraves and corrupts minds that are susceptible to immoral influences. This, in turn, was the basis for the famous United States Comstock Law of 1873, which established penalties for anyone mailing or receiving obscene, lewd, or lascivious publications.

A famous application of the obscenity laws to literature was the attempt by the federal government to stop the importation of James Joyce's *Ulysses* (1922), resulting in a decision by the U.S. district court in New York in 1933 that the novel is not obscene. D. H. Lawrence's *Lady Chatterley's Lover* (1928) was suppressed in the United States until 1959, and Henry Miller's *Tropic of Cancer* (1934) until 1961. In 1948, the Supreme Court affirmed that Edmund Wilson's *Memoirs of Hecate County* (1946) is obscene. In 1967, Congress established the Commission on Obscenity and Pornography, which recommended the repeal of all general obscenity legislation, finding that there is no evidence that obscenity causes antisocial behavior. President Richard M. Nixon and the U.S. Senate rejected the findings.

After various obscenity trials, the legal test involved came to be whether the dominant theme of the materials would appeal to the prurient interest of the average person, under contemporary community standards. In *Miller v. California* (1972) a three-part test was established. First, does the dominant theme as a whole appeal to a prurient interest in sex? Second, is the material offensive to community standards as defined by state law, regarding depictions of sexual conduct? Third, is the material without redeeming literary, artistic, political, or scientific value? This three-part test, which made prosecutions of obscenity more difficult than they had been before, reduced the number of attempts to censor literature significantly. This reduction is the result of the third part of the test; it is difficult to show that a novel has no literary value.

Since *Miller v. California* and since a marked polarization of society into groups of different and antagonistic philosophies after the social upheavals of the 1960's, incidents have highlighted the censorship of literature taking place in schools. A dramatic example of schoolbook censorship took place in Kanawha County, West Virginia. In December, 1973, the West Virginia Board of Education decided that all school districts must select school materials that accurately represent ethnic and minority contributions to American culture and demonstrate the intercultural quality of American society. On March 12, 1974, the Kanawha County English Language Arts Textbook Committee made recommendations of 325 titles to the board, including textbooks from various major publishers, and the board ratified them.

Alice Moore, a Kanawha County School Board member and wife of a Fundamentalist minister, took some of the books home and then contacted Mel Gabler and Norma Gabler, heads of Educational Research Analysts, a self-appointed textbook evaluating corporation. The Gablers mailed Moore back reviews of the books. She, in turn, supplied the other board members and a local newspaper with the reviews, and the community began gathering momentum against use of the books.

This led to a school board meeting, at which Moore charged that the books were filthy, unpatriotic, and overly sympathetic to blacks. She garnered some support, and another meeting was scheduled. Before it took place, Moore began a publicity campaign to get the books banned. This prompted the local PTA to oppose several of the books as antireligious, anti-American, and sexually explicit. The Magic Valley Mother's Club joined in and circulated a petition to ban the materials.

The next school board meeting attracted an audience of more than 1,000 people and resulted in a board vote to keep all of the books except for eight titles from one series. The battle was to grow larger.

The Christian-American Parents organization and the Concerned Citizens organization initiated campaigns against the books, including a Labor Day rally at which the Reverend Marvin Horan implored a crowd to boycott the schools. These campaigns resulted in students being kept out of school for the first week of classes. The school board announced on September 11, 1974, that the offending books would be removed for a thirty-day review. The Reverend Marvin Horan, joined by Reverend Graley, Reverend Hill, and Reverend Quigley, asked Christians to pray to God to kill the board members who voted to keep the books. Numerous other voices joined in on the anticensorship side; national organizations opposing censorship helped the involved local citizens. On February 10, 1975, most of the original textbooks were reinstated, but they were not used.

Two major concerns of school censorship have always been those surrounding religion and sex. In 1985, *Grove v. Mead School District 354* rejected a claim that *The Learning Tree* (1963) by Gordon Parks be removed from an eighth-grade class because it fostered a belief in secular humanism. A more famous case, *Mozert v. Hawkins County School District* (1987), led to the decision that "The First Amendment does not protect the plaintiffs from exposure to morally

Censorship of Literature
Milestones

A.D. 391 — The great library of Alexandria is burned by Christians.

1559-1966 — The *Index Librorum Prohibitorum* (Index of Forbidden Books). During the time of the index's enforcement, Catholics are forbidden to read, translate, own, or print a book on the list.

1865 — *Alice's Adventures in Wonderland*, Lewis Carroll's famous book for children, is published. Some critics hold that the book should be kept away from children because it is riddled with material that causes anxiety.

1922-1933 — *Ulysses*, by James Joyce, is published and put on trial in various countries. In 1922 imported copies of *Ulysses* are burned in Ireland and Canada, and five hundred copies are burned by the U.S. Post Office. The following year sees the destruction of another five hundred copies at the port of Folkstone by British customs officers. A U.S. trial of *Ulysses* leads to a great change of the legal definition of what can be considered obscene. Margaret Anderson and Jane Heap, who publish *The Little Review* in New York City's Greenwich Village, are the first to try putting Joyce's new work—chapter by chapter—into print in the U.S. The U.S. Post Office seizes the magazine. On October 4, 1920, John Sumner, head of the New York Society for the Suppression of Vice, has Anderson and Heap arrested and charged with publishing obscene material. Eventually Random House, an American publisher, decides to force a test case. After signing a contract with Joyce in 1932, Random House arranges to have a copy of *Ulysses* seized by customs officials in New York. In *The United States of America v. One Book Called Ulysses*, the government argues that the book is obscene under the terms of the Tariff Act of 1930. Judge John M. Woolsey presides over the book's trial, which opens in the fall of 1933 and closes with a decision lifting the ban in early December. Woolsey argues that a book needs to be read as a whole before being judged obscene; the previous standard was that a book could be judged obscene based on any of its sections.

1928 — *The Well of Loneliness*, by Radclyffe Hall, a book with lesbian themes, is published. Sir Charteres Biron presides over the book's obscenity trial and refuses to allow testimony on the book's literary merit. Biron then orders *The Well of Loneliness* burned.

1929 — *A Farewell to Arms*, by Ernest Hemingway. From its publication onward, the book is perennially challenged for three primary reasons: sex; violent deaths and senseless brutality; and belief in a universe indifferent to people's suffering.

1934 — *Tropic of Cancer*, by Henry Miller, is published by Obelisk Press in Paris. U.S. Customs officials confiscate a copy the year of its publication. Grove Press issues the book in 1961. The publisher is deluged with trials as various states declare the work obscene. The book wins its court war decisively in 1964, when the U.S. Supreme Court declares the book not obscene.

1939 — *The Grapes of Wrath*, by John Steinbeck, is one of the most widely suppressed and censored modern novels in American literature. Critics have attacked its alleged atheistic beliefs and profane language.

offensive value systems or from exposure to antithetical religious ideas." In this case, Vicky Frost, a Fundamentalist, was sparked to protest by a passage at the end of a story in the 1983 edition of a basic reading series that mentioned mental telepathy, which she considered contrary to her religious beliefs, God alone having such powers. Obscenity and vulgarity, on the other hand, have generally been considered legitimate reasons for limiting children's access to books.

In general, court decisions in the 1990's involving censorship have placed the decision in the hands of the local communities. Community standards therefore remain a key in the censorship of literature. National organizations often are involved, however, in the battles taking place on the local level.

SUGGESTED READINGS

American Library Association. *Banned Books, 1995*. Chicago: World Book, 1995. Publication of current issues.

_____. *Censorship Litigation and the Schools*. Chicago: World Book, 1983. Proceedings of an important colloquium.

Censorship of Literature Milestones — CONTINUED

1951 *The Catcher in the Rye*, by J. D. Salinger, is another one of the most frequently attacked books. The book has been a target of censorship by critics who have found its central character, Holden Caulfield, a poor role model who uses foul language, among other things.

1955 In *Lolita*, by Vladimir Nabokov, a European émigré falls in love with and seduces a twelve-year-old American girl nicknamed Lolita. Nabokov mocks the moralizing smugness and pretensions to family values of the 1950's United States. The book is widely attacked for its portrayal—which many mistake for advocacy—of sexual perversion.

1956 *Giovanni's Room*, by James Baldwin, treats homosexuality openly. Baldwin's agent, Helen Strauss, suggests that he burn his manuscript. Following the novel's acceptance for publication in England, Dial Press contracts with Baldwin to publish the book in the United States.

1957 Allen Ginsberg's obscenity trial in San Francisco. On October 13, 1955, Ginsberg gives a reading of "Howl," a long poem, at Six Gallery. Lawrence Ferlinghetti, a local poet and publisher, hears Ginsberg's reading and offers to publish "Howl." The second printing of the book *Howl* is seized by customs officials on March 25, 1957.

1960 *To Kill a Mockingbird*, by Harper Lee, one of the most widely read novels in American junior high and high schools, is challenged frequently by parents and school boards and even banned in some areas.

1970 *I Know Why the Caged Bird Sings*, by Maya Angelou, is honored as a modern African American classic. The book ranks as one of the most frequently challenged books of the late twentieth century. Offended parents and pressure groups object to the book's descriptions of child molestation, its sex scenes, its coarse language, its irreverent attitude toward institutional religions, and its pervading bitterness toward whites and the racism of the 1930's.

1982 *The Color Purple*, by Alice Walker, is criticized for its realistic depictions of domestic violence, incestuous and homosexual relationships, and its ostensibly irreligious themes. Ishmael Reed and Charles Johnson complain that both the novel and the film version do harm by helping to perpetuate negative stereotypes of African American men. They suggest that Walker should focus her work on intercultural rather than intracultural conflicts.

1987 The *Impressions* Language Arts textbook series is published by Holt, Rinehart and Winston and Harcourt Brace Jovanovich. The most frequently banned (and litigated) books of the 1990's are the *Impressions* readers. The *Impressions* series has anthologized works by C. S. Lewis, Laura Ingalls Wilder, Martin Luther King, Jr., Rudyard Kipling, A. A. Milne, Dr. Seuss, Jan Slepian, Katherine Paterson, and other classic and award-winning authors and illustrators. Teachers call *Impressions* a great improvement over other readers with bland reading selections chosen with the intention of offending no one. Protests against *Impressions* begin immediately. Parents in several small communities in Washington and Oregon protest, for example, that the *Impressions* books contain traces of witchcraft, mysticism, and fantasy, as well as themes encouraging rebellion against parents and authority figures.

1991 *American Psycho*, a novel by Bret Easton Ellis about a Wall Street investment banker who leads a double life as a sadistic serial killer, is attacked for the misogyny of its protagonist.

_____. *Intellectual Freedom Manual*. 4th ed. Chicago: World Book, 1992. A discussion of issues and procedures concerning library and school selection of materials.

_____. *Newsletter on Intellectual Freedom*. Chicago: World Book. Published every other month. Deals with current events, publications, and court cases involving censorship, mainly in schools and libraries.

Clor, Harry M. *Obscenity and Public Morality*. Chicago: University of Chicago Press, 1985. Places censorship of literature in the larger context of the culture views of morality, centering on questions about the definition of obscenity.

Davis, James, ed. *Dealing with Censorship*. Chicago: National Council of Teachers of English, 1979. Dated but still useful collection of essays on aspects of censorship in public schools.

Foerstel, Herbert N. *Banned in the U.S.A.: A Reference Guide to Book Censorship in Schools and Public Libraries*. Westport, Conn.: Greenwood Press, 1994. An overview of important incidents, pertinent laws, views of a few important authors on censorship. Contains a synopsis of the most frequently banned books in the 1990's.

Gregorian, Vartan, ed. *Censorship: Five Hundred Years of Conflict*. New York: Oxford University Press, 1984. A survey of the historical context.

—Harry Edwin Eiss

See also Abortion and birth control; Antiwar literature; Erotic identity; Religion and identity

Centaur, The

AUTHOR: John Updike (1932-   )
FIRST PUBLISHED: 1963
IDENTITIES: European American; family; men

The Centaur, John Updike's third novel, won for him his first National Book Award. Its story is of George Caldwell, a science teacher in a small Pennsylvania town, and his fifteen-year-old son, Peter. Updike's own father was a teacher in the high school in Shillington, Pennsylvania, and the book was in part intended to be a tribute to his father.

In January of 1947, George fears he may have cancer and goes after school for X rays. He and Peter then drive to a swim meet in a nearby town; their 1936 Buick breaks down, forcing them to spend the night. The next night a snow storm sets in during a basketball game, and the repaired Buick cannot get them all the way home. They walk the rest of the way through the snow and find out that the doctor has called—George does not have cancer. Peter has developed a severe fever, so he stays home the next day as George goes through the snow to school, realizing that his fate is not to die, but to live.

Peter is remembering these events fifteen years later, and the reader realizes that they were not just ordinary trials of a schoolteacher and his son, but crucial experiences in one boy's undertaking the universal task of finding one's father—and one's own identity. To reinforce this universality, Updike utilizes myth.

The book's title comes from the identification of George Caldwell with Chiron, the noble centaur (half-man, half-horse) who gave his life so Prometheus might be freed from punishment for giving humanity fire. Peter is identified with Prometheus; Hummel, the garage mechanic, represents Vulcan, god of the forge; the principal of the school is also the king of the gods, and so on.

The first and last chapters of the novel shift between describing a two-legged high school teacher and a four-legged centaur. Chapter 3 is entirely mythical, describing children under Chiron's instruction on Mt. Olympus. Chapter 5 is objectively narrated; chapter 7 is an impressionistic variety of scenes. Chapters 2, 4, 6, and 8 are told in the first person by Peter, with only tangential mythological references.

The mythical parallels give the book a quality of surprise and suggest a multilayered reality, but Updike recognized that many readers would not immediately recognize the different layers, so he provided an index that identifies specific allusions. As an adult, Peter recalls the daily sacrifices his father made for him; George's task, however, was not to die like Chiron, but to live; "he discovered that in giving his life to others he entered a total freedom."

SUGGESTED READINGS

Campbell, Jeff H. *Updike's Novels: Thorns Spell a Word*. Wichita Falls, Tex.: Midwestern State University Press, 1987.

Detweiler, Robert. *John Updike*. New York: Twayne, 1984.

Greiner, Donald. *John Updike's Novels*. Athens: Ohio University Press, 1984.

McNaughton, William, ed. *Critical Essays on John Updike*. Boston: G. K. Hall, 1982.

—Jeff H. Campbell

See also Adolescent identity; European American identity; School

Chávez, Denise Elia

BORN: Las Cruces, New Mexico; August 15, 1948

PRINCIPAL WORKS: *The Last of the Menu Girls*, 1986; *Face of an Angel*, 1990

IDENTITIES: Latino; West and Southwest; women

SIGNIFICANT ACHIEVEMENT: Chávez's poetry, fiction, and numerous plays show Mexican American women searching for personal identity and space in a complex cultural environment.

Denise Chávez was born in the desert Southwest, and she writes about the Native Americans, Mexican Americans, Anglo-Americans, and others who provide the region's rich cultural tapestry. Her works consistently focus on the strength and endurance of ordinary working-class Latino women.

Chávez had twelve years of Catholic schooling and started writing diaries and skits while still in elementary school. She received her bachelor of arts degree in theater from New Mexico State University in 1971, her master of fine arts in theater from Trinity University in San Antonio, Texas, in 1974, and her master of arts in creative writing from the University of New Mexico in 1984. During her school years she worked in a variety of jobs—in a hospital, in an art gallery, and in public relations. She also wrote poetry, fiction, and drama, always with emphasis on the lives of women. She taught at Northern New Mexico Community College, the University of Houston, Artist-in-the-Schools programs, and writers' workshops.

Chávez has written numerous plays and literary pieces, which she often performed or directed, including a national tour with her one-woman performance piece. Her plays have been produced throughout the United States and Europe. Her plays (mostly unpublished), written in English and Spanish, include *Novitiates* (1971), *The Flying Tortilla Man* (1975), *Rainy Day Waterloo* (1976), *The Third Door* (1978), *Sí, hay posada* (1980), *The Green Madonna* (1982), *La morenita* (1983), *El más pequeño de mis hijos* (1983), *Plague-Time* (1984), *Novena Narrativas* (1986), and *Language of Vision* (1987).

The Last of the Menu Girls, interrelated stories about a young Chicana, and the novel *Face of an Angel* have established Chávez's high reputation as a fiction writer. Both works address critical questions of personal and cultural identity with extraordinary wit and compassion. Chávez has a striking ability to create a sense of individual voice for her characters, and she makes that voice resonate for readers who may or may not be familiar with the places and people about whom she writes.

SUGGESTED READINGS

Balassi, William, John F. Crawford, and Annie O. Eysturoy, eds. *This Is About Vision: Interviews with Southwestern Writers*. Albuquerque: University of New Mexico Press, 1990.

Farah, Cynthia. *Literature and Landscape: Writers of the Southwest*. El Paso: Texas Western Press, 1988.

Reed, Ishmael. *Hispanic American Literature*. New York: HarperCollins, 1995.

—Lois A. Marchino

See also *Face of an Angel*; *Last of the Menu Girls, The*; Latino American identity

Cheever, John

BORN: Quincy, Massachusetts; May 27, 1912

DIED: Ossining, New York; June 18, 1982

PRINCIPAL WORKS: *The Way Some People Live*, 1943; *The Enormous Radio and Other Stories*, 1953; *The Wapshot Chronicle*, 1957; *The Housebreaker of Shady Hill and Other Stories*, 1958; *The Wapshot Scandal*, 1964; *Bullet Park*, 1969; *Falconer*, 1977; *The Collected Stories of John Cheever*, 1978; *Oh, What a Paradise It Seems*, 1982

IDENTITIES: Disease; European American; Northeast

SIGNIFICANT ACHIEVEMENT: Cheever's short stories and novels satirize upper-middle-class families living in the suburbs north of New York City and in New England.

John Cheever's father, a successful shoe salesman, and his mother, born in Sheffield, England, provided for his education at Thayer Academy. Cheever was eventually expelled. This dismissal led to his story "Expelled," which was published in *The New Republic* in October, 1930. In New

John Cheever, author of Oh, What a Paradise It Seems *(1982), a critical portrait of life in suburbia.* (© Nancy Crampton)

York in 1932, Cheever worked with Malcolm Cowley and for *The New Yorker*, a magazine which published 120 of Cheever's stories.

In 1951, Cheever moved to Scarborough, a community about twenty-five miles north of New York City. In this environment, Cheever's interpretation of suburbanites developed, and Cheever gained a reputation for stylish satire of manners and customs in communities named variously as St. Botolph's, Bullet Park, Talifer, Remsen Park, Proxmire Manor, Shady Hill, and Gorey Brook. Typically the residents are white Protestants who suffer through love and loneliness, often facing the destruction of their families. In many cases, characters abuse alcohol and engage in sexual promiscuity while financial pressures threaten their social position and technological development threatens their humanity.

In "The Country Husband," the superficiality of Shady Hill is satirized as Francis Weed endures a family and community that refuse to acknowledge his individuality. In "The Swimmer," Neddy Merrill swims across his community by advancing from the pool of one neighbor to the pool of the next. The journey allows Cheever to reveal the identity of the neighbors, and Neddy stumbles home at the end to realize that his protracted drunkenness has led his wife to abandon him. In *The Wapshot Scandal*, suicidally alcoholic characters descend into episodes of sexual depravity. The community has the atmosphere of a wasteland, with nuclear holocaust looming ominously.

John Cheever's career was illustrious, but his personal life, like the lives of many of his characters, was marred by alcoholism, infidelity, and family crises. Cheever won the O. Henry Award, the Pulitzer Prize, and the National Book Critics Circle Award, among others, for his fiction.

SUGGESTED READINGS

Bosha, Francis J., ed. *The Critical Response to John Cheever*. Westport, Conn.: Greenwood Press, 1994.

Collins, Robert G. "From Subject to Object and Back Again: Individual Identity in John Cheever's Fiction." *Twentieth Century Literature* 28 (Summer, 1982): 1-13.

Hunt, George W. *John Cheever: The Hobgoblin Company of Love.* Grand Rapids, Mich.: W. B. Eerdmans, 1983.

Meanor, Patrick. *John Cheever Revisited.* New York: Twayne, 1995.

—*William T. Lawlor*

See also Alcoholism; "Country Husband, The"; *Wapshot Scandal, The*

Chicago Poems

AUTHOR: Carl Sandburg (1878-1967)
FIRST PUBLISHED: 1916
IDENTITIES: European American; Midwest

Chicago Poems, Carl Sandburg's first published book of poetry, is a collection of nearly 150 poems. In it, Sandburg revitalized the subject matter and the form of poetry. His poetry is of the people and cities of the Midwest. The people of his cities, the laboring masses who migrated there in search of a better life, speak in the often slangy, colloquial words of the laboring classes. His nature images are taken from the wide rolling prairies.

Sandburg first attacks then praises the people about whom he writes. In "Chicago," the opening poem, Sandburg is explaining that the city has a terrible side to it, with its prostitutes and its killers who are set free; it is a ruthless city that allows women and children to starve. Chicago also is a metropolis that affirms life by industriousness and joy in the face of destiny. It is a city that is made up of people who may not be well educated or have fine manners, but who exhibit energy and pride, and these, according to Sandburg, are the necessary foundations of a healthy society.

Social idealism is apparent on almost every page of *Chicago Poems*. An especially telling example is the poem "I Am the People, the Mob." In it, Sandburg defines the masses as laborers and as witnesses to history. From the very beginning of the book, Sandburg focuses upon the concept of the ultimate power of the people, diminishing the position of the well-to-do in order to accentuate his compassion for the laboring classes. No poem in the book exhibits any sympathy for the problems of the upper or middle classes. Other themes in *Chicago Poems* include the limitations of the written word, the certainty of change, and death as a final silence. For example, the people as a force might move on through the centuries, but as individuals they must undergo the same fate as their politicians and leaders. The theme of this burden of time permeates the entire book. It is especially apparent in "Losses," in which a sweetheart, a child, and a strumming banjo all become a part of that inevitable river of time. Only shadows will be left.

Chicago Poems exemplifies Sandburg's humanitarianism, his great empathy for and defense of the masses. It is his presentation of the profoundly sincere American: He demonstrates not only that people who are but a part of the masses have problems, but that within that mob of people each individual has his or her own set of problems, as well as pleasures and ecstasies. As a result of this, Sandburg is given the distinction of being the American poet who can speak clearly in an authentic voice for the American people.

SUGGESTED READINGS

Crowder, Richard. *Carl Sandburg.* New York: Twayne, 1964.

Golden, Harry. *Carl Sandburg.* Cleveland: World Publishing, 1961.

Lowell, Amy. *Tendencies in Modern American Poetry.* New York: Octagon Books, 1971.

—*Lela Phillips*

See also American identity: Midwest; Sandburg, Carl

Chicano identity

IDENTITIES: Latino

When historians and other scholars began to assess the impact of the Chicano Renaissance of the 1960's and early 1970's, they soon realized that the social and political upheaval of the time also produced an explosion of artistic creation which needed to be understood. Literary works in particular became the subject of intense scrutiny because for many, they held the secret to understanding the Chicano experience in that age of growing awareness. The process of discovering Chicano literature, to a large extent, also became a process of defining Chicano identity.

History

The history of Chicano identity in literature can trace its beginnings to José Antonio Villarreal's novel *Pocho* (1959), which is generally regarded as the first Chicano novel. In it, Richard Rubio, the protagonist, undergoes the rites of passage that all children and adolescents experience in the process of maturation. Paralleling this transition is another one featuring a movement away, by the protagonist, from the Mexican world of his father, who had been a colonel in Pancho Villa's army during the Mexican Revolution of 1910. Richard is symbolically transformed into a *pocho* (Spanish for "rotten," used pejoratively to describe someone of Mexican descent who has adopted Anglo customs and values). Richard occupies, as one born in the United States to his Mexican parents, a new identity, one based on an American cultural landscape. In *Pocho*, Richard discovers that cultural identity is no longer simply an extension of Mexican nationality or of the American mainstream.

The rather confusing and sometimes conflicting tendencies of Richard's identity result from his being Mexican, being American, and being neither of those things. These tendencies affect Richard's concept of identity in *Pocho*. These issues continue to be an important part of the Chicano experience. Rudolfo Gonzales' *I Am Joaquín* (1967), the epic poem of the Chicano Renaissance, takes the cultural confusion first expressed in *Pocho* and attempts to resolve it in the person of Joaquín, a collective hero who represents the Chicano people.

Pocho and *I Am Joaquín* ushered in a variety of dynamic Chicano voices. Memorable voices of the Chicano Renaissance, such as Alurista, Luis Omar Salinas, Gloria Pérez, and Abelardo Delgado brought a greater understanding of the dimension of the Chicano experience. Although these writers began by dealing with personal questions about their existence, they also strived to establish a context for their roots in a historical and cultural Chicano reality.

1970's

The 1970's witnessed an explosion of literary production which firmly established the foundation of Chicano identity in literature. It began in 1970, with Ricardo Sánchez's book of poetry *Canto y grito mi liberación*, Luis Omar Salinas' *Crazy Gypsy*, and a new edition of Villarreal's *Pocho*. Then, in 1971, Alurista published *Floricanto en Aztlán*, a book of poetry that became a classic. It speaks about the American Southwest as Aztlán, the mythical place of origin of the Aztecs. The book affirmed the Southwest as a geographical home and a literary space for the Chicano. Also in 1971, Tomás Rivera published *And the Earth Did Not Part*, a landmark novel about migrant workers from Southern Texas who harvest the crops for the rest of the world. Rivera's work brought the farmworker, an important part of Chicano society, into the literary landscape. Finally, Luis Valdez published a collection of plays, *Actos*, which had been written and performed for César Chávez's farmworkers' movement in California. The plays were used as teaching tools that graphically explain the plight of the Chicano underclass and the social, historical, and economic reasons for that plight.

In 1972, Rudolfo Anaya published his first novel, *Bless Me, Ultima*. *Bless Me, Ultima* brings a powerful message about the land and how those who work it and live on it are affected by its unchanging character. That same year, Antonio Castañeda Shular, Tomás Ybarra-Frausto, and Joseph Sommers published *Literatura Chicana: Texto y Contexto* (Chicano literature: text and context), an anthology that received immediate recognition in Chicano letters. In 1973, Rolando Hinojosa published *Estampas del valle y otras obras-Sketches of the Valley and Other Works*, a humorous novel that presents a series of sketches about the Spanish-speaking communities along the Rio Grande River in Southern Texas.

After *Pocho*, Villarreal published his second and third novels *The Fifth Horseman* (1974) and *Clemente Chacón* (1979), which seek to integrate the epic experience of the Mexican Revolution of 1910 into the Chicano cultural landscape. Anaya's second and third novels, *Heart of Aztlán* (1976) and *Tortuga* (1979), complete the trilogy begun by *Bless Me, Ultima* and deepen the discussion of Chicano identity by alluding to the pre-Columbian Aztec world and its homeland of Aztlán. The literature of Chicano experience developed its own mythos.

During the 1980's, the important writers of the 1970's continued to produce and were joined by new voices, including Nash Candelaria, Arturo Islas, Jr., Eliud Martínez, and Carlos Morton. Chicano identity in literature took an important turn with the arrival of Chicana writers at the forefront of the literary stage. They brought new points of view that enriched the Chicano perspective and effectively changed the tone of the discussion about identity to include gender and the problems in the relationship between Chicanos and Chicanas.

Among the many women who came forward in the 1980's were Ana Castillo, Denise Elia Chávez, Sandra Cisneros, and Mary Helen Ponce. Castillo published her first book of poetry in 1976, but her first novel, *The Mixquiahuala Letters* (1986), defined her to the public. The novel is structured as a series of letters from one woman to another. The letters delve into the love and gender conflicts between Chicanos and Chicanas. It is an indictment of Chicano men's inability to treat women fairly. Chávez is a playwright who also writes poetry and prose. She first published a play in 1973. Her first novel, *The Last of the Menu Girls* (1986), however, attracted special attention because of its delicate prose and the portrayal of a woman's developing identity outside the traditional order.

Chicana writers

Cisneros is a poet who turned to narrative to describe the life of an adolescent girl in *The House on Mango Street* (1983), a novel that received excellent critical reviews. Mary Helen Ponce published her first book of short stories in 1983; her first major work is another collection of short stories, *Taking Control* (1987), which features women as victims, then survivors, then people who, at the end of their stories, are able to take control. This message is confirmed in her first novel, *The Wedding* (1989), which sees life in a Chicano neighborhood through the eyes of a pregnant bride-to-be. The novel is an amusing rendition of traditional customs and mores that hinder women's development.

The 1990's have witnessed an expansion on the themes that have shaped Chicano identity. These themes include Aztlán as a Chicano homeland and its connection to the pre-Columbian past, the past and present relationship of the Chicano with the Mexican, and the relationship of the Chicano to the American mainstream, to the land, and to the Catholic church. Chicano literature of the 1990's also continues to explore the relationship between the Chicano and the Chicana. The last theme sometimes involves a painful reevaluation of cultural values.

1990's

Anaya's contribution to this expansion has come, among other things, in the form of three novels, *Alburquerque* (1992), which explores the Indo-Hispanic genealogy of the city (beginning with the correction in the spelling of its name), *Zia Summer* (1995), a novel that looks for clues in Chicano culture to unravel its mystery plot, and *Jalamanta* (1996), a novel that conveys a message about the apocalyptic destruction of a mythical world that desperately needs to return to the path of the sun. The implication is that the mythical world could very well be this one.

Castillo returned with two novels, *Sapogonia* (1990) and *So Far from God* (1993), which reverse the patriarchal structure of valuing men over women and create a new universe. Castillo's collection of feminist-oriented poetry, *My Father Was a Toltec* (1995), and a collection of essays, *Massacre of the Dreamers: Essays on Xicanisma* (1994), delineates her feminist philosophy and helps explain the themes in her literary production.

Chávez's long novel *Face of an Angel* (1990) depicts the life of a waitress who makes the best of a bad situation and redefines the concept of service, eliminating its demeaning context. Cisneros published, in 1991, a book of short stories, *Woman Hollering Creek and Other Stories*, which deal with how love is idealized by women, who are subsequently disappointed. Mary Helen Ponce reveals life in her neighborhood with her family in *Hoyte Street* (1994), an autobiography that reads like a novel.

Chicano writers have built an awareness of identity for Chicanos that begins in the pre-Columbian past and continues in a present that is filled with male and female voices. In the process they have built a body of Chicano literature.

Implications for identity   The history of Chicano literature reveals an expanding search for identity that goes hand in hand with the Chicano's increasing sense of self-awareness. Villarreal's *Pocho* provides a beginning by delineating the new context of what it is to be Chicano. Gonzales' *I Am Joaquín* connects the Indo-Mestizo world to contemporary Chicano reality. Anaya and his contemporaries orchestrate history, land, and people into a worldview and a new literary landscape. Finally, women writers such as Castillo, Chávez, Cisneros, and Ponce bring the feminine point of view, the plight of Chicanas, and their insistence on change into focus. The Chicana issues represent the latest in the expansion of Chicano awareness and identity.

SUGGESTED READINGS

Bruce-Novoa, Juan. *Chicano Authors: Inquiry by Interview*. Austin: University of Texas Press, 1980. Includes interviews of major Chicano authors.

Eger, Ernestina N., ed. *A Bibliography of Criticism of Contemporary Chicano Literature*. Berkeley: Chicano Studies Library Publication Series, University of California, 1980. Includes names and addresses of Chicano literary presses. Most useful in the search for information.

Jiménez, Francisco, ed. *The Identification and Analysis of Chicano Literature*. New York: Bi-lingual Press/Editorial Bilingüe, 1979. Puts Chicano literature into perspective.

Martínez, Julio, and Francisco A. Lomelí, eds. *Chicano Literature: A Reference Guide*. Westport, Conn.: Greenwood Press, 1985. A good starting point for selecting Chicano authors to read. It includes biographical essays on Chicano writers.

Tatum, Charles M. *Chicano Literature*. Boston: Twayne, 1982. Includes summaries of literary works.

—David Conde

See also Anaya, Rudolfo A.; Chávez, Denise Elia; Chicano Renaissance; Cisneros, Sandra; Hinojosa, Rolando; *Last of the Menu Girls, The*; Rivera, Tomás; Villarreal, José Antonio

Chicano Renaissance

IDENTITIES: Latino

History   During the 1960's and 1970's, when the United States was experiencing profound sociopolitical changes, Chicanos experienced a rebirth in culture and the arts. Chicanos, long exploited and awaiting their turn for recognition and justice, began to create a proliferation of artistic and literary works. Chicanos began their own presses, journals, art, theater, and literature. Philip D. Ortego y Gasca first labeled this burst of creativity as the Chicano Renaissance. Ortego's pronouncement came in conjunction with the publication of Tomás Rivera's *. . . y no se lo tragó la tierra-And the Earth Did Not Part* (1971). Conferences held in Denver in 1969 and in 1970, which led to written goals for the creation of the field of Chicano studies, also may be used as markers of the beginning of the Chicano Renaissance.

Creativity   Annual national art and literary festivals were created. These festivals were modeled after Aztec festivals and reestablished tradition. They upheld a new consciousness that went beyond the aesthetic to the political. Poetry, murals, sculpture, and prose works flowered. New Chicano student organizations and journals also came into being. Organizations created newsletters, activist newspapers, and publications, including *El Chicano*, *Con Safos*, *El Gallo*, *El Grito*, and *El Grito del Norte*. Anthologies of Chicano literature include *El Espejo* (1969) and *La Cosecha* (1977).

Themes   Chicano literature during this rebirth was concerned with the plight of the Chicano and with the minority experience. The works of the 1970's are often in Spanish. Later works are often in English. The Chicano Renaissance has sustained itself—many books, festivals, and artistic works continue to be produced. In either language, Chicano literature is often concerned with inhumanity, death, *curanderismo*, Aztec heritage, Catholicism, machismo, racism, exploitation, feminism, and the tenacity of the Chicano family. Leading poets and writers of the Chicano Renaissance include Alurista, Rudolfo Anaya, Lorna Dee Cervantes, Sandra Cisneros, Rolando Hinojosa, Pat Mora,

Tomás Rivera, Ricardo Sánchez, and Alma Luz Villanueva. Theater of the Chicano Renaissance originated with the Teatro Campesino of Luis Valdez in 1965. This theater presented politically charged short plays to audiences of farmworkers. Valdez's *Zoot Suit* (1978) was a stage and film success.

In music, the Chicano Renaissance frequently adapted traditional Mexican music to the popular **Music and cinema** sounds of 1970's. Chicano music has always been a rich hybrid of Mexican and American styles—music of the Chicano Renaissance is often affirming of Chicano identity and openly political. Musical styles and forms created in Spanish and in English reached national and international audiences. Chicano *conjunto* music additionally became popular across social and cultural lines, reaching as far as Japan. The Chicano Renaissance eventually reached mainstream cinema, resulting in *La Bamba* (1987), *The Milagro Beanfield War* (1988), the film version of *Zoot Suit* (1981), *Stand and Deliver* (1988), and *American Me* (1992). Robert Rodriguez and Carlos Gallardo made waves in the motion picture industry in 1993 when their thriller *El Mariachi,* made for seven thousand dollars, was picked up for distribution by Columbia Pictures.

SUGGESTED READINGS

Bruce-Novoa, Juan. "History as Content, History as Act: The Chicano Novel." *Aztlán: A Journal of Chicano Studies* 24, no. 1 (Spring, 1987): 29.

Klein, Dianne. "Coming of Age in Novels of Rudolfo Anaya and Sandra Cisneros." *English Journal* 81 (September, 1992): 21.

Saldívar, José, and H. Calderón, eds. *Criticism in the Borderlands: Studies in Chicano Literature, Culture, and Ideology.* Durham, N.C.: Duke University Press, 1991.

—*Arnoldo Carlos Vento*

See also Chicano identity

Chicanos. *See* **Chicano identity**

Chickencoop Chinaman, The

AUTHOR: Frank Chin (1940-   )
FIRST PERFORMED: 1972; first published, 1981
IDENTITIES: Chinese American

The Chickencoop Chinaman is a subtle depiction of the experiences of a Chinese American writer who loses and then regains his racial identity and cultural heritage. Laced with historical allusions to legislative and euphemized discrimination against Chinese Americans, the play centers on a visit the writer, Tam Lum, makes to Pittsburgh to collect materials for a documentary film about a famous black boxer. The events that take place during his visit make him realize that what he should do is pursue the lonely mission of telling stories to the unassimilated children of the Chinese railroad builders and gold miners.

The play begins with Tam telling an airline hostess that he was born to be a writer for "the Chinamans sons of Chinamans." As the ensuing scenes show, he has never had a chance to write about the heroism of his people. When a boy, he used to sit in the kitchen, listening to his grandmother's stories of the Chinese railroaders, but he heard no such stories on the radio. In his desperate search for a hero of his own race, he imagined that the Lone Ranger with his mask was a Chinese American in disguise. To his dismay, the Ranger turned out to be a decrepit white racist who ordered Tam to go back to Chinatown to preserve his culture.

Ironically, there was no Chinatown to which Tam could return to preserve his culture, for the old people there were trying to forget their history in order to survive. They urged him to destroy the past and get assimilated. Thus, he turned his back on his father, eradicated his memory of the railroaders, and married a white woman. A few years later, he found himself incompetent as a writer, deserted by his wife, and forgotten by his children. In order to keep himself busy and give his children a gift, he decided to make a film about a black former boxer and his father, Mr. Popcorn, who lived in Pittsburgh.

In Pittsburgh, Tam discovers that the boxer has invented a father. Mr. Popcorn adamantly refuses to play a fake father in a documentary film and chastises Tam for betraying his real father. Tam's plan for the film collapses; however, he learns that he must be true to his own identity and fulfill his destiny. The play ends with Tam standing in a kitchen, asking a group of children to turn off the radio and listen to the stories that his grandmother used to tell him about the Chinese railroaders in the Old West.

SUGGESTED READINGS

Chen, Jack. *The Chinese of America*. San Francisco: Harper & Row, 1980.

Davis, Robert Murray. "Frank Chin: Iconoclastic Icon." *Redneck Review of Literature* 23 (Fall, 1992): 75-78.

McDonald, Dorothy Ritsuk. "An Introduction to Frank Chin's *The Chickencoop Chinaman* and *The Year of the Dragon*." In *Three American Literatures: Essays in Chicano, Native American, and Asian American Literature for Teachers of American Literature*, edited by Houston A. Baker, Jr. New York: Modern Language Association of America, 1982.

Samarth, Manini. "Affirmations: Speaking the Self into Being." *Parnassus: Poetry in Review* 17, no. 1 (1992): 88-101.

—Chenliang Sheng

See also Asian American identity: China, Japan, and Korea; Chin, Frank; *Donald Duk*; *Year of the Dragon, The*

Children of a Lesser God

AUTHOR: Mark Medoff (1940-   )
FIRST PRODUCED: 1979; first published, 1980
IDENTITIES: Disability; European American; family; women

Set in a state school for the deaf, *Children of a Lesser God* depicts several key issues facing the hearing-impaired community. It proclaims the right of deaf individuals to determine their own role in society. James Leeds, a new speech teacher, is assigned to Sarah Norman, a twenty-six-year-old deaf woman who prefers to communicate exclusively in American Sign Language (ASL). She informs James that it is a waste of time trying to force deaf people to speak and read lips so that the deaf can pass for hearing. When James counters that ASL is only good among the deaf, Sarah accuses him of wanting to be God, wanting to make her over in his own image. Deaf students do not want to be changed simply because hearing teachers want to change them. Sarah confides that she dreams of becoming a teacher for the deaf and having deaf children. They eventually realize that they want to communicate with each other no matter what the language and decide to get married. Orin, a hearing-impaired student, tries to convince Sarah that their marriage cannot work. The schoolmaster tries to convince James that the marriage is unwise. While arguing, James catches himself trying to censor the conversation for Sarah and realizes that he has no right to decide what she can or cannot "hear."

They are married and Sarah begins to enjoy life with her hearing husband, but Orin urges her not to turn her back on the deaf, arguing that "deaf rights" are more important than her marriage. As Orin brings a civil rights suit against the school, Sarah feels caught between the deaf and hearing worlds. Sarah realizes that James still wants to change her into a hearing person, Orin wants her to remain "pure deaf" for his political agenda, and his lawyer wants the commission to pity her. Sarah becomes outraged by the hypocrisy and erupts in a passionate, unintelligible voice that shocks and repulses James. Humiliated by his reaction, she explodes in ASL and runs away.

When James finds her, Sarah explains that she finally realizes that it is she who does not have the right to change him and that she no longer wants deaf children because no one has the right to create someone in his or her own image. James is left alone, hoping that someday they might be able to help each other.

Children of a Lesser God portrays the diversity of the deaf community and its struggle to achieve its own identity against a paternalistic system. A feminist statement against male suppression, the play is primarily the story of an emerging culture demanding the right to speak for itself.

SUGGESTED READINGS

Erben, Rudolf. *Mark Medoff*. Boise, Idaho: Boise State University Press, 1995.
Gill, Brendan. "Without Speech." *The New Yorker*, April 14, 1980, 101-106.

—*Gerald S. Argetsinger*

See also Feminism; Keller, Helen; *Miracle Worker, The*; Physical disabilities and identity

Children's Hour, The

AUTHOR: Lillian Hellman (1905-1984)

FIRST PRODUCED: 1934; first published, 1934

IDENTITIES: European American; gay, lesbian, and bisexual; women

The Children's Hour, Lillian Hellman's first successful drama, was an immediate sensation because it concerns lesbianism, a subject that the American theater had previously ignored. For Hellman, however, the intended focus was the maliciousness of society in its rush to judgment and its willingness to condemn and ostracize those who are wrongfully accused.

In the play, two young women friends, Martha Dobie and Karen Wright, run a New England girls' school. Mary Tilford, a student, determines to avenge herself on the women for what she sees as unnecessary discipline. Mary leads her grandmother, the influential Mrs. Amelia Tilford, to believe that Martha and Karen have an "unnatural affection" for each other.

Parents believe the unproved accusations and pull their children out of school. In a confrontation scene with Mrs. Tilford, Martha attacks Mary's credibility and maintains that Karen and she are innocent of the accusations. They are defended to no avail by Karen's fiancé, Dr. Joseph Cardin, who is Mrs. Tilford's nephew. By act 3, the women have lost their court case against Mrs. Tilford and have no hope of reopening their school. Although Dr. Cardin offers escape by starting a new life in Europe, his doubts about the relationship between the two women surface, and he and Karen part. Martha, who has vehemently denied any reality to the lesbian accusations, finally admits to Karen that she has been in love with her and has been jealous of Dr. Cardin. This admission and its accompanying guilt spur her to suicide, leaving Karen alone at play's end, listening listlessly, though perhaps mercifully, to Mrs. Tilford's admission of guilt after her discovery of Mary's lies.

The play's title is an ironic echo of a sentimental poem about childhood innocence by Henry Wadsworth Longfellow. Hellman's drama underscores the wickedness of children and the society in which they are reared. Characteristic of Hellman's dramas is the portrayal of the two strong women at the center of the plot. Martha is an outspoken and emotionally charged critic of society. She is destroyed by guilt over her long-denied "immoral" affection for Karen. In contrast, Karen is the voice of reason, slow to act and careful to digest and consider all alternatives. She has not shared Martha's "unnatural" love, but realizes that she cannot find happiness with the well-intentioned but ineffectual Dr. Cardin. Although Karen's future is unclear at play's end, it seems likely she will survive in a muted and isolated existence, perhaps more mature, but clearly forever changed by the false accusations, the rumors, and Martha's admission and death.

SUGGESTED READINGS

Armato, Philip M. " 'Good and Evil' in Lillian Hellman's *The Children's Hour*." In *Critical Essays on Lillian Hellman*, edited by Mark W. Estrin. Boston: G. K. Hall, 1989.
Falk, Doris. *Lillian Hellman*. New York: Frederick Ungar, 1978.
Lederer, Katherine. *Lillian Hellman*. Boston: Twayne, 1979.
Rollyson, Carl. *Lillian Hellman: Her Legend and Her Life*. New York: St. Martin's Press, 1988.

—*Delmer Davis*

See also Feminism; Hellman, Lillian; Lesbian identity; *Little Foxes, The*

Chin, Frank

BORN: Berkeley, California; February 25, 1940

PRINCIPAL WORKS: *Aiiieeeee! An Anthology of Asian-American Writers*, 1974 (coeditor); *The Chickencoop Chinaman*, pr. 1972, pb. 1981; *The Year of the Dragon*, pr. 1974, pb. 1981; *The Chinaman Pacific and Frisco R. R. Co.*, 1988; *Donald Duk*, 1991; *Gunga Din Highway*, 1994

IDENTITIES: Chinese American

SIGNIFICANT ACHIEVEMENT: Author of the first Asian American play produced on the New York stage, Chin is among the first few writers to present the experiences of Chinese Americans.

A fifth-generation Chinese American, Frank Chin has been witness to a most dramatic chapter in the history of his people. The chapter started with the 1943 repeal of the racially discriminatory Chinese Exclusion Act of 1882. Chin has lived in a social and cultural environment that tends to distort the image of his people and to ignore their history. Chin sees it as his mission to restore their image and remember the heroism, the pioneering spirit, and the sufferings of his people by writing about them from a Chinese American perspective. His plays and novels are informed by his knowledge of the history of Chinese Americans, his understanding of their cultural heritage, and his vision of their future.

Chin believes that the history of Chinese Americans constitutes a heroic and vital part of the history of the American West. In the 1970's, his sense of history was accompanied by a pessimistic prediction. Chin was aware that legislative racism had turned the Chinese American community into a bachelor society in the past and that euphemized discrimination was luring many young Chinese Americans toward assimilation. Hence, he declared in an essay, "Yellow Seattle," that Chinese America was doomed to extinction. This kind of pessimism permeates the two plays that he wrote in the 1970's: *Chickencoop Chinaman* and *The Year of the Dragon*. Pervading these works is an atmosphere of gloom, decay, and death, with bitter young people full of self-contempt renouncing their racial identity and with their families and communities falling apart. The apparent revival of Chinatown and the growth of the Chinese community in the 1980's seem to have helped change Chin's view. Such a change is discerned in *Donald Duk*, in which an atmosphere of renewal

Asian American dramatist, writer, and editor Frank Chin. (Corky Lee)

and jubilant celebration prevail. In the play, a family and a community conscientiously and successfully pass on their heritage from one generation to another in San Francisco's Chinatown.

SUGGESTED READINGS

Chen, Jack. *The Chinese of America.* San Francisco: Harper & Row, 1980.

Davis, Robert Murray. "Frank Chin: Iconoclastic Icon." *Redneck Review of Literature* 23 (Fall, 1992): 75-78.

Samarth, Manini. "Affirmations: Speaking the Self into Being." *Parnassus: Poetry in Review* 17, no. 1 (1992): 88-101.

Sechi, Joanne Harumi. "Being Japanese-American Doesn't Mean 'Made in Japan.'" In *The Third Woman: Minority Women Writers of the United States*, edited by Dexter Fisher. Boston: Houghton Mifflin, 1989.

—*Chenliang Sheng*

See also *Aiiieeeee!*; Asian American identity: China, Japan, and Korea; *Chickencoop Chinaman, The*; *Donald Duk*; *Year of the Dragon, The*

China Men

AUTHOR: Maxine Hong Kingston (1940-   )

FIRST PUBLISHED: 1980

IDENTITIES: Chinese American

In *China Men*, Maxine Hong Kingston tells the stories of her male relatives who came to America. The opening chapter, "Our Fathers," signals her intention to embrace the community of Chinese immigrants. She challenges readers to reconsider the Eurocentric version of American history by bringing to their attention the contributions of Chinese to the building of America.

Kingston weaves her narrative from a poetic association of folklore, fantasy, and fact. In "On Discovery," she relates a Chinese legend: the arrival in North America of Tang Ao during the reign of the Empress Wu (694-705). Captured and forced to become a transvestite, feet bound, face powdered and rouged, ears studded with jade and gold, Tang Ao was forced to serve meals to the court. The bewildering experience of this precursor is a metaphor for the emasculation of Chinese men in America as racism disempowered them, forcing them to perform women's tasks: laundering and cooking.

In America, Kingston's forefathers find themselves off center as they are marginalized by U.S. laws. A chapter on laws, in the middle of *China Men*, documents the legislation and court decisions that, beginning in 1868, systematically excluded Chinese immigrants from normal treatment until 1958. Particularly dehumanizing was the law prohibiting the immigration of the wives and children of Chinese men working in America.

Through the portraits of her many forefathers, Kingston describes a multitude of immigration experiences. Great-grandfather Bak Goong sails to Hawaii in the hold of a ship and works for endless years under the whip on a sugar plantation. His dream of saving enough money to reach Gold Mountain is a mirage. The story of grandfather Ah Goong details the courage and skills of the Chinese who built the most difficult and dangerous section of the transcontinental railroad. They worked for lower wages and endured longer hours than white laborers but were denied the right to own property and become citizens. Nevertheless, Ah Goong prophesies: "We're marking the land now. The tracks are numbered."

Kingston's father, Baba, a man of scholarly accomplishment in China, enters America full of hope, only to be reduced to washing other people's clothes. Then, demonstrating the changing status of the Chinese in America after World War II, his son, drafted into the U.S. Navy to serve in the Vietnam War, receives the highest level of security clearance. "The government was certifying that the family was really American, not precariously American but super-American." Kingston's brother declines the invitation to attend language school, however, because he fears his improved Chinese will be used by intelligence to "gouge Viet Cong eyes, cattleprod their genitals."

Kingston thus ends her chronicle of Chinese American history on a questioning note. The Chinese American is now a full citizen but must share in all that is questionable in American culture.

SUGGESTED READINGS

Chan, Jeffrey Paul, et al., eds. *The Big Aiiieeeee! An Anthology of Chinese American and Japanese American Literature*. New York: Penguin, 1991.

Kingston, Maxine Hong. "Talk with Mrs. Kingston." Interview by Timothy Pfaff. *The New York Times Book Review*, June 18, 1980, 1, 26-27.

Li, David Leiwei. "China Men: Maxine Hong Kingston and the American Canon." *American Literary History* 2 (Fall, 1990): 482-502.

—Joseleyne Ashford Slade

See also Asian American identity: China, Japan, and Korea; Emigration and immigration; Kingston, Maxine Hong; *Woman Warrior, The*

Chinaberry Tree: A Novel of American Life, The

AUTHOR: Jessie Redmon Fauset (1882-1961)
FIRST PUBLISHED: 1931
IDENTITIES: African American; women

The Chinaberry Tree, Jessie Redmon Fauset's third novel, is her attempt to illustrate that "to be a Negro in America posits a dramatic situation." Believing that fate plays an important role in the lives of blacks and whites, Fauset depicts the domestic lives of African Americans who are not struggling with the harsh realities of day-to-day existence.

The Chinaberry Tree relates the story of two cousins, Laurentine Strange and Melissa Paul. Because Laurentine is the product of an illicit romantic relationship between a former slave and her master, Laurentine accepts the community's opinion that she has "bad blood." Rejection from a male suitor reinforces her feelings of inadequacy and propels her to further isolation from the community. The young Melissa, although the daughter of an adulterous relationship between Judy Strange and Sylvester Forten, believes herself superior. Sent to Red Brook to live with her relatives, Melissa meets and falls in love with Malory Forten, who, unknown to her, is her half brother. The "drama" of the novel is the exploration of both women's responses to being innocent victims of fate. Laurentine overcomes her feelings of inadequacy, and Melissa learns that she too is a product of "bad blood."

The Chinaberry Tree is also Fauset's attempt to prove that African Americans are not so vastly different from any other American. To illustrate this, Fauset creates characters such as Dr. Stephen Denleigh (whom Laurentine eventually marries) and Mrs. Ismay and Mrs. Brown, wives of prominent physicians, who enjoy the leisurely pursuits of bridge and whist and travel to Newark or Atlantic City to view moving pictures or to shop. There are also their offspring, children who attend private schools, enjoy winter sports, and have servants. Fauset's characters are not very different in their daily lives from financially comfortable whites.

Fauset's characters experience the joys and sorrows of love. Sarah's and Colonel Halloway's was a forbidden love; they were denied marriage because of the times in which they lived. He could not marry Sarah, but Colonel Halloway provided a comfortable home for Sarah and Laurentine. Although Laurentine experiences rejection by her first suitor, she attains love and happiness after she learns to accept herself. Melissa, who cannot marry Malory, is loved by Asshur Lane, someone she initially rejects because he aspires to be a farmer. Fauset argues that the African American is "endowed with the stuff of which chronicles may be made." In this novel Fauset addresses issues of identity in terms of race and social standing amid the disorder of her characters' daily lives.

SUGGESTED READINGS

Feeney, Joseph. "Greek Tragic Patterns in a Black Novel: Jessie Fauset's *The Chinaberry Tree*." *CLA Journal* 18 (December, 1974): 211-215.

Lupton, Mary. "Bad Blood in Jersey: Jessie Fauset's *The Chinaberry Tree*." *CLA Journal* 27 (June, 1984): 383-392.
Sylvander, Carolyn. *Jessie Redmon Fauset: Black American Writer*. Troy, N.Y.: Whitston, 1981.
—*Paula C. Barnes*

See also African American identity; Fauset, Jessie Redmon; Harlem Renaissance

Chinese Americans. *See* Asian American identity: China, Japan, and Korea

Choices
Author: Mary Lee Settle (1918-   )
First published: 1995
Identities: European American; family; South; women

Choices, Mary Lee Settle's thirteenth novel, begins and ends in April, 1993, on a small island off the coast of Italy. The protagonist, Melinda Kregg, is eighty-two years old. Her two adopted children, Maria, who escaped with her from Spain in 1938, and Aiken, an African American who fled Louisiana in 1964, have come to be with her on the last day of her life. Melinda faces the end cheerfully, satisfied with her life and with the identity she has developed for herself, as a political liberal and a woman who has made a difference in the troubled times through which she has lived. The novel chronicles her adventures and her choices, often made at three o'clock in the morning, when she finds that the difference between right and wrong is particularly clear.

Starting out as a wealthy debutante in Richmond, Virginia, near the end of the 1920's, Melinda soon finds her comfortable world upset. The stock market crash of 1929 ruins her father, who commits suicide, hoping his life insurance will let his wife and daughter keep their places in Richmond society. Melinda, however, resolves to find her own identity without relying on her inheritance.

Beginning as a volunteer with the Red Cross during the labor troubles of the early 1930's in Kentucky, where she first becomes aware of class struggle, Melinda goes on to participate in many of the key events of the century. She is with the Republicans in the Spanish Civil War, nurtures the hurt and homeless in London during the Battle of Britain (Settle served in the Women's Auxiliary of the Royal Air Force at about the same time), and demonstrates for integration in the U.S. South in the 1960's. She is first called a liberal in Kentucky by a hostile Communist organizer. As such, she works for individual freedom against powerful oppressors: capitalists, communists, fascists, Nazis, and segregationists, among others. She works hard to make herself useful to the cause; although she never fires a weapon or makes a speech, she acquires an identity for herself as a woman warrior, capable of repairing a truck and driving it through enemy lines, dressing wounds, maintaining inventories, or cheering her fellow resisters.

At the end, at home on her island, Melinda remembers her life convinced that, although values she and her friends fought for are still at risk, the world she is leaving is better than the one she came into. She identifies herself not by her place in Richmond society but by her struggles to make all society more equitable and less oppressive.

Suggested readings
Garrett, George. *Understanding Mary Lee Settle*. Columbia: University of South Carolina Press, 1988.
Leonard, John. "*Choices* by Mary Lee Settle." *The Nation*, July 10, 1995, 67-68.
Rosenberg, Brian. *Mary Lee Settle's Beulah Quintet: The Price of Freedom*. Baton Rouge: Louisiana State University Press, 1991.
—*William T. Hamilton*

See also Civil Rights movement; Class and identity; Spanish Civil War; World War II

Chopin, Kate

BORN: St. Louis, Missouri; February 8, 1851
DIED: St. Louis, Missouri; August 22, 1904
PRINCIPAL WORKS: *At Fault*, 1890; *Bayou Folk*, 1894; *Night in Acadie*, 1897; *The Awakening*, 1899
IDENTITIES: European American; South; women
SIGNIFICANT ACHIEVEMENT: Chopin's regionalist short stories and novels are among the earliest and best American feminist fiction.

Kate Chopin began writing in 1888, at the age of thirty-seven; even her early work is thus informed by a range of experience that shaped the thoughts, feelings, and actions of a host of convincing characters. The child of a prominent St. Louis family, she was reared in a privileged environment. From ages nine through seventeen, she was educated at an elite Catholic school. At nineteen, she married Oscar Chopin, a New Orleans banker seven years her senior.

Chopin was independent to a degree unusual for a woman of her time. Her diary, for example, records her delight in her physical accomplishments such as rowing and walking, her sorrow for women who were less active, and her bemusement at reactions to her behavior. Oscar appears to have been sympathetic to his young wife's unconventional nature; still, stories such as "A Point at Issue" (1889) reflect Chopin's yearning for a relationship in which wife and husband could each "remain a free integral of humanity, responsible to no dominating exactions of so-called marriage laws."

The couple settled in New Orleans, where Chopin bore six children in less than a decade. The frustrations Chopin felt as a strong-willed woman in a patriarchal culture are clearly reflected in much of her writing. In "The Story of an Hour" (1894), for example, a young woman informed of her husband's death regrets his loss but cannot help but be pleased that "there would be no one to live for her during those coming years; she would live for herself." When Oscar's cotton ventures failed, the family moved to Natchitoches Parish, where he died in 1882. Chopin assumed responsibility for the family business, moving back to St. Louis.

A physician friend, Frederick Kolbenheyer, introduced her to the works of radical *fin de siècle* writers and urged her to write as a way of dealing with her sense of "otherness." Her familiarity with the Bayou culture and her reading of regionalist writers led Chopin to produce "local color" stories set in southern Louisiana. Her keen renderings of aristocratic Creoles and rustic Acadians—often infused with subtle observations on the region's racial and social divisions—earned for her a national reputation. Chopin was influenced by Guy de Maupassant, whom she translated into English.

Women's experience is at the heart of all Chopin's work, from Paula's rejection of a marriage proposal because "it doesn't enter into the purpose of my life" ("Wiser than a God," 1889) to Aurélie's discovery that her decision not to have children has left a void in her life ("Regret," 1897). Chopin's editors continually requested that she tone down her women characters; in 1899, her masterpiece *The Awakening* was condemned by critics and banned from libraries for its frank presentation of women's sexuality. Deeply hurt by the experience, Chopin wrote little more before her death. In the 1970's, however, her reputation was resurrected, and she was recognized as a master of realism and a pioneering feminist.

SUGGESTED READINGS

Bloom, Harold. *Kate Chopin*. New York: Chelsea House, 1987.
Seyersted, Per. *Kate Chopin: A Critical Biography*. Baton Rouge: Louisiana State University Press, 1969.
Skaggs, Peggy. *Kate Chopin*. Boston: Twayne, 1985.
Toth, Emily. *Kate Chopin*. New York: William Morrow, 1990.

—Thomas D. Petitjean, Jr.

See also *Awakening, The*; Creole and Acadian literature; Erotic identity; Feminism

Christianity and Christian Fundamentalism

IDENTITIES: Religion

DEFINITION: Christianity is religion based on belief in Jesus Christ. Christian Fundamentalism concentrates on the idea that the Bible is infallible concerning the history of the world.

Christianity

Christianity is the religion that focuses on Jesus Christ as Savior to all followers. There are three primary divisions in the Christian religion, which are the Roman Catholic church, the Protestant churches, and the Holy Orthodox Catholic Apostolic Eastern church. All of these three divisions practice various rituals and beliefs, but as a whole, the followers of Christianity adhere to three basic elements of faith. The first element is that a story is told, which is the Gospel. The Gospel details and narrates the events and various aspects of Jesus' life and teaching. The second element is doctrine, which followers accept as stemming from the belief that Jesus is God. Third, followers use Jesus' life as an example for their own lives.

Christianity relies on God the Father, Jesus Christ, and the Holy Spirit as divine forces who guide their followers' lives by emphasizing virtues such as patience, forgiveness, and love. Christians believe that perfection and happiness are found through God's love. Christianity also strives toward universalism in that the followers and teachers of the religion and the Gospel act as witnesses, or examples for others, and in that way they spread the Gospel. Christianity seeks converts. It is unnecessary to point out how essential the written mode of communication is in spreading information to readers. Christianity is often found in literature for the objective of spreading knowledge of the religion. Christianity came to be in a time of the written word; hence, the Word is central to Christianity. Believers hold the Scripture, or the Old and New Testaments of the Bible, as the primary source of reference in their beliefs, and therefore the Scripture is instrumental in the spreading and informing of the religion to others. In the New Testament, Matthew 28:19-20 contains a Scripture in which Jesus tells his disciples: "Go ye therefore, and teach all nations, baptizing them in the name of the Father, and of the Son, and of the Holy Ghost: Teaching them to observe all things whatsoever I have commanded you." The followers, or disciples, of Christianity therefore welcome and use literature as a communicating tool.

Major Protestant denominations within the Christian religion include Lutheranism, Presbyterianism, Congregationalism, Baptist churches, and Methodism. In Christianity, baptism is the sacrament of admitting a person into Christianity by immersing the individual in water or by sprinkling water on the individual's head, thereby washing away sin and allowing purification of the person's spirit. Lutheranism distinctively allows the baptism to be performed on infants. A baptized infant remains purified, unless as an adult the person renounces the faith. Presbyterianism stresses the absolute sovereignty of God in deciding whom he will save. This sovereignty is known as predestination. There are some divisions in the Presbyterian church as well, and there are some congregations that advocate that it must be the individual's choice in allowing God into one's life, by giving that life to God completely. Only then will God administer his doctrine and direction to eternal salvation. Baptist churches distinctively teach that only adults can be baptized, having made the educated choice to accept salvation.

Christian Fundamentalism

Fundamentalists are Christians who follow the fundamental aspects of faith. The movement of Fundamentalism is a reaction against other movements that criticize the Bible (that is, treat it more as a historical document than as the revealed Word of God) and that stress a rational, objective approach to Christianity. Revelations coming from research in astronomy, geology, and evolution led to the widespread belief among Christians that the Bible is not always literally true. Fundamentalists believe that it is. Fundamentalists vehemently oppose the modern critical approach to religion, doctrine, and Scripture.

The primary articles of Fundamentalist faith, dating from the beginning of the twentieth century and still followed as a general rule, are that Jesus Christ is God, that he was born of a virgin (Mary), that he died on the cross for all followers' sins, that he was resurrected from the dead, and that he will return again in bodily form. The Trinity, or concept of the Father, the Son, and the Holy Ghost as one composition of God, is another belief. The existence of Satan is acknowledged, as is the original sin of Adam and Eve. Salvation through grace and baptism is another commonly held belief. Most central to these beliefs, however, is that all final authority for faith lies in the Bible. To Fundamentalists, the Bible provides the answers to all questions. The examples of Jesus' work and the lives in the Bible are to be used and embodied in one's own life. Fundamentalists believe that events occur in history as they are foretold in Scripture and that scientific evidence that challenges literal interpretation of the Bible is only theory.

Another Fundamentalist belief is that of God's salvation of sinners through the death and resurrection of Jesus Christ. Some of the most adamant supporters of the Fundamentalist movement are the Evangelicals, who believe that salvation holds the key to virtue. Consequently, if one does not believe in salvation, one will go to Hell. Certainly this is an extreme view, and not held so seriously by all Fundamentalists, although it is condoned.

Fundamentalists are sensitive to scientific criticism of the Bible, even when the criticism is of occurrences such as the parting of the Red Sea, which do not take place any longer and have not since biblical times. Most Fundamentalists agree that supernatural occurrences have happened since then and insist on their truth in the Bible. Fundamentalists defend the Creation of humanity as told in Genesis in the Bible. Those who challenge this version of human development defend the scientific theories, such as Charles Darwin's evolution theory. There are many branches within the Fundamentalist camp, as there are in other large religious groups. Positions have evolved over time as society and culture have changed.

History of Christianity

The first recorded writings of the Old Testament date back to approximately 1000 B.C. Jesus was born approximately 4 B.C., and crucified approximately A.D. 30. Converts began to spread the Word through the Roman Empire. Within three hundred years of its beginning, Christianity became the dominant religion in the Roman Empire, and in the approximately two thousand years since then it has become the world's most populous religion.

As an organized religion Christianity began with the small band of disciples who followed Jesus Christ during his teaching in Palestine in the first century. The history of the Church can be divided into three major time periods, which are the ancient, the medieval, and the modern. In the early fourth century under Constantine I, Christianity became accepted in the Roman Empire. The medieval period was marked by relations between Church and state in which the Church exerted considerable authority. The Renaissance and the Reformation marked the beginning of the modern period of the Christian church; a date that may be selected to mark the change is 1517, when Martin Luther posted his ninety-five theses.

Denominations formed as more questioning of Rome's supremacy took place. This pattern continued into the nineteenth century, when people were disillusioned with religion as a means to improve the human condition. In the seventeenth century, a group of dissenters from the Anglican church, called Puritans, sparked the creation of Protestant denominations such as the Anglicans, Presbyterians, Congregationalists, Quakers, and Baptists. The Puritans brought their set of beliefs to America, and it would not take long for other denominations to emigrate to America for the same reason as the Puritans, who sought religious freedom.

From the nineteenth century onward, people experienced disillusionment with religion in an age faced with scientific research, discovery, questioning, and diverse theory. A group of faithful Christians emerged that defended the Scripture when it was undermined as literal truth by many types of criticism. This group was the Christian Fundamentalists. Their influence in America was felt markedly beginning in the 1920's and continued for many years. The Fundamentalist movement lost dominance among thinkers and theologians as an age of open-mindedness concerning all things arose, especially in matters of religion. Fundamentalism remained powerful in political and social settings, however.

History of Christian Fundamentalism

The movement began in the early 1900's, in reaction to a time in which even clergy and those in other respected religious positions and offices began to question the text of the Bible and some of its doctrines. This allowed for a historical study of the Bible and prompted more questioning brought on by modern knowledge and thought. Many of these Fundamentalists became quite vigorous in denouncing this historical examination of aspects of the Christian belief system and went so far as to have the clergymen and theologians who embraced the criticism dismissed from their positions.

The popularity of Christian Fundamentalism flourished in the early twentieth century. About this time, Fundamentalism was beginning to be taught in schools so that the young people of the country would be prepared to resist modern temptations and defend Christianity, its doctrines, Scripture, and Fundamentalism. One institution of this type of teaching was the Los Angeles Bible Institute. As the retaliation against modern thought took a forceful role in Fundamentalism, the secular world retaliated when Fundamentalists went so far as to try to pass legislation that would forbid the teaching of evolution in the schools. In addition to some Southern states and border states, Tennessee passed such laws. A trial took place in 1925 in which high school teacher John Thomas Scopes was convicted (later acquitted on a technicality) of teaching evolution. Orator and politician William Jennings Bryan acted as a prosecuting attorney at the trial. Bryan became known as a defender of the faith. He was one of the most active and fervent supporters of the Fundamentalist movement and gave many speeches and wrote many tracts defending the Fundamentalist position.

Bryan believed that God was his divine Savior and that the Bible was irrefutably the Word of God. Already a political public figure, it is natural that he verbally denounced the modernism that challenged his own personal belief system. He failed, however, at being a credible expert on the Fundamentalist side. During the trial in 1925, a defense attorney named Clarence Darrow verbally bested Bryan and revealed in the courtroom that Bryan was not as knowledgeable in the points of Fundamentalism as was generally thought. It is reasonable that this embarrassment not only contributed to Bryan's death shortly after the trial, but also to the decline of the Fundamentalist movement in the 1930's.

Continuing acceptance of scientific theory by the Christian American public caused the movement to lose its momentum. The movement revived again when faced with two new theological movements, ecumenicity and neo-orthodoxy. Ecumenicity is a movement in which a better understanding of all religions and faiths around the world is prompted, along with a unification of Christian churches. Neo-orthodoxy is a movement in Protestantism that stresses the traditional doctrines of the Reformation, which in turn are against the doctrines of Fundamentalism. Resistance to these two movements began in the 1940's. Since this time, a number of associations have been developed, such as the American Council of Christian Churches and the National Association of Evangelicals. In 1948, an international Fundamentalist group was also formed. The Fundamentalist movement is still in existence and promises to remain a part of America's social and religious landscape.

In American literature, Christianity and Christian Fundamentalism are widespread themes, **Important works** especially in early American literature. In the early 1600's, John Winthrop was an influential writer. His work of 1630 (the year of his arrival in America), entitled *A Model of Christian Charity*, is of lasting importance in American history and religion. The work clearly sets out the ideals of a harmonious Christian community. Cotton Mather referred to Winthrop as the embodiment of a perfect earthly ruler.

William Bradford wrote a Puritan work entitled *History of Plymouth Plantation*, which was published in 1856. It relates events to 1646. This work details the Reformation in England and describes the oppression the Puritans suffered after their break from the Anglican church. This work provides an example of the questioning of religion that was taking place in the 1600's.

Michael Wigglesworth saw in his own day unfortunate occurrences and, considering the approach of Judgment Day and the Second Coming of Christ, wrote a poem, "The Day of Doom" (1662). He gives examples from the Scripture as answers to his questions of religion and the motives of God. As Fundamentalists believe strongly in the Second Coming, they also use the Scripture as a reliable reference.

Mary Rowlandson, a Puritan woman, was captured by Indians in 1675 on one of the Indian chief Metacomet's raids. She was held captive for almost eight weeks. After her release she wrote an account of the captivity. This was published in 1682 as *Narrative of the Captivity and Restauration of Mrs. Mary Rowlandson*, and she revealed her heavy reliance on the Scripture, specifically the book of Psalms, to endure the experience. Throughout the work she makes constant reference to God and the Scripture.

Cotton Mather was pastor of the Second Church of Boston from 1685 until his death in 1728. He was a skillful preacher and theologian and secured a very important place in American literature through his historical accounts of the time. He lived during the time of the Salem witch trials. Mather wrote *Magnalia Christi Americana* (1702), which details the struggles of religion during his time, and provides a reference, based on Scripture, for Christian lives.

Jonathan Edwards welcomed the responsibility and opportunity to approach a disillusioned mass of people who had lost a sense of commitment with God. He wanted to reform these people into believers and followers who understood the doctrines and beliefs of Christianity and followed them. He wrote a work entitled *The Nature of True Virtue* (1765) in which he depicts the Fundamentalist view of the complete sovereignty of God. This tract was valuable to Fundamentalists during the middle of the twentieth century. He also delivered the sermon "Sinners in the Hands of an Angry God" (1741), which goes step by step through Scripture so he may define the beliefs to the people, and in it he provides methods of application so that the people can see how to mold their lives to the Scripture.

Thomas Paine, the son of a Quaker father and an Anglican mother, came to America when he was thirty-seven years old. He was an active journalist and anonymously published *Common Sense* in 1776, which is a pamphlet encouraging an American break from England. This break was political as well as religious. He later wrote a larger work entitled *The Age of Reason* in 1794, attempting to defend his beliefs, which at the time were seen as attacks on Christianity. He does challenge the validity of the Scripture, perhaps writing the beginnings of modernist thought in American literature.

Phillis Wheatley, once a slave, was intellectually encouraged as a young woman in her studies of religion and the status of the world. In 1773, her *Poems on Various Subjects, Religious and Moral* was published in London. Her literary genius, intelligence, and piety serve as an example of a righteous believer in God and follower of Christianity. In her poem "Thoughts on the Works of Providence," she gently speaks to the people of her day of the grandness of God, once describing him as the light that the world cannot function without. She reveals the emotions of an age filled with religious spirit.

Nathaniel Hawthorne

Another great voice of Christianity in American literature, if not the greatest, is Nathaniel Hawthorne. In his short stories and in a more famous novel, *The Scarlet Letter* (1850), Hawthorne depicts the Puritan ethos. Perhaps the most recognizable short story dealing with the topic of religious faith is his "Young Goodman Brown." The main character's faith in God is questioned when he faces realizations concerning corruption and hypocrisy in a supposedly perfect church. Hawthorne never gives an answer or solution to the issue. People of Hawthorne's time were immersed in doubt, speculation, suspicion, and disillusionment. Yet, he contributed to the view that answers must be sought, or like Goodman Brown, people will live out bitter and spiritually empty lives. Another short story, "The Minister's Black Veil," questions not those involved in positions within the church but those of the congregation. Hawthorne challenges his readers to avoid becoming Reverend Hooper's congregation by removing their own superficial veils and allowing religion into their lives.

From Hawthorne's writings, there is a gap in American literary history in which there were no major writings concerned with Christianity. Most of the writings addressed social issues apart from religion. This is significant because the steady strong line between religious devotion and the socially aware individual has been bent or in some cases, completely severed. Wallace Stevens, in the twentieth century, revealed the transition across this line. He began writing when popular religious poetry was losing popularity. He embraced a modernist ideology and his new faith shows especially in his later poems. In his poem "A High-Toned Old Christian Woman," he criticizes her rigid Christian Fundamentalist views, showing how the woman is so restricted in her beliefs and her views that she winces at even winking her eye. The winking of her eye would mean looking out the windows and acknowledging the modernist challenge, and she, as the Fundamentalist, simply cannot wink. Stevens wrote this during the height of the Fundamentalist debate leading to the trial in 1925. Since that time, many essays and nonfiction books have been written in American literature, discussing all sides of both movements.

An individual looking for identity, specifically religious identity, can easily go to the great works and eras of American history and find perhaps what best suits that individual. A survey of Christianity and Fundamentalism in literature provides an educated, intellectual, and broad knowledge of the identities of believers, followers, and those in opposition of religious faith and doctrine from the time of the Roman Empire to present. The role that religion has played in history is primary. Ages have been shaped and identities have been found through eras of strong religious devotion, of questioning and unrest, and of religious resistance. The most important mode of communication for this world, the written word, continues to provide a source of religious and social history, as well as a source for an individual's search for religious identity and existence. American literature depicts all identities on both sides of the religious debate, so that future generations may draw on them in pursuit of their own.

Finding identity

SUGGESTED READINGS

Evans, Rod L., and Irwin M. Berent. *Fundamentalism: Hazards and Heartbreaks*. La Salle, Ill.: Open Court, 1988. Defines Fundamentalism, presents the movements challenging Fundamentalism, various interpretations of the Bible, and includes bibliography.

Levine, Lawrence W. *Defender of the Faith: William Jennings Bryan—The Last Decade, 1915-1925*. Cambridge, Mass.: Harvard University Press, 1965. Chronicles the political and religious life of Bryan, and his active involvement in the Fundamentalist debate.

Marsden, George M. *Fundamentalism and American Culture: The Shaping of Twentieth Century Evangelicals, 1870-1925*. New York: Oxford University Press, 1980. Discusses American status before Fundamentalism, the debate, Christianity and culture, and interpretations.

Novak, Philip. *The World's Wisdom*. New York: HarperCollins, 1994. Introduction to the world's religions and each religion's sacred texts.

Williams, Paul J. *What Americans Believe and How They Worship*. Rev. ed. New York: Harper & Row, 1962. Survey of the Christian church and all denominations, innovations, and movements. Also includes a survey of the role of religion in shaping American identity.

—Holly K. Henson

See also Religion and identity

Chu, Louis H.

BORN: Toishan, Kwangtung Province, China; October 1, 1915
DIED: New York, New York; 1970
PRINCIPAL WORK: *Eat a Bowl of Tea*, 1961
IDENTITIES: Chinese American; family; Northeast
SIGNIFICANT ACHIEVEMENT: Chu is acknowledged as the first Chinese American novelist to depict Chinatown life realistically.

Born in China, Louis Chu emigrated to America when he was nine years old. Thus Asia and America played significant roles in his formative experience. In *Eat a Bowl of Tea*, Chu's only published novel, he writes knowledgeably and feelingly about life in a rural community of South China as well as about life in New York's urban Chinatown. Chu's life and career in the United States followed a pattern of education and employment that many immigrants would envy. After completing high school in New Jersey, Chu attended Upsala College, earning his degree in 1937.

He then attended New York University, obtaining an M.A. in 1940. Two years of graduate study at the New School for Social Research in New York rounded off his formal education. During World War II, Chu served in the Signal Corps of the U.S. Army. In 1940, he married Pong Fay, who had been born and raised in China; they brought up four children in Hollis, New York, a Queens suburb, where they made a Chinese-speaking home.

Things Chinese American were very much a part of Chu's career. From 1951 to 1961, he was a disc jockey for radio station WHOM in New York City (he was the only Chinese American disc jockey in the city). His radio show, called *Chinese Festival*, could be heard four evenings a week. In 1961, Chu went to work for the city's Department of Welfare and became the director of a center in New York's Chinatown. He was also an entrepreneur, being the owner of the Acme Company, and played an active role in the Chinatown community, holding the post of executive secretary of the Soo Yuen Benevolent Association for more than a decade.

Chu's experience and observation provided ample grist for the mill of his novel, *Eat a Bowl of Tea*, whose protagonist wrestles with issues of traditional Confucian filial duty, marital infidelity, and his identity as a Chinese in America during the 1940's.

SUGGESTED READINGS

Chua, Cheng Lok. "Golden Mountain: Chinese Versions of the American Dream in Lin Yutang, Louis Chu, and Maxine Hong Kingston." *Ethnic Groups* 4 (1982): 33-57.

Hsiao, Ruth. "Facing the Incurable: Patriarchy in *Eat a Bowl of Tea*." In *Reading the Literatures of Asian America*, edited by S. Lim and A. Ling. Philadelphia: Temple University Press, 1992.

Kim, Elaine. *Asian American Literature*. Philadelphia: Temple University Press, 1982.

Ling, Jinqi. "Reading for Historical Specificities: Gender Negotiations in Louis Chu's *Eat a Bowl of Tea*." *MELUS* 20, no. 1 (1995): 35-51.

—*C. L. Chua*
—*Janet Fujimoto*

See also Asian American identity: China, Japan, and Korea; *Eat a Bowl of Tea*; Lee, Gus

Cisneros, Sandra

BORN: Chicago, Illinois; December 20, 1954

PRINCIPAL WORKS: *The House on Mango Street*, 1983; *My Wicked, Wicked Ways*, 1987; *Woman Hollering Creek and Other Stories*, 1991; *Loose Woman*, 1994

IDENTITIES: Family; Latino; Midwest; women

SIGNIFICANT ACHIEVEMENT: Cisneros' work introduced a powerful and zestful Latina voice to American literature.

Sandra Cisneros had a library card before she could read. Her mother insisted that Sandra and her six brothers know books, although the family was too poor to buy them. Her father was Mexican, her mother American-born. Cisneros spoke Spanish with her father and English outside the home and always identified herself as American. Her family moved frequently, and as a result she was shy, turning inward and to books. Not a distinguished student in schools where little was expected of Chicanas, she read voraciously, and she began to write when she was ten. After being graduated from Loyola University in Chicago, she enrolled at the University of Iowa Writers' Workshop, where she completed her master of fine arts in 1978.

At the writers' workshop she experienced an identity crisis that led to her finding her voice. She found this voice in her childhood and in the stories that became *The House on Mango Street*. This book is based on memories of her life after her family settled into their first house, a time important to her identity, because she then began to observe critically the kinds of feminine identity her culture offered. Cisneros found a voice by creating the voice of Esperanza (hope).

The success of *The House on Mango Street* led to Cisneros' teaching writing, to international lectures, and to awards and grants, including a writing grant from the National Endowment for the

Arts. In most of her work, a woman's struggle for self-determination is a central theme. Obstacles include confining Mexican American traditions of feminine identity and the racism and sexism that confront a Chicana in a white-dominated society. Although Cisneros takes this struggle seriously and some of her pieces are deeply bitter, the overall tone of her work is exuberant, as reflected in the longest poem title in *Loose Woman*: "I Am So Depressed I Feel Like Jumping in the River Behind My House but Won't Because I'm Thirty-Eight and Not Eighteen."

Suggested readings

Hoffert, Barbara. "Sandra Cisneros: Giving Back to Libraries." *Library Journal* 117, no. 1 (January, 1992): 55.

Tabor, Mary B. W. "A Solo Traveler in Two Worlds: At the Library with Sandra Cisneros." *The New York Times*, January 7, 1993, B2, C1.

—*Terry Heller*

See also Chicano identity; Feminism; *House on Mango Street, The*; Urban life; *Woman Hollering Creek and Other Stories*; Women and identity

Sandra Cisneros, author of Loose Woman *(1994), a rebellious look at the roles assigned to Chicanas.* (© Rubén Guzmán)

City of God

Author: Gil Cuadros (1962-1996)

First published: 1994

Identities: Gay, lesbian, and bisexual; Latino

Gil Cuadros' *City of God* reveals to readers a gay's life from a twofold perspective. The narrative center draws heavily from Cuadros' memories as a Latino child with gay tendencies. Cuadros' family was working class, his parents Mexican. *City of God* consists of two distinct parts. The first part uses short narrative, the second, poetry. This choice is significant. The short stories re-create Cuadros' childhood world. Their main characters are children who are expected to display a strong masculine behavior, but these children are sensitive individuals who are struggling with their first gay experiences. Following the traditional pattern of a diary, the narration focuses on sexual incidents as centers of the action, which, in turn, serve as material for the second part.

Sexual desire is a main theme and cohesive leitmotif of these stories. The main character confronts physical changes at the beginning of his teenage years and his discovery of sexual pleasure. As an adult, besides dealing with his family's disapproval of his gay lifestyle, he must struggle against the racist attitude of a predominantly white gay community that views him as a sexual object. In addition, he must deal with the imminent death of his white gay lover and his own HIV-positive status. Of particular interest is the main character's coming out to his family at age twenty-three, disclosing to them that he has a white lover. This stand clashes with the traditional Hispanic treatment of gay life, which, as reflected in another short story, is to cover it up with a marriage.

The poetic second part continues Cuadros' adult recall of the most memorable events in his gay life. This section contains a remarkable view of life with acquired immune deficiency syndrome (AIDS), which serves as catalyst for self-analysis by means of specific recurrent themes (the strong father figure and gay sexual practices). Through the protagonist's anguish, the reader faces starkly the immediacy of death and the necessity of preparing for it at the peak of one's life.

Cuadros' work fulfills several purposes. It introduces into Latino literature taboo issues such as the painful recognition of being gay and frank descriptions of gay sexual acts. Cuadros' major contribution, however, is his open treatment of AIDS in a positive light. His characters are normal Latino gay men who are forced to examine their lives as they fight their survival.

SUGGESTED READINGS

Publishers Weekly. Review of *City of God*, by Gil Cuadros. 241, no. 44 (October 31, 1994): 59.

Tavis, Thomas. Review of *City of God*, by Gil Cuadros. *Library Journal* 119, no. 18 (November 1, 1994): 80.

—*Rafael Ocasio*

See also AIDS; Chicano identity; *City of Night*; Coming out; Gay identity; Latino American identity

City of Night

AUTHOR: John Rechy (1934-   )
FIRST PUBLISHED: 1963
IDENTITIES: European American; gay, lesbian, and bisexual; Latino; religion; West and Southwest

Based on the author's experiences, *City of Night* explores sexuality and spirituality as they develop during the protagonist's quest for salvation. Combining Chicano heritage, autobiographical material, and a poetic rendering of the restless loneliness of America's sexual underground, *City of Night*—John Rechy's first and best-known novel—investigates difficulties and rewards of an individual's search to claim the many identities that intersect in a single life.

The unnamed protagonist's "journey through nightcities and nightlives—looking for . . . some substitute for salvation" begins with his childhood in El Paso, Texas. Rechy draws on stark, lonely imagery (the fiercely unforgiving wind, the father's inexplicable hatred of his son, the mother's hungry love) to portray a childhood and adolescence denied any sense of connection and certainty. Disconnected and detached from his home, the protagonist stands before the mirror confusing identity with isolation. He asserts a narcissistic removal from the world ("I have only me!") that his quest at first confirms, then refutes.

The first-person narrative chronicles the protagonist's wanderings through New York City, Los Angeles, Hollywood, San Francisco, Chicago, and New Orleans. For Rechy, these various urban settings are "one vast City of Night" fused into the "unmistakable shape of loneliness." Working as a male prostitute, the protagonist navigates this landscape, portraying the types of sexual and spiritual desperation he encounters along the way. His journey is a pilgrimage first away from home and then back to it, as he accepts the possibility that he might come to terms with his family, his childhood, and himself.

City of Night interweaves chapters that describe the geographies of the cities the protagonist passes through with chapters that portray people condemned to these dark cities. Sometimes humorous, sometimes bitter, sometimes indifferent, these portraits of people trapped in the loneliness and cruelty of the cities mirror the protagonist's quest. He is like and unlike the denizens of this world.

In New Orleans during Mardi Gras, the protagonist encounters and rejects his first sincere invitation to love: the "undiscovered country which may not even exist and which I was too frightened even to attempt to discover." This invitation nevertheless triggers the narrator's search for redemption and salvation. The memory of his rejection of Jeremy's love haunts him. Caught up in the festivity of the carnival, surrounded by masked revelers and cathedrals, the protagonist affirms the possibility for change.

He returns to El Paso. Exposed to the West Texas wind, "an echo of angry childhood," the protagonist acknowledges uncertainty, the need for hope, and renewal. Rechy leaves the culmination of this search unresolved, a matter of existential self-definition. Combining ethnic, sexual, and spiritual identities, *City of Night* establishes important themes that Rechy explores in greater depth in later works. *City of Night* represents a pioneering look at the interdependency of multiple identities in an individual's search for meaning.

SUGGESTED READING

Moore, Harry T., ed. *Contemporary American Novelists*. Carbondale: Southern Illinois University Press, 1964.

—Daniel M. Scott III

See also Chicano identity; Gay identity; Prostitution; Rechy, John; Religion and identity; *This Day's Death*

Civil Disobedience

AUTHOR: Henry David Thoreau (1817-1862)
FIRST PUBLISHED: 1849
IDENTITIES: European American

One night in July, 1846, while Henry David Thoreau was living a quiet life on the shores of Walden Pond, near Concord, Massachusetts, he was jailed for failing to pay his taxes. He was released the next day because someone, probably his aunt, paid the tax. He gave a public lecture in 1848 at the Concord Lyceum to explain to his community his reasons for refusing to pay the tax. The text of that lecture was first published in 1849, under the title "Resistance to Civil Government." The essay, now known as "Civil Disobedience," was written to argue the moral necessity of resisting the institution of slavery, which the United States' war against Mexico sought to extend. "Civil Disobedience" has become one of the ethical cornerstones of nonviolent resistance movements. It is known to have been an inspiration to Mohandas Gandhi, who led the passive resistance movement for the liberation of India from British colonial rule. Thoreau's ideas also influenced Martin Luther King, Jr.'s Civil Rights movement and the American struggle to end the Vietnam War.

Thoreau did not find his identity in association with other people who shared his background. Rather, he believed his truest identity would be found in differentiating himself from the common herd of humanity, which he saw as mediocre, morally lazy, and cowardly. He was an individualist; he held that each person's responsibility is to follow the highest leadings of personal conscience. Ultimate moral authority emanates from individual judgment, and getting "out of its way" is one of the most important things a just government can do. Civil law and the power of the democratic majority are secondary to the higher moral law as it is discerned by the individual. In cases in which civil government conflicts with personal conscience, Thoreau advocates withdrawing all support from that government immediately, without waiting to change the law or public opinion. Withdrawal of support—such as the refusal to pay taxes or to serve in the military—is likely to be met with punishment, and Thoreau advocates accepting the penalty imposed. Even if that penalty involves imprisonment, he claims that bodily confinement is trivial when compared to the spiritual liberty of thought and conscience that comes from following the higher law. Persons who obey a law or fight a war that they think is wrong become less than fully human—they lose their identities, they become machines.

SUGGESTED READINGS

Harding, Walter. *The Days of Henry Thoreau*. New York: Alfred A. Knopf, 1965.

_____. *Thoreau: A Century of Criticism*. Dallas: Southern Methodist University Press, 1954.

—Donna Glee Williams

See also American identity: Northeast; Civil Rights movement; Slavery; *Walden*

Civil Rights movement

IDENTITIES: African American

Rosa Parks's refusal in 1955 to move to the back of the bus in Montgomery, Alabama, signaled the birth of the Civil Rights movement. Under Martin Luther King, Jr.'s leadership, African Americans began to demand their rights as American citizens. The African American struggle for

Background

The Civil Rights movement worked to overthrow a pervasive and ingrained system of second-class citizenship. (Library of Congress)

civil rights followed a variety of approaches, including the nonviolent tactics of King, the more aggressive methods of Malcolm X and the Nation of Islam, and the direct militancy of the Black Panther Party (which favored a self-defense agenda). Groups such as the Student Nonviolent Coordinating Committee (founded in 1960) initially subscribed to peaceful methods but gradually espoused more combative techniques. As slogans such as Black Is Beautiful and Black Power became prevalent, African American literature became more attuned to the events of the decade, demonstrating theoretical approaches that, resembling the disparity in political ideology, were either conciliatory and encouraged dialogue or were bitterly irate and sought vengeance and revolutionary change.

Literature   Poets such as Gwendolyn Brooks, who won a Pulitzer Prize in 1950 for *Annie Allen* (1949), Margaret Danner, Langston Hughes, Robert Hayden, Melvin B. Tolson, Sterling Brown, and Mary Elizabeth Vroman expressed their feelings and concerns about the civil rights conflict in their poetry. Others expressed themselves in short stories, plays, novels, and essays. They include Ralph Ellison, author of the celebrated novel *Invisible Man* (1952), James Baldwin, author of *Go Tell It on the Mountain* (1953), Paule Marshall, author of *Brown Girl, Brownstones* (1959), Lorraine Hansberry, Mari Evans, William Melvin Kelley, and Ernest J. Gaines. Hansberry's *A Raisin in the Sun* (1959), which addresses segregated housing policies of the time, was the first play by an African American woman to reach Broadway. Considered by some as integrationist drama, much like the drama of Loften Mitchell and Alice Childress, the play also earned Hansberry the honor of being the youngest American to receive the New York Drama Critics Circle Award in 1959.

In a cultural outburst rivaled only by the Harlem Renaissance of the 1920's, black writers of the 1960's explored the beauty and uniqueness of African American culture. African American writers such as Hansberry, Hughes, and Amiri Baraka openly celebrated and incorporated into their lives and their writings the stories, rituals, songs, and customs of their African and African American ancestry. In addition to reclaiming and tapping from lost or disregarded black aesthetic and social values, these and other writers insisted that black literature be functional, express positive black images, cater primarily to the well-being of blacks, and connect with the goals of the civil rights agenda and with the black power ideology.

After riots in urban ghettoes in the 1960's, African American poetry was used as a political weapon. Poets such as Hayden, Lucille Clifton, Etheridge Knight, Sonia Sanchez, Baraka, Alice Walker, Nikki Giovanni, and Dudley Randall employed their poetry for communal purposes, as a dramatic voice primarily for all African Americans and sometimes expressing universal themes. Effects of the Black Power movement on the novelist are evident in the works of William Melvin Kelley (*dem*, 1967), Ishmael Reed (*The Free-Lance Pallbearers*, 1967), and Gaines (*Of Love and Dust*, 1967). Marshall, Gaines, Charlie Cobb, and Julia Fields also expressed the movement in short stories. Autobiographies and biographies of the time were powerful and insightful. Malcolm X's *The Autobiography of Malcolm X* (1964), Eldridge Cleaver's *Soul on Ice* (1968), and Maya Angelou's *I Know Why the Caged Bird Sings* (1969) became classic works on African American experience. In the field of theater, Baraka's play *Dutchman* (1964) launched him into theatrical prominence. Charles Gordone and his celebrated *No Place to Be Somebody: A Black Comedy* (1967) and Ed Bullins, acclaimed for his *In Wine Time* (1968), brought the new political awareness to the stage.

Some of the writers of this era were more radical than others, moving away decisively from the integrationist themes of the 1950's. Having abandoned deliberation and nonviolent methods that had proven insufficient, they sought more antagonistic styles and themes, dictating immediate and severe steps toward handling the crisis. Baraka and Larry Neal published *Black Fire: An Anthology of Afro-American Writing* in 1968, a collection of essays, poetry, fiction, and drama. The editors, describing African American writers as warriors in the foreword, declare the arrival of a new era for black art. Their anthology marks the birth of the Black Arts movement, which, Neal notes, condemns any principle that separates African American writers from their communities. African American art is to be considered an instrument for self-determination, justice, self-pride, and the revival of aesthetic and cultural values that derive from the black heritage. Many African Americans upheld and advanced the proposals of the movement, but other more conservative black critics faulted it, claiming that it was creatively restrictive. The Black Arts movement undoubtedly promoted black literature, however, and attracted a lot of attention to the Civil Rights movement. More and more independent publishers, black and white, began to explore and publish literature by African American writers. With the increased availability of this literature, its readership—black, white, and beyond—grew.

**Civil Rights Movement
Six Key Events**

1955   Rosa Parks refuses to surrender her seat on a bus in Montgomery, Alabama, to a white passenger, as required by law. The enforcement of the law against her leads to a long but successful boycott of the bus system by African Americans.

1956   The U.S. Supreme Court declares segregation laws unconstitutional.

1957   Despite harsh opposition, mostly from Southern legislators, President Eisenhower signs a civil rights bill into law, creating the Commission on Civil Rights.

1964   The Civil Rights Act becomes law.

1964   Martin Luther King, Jr., is awarded a Nobel Peace Prize for his continuing efforts on behalf of civil rights.

1968   Assassinations of Martin Luther King, Jr., and of Robert F. Kennedy mark a major setback in the struggle for civil rights.

SUGGESTED READINGS

Baraka, Imamu Amiri, and Larry Neal, eds. *Black Fire: An Anthology of Afro-American Writing.* New York: William Morrow, 1968.

Davis, Arthur P., J. Saunders Redding, and Joyce Ann Joyce, eds. *The New Cavalcade: African American Writing from 1760 to the Present.* Washington, D.C.: Howard University Press, 1991-1992.

Emanuel, James A., and Theodore L. Gross, eds. *Dark Symphony: Negro Literature in America.* New York: Free Press, 1968.

Smith, Valerie, et al., eds. *African American Writers.* New York: Macmillan, 1991.

—*Philip Uko Effiong*

See also African American identity; Baraka, Amiri; Giovanni, Nikki; Malcolm X; *Testament of Hope, A*

Civil War, Spanish. *See* Spanish Civil War

Class and identity

DEFINITION: "Class" refers to an economic or social stratum.

Those who study the role of class in American culture face an essential dilemma. For many Americans, past and present, class has seemed a foreign concept, more applicable to the European nations, which have a history of feudalism, than to North American social structures. In its promise of life, liberty, and the pursuit of happiness, the Declaration of Independence of the United States clearly condemns the stifling class structures of Britain and the European continent. Those who founded the United States envisioned a future full of economic and social opportunity. Despite slavery, a disparity of income, and the presence of wage labor during and after the nineteenth century industrial revolution, many Americans have agreed with Abraham Lincoln's optimistic description of American economic and social mobility: "The man who labored for another last year, this year labors for himself, and next year he will hire others to labor for him."

Since the mid-nineteenth century, however, rapid industrialization, an influx of unskilled immigrant workers, and the full development of market structures have provoked challenges to the belief in America's immunity, always more an ideal than a fact, from class segmentation. There has always been a dissenting tradition of intellectuals and writers who warned of America's propensity to mirror the class structures of Europe; they have more recently been joined by labor unionists, social scientists, and members of the working classes, who insist upon the reality of class identities in American culture, literature, and history. For writers such as Rebecca Harding Davis, Stephen Crane, Theodore Dreiser, Upton Sinclair, Jack London, Mike Gold, John Steinbeck, and Tillie Olsen, what America lacks is not class structures but class consciousness. According to these authors, the pervasiveness of the false understanding that America has no class structure has prevented Americans from understanding the way in which their identities have been influenced by socioeconomic forces.

Class mobility and literature
In general terms, there are two different ways in which writers have depicted class in literature, each tradition roughly correlative to different attitudes about class in America. Though rarely considered a literature of class identity, the more popular of these traditions, the rags-to-riches plot, clearly demonstrates an affinity with Abraham Lincoln's belief in class mobility and boundless opportunity. Horatio Alger, Jr., the best-known executor of this literary theme, wrote almost 120 popular children's books in the late nineteenth century, all based on the principle that a struggle against poverty and temptation inevitably leads to wealth and fame. In these novels, and in others that followed, class appears as a momentary disability to be transcended rather than as an identity to be explored. Like childhood, class is universal but ephemeral.

While this plot has functioned as a mainstay of popular and genre fiction since Alger's era, more canonical literature (that is, literature accepted as having high artistic merit) has also adopted this theme, reworking the rags-to-riches story through various contexts in the nineteenth and twentieth centuries. William Dean Howells' *The Rise of Silas Lapham* (1885) is an early, almost paradigmatic example of literary class mobility. Charting Lapham's rise from Vermont farmer to Boston businessman, Howells portrays the social difficulties of the newly rich. Three decades later, one of Howells' protégés, Abraham Cahan, adapted this theme to the context of Jewish immigrant life. In *The Rise of David Levinsky* (1917), the title character loses not only working-class solidarity but also ethnic community in his rise from poor tailor to wealthy sweatshop owner. The apotheosis of this tradition, F. Scott Fitzgerald's *The Great Gatsby* (1925), is similarly ambivalent about the legacy of class mobility. Jay Gatz's struggle to become the Great Gatsby leaves him lonely, wrecked, and romantically unfulfilled. His failed union with Daisy Buchanan indicates the ultimate irreconcilability of class mobility and social acceptance. These canonical renditions of the rags-to-riches plot are less sanguine about class ascension, but, as do Alger's novels, they portray class as fluid, dynamic, and ultimately unrestrictive.

Class identity and social realism

Although less popular in both canonical and noncanonical spheres, the other literary tradition of class, social realism, has always been more invested in a cultural exploration of class identities. Borrowing from British realists such as Charles Dickens and French naturalists such as Émile Zola, American social realists have focused on the interaction between classes rather than on the singular rise of a protagonist. Unlike Alger and his followers, realists such as Davis, Dreiser, Sinclair, and Steinbeck explore the permanent presence of class stratification in the land of plenty. For them, American class mobility was an economic circumstance for some, but to those politically opposed to class inequity, the absence of a class system in America was a promise yet to be fulfilled. America might still become an exception to the worldwide rule of class systems, but achieving this goal would require a literature that was realistic in vision and critical in attitude.

Rebecca Harding Davis

The first realist of note to comment on the developing conditions of class segmentation was Rebecca Harding Davis, whose 1861 novella "Life in the Iron Mills" inaugurated the labor narrative genre in America. Clearly derivative of British novels about industry in general and of Dickens' *Hard Times* (1854) in particular, "Life in the Iron Mills" nevertheless broke new ground in its attempt to find a literary language appropriate to the condition of wage labor in the antebellum United States. Davis' depiction of a Welsh mill hand in a multiracial town on the eve of the Civil War demonstrates that American labor literature had to account continually for the conditions of both immigration and slavery. Anticipating women labor novelists of the latter nineteenth century, such as Elizabeth Stuart Phelps (*The Silent Partner*, 1870) and Mary Wilkins Freeman (*The Portion of Labor*, 1901), Davis suggests that female cross-class alliance could resolve the multiple tensions of class, race, and ethnicity.

Although the major social realists of the postbellum era seldom acknowledged Davis' precedent and explicitly rejected the sentimentality of "women's fiction," they nevertheless continued to explore many of the same political concerns and literary themes. In particular, authors such as Howells and Jacob Riis (author of *How the Other Half Lives*, 1890) focused on the problems and promises of cross-class relations. For Howells, who again provides a paradigmatic example, the issue of relations between the middle and lower classes would become a central literary motif. Soon after writing his relatively blithe portrayal of class mobility in *The Rise of Silas Lapham*, Howells became alarmed by the judicial mistreatment of the anarchists involved in the Haymarket Riot. Morally chastened and politically inspired, Howells wrote *A Hazard of New Fortunes* (1890), a sprawling social novel about class relations in New York City. Although *A Hazard of New Fortunes* remains unconvincing in its resolution of class tension into moral doctrine, its concluding depiction of a strike and its sympathetic characterization of a working-class socialist greatly influenced social realists of the next five decades.

Naturalism

Howells' immediate successors—Dreiser, Crane, Frank Norris, Jack London, and Sinclair—followed his example by focusing on relations among classes, although they rejected much of his moral and sentimental message. For writers in the realistic tradition who came after Howells, class identity had little to do with morality and everything to do with the massive economic and social forces of the late nineteenth century. The social realism tradition of the nineteenth century often used moral and sentimental appeals; these later fell out of favor. Under the influence of such thinkers as Herbert Spencer, who took Charles Darwin's theories of biology and applied them to society, writers in the last decade of the nineteenth century and in the early twentieth century eschewed moralizing, preferring instead to depict the large social and economic forces that affect the individual. Faced with growing unemployment, immigration, and urbanization, these writers felt a duty to explore issues of class and identity using "objective" and "scientific" standards. In this respect, they were followers of the naturalist tradition. The results of this artistic strategy have often struck contemporary readers as overly reliant on clichéd images and well-worn plots, but the naturalists' unblinking depictions of the streets, the ghettos, the shop floors, and the working-class home revolutionized the literary depiction of class. One of the first such texts, Crane's *Maggie: A Girl of the Streets* (1893), exemplifies this new dynamic. Davis and Howells studied their subjects from afar, either reluctant or unable to enter into the world of another class, but Crane researched his first novel by taking up residence in New York's Bowery district. Thus, although the novel's plot is anything but original—charting the seduction, betrayal, and suicide of a working-class woman—its attention to detail, its focus on familial relations under the pressure of poverty, and its grim view toward its protagonist's efforts to rise make it a singular achievement in the literature of class identity.

The 1930's and beyond   With the notable exceptions of Upton Sinclair (*The Jungle*, 1906; *King Coal*, 1917) and David Graham Phillips (*Susan Lenox: Her Fall and Rise*, 1917), social realism in its various forms waned during the first two decades of the twentieth century, replaced by the aesthetic dictates of the ascendant school of literary modernism. Writers generally did not return to the theme of class and identity until the tumultuous years of the Great Depression, when newly visible class injustice virtually insisted upon literary representation. For the realists of that decade—John Dos Passos, Meridel LeSueur, John Steinbeck, Olsen, and others—the class structures underlying American capitalism needed representational critique; their efforts in this direction reformed the way in which class would be depicted in most subsequent literature. What differentiated their writings from earlier efforts was a greater understanding of the political dimensions of class identity and a fuller appreciation for the literary tools of modernism. Dos Passos, for instance, combined the realists' concern for characterization with an entirely new sense of modern existence, surrounding the multiple protagonists of the *U.S.A.* trilogy (1938) with newsreel headlines, minibiographies, and stream-of-consciousness autobiography. The resulting literary aesthetic captures, without the sentimentality or the clichés of previous literary eras, the process through which economic and social factors construct class identity.

The other major literary development of the 1930's was the influx of literature written by working-class writers. Agnes Smedley, Jack Conroy, Mike Gold, and numerous followers added a much needed personal perspective to literary explorations of class identity. In their mostly autobiographical novels and sketches, class was not an abstract category to be understood, but a lived set of oppressive relations to be struggled against. The legacy of such writers would later be occluded, but their model has effectively inspired a generation of contemporary writers attuned to class in America.

SUGGESTED READINGS

Blake, Fay M. *The Strike in the American Novel.* Metuchen, N.J.: Scarecrow Press, 1972. Historical account of depictions of class struggles in the nineteenth and twentieth century American novel—an excellent bibliographic source.

Denning, Michael. *Mechanic Accents: Dime Novels and Working-Class Culture in America.* New York: Verso, 1987. Argues that representations of the working classes in nineteenth century popular fiction are multifaceted.

Dimock, Wai Chee, and Michael T. Gilmore, eds. *Rethinking Class: Literary Studies and Social Formations.* New York: Columbia University Press, 1994. Articles by a number of scholars use poststructuralist theory to revitalize the literary study of class formations.

Foley, Barbara. *Radical Representations: Politics and Form in U.S. Proletarian Fiction, 1929-1941*. Durham, N.C.: Duke University Press, 1993. A reevaluation of the class-based literature of the Depression.

Fussell, Paul. *Class: A Guide Through the American Status System*. New York: Ballantine, 1983. A humorous account of America's difficulties acknowledging the presence of class structures.

Hapke, Laura. *Tales of the Working Girl: Wage-Earning Women in American Literature, 1890-1925*. New York: Twayne, 1992. Chronicles the debate on women's labor carried out in the sentimental fiction of the end of the nineteenth century and the beginning of the twentieth.

Herreshoff, David Sprague. *Labor into Art: The Theme of Work in Nineteenth-Century American Literature*. Detroit: Wayne State University Press, 1991. Argues for the centrality of work in canonical antebellum literature.

Wilson, Christopher. *White Collar Fictions: Class and Social Representation in American Literature, 1885-1925*. Athens: University of Georgia Press, 1992. An excellent example of the new scholarly focus on the social structures of middle-class fiction.

—*Eric Schocket*

See also American Dream; Economics of identity; Homelessness; Migratory workers; Poverty

Cleaver, Eldridge

BORN: Wabbaseka, Arkansas; August 31, 1935

PRINCIPAL WORKS: *Soul on Ice*, 1968; *Soul on Fire*, 1978

IDENTITIES: African American

SIGNIFICANT ACHIEVEMENT: *Soul on Ice*, an electrifying mixture of confessional writing and social commentary, is one of the major documents of the 1960's.

Eldridge Cleaver was born in the small village of Wabbaseka, Arkansas, near Little Rock. In 1946, he moved with his family to Rose Hill, a mainly Chicano neighborhood in the Los Angeles area. Cleaver was first arrested, for stealing bicycles, in 1947, and in 1949 he was sent to reform school, where he became a Roman Catholic. He explains in *Soul on Ice* that he chose the Catholic church because "all the Negroes and Mexicans went there."

Eldridge Cleaver speaks at a rally in 1968 in Washington, D.C. (Library of Congress)

In 1954, Cleaver was sent to prison for selling marijuana. Four years later he was charged with attempted rape and assault with intent to kill and was sent to Folsom Prison, from which he was paroled in November, 1966. A year later, Cleaver married Kathleen Neal. The publication of *Soul on Ice* in February, 1968, marked Cleaver's appearance as a self-educated intellectual to be reckoned with. In the work he speaks fluently on issues that were sensitive among blacks and whites. He attacks writer James Baldwin for his alleged bowing to whites, condemns homosexuality as a "sickness," and reviles black women. *Soul on Ice* began a crucial year for Cleaver. On April 6, Cleaver was wounded in a shoot-out with the Oakland police that resulted in Bobby Hutton's death. As a result of this incident, Cleaver's parole was revoked. Faced with return to prison, Cleaver fled to Montreal and on to Havana.

Cleaver was kept under guard for seven months in Cuba before being sent in 1969 to Algiers, where his hatred for capitalism intensified. In 1970, he led a group of eleven on a trip to Pyongyang, North Korea, and on to Hanoi and Peking. When two groups of black Americans hijacked planes to Algiers, Algeria forced the Cleavers to move to Paris, where they obtained legal residence in 1974.

The two years he spent in Paris proved crucial to Cleaver; his thinking turned conservative, and in late 1975, he returned to America as an evangelical Christian. He was arrested but released in 1976 on $100,000 bail. His active career as an evangelist faltered in the 1980's.

SUGGESTED READINGS

Anderson, Jervis. "Race, Rage, and Eldridge Cleaver." *Commentary* 46 (December, 1968): 63-69.
Foner, Philip. *The Black Panthers Speak*. Philadelphia: Lippincott, 1970.
Rout, Kathleen. *Eldridge Cleaver*. Boston: Twayne, 1991.
Schanche, Don A. *The Panther Paradox: A Liberal's Dilemma*. New York: David McKay, 1970.

—*Frank Day*

See also African American identity; Baldwin, James; Malcolm X; *Notes of a Native Son*; *Soul on Ice*

Clifton, Lucille

BORN: Depew, New York; June 27, 1936

PRINCIPAL WORKS: *Good Times*, 1969; *Good News About the Earth: New Poems*, 1972; *An Ordinary Woman*, 1974; *Generations: A Memoir*, 1976; *Two-Headed Woman*, 1980; *Good Woman: Poems and a Memoir, 1969-1980*, 1987; *Next: New Poems*, 1987; *Quilting: Poems 1987-1990*, 1991; *The Book of Light: Poems*, 1993

IDENTITIES: African American; family; women

SIGNIFICANT ACHIEVEMENT: Clifton's unique strength in poetry is her understated complexity in celebrating all life as an African American woman.

Lucille Clifton's parents had little education but were avid readers, and she grew to love books. Her father's stories steeped her in ancestral heritage, going back to Mammy Caroline, who was born in 1822 in Dahomey, Africa, seized as a child, and enslaved in the United States for much of her life. Caroline and other family members appear in *Generations: A Memoir* and in many of Clifton's poems.

Clifton's mother wrote and recited poetry. At age ten, Clifton became interested in writing, having learned from her mother that it is a means of self-expression. Being a writer never occurred to Clifton; she simply wrote. The first in her family to attend college, she had intellectual black friends, studied drama, and performed in plays—developing her voice and lyricism, and, in her writing, experimenting with sparse punctuation. In 1958, she married Fred Clifton, a philosophy professor. Continuing to write, Clifton did not attempt to have any poems published until her work was solicited. This happened when she was thirty-three, happily married, and with six children under the age of ten.

By then, Clifton had a wealth of education, experiences, and a growing family from which to draw for her writing. Her first published book of poetry, *Good Times*, focuses on difficulties in urban life. The book also celebrates strength and celebration in the face of adversity. In Clifton's second volume, she turns away from "white ways" to affirm "the Black." She celebrates her religious heritage and joins many contemporaries in celebrating racial heritage. With succeeding years and poetry volumes, Clifton's themes, subjects, and style have changed little.

Clifton has also achieved acclaim, and has been more prolific, in writing children's books. Some themes, ideas, and points of view found in her poetry are also found in her children's literature. In her children's books too, Clifton cultivates identity, values, and pride.

SUGGESTED READINGS

Beckles, Frances N. *Twenty Black Women: A Profile of Contemporary Maryland Black Women.* Baltimore: Gateway Press, 1978.

Madhubuti, Haki. "Lucille Clifton: Warm Water, Greased Legs, and Dangerous Poetry." In *Black Women Writers, 1950-1980: A Critical Evaluation,* edited by Mari Evans. New York: Doubleday, 1984.

Sims, Rudine. "Profile: Lucille Clifton." *Language Arts* 59, no. 2 (February, 1982): 160-167.

—*Sandra F. Bone*

See also African American identity; Black English; Women and identity

Clifton, Lucille, poetry of

AUTHOR: Lucille Clifton (1936-   )

PRINCIPAL WORKS: *Good Times*, 1969; *Good News About the Earth: New Poems*, 1972; *An Ordinary Woman*, 1974; *Two-Headed Woman*, 1980; *Good Woman: Poems and a Memoir, 1969-1980*, 1987; *Next: New Poems*, 1987; *Quilting: Poems 1987-1990*, 1991; *The Book of Light: Poems*, 1993

IDENTITIES: African American; family; women

Hesitant to call herself a poet in spite of wide literary acclaim, Lucille Clifton has noted that poetry is her heart. She has unassumingly identified herself as a black woman, a wife, and mother who "makes poems." Her poems celebrate all of life—its daily realities, its mysteries, and, most significantly, its continuity. She has claimed that celebrating life is what she is about; her poems validate the claim.

Beginning with *Good Times*, Clifton has capitalized on what she knows best. Virtually all her poems fall into one or more of three broad areas of focus: family, African American experience, and female sensibility.

Clifton is a lyric poet whose work is unpretentious and has little rhyme. She continually achieves her goal of rendering big ideas in simple ways. Through short poems of simple language she relates brief portraits, encounters, or disturbances that are neatly presented in a few lines. Clifton seems more guided by consciousness or heart than form or structure. Her use of precise, evocative images is masterful, as evidenced in "miss rosie," which describes the title character as "a wet brown bag of a woman." In that poem, and many others, what Clifton does not say is part of the poem's power. Always significant are her use of spaces, few capital letters, and vernacular. In "homage to my hair," the poet changes from standard English to a black dialect with great effect; in "holy night," Mary speaks in a Caribbean dialect. Clifton's use of metaphor is frequent, compelling, and nowhere better than in "lucy and her girls," relating the power of family ties to natural phenomena. The contrast and tension Clifton achieves through frequent juxtaposition of concepts, as in "inner city," is laudatory. Many of her lines are memorable, as "my mouth is a cave of cries" in "chemotherapy." Only occasionally didactic, sometimes humorous, typically subtle or understated, Clifton's poetry has emotion, conviction, moral stance, Christian tenets, and hope. It has changed little through the years, except to sometimes reflect aging and all that that implies. Always, Clifton defines and affirms the African American experience, politically and aesthetically, with originality, voice, dignity, and pride. She has twice been nominated for the Pulitzer Prize in poetry.

SUGGESTED READINGS
Clifton, Lucille. *Generations: A Memoir*. New York: Random House, 1976.
Madhubuti, Haki. "Lucille Clifton: Warm Water, Greased Legs, and Dangerous Poetry." In *Black Women Writers, 1950-1980: A Critical Evaluation*, edited by Mari Evans. New York: Doubleday, 1984.

—Sandra F. Bone

See also African American identity; Black English; Christianity and Christian Fundamentalism; Women and identity

Coal

AUTHOR: Audre Lorde (1934-1992)
FIRST PUBLISHED: 1976
IDENTITIES: African American; gay, lesbian, and bisexual; women

Coal explores Audre Lorde's identities as a black woman, mother, wife, and lover of women. Several of her life issues are examined and refracted in the poems. Lorde's lifelong journey toward claiming her West Indian, African American heritage is given voice in "Coal"; her motherhood is the subject of "Now That I Am Forever with Child"; and her women-centered existence is described in "On a Night of the Full Moon."

As a black woman of West Indian heritage, Audre Lorde knew the struggles of black Americans to claim their place and voice in American society. Raised in Harlem during the 1930's and 1940's, Lorde became aware of racism at an early age. The poem "Coal" claims a positive, strong voice for Lorde—a voice deeply embedded in her black heritage.

In "Coal," Lorde effectively transforms black speech into poetry: "I/ is the total black, being spoken/ from the earth's inside." Lorde defines poetic speech as a force that embraces blackness; then, she goes on to question how much a black woman can speak, and in what tone. Yet "Coal" defines Lorde as a black female poet who breaks the boundaries of silence and proclaims the sturdiness of power of her own words: "I am Black because I come from the earth's inside/ now take my word for jewel in the open light."

Fire imagery suffuses the book. The fire that marks the edges of many poems defines the anger and hostility engendered by a patriarchal and racist society. Lorde learns to empower herself by using the fire of anger and despair to create her own vision of spiritual and sexual identity. Embarked on her own journey toward truth, Lorde proclaims in the poem "Summer Oracle" that fire—which she equates with a warming agent in a country "barren of symbols of love"—can also be a cleansing agent. Fire burns away falsehoods and lets truth arise.

Lorde was widely praised by her contemporaries for her determination to see truth in everyday life. *Coal* could be called an uneven book, but her portraits of city life, love, anger, and sorrow make *Coal* a book of poetic transition from which Lorde would emerge into a life of more radical feminism and richer fulfillment.

SUGGESTED READINGS
Bloom, Harold, ed. *Black Women Poets and Dramatists*. New York: Chelsea House, 1996.
Evans, Mari, ed. *Black Women Writers (1950-1980): A Critical Evaluation*. Garden City, N.Y.: Doubleday, 1984.
Tate, Claudia. *Black Women Writers at Work*. New York: Continuum, 1983.

—R.C.S.

See also African American identity; *Cancer Journals, The*; Lesbian identity; Lorde, Audre; *Zami*

Coe, Christopher

BORN: Bethlehem, Pennsylvania; November 27, 1953
DIED: New York, New York; September 6, 1994
PRINCIPAL WORKS: *I Look Divine*, 1987; *Such Times*, 1993

IDENTITIES: Disease; European American; gay, lesbian, and bisexual

SIGNIFICANT ACHIEVEMENT: In his short writing career, Coe created two masterpieces of the gay experience.

Born in Pennsylvania but raised in Portland, Oregon, Christopher Coe divided his adult residency between New York City and Paris. His professional life combined a number of interests, including photography, cabaret singing, and writing. For a time, at Columbia University, Coe was a student of novelist and editor Gordon Lish, whose predilection for semiautobiographical material and self-revealing first-person narration can also be traced in Coe's work. Coe's first novel *I Look Divine*, for example, chronicles the life of a character named Nicholas, for whom identity resides in physical beauty, as embodied especially in the face. Coe seems to have shared his character's preoccupation about appearance. In a 1987 interview, the writer half-jokingly asserted that he dropped out of Columbia University partially because of his personal dismay over a bad photograph on his student identification card. As the character Nicholas avows, "Inner beauty is what counts, but outer beauty is what shows."

Significant autobiographical elements can also be found in Coe's second and most celebrated work, *Such Times*. Like the narrator Timothy, Coe was devoted for a number of years to an older lover, with whom he purchased an apartment in Paris. Timothy measures the beginning of his life from the time that he met Jasper, but the "control" that he exercises in his career as a photographer does not extend to his romantic life. Despite the younger man's desire for an exclusive relationship, Jasper argues that monogamy is "antithetical to the homosexual life" and, consequently, indulges in episodes of anonymous sex.

Timothy's reconciliation to this state of affairs is the dramatic heart of the book. "Everything that has come to me has come because I loved without demands," he asserts. From Jasper, he acquires a taste for fine clothing and haute cuisine, the experience of "ecstatic sex," and, perhaps, acquired immune deficiency syndrome (AIDS). To preserve his idealized image of their relationship, Timothy has unsafe sex with a stranger so that if he does test positive for the human immunodeficiency virus, he will not know for sure whether Jasper infected him.

Timothy does test seropositive and so did Christopher Coe. Character and author, because they lacked medical insurance, were also virtually bankrupted by the costs of their health care. That Timothy's fictional life partially mirrored Coe's adds poignancy to the narrative.

SUGGESTED READINGS

Burgin, Richard. "Not Just a Pretty Face." *The New York Times Book Review*, August 30, 1987, 11.

Hempel, Amy. "Talking to Christopher Coe." *Vogue* 438 (September, 1987): 455-458.

Nelson, Emmanuel S., ed. *Contemporary Gay American Novelists*. Westport, Conn.: Greenwood Press, 1993.

—*S. Thomas Mack*

See also AIDS; Appearance and identity; Erotic identity; Gay identity

Collected Poems, 1948-1984

AUTHOR: Derek Walcott (1930-   )

FIRST PUBLISHED: 1986

IDENTITIES: Caribbean

Collected Poems, 1948-1984 is a selection of 132 poems from nine of Derek Walcott's books: *In a Green Night: Poems 1948-1960* (1962), *Selected Poems* (1964), *The Castaway and Other Poems* (1965), *The Gulf and Other Poems* (1970), *Another Life* (1973), *Sea Grapes* (1976), *The Star-Apple Kingdom* (1979), *The Fortunate Traveller* (1981), and *Midsummer* (1984).

To establish his poetic voice, Walcott began using the lens of classical myth along with European and African influences. The book's images of wanderers, nature, and animals show a complex political and historical view across a thirty-six-year span of writing. The major connecting theme is the traveler.

The poem "Prelude," from *In a Green Night*, presents the young poet and traveler sitting cross-legged over the "uncouth features" of his "prone island," attempting to learn how to suffer "in accurate iambics." The 1948 poem typifies Walcott's major theme. The plaintive "A Far Cry from Africa" identifies Walcott as the traveler continuing his search by asking "Where shall I turn, divided to the vein?" The division to which Walcott alludes is characteristic of the poems in the opening of this collection, especially the bitter "Return to D'Ennery: Rain" that asks God "where is our home? For no one will save/ The world from itself."

Nature images enhance the traveler theme in "The Banyan Tree, Old Year's Night." In the poem, the tree attempts to explain responsibility as what "age could not" identify and so remains "blank," unable to "keep the homeless wind." Hence, for Walcott, nature is an impotent environment and character appearing orphaned and alone, as is the traveler.

Collected Poems, 1948-1984 reflects not only themes of search and nature but also history and politics. Walcott explores what he calls "history as myth" and "history as time." Working within myth and time oppositions, Walcott utilizes his classical education and multicultural background that some critics claim is a fault. The collection is, however, an honest and controlled answer to these people as its author moves gracefully from one cultural image to another.

Whatever the approach, as poems of search, nature, or cultural images, a wide variety of themes await the reader. The poems in the collection make complete the longing of the young poet in "Prelude" to the older, world-wise poet of "LII" from *Midsummer* who hears the younger artisan's "iambics" that now are "marching the leaf-wet roads of my head." The deconstructed world of diametrically opposed islanders shows the interior struggle of the poet with his themes: "one troop black, barefooted,/ the other in redcoats bright as their sovereign's blood . . . the bare soles with the shod./ One fought for a queen, the other was chained in her service,/ but both, in bitterness, travelled the same road."

SUGGESTED READINGS

Brown, Stewart, ed. *The Art of Derek Walcott*. Chester Springs, Pa.: Dufour Editions, 1991.

Hamner, Robert D., ed. *Critical Perspectives on Derek Walcott*. Washington, D.C.: Three Continents Press, 1993.

_____. *Derek Walcott*. New York: Twayne, 1993.

—*Dennis L. Weeks*

See also Caribbean American literature; Colonialism; Multiculturalism

Collected Poems: 1957-1982

AUTHOR: Wendell Berry (1934-   )
FIRST PUBLISHED: 1985
IDENTITIES: European American; family; South

Containing nearly two hundred poems from eight previous volumes, *Collected Poems: 1957-1982* has helped to establish Wendell Berry as a major American poet. The collection illustrates the ideas Berry develops in his fiction and substantiates in his autobiographical and polemical essays. Unifying his poetry are the principles and rewards of small-scale, hands-on, community-based, multigenerational farming, which Berry has found to be an exemplar of a continuous harmony between people and land. *Collected Poems* stands as one of the most substantial poetic explorations of the links between family, community, farming, and nature.

Central to Berry's poetry is the view of nature as the primal and ruling character of place—the genius of the place, to use the phrase he borrows from British poet Alexander Pope. Always particular and not abstract, nature in *Collected Poems* is often Berry's ancestral hill farm in Port Royal, Kentucky. This nature—and the ancestors who once lived in and enriched the place—is portrayed as a teacher, a conveyor of knowledge, and a clarifier of truths about oneself and the world.

Many of the poems illustrate the mysteries and lessons Berry has learned as a fifth-generation farmer. At the heart of nature's teachings, and thus at the heart of Berry's poetry, is the natural cyclic process of birth, growth, maturity, death, and rebirth. This wheel of life is a controlling metaphor throughout the poetry, especially in *The Wheel* (1982), in which themes and images hinge on a cyclic balance between use of and care for the land, growth and decay, life and death. The earth in *Collected Poems* is the source and the destiny of life, and thus life is portrayed as a cycle of departures and returns. In "Rising," Berry writes:

> And that is our story,
> not of time, but the forever
> returning events of light,
> ancient knowledge seeking
> its new minds. The man at dawn
> in spring of the year,
> going to the fields,
> visionary of seed and desire,
> is timeless as a star.

Related to this theme of cyclic harmony is another of Berry's central metaphors: the marriage between a farmer and the land. The ingredients of marriage—love, intimacy, understanding, patience, hope, responsibility, fidelity—form the substance of many of his poems. The joy, rhythm, and fecundity of a life wedded to the earth are focal in the volumes *Farming: A Handbook* (1970) and *The Country of Marriage* (1973). In Berry's "The Man Born to Farming," to the husbandman, "whose hands reach into the ground and sprout," the "soil is a divine drug. He enters into death/ yearly, and comes back rejoicing."

SUGGESTED READINGS

Angyal, Andrew J. *Wendell Berry*. New York: Twayne, 1995.

Lang, John. " 'Close Mystery': Wendell Berry's Poetry of Incarnation." *Renascence* 35, no. 4 (Summer, 1983): 258-268.

Merchant, Paul, ed. *Wendell Berry*. Lewiston, Idaho: Confluence Press, 1991.

—Morris Allen Grubbs

See also Berry, Wendell; Environment and identity; Rural life

Collected Stories of Eudora Welty, The

AUTHOR: Eudora Welty (1909-   )

FIRST PUBLISHED: 1980

IDENTITIES: European American; South; women

The Collected Stories of Eudora Welty contains forty-one stories—the distinguished Southern writer's complete short fiction—in which, by focusing brilliantly on the Mississippi milieu she knew from her life experiences, Welty creates symbolic situations that transform the ordinary into the mythical. Although Welty's stories do not often focus on realistic social situations that emphasize the external life of women in Southern society, they are filled with strong and independent women who memorably assert their unique identity.

Typical is Ruby Fisher in "A Piece of News," who is trapped in a marriage that allows her no sense of herself as an independent person. When she sees a story in a newspaper describing how a woman named Ruby Fisher was shot in the leg by her husband, her elaborate fantasy of her own death and burial is an ironic effort to find a sense of identity. When her husband tells her that the newspaper is from another state, she feels a puzzling sense of loss.

In "Clytie," the main character is a stereotyped old maid, exploited by her family and laughed at by the townspeople for her eccentricity. Just as Ruby Fisher sees herself in the newspaper story, Clytie achieves a similar recognition when she looks into the mirrored surface of a rain barrel and can think of nothing else to do but thrust her head into the "kind, featureless depth" of the water and hold it there. It is not simply social isolation that plagues Welty's women, but also a primal sense of separateness. It is not mere social validation that they hunger for but a genuine healing love that will give them a sense of order and meaning.

Other memorable women in Welty's stories caught in a quest for their own identity include Leota and Mrs. Fletcher who, Medusa-like in a beauty parlor in "Petrified Man," metaphorically turn men into stone; Phoenix Jackson, the indefatigable grandmother who in "A Worn Path" goes on a heroic journey to seek relief for her suffering grandson; and Livie, in the story that bears her name, who dares to leave the control and order of the paternalistic Solomon for the vitality of Cash McCord.

Welty's stories focus on women defined less by their stereotypical social roles than they are by their archetypal being. As a result, they do not so much confront their social self as they reveal what Welty sees as their nature as isolated human beings.

SUGGESTED READINGS

Appel, Alfred. *A Season of Dreams: The Fiction of Eudora Welty*. Baton Rouge: Louisiana State University Press, 1965.

Desmond, John F., ed. *A Still Moment: Essays on the Art of Eudora Welty*. Metuchen, N.J.: Scarecrow Press, 1979.

Prenshaw, Peggy Whitman, ed. *Eudora Welty: Critical Essays*. Jackson: University Press of Mississippi, 1979.

Vande, Kieft. *Eudora Welty*. 1962. Rev. ed. Boston: Twayne, 1987.

—*Charles E. May*

See also American identity: South; Feminism; Welty, Eudora

Collected Stories of Katherine Anne Porter, The

AUTHOR: Katherine Anne Porter (1890-1980)

FIRST PUBLISHED: 1965

IDENTITIES: European American; religion; South; women

The Collected Stories of Katherine Anne Porter is a compilation of Katherine Anne Porter's finest short stories and short novels. The collection, first published in 1965, brings together work from three previous collections and four stories not available elsewhere in book form. In 1966, Porter received a Pulitzer Prize in fiction and a National Book Award for *The Collected Stories of Katherine Anne Porter*.

The first section contains the stories from *Flowering Judas and Other Stories* (1930). Included in this section are stories such as "The Jilting of Granny Weatherall," "Theft," and "Flowering Judas." Many stories in this section are set in Mexico. "María Concepción," the first story in the section, is one of these stories. In "María Concepción," the classic struggle between the "traditional" woman and the "new" woman is carried on in the Mexican countryside, where the people are poor and are continually threatened by war. María Concepción, a woman who is honest and a loyal supporter of traditions, triumphs over María Rosa, an aggressive woman who makes a nuisance of herself by ignoring convention. The primitive Mexican setting in "María Concepción" and the other Mexico stories highlights the brutality and irony of the human condition.

Three longer pieces, "Old Mortality," "Noon Wine," and "Pale Horse, Pale Rider," constitute the second section. "Old Mortality" and "Pale Horse, Pale Rider" are about Miranda, Porter's autobiographical heroine who figures prominently in many of her stories. The child Miranda is the central character of "Old Mortality"; "Pale Horse, Pale Rider" is about the adult Miranda. "Noon Wine" is less autobiographical, and its focus is less limited. The main characters are the Thompson family, and the theme of this work concerns their efforts to cope with evil. These three works were originally collected under the title *Pale Horse, Pale Rider: Three Short Novels* (1939).

The third section is "The Leaning Tower and Other Stories." The stories "The Source," "The Journey," "The Witness," "The Circus," "The Last Leaf," "The Fig Tree," and "The Grave" are from a series Porter called "The Old Order." These stories introduce the character Sophia Jane

Rhea and her family. The stories provide a fascinating account of a Southern girl growing up in the country. The other stories in this section have more universal themes. For example, "A Day's Work," set in the slums of New York City, is a black comedy that dramatizes the battle of the sexes.

Each story in the collection is a gem, and in Porter's words, the collection of stories as a whole is "a renewal of their life, a prolonging of their time under the sun."

SUGGESTED READINGS

DeMouy, Jane Krause. *Katherine Anne Porter's Women*. Austin: University of Texas Press, 1983.

Hendrick, Willene, and George Hendrick. *Katherine Anne Porter*. Boston: G. K. Hall, 1988.

Unrue, Darlene Harbour. *Truth and Vision in Katherine Anne Porter's Fiction*. Athens: University of Georgia Press, 1985.

—Traci S. Smrcka

See also American identity: South; Feminism; *Pale Horse, Pale Rider*; Porter, Katherine Anne; Women and identity

Colón, Jesús

BORN: Cayey, Puerto Rico; 1901
DIED: New York, New York; 1974
PRINCIPAL WORK: *A Puerto Rican in New York and Other Sketches*, 1961
IDENTITIES: Caribbean; Latino
SIGNIFICANT ACHIEVEMENT: Colón's sketches stand out as firsts in the literature in English that deals with the Puerto Rican experience.

Jesús Colón was involved as an activist with the Puerto Rican and Latino communities in New York City. He understood the plight of the poor, working-class immigrant, since he had held a variety of odd jobs, from dishwasher to dockworker. A committed socialist, Colón wrote from New York for a socialist newspaper, *Justicia*, published in Spanish in Puerto Rico. He also contributed articles in English to the New York-based socialist newspapers *The Daily Worker* and *The Worker*. His publications denounced violations against the working class, and they opposed biased attitudes against the Puerto Rican, the Latino, and the African American populations. His 1961 anthology gathers together some of those articles, some of them published for the first time in English.

Colón's background as a newspaper reporter directly influenced his sketches. Born to a humble peasant family, Colón aims to offer a kinder view of the Puerto Rican experience by recapturing key moments of his own life and stressing particular folk traditions as representative of Puerto Rican culture. His struggle to succeed in New York City, where he arrived at sixteen, illustrates the saga of the Puerto Ricans generally, who since the 1920's have come to that city by the thousands. In spite of the sizable importance of the Puerto Rican population, Colón protests a generally negative attitude toward Puerto Ricans. Colón offers, instead, his own life as example of the Puerto Rican experience in New York, a life that is a combination of strong, fulfilling, and discouraging emotions.

Colón's sketches place the writer as protagonist in stories that attempt to illustrate specific traits of the Puerto Rican personality. His narrative is highly dependent upon his memories, which go back to his childhood in rural Puerto Rico during the first decade of the twentieth century. Displaying his ability to remember incidents from several decades before, Colón recalls the readers who entertained tobacco wrappers, some of whom were so well read that they could recite long literary passages from memory. Listening to men reading and commenting on literature made the boy Colón aware of social injustice toward the working class.

Colón's stories bring together a number of colorful characters who inhabit the Puerto Rican barrios of New York. His book, with its commitment to document the Puerto Rican immigrant experience, stands out as a rich sociological treatise. Colón's major contribution may be his ability to validate the role of average Puerto Rican immigrants as protagonists of their own stories. For Colón, the history of the Puerto Rican community is not to be found in the "sentimental, transient and ephemeral, or bizarre and grotesque in Puerto Rican life" but in "the deep traditions of striving for freedom and progress that pervade our daily life."

SUGGESTED READING

Colón, Jesús. *The Way It Was, and Other Writings*. Edited with an introduction by Edna Acosta-Belen and Virginia Sanchez Korrol. Houston, Tex.: Arte Público Press, 1993.

—Rafael Ocasio

See also American identity: Northeast; Caribbean American literature; Chicano identity; Latino American identity

Colonialism

DEFINITION: Colonialism is governmental and economic domination of one country by another.

History

World history is filled with tales of conquest and foreign domination. Mercantile expansion in the fifteenth and sixteenth centuries, as well as a Western commitment to exploration, laid the groundwork for modern colonialism, which reached its height at the end of the nineteenth century. At that time, vast Western empires (such as the British and the French) reached around the earth, forcefully tying disparate cultures and societies to Western civilization. The age of empire officially ended after World War II, but colonialism has remained. First World countries, such as Great Britain, France, and the United States, continue to dominate Third World countries.

Colonial literature

Colonial expansion inspired interest and generated writing during the age of the empire. Novels of exploration and exotic locales, such as Rider Haggard's or Rudyard Kipling's work, enjoyed great popularity. Even domestic tales were tinged by colonialism. For example, Jane Austen's *Mansfield Park* (1814) describes a family that owns plantations in Antigua. The madwoman in the attic in Charlotte Brontë's *Jane Eyre* (1847) is a woman from Jamaica. Colonialism figured heavily in the popular Western imagination and thus found its way into literature.

During the age of empires, linguists, philosophers and historians were also studying, labeling, and categorizing different cultures. As Edward Said has noted in *Orientalism* (1979), Western scholars made a virtual occupation of Asia, gaining fame from publishing work on the East. While this occupation was sometimes well-meaning, and did differ in form from area to area, it was usually appropriative. The natives were to be known and classified within a Western paradigm.

Postcolonial literature

Colonialism was not without its opposition. Many people within and outside the colonial center began to critique the practice, engendering postcolonial literatures. Although the term "postcolonial" can correctly be applied to any writing that resists or questions colonialism, it is usually reserved for writings by colonized or formerly colonized peoples. For example, the fiction of Salman Rushdie is more readily accepted as postcolonial than is E. M. Forster's *A Passage to India* (1924) or Joseph Conrad's *Heart of Darkness* (1899). It is also important to note that "postcolonial" does not necessarily imply national independence, for not all postcolonial writers are from decolonized areas. Seamus Heaney (Northern Ireland), for example, can be considered postcolonial.

The primary way in which postcolonial literatures resist colonization is through the creation of an autonomous identity. Instead of looking toward the colonial center, Europe, for models, these works show the perspective of the colonized. Chinua Achebe's *Things Fall Apart* (1959) shows the havoc and destruction Western missionaries bring when they civilize Africa. Margaret Atwood's *Survival: A Thematic Guide to Canadian Literature* (1972) attempts to recognize a Canadian tradition that is neither co-opted by the Commonwealth nor overshadowed by U.S. culture. Hanif Kureshi, in his screenplay *My Beautiful Laundrette* (1984), demonstrates how Pakistani people cope with life in England.

Differing perspective alone is not always enough for some writers of postcolonial literature. Some think that the language of the literature itself must be rethought. Irish poets, such as Nuala Ni Dhomhnaill, publish work in Gaelic. Ngugi wa Thiong'o, a writer from Kenya, began his career writing in English but then chose to write in Gikuyu. Believing, as Audre Lorde does, that the master's tools cannot dismantle the master's house, these writers manipulate their own language to combat colonization and create a separate postcolonial identity.

Postcolonial writers who continue to write in the colonizer's language have been subject to criticism, but they have helped to create important postcolonial literature. Many African, Caribbean, and Indian writers have chosen to write in their colonial languages, and their work raises important issues about national identity and colonial power. Ama Ata Aidoo may write in English, but *Our Sister Killjoy* (1977) is a vigorous rejection of Western ideals and colonization. Jamaica Kincaid uses her prose to decry what she sees as the commodification of the Caribbean in *A Small Place* (1988). Manipulating abrogation (a refusal of correct or standard usage) and appropriation, these authors make the colonial language represent the colonized's experience.

Colonialism has been and remains an important issue in literature. Since national or cultural identity is partially created through such artifacts as literature and art, it seems plausible that colonization, a practice that appropriates cultures, would figure prominently within those artifacts. Whether writers have justified colonization (and upheld the supremacy of empire, or have worked toward decolonization and the assertion of an autonomous postcolonial identity, they have had to deal with the issue of colonialism in literature.

SUGGESTED READINGS

Ashcroft, Bill, Gareth Griffiths, and Helen Tiffin. *The Empire Writes Back: Theory and Practice in Post-Colonial Literatures*. London: Routledge & Kegan Paul, 1989.

_____, eds. *The Post-Colonial Studies Reader*. London: Routledge & Kegan Paul, 1995.

Bhabha, Homi, ed. *Nation and Narration*. London: Routledge & Kegan Paul, 1990.

Boehmer, Elleke. *Colonial and Postcolonial Literature*. New York: Oxford University Press, 1995.

Hobsbawm, Eric. *The Age of Empire 1875-1914*. New York: Vintage, 1989.

Ngugi wa Thiong'o. *Decolonising the Mind: The Politics of Language in African Literature*. London: Heinemann, 1986.

Said, Edward. *Orientalism*. New York: Vintage, 1979.

Thomas, Nicholas. *Colonialism's Culture: Anthropology, Travel, and Government*. Princeton, N.J.: Princeton University Press, 1994.

—*Ann Marie Adams*

See also Canadian identity; Caribbean American literature; Creole and Acadian literature

Color Purple, The

AUTHOR: Alice Walker (1944-   )
FIRST PUBLISHED: 1982
IDENTITIES: African American; family; women

The Color Purple, awarded the Pulitzer Prize in fiction in 1983 and made into a successful film, is ultimately a novel of celebration. Initially, however, it is the tragic history of an extended African American family in the early and middle years of the twentieth century. Its tragedy is reflective of the country's and its characters' illness, and its celebration is of the characters' and the country's cure.

The story is written as a series of letters by two sisters, Celie and Nettie. The first letters reveal the fourteen-year-old Celie's miserable existence as caretaker of her parents' household. She bears two children to the man she believes to be her father (he is her stepfather), who immediately takes the children from her.

Celie is given into the same situation in marriage: She is made caretaker of another, now-deceased, woman's children and a stand-in sexual partner for yet another woman. When Celie and Nettie's father seeks to make Nettie his next victim, Nettie follows Celie to her new home, only to be victimized there by Celie's husband.

Nettie finds a home with the minister and his wife, who have become parents to Celie's children, Adam and Olivia. The five move to Africa to bring their Christian message to the Olinka. When the woman for whom Celie is stand-in partner enters her home, the note of harmony which will swell to the final chorus of celebration is sounded. Celie comes to love and to learn from Shug. She learns that she must enter Creation as loved creature of her Creator, who, neither white nor male, creates out of love and a desire to please "Its" creatures. Reverence for all of Creation—trees, the color purple, humanity—is the cure, finally, to her and the novel's ills. Nettie's letters show Celie that she and her minister husband have come independently, in Africa, to know the same loving Creator who loves all and repudiates no part of Creation.

Celie leaves her abuser, Albert, who is slow to learn and sing the novel's song. He finally helps to bring Nettie, Samuel, Adam, Olivia, and Tashi, Adam's wife, back to Celie. He tells Celie, as they, finally, establish a friendship, that the more he wonders at and about Creation the more he loves. Celie, now lover of self and Creation, is reunited in middle age with her sister and grown children.

SUGGESTED READINGS

Christophe, Marc-A. "*The Color Purple*: An Existential Novel." *CLA Journal* 36, no. 3 (March, 1993): 280-291.

Marvin, Thomas F. "Preachin' the Blues: Bessie Smith's Secular Religion and Alice Walker's *The Color Purple*." *African American Review* 28, no. 3 (Fall, 1994): 411-422.

Taylor, Carole Anne. "Humor, Subjectivity, Resistance: The Case of Laughter in *The Color Purple*." *Texas Studies in Literature and Language* 36, no. 4 (Winter, 1994): 462-483.

—*Judith K. Taylor*

See also African American identity; Erotic identity; Walker, Alice

Columbus, Christopher, literature about

IDENTITIES: European American

Christopher Columbus' encounters with the New World quickly inspired writers in Europe, providing the material for three Italian epic poems in the sixteenth century alone, as well as several Spanish and French tributes. Most of the early North American colonists thought of themselves as British subjects, and the figure of an Italian explorer in the service of Spain (the enemy of Protestantism) who had never actually landed on North America did not immediately attract English-language writers. The momentous events of the Declaration of Independence and the Revolutionary War, however, led North American colonists to think of themselves as Americans, and suddenly Columbus seemed to provide an alternative source of national identity and a founding myth for the new nation. The practice of referring to the colonies as Columbia, which had occurred occasionally before, took on a revolutionary significance in such patriotic poems as "American Liberty, a Poem," by Philip Freneau, published in 1775, and "To His Excellency General Washington," published in 1776 by Phillis Wheatley, a former slave.

Freneau wrote two poems specifically about Columbus, "Columbus to Ferdinand" (1770), a dramatic monologue in which Columbus petitions the king of Spain for support for his voyage, and *The Pictures of Columbus* (1774), a sequence of eighteen poems covering Columbus' life from before the first voyage through his final days. The works are unusual for the period because they concentrate more on building a psychological portrait of a complex and tragic character, who was visionary and victim, than on presenting a one-dimensional heroic figure to satisfy patriotism. More typical of early treatments is Joel Barlow's *The Vision of Columbus* (1787), later revised and expanded as *The Columbiad* (1807). Barlow set out to write a national epic glorifying the country's past, present, and future, with a narrator (an angel in the first version, a mythological guide in the second) who unrolls the panorama of American history before the eyes of the virtuous Columbus. While Barlow's poem was more successful at the time, Freneau's anticipates the darker view of Columbus often taken by modern writers.

Although nominally a biography, Washington Irving's enormously popular *A History of the Life and Voyages of Christopher Columbus* (1828) includes a large proportion of imaginative material along with its historical facts and is now seen as more important as a work of literature, providing a heroic, romanticized version of Columbus that became the model for generations of later writers. While Irving did note the negative aspects of Columbus' life story, including the explorer's advocacy of slavery, the overall image presented is positive, with Columbus, embodying virtues such as independence and courage that "singularly combined the practical and the poetical," depicted as a distinctively American blend of the man of action and the man of vision.

This symbolic Columbus proved durable and was readily adapted to a wide range of poetic purposes throughout the nineteenth century, for mainstream poetry such as Lydia Huntley Sigourney's "On the Meeting of the Old and New Worlds, 1492" (1834) and James Russell Lowell's "Columbus" (1844) as well as for Walt Whitman's "Prayer of Columbus" (1874). Columbus proved a viable symbol of the American melting pot, inspiring Jewish spokeswoman Emma Lazarus' "1492" (1883) and African American poet Paul Laurence Dunbar's "Columbian Ode" (1893).

Twentieth century writers have continued to find Columbus a malleable image to represent America's diverse cultural identity. Columbus is apt as an illustration of America's history of violence and racism; he also serves as a symbol of its idealism and multiculturalism. Columbus appears in William Carlos Williams' *In the American Grain* (1925) as lethal conqueror and helpless victim, in Hart Crane's poem *The Bridge* (1930) as a prophet of unity, in Joseph Chiari's *Christopher Columbus: A Play* (1979) as the man responsible for slavery in America, and in *The Double Reckoning of Christopher Columbus* (1992), Barbara Helfgott Hyett's collection of forty-seven poems arranged around Columbus' journal entries, as pure enigma, the image of moral and ethical paradox.

SUGGESTED READINGS

Bushman, Claudia L. *America Discovers Columbus: How an Italian Explorer Became an American Hero.* Hanover, N.H.: University Press of New England, 1992.

Elliott, Emory. *Revolutionary Writers: Literature and Authority in the New Republic, 1725-1810.* New York: Oxford University Press, 1982.

Greenfield, Bruce. *Narrating Discovery: The Romantic Explorer in American Literature 1790-1855.* New York: Columbia University Press, 1992.

Martin, Terence. *Parables of Possibility: The American Need for Beginnings.* New York: Columbia University Press, 1995.

Spengemann, William. *The Adventurous Muse: The Poetics of American Fiction, 1789-1900.* New Haven, Conn.: Yale University Press, 1977.

_____. *A New World of Words: Redefining Early American Literature.* New Haven, Conn.: Yale University Press, 1994.

Todorov, Tzvetan. *The Conquest of America: The Question of the Other.* Translated by Richard Howard. New York: Harper & Row, 1984.

—William Nelles

See also Colonialism; Melting pot; Multiculturalism; Racism and ethnocentrism; Slavery

Coming-of-age stories. *See* Bildungsroman and Künstlerroman

Coming out

IDENTITIES: Gay, lesbian, and bisexual

DEFINITION: "Coming out" used to refer exclusively to a debutante's presentation to society; the phrase is now more widely recognized as referring to a homosexual's proclaiming, rather than hiding, sexual preference. The phrase's newer meaning refers to the figure of speech "coming out of the closet."

As people begin to identify themselves as homosexual, they must deal with societal beliefs that this sexual preference is shameful, sinful, or pathological. From fear, often but not always justified, that revelation of homosexuality will lead to ostracism, many homosexuals keep their sexual preference secret from friends and family. Keeping such a secret is often called living in the closet; to proclaim one's homosexuality is to come out of the closet. In the cultural mainstream generally, history, religion, educational institutions, and cultural values and mores all maintain that people are naturally heterosexual and that homosexuality is a failing. As a result, homosexual women and men have powerful reasons not to acknowledge their sexual preferences. As the individual gay or lesbian begins to accept his or her identity, however, the coming out process becomes more compelling. In this sense, the metaphor of "coming out" is quite accurate, since coming out is a process of taking what is within (unspoken sexual identity) and bringing it out to the attention of others. Coming out can be difficult and dangerous, so many people live in the closet, acting as if they are attracted to members of the opposite sex. The distressing feelings of alienation that result from trying to be someone that one is not can motivate one to come out.

History   Literature shows that coming out is a new concept and word usage. The original usage of the term was associated with the debutante ball, usually given in the spring. The ball was a social event held to announce to society that each of the families involved had a daughter who was eligible as a potential wife. When the custom of such balls was established, a girl of sixteen or so was not considered too young to be engaged. In the later twentieth century, the custom continued, although the debutantes were considered eligible for dating and social autonomy rather than marriage.

Coming out for homosexuals was not mentioned in literature until gay and lesbian novels began to appear in numbers in the late 1960's and after. After the later 1960's there was a large increase in writing and publishing of gay, lesbian, and bisexual literature. Coming out (or failing to do so) is perhaps the most universal theme of gay, lesbian, and bisexual literature. Although a work may not recount directly such an event as telling one's family that one is gay (although many works do relate such stories), it is the rare work in this field that does not deal with the issue of characters' recognizing and finally either acknowledging or denying their homosexuality.

SUGGESTED READINGS

Caffey, John. *The Coming-out Party*. New York: Pinnacle Books, 1982.

Gantz, Joe. *Whose Child Cries: Children of Gay Parents Talk About Their Lives*. Rolling Hills Estates, Calif.: Jalmar Press, 1983.

Herdt, Gilbert H. *Children of Horizons: How Gay and Lesbian Teens Are Leading a New Way out of the Closet*. Boston: Beacon Press, 1993.

Jay, Karla, and Allen Young, eds. *Out of the Closets: Voices of Gay Liberation*. New York: Pyramid Books, 1972.

Katz, Jonathan. *Coming-Out: A Documentary Play About Gay Life and Liberation*. New York: Arno Press, 1975.

Nolder, Gay A. *The View from the Closet: Essays on Gay Life and Liberation*. Boston: Union Park Press, 1978.

Pharr, Suzanne. *Homophobia: A Weapon of Sexism*. Little Rock, Ark.: Chardon Press, 1988.

Rodi, Robert. *Closet Case: A Novel*. New York: E. P. Dutton, 1993.

Sutton, Roger. *Hearing Us Out: Voices from the Gay and Lesbian Community*. Boston: Little, Brown, 1994.

—Sandra J. Parsons

See also Bisexual identity; Erotic identity; Gay identity; Identity crisis; Lesbian identity

Coming Up Down Home: A Memoir of a Southern Childhood

AUTHOR: Cecil Brown (1943-   )
FIRST PUBLISHED: 1993
IDENTITIES: African American; family; South

In *Coming Up Down Home: A Memoir of a Southern Childhood*, Cecil Brown presents a child shaped by the clash between agricultural and urban living and by the omnipresent tension of racism in the South. Morris, the first-person narrator of *Coming Up Down Home*, is reared primarily by his aunt and uncle, who teach him the value of education and hard work. As teenagers, Morris and his brother are returned to their father, who has been released from prison. Culphert (Cuffy) Brown is a violent man who rejects the importance of education and culture but who supports Morris in surprising ways, such as buying him a new, top-of-the-line saxophone when Morris has the opportunity to join the high school band. Morris has the skills of a farmer but combines them with knowledge gleaned from school in order to move beyond his father's limitations. Morris notes that "I found the hard life of being a farmer's son alleviated by the ability to attach words and values to previously mundane surroundings. It opened up a whole new world for me."

Morris consistently attempts to escape his agricultural roots and his violent home life. At sixteen, he spends a summer in New York, where he discovers that the same racism he took for granted as a child in the South is present in New York, but in subtler forms. Upon his return to Bolton, Morris realizes that he can no longer live the life of a sharecropper's son. He discovers the strength to defy his often-abusive father, ultimately winning a college scholarship without Cuffy's knowledge. The main body of the memoir ends with Morris' departure, when Cuffy presents him with a typewriter, foreshadowing Brown's successful career as an author.

Coming Up Down Home, like many of Brown's works, makes frequent use of African American folk traditions. The reader experiences a sermon in a black church, numerous toasts, gospel songs, and other elements of the African American oral tradition. Morris includes these in his narrative without comment, implying that such forms are integral to growing up African American.

SUGGESTED READING
Thomas, H. Nigel. *From Folklore to Fiction: A Study of Folk Heroes and Rituals in the Black American Novel*. Westport, Conn.: Greenwood Press, 1988.

—Abby Zidle

See also African American identity; American identity: South; Black church; Racism and ethnocentrism

Complete Poems, The

AUTHOR: Anne Sexton (1928-1974)
FIRST PUBLISHED: 1981
IDENTITIES: European American; women

Anne Sexton was an extremely prolific poet, especially considering that she started writing in the middle of her life. Once she got started, Sexton published books of poems every two years and sometimes as often as every year. All of the books share Sexton's enthusiasm for confession, but many of the books present different types of poems: long poems, elegies, lyrics, narratives, reworked fairy tales, poems for children.

Even three years after her death, books of original verse continued to be published, as Sexton had arranged before her suicide. Afterward, one of her daughters, Linda Gray Sexton, wrestled with the difficult task of assembling poems from books (including books published in Great Britain but not in the United States), poems in myriad draft forms, and poems that appeared complete but were unpublished. The result was *The Complete Poems*.

In *Searching for Mercy Street* (1994), Linda Gray Sexton mentions that almost all of her mother's literary papers and poems are stored in the Harry Ransom Humanities Research Center at the University of Texas in Austin and have been there for some time. The collection includes drafts and revisions that are not in *The Complete Poems*. *The Complete Poems* includes some poems not present in Anne Sexton's many books.

Sexton strove in her poetry to understand her identity; she also wished to present herself as the witty, urbane woman of the suburbs who controls her madness, her abortions, her affairs, even her suicide attempts. One cannot believe that she controlled these things; *Searching for Mercy Street* makes clear how desperate Anne Sexton truly was.

SUGGESTED READINGS

George, Diana Hume. *Oedipus Anne: The Poetry of Anne Sexton*. Champaign: University of Illinois Press, 1987.

Middlebrook, Diane Wood. *Anne Sexton: A Biography*. Boston: Houghton Mifflin, 1991.

Sexton, Anne. *Anne Sexton: A Self-Portrait in Letters*. Boston: Houghton Mifflin, 1977.

Wagner-Martin, Linda, ed. *Critical Essays on Anne Sexton*. Boston: G. K. Hall, 1989.

—John Jacob

See also *Awful Rowing Toward God, The*; Mental disorders; *Searching for Mercy Street*; Sexton, Anne; *To Bedlam and Part Way Back*

Concubine's Children: Portrait of a Family Divided, The

AUTHOR: Denise Chong

FIRST PUBLISHED: 1994

IDENTITIES: Canada; Chinese American

Denise Chong begins her memoir with her grandparents. Her grandfather, Chan Sam, was one of the many Chinese who left their homeland to seek their fortune in the Americas. After many years alone in Vancouver, Canada, Chan decided to have a second wife, a concubine, sent over from China. May-ying arrived in Vancouver in 1924, using a false Canadian birth certificate procured for the occasion. Thus began the family history detailed in *The Concubine's Children: Portrait of a Family Divided*.

Throughout his life Chan Sam maintained two families—his Chinese family with Huangbo, and his Canadian family with May-ying, by whom he had three daughters. Two of May-ying's daughters, Ping and Nan, remained in China after a visit; Chan returned to Canada for the birth of their third child, foretold to be the son Chan longed for. They were disappointed with a third daughter, Hing, who later took the American name Winnie. May-ying's disappointment was so great that for a time she dressed Hing as a boy, and later "adopted" a son, Leonard. On one of his visits home Chan conceived a son with Huangbo, but the boy, Yuen, had horribly deformed feet that "looked to be on backwards."

The Canadian branch of the family provided for much of the Chinese family's needs. As commanded by her husband, May-ying worked as a waitress in Chinatown tea houses, but she grew to enjoy the waitressing life and its freedom. She drank and gambled at mah-jongg and, after separating from Chan, followed her lover Guen from place to place, often leaving her daughter Winnie alone or in the care of strangers. Winnie reared herself in loneliness, married John Chong, and had several children, Denise among them. Denise's mother told her, "You're Canadian, not Chinese," but Denise's two years in Peking with her future husband, Roger Smith, stimulated her curiosity about her Chinese roots. She traveled the past with her mother, visiting her grandfather's village and Winnie's sisters and brother, with whom they shared the same Chinese dialect. They stayed in the large house built with May-ying's waitress earnings. The sweeping history of China serves as background for the personal traumas and tragedies of the divided family, whose Chinese branch survived the Japanese invasion of World War II, the Cultural Revolution of Mao Zedong, and the massacre in Tiananmen Square. Denise Chong is the author of this memoir, but it is her mother, Winnie, who finds her identity. Winnie's visits to China reveal that, despite the difficulties of her childhood, her life was in many ways more secure and less tragic than that of her siblings in China. For Denise, her recovered history imbues the past with new meaning, "perhaps enough to be a compass" for her own children.

SUGGESTED READINGS

Chiu, Monica. Review of *The Concubine's Children*, by Denise Chong. *Amerasia Journal* 21, no. 3 (Winter, 1995): 215.

Guterson, David. Review of *The Concubine's Children*, by Denise Chong. *The New York Times Book Review*, January 15, 1995, 24.

—*Linda Ledford-Miller*

See also Asian American identity: China, Japan, and Korea; Canadian identity

Conjure-Man Dies: A Mystery Tale of Dark Harlem, The

AUTHOR: Rudolph Fisher (1897-1934)
FIRST PUBLISHED: 1932
IDENTITIES: African American; Northeast

In *The Conjure-Man Dies: A Mystery Tale of Dark Harlem*, Rudolph Fisher combines his talent and comedic wit with his knowledge of medicine to produce the first known detective novel by an African American. Fisher introduces a variety of Harlem characters, including Jinx Jenkins and Bubber Brown, unemployed furniture movers who also appear in *The Walls of Jericho* (1928). Other characters include John Archer, the doctor who helps Harlem police solve the murder.

The complex plot highlights characters and settings popularized in Fisher's works. When Jinx and Bubber discover the murdered conjure man, they become suspects with several others: a numbers-runner, Spider Webb, who works in Harlem's illegal lottery system; a drug addict named Doty Hicks; a railroad worker; and a church worker. Mr. Crouch, mortician and owner of the building in which the conjure man is a tenant, and Crouch's wife Martha are quickly dismissed as suspects. When the corpse disappears and reappears as the live conjure man, Archer and Detective Dart know that there has been a murder but are unable to find the corpse. The conjure man is seen burning a body in the furnace. The body is of his servant, who was mistakenly killed instead of the conjure man. The conjure man adamantly insists he is innocent and helps to set a trap for the real murderer, but the conjure man is fatally shot by the railroad worker. Distraught that he has killed her lover, Martha assaults the railroad man, and all discover he is none other than the avenging Mr. Crouch, in disguise.

The detective story framework of *The Conjure-Man Dies* does not overshadow Fisher's depiction of several issues of Harlem life. Residents of Harlem resort to creative means to survive as the Depression makes their difficult economic situations worse. Bubber becomes a self-appointed detective for spouses who suspect their partners are being unfaithful. The numbers racket provides a living for many, including the conjure man. African Americans who are "firsts" to achieve a specific rank are under pressure to prove themselves worthy. Such is the case for detective Dart, who privately thanks Dr. Archer for promising that the city administration will be informed that Dart solved the murder.

Although Fisher's development of the hard-boiled character may have been influenced by the detective fiction of Dashiell Hammett, his most remarkable character is the conjure man, N'Gana Frimbo, a Harvard-educated West African king who imparts the traditions of his culture to Dr. Archer. Frimbo reflects Fisher's interest in the connections among blacks in Harlem, the Caribbean, and Africa. In the spirit of the Harlem Renaissance, Fisher creates a new path with *The Conjure-Man Dies*, one that would influence later writers such as Chester Himes and Walter Mosley.

SUGGESTED READING
Gloster, Hugh M. *Negro Voices in American Fiction*. Chapel Hill: University of North Carolina Press, 1948.

—*Australia Tarver*

See also African American identity; Fisher, Rudolph; Harlem Renaissance; Himes, Chester

Content of Our Character: A New Vision of Race in America, The

AUTHOR: Shelby Steele (1946-   )
FIRST PUBLISHED: 1990
IDENTITIES: African American

With *The Content of Our Character: A New Vision of Race in America*, Shelby Steele created a debate on the merits of affirmative action, the direction of the Civil Rights movement, and the growing ranks of African American political conservatives. Although certainly not the first to challenge views held by African American leaders, Steele pushed his challenge onto center stage more forcefully than others had before. Coming at a time when the United States was awash in conservative radio and television talk shows, the book quickly became a source of contention among political groups of all races and philosophies. Steele, through his television appearances, became a familiar figure throughout America as he explained and defended his ideas on race problems in America.

The book, titled after a line in Martin Luther King, Jr.'s famous speech, is a collection of essays, most of which appeared earlier in various periodicals. Central to Steele's book is a call for the African American community to examine itself and look to itself for opportunities. He calls for African Americans to look not to government or white society but to itself for the solutions to its problems. Steele contends that African Americans enjoy unparalleled freedom; they have only to seize their freedom and make it work for them. He suggests that such programs as affirmative action contribute to the demoralization or demeaning of African Americans because preferential treatment denies them the opportunity to "make it on their own."

Steele, calling for a return to the original purpose of the Civil Rights movement, says that affirmative action should go back to enforcing equal opportunity rather than demanding preferences. The promised land is, he writes, an opportunity, not a deliverance. Steele's ideas were strongly challenged by African Americans who believe that affirmative action and other civil rights measures are necessary for minority groups to retain the advancements that have been forged and to assure an open path for further progress. Steele's opponents believe that progress for minorities will not happen without civil rights laws and affirmative action. Opposition to Steele and other African American conservatives has led to charges that traditional African American civil rights leaders' intolerance of different voices within the black community is itself a form of racism.

SUGGESTED READINGS

Drake, William Avon, and Robert D. Holsworth. *Affirmative Action and the Stalled Quest for Black Progress*. Champaign: University of Illinois Press, 1996.

Little, Malcolm. *The Autobiography of Malcolm X*. New York: Ballantine, 1965.

Lokos, Lionel. *The New Racism: Reverse Discrimination in America*. New Rochelle, N.Y.: Arlington House, 1971.

—*Kay Hively*

See also African American identity; Civil Rights movement; Malcolm X; Martin Luther King, Jr.; Steele, Shelby

Continents of Exile

AUTHOR: Ved Mehta (1934-   )
FIRST PUBLISHED: 1972-1993
IDENTITIES: Disability; family; South Asian

In *Continents of Exile*, Ved Mehta has set himself the task of remembering and interpreting his life. In the seven volumes published before 1994, he examined his own development up to his graduation from the University of Oxford. Mehta's quest for self-understanding is also an introduction to the several different cultures through which Mehta has passed. From childhood Mehta has been an outsider seeking to understand worlds of which he is not fully a part. The loss of his eyesight at age three made him an exile in the world of the sighted, and his almost heroic struggle to secure an education sent him into exile—to Bombay from his native Punjab, to the United States, and to England. In describing his experiences, Mehta also gives the reader the flavor of different worlds, including India before and after its partition into India and Pakistan in 1947, Arkansas during segregation, suburban California in the tranquil 1950's, Oxford before the upheavals of the 1960's, and the world of blindness.

Continents of Exile is in some ways a sequel to Mehta's first book, *Face to Face* (1957). That book, written while Mehta was still an undergraduate, tells the story of his life up to almost the point reached in the seven later volumes. It lacks, however, the breadth, frankness, and detachment of the later volumes. In *Continents of Exile*, Mehta explores the power of memory. He has discovered that, with the aid of some research, memory yields much more than one might think. He also can analyze his experience with more detachment than his younger self could.

The series begins with biographies of Mehta's father and mother, *Daddyji* (1972) and *Mamaji* (1979). Mehta's father's family embraced Western influences, the English language, and an "unsuperstitious" form of Hinduism. Mehta's mother's family was more resistant to Western influences, and Mehta's mother often sought cures through charms and native treatments. In telling the stories of his very different parents and their nevertheless successful marriage, Mehta recalls the world of a close-knit family. He left the family to seek an education. *Vedi* (1982) and *The Ledge Between the Streams* (1984) describe Mehta's childhood, including his first experience of exile at a boarding school for the blind in Bombay and his family's flight from their home during the chaos following partition.

The next three volumes chronicle Mehta's education in America and England. In *Sound-Shadows of the New World* (1985) Mehta recounts his years at the Arkansas School for the Blind. *The Stolen Light* (1989) takes Mehta to Pomona College in California, where he is a great success and an outsider. *Up at Oxford* (1993) describes Mehta's years at Balliol College and sketches portraits of some promising minds he met there.

SUGGESTED READINGS

Slatin, John M. "Blindness and Self-Perception: The Autobiographies of Ved Mehta." *Mosaic* 19, no. 4 (Fall, 1986): 173-193.

Sontag, Frederick. "The Self-Centered Author." *New Quest* 79 (July-August, 1989): 229-233.

—*Brian Abel Ragen*

See also Asian American identity: India; Mehta, Ved

Conversion, religious

IDENTITIES: Religion

DEFINITION: Religious conversion is transformation of identity that embraces new religious beliefs.

Religious conversion is one of the great themes of literature. North American writers of diverse identity have described acts of conversion to the world's major religions—Christianity, Judaism, Islam, and many Eastern and Native American faiths. Religious conversion is radical change of identity. It involves rejecting accepted ways in order to nurture a connection with the spiritual. This conversion may be sudden or a slow, meditative process. People experiencing conversion grow into a spiritual life, sometimes alienating themselves from their community.

Historical roots

Settlers from England came to America to escape the hypocrisy of established churches. Early American Puritans such as John Winthrop and Jonathan Edwards describe intense religious experiences, insisting on personal conversion in order to fully sanctify oneself and accept God's will. Winthrop's *A Model of Christian Charity* (1629) describes the hope that colonial New England might become a "city upon a hill" upholding high standards of Christian behavior before the rest of the world. Edwards' *Divine and Supernatural Light* (1734) argues that saving grace comes only from the mind's supernatural illumination.

Native American literature contains many vision quests analogous to Christian conversions. Black Elk and John G. Neihardt's *Black Elk Speaks* (1932) tells the story of the Oglala Sioux holy man's instruction in sacred lore by medicine men who strived to retain the sacred identity of his nation. Black Elk's book also describes his conversion to Catholicism.

Modern expressions

John Steinbeck's *The Grapes of Wrath* (1939) describes tenant farmers from Oklahoma on an arduous westward journey. Accompanying them is Jim Casy, a former preacher who recounts being transformed by God. Although Casy has lost his faith, he functions as a spiritual healer and shows the powerful influence of his conversion. Some writers move away from tradition in their religious conversions while others move toward orthodoxy. T. S. Eliot's cycle of poems *Four Quartets* (1943) is composed of religious and philosophical meditations. Especially in one quartet, "Little Gidding," the poet undergoes a dramatic reevaluation of his concepts of time, faith, and God at the site of a seventeenth century Anglican community.

Thomas Merton converted to Roman Catholicism and became a Trappist monk at a Kentucky monastery. Merton depicts his conversion in *The Seven Storey Mountain* (1948). Flannery O'Connor's novels and stories describe many ecstatic religious experiences, especially those that are grotesque in nature. *Wise Blood* (1952) concerns a young fanatic who tries to establish a church in rural Georgia. *The Violent Bear It Away* (1960) presents the fanatical mission of a boy intent on baptizing another boy. Many of O'Connor's short stories, such as "A Good Man Is Hard to Find" or "Everything That Rises Must Converge," show the inner turmoil of characters searching for a mystical revelation.

Many conversions correspond to ethnic and racial identity. Malcolm X, a civil rights leader and preacher, describes his conversion in *The Autobiography of Malcolm X* (1965). The book movingly tells of Malcolm's self-education while in prison and how his sense of self-worth was enhanced by his conversion to Islam. N. Scott Momaday's *The Way to Rainy Mountain* (1969) describes the Kiowa creation story. Torn between two worlds of Native American and white, Momaday's vision quest is a conversion and an attempt to recover his tribal identity.

Conversions need not be ethnic or orthodox. Peter Matthiessen describes his trek to Tibet in quest of spiritual fulfillment and enlightenment in *The Snow Leopard* (1978). The animal is considered sacred by Buddhists. Maya Angelou's *All God's Children Need Traveling Shoes* (1986) is an autobiographical account of her stay in Ghana at the time it won its political independence. Angelou's spiritual journey to Africa strengthens her identity as an African American. Anne Tyler's *Saint Maybe* (1991) tells the story of Ian Bedloe's conversion in the Church of the Second Chance, where he seeks a personal salvation.

SUGGESTED READINGS

Ahlstrom, Sydney E. *A Religious History of the American People*. 2 vols. Garden City, N.Y.: Image Books, 1975.

Eliot, T. S. "Religion and Literature." In *Religion and Modern Literature: Essays in Theory and Criticism*, edited by G. B. Tennyson and Edward E. Ericson. Grand Rapids, Mich.: Wm. B. Eerdmans, 1975.

Gallagher, Susan, and Roger Lundin. *Literature Through the Eyes of Faith*. New York: HarperCollins, 1989.

Hatch, Nathan, and Mark Noll, eds. *The Bible in America*. New York: Oxford University Press, 1982.

O'Connor, Flannery. "Catholic Novelists and Their Readers." In *Mystery and Manners*, edited by Sally Fitzgerald and Robert Fitzgerald. New York: Farrar, Straus & Giroux, 1961.

—*Jonathan L. Thorndike*

See also Black church; Catholicism; Christianity and Christian Fundamentalism; Eastern religion and philosophy; Islamic literature; Jewish American identity; Puritan and Protestant tradition; Religious minorities

Conversion narratives. *See* Conversion, religious

Countercultures

DEFINITION: Groups consciously opposed to the prevailing culture.

Literature has always given a voice to those disenchanted with their cultures. The word "countercultures" in the context of North American literature, however, refers primarily to the youth movements of the late 1960's, which strove for an alternative to the established culture. Members of this counterculture valued experience, personal expression, egalitarianism, self-examination, and authenticity; their literature blends high and low culture, multicultural influences, Americana, avant-garde forms, and voices from the past.

The counterculture combined a quest for intense experience with a utopian desire to renew the world. These desires were expressed in art, music, and literature, and in activities such as antiwar and civil rights protests, mystical exploration, drugs, and the sexual revolution. The counterculture experienced considerable success in redefining culture, changing perceptions and practices in the realms of art, music, politics, education, religion, and social mores. Political protest, street theater, and communally produced art reflected the democratic and antiauthoritarian impulse of the counterculture's artistic acts. There is a literature of the counterculture: produced by it, written about it, or adopted by it.

Jay Stevens writes in *Storming Heaven: LSD and the American Dream* (1987): "in many respects the hippies were second-generation Beats." Although the counterculture generation was more colorful, more optimistic, and more political, it shared with the Beats a distaste for authority and conformity. Allen Ginsberg and William S. Burroughs, major Beat writers, became leading counterculture figures. **Influences, roots, and borrowings**

The counterculture also brought popularity to kindred spirits from the past. Ginsberg drew attention to English Romantic poets William Blake and Percy Bysshe Shelley. Even more popular was Hermann Hesse, a German novelist and poet whose antiwar sentiments, Eastern mysticism, and psychological probings appealed to the counterculture.

The fantasy books of J. R. R. Tolkien (*The Hobbit*, 1937, and *The Lord of the Rings*, 1954-1955) were favorites in the counterculture; in general, fantasy and science fiction appealed to the counterculture's exuberant imagination. The counterculture was influenced by the Beats, the literature the Beats advocated, and by such writers as Tolkien; in turn, the counterculture influenced such fanciful works as *The Butterfly Kid* (1967) by Chester Anderson, and Robert Shea and Robert Anton Wilson's *The Illuminatus Trilogy* (1974).

The most innovative literature produced by the counterculture was passionately personal and experimental nonfiction. In the 1960's, this nonfiction flourished in the underground newspapers, in rock-and-roll magazines such as *Rolling Stone*, and in satiric publications such as Paul Krassner's *The Realist*. This nonfiction, in a bold stroke, dropped the mask of objectivity in journalism and used the personal voice and point of view of the journalist in describing events. Counterculture journals published manifestos, guerrilla journalism (ranging from political exposé to advice on finding free food), and personal narrative. The late 1960's and early 1970's saw the book equivalents of underground journalism: *Revolution for the Hell of It* (1968) and *Steal This Book* (1971) by Abbie Hoffman; James S. Kunen's *The Strawberry Statement: Notes of a College Revolutionary* (1969); and *Do It: Scenarios of the Revolution* (1970) by Jerry Rubin. Important memoirs also chronicle the time, from Emmett Grogan's *Ringolevio: A Life Played for Keeps* (1972) to *Heavenly Breakfast* (1979) by Samuel R. Delany. Personal and subjective narration mixed with factual reporting became known as new journalism. Classic examples may be found in the works of Tom Wolfe, Norman Mailer, Joan Didion, and Hunter S. Thompson. **New nonfiction**

Major public figures of the counterculture produced little fiction; Ken Kesey's popular *One Flew over the Cuckoo's Nest* was published as a novel in 1962. Burroughs continued steady publication of his antiestablishment works. Three major writers who participated little in public events of the counterculture but who examine countercultural themes are Kurt Vonnegut, Richard Brautigan, and Thomas Pynchon. Vonnegut's novels, especially *Cat's Cradle* (1963) and *Slaughterhouse-Five: Or, The Children's Crusade, a Duty-Dance with Death* (1969), offer satire, imagination, and hope in an absurd world. Brautigan's poetry and prose use evocative and surreal imagery to critique everyday life. Pynchon, the best and most challenging writer of the counterculture, makes brilliant, encyclopedic observations about the society of his time in *V.* (1963), *The Crying of Lot 49* (1966), and *Gravity's Rainbow* (1973). Pynchon's *Vineland* (1990) is a bittersweet look at the graying **Fiction** members of the counterculture and their challenge to find hope in the years of the Reagan Administration.

SUGGESTED READINGS

Dickstein, Morris. *Gates of Eden: American Culture in the Sixties*. New York: Basic Books, 1977.

Peck, Abe. *Uncovering the Sixties: The Life and Times of the Underground Press*. New York: Pantheon Books, 1985.

Sayres, Sohnya, et al., eds. *The Sixties Without Apology*. Minneapolis: University of Minnesota Press, 1984.

Stevens, Jay. *Storming Heaven: LSD and the American Dream*. New York: The Atlantic Monthly Press, 1987.

Whitmer, Peter O., with Bruce Van Wyngarden. *Aquarius Revisited: Seven Who Created the Counterculture That Changed America*. New York: Macmillan, 1987.

—Bernadette Lynn Bosky

See also Antiwar literature; Brautigan, Richard; Delany, Samuel R.; Didion, Joan; Drugs; Ginsberg, Allen; Kesey, Ken; Mailer, Norman; Pynchon, Thomas; Vonnegut, Kurt; Wolfe, Tom

Country Husband, The

AUTHOR: John Cheever (1912-1982)

FIRST PUBLISHED: 1954

IDENTITIES: European American; family

"The Country Husband" exemplifies John Cheever's interpretation of life, values, and futile rebellion among neighbors and families. In Shady Hill, a suburb within commuting distance of New York, wives are concerned with dinners, social gatherings, and social status; daughters are absorbed in romance magazines; children bicker on household battlefields; and husbands delude themselves with fantasies of romance as they struggle merely to be acknowledged.

Clayton Thomas, who is engaged to Anne Murchison, a baby-sitter, offers a summary of Shady Hill: "What seems to me really wrong with Shady Hill is that it doesn't have any future. So much energy is spent in perpetuating the place—in keeping out undesirables, and so forth—that the only idea of the future anyone has is just more and more commuting trains and more parties."

Francis Weed, the story's central character, seems to agree, for he thinks that there is "no turpitude." Life seems "arranged with more propriety even than in the Kingdom of Heaven." The story begins as Francis survives a plane's emergency landing, but upon his return to Shady Hill, he can find no one to listen to his harrowing experience. The superficiality of life in Shady Hill becomes especially clear when Francis sees a maid at a party and realizes that he saw her in France during World War II: She was publicly humiliated for being a collaborator with the Germans. Shady Hill residents consider drama, memory, and war to be not nice; Francis does not recount the story.

Wanting to go beyond social limitations, Francis seeks romance with Anne Murchison. He fantasizes but is grounded in the world of his wife, who plans a session for family photographs. Rejecting Shady Hill, Francis turns a chance meeting with Mrs. Wrightson, the neighborhood ruler of social affairs, into an occasion for a rude outburst. When Julia, Francis' wife, confronts Francis about his behavior, Francis hits her across the face, yet her threat to abandon him dissolves into a pledge to stay "a little while longer." Obsessing about Anne, Francis becomes crudely jealous of Clayton and, when asked to provide a helpful reference, besmears his name.

In the end, Francis seeks psychological help from Dr. Herzog, who instructs Francis to find solace in doing woodworking projects in his basement. Ironically, Francis, who at the outset bemoans the sterility of Shady Hill, ultimately betrays Clayton, the one resident aware of the community's weaknesses, and retreats to the community's superficiality. In the end, Jupiter, a romping dog who rambles through gardens, has more freedom and happiness than Francis, yet the dog's destiny, Francis knows, is to be poisoned by an irritated householder.

SUGGESTED READINGS

Bosha, Francis J., ed. *The Critical Response to John Cheever*. Westport, Conn.: Greenwood Press, 1994.

Collins, Robert G., ed. *Critical Essays on John Cheever*. Boston: G. K. Hall, 1982.

Hunt, George W. *John Cheever: The Hobgoblin Company of Love*. Grand Rapids, Mich.: Wm. B. Eerdmans, 1983.

Meanor, Patrick. *John Cheever Revisited*. New York: Twayne, 1995.

—*William T. Lawlor*

See also Alcoholism; Cheever, John; *Wapshot Scandal, The*

Country of the Pointed Firs, The

AUTHOR: Sarah Orne Jewett (1849-1909)

FIRST PUBLISHED: 1896

IDENTITIES: European American; Northeast; women

In *The Country of the Pointed Firs*, Sarah Orne Jewett focuses on a topic similar to that found in *Deephaven* (1877); in both books, summer visitors from the city meet the sometimes-eccentric local population of a remote Maine village. The narrator in *The Country of the Pointed Firs*, a middle-aged female writer, has come to the village for the solitude she has associated with the place since an earlier brief visit. She boards with Mrs. Todd, a widow with mystical powers, who gathers and sells curative herbs. Mrs. Todd's rural ways contrast sharply with those of the urban narrator. Although these women characters have little in common, Jewett describes, with exceptional sensitivity, how a touching relationship between the two develops. They come to understand and appreciate each other. From annoyance grows mutual respect and interdependence.

The annoyance is that the narrator counts on having her mornings alone to write while Mrs. Todd is gathering herbs in the surrounding countryside. Such, however, is not the case: While Mrs. Todd is away, customers bang on her door. The narrator attends to their needs. In desperation, she rents a small schoolhouse to which she transfers her morning writing activities. There she begins to feel isolated. She realizes, as she watches a funeral in which much of the community participates, that her urban identity separates her from the townspeople. Soon, wishing to feel more integrated into the community, she resumes her morning duties at Mrs. Todd's, to her landlady's great delight.

Gradually, Mrs. Todd reveals to the narrator her inmost feelings, confessing that she had a lover who married someone else and then died and that she did not really love her husband, who also died, causing her to experience an intermixture of guilt and relief. The bond between these women is cemented when the narrator treats Mrs. Todd's old friend, the demented Captain Littlepage, respectfully. Mrs. Todd takes the narrator to Green Island to meet her mother, Mrs. Blackett, a remarkable woman often called upon to comfort the dying as her daughter is called upon to cure the ailing. Mrs. Todd's shy son, William, takes the two women to the island, but he remains aloof until the narrator wins him over by a simple act.

SUGGESTED READINGS

Blanchard, Paula. *Sarah Orne Jewett: Her World and Her Work*. Cambridge, Mass.: Radcliffe Biography Series, 1994.

Cary, Richard, ed. *Appreciation of Sarah Orne Jewett*. Waterville, Maine: Colby College Press, 1973.

Nagel, Gwen, ed. *Critical Essays on Sarah Orne Jewett*. Boston: G. K. Hall, 1984.

Pryse, Marjorie. Introduction to *The Country of the Pointed Firs*, by Sarah Orne Jewett. New York: W. W. Norton, 1982.

Roman, Margaret. *Sarah Orne Jewett: Reconstructing Gender*. Tuscaloosa: University of Alabama Press, 1992.

—*R. Baird Shuman*

See also American identity: Northeast; *Deephaven*; Feminism; Jewett, Sarah Orne

Creole and Acadian literature

IDENTITIES: European American; South

DEFINITION: Creoles are the descendants of French settlers in Louisiana, as are Acadians, or Cajuns, whose ancestors were exiled in 1755 and 1758 from the formerly French territory of Acadia, which included Nova Scotia and its environs.

Background
Historically, Louisiana has enjoyed a rich cultural and literary heritage. Motivated by the threat of assimilation, the people of Louisiana, most notably the Creoles and Acadians, held fast to their French and Spanish roots. In so doing, they developed unique cultural, linguistic, culinary, and religious patterns that gave them strong definition in a country that was becoming increasingly homogeneous.

There has always been an impulse to group the Acadians and Creoles together, but it is necessary to distinguish between the two societies. Finding it difficult to make a productive living in France, the Acadians, an agrarian community, immigrated to what is now known as Nova Scotia, Canada, in the early seventeenth century. Primarily a peasant class, the Acadians found little comfort in their new land, as it was mercilessly cold. Geographic isolation forced this small band of French pioneers to work together in order to survive, fostering in them a strong sense of kinship. When the English (who were in constant conflict with France), suspicious of the French heritage of the Acadians, insisted they assimilate into English society, the result was a sense of Acadian national identity that outlasted the numerous assaults upon Acadian culture. After repeated skirmishes with the British, the Acadians were expelled from Nova Scotia. One literary version of the Acadian experience is American poet Henry Wadsworth Longfellow's long narrative poem *Evangeline: A Tale of Acadie* (1847).

Some Acadians relocated further into the Canadian interior, some to the northern United States, some to France, and some, hoping to reunite with their French countrymen, immigrated to Louisiana. Settling along the southwestern Mississippi coast, the Acadians established a unique agrarian culture based upon strong familial, linguistic, and historical ties with their native France. Over time, they, much like the Creoles, were forced to redefine certain practices in order to accommodate the unique geographical features of their new land. This is especially seen in their culinary practices, which, accordingly, incorporate those foods that are most easily grown along the Mississippi coast. More than 500,000 Acadians are estimated to be living in Louisiana, many of whom are making a concerted effort to preserve their ancestral ways.

The Creoles, unlike the Acadians, are the direct descendants of the French and Spanish immigrants who first came to New Orleans. These early immigrants were mainly aristocrats, who attempted to forge for themselves a feudal society closely resembling the one they left behind. Unlike the Acadians, the Creoles were generally merchants and plantation owners; they dictated public policy until Louisiana came under American authority in 1803. By the time Americans began settling in Louisiana, however, the Creoles had already established a solid identity and, like their Acadian brethren, were determined not to bow to the threat of assimilation. Although Creoles

---

Creole and Acadian Literature
Eight Key Works

1847	Henry Wadsworth Longfellow's long narrative poem *Evangeline: A Tale of Acadie*.	1897	Kate Chopin's *A Night in Acadie*.
		1936	William Faulkner's *Absalom, Absalom!*
1879	George W. Cable's *Old Creole Days*.	1962	Translator Corrine L. Saucier's *Folk Tales from French Louisiana*.
1880	George W. Cable's *The Grandissimes*.		
1888	Grace Elizabeth King's *Monsieur Motte*.	1965	George W. Cable's *Creoles and Cajuns: Stories of Old Louisiana, by George W. Cable*.

---

lost their political power, they maintained social and cultural control of the territory. As was the practice, Creole children continued to be educated in France, returning to Louisiana to marry within their class.

In addition to these two groups are the Creole people of color, brought onto the plantations from Africa and Haiti. The fusing of the African and French cultures brought about a new and distinct society, whose dialect and customs are different from those of their predecessors. In a Southern state that had more free blacks than any other, intimacy between Creole men and free black women was accepted and recognized within the community at large. Such relationships were, to a certain extent, legitimized, and the offspring of these unions took their appropriate place within the Creole hierarchy. This type of relationship is depicted in William Faulkner's *Absalom, Absalom!* (1936). Both cultures have continued to flourish in South Louisiana, especially the areas of New Orleans, Baton Rouge, and Lafayette.

Literary concerns
One of the most important tasks in defining identity is recognizing Creoles and Acadians as distinct groups. One should avoid the temptation to consider all Louisiana francophone societies as one. Much Creole and Acadian history is contained in oral tradition, and most recently, historians and writers alike are recognizing the importance of Creole and Acadian narratives, transcribing them and publishing collections. Although there are still an enormous number of stories to hear, much work has been done already, and several good editions have emerged.

The emphasis on protecting the Acadian and Creole experiences from extinction flourished during the Civil War, for it was during this time that the Southern identity in general became most vulnerable. One of the most important writers to take up the challenge of preserving the Creole and Acadian way of life during this time was George Washington Cable. Born and reared in New Orleans, Cable realized the rich material his world presented and wrote stories reflecting the customs and language of the Creole and Acadian people. Placing emphasis on accuracy, Cable amassed a tremendous amount of historical data (and learned French), which he carefully incorporated into his literature. The beauty and seriousness of his work forced the literary community to take notice of these societies, and a new area of study was born. His works include *Old Creole Days* (1879), a collection of stories, and *The Grandissimes* (1880).

Noted Southern author Kate Chopin relied heavily on local color for her sensitive depictions of Creole and Acadian women. The popularity of her fiction, originally published in the late nineteenth century, epitomizes the interest the literary world has taken in literature by and about Creoles and Acadians. Her works featuring Creole and Acadian characters include *A Night in Acadie* (1897) and *The Awakening* (1899).

SUGGESTED READINGS

Brasseaux, Carl A. *The Founding of New Acadia: The Beginnings of Acadian Life in Louisiana, 1765-1803*. Baton Rouge: Louisiana State University Press, 1987.

Brown, Dorothy H., and Barbara C. Ewell, eds. *Louisiana Women Writers: New Essays and a Comprehensive Bibliography*. Baton Rouge: Louisiana State University Press, 1992.

Cable, George W. *Creoles and Cajuns: Stories of Old Louisiana, by George W. Cable*. Edited by Arlin Turner. Gloucester, Mass.: P. Smith, 1965.

Saucier, Corrine L., trans. *Folk Tales from French Louisiana*. New York: Exposition Press, 1962.

Turner, Arlin, ed. *Critical Essays on George W. Cable*. Boston: G. K. Hall, 1980.

Woods, Frances J. *Marginality and Identity: A Colored Creole Family Through Ten Generations*. Baton Rouge: Louisiana State University Press, 1972.

—Annemarie Koning Whaley

See also American identity: South; *Awakening, The*; Bilingualism; Cable, George Washington; Chopin, Kate; Mixed race and identity

Creoles. *See* Creole and Acadian literature

Crimes of the Heart

AUTHOR: Beth Henley (1952-   )
FIRST PRODUCED: 1979; first published, 1981
IDENTITIES: European American; family; South; women

Crimes of the Heart is a character study of three sisters, each attempting to discover her own identity. They collectively deal with family problems and individual challenges. The bizarre yet believable characters in Henley's Southern gothic comedy struggle to deal with despair, loneliness, and failure. Black humor enables the MaGrath sisters to find meaning and happiness in life, even if it is only momentary.

The sisters were abandoned by their father and then abandoned again when their mother hanged herself, along with her cat. The oldest sister, Lenny, has sacrificed her life to care for the grandfather who raised them. Her loneliness is deepened by her belief that she is undesirable because she cannot conceive. Meg, the totally self-centered middle sister, ran away to Hollywood but has since given up her dream of becoming a star. They are reunited in Hazelhurst, Mississippi, because the youngest sister, Babe, has shot her husband and is facing trial. The sisters confront their pasts in ways that enable them to redefine their own identities as stronger, independent women.

When their grandfather slips into a coma, Lenny finally realizes that she does not have to spend her life as a lonely spinster. Meg is invited out by the lover whom she abandoned in the devastation of Hurricane Camille, a metaphor for the disaster of the sisters' past lives. When he does not beg her to run away with him, she realizes that she can love unconditionally. Babe brings understanding to the sisters and self-realization to herself. She shot her husband because he discovered her affair with a fifteen-year-old black boy. Considering suicide, she realizes she actually wanted her husband, not herself, to die. She also realizes that her mother did not want to die and that her mother killed the cat not because she hated it but because she was afraid to face death alone. Babe's lawyer, motivated beyond his natural abilities by a personal vendetta, establishes that Babe was a battered wife and that it is in everyone's best interest not to charge her with any crime. As the play ends, the three sisters are, for the moment, laughing.

The MaGrath sisters deal with crises as required by their identities as faded Southern gentry. No longer wealthy, the family still values manners, education, and appearances. With the ugly business of the past put more or less to right, the sisters, in their solidarity, uphold, or perhaps demolish, their identities as Southern ladies.

SUGGESTED READINGS

Guerra, Jonnie. "Beth Henley: Female Quest and the Family-Play Tradition." In *Making a Spectacle: Feminist Essays on Contemporary Women's Theater*, edited by Lynda Hart. Ann Arbor: University of Michigan Press, 1989.

Harbin, Billy J. "Familial Bonds in the Plays of Beth Henley." *Southern Quarterly* 25 (Spring, 1987): 81-94.

—*Gerald S. Argetsinger*

See also Adultery; American identity: South; Feminism

Crown of Feathers, A

AUTHOR: Isaac Bashevis Singer (1904-1991)
FIRST PUBLISHED: 1973
IDENTITIES: European American; Jewish; religion; women

"A Crown of Feathers" is the title story of a collection which won the National Book Award for 1973. Like many of Isaac Bashevis Singer's stories, it depicts an individual pulled between belief and disbelief, between the religious and the secular, and between self and others. The story concerns an orphan, Akhsa, whose own emerging identity becomes entangled with the conflicting values of her wealthy grandparents.

Her grandfather is a traditionally religious man, a community leader in the Polish village of

Krasnobród, while her grandmother, from the sophisticated city of Prague, is more worldly and possibly, it is learned after her death, a follower of false messiahs. These differences, presented very subtly at first, become more pronounced when, after her grandparents' deaths, Akhsa internalizes their warring voices.

Each voice accuses the other of being a demon, while both battle over Akhsa's soul. Her grandmother assures her that Jesus is the Messiah and encourages Akhsa to convert. As a sign, she has Akhsa rip open her pillowcase, where she finds an intricate crown of feathers topped by a tiny cross. Akhsa converts, makes an unhappy marriage with an alcoholic Polish squire, and sinks into melancholy. Her despair is not mere unhappiness, but a continuing crisis of faith. A demon tells her, "The truth is there is no truth," but her saintly grandfather appears and tells her to repent.

Her grandfather's advice leads Akhsa to return to Judaism and to seek out and marry the man her grandfather had chosen for her years before. This embittered man, however, humiliates her mercilessly. On her deathbed, Akhsa tears open her pillowcase and finds another crown of feathers, this one with the Hebrew letters for God in place of the cross. "But, she wondered, in what way was this crown more a revelation of truth than the other?"

Akhsa never grasps with certainty the truth she has sought, nor is she ever able, like Singer's Gimpel the Fool, to accept the ambiguity of uncertainty. Akhsa's conversion and subsequent exile, her repentance and journey back to her grandfather's faith—her entire life—have constituted an agonized quest for truth. Torn between two voices of authority, Akhsa has never been certain of her own voice, has never understood her own wants, needs, or beliefs. While Gimpel, when finding his vocation as wandering storyteller, ultimately finds a faith to which he can firmly adhere, Akhsa finds neither self nor truth. Moving from one pole of certain faith to its opposite, and back again, Akhsa never accepts Singer's own truth, which is that "if there is such a thing as truth it is as intricate and hidden as a crown of feathers."

SUGGESTED READINGS

Alexander, Edward. *Isaac Bashevis Singer: A Study of the Short Fiction*. Boston: Twayne, 1990.

Friedman, Lawrence S. *Understanding Isaac Bashevis Singer*. Columbia: University of South Carolina Press, 1988.

Wood, Michael. "Victims of Survival." *The New York Review of Books*, February 7, 1974, 10-12.

—*Grace Farrell*

See also *Gimpel the Fool*; Jewish American identity; Singer, Isaac Bashevis

Crucible, The

AUTHOR: Arthur Miller (1915-   )
FIRST PRODUCED: 1953; first published, 1953
IDENTITIES: European American; family; religion

Set in Salem, Massachusetts, during the witch-hunts of 1592 but full of allusions to Senator Joseph McCarthy and the House Committee on Un-American Activities' persecutions of the 1950's, Arthur Miller's *The Crucible* is a masterful play that ultimately transcends both historical contexts with its message of resistance to tyranny. The play focuses on the moral struggles of John Proctor, a New England farmer, who is sucked into a witch-hunt that rages through his Puritan society. By deftly juxtaposing the religious paranoia that permeates a Fundamentalist community suddenly convinced that the devil is loose in its village with the less lofty but more powerful forces of human greed, envy, and revenge, Miller exposes the core of hypocrisy that is cloaked by the guise of authority.

The play opens in the attic bedroom of the Reverend Samuel Parris, minister of Salem, the night after Parris surprised his daughter Betty, his beautiful and sensual niece Abigail, and a number of other girls from Salem village dancing in the woods (a forbidden act). Parris all too quickly assumes that the girls have been bewitched, and soon Parris' bedroom is packed with Salemites convinced that witchcraft is afoot. As the act closes, the logic and sense of Proctor's doubts are overwhelmed by hysteria as Abigail and Betty launch the witch-hunt by screaming out the names of those who have supposedly consorted with the devil. They initially name, for the most part, those of the community who are vulnerable, and they name names in order to escape punishment. This pattern of accusation and betrayal has a close resemblance to McCarthy's anti-communist tactics.

The remainder of the play pits Salem's authority structure, as typified by Deputy Governor Danforth with his smug self-righteousness, against its helpless individual victims. Since "the accuser is always holy," the innocent—Proctor, Proctor's wife Elizabeth, and the saintly Rebecca Nurse—have no defense. It is clear that the accusations have nothing to do with witchcraft but are the result of long-standing animosities. Abigail, who has had a sexual relationship with Proctor, wants Proctor for herself, and so Elizabeth is named a witch. The play's climax comes as Proctor, who has long struggled with the guilt over his infidelity and with his powerlessness to assert his innocence in the face of an implacable and tyrannous authority, realizes that he cannot destroy his true identity by signing a false confession: "Because it is my name! Because I cannot have another in my life!" The play's final image of an innocent Proctor going to his unjust hanging was to be uncannily echoed three years after the play was written when Miller was called before the House Committee on Un-American Activities and convicted of contempt of Congress.

SUGGESTED READINGS

Bigsby, C. W. E. "Arthur Miller." *Williams, Miller, Albee*. Vol. 2 in *A Critical Introduction to Twentieth-Century American Drama*. Cambridge, England: Cambridge University Press, 1984.
Martine, James J. *The Crucible: Politics, Property, and Pretense*. New York: Twayne, 1993.
Miller, Arthur. *Timebends: A Life*. New York: Grove Press, 1987.

—Gregory W. Lanier

See also Censorship of literature; *Death of a Salesman*; Miller, Arthur; Puritan and Protestant tradition

Cruelty

AUTHOR: Ai (1947-   )
FIRST PUBLISHED: 1973
IDENTITIES: African American; Asian American; European American; multiracial; Native American

Ai is more concerned with social class than with racial identity or gender in *Cruelty*. The book is a series of poetic dramatic monologues spoken by members of the underclass in America. It is a searing indictment of societies that permit the existence of poverty.

Life, itself, is cruel for the speakers in *Cruelty*. The speaker in "Tenant Farmer" has no crops. The couple in "Starvation" have no food. In "Abortion," a man finds the fetus of his son wrapped in wax paper and thinks: "the poor have no children, just small people/ and there is room for only one man in this house." Men and women become alienated from each other in these conditions. The speaker in "Young Farm Woman Alone" no longer wants a man. In "Recapture," a man finds and beats a woman who has run off from him. In "Prostitute," a woman kills her husband, then goes out to get revenge on the men who use her.

Out of the agony of their lives, some of Ai's characters achieve transcendence through love. The couple in "Anniversary" has managed to stay together, providing a home for their son for many years, in spite of never having "anything but hard times." In "The Country Midwife: A Day," the midwife delivers a woman's child for "the third time between abortions." Beneath the mother "a stain . . . spreads over the sheet." Crying out to the Lord, the midwife lets her bleed. Ending the cycles of pregnancy for the woman, in an act of mercy, the midwife takes upon herself the cross of guilt and suffering.

Ai extends her study of the causes and consequences of poverty to other times and places in the second half of *Cruelty*. The figure in "The Hangman" smells "the whole Lebanese coast/ in the upraised arms of Kansas." In "Cuba, 1962" a farmer cuts off his dead wife's feet, allowing her blood to mix with the sugar cane he will sell in the village, so everyone can taste his grief. Medieval peasants are evoked by "The Corpse Hauler's Elegy," although the plague victims he carries could also be contemporary.

Violence increases in the final poems of the book, a sign of the violence in societies that perpetuate social injustice. In "The Deserter," a soldier kills the woman who gave him shelter in order to leave everything of himself behind. In "The Hitchhiker," a woman is raped and killed by a psychopath in Arizona. In "The Child Beater," a mother beats her seven-year-old daughter with a belt, then gets out her "dog's chain leash." Ai has compassion for all of these people—including the killers—and she demands compassion for them from her readers.

SUGGESTED READINGS
Ai. "On Being One-Half Japanese, One-Eighth Choctaw, One Quarter Black, and One-Sixteenth Irish." *Ms.* 6 (May, 1978): 58.
Cuddihy, Michael, and Lawrence Kearney. "Ai: An Interview." *Ironwood* 12 (Winter, 1978): 27-34.
—*James Green*

See also Ai; *Greed*; Mixed race and identity

Crusade for Justice: The Autobiography of Ida B. Wells
AUTHOR: Ida B. Wells-Barnett (1862-1931)
FIRST PUBLISHED: 1970
IDENTITIES: African American; women

Crusade for Justice: The Autobiography of Ida B. Wells is the inspiring story of an African American feminist and civil rights leader. She documents her individual struggles, her accomplishments, and her major activities to promote equality for women and African Americans. Born into slavery in 1862, she lived through the Reconstruction era after the U. S. Civil War, the battle for suffrage, World War I, and its aftermath. Ida B. Wells-Barnett's reflections provide a critical review of American racial and sexual relations. She did not simply observe the American scene; she also altered it as a leader in the women's movement and the African American Civil Rights movement.

The autobiography is especially important in documenting the widespread patterns of lynchings of African American men by white mobs. In protests and writings about these horrors, Wells-Barnett fought against any acceptance of these illegal and violent acts. She struggled with many people to have her radical and unflinching stands represented. Her struggles included arguments with other leaders such as the suffragist Susan B. Anthony, the civil rights activist W. E. B. Du Bois, and the African American leader Booker T. Washington. She presents her side of these differences in the autobiography, which reflects her occasional unwillingness to compromise and her hot temper.

Wells-Barnett published in formats such as small-circulation newspapers, pamphlets, and journals, so the autobiography is vital in providing obscure information about her life and ideas. She did not complete the autobiography, however, and her daughter Alfreda Duster helped fill in many missing pieces for the publication of the manuscript almost four decades after her mother's death. In addition, Wells-Barnett lost many of her writings in two different fires, so her daughter did not have access to the full range of her mother's publications and thoughts. As a result, major areas of Wells-Barnett's life and ideas that are not covered or explained. Wells-Barnett's life is remarkable in its courage and influence. She refused to be limited by her battles with personal poverty, sexism, and racism, and her valiant spirit is apparent in her life story.

SUGGESTED READINGS
Aptheker, Bettina. Introduction to *Lynching and Rape: An Exchange of Views*, by Jane Addams and Ida B. Wells-Barnett. Occasional Papers Series 25. San Jose, Calif.: American Institute for Marxist Studies, 1977.

Wells-Barnett, Ida B. *The Memphis Diary of Ida B. Wells*. Edited by Miriam DeCosta-Willis. Boston: Beacon Press, 1995.

—Mary Jo Deegan

See also African American identity; American identity: Midwest; Civil Rights movement; Feminism

Cruz, Sor Juana Inés de la (Juana Inés de Asbaje y Ramírez de Santillana)

BORN: San Miguel Neplanta, Mexico; November, 1648
DIED: Mexico City, Mexico; April 17, 1695
PRINCIPAL WORKS: *Inundación castálida*, 1689 (Castalian flood); *Segundo volumen de las obras*, 1692 (second volume of the works); *Fama y obras póstumas*, 1700 (fame and posthumous works)
IDENTITIES: Latino; religion; women
SIGNIFICANT ACHIEVEMENT: Sor Juana is considered the major lyric poet of colonial Spanish America and was the first author in the New World to express belief in the intellectual rights and dignity of women.

Juana Inés de Asbaje y Ramírez de Santillana was born in colonial Mexico, a closed society dominated by the Catholic church and by men. There was little room for an intelligent, educated woman. Reading by the age of three, as a child she pestered her mother, pleading to be dressed as a boy and sent to Mexico City to study at the university. Sor Juana was, however, obliged to educate herself by reading in her grandfather's library.

Sent to Mexico City to live with relatives at age eight, Sor Juana was invited into the court of the viceroy as an intellectual companion for his wife. At court, Sor Juana wrote poetry for social and political events associated with the court and the clergy. From the beginning she displayed mastery of all forms of baroque poetry, using metaphors from her studies in music, painting, mathematics, logic, theology, and physics. The poetic style of her time was learned and complex; she was able to meet this challenge.

At seventeen, Sor Juana entered the convent of St. Jerome, taking her religious name, by which she would be best known. At the convent she enjoyed some freedom to continue her education through reading. She eventually amassed a library of four thousand volumes. She also continued writing poetry, prose, and drama. From the first, her writing expressed her strong belief in the moral and intellectual equality of women and their right to an education. A famous quatrain accuses "Stupid men who accuse/ Women without any grounds,/ Without seeing that you are the cause/ Of the very thing that you blame." In a love poem she claims: "Neither being a woman nor absent/ Keeps me from loving you,/ For you know that souls/ Ignore distance and sex." In poems written for the feast of the Virgin Mary, Sor Juana presents the mother of Jesus as a "professor in the highest theological chair," and "the great female astronomer."

In 1690, Sor Juana wrote a criticism, in the form of a letter, of a sermon delivered by a famous Jesuit scholar. She contradicts his interpretation of a difficult and minor theological point and cannot restrain herself from commenting, "just for me to dare to criticize Father Viera's sermon must be quite mortifying, for so famous a man . . . to see that an ignorant woman is so daring, a woman for whom theology is so alien a style of thought, so far removed from females." Her words drew tremendous criticism, particularly of her daring as a woman, but the bishop of Puebla wrote a letter in her defense in the guise of an admirer, a nun by the name of Sister Filotea. Sor Juana's famous response to him defended her right to an intellectual life, even as a woman and a nun. Nevertheless, shortly afterward, pressured by religious authorities, she sold her books, jewels, and musical and scientific instruments and devoted herself to the religious life. Two years later, after nursing some nuns who were dying during an epidemic, Sor Juana died.

SUGGESTED READINGS

Marting, Diane E. *Women Writers of Spanish America*. Westport, Conn.: Greenwood Press, 1987.

Paz, Octavio. *Sor Juana: Or, The Traps of Faith*. Translated by Margaret Sayers Peden. Cambridge, Mass.: Harvard University Press, 1988.

Sole, Carlos A., and Maria Isabel Abreu. *Latin American Writers*. New York: Charles Scribner's Sons, 1989.

—Robert H. Schwarz

See also Catholicism; Censorship of literature; Feminism; Intelligence; Religion and identity; Women and identity

Cruz, Sor Juana Inés de la, poetry of

AUTHOR: Sor Juana Inés de la Cruz (Juana Inés de Asbaje y Ramírez de Santillana, 1648-1695)

FIRST PUBLISHED: *Inundación castálida*, 1689 (castalian flood)

IDENTITIES: Latino; religion; women

Sor Juana Inés de la Cruz was known throughout seventeenth century Mexico and Spain for her skill in almost all forms of baroque poetry: pastoral poems, sonnets, love poems, romances, religious poetry in several traditional forms, portrait poetry, and drama. In poetry written mostly for religious and civil ceremonies, she cleverly displays the customary poetic devices of the age—parallelism, oxymoron, paradox, mythological allusion (even in her religious poetry), and metaphors drawn from physics, mathematics, and music. A birthday poem states: "Let your age, my lord, so greatly exceed/ The capacity embraced by zero/ That the *ars combinatoria* of Kircher/ Are unable to multiply its quantity." Even her love poetry is intellectual and expressed in careful, mannered, and elegant language. A love poem begins: "Halt, reflection of my elusive love,/ Image of the charm I most adore,/ Lovely illusion for whom I gaily die,/ Sweet fiction for whom I sadly live."

What sets her poetry apart from all other of the time is her theme: the equality of women and their right to an education and an intellectual life. A love poem that begins in a very traditional way: "Feliciano adores me, and I abhor him;/ Lisardo abhors me, and I adore him" ends with a surprisingly feminist declaration: "But I, as the better alternative, choose/ To serve him whom I don't love, against my will/ Rather than be, of him who doesn't love me, the despised victim."

Even in her religious poetry, Sor Juana employs intellectual metaphors and declares a feminist theme. A poem dedicated to Saint Catherine, a martyr of the church, declares: "By a woman they are convinced,/ All the sages of Egypt,/ By her proof that sex/ Is not the essence of sense . . . / She studies, argues, and teaches/ And is of service to the Church,/ For God doesn't want her to be ignorant/ Since He made her a rational being." Sor Juana's insistence on an intellectual and rational view of life, divorced from emotional and sexual bias, shapes her long poem *First Dream*. In this philosophical discourse, the soul, after the body has fallen asleep, attempts to grasp creation intuitively. Failing this, it tries again, using Aristotle's dialectical method, moving from the simple to the more complex. Failing again, the soul admits the impossibility of complete comprehension of the universe, but in its failure recognizes the value of intellectual effort in giving meaning to life, as Sor Juana herself recognized.

SUGGESTED READINGS

Cohen, J. M. *The Penguin Book of Spanish Verse*. New York: Penguin, 1956.

Flynn, Gerard. *Sor Juana Inés de la Cruz*. New York: Twayne, 1971.

Paz, Octavio. *Sor Juana: Or, The Traps of Faith*. Translated by Margaret Sayers Peden. Cambridge, Mass.: Harvard University Press, 1988.

—Robert H. Schwarz

See also Catholicism; Feminism; Women and identity

Cuban Americans. *See* Caribbean American literature

Cullen, Countée

BORN: New York, New York, or possibly Louisville, Kentucky; May 30, 1903
DIED: New York, New York; January 9, 1946
PRINCIPAL WORKS: *Color*, 1925; *The Ballad of the Brown Girl: An Old Ballad Retold*, 1927; *Copper Sun*, 1927; *Caroling Dusk: An Anthology of Verse by Negro Poets*, 1927 (editor); *The Black Christ and Other Poems*, 1929; *One Way to Heaven*, 1932; *The Medea and Some Poems*, 1935; *The Lost Zoo (A Rhyme for the Young, but Not Too Young)*, 1940; *On These I Stand: An Anthology of the Best Poems of Countée Cullen*, 1947
IDENTITIES: African American; Northeast
SIGNIFICANT ACHIEVEMENT: Cullen, one of the most prolific poets of the Harlem Renaissance, combined English poetic styles with racial themes and identities.

Countée Cullen recognized early in his life that he wanted to use poetry to express his belief that a poet's skin color should not dictate style and subject matter in a poem. He began writing poetry while in high school. Cullen, a Phi Beta Kappa honoree from New York University, had already published *Color* by the time he entered graduate school at Harvard University. With a master's in English and three additional books of poetry, Cullen was widely known as the unofficial poet laureate of the Harlem Renaissance.

In his introduction to *Caroling Dusk: An Anthology of Verse by Negro Poets*, Cullen set forth many of the ideas that shaped his identity as a poet and an African American. He believed that poetry elevated any race and that African American poets could benefit from using the rich traditions of English and American verse. Cullen also chose not to include dialect poetry in his anthology, viewing this style as out-of-date, restrictive, and best left to the white poets who were still using it.

Cullen was not ashamed of his race, nor did he deliberately seek white approval. He did feel that he should be receptive to many ideas to enhance his poetry. Many of his poems, such as "Incident," "From the Dark Tower," and "Colors," protest racism and bigotry. However, in his collection *The Black Christ and Other Poems*, themes of love and death prevail. Such themes show the influence of the British Romantic poets John Keats and Percy Bysshe Shelley. Keats especially was Cullen's artistic mentor. Cullen records his response to having visited Keats's grave in "Endymion," a poem celebrating the power of Keats's lyricism.

Cullen's use of genteel traditions and the black experience caused dilemmas and conflicts throughout his writing career. Critics praised Cullen for his skillful use of the sonnet form, but they castigated him when he did not use racial experiences as the primary source of his themes. However, even as he cautioned Harlem Renaissance poets about excessive use of racial themes, he published a novel about Harlem characters, *One Way to Heaven*.

From 1934 until his death, Cullen taught French and English at Frederick Douglass Junior High School, guiding students in the traditions that made him a celebrated poet.

SUGGESTED READINGS

Davis, Arthur P. *From the Dark Tower: Afro-American Writers, 1900-1960*. Washington, D.C.: Howard University Press, 1974.

Huggins, Nathan. *Harlem Renaissance*. New York: Oxford University Press, 1971.

Lewis, David Levering. *When Harlem Was in Vogue*. New York: Alfred A. Knopf, 1981.

Turner, Darwin T. *In a Minor Chord: Three Afro-American Writers and Their Search for Identity*. Carbondale: Southern Illinois University Press, 1971.

—*Australia Tarver*

See also African American identity; Harlem Renaissance; *On These I Stand*

D

Daggers and Javelins: Essays, 1974-1979

Author: Amiri Baraka (LeRoi Jones, 1934-   )
First published: 1984
Identities: African American

The essays and lectures collected in *Daggers and Javelins: Essays, 1974-1979* represent Amiri Baraka's vigorous attempt to identify an African American revolutionary tradition that could parallel anticolonial struggles in Third World countries of Africa, Asia, and South America. Baraka applies a Marxist analysis to African American literature in these essays.

Having become disappointed with the progress of the Black Power movement and its emphasis on grassroots electoral politics, Baraka came to Marxism with the zeal of a new convert. "The essays of the earliest part of this period," he writes, "are overwhelmingly political in the most overt sense." While some of the essays in *Daggers and Javelins* address jazz, film, and writers of the Harlem Renaissance, all of them do so with the purpose of assessing what Baraka calls their potential to contribute to a revolutionary struggle.

In "The Revolutionary Tradition in Afro-American Literature," Baraka distinguishes between the authentic folk and vernacular expression of African American masses and the poetry and prose produced by middle-class writers in imitation of prevailing literary standards. Considering the slave narratives of Frederick Douglass and others as the beginnings of a genuine African American literature, he criticizes works that promote individualism or are merely "a distraction, an ornament." Similarly, "Afro-American Literature and Class Struggle" and other essays consider how the economic structure of society affects the production and the appreciation of art. "Notes on the History of African/Afro-American Culture" interprets the theoretical writings of Karl Marx and Friedrich Engels and draws parallels between colonized African societies and the suppression of African American artistic expression by the American cultural mainstream.

Broadening his scope in essays on African and Caribbean authors, Baraka suggests that figures such as the Kenyan novelist Ngugi wa Thiong'o and the poet Aimé Césaire from Martinique can provide models for how African American artists can escape being co-opted into an elite that supports the status quo and, instead, produce art that offers a "cathartic revelation of reality" useful in promoting social change.

Suggested readings

Reilly, Charlie, ed. *Conversations with Amiri Baraka*. Jackson: University Press of Mississippi, 1994.

Tate, Greg. "Growing Up in Public: Amiri Baraka Changes His Mind." *Flyboy in the Buttermilk: Essays on Contemporary America*. New York: Simon & Schuster, 1992.

—Lorenzo Thomas

See also African American identity; Baraka, Amiri; *Blues People*; *Dutchman*; *Selected Poetry of Amiri Baraka/LeRoi Jones*

Dakota: A Spiritual Geography

Author: Kathleen Norris (1947-   )
First published: 1993
Identities: European American; Midwest; religion

In *Dakota: A Spiritual Geography*, Kathleen Norris writes about the stark, scarcely populated landscapes of western North and South Dakota. Norris writes of a harsh and beautiful country, of small towns rich in immigrant traditions, of a Benedictine monastery as sacred as the grasslands surrounding it, and of her journey toward constructing a literary and spiritual life.

Dakota, a nonfiction work, is part autobiography, part religious meditation, and part social history. The book captures the specific character of the European American immigrants who settled and still inhabit the western Dakotas. The western Dakotas share a terrain and an identity different than their eastern counterpoints. These isolated places share particularly barren winters and fierce summers. The people who live there are insular and fiercely independent. According to Norris, the western Dakotas are often presented as lacking physical beauty and culture.

Without ever leaving the landscape behind, Norris subtly inverts what is commonly regarded as lack and reveals the area's hidden plenitude. What others might call deprivation—isolation, lack of airports and symphony halls, small town life, harsh winters, monastic discipline—she reimagines as privilege. Norris' definition of spiritual identity and conversion is hard-won and perhaps unsurpassed in contemporary American letters. Norris writes about being an oblate, a lay member of a Benedictine monastery in western North Dakota, offering a rare and honest glimpse into American Catholic, monastic spiritual traditions. Norris also writes about her work as a lay preacher in a small, Protestant church in South Dakota, affirming the importance of such communities. *Dakota* is almost an elegiac work, written about communities that have survived rigorous demands of weather, landscape, and the changing American culture. She writes with an awareness, however, of what the threatened loss of western Dakota communities, and perhaps communities like them all over the country, might mean.

For Norris, external geography shapes internal geography. One's external landscapes shape one's internal senses of time and place, influence one's view of material goods, and shape one's ways of talking and acting. The landscapes of the western Dakotas are different from any other American landscapes—so, too, must be the inner landscapes of those who live there. *Dakota* speaks of an American need to construct a sense of soul or identity somehow at peace with the geographical places and the human communities where one lives.

SUGGESTED READINGS

Klinkenborg, Verlyn. "The Prairie as an Act of Devotion." Review of *Dakota: A Spiritual Geography*, by Kathleen Norris. *The New York Times Book Review*, February 14, 1993, 8.

New Yorker, The. Review of *Dakota: A Spiritual Geography*, by Kathleen Norris. March 15, 1993, 123.

—*Jane Hoogestraat*

See also American identity: Midwest; American identity: West and the frontier; Catholicism; Environment and identity; Religion and identity; Rural life

Dance and the Railroad, The

AUTHOR: David Henry Hwang (1957-   )
FIRST PRODUCED: 1983; first published, 1981
IDENTITIES: Chinese American; West and Southwest

The Dance and the Railroad is a history play based on the Chinese railroad workers' strike of 1867. It reveals a significant event in the Chinese American past, rejecting the stereotype of submissive coolies and depicting assertive men who demanded their rights in spite of great personal risk. Originally intended as a contribution toward the reclaiming of the Chinese American past, it accomplished much broader artistic goals.

Ma, a young Chinese emigrant who has been in America only four weeks, comes to warn Lone, a performer, that the other Chinese do not like his superior attitude. Hired to build the railroad across the Sierras, they are now in the fourth day of a strike against the labor practices of the "white devils." The Chinese have demanded an eight-hour workday and a fourteen-dollar-a-week increase in pay.

Lone is estranged from the other Chinese because he refuses to waste time drinking and gambling and instead practices the traditional Chinese opera. Captivated by Lone's beautiful dance, Ma decides to become a performer when he returns to China a wealthy man. Lone scoffs at Ma's naïve beliefs that America is a place with a mythical Gold Mountain, that his cheating Chinese coworkers are his friends, and that he will ever be able to portray the great Gwan Gung, god of fighters. Lone tells Ma that if he is to succeed he must face reality and willingly accept being shunned by the "already dead" Chinese men. Undaunted by this challenge, Ma begins to practice Chinese opera. Ma is subsequently shocked, however, to learn that if he works hard, he might successfully portray the Second Clown. Lone reveals how he spent eight years in opera school training to play Gwan Gung, only to be "kidnapped" by his parents and sent to the Sierras to work. Ma is determined and practices by spending the night in the "locust" position, a metaphor for the emigrant awakening. Lone returns, reporting that the strike is over. The Chinese have achieved their eight-hour day but only an eight-dollar-a-week raise. Ma finally realizes that, although a few Chinese men in America might achieve their dreams, most become dead to China. Ma and Lone improvise a Chinese opera revealing their voyages to America and experiences on the Gold Mountain. When the mountain fights back, Lone is exhilarated but Ma falls, his spirit broken. Now a realist, Ma returns to work with the "already dead" men, while Lone continues practicing for the Chinese opera.

David Henry Hwang contrasts two portraits of emigrant Chinese becoming Americans. Ma loses his innocence, discards his traditions, and joins the "already dead" laborers. Lone adapts Chinese mythology and tradition to his American experience. The Asian community has lauded Hwang's work, praising its depiction of the lives of Chinese Americans.

SUGGESTED READINGS

Gerard, Jeremy. "David Hwang: Riding the Hyphen." *The New York Times Magazine*, March 13, 1988, 44, 88-89.

Hwang, David Henry. Introduction to *FOB and Other Plays*, by David Henry Hwang. New York: Plume, 1990.

Street, Douglas. *David Henry Hwang*. Boise, Idaho: Boise State University Press, 1989.

—*Gerald S. Argetsinger*

See also Asian American identity: China, Japan, and Korea; Emigration and immigration; *Family Devotions*; Hwang, David Henry

Dangerous Music

AUTHOR: Jessica Tarahata Hagedorn (1949-   )
FIRST PUBLISHED: 1975
IDENTITIES: Pacific Islander; women

The poems in *Dangerous Music* were composed after Jessica Tarahata Hagedorn began "discovering myself as a Filipino-American writer" in California. Orientalist Kenneth Rexroth had placed five of her early poems in his 1973 anthology, *Four Young Women*. "The Death of Anna May Wong," included in that edition, signified the poet's rejection of Hollywood stereotypes of Asian women as demure or exotically sinister. *Dangerous Music* continues the author's search for authentic images of non-Europeans that describe her own situation as well as those of other minorities. The intensity of many of these lyrics, written while she was performing with her West Coast Gangster Choir, became a way of expressing whole dimensions of society largely ignored or misunderstood by generations of European Americans. Although on the page such poems resemble songs without music, their occasional arrangement in ballad quatrains sometimes imitates blues music. The influence of Latino or African music is visible in the more jagged, syncopated lines of such poems as "Latin Music in New York" or "Canto Negro."

The cultural environment that is so much a part of the voices she assumes in *Dangerous Music* can readily be imagined. "Something About You," for example, affectionately connects Hagedorn with fellow artists Ntozake Shange and Thulani Davis, with whom she performed poems set to music for New York's Public Theater. Other poems identify her with Puerto Rican or Cuban musicians. More typical poems, however, describe a love-hate relationship with the American Dream. In "Natural Death," a Cuban refugee seems satisfied with fantasies of cosmetic splendor, though warned about bodies buried in saran wrap on a California beach. Loneliness and anger are conveyed by the mocking refrain: "o the grandeur of it." Yet the Philippines, which is remembered in "Sometimes" ("life is very cheap"), is equally far from being ideal. "Justifiable Homicide" warns of urban dangers anywhere in the world, when differences among people become cause for mutual indifference.

The only defense against the insanity that comes from cultural and economic stress is found in singing, according to "Sorcery" and "Easter Sunday," even if the songs themselves are passionate outcries of pain, not lullabies. The unacceptable alternative to release through song is to surrender one's memories of better dreams or, as in the case of "The Blossoming of Bongbong," the one prose fantasy included with these poems, total forgetfulness of one's personal identity.

SUGGESTED READINGS

Casper, Leonard. *Sunsurfers Seen from Afar: Critical Essays 1991-1996*. Metro Manila, Philippines: Anvil, 1996.

Zapanta Manlapaz, Edna. *Songs of Ourselves*. Metro Manila, Philippines: Anvil, 1994.

—Leonard Casper

See also Asian American identity: Pacific Islands; Brainard, Cecilia Manguerra; Multiculturalism; Rosca, Ninotchka

Darkness Visible: A Memoir of Madness

AUTHOR: William Styron (1925-   )
FIRST PUBLISHED: 1990
IDENTITIES: Disease; European American

Toward the end of 1985, Pulitzer Prize-winning author William Styron slowly fell into a deep state of depression. He first made his condition public in 1988, when he published an editorial in *The New York Times* on the suicide of Auschwitz survivor and noted author Primo Levi. In the editorial, Styron makes the case that Levi's death does not have moral implications and that depression can lead inexorably to suicide.

Styron also further argues that many people do survive depression, even its most devastating forms. Time, he claims, is the key. After publishing several articles in *Vanity Fair* in 1989 on his bout with depression, Styron completed his writings on depression with a longer personal narrative, *Darkness Visible: A Memoir of Madness*. A concise, harrowing recounting of his ordeal, *Darkness Visible* employs an artist's dexterity with language to attempt to describe, understand, and delineate the many facets of depression.

Depression affects people across boundaries of sex, race, age, and class. It has different manifestations and different origins—perhaps as many as it has sufferers. Understanding that, Styron avoids making grand claims and generalizations about the illness. Instead, he tells his story, and the stories of a few famous writers—Albert Camus, Randall Jarrell, Art Buchwald, and others—trying to illustrate by example the experience of the disease.

Darkness Visible discusses possible causes of depression, and it describes various forms of treatment, including psychotherapy, drug therapy, and hospitalization. Usually, a combination of these treatments are used to fight depression, but since time is a key element in overcoming and in succumbing to depression, fighting it is a perilous, anxious battle.

Feeling on the verge of suicide, Styron had himself institutionalized near the end of December, 1985. After more than six weeks in the hospital, which he likens to a stay in Purgatory, he emerged, no longer a threat to himself and ready to continue the lifelong struggle against depression, a condition that recurs with some regularity in its sufferers.

Darkness Visible is addressed to people who have been affected, directly or indirectly, by depression. It is not a medical book, and it is not a guide to surviving or beating depression. Rather, it is a story, told by one of America's most gifted writers, of how a person can, almost unwittingly, sink into the depths of emotional darkness and how one person came through it, alive, stronger, and determined to continue to fight the disease for the rest of his life. Styron's great message in *Darkness Visible* is that depression is conquerable. This message is reassuring not as a promise or an admonition but as a heartfelt testament of his own experience.

SUGGESTED READINGS

Cronkite, Kathy. *On the Edge of Darkness: Conversations About Conquering Depression*. New York: Doubleday, 1994.

Karp, David Allen. *Speaking of Sadness: Depression, Disconnection, and the Meanings of Illness*. New York: Oxford University Press, 1996.

Wurtzel, Elizabeth. *Prozac Nation: Young and Depressed in America*. Boston: Houghton Mifflin, 1994.

—*Chris Freeman*

See also Mental disorders; Plath, Sylvia; Sexton, Anne

Daughters, I Love You

AUTHOR: Linda Hogan (1947-   )

FIRST PUBLISHED: 1981

IDENTITIES: Native American; women

Daughters, I Love You is a small, tightly interwoven collection of nine poems addressing the issue of the nuclear age. The work might even be considered a single long poem in several parts all thematically centered on this issue. Linda Hogan's dedication offers the book to Navajo women fighting environmental exploitation, to Sister Rosalie Bertell, a fellow participant at a protest encampment in South Dakota, to gentle women throughout the world, and to the author's daughters. References to all of these women recur throughout the poems. In two of the poems the author ends with the title phrase, "Daughters, I love you." The poems celebrate gentleness as the speaker sees gentleness as a paradoxical source of strength in opposing all forms of violence, and especially the mammoth violence of the nuclear age. Consistently the poems celebrate the peacemaking and nurturing qualities of women of all ages and throughout the world.

The poems in *Daughters, I Love You* frequently refer to specific events. For instance, many allude to the atomic bombing of Japan. One focuses on the site of an accident at an atomic reactor in Idaho, and at least one grew directly out of the experience of a peace encampment to protest the presence of nuclear missiles and bombs in the sacred Black Hills of South Dakota. The poet's strategy in most of the poems is to weave related images around a central theme. For example, in "Black Hills Survival Gathering, 1980," the image and feeling of sunrise are associated with historical memory of Hiroshima, the presence of a Buddhist monk protesting nuclear war, and the appearance of a bomber flying overhead.

While they might loosely be categorized as poems of protest, the works in *Daughters, I Love You* are strongly unified in the underlying spiritual dimension the author sees as the most significant response she can make to the evil of pure destructiveness represented by the nuclear world. Thus, in "A Prayer for Men and Women" the speaker counters the dreams of men for power and poison with women's quiet work and prayers. Likewise, in "Idaho Falls, 1961" the speaker contrasts the violence of the nuclear explosion with the gentle approach of a woman going into a barn and caring for animals. This poem is also one that could be termed a poem of witness, for it records and brings to light a nuclear explosion that was downplayed in the media at a time when nuclear power was promoted as a miracle technology.

SUGGESTED READINGS

Ackerberg, Peggy Maddux. "Breaking Boundaries: Writing Past Gender, Genre, and Genocide in Linda Hogan." *Studies in American Indian Literatures* 6, no. 3 (1994): 7-14.

Hogan, Linda. " 'A heart made out of crickets': An Interview with Linda Hogan." Interview by Bo Scholer. *The Journal of Ethnic Studies* 16, no. 1 (1988): 107-117.

_____. "An Interview with Linda Hogan." *The Missouri Review* 17, no. 2 (1994): 109-124.

_____. "Linda Hogan." Interview by Patricia Clark Smith. In *This Is About Vision: Interviews with Southwestern Writers*, edited by William Balassi, John F. Crawford, and Annie O. Esturoy. Albuquerque: University of New Mexico Press, 1990.

—Helen Jaskoski

See also *Calling Myself Home*; Feminism; Native American identity; Poverty; World War II

Davies, Robertson

BORN: Thamesville, Ontario, Canada; August 28, 1913
DIED: Toronto, Canada; December 2, 1995
PRINCIPAL WORKS: The Salterton trilogy: *Tempest-Tost*, 1951; *Leaven of Malice*, 1954; *A Mixture of Frailties*, 1958; the Deptford trilogy: *Fifth Business*, 1970; *The Manticore*, 1972; *World of Wonders*, 1975; the Cornish trilogy: *The Rebel Angels*, 1981; *What's Bred in the Bone*, 1985; *The Lyre of Orpheus*, 1988
IDENTITIES: Canada; religion
SIGNIFICANT ACHIEVEMENT: Davies was a major Canadian novelist of the postwar era.

Son of a widely influential and prominent newspaper publisher, Robertson Davies was raised in a creative and intellectual family, which contrasted with the culturally impoverished small town in which he spent his early years. Davies succeeded in overcoming these two early obstacles—a

Canadian author Robertson Davies has written about spiritual identity in a modern context.
(Jerry Bauer)

hugely successful father and a narrow-minded, provincial society—to forge his own identity within a newly cosmopolitan Canada.

As a young adult, Davies made his way to Toronto and then to England, where he took a degree from Oxford and joined the prestigious Old Vic theater company. He and his new wife returned to Canada in 1940, where he began to form his identity as a Canadian man of letters, writing a popular newspaper column as the fictive Samuel Marchbanks. This column, which examined the foibles of Canadian society, assumed a Canadian readership that was growing less narrow and provincial. Although Davies also made a significant contribution to indigenous Canadian theater as a playwright and producer, his identity as a man of letters took precedence when he was appointed the first master of the newly established Massey College, which was part of a general expansion of educational and cultural life in Canada.

Davies' identity as a satiric author underwent a significant change with *Fifth Business*, arguably his greatest novel, and one which not only established him as a major Canadian novelist but also brought him a cult following in the United States. With this novel, the first of the Dept ford trilogy, Davies revealed a deep interest in the dark side, forging an identity as a serious romancer and as a mage or latter-day Merlin, complete with flowing silver beard and magisterial cane. Davies' later novels, featuring strange characters and Gothic doings, jolted Canadian literature out of its previously conventional realism. Deploying Jungian psychology to explore what he felt was the neglected spiritual side of the Canadian psyche, Davies was also inspired by the Jungian concept of individuation, which he used to develop his idea of the emergent self, that is, the self that comes into its own. This theme of individuation was important for Canadian society, whose ties to England and proximity to the United States frequently overwhelmed its sense of national identity.

SUGGESTED READINGS

Davis, J. Madison, ed. *Conversations with Robertson Davies*. Jackson: University Press of Mississippi, 1989.

Grant, Judith Skelton. *Robertson Davies, Man of Myth*. New York: Viking Press, 1994.

Peterman, Michael. *Robertson Davies*. Boston: Twayne, 1986.

—*Margaret Boe Birns*

See also Atwood, Margaret; Canadian identity; Jung, Carl Gustav

Davis, Angela Y.

BORN: Birmingham, Alabama; January 26, 1944

PRINCIPAL WORKS: *If They Come in the Morning: Voices of Resistance*, 1971 (with others); *Angela Davis: An Autobiography*, 1974; *Women, Race, and Class*, 1981; *Women, Culture, and Politics*, 1989

IDENTITIES: African American; women

SIGNIFICANT ACHIEVEMENT: Davis' autobiographical work explores the development of the African American political consciousness in the late twentieth century.

Primarily known as a political activist, Angela Davis began writing as a result of her activities within the Black Liberation movement of the late 1960's and early 1970's. Her work consistently explores the destructive influences of racism, sexism, and economic inequality on the development of African Americans, women, and the poor. Davis felt the full impact of racism beginning with her childhood, having been born and raised in segregated Birmingham. The racial inequality that prevailed particularly in the American South did much to shape her consciousness as an African American. In her autobiography, for example, she expresses her determination as a child to "never harbor or express the desire to be white" in spite of the fact that most whites lived what in comparison to hers was a privileged life.

Davis attended Elizabeth Irwin High School in New York. She studied philosophy at Brandeis University, the Sorbonne in Paris, the University of Frankfurt, and the University of California at

San Diego. In 1968, she officially joined the Communist Party, having concluded that "the emancipation of all oppressed groups" could be achieved through the emancipation of the proletariat.

As a result of her membership in the Communist Party, the Board of Regents of the University of California fired Davis from her teaching position at UCLA in 1969; she was reinstated after a trial. Charged with murder and kidnapping in connection with an escape attempt from a California courthouse, Davis was arrested and imprisoned in 1970 after spending several months on the run. She was tried and acquitted in 1972.

Davis' early writings center on the difficulties African Americans face in trying to establish a positive African American identity and political consciousness within a system that is racially oppressive. In *If They Come in the Morning: Voices of Resistance* and *Angela Davis: An Autobiography*, Davis presents a personal account of the ways the legal and penal systems stifle the African American community and political expression. In her autobiography, she touches on what it means to be an African American woman in a racially and sexually divided society. She explores this issue in greater detail in her works on the problems of racial division within the women's movement, *Women, Race, and Class* and *Women, Culture, and Politics*. Many critics claim that in presenting her ideas from a decidedly Marxist perspective, Davis deprives her writing of personal insight. Most contend, however, that in spite of her ideological viewpoint, she gives a unique and passionate voice to the experience of African American women.

SUGGESTED READINGS

Ashman, Charles R. *The People vs. Angela Davis*. New York: Pinnacle, 1972.
Jackson, George. *Soledad Brother*. New York: Coward-McCann, 1970.
Smith, Nelda J. *From Where I Sat*. New York: Vantage, 1973.

—*Lisa R. Aunkst*

See also African American identity; *Angela Davis: An Autobiography*; Civil Rights movement; Feminism

Day of the Locust, The

AUTHOR: Nathanael West (Nathan Weinstein, 1903-1940)
FIRST PUBLISHED: 1939
IDENTITIES: Disease; Jewish

At first titled *The Cheated*, Nathanael West's final work, *The Day of the Locust*, takes its title from the plague of locusts set upon the pharaoh in the Book of Exodus. *The Day of the Locust* leaves the reader with a pervasive sense of horror that civilization is being destroyed. All the characters in the novel are cheated; they swarm to 1930's Hollywood in search of cinematic dreams. When these dreams prove to be bogus, these characters, mostly from the lower middle class, turn violent.

The characters in *The Day of the Locust* are unreal constructions from low-budget movies. In the Hollywood "dream factory," nothing is what it appears to be. A fat lady in a yachting cap is really a housewife going shopping. An insurance agent is disguised by his Tyrolean hat. Women in slacks, bandannas, and sneakers are office workers. Faye Greener, a main character, is a trashy imitation of the 1930's Hollywood sex goddesses. Homer Simpson, another main character, is a Midwestern innocent, signified ironically by his powerful hands, which are likened not to hands of creation, building, or strength but rather to rapists' or stranglers' hands. The aspiring child star Adore Loomis is also a construction of movie imagery. His grotesque song-and-dance of sexual pain is ludicrous and painful to watch.

The identities of all characters in *The Day of the Locust* have been formed by media images. Harry Greener, Faye's father, has become "a mechanical toy that has been overwound." Greener's actions are those of a performing clown. Faye, consumed by her own dreams, continues to create them but is stopped by her own vagueness. A Tarzan-like male, a spoiled young female, and the dangers of a storm and snake are clichés of a proposed unfinished screenplay.

Even the book's personification of Satan is reduced to a media image. The dwarf Abe Kusich carries a rolled copy of *Daily Running Horse* instead of a crooked thorn stick. Abe's violence is grossly comic. When Faye's cowboy lover Earle kicks him in the stomach, Abe responds by squeezing Earle's testicles until he collapses.

The protagonist Tod Hackett is a painter and observer of the Hollywood scene. His proposed work, *The Burning of Los Angeles*, foreshadows the terrible ending of the novel, in which a crowd of the cheated are waiting for a world premier of a new film. West foreshadows the apocalyptic ending with his description of the searchlights by the theater: "great violet shafts of light moving across the evening sky in wide crazy sweeps." The crowd becomes a vicious mob and Tod is caught in the frenzy; he can no longer speak but only imitate the sound of screaming sirens. West's prophetic vision of the rage that wells up when people's identities are found to be a sham remains terrifying.

SUGGESTED READINGS

Fiedler, Leslie A. "Master of Dreams." *Partisan Review* 34, no. 3 (Summer, 1967): 339-356.

Gehman, Richard B. Introduction to *The Day of the Locust*, by Nathanael West. New York: New Directions, 1950.

Malin, Irving. *Nathanael West's Novels*. Carbondale: Southern Illinois University Press, 1972.

Reid, Randall. *The Fiction of Nathanael West*. Chicago: The University of Chicago Press, 1967.

—*Helen O'Hara Connell*

See also American identity: West and the frontier; *Catch-22*; *Miss Lonelyhearts*; *Natural, The*; West, Nathanael

Death Comes for the Archbishop

AUTHOR: Willa Cather (1873-1947)

FIRST PUBLISHED: 1927

IDENTITIES: European American; Latino; Native American; religion; West and Southwest; women

Willa Cather populates *Death Comes for the Archbishop* with characters who seem features of the landscape. They have depth but they represent types rather than particular personalities. They do not develop and change so much as they reflect a movement by the Catholic church in the mid-1800's to reinforce its teachings and to locate potential converts.

One New Mexico missionary, Jean Latour, is reflective and intellectual. Another, Joseph Vaillant, is impulsive, enthusiastic, adept at garnering funds for the cause. Latour has admirers, but Vaillant is able to get closer to the people. Cather sees them as two wings of the church, different but each respectful of the other, united in a common goal.

In her treatment of the natives of the region, Cather shows some bias. Certainly she was influenced by some widespread misconceptions of the times. Throughout the novel, Mexicans are portrayed less favorably than are Indians. Father Vaillant's attitude toward Mexicans underlies much of the work. He thinks of them as little children, but says "their foolish ways no longer offend, their faults are dear." Bishop Latour also infantilizes Mexicans, suggesting they have not "room in their minds for two ideas." The Mexican padres are disreputable. Far from having a disciplined commitment to the church, they are boozing womanizers who seek personal gain while ruling their parishioners with an iron fist.

Cather puts the reader on notice at the outset that the novel takes place during a period of native uprisings, but shows only one element of violence: The Acoma Indians throw their padre over the side of the mountain for inadvertently killing a boy. Even then, they do so gently, with a sense of exacting a just punishment for a crime. It may be the element of threat that fascinated Cather about the Native Americans of the region. In any event, she treats the Indian with a kind of respectful awe.

Cather's appreciation of the essence of Indian culture is captured in Father Latour's travels with

Esabio, the Navajo guide who accepts all elements of nature and weather. When leaving an encampment, he is "careful to obliterate every trace" of their stay. He buries the "embers of the fire and the remnants of food, unpile[s] any stones he had piled together, fill[s] up the holes he had scooped in the sand." Latour observes that "just as it was the white man's way to assert himself in any landscape, to change it, make it over a little [as some] mark of memorial . . . it was the Indian's way to pass through a country without disturbing anything; to pass and leave no trace, like fish through the water, or birds through the air."

Despite some elements of bias, *Death Comes for the Archbishop* lovingly captures the inhabitants of the Southwest in the 1850's. Cather's characters have a vitality that impresses them on the reader's memory long after reading the novel. Her book makes palpable a time and a place in the United States.

SUGGESTED READINGS

Brown, E. K. *Willa Cather*. New York: Alfred A. Knopf, 1953.

Gilbert, Sandra M., and Susan Gubar. *Sexchanges*. Vol. 2 in *No Man's Land: The Place of the Woman Writer in the Twentieth Century*. New Haven, Conn.: Yale University Press, 1989.

Woodress, James. *Willa Cather: A Literary Life*. Lincoln: University of Nebraska Press, 1987.

—*Gay Zieger*

See also American identity: Southwest; Cather, Willa; Native American identity; Religion and identity

Death in the Family, A

AUTHOR: James Agee (1909-1955)

FIRST PUBLISHED: 1957

IDENTITIES: European American; family; religion; South

James Agee's autobiographical novel, *A Death in the Family*, recalls his tranquil childhood in Knoxville, Tennessee, and the tragic event that hastened his loss of innocence and security—the death of his father, Hugh James (Jay) Agee. The novel's manuscript, on which its author had been working for years, was left incomplete at Agee's sudden death in 1955. Edited and published in 1957, it was awarded a Pulitzer Prize in fiction.

A Death in the Family offers a compelling look at the Follet family's reaction to the death of a young father, exploring the loneliness of the self and contentment brought about by family members. The fundamental differences in the character and personality of Mary and Jay Follet are revealed early in the novel; the mother's religiosity and serious disposition is contrasted with her husband's more independent and spontaneous nature. Much of the action is filtered through the experience, perception, and sense impressions of Rufus, their six-year-old son, whose loving relationship with his father is powerfully evoked in the novel's opening chapter.

In the middle of the night, Jay receives a phone call that summons him to the country and to his ailing father. Rufus and his younger sister, Catherine, are asleep when the telephone rings; their father decides not to wake them for he plans to return in time for supper. The ties of family relationships—trivial, intimate, tender—are evoked as Jay prepares to leave before daybreak and his wife, Mary, awakens to cook his breakfast. Once again, the children are asleep the following evening when a stranger calls to tell Mary that her husband has been in an accident. On the way back from the country, the steering mechanism of his car broke and Jay was killed instantly.

The simplicity of the novel's plot belies a complex exploration of the emotional effect of Jay's death on family members and the flavor of life in Tennessee during the early decades of the twentieth century. In her grief, Mary turns to religion for consolation. Catherine, Rufus' sister, is too young to understand her loss or her mother's sorrow. For young Rufus, however, much about life is mysterious; the death of his father is yet another baffling puzzle that he struggles to understand. Other family members give the novel its texture and regional emphasis, establishing the world in which adults and children confront the fact of death.

SUGGESTED READINGS

Barson, Alfred T. *A Way of Seeing: A Critical Study of James Agee*. Amherst: University of Massachusetts Press, 1972.

Kramer, Victor A. *Agee and Actuality: Artistic Vision in His Work*. Troy, N.Y.: Whitston, 1991.

Lofaro, Michael, ed. *James Agee: Reconsiderations*. Knoxville: University of Tennessee Press, 1992.

Moreau, Genevieve. *The Restless Journey of James Agee*. New York: William Morrow, 1977.

—Michelle A. Balée

See also Agee, James; American identity: South; *Let Us Now Praise Famous Men*

Death of a Salesman

AUTHOR: Arthur Miller (1915-   )
FIRST PRODUCED: 1949; first published, 1949
IDENTITIES: European American; family

Death of a Salesman, widely regarded as Arthur Miller's best and most important play, chronicles the downfall and suicide of Willy Loman, a ceaselessly struggling New England salesman driven by dreams of success far greater than he can achieve. Almost a classical tragedy in its form, *Death of a Salesman* has provoked much controversy due to the unheroic nature of its protagonist. Although the play, like its Greek forebears, conveys a sense of the inevitability of fate, Willy himself possesses no greatness in either achievement or status. Willy's sheer commonness, rather, gives the play its power. In *Death of a Salesman*, Miller shows that tragedy comes not only to the great but also to the small.

On its most fundamental level, *Death of a Salesman* depicts the disintegration of Willy's personality as he desperately searches for the moment in his memory when his world began to unravel. The play's action is driven primarily by Willy's volcanic relationship with grown son Biff, who is every inch the failure that his father is. Willy's grandiose dreams of happiness and material success conflict with the reality of his failures as a salesman, as a husband to his wife Linda, and as a father to his two boys, Biff and Happy. The alternation between present action and presentations of Willy's delusional "memories" forms the play's thematic center. Willy's memory is populated by figures who idealize success, most notably his brother Ben, who became rich, Dave Singleman, a fabulously successful and well-liked salesman, and the woman in Boston with whom Willy has had an affair. Countering those empty fantasies are the realities of Howard, Willy's unsympathetic boss; Charley, Willy's best friend and neighbor (who gives Willy the money he needs to pay his bills), Charley's successful son Bernard, and of course Biff, who refuses to accept Willy's delusions. "We never told the truth for ten minutes in this house!" Biff says at one point. Willy cannot accept the piercing truth of Biff's description: "You were never anything but a hard-working drummer who landed in the ash can like all the rest of them!" Rather, Willy commits suicide by crashing his car. The play's final tragic irony comes out in the play's last scene: Although Willy strove all his life to be well-liked and remembered, his funeral is attended only by his close family and friends. Neither he nor they are finally free, but only alone.

SUGGESTED READINGS

Bloom, Harold. *Modern Critical Interpretations: Arthur Miller's "Death of a Salesman."* New York: Chelsea House, 1988.

_____. *Major Literary Characters: Willy Loman*. New York: Chelsea House, 1991.

Miller, Arthur. *Timebends: A Life*. New York: Grove Press, 1987.

Murphy, Brenda. *Miller: "Death of a Salesman."* Cambridge, England: Cambridge University Press, 1995.

Nelson, Benjamin. *Arthur Miller: Portrait of a Playwright*. New York: David McKay, 1970.

—Gregory W. Lanier

See also American Dream; Class and identity; *Crucible, The*; Jewish American identity; Miller, Arthur; Psychological theories of identity

De Burgos, Julia

BORN: Carolina, Puerto Rico; February 17, 1914?

DIED: New York, New York; July 6, 1953

PRINCIPAL WORKS: *Poema en veinte surcos*, 1938 (poem in twenty furrows); *Canción de la verdad sencilla*, 1939 (song of the simple truth); *El mar y tú*, 1954 (the sea and you)

IDENTITIES: Latino; women

SIGNIFICANT ACHIEVEMENT: De Burgos' poetry promotes a strong feminist sentiment and includes reflections on her political activism in favor of the independence of Puerto Rico.

Born into a poor peasant family in rural Puerto Rico, Julia de Burgos, a remarkably intelligent girl, received schooling because of money collected among her equally poor neighbors. Eventually she earned a teaching degree. Her experiences as a rural teacher and her agrarian background added to her deep concern for the exploited workers and for the women subjected to male-chauvinist cultural patterns. Her contact with common people also ignited her interest in local politics, especially in independence-seeking revolutionary movements.

De Burgos is best known for her strongly feminist poems. Her poetry is thematically diverse; it includes an inclination to the erotic and to social activism. De Burgos' feminist poems present a philosophical consideration of the role of women in Puerto Rican society. By such questioning, de Burgos explores womanhood issues in her efforts to break away from restrictive social patterns. Her definition of womanhood encompasses multiple facets: the woman yearning for motherhood (which she herself never fulfilled), the social nonconformist who openly challenges sexist traditions, and the devoted citizen and political activist.

Her political involvement with the Puerto Rican Nationalist Party, which aggressively promoted the independence of Puerto Rico by means of revolutionary guerrilla warfare, added to her poetry a marked sense of patriotism. Her idea of a pure, lush countryside clashed with the realities of an increasingly urbanized and, therefore, Americanized Puerto Rico. Committed to international activism, de Burgos also wrote against Fascism in Spain during that country's civil war.

De Burgos' life can be examined as an example of a commitment to fight social injustice. At a time when racial discrimination was rampant, de Burgos, a woman of black descent, fought such restrictions. Racism was certainly her major problem upon arriving in New York City in 1942, where she lived until her death. In New York, although she was a renowned poet and fully bilingual, de Burgos was obliged to take menial jobs. She fought back, however, by writing against such oppression. Her alcoholism led to her early death.

De Burgos stands out as a early feminist activist at a time when Puerto Rican culture restricted women to the traditional roles of spouse and mother. The inclusion of feminism in her poetic production, which she links to political activism, puts de Burgos on the cutting edge of an incipient movement in Puerto Rico and in the United States. It may be more significant, however, that her life reflected her cherished beliefs.

SUGGESTED READING

Kattau, C. "The Plural and the Nuclear in 'A Julia de Burgos.'" *Symposium—A Quarterly Journal in Modern Foreign Literatures* 48, no. 4 (Winter, 1995): 285-293.

—*Rafael Ocasio*

See also Alcoholism; Caribbean American literature; Feminism; Latino American identity; Rural life; Spanish Civil War

Deep South: Memory and Observation

AUTHOR: Erskine Caldwell (1903-1987)

FIRST PUBLISHED: 1968

IDENTITIES: European American; family; religion; South

In this nonfiction work, Erskine Caldwell reflects on his life as a minister's son in the American South. He describes the social norms of white, rural, Fundamentalist sects that—while varying widely in their religious practices—share an unwavering faith in the virgin birth, the second coming of Christ, the direct creation of humanity by God, miraculous healing, answers to prayers, personal salvation, and physical life after death.

Caldwell sets his reflections against the landscape of the South so vividly portrayed in his best-known novels, *Tobacco Road* (1932) and *God's Little Acre* (1933). This is a land of muddy, rutted roads lined with tumbledown shacks and trod by impoverished tenant farmers. Once-white paint peels on sagging country churches where wasps buzz under the eaves. The region's only change between the 1920's and the 1960's was the displacement of the horse by the automobile.

Caldwell's reminiscences focus on his father, Ira Sylvester, a pastor of the Associate Reformed Presbyterian faith who, at various times, held church posts throughout the South. Wherever they went, father and son attended religious observances: all-night camp meetings, baptismal immersions in streams, foot-washings, blood-drinking communions, snake-handlings, and speaking in tongues. Ira Sylvester hoped the wide-ranging experience would protect his son against the tyranny of dogma and prejudice.

A dignified clergyman of conservative nature, Ira Sylvester found himself in perpetual conflict with Fundamentalism. On one occasion, Florida church elders demanded that he resign because dark-skinned Cubans were attending services. At other churches, he was condemned for failing to preach "old time religion." His assistance to poverty-stricken families of all colors and denominations earned him disapproval in several locales.

A moderate man—restrained in temperament and intellectual by nature—he condemned religious ecstasy as a dangerously addictive narcotic for those gripped by poverty and despair. He advocated the Ten Commandments as a code of conduct and denounced evangelists who incited feverish emotionalism among their congregations.

Fundamentalist religion and states' rights politics were synonymous in Caldwell's South, and from their proponents the Ku Klux Klan drew its members. The Klan used terrorist tactics to crusade for the preservation of white, Protestant supremacy. Both Caldwells scorned the night-riding violence of those who, while faithful in their attendance at Sunday worship, betrayed the biblical principle of brotherhood. Many good people lived in the South, Erskine Caldwell wrote, but they were well hidden amid what he called a "miasma of prejudice."

This book counterpoints two identities. The stereotypic, sweat-dripping, voice-quavering evangelist stands in stark contrast to Ira Sylvester, a rational man forever embattled against irrationality.

SUGGESTED READINGS

Arnold, Edwin T., ed. *Conversations with Erskine Caldwell*. Jackson: University Press of Mississippi, 1988.

Cook, Sylvia Jenkins. *Erskine Caldwell and the Fiction of Poverty*. Baton Rouge: Louisiana State University Press, 1991.

Klevar, Harvey L. *Erskine Caldwell: A Biography*. Knoxville: University of Tennessee Press, 1993.

—*Faith Hickman Brynie*

See also American identity: South; Christianity and Christian Fundamentalism; Religion and identity; *Tobacco Road*

Deephaven

AUTHOR: Sarah Orne Jewett (1849-1909)

FIRST PUBLISHED: 1877

IDENTITIES: European American; gay, lesbian, and bisexual; Northeast; women

In *Deephaven*, Sarah Orne Jewett presents two American identities in the hope that they could explain each to the other. Deephaven is a sleepy Maine village more akin to York and Wells than to the South Berwick in which the author grew up and lived for much of her life. The town is twelve miles from the railroad and is described as being more English than American, the result perhaps of Jewett's having, in 1874, read and been much influenced by Elizabeth Gaskell's *Cranford* (1853).

Deephaven is a composite of thirteen sketches that Jewett revised considerably and wove into a novel. The narrative is supplied by two summer visitors from the city, Helen Denis and Kate Lancaster, each twenty-four years old. Katherine Brandon, Kate's great-aunt, has died and left her house in Deephaven to Kate's mother, who grants the two young ladies use of it for the summer. In the course of the summer, Kate and Helen come to know a considerable gallery of locals, whom Jewett presents in authentic detail. They range from two retired sea captains to a fisherman to the widow Patton to Mrs. Kew, an earth mother who lives in the lighthouse, to Miss Honora Carew, who expresses her gratitude that Deephaven has "no disagreeable foreign population," to Olive Grant, the obligatory gossip who serves the author's need to reveal many facts.

The result of this summer is that two disparate camps begin to know, understand, and sympathize with each other. Recent critics have also suggested that the book has to do with the sexual identities of Kate and Helen, who might be inferred to have sexual feelings for each other, much as Jewett is thought to have had for many of her female friends.

Many of the characters in *Deephaven* are grotesques when compared with people in mainstream society. In Deephaven, however, they have established their identities and are accepted on an equal basis with their less eccentric fellow citizens. The people in town have been raised around one another and accept one another, each according to his or her own singular identity.

SUGGESTED READINGS

Blanchard, Paula. *Sarah Orne Jewett: Her World and Her Work*. Cambridge, Mass.: Radcliffe Biography Series, 1994.

Cary, Richard. *Sarah Orne Jewett*. New York: Twayne, 1962.

Donovan, Josephine. *New England Local Color Literature: A Woman's Tradition*. New York: Continuum, 1988.

Matthiessen, Francis Otto. *Sarah Orne Jewett*. Boston: Houghton Mifflin, 1929.

Roman, Margaret. *Sarah Orne Jewett: Reconstructing Gender*. Tuscaloosa: University of Alabama Press, 1992.

—*R. Baird Shuman*

See also American identity: Northeast; *Country of the Pointed Firs, The*; Gay identity; Jewett, Sarah Orne; Lesbian identity; Women and identity

Delany, Samuel R.

BORN: New York, New York; April 1, 1942

PRINCIPAL WORKS: *The Jewels of Aptor*, 1962; *Babel-17*, 1966; *The Einstein Intersection*, 1967; *Nova*, 1968; *Dhalgren*, 1975; *Triton*, 1976; *The Jewel-Hinged Jaw*, 1977; *The American Shore*, 1978; *Heavenly Breakfast*, 1979; *Tales of Nevèrÿon*, 1979; *Nevèrÿona*, 1983; *Flight from Nevèrÿon*, 1985; *The Bridge of Lost Desire*, 1987; *The Motion of Light in Water*, 1988; *Silent Interviews*, 1994; *Atlantis: Three Tales*, 1995

IDENTITIES: African American; gay, lesbian, and bisexual

SIGNIFICANT ACHIEVEMENT: Delany is an intensely self-analytical explorer of the linguistic and imaginative possibilities of science fiction.

Samuel Delaney's early science fiction is remarkable for its vivid imagination, its pyrotechnic style, and its interest in linguistic science. Several essays collected in *The Jewel-Hinged Jaw* began an analysis of the distinctive ways in which meaning is generated in texts that refer to imaginary worlds. This analysis is a central preoccupation of his academic writing and played a vital part in shaping his later fiction. *The Einstein Intersection* is the first of his novels that makes the creator visible within the text and that links the process of fictional creation to his parallel life experiences.

The increasing openness of the science-fiction field allowed Delany to move on to an explicit and very elaborate examination of homosexual identity in *Dhalgren*. The intense introspective analysis of *Dhalgren* is inverted in *Triton*, which extrapolates the personal into the political with flamboyance in its analysis of a future "heterotopia" in which all kinds of sexual identities are readily accommodated and available for sampling.

Delany began to subject his life to an unusually candid and thoughtful analysis. The primary product of this analysis is *The Motion of Light in Water*, a detailed autobiographical account of his life between 1957 and 1965. The semiautobiographical novella *Heavenly Breakfast* deals with an experiment in communal living in the late 1960's. "Citre et Trans" (in *Atlantis*) describes a black American writer's erotic experiences in Greece in the mid-1960's. *Silent Interviews* is a collection of dialogues in which Delany responds in detail to various inquisitors. The remarkable fiction "The Tale of Plagues and Carnivals" (in *Flight from Nevèrÿon*), which offers a searching part-allegorical and part-autobiographical analysis of the advent of acquired immune deficiency syndrome (AIDS), is the most complex and powerful of his works in this introspective vein.

The hallmark of all Delany's self-analytical work is a remarkable frankness, especially in matters of sexuality, although there is nothing self-aggrandizing in his examinations of his own sex life or the imaginary sex lives of characters like him. His curiosity about his experience as a gay black man is utterly scrupulous in its quest for honest expression and true explanation, and his attempts to understand and explain the different experiences of others are marked by great generosity of spirit and critical insight. His occasional adventures in pornography, recounted without embarrassment, demonstrate that his attempts to understand the erotic workings of the human mind are uninhibited by fear of stigmatization.

SUGGESTED READINGS

Barbour, Douglas. *Worlds out of Words: The SF Novels of Samuel R. Delany*. Frome, England: Ban's Head, 1979.

McEvoy, Seth. *Samuel R. Delany*. New York: Frederick Ungar, 1983.

—*Brian Stableford*

See also African American identity; Erotic identity; Gay identity; *Motion of Light in Water, The*; *Triton*

Demographics of identity

DEFINITION: Demographics are the characteristics of a population that can be considered statistically.

Immigrants have played a key role in the settlement, economic development, and history of North America. Most immigrants have been drawn to the United States and Canada by the prospect of employment and freedom. Although the factors underlying this migration have essentially remained unaltered since each country's foundation, the primary sources of immigrants to each country have changed. Europe, until the latter half of the twentieth century, supplied the majority of immigrants to both countries, but toward the end of the twentieth century, Asia became the principal supplier of immigrants.

The United States has experienced four major waves of immigration. In the first wave, between 1790 and 1820, most immigrants came from Great Britain and spoke English. During the second wave, from 1840 to 1860, the majority of immigrants were from Northern and Western Europe, most particularly Ireland and Germany. The third wave, from 1880 to 1914, is characterized by a transition in sources from Northern and Western Europe to Southern and Eastern Europe. This wave is associated with a peak period of U.S. immigration. In 1907, a record 1.3 million immigrants entered the country, with Italy accounting for more than 20 percent of this total. The outbreak of World War I effectively ended European immigration—numbers declined from 1 million in 1914 to 31,000 in 1918.

United States immigration

The transition in immigrant sources aroused nativist sentiments among older immigrant groups. Fear of Asian immigration, for example, led the U.S. Congress to enact the Chinese Exclusion Act in 1882. Other Asian groups were added to the exclusion list with the creation of the Asiatic Barred Zone in the 1917 Immigration Act. The justification for excluding these groups was found in racist theories of Anglo-Saxon superiority. The U.S. Congress responded to public pressure to curtail immigration from Southern and Eastern Europe by enacting the National Origins Quota system in 1924. Under this system, immigrant visas were apportioned for each country according to its contribution to the U.S. population in 1910. Since Britain, Ireland, and Germany had provided the largest number of immigrants, they received the largest quotas. No restrictions were placed on immigration from the Western Hemisphere, largely in response to U.S. agricultural interests that wanted access to cheap Mexican labor that could be recruited when needed. In 1952, the so-called Texas Proviso was added to immigration law; the proviso exempted employers from sanctions for hiring undocumented workers. This had the effect of increasing illegal immigration after the United States ended its formal system of hiring agricultural workers, the Bracero Program, in 1964. The 1986 Immigration Reform and Control Act made it illegal for employers to hire an undocumented worker.

Immigration levels declined from 1924 to 1945 as a result of the National Origins system, the Great Depression, and World War II. After 1945 U.S. concerns with immigrant origins (that is, worries about race) were replaced with concerns about immigrant skills and educational background (the United States, amply populated, began to wish only for immigrants who could contribute to the economy). In 1965, the secretary of state testified before the House Judiciary Committee that "the significance of immigration to the U.S. now depends less on the numbers than on the quality of immigrants. . . . We are in the international market of brains." Restrictions on immigration from Asia and Southern and Eastern Europe were gradually removed during and after World War II. The National Origins system was formally replaced by the 1965 Amendments to the Immigration and Nationality Act, which allocated an annual ceiling of 170,000 immigrants for the Eastern Hemisphere and 120,000 for the Western Hemisphere. Within this overall ceiling, a system of priority categories was established based upon family reunification criteria and labor requirements, with the immediate relatives of U.S. citizens being exempt from the numerical cap. In 1990, a global quota of 714,000 immigrants was established

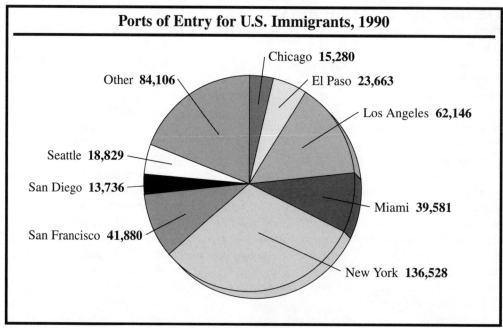

Ports of Entry for U.S. Immigrants, 1990

Chicago **15,280**
El Paso **23,663**
Los Angeles **62,146**
Other **84,106**
Miami **39,581**
Seattle **18,829**
San Diego **13,736**
San Francisco **41,880**
New York **136,528**

Source: U.S. Immigration and Naturalization Service, *Statistical Yearbook of the Immigration and Naturalization Service, 1990.* Washington, D.C.: U.S. Government Printing Office, 1991.

for 1992 to 1994, and 675,000 beginning in 1995, with the majority of visas being allocated to spouses, children, and other relatives of U.S. citizens. In addition to this global quota are refugees, who are admitted under the 1980 Refugee Act, which had a 1992 ceiling of 142,000 persons and a series of smaller quotas designed for particular groups which have been adversely affected by earlier immigration laws.

These changes in legislation have coincided with a fourth wave of immigration. Since 1970 immigration has gradually increased to approach the record levels, in raw numbers, that were reached at the beginning of the twentieth century. The number of immigrants in the fourth wave relative to the rest of the population, however, is far less than at the beginning of the twentieth century. During the 1970's the United States admitted 4.4 million immigrants. The following decade this figure increased to 7.3 million. In 1993, a total of 904,300 immigrants legally entered the country. Concurrent with this boost in immigration has been a change in immigrant sources from the "developed" to the "developing" world. During the 1960's, the six leading suppliers of U.S. immigrants were Mexico (443,300), Canada (286,700), Cuba (256,800), United Kingdom (230,500), Italy (206,700) and Germany (200,000). The comparable figures for the 1980's were: Mexico (1,653,300), Philippines (495,300), Vietnam (401,400), China (388,800), Korea (338,800) and India (261,900).

This transformation in immigrant sources is also associated with a change in immigrant settlement patterns. During the third wave of immigration, the United States was undergoing industrialization, which meant a large demand for factory labor in cities. European immigrants settled in Northeastern and Midwestern industrial cities and transformed the urban landscape. Italian, Polish, and Greek neighborhoods, for example, grew up around Chicago's downtown district. Since the 1950's, factory closures in such traditional industries as textiles, automobiles, and steel have reduced the demand for labor and brought long-term economic decline to the region. Economic growth and the demand for labor have shifted to the rapidly growing service-based economies of the so-called Sunbelt states, which stretch from Southern California to Florida. Many of the new immigrant groups have settled in the rapidly growing cities of this region. The resulting ethnic diversity from this settlement can be seen in Los Angeles, Houston, and Miami.

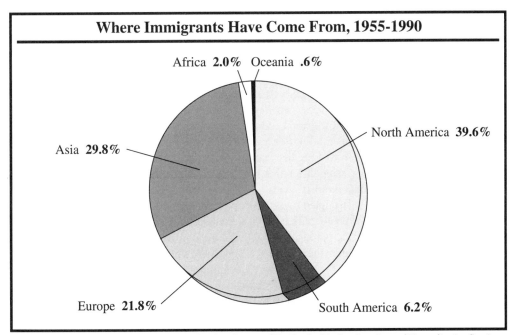

Where Immigrants Have Come From, 1955-1990

Africa **2.0%**   Oceania **.6%**
Asia **29.8%**
North America **39.6%**
Europe **21.8%**
South America **6.2%**

Source: U.S. Immigration and Naturalization Service, *Statistical Yearbook of the Immigration and Naturalization Service, 1990.* Washington, D.C.: U.S. Government Printing Office, 1991.

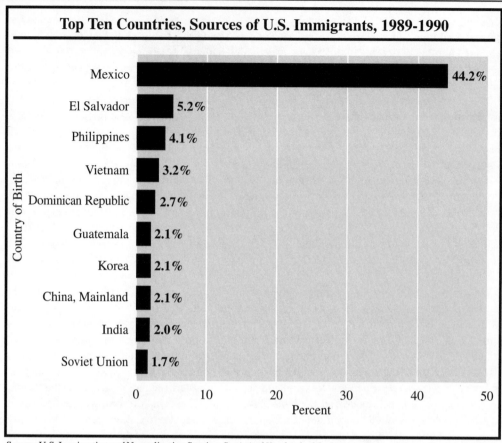

Top Ten Countries, Sources of U.S. Immigrants, 1989-1990

Mexico — 44.2%
El Salvador — 5.2%
Philippines — 4.1%
Vietnam — 3.2%
Dominican Republic — 2.7%
Guatemala — 2.1%
Korea — 2.1%
China, Mainland — 2.1%
India — 2.0%
Soviet Union — 1.7%

Source: U.S. Immigration and Naturalization Service, *Statistical Yearbook of the Immigration and Naturalization Service, 1990.* Washington, D.C.: U.S. Government Printing Office, 1991.

Note: Data show number of persons admitted as legalization immigrants under the Immigration Reform and Control Act and as non-legalization immigrants. A legalization applicant is an alien who has been in the U.S. unlawfully since January 1, 1991.

Adding to the immigrant population in the early 1990's was an annual flow of an estimated 250,000 illegal immigrants. Illegal immigrants include those who overstay a visa (often a student visa) and those who simply walk across the border. Mexico is the leading source of these migrants, followed by El Salvador and Guatemala, two Central American countries torn, especially in the 1980's, by terrorism and warfare. California contains the largest number of illegal migrants. The net effect of the fourth wave of immigration has been to accelerate—not cause—the cultural transition of the United States from a predominantly white population rooted in western culture to a diverse society comprising many different ethnic and racial minorities.

Canadian immigration

In 1867, at the time of Confederation, Canada had a population of 3.2 million. For the following thirty years the young country struggled to obtain population growth as thousands of Canadians moved to the United States. The post-Confederation National Policy was designed to help establish the new country. Two aims of the National Policy were the construction of the transcontinental railroad and homestead settlement in the West. The Canadian government was fearful of American northward expansion and annexation, and so viewed immigration to the prairies as an essential component of nation building. As in the United States, there were concerns about who immigrated. Chinese workers, for example, had been recruited to work on the railroad and in lumber camps, and their presence in British Columbia aroused racist fears. Opposition to the Chinese was particularly pronounced in Vancouver, where a dilapidated Chinatown had been established. The federal government responded to these nativist sentiments by taxing Chinese immigration; later, the Canadian government pressured Japan into voluntarily limiting its emigrants to four hundred per year.

The beginning of the twentieth century was a boom period in Canadian immigration; 1.5 million immigrants entered the country between 1900 and 1914. In 1913 a record 400,000 arrived in the country. Many of these immigrants were from Eastern and Central Europe and were responding to the same factors that led their counterparts to settle in the United States. Instead of settling in urban areas, as in the United States, the Canadian immigrants generally settled on the prairies in rural ethnic communities. The relative isolation of these small towns and villages helped the immigrants sustain their cultural identity and in effect laid the foundation for the so-called Canadian mosaic and later multiculturalism.

After World War I, Canada established a national origins system, classifying prospective immigrants into ethnic categories: British and Northwest Europeans were classified as "preferred"; Central and Eastern Europeans "non-preferred," while in the "restricted" category were Italians, Greeks, and Jews. The responsibility for administering this system was transferred to the Canadian Pacific and Canadian National Railways in 1925. These companies owned vast tracts of land in the West and it was in their interest to sell off this land to new settlers. As a result, the preference categories were ignored. By the late 1920's, the majority of Canadian immigrants were from the non-preferred and restricted categories. The Great Depression and World War II all but ended immigration to Canada.

Canadian immigration policy changed after World War II. Non-Jewish displaced persons from Europe who had been made homeless by the war were admitted in 1946; Jews were allowed to immigrate two years later. The expanding industrial economies of Ontario and Quebec needed labor that could not be supplied from Britain, so the government began an active pro-immigration policy in 1949. Europe continued to supply most of Canada's immigrants during the 1950's and 1960's, but the majority of them came from Italy, Greece, and Portugal. Amendments to the 1952 Immigration Act in 1962 and 1966 formally abolished the previous exclusions of particular racial groups and established a universalistic point system for admission into the country. Points were awarded for educational attainment, for the ability to speak the major languages, and for having Canadian family members. These reforms stemmed from the need to attract professionals to the expanding scientific, educational, governmental and health care sectors, from a reduction in racist attitudes, and from an increasing acceptance of Canada's multicultural character.

Since 1971, the federal government has actively promoted multiculturalism by providing grants for ethnic histories and promoting cultural heritage. The new admissions policy resulted in a shift away from Europe as the country's principal supplier of immigrants. Canadian support for diversity has also included the appointment in 1972 of the first Minister of State for Multiculturalism and the passage in 1988 of the Canadian Multiculturalism Act. In 1992, Hong Kong, Sri Lanka, India, and the Philippines were the four leading sources of Canadian immigrants.

In 1994, the province of Ontario, with 37 percent of Canada's population, received 52 percent of Canada's immigrants, while the comparable figures for British Columbia were 12 percent and 22 percent respectively. Most immigrants of the late twentieth century have settled in urban areas. The 1991 census reported that 38 percent or 1.5 million residents of the Toronto metropolitan area were immigrants, while the comparable figures for Vancouver and Montreal were 30 percent and 17 percent respectively.

SUGGESTED READINGS

Epenshade, Thomas J. "Unauthorized Immigration to the United States." *Annual Review of Sociology* 21 (1995): 195-216.

Higham, John. *Strangers in the Land: Patterns of American Nativism, 1896-1925.* New York: Atheneum, 1963.

Massey, Douglas S. "The New Immigration and Ethnicity in the United States." In *Population and Development Review* 21, no. 3 (September, 1995): 631-652.

Rumbaut, Rubén G. "Origins and Destinies: Immigration to the United States Since World War II." *Sociological Forum* 9, no. 4 (December, 1994): 583-621.

Thompson, John H., and M. Weinfeld. "Entry and Exit: Canadian Immigration Policy in Context." In *The Annals of the American Academy of Political and Social Sciences* 538 (March, 1995): 185-198.

—*Michael Broadway*

See also Emigration and immigration; Ethnic composition of universities; Multiculturalism, statistics of; Pluralism versus assimilation

De Vries, Peter

BORN: Chicago, Illinois; February 27, 1910
DIED: Norwalk, Connecticut; September 28, 1993
PRINCIPAL WORKS: *But Who Wakes the Bugler?*, 1940; *The Handsome Heart*, 1943; *Angels Can't Do Better*, 1944; *No, but I Saw the Movie*, 1952; *The Tunnel of Love*, 1954; *Comfort Me with Apples*, 1956; *The Mackerel Plaza*, 1958; *The Tents of Wickedness*, 1959; *Through the Fields of Clover*, 1961; *The Blood of the Lamb*, 1962; *Reuben, Reuben*, 1964; *Let Me Count the Ways*, 1965; *The Vale of Laughter*, 1967; *The Cat's Pyjamas and Witch's Milk*, 1968; *Mrs. Wallop*, 1970; *Into Your Tent I'll Creep*, 1971; *Without a Stitch in Time*, 1972; *Forever Panting*, 1973; *The Glory of the Hummingbird*, 1974; *I Hear America Swinging*, 1976; *Madder Music*, 1977; *Consenting Adults: Or, The Duchess Will Be Furious*, 1980; *Sauce for the Goose*, 1981; *Slouching Towards Kalamazoo*, 1983; *The Prick of Noon*, 1985; *Peckham's Marbles*, 1986
IDENTITIES: European American; family; religion
SIGNIFICANT ACHIEVEMENT: De Vries' novels feature droll wordplay and are generally plotted as quest narratives in which the protagonist abandons or subverts the traditional conventions of marriage, family, and religious faith only to recognize the value of these institutions, or some version of them, after a loose series of incidental comic and erotic adventures.

Four elements are common in the fiction of Peter De Vries: a fascination with metaphysics, especially questions relating to religious issues and to meaning in life; a sympathetic presentation of ordinary domestic arrangements; poking fun at ordinary Midwest and Northeast suburban society; and an amazing skill with the English language.

De Vries was born into a family of Dutch Calvinists and reared in their strict faith. He was graduated from Calvin College in 1931. As a novelist, he often weaves questions of faith into the musings of his characters and the comic transformations they undergo. While exploring religious and existential questions in this way, he satirizes aspects of contemporary life. De Vries celebrates domestic life without sentimentalizing it. He eventually settled with his wife, the writer Katinka Loeser, in suburban Connecticut and fathered five children. A daughter died of leukemia in 1960, a tragedy commemorated in *The Blood of the Lamb*. In comic novels, his characters usually take a circuitous route to domestic bliss, sometimes exploring unconventional paths along the way. Ultimately, however, they reconcile themselves to conventional happiness.

De Vries devoted his life to language. He held several editorial positions: on small newspapers, at *Poetry* magazine (1938-1944), and as a staff contributor to *The New Yorker* (1944-1987). His wit has been placed in the company of that of such noted humorists as S. J. Perelman, Oscar Wilde, Evelyn Waugh, and others.

SUGGESTED READINGS

Bowden, J. H. *Peter De Vries*. Boston: Twayne, 1983.
Campion, Dan. *Peter De Vries and Surrealism*. Cranbury, N.J.: Bucknell University Press, 1995.
Jellema, Roderick. *Peter De Vries: A Critical Essay*. Grand Rapids, Mich.: Wm. B. Eerdmans, 1966.

—*Victoria Gaydosik*

See also Adolescent identity; American identity: Midwest; American identity: Northeast; Erotic identity; Religion and identity; *Slouching Towards Kalamazoo*

Dharma Bums, The

AUTHOR: Jack Kerouac (1922-1969)

FIRST PUBLISHED: 1958

IDENTITIES: European American; religion

Jack Kerouac's *The Dharma Bums*, relatively upbeat and often humorous, is a fictional account of Kerouac's attempt to unify his identity through Buddhism. The main character, Ray Smith, is accompanied on this quest by the physically and mentally agile savant Japhy Ryder (the poet Gary Snyder), a young yet accomplished Buddhist. The flower children of the 1960's appreciated the novel's sexual freedom and used *The Dharma Bums* as a guide to the "rucksack revolution" predicted by Ryder.

Dharma bums, as the name implies, roam in solitude, unencumbered by material goods, seeking instruction (dharma), taking some risks, and learning through meditation. Smith climbs a mountain in California with Ryder, meditates in the woods in North Carolina, parties in Ryder's cabin, and finally takes over Ryder's solitary fire lookout job in Washington State. Smith drinks excessively, but he struggles to control his appetites. He believes he practices a devout Buddhist lifestyle. His ideas, dreams, and visions express Buddhist dogma, and his friends are other dharma bums who contribute their own interpretations, expanding Smith's own views and creating a noteworthy general discussion of Buddhist philosophy.

Another novel, *Desolation Angels* (1965), reveals more fully the rigorous self-examination that Kerouac conducted. The unique relevance of *The Dharma Bums* to literary identity, however, is enhanced by the circumstances surrounding its publication. When Kerouac wrote *The Dharma Bums*, a commissioned work that he never revised, his interest in Buddhism was waning. Kerouac's change of heart complicated Ray Smith's narrative voice. At times an omniscient narrator appears in the novel offering opinions more like those of Kerouac at the time of the novel's writing. This narrator is identified early on when he states that he is no longer "very devout" like Smith in the novel, but rather "a little tired and cynical," no longer persisting in the beliefs of the "perfect religious wanderer" that he once was. He bluntly recounts friends' thoughtful criticisms of the character Smith. At times, he subtly derides his past self; at others, he openly portrays his past self as embarrassing or hypocritical, even scandalously insensitive. Though he recaptures the positive spirit of the experience to a great degree, he also feels superior to the character and tries on occasion to separate his present self from that of his past. Such narrative intrusions reveal much about how identity changes over time while only beginning to explain the complex identity of the persona who haunts and controls this narrative.

SUGGESTED READINGS

Feied, Frederick. *No Pie in the Sky: The Hobo as American Cultural Hero in the Works of Jack London, John Dos Passos, and Jack Kerouac.* Secaucus, N.J.: Citadel Press, 1964.

Hart, John E. "Future Hero in Paradise: Kerouac's *The Dharma Bums*." *Critique: Studies in Modern Fiction* 14, no. 3 (1973): 52-62.

Hull, Keith N. "A Dharma Bum Goes West to Meet the East." *Western American Literature* 11, no. 4 (1977): 321-329.

Nicosia, Gerald. *Memory Babe*. New York: Grove Press, 1983.

Rexroth, Kenneth. "San Francisco's Mature Bohemians." *The Nation* 184 (February 23, 1957): 159-162.

Tytell, John. "The Beat Generation and the Continuing American Revolution." *American Scholar* 42 (Spring, 1973): 308-317.

—*Mary L. Otto Lang*

See also Alcoholism; Countercultures; Eastern religion and philosophy; Kerouac, Jack; *On the Road*; Snyder, Gary

Diaries and journals: literary legacies

DEFINITION: Diaries and journals are daily accounts of and reflections upon the events of the writers' lives.

A survey   Diaries and journals (the terms are interchangeable, both denoting a daily record) are fundamental reflections of American identity from colonial times to the present. America's first diary writers often began their accounts on the ships that brought colonists to the New World and continued to record their experiences and reactions once they arrived. The early diaries often reflect the writers' perceptions of themselves as religious and political pioneers in a land blessed by Providence and destined for greatness. The religious element continues in many diaries that record America's development through revolution, industrialization, the westward movement, and wars. While for a few the diary becomes a record of spiritual development, for others the diary records the writers' reactions to momentous experiences, such as a long journey through strange terrain, or participation in a war. Another common motivation for diaries is primarily literary, with writers such as Henry David Thoreau, Ralph Waldo Emerson, Mark Twain, Nathaniel Hawthorne, Louisa May Alcott, Henry L. Mencken, and May Sarton recording the daily observations that might later be included in literary works.

Journals motivated to some degree by travel include that of Sarah Kemble Knight, whose round trip in 1704 from Boston to New York reveals the primitive conditions for travel. Washington Irving's travel diaries provide substance for his literary tales. John Early, a circuit-riding minister in the early 1800's, wrote an important diary. William Clark and Meriwether Lewis' journals of an expedition (1804-1806) to the mouth of the Columbia River reveal new flora and fauna, the vast expanses of the continent, and a view of western native people. John C. Frémont, whose explorations and mapping of the American west prepared the way for further westward expansion, also kept a journal. Caroline Seabury, whose travels from Brooklyn, New York, to Columbus, Mississippi, where she taught the daughters of plantation owners prior to and during the Civil War, writes with a Northern bias about Southern social, political, and military conditions.

Numerous diaries record travel to gold fields in the 1850's and after. The westward migration to Oregon and California, beginning in the 1840's, inspired many diaries, and Lillian Schlissel has excerpted from over one hundred of them in *Women's Diaries of the Westward Journey* (1982).

War diaries   Diaries record all American wars from the Revolutionary War onward. They reflect their writers' political sympathies, the sufferings and apprehensions of wartime, and frequently their writers' dependence on God for safety and victory. During the Revolutionary War, Lewis Beebe, a surgeon, deplored the conditions and sufferings of colonial troops. Sally Wister, a Quaker teenager in Pennsylvania, met many officers of the colonial army and, true to her upbringing, avoided discussing politics with them. She does, however, show romantic interest in some. The Civil War produced many diaries from both sides of the conflict. John Ransom tells of his imprisonment at Andersonville and his eventual escape to Union lines. A more comprehensive view of the war is Elisha Hunt Rhodes' *All for the Union: The Civil War Diary and Letters of Elisha Hunt Rhodes* (1992). Rhodes joined the army in Rhode Island and fought in nineteen major battles. Rhodes rose through the ranks and commanded his regiment by the war's end. Southern views are well represented in Mary Chesnut's *A Diary from Dixie* (1905). Since Chesnut and her husband James were intimate acquaintances of Jefferson Davis, president of the Confederacy, and his wife Varina, Chesnut's diary presents an articulate view of those in power in the South. Two diaries from World War II, *Guadalcanal Diary* (1943) by Richard Tregaskis and *Pacific War Diary* (1993) by James Fahey, reveal the stresses and carnage of battle. The diary of Charles Kikuchi shows the effects of internment in California on Japanese Americans during World War II. Kikuchi's diary also emphasizes a continuing loyalty to the United States.

Themes   American diaries present universal themes. Love is a frequent theme. Sexuality appears in various modes (see William Byrd's diaries from the early eighteenth century for heterosexual accounts or John Cheever's from the twentieth century for experiences involving homosexuality). Racial themes are frequent in plantation diaries and those relating to the Civil War. Charlotte L. Forten, from a prominent African American family in Philadelphia, was a teacher; her diary reflects her efforts to educate former slaves in South Carolina. Religious themes, like the revivals that swept some military units during the Civil War and accounts of missions among Indians, are common. Money and its acquisition are important to many diarists.

Politics, courage, patriotism, spiritual introspection, death, family and relational values, optimism, depression, health, education, feminism, adventure—these themes reflect the universal tendencies of American diaries.

SUGGESTED READINGS

Billington, Ray Allen, ed. *The Journal of Charlotte Forten*. New York: Dryden Press, 1953.

Hughes, Ted, and Frances McCullough, eds. *The Journals of Sylvia Plath*. New York: Dial Press, 1982.

Mallon, Thomas. *A Book of One's Own: People and Their Diaries*. New York: Ticknor & Fields, 1984.

Miller, Randall M., and Linda Patterson Miller, eds. *The Book of American Diaries*. New York: Avon Books, 1995.

Modell, John, ed. *The Kikuchi Diary: Chronicle from an American Concentration Camp—The Tanforan Journals of Charles Kikuchi*. Champaign: University of Illinois Press, 1973.

Rhodes, Robert Hunt, ed. *All for the Union: The Civil War Diary and Letters of Elisha Hunt Rhodes*. New York: Vintage Books, 1992.

Schlissel, Lillian. *Women's Diaries of the Westward Journey*. New York: Schocken Books, 1982.

Ulrich, Laurel Thatcher. *A Midwife's Tale: The Life of Martha Ballard, Based on Her Diary, 1785-1812*. New York: Alfred A. Knopf, 1990.

Woodward, C. Vann, ed. *Mary Chesnut's Civil War*. New Haven, Conn.: Yale University Press, 1981.

Wright, Louis B., and Marion Tinling, eds. *The Secret Diary of William Byrd of Westover, 1709-1712*. Richmond, Va.: Dietz Press, 1941.

—*Ray Leadbetter*

Anaïs Nin, whose diary caused a literary sensation. (Christian Du Bois Larson)

See also Christianity and Christian Fundamentalism; Erotic identity; Feminism; Gay identity; Japanese American internment; Puritan and Protestant tradition; Slavery

Diary of Frida Kahlo: An Intimate Self-Portrait, The

AUTHOR: Frida Kahlo (1907-1954)

FIRST PUBLISHED: 1995

IDENTITIES: Disability; Latino; women

The Diary of Frida Kahlo: An Intimate Self-Portrait was drawn, painted, and written during the last decade of the Mexican painter's life. During these years, her health, precarious since a 1925 accident, declined precipitously. She spent the years from 1944 until her death encased in a series of eight surgical corsets, often bedridden or confined to a wheelchair. In 1953, she was forced to have her gangrenous left leg amputated; her spirit never entirely recovered, and she died on July 13, 1954. The evidence of Kahlo's declining physical and mental state is evident as the exuberant free associations and humor of the earlier pages of the diary give way to reflection and more painful images.

The entire written part of the journal is suffused with her relationship with her husband, the Mexican muralist Diego Rivera. One of the most potent images, which she repeats through the journal, in defining their relationship is that of the chemical groups auxochrome and chromophore: "You were called AUXOCHROME, the one who captures color. I CHROMOPHORE—the one who gives color." The one sketch in the diary that led to a painting depicts her vision of their relationship: She cradles Diego in her arms as he holds the fire of creativity in his hands; both are embraced by the Mexican earth goddess and the spirit of the universe.

In the six-page "Outline of my life," Kahlo describes a battle during the Mexican Revolution that she witnessed at the age of four. She credits her early exposure to the spirit of revolution for her political beliefs. Throughout the latter part of the journal Kahlo is engaged with analyzing and reaffirming her faith in communism. The party's dialectical materialism appealed to her, and its revolutionary fervor gives her a purpose to survive.

On facing pages of the journal she pairs a poster drawing of a hammer and sickle, inscribed with the names of Karl Marx, Friedrich Engels, Vladimir Ilich Lenin, Joseph Stalin, and Mao Zedong, with a pictographic painting of an Aztec pyramid rising into a sky containing the painted words *luna* (moon) and *sol* (sun). In the foreground of the painting is a female figure dressed in traditional Mexican clothes which Kahlo labels *yo?* (me?). The juxtaposition of revolutionary Marxism with traditional symbols of Aztec culture is typical of Kahlo's idealization of Mexico's past and what she hoped was its future.

The other predominant images in the final pages of the journal are of broken and disconnected body parts, especially feet. Other recurring images are her dog, Mr. Xolotl, and winged figures, often identified with Kahlo. The images reflect her vulnerability. The disembodied feet reflect her preoccupation with her disintegrating body. On one page she addresses her beloved pet as "The Lord Xolotl AMBASSADOR of the Universal Republic of Xibalba Mictlan," the Mexican underworld. His presence symbolically represents her own journey toward death. The winged figures serve as symbolic images of her desire for release. The final drawing in the journal, probably the last painting she made, is a green winged creature with blackened legs. It leaves a trail of blood. She wrote: "I hope the leaving is joyful—and I hope never to return—FRIDA."

SUGGESTED READINGS

Herrera, Hayden. *Frida: A Biography of Frida Kahlo*. New York: Harper & Row, 1983.
_____. *Frida Kahlo: The Paintings*. New York: HarperCollins, 1991.
Lowe, Sarah M. *Frida Kahlo*. Universe Series on Women Artists. New York: Universe, 1991.

—Jane Anderson Jones

See also Diaries and journals: literary legacies

Didion, Joan

BORN: Sacramento, California; December 5, 1934

PRINCIPAL WORKS: *Slouching Towards Bethlehem*, 1968; *Play It as It Lays*, 1970; *The White Album*, 1979; *After Henry*, 1992; *The Last Thing He Wanted*, 1996

IDENTITIES: European American; family; West and Southwest; women

SIGNIFICANT ACHIEVEMENT: Didion's intelligent and careful reporting on American mythmaking is unique in modern journalism, and her novels describe the emptiness that results when these myths are no longer believed.

Joan Didion is a California native, and she writes novels about California women. Her women are often lost and lonely and unhappy. When they leave their native state, they wander into a Third World country and remain there, victims of the lack of any real home in the fragmented society of late twentieth century America. Although Didion claims that her novels are the most important part of her work, it is her essays which have received the most praise from critics. Her earliest recognition came when she won the *Vogue* magazine Prix de Paris for an essay on a California architect, William Wilson Wurster. She has since covered political campaigns, interviewed famous people, recorded social phenomena such as the hippie movement in San Francisco, and written

Joan Didion's essays and novels address such issues as alienation and disempowerment. (Quintana Roo Dunne)

about places she has been. Although she has described Honolulu, El Salvador, Miami, New York, and Washington, D.C., it is her native state that is most often the subject or the setting for her highly praised nonfiction.

Didion grew up in Sacramento and attended the University of California at Berkeley. Her writing career began there with a short story published in a campus magazine. After graduation, she moved east to work on *Vogue* and to live in New York City for almost ten years. There she met John Gregory Dunne, a fellow writer, and they married and came back to live in Los Angeles. Didion continued to write novels and articles for a variety of prominent national magazines. At the same time, she collaborated with her husband on a magazine column and wrote screenplays.

Didion's personal world is the source for her writing. A daughter of pioneers, her outlook is radically individualist and she finds no comforting systems to explain the scattered chaos of events in her home state. She questions all group allegiances and all party lines, including the women's movement, for which she has drawn criticism from its members.

In three collections of her journalism, *Slouching Towards Bethlehem*, *The White Album*, and *After Henry*, her description of current events of the time is often highly personal. In the novels, readers have suspected, the sad heroines are Didion without the consolation of a career. In Didion's nonfiction she records her bouts with migraines and depression. Although she has written about other places, Didion seems to take California with her when she travels, and California is her subject. In her book *After Henry* there are twelve essays; seven are about California. As a social critic, Didion is pessimistic. She believes that American myths have little or nothing to do with what happens in most people's lives. In her opinion, mythmaking from unsuitable facts is a dangerous business engaged in largely by politicians and the media. She offers no cure except her own intensely concrete writing, a record of observable facts without, as she insists, a narrative.

Suggested readings

Didion, Joan. *Joan Didion: Essays and Conversations*. Edited by Ellen G. Friedman. Ontario: Ontario Review Press, 1984.

Winchell, Mark Royden. *Joan Didion*. Boston: Twayne, 1980.

—Lucy Golsan

See also American identity: West and the frontier; *Play It as It Lays*; Television and identity; *White Album, The*

Disability. *See* Physical disabilities and identity

Divorce

Identities: Family; men; women

Definition: Divorce is the legal dissolution of a marriage.

At issue   Since divorce is a legal process, it constitutes a socially sanctioned transformation of one kind of social unit into another. Divorce is significantly different from a dissolution of the family through the desertion or abandonment of one partner by the other, or of one or both partners of their children, because desertion is not sanctioned by society. On the contrary, abandonment is generally perceived as a socially unacceptable action, one which breaks with the culture's established norms of order and moral value. Therefore, the legitimate return of married people to the legal status of a single individual is important because it means that society accepts that the rights and interests of the individual can be more important than those of the family or of social stability in general. Divorce has figured in North American literature, with some significant exceptions, as a powerful means of dramatizing a married woman's struggle to attain an identity of her own. A man's marital status has not, traditionally, been as important to his identity as it has been for a woman; hence the emphasis on the woman's experience with divorce.

Literature to 1900   Until the middle of the nineteenth century, divorce was conspicuously absent from the literary work produced in North America. Such writers as James Fenimore Cooper and Washington Irving idealized marriage but never dealt with it directly in their fictions, and earlier writers tended to be conventional, moralistic, and provincial regarding public morality in general and the sanctity of the marriage bond in particular. Beginning with Nathaniel Hawthorne's *The Scarlet Letter* (1850), however, North American writers began to present strong female characters entangled in troubled, inadequate, or unsatisfactory marriages, and more than that, to suggest women could replace these failed relationships with a more satisfactory life as emancipated individuals, with or without a more suitable partner. Hawthorne's Hester Prynne marks the first example in American literature of this kind of female character. Although she endures physical punishment and social rejection by a society that judges her adversely for having a child during her husband's extended absence, and for refusing to identify the father, she is undaunted and self-reliant, urging her lover to elope with her to Europe, where they can live together outside the laws that govern them in America. Her lover, the highly respected young minister Arthur Dimmesdale, can neither bring himself to make public admission of what he has done nor escape with her to Europe and make a new start. Instead he punishes himself for years in private before making a humiliating public admission of his sin and finally dying in Hester's arms, a broken man. After Dimmesdale's death, Hester goes to Europe with her daughter and enjoys the fruits of her strong-minded individuality in peace, free from the social stigma that was her lot in New England. Since social norms in the mid-nineteenth century strictly forbade divorce on any grounds but adultery, and since such divorces were considered scandalous and socially unacceptable, the position Hawthorne takes in this novel is a radical one, for he makes it clear that an inflexible insistence on maintaining marriage at any cost is incompatible with individual happiness.

The conflict between marriage and a woman's individual identity Hawthorne suggested in *The Scarlet Letter* was specifically linked to divorce later in the century by such writers as Henry James in *The Portrait of a Lady* (1881) and *What Maisie Knew* (1897). In *The Portrait of a Lady* James's heroine, Isabel Archer, openly considers and rejects divorce from Ormond, her sophisticated but immoral husband. Eventually Isabel asserts her independence by disobeying her husband's direct command to remain with him in Italy; she goes to tend to her dying cousin in England. When she is offered a chance to elope with one who truly loves her (and whom she loves in return), she refuses to be the possession of any man and returns to Rome and to the husband whom she no longer loves. Because she does not love him, he no longer has the power to control her actions or limit her growth as a mature individual.

The Portrait of a Lady does not present readers with an actual divorce or with a protagonist who was divorced. Nearly twenty years later James addressed this issue in *What Maisie Knew* (1897), a powerful, subtle, and at times disturbingly funny portrait of a high-society divorce and the ensuing vicissitudes of custody squabbles, love affairs, remarriages, and parental neglect, as seen through the eyes of the only child of the divorced couple. This novel was revolutionary in its frank, detailed, and explicit treatment of divorce. The novel also broke new ground in its perspective, for James focuses on the identity of the child of the divorced couple rather than on that of one or the other of the partners in the marriage. As Maisie watches her parents divorce, remarry, and divorce again, she finds that she is manipulated, flattered, and used by each of them in turn, and develops not only a substantial aversion to her natural parents but also a deep conviction that marriage and individuality are incompatible. The novel ends with another round of marriages—this time the former spouses of Maisie's parents are marrying each other, and Maisie refuses to live with anyone but Mrs. Wix, the faithful nurse and governess who was hired soon after her parents were first divorced and who has proved to be the only person in Maisie's life who is truly devoted to her. By shifting the focus from the persons getting a divorce to the child of divorce, James poses the problem of the compatibility of individual identity and marriage with greater intensity—and considerably less optimism—than Hawthorne does.

The fictional landscape of divorce and the question of the compatibility of individual female identity and marriage are brilliantly explored by Edith Wharton in *The Custom of the Country* (1913). The custom referred to in the title is divorce, the country is the United States, and the novel recounts the rise of Undine Spragg, through a series of marriages and divorces, to social prominence in New York and later Parisian society. Along the way she acquires a son, has an affair, converts to Catholicism, marries a French count, and finally marries Elmer Moffatt, a self-made railroad tycoon who had been her first husband years before when he was poor and unsuccessful. The power to obtain a divorce is linked to a positive personal benefit in terms of freedom, happiness, and self-realization. Divorce is depicted as the "wave of the future," a vigorous practice of the young and economically booming Midwest which, in the person of Undine, invades and conquers the conservative bastions of the old aristocratic order. Undine's career is paralleled throughout the novel by the steady rise of Elmer (whose identity as her first husband is hinted at early in the story, but not revealed until its final chapters), and their joint victory over old-fashioned ideas and customs is symbolized by their marriage and by the fact that they finally take up residence in a mansion, in a new section of Paris, furnished in part with heirloom tapestries surreptitiously purchased from the impecunious French count who had been Undine's previous husband. Wharton's attitude toward her heroine's success is more complex than a simple summary of the plot may make it appear. The universal stupidity, frivolity, and complacency of the upper-class elites on both sides of the Atlantic attest a moral and spiritual weakness that deserves to be exploited. Undine, however, is undoubtedly shallow and insatiably ambitious. She neglects her son, and for all her success she never seems to know who she really is or what she really wants to become. When her husband tells her he can never be an ambassador because Undine had been divorced, she is convinced that she was meant to be an ambassador's wife. Wharton is too realistic to believe that divorce will necessarily lead to complete happiness, but she is also too sensible not to see that divorce gives a woman an opportunity to develop an identity that is suited to herself and to the times in which she lives. The right for a woman to pursue opportunity is what Undine, for all her flaws, triumphantly represents.

**Literature from
1900 to 1950**

Literature since 1950

Despite the example of *The Custom of the Country*, until the mid-1920's most literature that treated the theme of individual identity in relation to marriage relied on the affair. Divorce itself was becoming more common, and eventually mainstream novelists began to depict divorced people with regularity as a facet of urban life, particularly among the rich, the intelligentsia, and artists. Examples of novels that treat divorce in such a way include John Dos Passos' *Manhattan Transfer* (1925), his *U.S.A.* trilogy (1937), and later stories and novels by F. Scott Fitzgerald, especially *Tender Is the Night* (1934). Divorce is not the central or crucial experience depicted in these later novels, as it is in *What Maisie Knew* or *The Custom of the Country*, but divorce in the later novels remains linked to a search for individual identity, especially for strong-minded and talented women who find that marriage prevents them from fully realizing themselves.

Divorce became much more prevalent in North American society during the second half of the twentieth century, especially from the 1960's on, and its appearance in fiction increased correspondingly. The focus of interest shifted from the question of the effect of divorce on the identities of women to the effect of divorce on the identities of men. In the powerful climax of John Updike's *Rabbit, Run* (1960), for example, Rabbit Angstrom, unable to decide whether to divorce his wife and marry his pregnant girlfriend or desert the girlfriend and stay with his wife and child, abandons them all, literally running away from his past life. Divorce propels Saul Bellow's protagonist in *Henderson the Rain King* (1959), a middle-aged Connecticut millionaire, to go to Africa in an attempt to quell an inner voice that continually cries "I want, I want." After extraordinary adventures in a world "discontinuous with civilization" he achieves self-knowledge and, at peace with himself at last, returns to America. In Arthur Miller's *After the Fall* (1964) the audience is forced to enter the mind and experience the memories of a middle-aged man as he relives two failed marriages in an effort to gain a better sense of his true personal identity. Not only do these works, for the first time, make the male experience of divorce a central theme in American fiction, but also they consistently deal with divorce's adverse effect on the male identity. For female literary characters up to the late twentieth century, divorce facilitates, or is necessitated by, a growth in personal identity. For male characters in the fiction of the 1950's and 1960's, divorce marks a painful collapse of traditional forms of personal identity.

During that late twentieth century female characters also began to experience divorce in terms of a collapse of identity along with the collapse of a marriage. This was not really parallel to the fictional presentation of the male experience of divorce in this period but rather was an extension of the earlier pattern: Women need freedom from the limitations of marital roles in order to gain individual identity. In Mary McCarthy's *The Group* (1963), for example, when Kay Strong's marriage ends in separation and she is on the verge of divorce when she dies in a sanatorium, it is clear that her failed marriage and death are a direct result of her inability successfully to separate her identity from that of her husband, Harald. Her classmate Norine, however, has a stronger sense of herself and terminates one unsatisfactory marriage and eventually makes a successful second marriage. This tendency to present both pros and cons to the project of promoting strong personal identities for women (but with the emphasis clearly on women's finding a way to succeed as individuals in a male-dominated world) continued in the 1970's. Marilyn French's autobiographical novel *The Women's Room* (1977) is a good example of realism in the handling of this theme, recounting the heroine Mira's transformation of herself from a repressed, vain, and shallow wife and mother who "slammed genteel doors in her head" into a divorced, independent, self-supporting individual who, despite having "opened all the doors in my head," still knows frustrations. Mira is willing to face the fact that the price of her independence has turned out to be loneliness, and she is ready to begin something new.

In the last two decades of the twentieth century, divorce became a standard part of the fictional landscape, as it had become a familiar part of the lives of North Americans in general. Short fiction, novels, and plays frequently contain characters who have been divorced or who are going through a divorce. Divorce no longer seems to be a primary vehicle for the theme of identity, which more frequently has been developed in terms of race, ethnicity, sexual orientation, or regional affiliation.

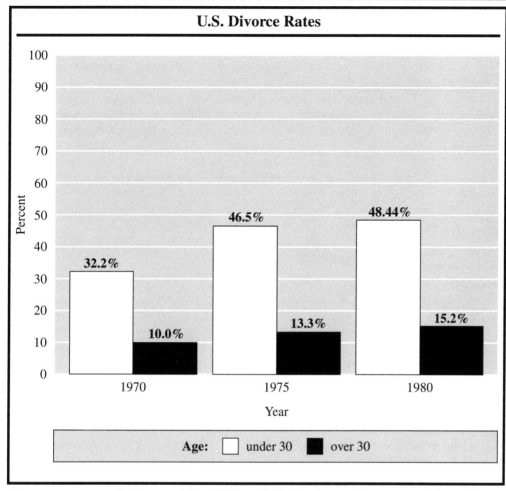

U.S. Divorce Rates

Divorce rates generally increased from 1970 to 1980. Marriages, often contracted in one's early twenties, are less likely to end in divorce after the initial years of marriage.

Source: National Center for Health Statistics.

Some of the stories in Bobbie Ann Mason's collection *Shiloh and Other Stories* (1982), for example, feature the breakup of a marriage or the visit of a divorced daughter to a holiday family dinner, but the identities that are explored in her fiction are founded on the shared life experiences, habits, and customs of southern rural America. Similarly, the central issue for Wendy Wasserstein's characters in the play *The Sisters Rosensweig* (1991) is not the multiple divorces of the oldest sister, the successful marriage of the second sister, or the failed relationships of the youngest, but rather their identities as successful Jewish women. Marriage is no longer a constant, a given, an enduring personal commitment, as it was in the days when Hawthorne wrote *The Scarlet Letter*, and as a result it has lost most of its ability to define the issue of individual identity.

SUGGESTED READINGS

Bell, Millicent. *Meaning in Henry James.* Cambridge, Mass.: Harvard University Press, 1991. A literary interpretation of James's most important novels, focusing on the subtleties of his development of character, including discussions of the construction of identity in *The Portrait of a Lady* and *What Maisie Knew.*

Bloom, Harold, ed. *Hester Prynne.* New York: Chelsea House, 1990. A collection of essays exploring a range of views of Hawthorne's heroine, from dangerous violator of social norms to healthy individualist.

Chase, Richard. *The American Novel and Its Tradition*. Garden City, N.J.: Anchor Press, 1957. An excellent introduction to the American novel.

Hook, Andrew. *Dos Passos*. Englewood Cliffs, N.J.: Prentice-Hall, 1974. A collection of essays that discuss the ways Dos Passos' fiction documents the social, sexual, and economic changes of early twentieth century urban America.

Joslin, Katherine. *Edith Wharton*. New York: St. Martin's Press, 1994. Compares Wharton to other women writers of the late nineteenth and early twentieth centuries, with emphasis on her unusual concern for the plight of the individual whose identity is too constrained by social ties and obligations.

—R. A. Martin

See also Erotic identity; Feminism; Nontraditional family; Patriarchy and matriarchy; Women and identity

Donald Duk

AUTHOR: Frank Chin (1940-   )
FIRST PUBLISHED: 1991
IDENTITIES: Chinese American

Donald Duk is a psychologically realistic depiction of a fifth-generation Chinese American boy who, by learning his family history and his cultural heritage, frees himself from the trauma caused by the racial stereotyping of his people. Set in San Francisco's Chinatown during a New Year's celebration, the novel delineates the initiation of its protagonist, Donald Duk, in a manner that interweaves history, legend, surrealistic dreams, and psychological realism.

Donald is troubled more by his racial identity than by his funny name. Repeatedly he has heard people at school and in the media say that his people are traditionally timid and passive, introverted and nonassertive; therefore, they are alien to American heroism and pioneering spirit. He is thus filled with self-contempt and tormented by everything Chinese. With the Chinese New Year approaching, he becomes more and more depressed and withdrawn, for the New Year will provide another opportunity for his schoolteachers to repeat in class the same thing that everybody else says about his people.

The New Year during which Donald completes the first twelve-year cycle of his life (there are twelve years in the Chinese zodiac) is the right time for the elders in his family and in the community to tell him what everybody has chosen not to say about his people. From these elders he learns that his people came from a land that had produced its own Robin Hoods, and that Chinese railroaders, his great-great grandfather among them, blasted their way through Nevada, lived in tunnels carved in deep frozen snow for two winters, set a world record in track-laying, and went on strike for back pay and Chinese foremen for Chinese gangs. He is so fascinated with these railroaders' heroism and pioneering spirit that scenes of their toil and struggle appear one after another in his dreams.

Through careful library research, Donald determines that his dreams are actually flashbacks to the real events that have been excluded in history books by the majority culture. With his newly gained understanding of the cultural heritage of his people, he is eager to go back to school to challenge the stereotype of his people with his story about their courage and assertiveness.

SUGGESTED READINGS

Chen, Jack. *The Chinese of America*. San Francisco: Harper & Row, 1980.

Davis, Robert Murray. "Frank Chin: Iconoclastic Icon." *Redneck Review of Literature* 23 (Fall, 1992): 75-78.

McDonald, Dorothy Ritsuk. "An Introduction to Frank Chin's *The Chickencoop Chinaman* and *The Year of the Dragon*." In *Three American Literatures: Essays in Chicano, Native American, and Asian American Literature for Teachers of American Literature*, edited by Houston A. Baker, Jr. New York: Modern Language Association of America, 1982.

Samarth, Manini. "Affirmations: Speaking the Self into Being." *Parnassus: Poetry in Review* 17, no. 1 (1992): 88-101

Sechi, Joanne Harumi. "Being Japanese American Doesn't Mean 'Made in Japan.'" In *The Third Woman: Minority Women Writers of the United States*, edited by Dexter Fisher. Boston: Houghton Mifflin, 1989.

—*Chenliang Sheng*

See also Asian American identity: China, Japan, and Korea; Chin, Frank; *Chickencoop Chinaman, The*; *Year of the Dragon, The*

Dorris, Michael

BORN: Louisville, Kentucky; January 30, 1945
DIED: Concord, New Hampshire; April 11, 1997
PRINCIPAL WORKS: *Native Americans: Five Hundred Years After*, 1977; *A Guide to Research on North American Indians*, 1983 (with Arlene B. Hirschfelder and Mary Gloyne Byler); *A Yellow Raft in Blue Water*, 1987; *The Broken Cord: A Family's Ongoing Struggle with Fetal Alcohol Syndrome* (1989; *The Broken Cord: A Father's Story*, 1990); *The Crown of Columbus*, 1991 (with Louise Erdrich)
IDENTITIES: African American; European American; family; Native American; religion; women
SIGNIFICANT ACHIEVEMENT: Dorris' works are among the best examples of fiction and nonfiction featuring Native Americans.

Michael Dorris' involvement with Native American affairs came quite naturally. The only child of a non-Native American mother and a Modoc father, Dorris spent childhood vacations with relatives who lived on reservations in Montana and Washington. His disdain for being called a Native American writer stemmed from these early experiences; he learned to think of people as human beings rather than as members of particular ethnic groups.

After his father's death, Dorris was raised by his mother, aunts, and grandmothers. The result of this feminine influence is apparent in his novel *A Yellow Raft in Blue Water*, a story about three generations of women, narrated in their own voices.

In 1981, Dorris married Louise Erdrich, another author of mixed ancestry. Dorris attributed his literary success to Erdrich, making her another of his women-as-mentors. Dorris and Erdrich collaborated as they wrote, producing works that authentically showcase Native Americans.

After his adopted son, Abel, was diagnosed with fetal alcohol syndrome, a preventable but debilitating condition caused by alcohol consumption during pregnancy, Dorris began writing *The Broken Cord: A Family's Ongoing Struggle with Fetal Alcohol Syndrome*. The book includes a touching autobiographical account provided by Abel.

The Broken Cord's focus on alcohol abuse reflects Dorris' concern that government policies are plunging Native Americans into a health and education crisis, and continues his work as a Native American activist. While a professor at Dartmouth, Dorris founded the Native American Studies Program and received the Indian Achievement Award. His empathy for Native Americans is apparent in his literary characters, who dramatize the often difficult living conditions of contemporary tribal members.

Despite the focus on Native Americans in his works, the common experiences of humanity fueled Dorris' passion for writing. As an anthropologist who valued differences, Dorris used his literary voice to promote acceptance of diversity, touching on the basic elements of life that connect all people.

SUGGESTED READINGS
Chavkin, Allan, and Nancy Feyl Chavkin, eds. *Conversations with Louise Erdrich and Michael Dorris*. Jackson: University Press of Mississippi, 1994.

Owens, Louis. "Erdrich and Dorris's Mixedbloods and Multiple Narratives." In *Other Destinies: Understanding the American Indian Novel*. Norman: University of Oklahoma Press, 1992.

Rayson, Ann. "Shifting Identity in the Work of Louise Erdrich and Michael Dorris." *Studies in American Indian Literatures* 3 (Winter, 1991): 27-36.

—*Lynne Klyse*

See also Alcoholism; Erdrich, Louise; Native American identity; *Yellow Raft in Blue Water, A*

Dostoevski, Fyodor

BORN: Moscow, Russia; November 11, 1821

DIED: St. Petersburg, Russia; February 9, 1881

PRINCIPAL WORKS: *Zapiski iz podpolya*, 1864 (*Letters from the Underworld*, 1913; better known as *Notes from the Underground*, 1918); *Igrok*, 1866 (*The Gambler*, 1949); *Prestupleniye i nakazaniye*, 1866 (*Crime and Punishment*, 1886); *Idiot*, 1868 (*The Idiot*, 1887); *Bratya Karamazovy*, 1879-1880 (*The Brothers Karamazov*, 1912)

IDENTITIES: Religion; world

SIGNIFICANT ACHIEVEMENT: Dostoevski examines the paradoxical nature of human identity, concluding that the suffering brought by free will is a necessary prerequisite to redemption.

At about four o'clock one morning in April, 1849, the twenty-seven-year-old Fyodor Dostoevski was awakened in his room and arrested by the czar's secret police. One of thirty-four members of the Petrashevsky circle to be arrested that night, Dostoevski was convicted of holding atheistic and antigovernment socialistic beliefs. After eight harrowing months in confinement, during which time many of his comrades died or went insane, he was led out to be publicly executed in late December. Waiting twenty minutes to be shot, Dostoevski was saved from death by a reprieve from the czar, granted much earlier but delayed for dramatic effect. This mock execution became the defining moment in Dostoevski's life, and the motif of the condemned person awaiting death reappears often in his works.

Instead of being executed, Dostoevski served eight years in penal servitude in Siberia, where for four years he worked in isolation, constantly shackled. His political and religious views changed dramatically at this time to embrace a form of mystical Christianity and conservative nationalism. *Zapiski iz myortvogo doma* (1861-1862; *Buried Alive: Or, Ten Years of Penal Servitude in Siberia*, 1881; better known as *The House of the Dead*, 1915) is based on this experience. In *The House of the Dead*, Dostoevski explores what effects isolation and punishment have on human identity, implying that the penal colony is a religious microcosm of humanity.

Upon his release, Dostoevski was assigned as a soldier in Mongolia. In 1859, he was permitted to return to Russia and St. Petersburg. There he resumed his writing, first begun before his imprisonment. In 1861, Dostoevski began to exhibit behavior that was to plague him most of the rest of his life: A compulsive gambler (*The Gambler* is semiautobiographical), his debts frequently forced him to flee creditors. Also, epileptic seizures made his life erratic and unpredictable. Finally, his emotional relationships with others resulted in periods of ecstasy followed by despair.

In the masterpiece *Crime and Punishment*, Raskolnikov, the protagonist, dares to think of himself as a superior human, committing what he believes is the perfect murder as an intellectual exercise demonstrating his point. He completes the act without immediate repercussions, but he soon suffers immobilizing guilt, which ultimately forces upon him the realization that he is no better than anyone else. At the end of the novel, Raskolnikov admits his crime and embraces his punishment, finally accepting an orthodox Christian belief.

Later in his life, Dostoevski traveled around Europe, writing and most frequently living in desperate poverty. It was only toward the end of his life, with the publication of *The Brothers Karamazov*, that fame and some prosperity came to him. He died early in 1881.

SUGGESTED READINGS

Ivanov, Vyacheslav. *Freedom and the Tragic Life: A Study in Dostoevsky*. New York: Farrar, Straus & Giroux, 1960.

Mochulsky, Konstantin. *Dostoevski: His Life and Work*. Translated by Michael A. Minihan. Princeton, N.J.: Princeton University Press, 1967.

Wasiolek, Edward. *Dostoevski: The Major Fiction*. Cambridge, Mass.: MIT Press, 1964.

—*Dana Anthony Grove*

See also Existentialism; *Notes from Underground*; Underground man: a literary archetype

Douglass, Frederick (Frederick Augustus Washington Bailey)

BORN: Tuckahoe, Talbot County, Maryland; February, 1817?

DIED: Washington, D.C.; February 20, 1895

PRINCIPAL WORKS: *Narrative of the Life of Frederick Douglass: An American Slave*, 1845; *My Bondage and My Freedom*, 1955; *The Life and Times of Frederick Douglass*, 1881

IDENTITIES: African American

SIGNIFICANT ACHIEVEMENT: Douglass wrote one of the most artistic, articulate, and insightful slave narratives and lived a life dedicated to championing black civil rights.

Frederick Augustus Bailey, who changed his name to Frederick Douglass after escaping slavery, was the son of a slave mother and a white man, probably his mother's master, Captain Aaron Anthony. He grew up in a variety of slavery conditions, some very harsh. He nevertheless taught himself to read and write and became a skilled caulker at the Baltimore shipyards.

In 1838, he escaped to New York disguised as a free sailor. After marrying Anna Murray, a freewoman who had helped him escape, they moved to Massachusetts. He took the name Douglass and began working for the abolitionist cause. For four years he was a popular and eloquent speaker for antislavery societies and in 1845 published his *Narrative of the Life of Frederick Douglass: An American Slave*, one of the finest slave narratives.

As a precaution against recapture following the publication of his autobiography, Douglass went to England to lecture on racial conditions in the United States. In late 1846, British friends purchased and manumitted Douglass, and the following year he returned to New York a free man.

Moving to Rochester, Douglass began an abolitionist newspaper, *The North Star* (later renamed *Frederick Douglass' Paper*), became an Underground Railroad agent, wrote in support of women's rights and temperance, and revised and expanded his autobiography. In 1859, he narrowly escaped arrest following John Brown's raid at Harpers Ferry. Although Douglass had not supported the raid, he was a friend of Brown. He fled to Canada, then England, returning months later when he learned of his daughter Annie's death.

During the Civil War, Douglass urged the recruitment and equal treatment of blacks in the military (his two sons were early volunteers) and became an unofficial adviser to Abraham Lincoln on matters of race. After Lincoln's death, he opposed Andrew Johnson's procolonization stance and worked for black civil rights, especially suffrage.

A loyal supporter of the Republican Party, he was appointed to various posts by five presidents. In 1881, Douglass again updated his autobiography. The following year Anna Murray Douglass died. Two years later, Douglass married Helen Pitts, his white secretary, a marriage that shocked many. In 1889, President Benjamin Harrison appointed Douglass minister to Haiti. Douglass retired in 1891 but remained a powerful voice

Frederick Douglass was a leader in the abolitionist movement. (Library of Congress)

speaking out for racial equality until his death in 1895. He is remembered as not only the most prominent black American of his era but also a man whose life of commitment to the concept of equality made him an outstanding American for all times.

SUGGESTED READINGS

Bontemps, Arna. *Free at Last: The Life of Frederick Douglass*. New York: Dodd, Mead, 1971.

McFeely, William S. *Frederick Douglass*. New York: W. W. Norton, 1991.

Preston, Diopkon J. *Young Frederick Douglass: The Maryland Years*. Baltimore: The Johns Hopkins University Press, 1980.

Quarles, Benjamin. *Frederick Douglass*. Washington, D.C.: Associated Publishers, 1948.

—*Grace McEntee*

See also *Narrative of the Life of Frederick Douglass*; Slave narratives; Slavery

Dove, Rita

BORN: Akron, Ohio; August 28, 1952

PRINCIPAL WORKS: *The Yellow House on the Corner*, 1980; *Museum*, 1983; *Fifth Sunday*, 1985; *Thomas and Beulah*, 1986; *The Other Side of the House*, 1988; *Grace Notes*, 1989

IDENTITIES: African American; women

SIGNIFICANT ACHIEVEMENT: Dove's poems give voice to the African American woman whose concerns are wider than region or race.

Rita Dove acknowledges that her writing is influenced by a range of experiences. Consequently, Dove consistently avoids being pigeonholed. As an undergraduate at Miami University in Oxford, Ohio, she spent a year on a Fulbright Scholarship at the University of Tübingen, in West Germany, where she realized that a writer cannot have a limited view of the world. Although her earlier work was influenced by African American writers of the 1960's, she stands apart from African American writers who write primarily of the politics of ethnicity. Well-educated, Dove allows her poetry to reflect her wide interests. Many poems allude to the visual arts and music. Poems in *Museum*

Rita Dove, author of several volumes of poetry describing the African American experience. (Fred Viebahn)

discuss Catherine of Alexandria, Catherine of Siena, William Shakespeare, Friedrich Hölderlin, and Giovanni Boccaccio. The cross-cultural thrust of her writing is indicative of the influence that Dove's European experience had on her.

Dove's poetry uses family history as material. In *Thomas and Beulah*, Dove mixes fact and imagination to describe the lives of her maternal grandparents. A book-length narrative, the story of her family employs two separate points of view, that of her grandfather and that of her grandmother. Race is central to the story, but Dove focuses on the relationship that they had, in spite of the difference between their families. Winner of the 1987 Pulitzer Prize in poetry, the volume shows her concern with the voices of ordinary people. Through these lives she addresses more communal concerns. Dove's work acknowledges the existence of race problems but allows the human spirit to triumph.

Marriage to Fred Viebahn in 1979 produced one daughter, Aviva Chantal Tamu Dove-Viebahn. Dove's poetry of the time explores mother-daughter relationships, especially when the child is biracial. Such poems are evident in *Grace Notes*. Dove experiments with other literary forms. She has produced a verse play, short stories, and a novel. *Through the Ivory Gate*, her first novel, explores the interplay between autobiography and artifice. Virginia King, a character reflecting Dove's experiences, returns to Akron to work with young students. Learning the stories of her family confirms Virginia in her desire for a career in the theater.

In 1993, Dove became poet laureate of the United States. In that role, she worked with emerging writers, encouraging them to gain the breadth and depth of experience that would fuel their writing.

SUGGESTED READINGS

Costello, Bonnie. "Scars and Wings: Rita Dove's *Grace Notes*." *Callaloo* 14, no. 2 (1991): 434-438.
Vendler, Helen. *The Given and the Made: Recent American Poets*. London: Faber & Faber, 1995.

—*Martha Modena Vertreace*

See also Feminism; Mixed race and identity; Multiculturalism

Down These Mean Streets

AUTHOR: Piri Thomas (1928-   )
FIRST PUBLISHED: 1967
IDENTITIES: Adolescence and coming-of-age; African American; Caribbean; Latino; multiracial

Down These Mean Streets, Piri Thomas' confessional autobiography, documents the brutal growing-up experiences of a young man of African and Puerto Rican descent in New York City. This testimonial depicts the Depression of the 1930's in Spanish Harlem and the struggle to achieve an identity in a society where inequality prevails.

The dark-skinned Piri, known as Johnny Gringo, encounters racial and social prejudice beginning in childhood. The son of Hispanic immigrants, he becomes aware of his parents' poverty at an early age. His father often submits the family to the humiliation of welfare, while the mother escapes reality by daydreaming about Puerto Rico. Piri, the oldest of five children, yearns for the love of his father, who favors the siblings with lighter skin. When the family moves to an Italian neighborhood, Piri is a victim of racial remarks and physical abuse. As an outsider, in his need to belong, he joins street gangs that walk down the streets "tall and tough," and becomes a burglar.

In 1944, the family moves to a suburb in Long Island; Piri's attempts to make friends fail because of discrimination. He moves back to Harlem on his own; unable to get a job, he starts dealing drugs. He achieves recognition and prestige among junkies and hoodlums.

Confused about his identity, Piri joins the merchant marine with his black friend Brew. Prejudice becomes intolerable after seven months around the world. He returns to Harlem. When Piri's mother dies, the streets become his world again. Although he is in love with Trina, he fathers a child with Dulcien. Addicted to heroin, in need of money, he gets involved in burglaries. Convicted of an attempted armed robbery, he is sentenced to five to fifteen years hard labor in prison. His adored Trina marries somebody else.

In his twenties, while in prison, Piri tries to find himself through learning. Eligible for parole after four years, he focuses on preparing for freedom. He earns a high school diploma, three or four certificates, and three diplomas for Bible studies. Through self-discovery, faith, and endurance, he finds redemption. A classic coming-of-age narrative, *Down These Mean Streets* portrays the survival strategies of underprivileged Latino youth in urban streets and in prison. Through the achievement of self-respect and dignity, there comes a new sense of identity.

SUGGESTED READINGS

Flores, Juan. *Divided Borders: Essays on Puerto Rican Identity*. Houston, Tex.: Arte Público Press, 1993.
Rivero, Eliana. "Hispanic Literature in the United States: Self-Image and Conflict." *Revista Chicano-Riqueña* 13, nos. 3-4 (1985): 173-192.

Rodriguez de Laguna, Asela, ed. *Images and Identities: The Puerto Rican in Literature*. New Brunswick, N.J.: Transaction, 1987.

Shorris, Earl. *Latinos: A Biography of the People*. New York: W. W. Norton, 1992.

—*Ludmila Kapschutschenko-Schmitt*

See also American identity: Northeast; Latino American identity; Racism and ethnocentrism

Dream of a Common Language, The

Author: Adrienne Rich (1929-   )
First published: 1978
Identities: European American; gay, lesbian, and bisexual; women

The Dream of a Common Language is a collection of poetry written by a woman, about women, for women. This book was the first that Adrienne Rich published after she publicly came out as a lesbian in 1976. In this book her life and work become an integrated whole; in lesbianism her most intimate personal relationships become a reflection of her political and social idealism.

The collection is divided into three sections. The first, "Power," is about the accomplishments of individual women. The opening poem about Marie Curie announces one of Rich's themes. Her ideology champions the common women. In "Power," about a famous or uncommon woman, Marie Curie's power, radiation, becomes the source of her wounds. Rich is searching in her poetry for a common language for the ordinary woman. In "Origins and History of Consciousness" she articulates this theme, as well as the theme of connection, a community of women. She concludes: "the true nature of poetry. The drive/ to connect. The dream of a common language."

The second section of the book, "Twenty-one Love Poems," is the open proclamation of Rich's sexual preference. The poems are filled with the yearning for a lasting mature relationship, as when she writes: "Since we're not young, weeks have to do time/ for years of missing each other." The language of this section is lyrical, even ecstatic, yet the poems also include the prosaic details of women's daily lives. They are also openly, radically, explicit about the love-making between women. Rich is brave, confident, about her newly acknowledged lesbianism. Her lesbianism is her conscious choice. "I choose to walk here. And to draw this circle."

In the final section, "Not Somewhere Else, but Here," Adrienne Rich continues her exploration of female relationships. In "Natural Resources," she lists some elements of the lives of common women, "the loving humdrum acts/ of attention to this house." In the final poem, "Transcendental Etude," Rich celebrates woman's power to create with common or ordinary materials in a metaphor of quilt-making. In this poem, two women create "a whole new poetry beginning here."

Throughout *The Dream of a Common Language*, Rich's language and poems express the knowledge that her art is based on her being a woman. She explores the nature of language and poetry with this concept as a basis for "a whole new poetry," "the dream of a common language."

Suggested readings

Cooper, Jane Roberta, ed. *Reading Adrienne Rich: Reviews and Re-Visions, 1951-81*. Ann Arbor: University of Michigan Press, 1984.

Keyes, Claire. *The Aesthetics of Power: The Poetry of Adrienne Rich*. Athens: University of Georgia Press, 1986.

Martin, Wendy. *An American Triptych: Anne Bradstreet, Emily Dickinson, Adrienne Rich*. Chapel Hill: University of North Carolina Press, 1984.

—*Susan Butterworth*

See also Lesbian identity; Rich, Adrienne; Rich, Adrienne, poetry of

Dreaming in Cuban

Author: Cristina Garcia (1958-   )
First published: 1992
Identities: Adolescence and coming-of-age; Caribbean; Latino; women

Dreaming in Cuban, Cristina Garcia's first novel, chronicles the lives of three generations of women as they strive for self-fulfillment. This bittersweet novel also illustrates the Cuban American immigrant experience in the United States, focusing on the search for cultural identity in exile. In Cuba, for twenty-five years, the matriarch Celia del Pino writes letters to Gustavo, a long lost lover. She never sends the self-revealing correspondence, and stops writing in 1959, at the time of the Cuban Revolution, when the family becomes divided by politics and her granddaughter Pilar is born.

Celia, who believes that "to survive is an act of hope," sublimates her unfulfilled romantic desires by imagining herself as a heroine of the revolution. In need of recognition, she supports Fidel Castro devotedly. As her husband Jorge del Pino leaves her to join their daughter Lourdes in the United States, she spends her days scanning the sea for American invaders and daydreaming about a more exciting life.

Felicia, Celia's youngest daughter, abused and abandoned by her first husband Hugo Villaverde, suffers from fits of madness and violence. A stranger to herself and her children, she seeks refuge in music and the Afro-Cuban cult of Santeria; after becoming a priestess, she finds peace in death. Lourdes, Celia's eldest daughter, raped and tortured by the revolutionaries, loses her unborn son. She escapes from Castro's Cuba with her husband Rufino del Puente and their daughter Pilar. Emotionally unfulfilled, she develops eating disorders; while her family dreams of returning to Cuba, she supports the anti-Castro movement, establishes a chain of Yankee Doodle bakeries, and focuses on achieving the American Dream.

Raised in Brooklyn, in conflict with her Americanized mother, Pilar identifies with her grandmother Celia in Cuba. She visits the homeland in search of her true identity and, as she receives Celia's legacy of letters and family stories, she becomes aware of the magic inner voice that inspires artistic creativity. Pilar returns to America with a positive self-image, accepting her double identity as a bilingual and bicultural Latina.

Dreaming in Cuban represents the coming-of-age memoir narrative. Through recollections and nostalgic remembrances, the novel illustrates issues of identity and separation, women's survival strategies, and cultural dualism.

SUGGESTED READINGS

Boswell, Thomas D. *The Cuban American Experience: Culture, Images and Perspectives*. Totowa, N.J.: Rowman and Allanheld, 1984.

Davis, Thulani. "Fidel Castro Between Them: *Dreaming in Cuban*." *The New York Times Book Review*, May 17, 1992, 14.

Pérez Firmat, Gustavo. *Life on the Hyphen: The Cuban American Way*. Austin: University of Texas Press, 1994.

Ugalde, Sharon Keefe. "Process, Identity, and Learning to Read: Female Writing and Feminist Criticism in Latin America Today." *Latin American Research Review* 24, no. 1 (1989): 222-232.

—*Ludmila Kapschutschenko-Schmitt*

See also Bilingualism; Caribbean American literature; Emigration and immigration; Latino American identity

Dreiser, Theodore

BORN: Terre Haute, Indiana; August 27, 1871

DIED: Hollywood, California; December 28, 1945

PRINCIPAL WORKS: *Sister Carrie*, 1900; *Jenny Gerhardt*, 1911; *The Financier*, 1912, 1927; *The Titan*, 1914; *The "Genius,"* 1915; *An American Tragedy*, 1925; *The Bulwark*, 1946; *The Stoic*, 1947

IDENTITIES: European American

SIGNIFICANT ACHIEVEMENT: As the son of a poor German immigrant, Dreiser created a new American realism that voiced the problems and concerns of people who had never before been represented in American fiction.

Theodore Dreiser began his writing career as a journalist, and his novels incorporate journalistic content and technique. By relying heavily on real experience, Dreiser was able to represent the longings of Americans, especially young, urban Americans, who, like himself, wanted success but often experienced failure. His father had been a skilled weaver, but by the time Dreiser was born, the ninth of ten children, his father had failed, and the family lived in poverty, moving from house to house, city to city. On one occasion the family was humiliated and forced to move when one of Dreiser's unmarried sisters became pregnant. Although his father was unable to support the family, he attempted to maintain a rigid Catholic morality that was out of touch with the experiences of Dreiser and his siblings. It was from these experiences that Dreiser drew the materials for novels, such as *Sister Carrie*, *Jenny Gerhardt*, and *An American Tragedy*.

In *The "Genius,"* Dreiser took his own experiences as a struggling artist and fictionalized them, creating a portrait of an artist, a realist painter, who is torn between financial and artistic success. In *The "Genius,"* as in all Dreiser novels, characters desire money and happiness—they desire the American Dream, but their struggles to maintain happy relationships or to gain wealth are thwarted. Dreiser was fascinated by wealth and by people who had money, which led him to write three novels, *The Financier*, *The Titan*, and *The Stoic*, about a millionaire, Frank Cowperwood.

While Dreiser attempted to capture the human condition in all of his novels, it is in *Sister Carrie* and *An American Tragedy* that he demonstrates his greatest power as a realist. This power derives from two strengths: Dreiser's sympathetic portrayal of characters who would not normally be considered sympathetically and his detailed description of the environment in which these characters existed. In giving voice to characters who had never before been represented (often poor people who live and act in ways more representative of reality than of literary and moral convention) Dreiser became a model for many twentieth century writers who employed fiction as a means to communicate their experiences.

SUGGESTED READINGS

Gerber, Philip L. *Theodore Dreiser Revisited.* New York: Twayne, 1992.

Gogol, Miriam, ed. *Theodore Dreiser: Beyond Naturalism.* New York: New York University Press, 1995.

Lingeman, Richard. *Theodore Dreiser: An American Journey, 1908-1945.* New York: Putnam, 1990.

_____. *Theodore Dreiser: At the Gates of the City, 1871-1907.* New York: Putnam, 1990.

—*Roark Mulligan*

See also *American Tragedy, An*; *Sister Carrie*; Urban life

Drugs

IDENTITIES: Disease

The nineteenth and early twentieth centuries

The exploration of drugs in literature is a time-honored subject that stretches backward in North American history at least to the early nineteenth century. The works of Edgar Allan Poe, for example, depict the use of opium in such short stories as "Ligeia," "The Fall of the House of Usher," and "Tale of the Ragged Mountain," published in the late 1830's and early 1840's. It was not until the twentieth century, however, that drugs, particularly their use and abuse, became a mainstay in literature. Alcohol is prominent in the works of F. Scott Fitzgerald and Ernest Hemingway, ranging from Fitzgerald's *The Great Gatsby* (1925) and *Tender Is the Night* (1934) to Hemingway's *The Sun Also Rises* (1926) and *A Farewell to Arms* (1929). Alcohol and drugs are central to such plays by Eugene O'Neill as *Long Day's Journey into Night* (1941) and *The Iceman Cometh* (1946). The main themes of all of these works include people coming to terms with the roles drugs play, or have played, in their lives and the lives of those around them.

The late twentieth century

Since the 1950's, drugs have increasingly become a part of everyday life, and the literature since that time has reflected this social change. Most prominent in celebrating the role of marijuana, heroin, and psychedelic drugs in defining individuality in the 1950's were the Beat generation writers, a listing of whom includes William Burroughs, Jack Kerouac, and Allen Ginsberg.

Burroughs' drug addiction and exploration provided the material for *Junkie* (1953) and *Naked Lunch* (1959); *The Wild Boys* (1971) celebrates an outlaw posse of hashish users at the close of the twentieth century. Kerouac's *On the Road* (1957), filled with tales of freedom and drug use, glorified by the underground counterculture, became the scripture for the Beat generation. Ginsberg expressed the terrible side of the world extolled by Kerouac in works including *Howl* (1956) and "Lysergic Acid."

The 1960's psychedelic era produced works dealing with drugs and their possibilities for transcendental or soul-changing experiences. Noteworthy authors include Timothy Leary, Ken Kesey, Tom Wolfe, and Carlos Castaneda. Leary's *The Psychedelic Experience* (1964) presents a guide to combining LSD use and Eastern, particularly Tibetan, philosophy. His *High Priest* (1968) and *The Politics of Ecstasy* (1968) both deal with hallucinogens and religious experiences. Kesey's *One Flew over the Cuckoo's Nest* (1962) presents an examination of institutional drug use and psychological therapy in fictional form. Narcotics and the 1960's hippie generation are the subject of Wolfe's *The Electric Kool-Aid Acid Test* (1968). Castaneda gives an account of hallucinogenic

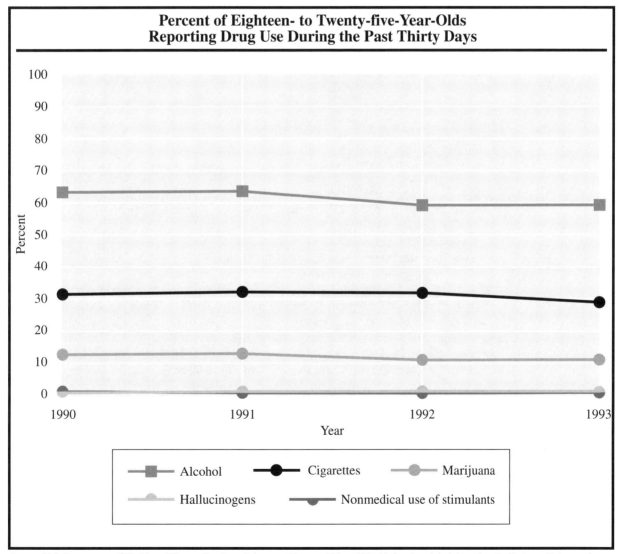

Percent of Eighteen- to Twenty-five-Year-Olds Reporting Drug Use During the Past Thirty Days

Legend: Alcohol, Cigarettes, Marijuana, Hallucinogens, Nonmedical use of stimulants

Source: U.S. Department of Health and Human Services, Substance Abuse and Mental Health Services Administration, *Preliminary Estimates from the 1993 National Household Survey on Drug Abuse.*

drug usage and Southwest Indian teachings in his Don Juan series, beginning with *The Teachings of Don Juan: A Yaqui Way of Knowledge* (1968).

The 1970's and 1980's produced some work dealing with drugs, but the heyday was mostly over. Notable in this last period are Hunter S. Thompson, Jay McInerney, and Bret Easton Ellis. Thompson, writing from the late 1960's onward, combines fact and fiction in his tales of massive drug usage in, among others, *Fear and Loathing in Las Vegas: A Savage Journey to the Heart of the American Dream* (1971), *Fear and Loathing: On the Campaign Trail '72* (1973), and *The Great Shark Hunt* (1979). McInerney describes cocaine usage among the East Coast yuppies of the 1980's in *Bright Lights, Big City* (1984). Ellis' work deals with drug usage among college students and dropouts on the West Coast of the United States in *Less Than Zero* (1985), and on the East Coast of the United States in *The Rules of Attraction* (1987).

SUGGESTED READINGS

Goodwin, Donald W. *Alcohol and the Writer*. New York: Penguin Books, 1988.

Kusinitz, Marc. *Drugs and the Arts*. New York: Chelsea House, 1987.

Lenson, David. *On Drugs*. Minneapolis: University of Minnesota Press, 1995.

Tytell, John. *Naked Angels: The Lives and Literature of the Beat Generation*. New York: McGraw-Hill, 1976.

Weiss, Allen S. *The Aesthetics of Excess*. Albany: State University of New York Press, 1989.

—Joshua Stein

See also Addiction; Alcoholism; Alienation; Countercultures; Eastern religion and philosophy; Twelve-step programs

Du Bois, W. E. B.

BORN: Great Barrington, Massachusetts; February 23, 1868
DIED: Accra, Ghana; August 27, 1963
PRINCIPAL WORKS: *The Philadelphia Negro: A Social Study*, 1899; *The Souls of Black Folk: Essays and Sketches*, 1903; *Darkwater: Voices from Within the Veil*, 1920; *Vospominaniia*, 1962 (*The Autobiography of W. E. B. DuBois: A Soliloquy on Viewing My Life from the Last Decade of Its First Century*, 1968)
IDENTITIES: African American
SIGNIFICANT ACHIEVEMENT: Du Bois was the foremost African American intellectual of the twentieth century and a leader in civil rights and pan-Africanism.

W. E. B. Du Bois was a towering intellectual who created a new language of protest and ideas to understand and guide the African American experience. He wrote fiction and nonfiction, infusing his writings with eloquence and anger. He envisioned a world with equality for all people, emphasizing social justice for Africans and their descendants throughout the New World.

Du Bois' chronicle of his childhood begins with a tale of small-town conventionality in rural Massachusetts, where he experienced a loving home. In 1888, he entered Fisk University and saw firsthand the "color line" dividing the South. After graduating from Fisk, he returned to Massachusetts, where he earned a doctorate in history at Harvard.

His first important academic position was a marginal one at the University of Pennsylvania, but it resulted in his brilliant exposition, *The Philadelphia Negro*. In that work he outlines the historical background of the black community in Philadelphia and documents its patterns of daily life.

In 1897, he accepted a position at the University of Atlanta, where he worked until 1910. He held a yearly conference, resulting in a series of edited books on such topics as African Americans and business, religion, and social life. In 1903, Du Bois published the literary masterpiece *The Souls of Black Folk*, the first of four autobiographies that connect his personal experience with that of his community.

In 1909, Du Bois helped organize the National Association for the Advancement of Colored People (NAACP). He became the first editor of their journal *Crisis* in 1910. For the next quarter century, Du Bois was a center of debate on pressing social issues, and he was personally responsible for many columns, opinions, and reviews in the journal.

By 1935, Du Bois was increasingly at odds with the leadership at the NAACP. He resigned his position there and returned to the University of Atlanta. He helped found the journal *Phylon*, which continues to provide an important voice for African American scholarship. Beginning in the 1920's, Du Bois turned his attention to international affairs, organizing pan-African conferences and observing the racist and classist practices of the Western nations. He became a Marxist, and was attacked by other intellectuals. Du Bois was indicted by the United States for being an agent of a foreign power; the indictment was the result of his peace activism and leftist politics during the Cold War. Although he was acquitted, the accusation that his government made against him remained a source of bitterness.

Du Bois traveled widely around the world—after at first being denied a passport—and eventually settled in Ghana, whose leader, Kwame Nkrumah, was his friend. In Ghana, in his nineties, he began work on an encyclopedia of African culture. Much of Du Bois' vision of racial equality and African American achievement remained unfulfilled at his death in 1963.

SUGGESTED READINGS

Andress, Lillian, ed. *Critical Essays on W. E. B. Du Bois*. Boston: G. K. Hall, 1985.

Lewis, David Levering. *W. E. B. Du Bois: Biography of a Race, 1868-1919*. New York: Henry Holt, 1993.

—*Mary Jo Deegan*

See also African American identity; *Autobiography of W. E. B. DuBois, The*; Civil Rights movement; *Souls of Black Folk, The*

Dunbar, Paul Laurence

BORN: Dayton, Ohio; June 27, 1872

DIED: Dayton, Ohio; February 9, 1906

PRINCIPAL WORKS: *Oak and Ivy*, 1893; *Majors and Minors*, 1895; *Lyrics of Lowly Life*, 1896; *Folks from Dixie*, 1898; *Lyrics of the Hearthside*, 1899; *The Strength of Gideon and Other Stories*, 1900; *The Sport of the Gods*, 1902; *Lyrics of Love and Laughter*, 1903; *The Heart of Happy Hollow*, 1904

IDENTITIES: African American

SIGNIFICANT ACHIEVEMENT: Dunbar was one of the most popular American poets of his time, and America's first professional black writer.

Paul Laurence Dunbar's creative genius and personal and professional tragedies have often been misunderstood by readers who neglect to consider the poet in the context of his time, which was not just marked, but defined, by all-encompassing racial politics. At the end of the nineteenth and beginning of the twentieth centuries, commonly referred to by scholars of African American history as the nadir, Dunbar was a singular phenomenon, trapped between his audience's demands that he be the voice of his race and his own creative mandate that he not be restricted to any given subject matter. Dunbar wrote not merely evocative but enduring work, particularly as a poet. In addition to six volumes of verse, he also wrote four collections of short stories and four novels in the twelve prolific years before his untimely death at the age of thirty-three. Best known for his poems and stories about the Southern rural black world from which he came, Dunbar also wrote verse in standard English, often on black themes. His "We Wear the Mask" is a classic revelation of what it means to be black and American, and his "Sympathy" ("I know why the caged bird sings!") is an ode to freedom with universal appeal.

Dunbar was the only surviving child of Joshua and Matilda Glass Burton Murphy Dunbar, former slaves who had taught themselves to read and write. They nurtured their son with stories of their Kentucky plantation years, the Underground Railroad, the Civil War, and emancipation. These accounts became an important part of Dunbar's consciousness of himself as an inheritor of a particular history and a voice for that identity. Ironically, however, white audiences exploited

Paul Laurence Dunbar, author of Lyrics of Lowly Life *(1896).* (Library of Congress)

this work, even as they championed it, seeing it as a black confirmation of their stereotypical plantation tradition. Despite Dunbar's apparent compromise in this regard, black audiences reveled in and memorized his verses, representing as they did the first national exposure of the black experience rendered in high art.

In 1898, Dunbar married Alice Ruth Moore, a Creole from New Orleans and a writer. The couple separated, however, in 1902, the result of tensions from within the marriage, including her family's disdain for the dark-skinned Dunbar and the demands of his professional life. These pressures contributed to Dunbar's failing health from tuberculosis and his general melancholy, from which his late work suffered. He died childless and broken in spirit in the house he shared with his mother in Dayton.

SUGGESTED READINGS

Braxton, Joanne M., ed. *The Collected Poetry of Paul Laurence Dunbar*. Charlottesville: University Press of Virginia, 1993.

Martin, Jay, ed. *A Singer in the Dawn: Reinterpretations of Paul Laurence Dunbar*. New York: Dodd, Mead, 1975.

Martin, Jay, and Gossie H. Hudson, eds. *Paul Laurence Dunbar Reader*. New York: Dodd, Mead, 1975.

Revell, Peter. *Paul Laurence Dunbar*. Boston: Twayne, 1979.

—*Cynthia Packard*

See also African American identity; Dunbar, Paul Laurence, poetry of

Dunbar, Paul Laurence, poetry of

AUTHOR: Paul Laurence Dunbar (1872-1906)

PRINCIPAL WORKS: *Oak and Ivy*, 1893; *Majors and Minors*, 1895; *Lyrics of Lowly Life*, 1896; *Lyrics of the Hearthside*, 1899; *Lyrics of Love and Laughter*, 1903; *Lyrics of Sunshine and Shadow*, 1905; *Complete Poems*, 1913

IDENTITIES: African American

The poetry of Paul Laurence Dunbar provided America with its first widely read view of black America in verse. Dunbar's poems may be considered America's first experience with an African American poet's perspective on himself and his people and his conflicts with his world. Most of Dunbar's poetry is written in standard English and recalls in form, subject matter, and language the influences of the classic English and American poets. The work most quoted and criticized, however, is that which reflects the identity and experience of African Americans. Dunbar's race-conscious work is influenced by his appreciation for the oral tradition, by black folklore and mores, by the beliefs and expressive language of the black church, and by the historical works of black scholars such as George Washington Williams. Against the prevailing social and literary stereotype of black people as ignorant, contented, and comic, as seen in the work of Southern white writers, Dunbar tried to present his people realistically, in the fullness of their humanity and culture, with their particularities, and in their own voices. Sometimes, however, Dunbar's character depictions were too gently deepened, and the poet was criticized for his alleged conciliatory tone, as in "Home Longings," in which the speaker claims to want to "Drop the pen an' take the plow," a symbolically antiprogressive wish that a white racist could, clearly, misread.

Common themes in Dunbar's dialect poetry include a longing for and celebration of the South as home for the black community ("Goin' Back," "Possum Trot," and "A Letter"), the affirmation of family and love relationships to be found there ("A Negro Love Song" and "Little Brown Baby"), and the celebration of black humanism and cultural gifts ("When Malindy Sings"). In "When Malindy Sings," rhythmic language, rhyme, and exaggeration combine to praise Malindy's innate ability and compare it favorably to Miss Lucy's questionable learned skills. Often Dunbar's more lighthearted poetry seems simply designed to amuse, but closer examination reveals his satiric awareness of social injustice ("Accountability" and "An Ante-Bellum Sermon").

Dunbar's race-conscious poems in standard English reflect the perils, heroism, and survival techniques that come from living in a potentially violent, rigidly segregated, and racist society. Some poems eulogize black heroes and white allies of the freedom struggle ("Frederick Douglass" and "Robert Gould Shaw"). Others expose and condemn those who perpetuate injustices toward black people ("The Haunted Oak" and "To the South"). Still others praise the glory of the African race ("Ode to Ethiopia"). Dunbar's most popular and enduring poems express his awareness of his dilemma as a black man and poet in a restrictive society ("We Wear the Mask" and "Sympathy").

SUGGESTED READINGS

Braxton, Joanne M. Introduction to *The Collected Poetry of Paul Laurence Dunbar*, by Paul Laurence Dunbar. Charlottesville: University Press of Virginia, 1993.

Martin, Jay, ed. *A Singer in the Dawn: Reinterpretations of Paul Laurence Dunbar*. New York: Dodd, Mead, 1975.

—*Cynthia Packard*

See also African American identity; Dunbar, Paul Laurence

Dust Tracks on a Road: An Autobiography

AUTHOR: Zora Neale Hurston (1891-1960)

FIRST PUBLISHED: 1942

IDENTITIES: African American; women

Dust Tracks on a Road: An Autobiography was written when Zora Neale Hurston was about fifty years old. The book poignantly describes what it was like to grow up poor, black, and female;

it shows an energetic woman who overcomes odds to achieve a liberated, rewarding life. Hurston was born in Eatonville, Florida, America's first incorporated black community. Her father was a driving force in the community; her mother died when she was nine. The liberating force for Hurston was her love of knowledge. While at the black grammar school, she won a reading contest, receiving books that ignited her imagination. In turn, she learned about real life at Joe Clarke's store, the meeting place of the men in town.

After her mother's death, she was moved from place to place. It was her own initiative that released her from her circumstances. When she learned that an actress in a traveling Gilbert and Sullivan troupe was looking for a lady's maid, she approached the woman with "I come to work for you." When her service ended—a service that had been a marvelous education in humanity and the arts—she went back to night high school, then to Howard University and Barnard College.

At Barnard, working under anthropologist Franz Boas, she studied the folklore of her people in Polk County, Florida. This began a lifelong interest in the roots of her people. Yet some of Hurston's greatest friends and confidants were the upper-class whites she met both in school and after. Author Fannie Hurst, singer Ethel Waters, and critic Carl Van Vechten were among the many who encouraged her and introduced her to other writers of her times. Hurston at times bemoans her own people and their plight. She sees their disillusionment and oftentimes ill-suited efforts to break out of a stereotype. She lovingly describes the black race as not a race chosen by God but "a collection of people who overslept our time and got caught in the draft."

Hurston's descriptions of her own dedication and hard work inspire the reader to see what a poor African American woman could achieve with forwardness and luck. Her sensitive pictures of her race show people who have the power to overcome obstacles and succeed. Her generous view of humanity and lack of prejudice against anyone because of background or color give the reader a hopeful vision for the future in which love, hope, and hard work make the American Dream possible for anyone.

SUGGESTED READINGS

Gates, Henry Louis, and Anthony Appiah. *Zora Neale Hurston: Cultural Perspectives Past and Present*. New York: Amistad, 1993.

Hemenway, Robert E. *Zora Neale Hurston: A Literary Biography*. Champaign: University of Illinois Press, 1977.

Yanuzzi, Della A. *Zora Neale Hurston: Southern Storyteller*. Springfield, N.J.: Enslow, 1996.

—Janine Rider

See also African American identity; American identity: South; Class and identity; Harlem Renaissance; Hurston, Zora Neale; *Their Eyes Were Watching God*; Women and identity

Dutchman

AUTHOR: Amiri Baraka (LeRoi Jones, 1934-   )
FIRST PRODUCED: 1964; first published, 1964
IDENTITIES: African American; men

A powerful one-act drama, *Dutchman* brought immediate and lasting attention to poet Amiri Baraka. The play is a searing two-character confrontation that begins playfully but builds rapidly in suspense and symbolic resonance. Set on a New York subway train, *Dutchman* opens with a well-dressed, intellectual, young African American man named Clay absorbed in reading a magazine. He is interrupted by Lula—a flirtatious, beautiful white woman a bit older than he. As Lula suggestively slices and eats an apple, she and Clay tease each other with bantering talk that becomes more and more personal. She reveals little about herself, but Lula is clearly in control of the conversation and the situation as she perceptively and provokingly challenges Clay's middle-class self image. Lula is, in fact, a bit cruel. "What right do you have to be wearing a three-button suit and striped tie?" she asks. "Your grandfather was a slave, he didn't go to Harvard." Aware of his insecurities, Lula dares Clay to pretend "that you are free of your own history."

Clay's insecurities about his race, social status, and masculine prowess—slowly revealed as his answers shift from machismo to defensiveness—become the targets for Lula's increasingly direct taunts. Eventually, Lula's attempt to force Clay to see in himself the negative stereotypes of the black male—as either oversexed stud or cringing Uncle Tom—goad him into an eloquently bitter tirade. Black music and African American culture, he tells her, are actually repressions of a justified rage that has kept African American people sane in the face of centuries of oppression. Clay seems as desperate to prove this to himself as he is to convince Lula. He does not seem to know whether the rage or the repression has taken the greater toll on African American sanity. The scene escalates in dramatic force until Lula unexpectedly stabs Clay to death.

Baraka has said that *Dutchman* "is about how difficult it is to become a man in the United States." Nevertheless, the ancient symbolism of apple and temptation, and the myth of the ghostly pirate ship, *The Flying Dutchman*, used in Richard Wagner's opera and other literary works, are carefully suggested in Baraka's play and amplify the dimensions of racial conflict.

SUGGESTED READINGS

Hudson, Theodore R. *From LeRoi Jones to Amiri Baraka.* Durham, N.C.: Duke University Press, 1973.

Neal, Larry. *Visions of a Liberated Future: Black Arts Movement Writings.* New York: Thunder's Mouth Press, 1989.

Sollors, Werner. *Amiri Baraka/LeRoi Jones: The Quest for a "Populist Modernism."* New York: Columbia University Press, 1978.

—*Lorenzo Thomas*

See also African American identity; Baraka, Amiri; *Blues People*; *Daggers and Javelins*; *Selected Poetry of Amiri Baraka/LeRoi Jones*

Dworkin, Andrea

BORN: Camden, New Jersey; September 26, 1946

PRINCIPAL WORKS: *Woman Hating: A Radical Look at Sexuality*, 1974; *Our Blood: Prophecies and Discourses on Sexual Politics*, 1976; *Pornography: Men Possessing Women*, 1981; *Right-Wing Women*, 1983; *Ice and Fire*, 1986; *Intercourse*, 1987; *Letters from a War Zone*, 1989; *Mercy*, 1990

IDENTITIES: Jewish; women

SIGNIFICANT ACHIEVEMENT: Dworkin, a radical feminist, presents alternative views of sexuality and gender roles in society.

Andrea Dworkin was born to left-wing Jewish parents. Inspired by the peace movement of the 1960's, Dworkin participated in a number of antiwar demonstrations. It was at one of these demonstrations that she had the experience that changed her life. At eighteen she was arrested and taken to the Women's House of Detention. Her treatment there was brutal: bullying, harsh internal examinations, and authoritarian contempt left her emotionally and physically scarred. Released after four days, Dworkin hemorrhaged vaginally for two weeks. She spoke out publicly about her trauma in an attempt to find out why any woman should be humiliated in so sexual a way. Her marriage to a Dutch anarchist awakened her to the reality of sexual violence in relationships; he beat her severely until she escaped from him with the help of feminist friends. She was an intelligent, educated woman who had been graduated from Bennington College, but she could not prevent herself from being hurt.

Dworkin describes her childhood as one that taught her to defy convention. As a Jewish child, she refused to sing Christmas carols such as "Silent Night" at school. When her brush with the law and her nightmarish marriage left her horrified by the status of women, she took action.

Woman Hating: A Radical Look at Sexuality, Dworkin's first major work, echoes the pain of her personal experiences of misogyny. Later books, such as *Our Blood: Prophecies and Discourses on Sexual Politics* and *Intercourse*, go further into the implications of the sexual act itself. Dworkin analyzes the historical perceptions of rape and possession and of the biology of sexual contact. She also studies pornographic magazines in an attempt to understand how women are demeaned by pornography. Since many critics, such as one reviewer from the *London Review of Books*, find Dworkin's lack of makeup, her unflattering clothes, and her heaviness to be unattractive, Dworkin has had to relate to a double standard of beauty that does not apply to male writers, no matter how polemic they may be. As do other feminist writers, Dworkin enlightens women about gender roles in society.

SUGGESTED READINGS

Blakely, Mary Kay. "Is One Woman's Sexuality Another Woman's Pornography?" *Ms.* 13 (April, 1985): 37-38.

Dworkin, Andrea. Letter to *The New York Times Book Review*, May 3, 1992, 15-16.

O'Driscoll, Sally. "Andrea Dworkin: Guilt Without Sex." *The Village Voice* 26, no. 29 (July 15-21, 1981): 26-29.

Rosenthal, Carole. "Rejecting Equality." *Ms.* 5, no. 8 (February, 1977): 68-79.

—*Julia M. Meyers*

See also Erotic identity; Feminism; *Intercourse*

E

East Is East

AUTHOR: T. Coraghessan Boyle (Thomas John Boyle, 1948-   )
FIRST PUBLISHED: 1990
IDENTITIES: European American; Japanese American

T. Coraghessan Boyle's fifth novel, *East Is East*, satirizes the intransigence of the American and Japanese cultures, exposing the ignorance and ethnocentrism fundamental to their mutual misunderstanding.

Hiro Tanaka, the illegitimate son of an American musician and a Japanese mother, jumps ship off the coast of Georgia, hoping to escape the stigma his half-breed heritage has earned him in his native Japan, and perhaps to track down the father whose act of abandonment drove Hiro's mother to suicide. Hiro has a romantic image of America: "He envisioned a city like Tokyo, with skyscrapers and elevated trains and a raucous snarl of traffic, but every face was different—they were white and black and yellow and everything in between and they all glowed with the rapture of brotherly love." His identity as a Japanese, however, has been shaped by the writings of nationalist Yukio Mishima, who extolled a code of personal conduct tragically untenable in the West.

Hiro washes up on the shore of Tupelo Island, where his contact with the locals leads to a series of comic misadventures aggravated by his poor grasp of English and their prejudices. When he accidentally scares a black man to death, he becomes the object of a manhunt led by the local sheriff and his bigoted assistant.

Hiro seeks refuge at Thanatopsis House, a writers' colony on the island, and is hidden away by Ruth Dershowitz, one of its writers-in-residence. Ruth's intentions are humanitarian at first but the competitive environment of the colony and her personal insecurities as a writer lead her to exploit her relationship with Hiro for raw material for a story.

Hiro is captured by the authorities but escapes into the nearby Okefenokee Swamp, where the primordial struggle of nature comes to symbolize the hell he has found the West to be. Reduced to primitive survival instincts, Hiro realizes he has been betrayed by his illusion of America as a place of brotherly love. He also feels betrayed by Ruth, who helps rescue him from the swamp but who schemes to write a journalistic account of Hiro's ordeal and recover the reputation that she has lost through her association with him.

At the novel's end, Hiro understands that being only half-American makes him as much an outcast in his adopted home as in Japan. In a final affirmation of his identity, he follows the samurai code to its inevitable extreme. His action acknowledges the implacable truth of the aphorism from which the title is taken: "East is east, west is west, and never the twain shall meet."

SUGGESTED READINGS

Dickinson, Charles. Review of *East Is East*. *Tribune Books*, September 9, 1990, 5.
Friend, Tad. "Rolling Boyle." *The New York Times Magazine*, December 9, 1990, 50, 64-68.
Godwin, Gail. Review of *East Is East*. *The New York Times Book Review*, September 9, 1990, 13.
Payne, David. Review of *East Is East*. *The Washington Post Book World*, September 2, 1990, 1.

—Stefan Dziemianowicz

See also American Dream; American identity: South; Asian American identity: China, Japan, and Korea; Boyle, T. Coraghessan; Eastern religion and philosophy; Mixed race and identity; Racism and ethnocentrism; Stereotypes and identity; *Tortilla Curtain, The*

Eastern religion and philosophy

IDENTITIES: Asian American; religion

American writers, particularly in the nineteenth and twentieth centuries, were strongly influenced by Asian and Indian texts. The influence of Asian and Indian thought on American literature was perhaps first manifested in the eighteenth century, when the rational philosophy of Confucius helped shape the thinking of the Framers of the Constitution. As would often be the case, Eastern thought came by way of European thinkers, particularly the French philosophers of the Enlightenment, who were influential in the era's neo-Confucianism. As was the case in later revivals of interest in Confucius, Western thinkers saw ideas in Confucius that paralleled their own prevalent Deistic emphasis on reason and benevolence. Thomas Jefferson's writings, for example, demonstrate his wide reading of such philosophers, notably Voltaire, and fellow Deist Benjamin Franklin advocated reading Chinese literature in his essays for the American Philosophic Society.

Eastern influence is more direct in the works of authors who participated in four major literary movements or groups in the nineteenth and twentieth centuries. The first group is the New England Transcendentalists of the 1830's and 1840's and writers influenced by them in the American Romantic period that occurred in the three decades before the Civil War (1861-1865). The most notable Transcendentalists who read such Hindu works as the widely circulated *Bhagavad Gītā* (first transcribed first or second centuries A.D.) and the works of Confucius (c. 551-c. 479 B.C.) in translation were Ralph Waldo Emerson, Henry David Thoreau, and Bronson Allcott. Margaret Fuller, editor of the Transcendental journal *The Dial*, published Elizabeth Peabody's translation of *The Lotus Sutra* as "The Teaching of Buddha" in 1844, the first known translation of a Buddhist text in America. These writers and thinkers integrated their reading of Eastern works with that of English, German, and Swedish philosophers, creating a synthesis of ideas that was not systematic but eclectic in its approaches. The entire intellectual and religious community of New England was influenced by Transcendentalist ideas, which fostered a popular vogue for Hindu and Chinese books. Poets such as Walt Whitman and Emily Dickinson, while not members of the Transcendentalist circle, became influenced both by their own occasional readings in Eastern writings and by Emerson's widely influential use of Eastern thought in his philosophical essays. Far afield from this trend was novelist Herman Melville, who, nevertheless, writing from personal experiences, describes Hindu-influenced religious ceremonies in *Moby Dick: Or, The Whale* (1851).

In the twentieth century, two related poetry movements looked eastward for form, content, and freshness of thought. The first movement was the Imagist school of Ezra Pound, William Carlos Williams, and other poets. These poets were primarily interested in haiku and related Chinese and Japanese forms; these writers sought a new emphasis on images in poetic form. While these writers were less interested in the philosophy of Asian texts than the poetic structures that conveyed them, their work still retains much of the philosophy of Chinese and Japanese poets whose beliefs were inherent in the poetic forms they created.

After World War II, the Beat generation looked to Oriental forms and philosophy as a means to express ideas outside the then mainstream forms of poetry advocated by colleges and literary critics. Writers Allen Ginsberg, Jack Kerouac, Gary Snyder, and Philip Whalen, in particular, called themselves Buddhists and actively used literature to convert Westerners to Buddhism. During the 1960's and throughout later decades of the twentieth century, Eastern thought remained an important focus in American letters. The Beats remained an important link between cultures, and widespread interest in multiculturalism led to increased awareness among Asian American writers who were exploring the duality of East-West approaches to life and literature. After the interest of the Imagists such as Pound in Eastern letters, and after the popularity and cultural phenomena of Beat literature, a worldwide synthesis of poetic interests became a constant, with a circle of influence that involved writers on both sides of the Pacific. This synthesis resulted in an important school of writers exploring Old World-New World cultural conflicts. Chinese American writers such as Maxine Hong Kingston, for example, wrote *Tripmaster Monkey: His Fake Book* (1989),

Eastern religious thought began to reach North America in the nineteenth century. (Library of Congress)

which became noted as a novel linking the Beat tradition with Chinese American identity.

In the latter decades of the nineteenth century into the first decade of the twentieth century, many American writers professed an interest in Chinese, Japanese, and Indian culture but were primarily exploiting racist stereotypes of Eastern cultures. These stereotypes were based on imaginative ideas of exotic foreigners and paralleled popular concepts of Native Americans. One example would be Bret Harte and Mark Twain's play *Ah Sin* (1877), which represented popular, comic concepts of Chinese Americans rather than making an attempt to explore the culture of the Asian immigrant population. Later, in his 1897 *Following the Equator*, Mark Twain described his tour of India and his reactions to Hindu religious practices. He claimed, with his typically acerbic skepticism, that Christianity could take no hold in India because Hindu miracles outweighed those in the Bible.

In 1893, the Chicago World's Fair featured a pavilion on Eastern cultures, and speeches made during that event led to the first widespread interest in college programs addressing comparative literature. During this period, more Eastern religious texts became available, including James Legge's widely read 1899 translation of the *I Ching*, an ancient Chinese text listed as part of the Confucian canon. This work inspired a host of other translations of Eastern texts, which influenced several ensuing generations of American writers.

Writers not connected with the schools of Imagism or Beat literature in the twentieth century also found Eastern religious texts a spiritual and creative muse for their philosophical approaches to literature. In 1934, expatriate American novelist Henry Miller claimed an awakening through Helena Petrovna Blavatsky, the founder of Theosophy, a Westernized system based on Buddhist and Hindu principles. Miller later claimed Blavatsky's *The Secret Doctrine* (1888) was one of the ten greatest books ever written.

Poet Wallace Stevens, who kept a picture of Buddha in his study, was also profoundly influenced by the Eastern-infused essays of Emerson, and his letters reveal a special interest in the art of India and Sri Lanka. Poems such as "Owl's Clover" (1935) incorporate the interconnected, natural Buddhist worldview into Stevens' own perceptions.

The Romantics   American philosopher Ralph Waldo Emerson and his more pragmatic colleague, Henry David Thoreau, were keenly interested in Eastern philosophies, although they tended to see Hindu philosophy as interchangeable with Buddhism, a religion little known or understood in the nineteenth century. Emerson integrated his reading of Hindu epics into his influential essays, notably *Nature* (1836), which discusses Emerson's mystical belief in an "Over-soul" that binds God and nature into one spiritual entity, a concept paralleling Hindu and Buddhist philosophy. Emerson was also taken with David Collie's translation of Confucius, whose stoic recommendations for pursuing an honorable life merged with Emerson's interest in self-reliance and personal discipline.

While Emerson's interest in the East came slowly and was lifelong, Thoreau was quickly infatuated with the Hindu epics he borrowed from Emerson's library but lost interest after the publication of his own significant works. In 1842, Thoreau contemplated writing an epic poem modeled on Hindu scriptures. His journal entries written in 1846 later developed into *A Week on the Concord and Merrimack Rivers* (1849), which includes long contemplative extracts from Hindu scriptures. An 1849 journal entry praises Hindu seers who counseled vision beyond death. In 1850, Thoreau read an English translation of "Transmigrations of the Seven Brahmans," an Indian parable of loss and restitution that influenced his notions of nature's cycles. In a May 6, 1851, journal entry, Thoreau notes his continuing interest in both Hindu and Chinese texts. He refers to them repeatedly in his *Walden: Or, Life in the Woods* (1854), particularly Confucius and the Indian epic poems the *Bhagavad Gītā*, the fifth century A.D. "Harivansa," and the Vedas, the Hindu texts detailing the myths surrounding the god Krishna. Thoreau used these Eastern scriptures as a counterpoint to Christian teachings he found lacking in spirituality, and throughout *Walden* he expresses values closely paralleling Taoist notions of living in the present moment, having an appreciation for simplicity, enjoying physical labor, and seeking spiritual immersion in natural settings and cycles.

While there is little direct evidence that Whitman read specific works by Eastern writers, there is clearly evidence in his work that he was interested in Eastern thinking. There are many parallels between his inclusive philosophy and the principles expressed in Hindu literature. Twentieth century Indian scholars became convinced that Whitman studied the *Bhagavad Gītā*, because *Leaves of Grass* (1855), the title of his collected verse, reflects the teachings of Vedanta, and they note that "Song of Myself" is a virtual echo of the sayings of Krishna and Persian writers. For example, his "Crossing Brooklyn Ferry" catalogs Eastern figures including Mandarins, Chinese fishermen, emperors, Confucius, and warriors from Tibet and China, along with representatives from European, Middle Eastern, Native American, and African backgrounds. He believed them all equally important in the human procession of history, and this belief is taught in Hindu and Buddhist religious texts.

Whitman also disavowed the body-soul hierarchy or duality of Western philosophy. For example, the Whitmanian idea of sharing atoms expressed in "Song of Myself" restates the Buddhist idea that distinctions between the self and the external world are illusions, that there is no separation between person and nature or between subject and object. Buddhist concepts also appear in "Twilight," in which Whitman refers to death as "haze-nirvana . . . oblivion" and in "Old Ireland," which addresses reincarnation. Hindu texts are evoked in "Passage to India," in which Whitman asks, "Soundest below the Sanskrit and the Vedas?" This line indicates his interest in merging Eastern and Western cultures.

The Imagists

In 1915, poet F. S. Flint said the Imagist school of poetry, which flourished between 1909 and 1918, came together out of a dissatisfaction with traditional English poetry that paralleled the group's interests in the sharp, simple images of Japanese haiku. These interests were crucial in the work of the group's leading figure, Ezra Pound, who was strongly influenced by the Japanese No play and haiku as well as Chinese ideograms. His *Cathay* (1915) is frequently cited as establishing the proper manner of rendering Chinese classic poetry into modern English using new cadences and diction, and his *Cantos* (1970) are filled with allusions to Eastern religions and mythology. Pound's study of Chinese and Japanese literature clearly helped develop his early haiku-influenced verse into important innovations in poetic style, notably his extended line structure, which changed the face of English poetry.

Pound's study also influenced fellow Imagists William Carlos Williams, John Gould Fletcher, H. D., and non-Imagists Carl Sandburg and T. S. Eliot. Editor and poet Amy Lowell listed the major tenets of Imagism in 1917, including the idea that poetry should not state a complete thought but should rather suggest one, an idea taken directly from Japanese philosophy. The Imagists also advocated that all subjects are of equal value, including the small, mundane matters of life, again, an ancient concept practiced by Chinese and Japanese poets. Imagists claimed that, like haiku, poetry should concentrate much meaning into few words in clear, vivid, and thought-provoking, memorable images, an idea reflected in numerous American poems, such as Williams' "The Red Wheelbarrow."

This credo, merging aspects of Eastern and Western craftsmanship, influenced all subsequent notable American poets, particularly the work of post-World War II writers who looked to the Romantics, the Imagists, and Eastern thought as sources for both style and content.

The Beats

In the first decade after World War II, American poets, influenced by Whitman, Thoreau, and the Imagists, looked to Eastern thought as more than a source of techniques and structures. A number looked to Buddhism as a religion; this influenced the form and message of their verse and fiction. Poet Lawrence Ferlinghetti believed this interest grew out of the West Coast's proximity to Eastern countries, the Asian communities of San Francisco, the presence of Eastern-influenced figures such Christopher Isherwood and Aldous Huxley on the West Coast, and the experiences of veterans in World War II. It is also true that many Buddhist texts became more available during this period, particularly the teachings of Zen master D. T. Suzuki, and that many members of the West Coast intellectual community knew at least one Asian language. One such important figure was poet Kenneth Rexroth, who had preceded the Beats in translating Chinese and Japanese texts.

He introduced the New York Beat writers to West Coast authors Gary Snyder and Philip Whalen, who shared an affinity for Buddhist texts. Rexroth is considered the father of the ensuing San Francisco Renaissance.

In turn, Beat writers became widely credited with bringing Eastern thought into popular culture, taking Asian literature beyond the domain of academics and translators. While key members of the group dived deeply into Buddhism, the movement also included writers such as William Everson and William Burroughs, who believed that Westerners could not fully understand a culture outside their own Christian tradition, and often urged their peers to reject dabbling in Buddhism. Burroughs specifically warned against reading Confucius. Still, on many levels, the Beat movement is often identified by its numerous Buddhist members, the major figures being Jack Kerouac, Allen Ginsberg, and Gary Snyder. Others who became part of the expanding circle of influence, creating the San Francisco Renaissance, were Diane di Prima, Lew Welch, Anne Waldman, Michael McClure, Harold Norse, Joanne Kyger, Albert Sajo, Lemore Kandel, Will Peterson, and Bob Kaufman. Cumulatively, this group has been credited not only with opening up new avenues in literature but also with fostering a religious and spiritual dimension in American culture.

For 1940's Columbia students Ginsberg and Kerouac, Buddhism was one aspect of their rebellion against mainstream white culture as they looked to African American, Native American, and Asian cultures for inspiration in an America that they felt was too materialistic and removed from spiritual values. Although he later renounced Buddhism, for most of his writing career Jack Kerouac's interest in Mahayana Buddhism—disavowing the intellectual wordsmanship of Zen— was profound and integral to his work. He first connected Buddhism to the Beat generation in his ecological *Dharma Bums* (1958), in which he expressed the expansionist Asian-Western fusion he believed would revolutionize Western thought.

Kerouac was steeped enough in Buddhism to work throughout 1955 on his *Wake Up*, a Buddhist "handbook for Western understanding of the ancient Law." The work, first published in 1994, retells the first Buddhist myths designed explicitly to convert Westerners. In 1956, Kerouac wrote his most Buddhist-influenced works, *Mexico City Blues* (1959), *Tristessa* (1960), and *Visions of Girrard* (1963). The closing pages of his 1959 *Dr. Sax* paraphrase concepts Kerouac read in Dwight Goddard's *A Buddhist Bible* (1932), a seminal influence on all Buddhist-oriented writers. Kerouac's *Desolation Angels* (1965) also focuses on Buddhist themes.

In his verse, Kerouac addresses poems to Chinese leader and poet Mao Zedong in which Kerouac urges modern China to go back to classical poets such as Li Po and Tao Yuan Ming for creative inspiration. He developed his Buddhist-influenced philosophy in *Book of Dreams* (1961) and *The Scripture of the Golden Eternity* (1960), which shows how Kerouac's interpretation of Buddhism supported his creative notion of spontaneity.

Poet Allen Ginsberg, who came to consider himself a "Buddhist Jew" after the prominence of his seminal work *Howl* (1956), also helped popularize the Beat generation. He became a major spokesman for Buddhism as an important aspect of his poetry and activist social philosophy. Ginsberg's devotion to Eastern thought deepened during various tours of India and the Far East in the 1960's, where he became interested in literary and musical religious forms, which he incorporated into his printed work and recordings of verse and songs. With poetic colleague Gary Snyder, Ginsberg met the Dalai Lama, and it was Ginsberg who introduced the Hindu Hare Krishna chant to American popular culture in the mid-1960's. He became an important icon in the counterculture movement, which eagerly embraced Eastern philosophies and religions, primarily from 1967 to 1969, when texts such as the *Bhagavad Gītā* and *I Ching* reached their height of popularity in America and Britain.

California poet Gary Snyder, the author of *Turtle Island* (1974), which won the Pulitzer Prize in poetry in 1975, became highly regarded as an American poet. He synthesized Asian and Native American philosophies. Snyder's first experiences with Buddhism occurred in the late 1940's and 1950's at Reed College, where, with poet roommate Philip Whalen, the two became enamored of the Imagists, Zen Buddhism, Chinese culture, and haiku verse.

On many levels, Snyder and Whalen's base in Buddhism ran deeper than that of Kerouac and other Beat devotees. After becoming a Buddhist monk in 1972, Whalen changed his name to the Buddhist Zenshin Ryufi, continuing to write poetry and teach Buddhism into the 1990's.

Snyder, the more prolific of the two Reed alumni, spent years in Buddhist monasteries and walked miles of Japanese and Indian country roads visiting Buddhist shrines. Snyder's literary synthesis began with his reading of Chinese and Indian vernacular texts as well as classic Sanskrit sources, which Snyder described in his *Myths and Texts* (1960) as part of the planetary heritage. He translated Japanese and Chinese poetry, lived in Buddhist communes in Japan, and married a Japanese woman. It was in Japan that Snyder became a mature poet, bringing to America Buddhist practices he attempted to implement in his daily life and social teachings.

Snyder's work, as in the prose collection *Earth House Hole* (1969), is often clearly an attempt to make Buddhism accessible to ordinary Westerners, using simple imagery and eschewing academic allusions. This is demonstrated in his 1986 collection, *Left Out in the Rain*. Like no other poet, Snyder's Buddhism is integral to his life and work, influenced by the psychology and philosophy of Zen (a fusion of Taoism and Buddhism), using Zen as source, inspiration, and subject matter of his verse and essays.

Post-Beat Eastern influences

In 1974, the Jack Kerouac School of Disembodied Poetics was established at the Naropa Institute, a Buddhist center in Boulder, Colorado. The institute, specifically founded to merge religion with modern poetry, became an influential center for post-Beat writers interested in East-West fusions of thought and art. Allen Ginsberg has served as Director Emeritus, and instructors for courses and workshops have included Michael McClure, Anne Waldman, Diane di Prima, and other alumni of the San Francisco Renaissance. Other Beat writers continued the Buddhist tradition, including poet and publisher Lawrence Ferlinghetti, whose 1994 "A Buddha in the Woodpile" is a poem addressing the Waco, Texas, tragedy surrounding the cult of David Koresh.

Other non-Beat writers also continued to look to Eastern themes, including Robert Pirsig, whose 1974 novel *Zen and the Art of Motorcycle Maintenance* uses Buddhist philosophy to give meaning to the author's experiences on the road. Popular novelist Tom Robbins demonstrated his interest in Eastern thought throughout his fiction, notably his *Even Cowgirls Get the Blues* (1976) and *Skinny Legs and All* (1990) as well as his nonfiction studies, including *Cults, Converts, and Charisma: The Sociology of New Religious Movements* (1988) and, with Dick Anthony, *In Gods We Trust: New Patterns of Religious Pluralism in America* (1989). Also noted for his readings of Eastern text was poet and fiction writer Richard Brautigan. His most influential work, *Trout Fishing in America* (1969), included the gentle themes and tone he later developed in such works as *Sombrero Fallout: A Japanese Novel* (1976) and *Tokyo Montana Express* (1980).

Asian American literature

Beginning in the 1970's, Asian American literature, primarily the works of Japanese, Chinese, and Korean writers living in the United States, became accepted as a new tradition in mainstream American literature. Works such as Kingston's *The Woman Warrior: Memoirs of a Girlhood Among Ghosts* (1976) and the writings of Shawn Wong, Hisaye Yamamoto, Wakako Yamauchi, and Mei Berssenbrugge explore Old World culture and values, immigrant history, race suffering, communal traditions, and what writer Frank Chin has called "neo-Confucianist ideology." Traditional ideas of the East became transplanted to a new setting, the United States, especially the West Coast area. Women writers such as Jeanne Wakatsuki Houston, Kim Ronyoung, Anzia Yezierska, and Jade Snow Wong examined the conflicts between Asian values and European American concepts, particularly on generational and gender lines. For these women writers, the stoicism and misogyny of Confucius led to male dominance in patriarchal, class-structured communities based on ancestor worship. Conflicts arose between ethnic and personal identity as feminist approaches to literature became a major issue in American thought, paralleling similar intellectual discussions in China.

In subsequent decades, American literary interests became dominated by writers from diverse backgrounds. Synthesis of various cultural heritages went from being something new and unusual to being something widespread and, in a sense, mandatory, as many Americans of diverse cultural backgrounds began to write of their experience and identity. Probably as a result of the revolutionary advances in communications and transportation of the twentieth century, synthesis became important in literature around the world, particularly among writers interested in fusions of East and West. For example, at a 1984 conference in Bejing, attended by Ginsberg and Kingston, Ginsberg observed that Chinese writers were enamored with Americans, hoping to interest American readers in new Chinese poetry. At the conference, Chinese poet Yuam Kejia claimed his primary influences were Whitman, T. S. Eliot, and Ginsberg. This circle of synthesis inspired Ginsberg, who wrote a series of poems including "One Morning I Took a Walk in China" and "China Bronchins," both poems echoing Gary Snyder's earlier *Riprap* (1959) and *Earth House Hole* poems set in Japan.

This productive event epitomized the 1980's and 1990's circle connecting cultures and traditions with such interesting results as college instructors teaching students of Chinese American literature the works of the Chinese poet Han Shan by way of Gary Snyder's translations. This synthesis of cultures has resulted in numerous anthologies of Eastern influenced writing, particularly poetry, and periodicals such as the Buddhist journal *Tri-cycle*, which publishes religious instruction and literature. Eastern philosophy's importance in American writing has not diminished since its first appearance in the nineteenth century.

SUGGESTED READINGS

Ames, Van Meter. *Zen and American Thought*. Honolulu: University of Hawaii Press, 1982. Explores Eastern thought in American literature from the Colonial period through the nineteenth century.

Chari, V. K. *Whitman in the Light of Vedantic Mysticism*. Lincoln: University of Nebraska Press, 1964. Examines Whitman's readings in Eastern religious texts and how they influenced his verse.

Ellwood, Robert S. *Eastern Spirituality in America: Selected Writings*. New York: Paulist Press, 1987. A historical overview of Eastern religions' growth in American intellectual and spiritual life. Contains writings of Eastern teachers who wrote in America.

Tonkinson, Carole. *Big Sky Mind: Buddhism and the Beat Generation*. New York: Riverhead Books, 1995. Overview and anthology of Buddhist-influenced writers, including the major Beat figures.

—Wesley Britton

See also Asian American identity: China, Japan, and Korea; Asian American identity: India; Ferlinghetti, Lawrence; Ginsberg, Allen; Kerouac, Jack; Kingston, Maxine Hong; Snyder, Gary

Eat a Bowl of Tea

AUTHOR: Louis H. Chu (1915-1970)
FIRST PUBLISHED: 1961
IDENTITIES: Chinese American; family; men

Widely acclaimed by Asian American writers and critics, Louis Chu's *Eat a Bowl of Tea* is the first Chinese American novel that realistically depicts New York's Chinatown bachelor society in the United States shortly after World War II. The novel focuses on the struggles of a young Chinese American who attempts to define his identity.

As the novel opens, it is revealed that the protagonist, Wang Ben Loy, a bridegroom of two months, has become impotent. Ben Loy is a Chinese American in his twenties, a filial son, obedient to his Confucian father, Wah Gay, who left him in China for twenty-five years while establishing himself in America.

Wah Gay, owner of a gambling establishment in Chinatown, sends for Ben Loy, who works as a waiter, joins the U.S. Army, then returns to waiting tables at a Chinese restaurant. Ben Loy alleviates his frustrations by regularly patronizing prostitutes; unfortunately, he contracts several venereal diseases. In 1948, Ben Loy fulfills his filial duty by marrying Mei Oi, a China-born daughter of Wah Gay's longtime friend.

Neglected by her husband, Mei Oi becomes pregnant by Ah Song, a notorious Chinatown philanderer. Chu appears sympathetic with women by implying that husbands must share blame for the infidelity of their wives when sexual and emotional needs are unsatisfied.

Mei Oi passes off the expected child as Ben Loy's, but when Ah Song is sighted sneaking from her apartment, Chinatown buzzes with gossip. Feeling disgraced, Wah Gay ambushes Ah Song after a tryst at Mei Oi's apartment and slices off his left ear. Justice is served when the unofficial Chinatown judicial system condemns Ah Song to five years' ostracism. Having lost face, Wah Gay exiles himself.

Ben Loy and Mei Oi go west to San Francisco, where Mei Oi has a baby whom Ben Loy accepts. They look forward to having others after Ben Loy's impotence is cured by a Chinese herbalist, who makes him "eat a bowl of tea" of medicinal herbs. Most important, Ben Loy breaks from the patriarchal control of his traditionalist Confucian father and becomes the arbiter of his Asian American identity.

SUGGESTED READINGS

Chua, Cheng Lok. "Golden Mountain: Chinese Versions of the American Dream in Lin Yutang, Louis Chu, and Maxine Hong Kingston." *Ethnic Groups* 4 (1982): 33-59.

Hsiao, Ruth. "Facing the Incurable: Patriarchy in *Eat a Bowl of Tea*." In *Reading the Literatures of Asian America*, edited by Shirley Geok-lin Lim and Amy Ling. Philadelphia: Temple University Press, 1992.

Kim, Elaine H. *Asian American Literature: An Introduction to the Writings and Their Social Context*. Philadelphia: Temple University Press, 1982.

Ling, Jinqi. "Reading for Historical Specificities: Gender Negotiations in Louis Chu's *Eat a Bowl of Tea*." *MELUS* 20 (1995): 35-51.

—*Janet Fujimoto*
—*C. L. Chua*

See also Adultery; Asian American identity: China, Japan and Korea; Chu, Louis; Erotic identity

Economics of identity

The issue

The question of identity, stated mathematically as $a = a$, is as old as philosophy. Western philosophy has long held to the argument that a does in fact always equal a, a philosophical tenet described as "essentialism." The essentialist belief holds that each individual has some unique characteristic, or "essence," that separates him or her from all other individuals. This essence, or soul, is viewed as being eternal and unchanging. The soul of the person at five is the soul of that person at fifty: $a = a$.

The literary convention of character follows a similar argument. An individual literary character is typically assumed to have an essential nature, by which means a reader or audience can distinguish that character from others. The most gripping fictional characters are, nevertheless, those who change in some form or another over the course of a narrative, who undergo a transformation and become something other than what they were at the beginning. Much of the appeal of narrative has to do with the tension between these two aspects of character.

Self-image derived from economic status has been one traditional means of determining both the type and importance of a literary character. Traditionally and historically, characters of low economic status are relegated to minor, static, roles. They are slaves, servants, fools, and the like, and usually remain in the background while the serious action goes on among those higher up the economic pyramid. This representation and stereotyping have been challenged throughout the history of literature.

History

The Greek philosopher Aristotle made original and famous statements concerning the economics of identity in literature. In the *Poetics* (c. 334-323 B.C.) Aristotle describes a tragic figure for Greek drama. The tragic hero needs to be an upper-class male Greek citizen who sees himself as a leader. Notably, the tragic character cannot be a Greek female (forbidden from holding property), a member of the lower class, or a slave. Dramatists who did not adhere to Aristotle's precepts, such as Euripides, were criticized for what Aristotle claimed to be a lack of dramatic skills. Aristotle's insistence that the tragic figure could only be a male of high position has been taken as a description and as a prescription. Lower-class figures have more often than not been relegated to the status of comic figures since then.

Roman literature, based on a more fluid class system, presented, relatively, a more flexible approach to the question of economic identity. It was not unknown in Roman society for slaves to be granted their freedom, and for them subsequently to gain great wealth. Roman comedy, especially the works of Plautus, frequently features narratives concerning escaped and freed slaves and their rise in good fortune. Even in these works, however, the characters are little more than caricatures, stock figures whose primary role is the advancement of often outlandish and obscene plots.

The medieval period in Europe brought about a great change in the treatment and idea of self-image. Literature became much more a method of instruction, and character became a means to an end, a way of relating moral precepts and standardized theology. The popular medieval play *Everyman* (first extant version, 1508) shows the change in philosophy and presentation. The teachings of the Christian church hold that poverty is a virtue, and thus Aristotle's classical precepts are turned around or ignored. The character of Everyman is a universal figure, and not intended to represent a particular class of people, such as the nobility. Furthermore, since Everyman is meant to be the average man, he has the characteristics of any man involved in redemption. As an allegorical figure, however, Everyman can hardly be said to represent an individual, changing character.

Giovanni Boccaccio's *The Decameron* (1349-1351) and Geoffrey Chaucer's *The Canterbury Tales* (1387-1400) mark an advance in literary depictions of economics and identity. Each work involves a storytelling contest among a group of people. *The Decameron* features a group of wealthy young people from the Italian city of Florence who seek to escape the plague by fleeing to the country. *The Canterbury Tales* features a cross-section of English society.

The contribution of each of these two works has to do with the use of a new idea of character, one concerning the tension between belief in a universal ideal of behavior, such as that found in *Everyman*, and examination of the effects of economic status on a character's self-image and behavior. The wealthy characters in *The Decameron* are castigated by Boccaccio in the introduction to the text for their selfish behavior. They abandon their city and surviving relatives in the midst of a deadly crisis. Their wealth allows them the freedom to detach themselves physically and emotionally from the suffering of their fellow citizens. *The Canterbury Tales*, on the other hand, presents characters from almost every English class, from bakers and millers to clerics, a knight, and Chaucer himself, who was a high-ranking commoner. Each character's tale reflects upon economic status and aspiration.

The novel   The novel is arguably the genre that places the greatest emphasis on wealth and self-image. The discursive form of the novel allows ample room for the description of clothing, surroundings, and furnishings, all of which serve as signs of economic status. As a genre associated with the middle and upper-middle classes from its inception, the novel in many ways reflects the concerns of its audience. The novel form also allows the writer to provide lengthy descriptions of thoughts and reactions, something that is out of the range of many literary genres.

The novel became the dominant literary mode in the United States after the Civil War. Whereas English novels often celebrate the possession of wealth, good taste, and manners, many American realist writers were skeptical about the effects of riches in a blatantly commercial economy. Perhaps the best-known of these antimoney novels is Mark Twain's *Adventures of Huckleberry Finn* (1884). Huck Finn refuses to be bound down with social concerns such as money or to allow his character to be defined by wealth. The price of such a choice is his inability to be assimilated into the economy of manners, rules, and cash. Huck would rather be floating down the Mississippi on a raft with his companion, the escaped slave Jim. At the novel's happy conclusion, Huck is planning to light out for the territories, away from civilization, one more time.

A subtle study of the effect of economic status on character is Henry James's *The Portrait of a*

Lady (1881). At the beginning of the novel the heroine, Isabel Archer, lives a comfortable middle-class life in upstate New York. A wealthy uncle dies and leaves her an enormous fortune, and overnight Isabel changes from a girl to a highly eligible lady. She rejects two wealthy suitors and instead marries a poor but titled Italian, operating on the assumption that poverty is necessarily ennobling. The choice turns out to be a mistake, as she soon discovers, and Isabel is left with the unhappy realization that her money gave her only the freedom to make foolish choices.

Later American writers have continued in this tradition of the theme of excess wealth's leading to unhappiness. Perhaps the most famous example of this is F. Scott Fitzgerald's *The Great Gatsby* (1925), one of the most popular novels of the early twentieth century. Set among the wealthy and newly wealthy of New York's Long Island, the novel is a tale of characters isolated and alienated by their drive for wealth and social status. Likewise, Janie, the protagonist of Zora Neale Hurston's novel *Their Eyes Were Watching God* (1937), finds wealth to be an isolating phenomenon. Janie finds herself married to the mayor of an all-black Florida town. He builds a big white house in order to show off his status to the populace. Only after Janie is married a second time—to a footloose character named Tea Cake—and lives among the migrant laborers of South Florida does she find fulfillment.

Although Janie finds escape from the confines of wealth, other fictional characters are not so fortunate. Naturalist writers often feature settings in which characters are ground down by overwhelming economic and social deprivation. This style of writing became popular in the United States in the 1930's and 1940's, partly as a reaction to the economic conditions of the Great Depression. Bigger Thomas, the ghetto-dweller who serves as the focus of Richard Wright's *Native Son* (1940), is surrounded by barriers seen and unseen. An African American growing up in a segregated Chicago, Bigger's poverty leads to economic servitude, reinforced by the fact that Bigger can only find work as a servant to wealthy white people. When Bigger accidentally kills the daughter of his employer, the resulting manhunt is a classic of naturalist fiction. Bigger's mistakes lead not only to his own capture but also to a fury unleashed toward all members of the urban underclass.

American works in the realist tradition continue in the dramatization of the isolating effects of money. Only writers in alternative genres, such as science fiction, have managed to imagine worlds in which economics does not constitute a primary defining factor for identity. Ursula K. Le Guin perhaps best illustrates such a world in *The Dispossessed* (1974). *The Dispossessed* is set on an anarchistic planet where property has been outlawed and identity is determined based on talent and personal predilection alone. Notably, the planet exists under constant threat from without, primarily from its capitalist sister planet, which bears a curious resemblance to Earth.

SUGGESTED READINGS

Aristotle. *Poetics*. Chicago: Henry Regnery, 1949. Essentially fragmentary notes from Aristotle's lectures, this text nevertheless establishes the foundation for much later literary criticism.

Jameson, Fredric. *The Political Unconscious: Narrative as a Socially Symbolic Act*. Ithaca, N.Y.: Cornell University Press, 1981. The most thorough current discussion of economic influence in narrative, with special emphasis placed on the novel.

Lauter, Paul, ed. *Reconstructing American Literature*. Old Westbury, N.Y.: The Feminist Press, 1983. Helped to reintroduce many neglected American writers, often highlighting the importance of economic status in narrative and canonization.

Williams, Raymond. *The Country and the City*. New York: Oxford University Press, 1973. A landmark work of literary history. Williams was one of the first English-speaking literary critics to emphasize the importance of wealth in the history of genre and characterization.

_____. *Keywords: A Vocabulary of Culture and Society*. New York: Oxford University Press, 1976. Features etymological and explanatory essays on the vocabulary of sociology and literary criticism. Extensive selection of terms dealing with the effects of economics on identity.

—Jeff Cupp

See also Anarchism; Class and identity; Hurston, Zora Neale; James, Henry; Wright, Richard

Education of Henry Adams, The

AUTHOR: Henry Adams (1838-1918)
FIRST PUBLISHED: 1907
IDENTITIES: Adolescence and coming-of-age; European American; family

The Education of Henry Adams is a study of the forces that shaped the life and mind of Henry Adams as well as many Americans of his generation. Adams describes a general identity crisis in the United States during its transformation from an agricultural society to an urban, industrial world power. Adams poses a question about himself: "What could become of such a child of the seventeenth and eighteenth centuries, when he should wake up to find himself required to play the game of the twentieth?" His autobiography shows how he fared in adjusting to "the game" or challenges of a modern scientific age.

In the opening chapter, "Quincy," Adams acknowledges that as a child in a famous family that includes two presidents, John Adams and John Quincy Adams, "probably no child born that year held better cards than he." Nonetheless, he considers himself "heavily handicapped" because the outdated values of his family would hinder him in the new age. During the Civil War, Adams assists his father, the minister to Great Britain, in gaining British support for the Union cause. Afterward, he works in Washington, D.C., as a political journalist. Ultimately, he realizes that his family creed of honest public service is obsolete in the era's politics of money, power, and self-interest: "The selfishness of politics was the earliest of all political education."

Adams withdraws from politics into the life of a scholar, another tradition of his family. After serving as a professor of history at Harvard, he concludes that history "has little use" in understanding modern America. The science exhibition at the Chicago World's Fair induces Adams to study modern science. His new studies in biology, mathematics, chemistry, and physics, coupled with his previous ones in law, history, and anthropology, reveal to him a universe that is rapidly disintegrating. Adams counters the American belief in progress with historical evidence of decline ending in chaos: "Chaos was the law of nature; Order was the dream of man."

The chapter "The Dynamo and the Virgin" illustrates symbolically the conflict of identities for Americans at the threshold of a new world. Adams regards the electric generator, the dynamo, with amazement as a "man before silent and infinite force." Though the dynamo is powerful and modern, it is inhuman and indifferent. Adams looks back into history and discovers that the Virgin Mary is "the highest energy ever known to man." By comparing the dynamo to the Virgin, Adams suggests that American society has declined spiritually. Adams concludes that his education and family identity have failed him, but he subtly poses the dilemma of whether one wins or loses by succeeding in a materialistic America.

SUGGESTED READINGS

Adams, James Truslow. *Henry Adams*. New York: Barnes & Noble Books, 1962.

Harbert, Earl N. In "The Education of Henry Adams." *The Force So Much Closer Home: Henry Adams and the Adams Family*. New York: New York University Press, 1981.

Hochfield, George. "The Education of Henry Adams." In *Henry Adams*. New York: Barnes & Noble Books, 1962.

—*David Partenheimer*

See also Adams, Henry; American identity: Northeast

Eliot, T. S.

BORN: St. Louis, Missouri; September 26, 1888
DIED: London, England; January 4, 1965
PRINCIPAL WORKS: *Prufrock and Other Observations*, 1917; *The Sacred Wood*, 1920; *The Waste Land*, 1922; *Murder in the Cathedral*, pr., pb. 1935; *Four Quartets*, 1943; *The Cocktail Party*, pr. 1949, pb. 1950; *Collected Poems, 1909-1962*, 1963
IDENTITIES: European American

SIGNIFICANT ACHIEVEMENT: Poet, critic, and essayist, Eliot was one of the most influential writers of the twentieth century.

T. S. Eliot began his career as a modernist poet, breaking with the traditions of nineteenth century literary standards and creating a new and innovative approach to the way poetry is written, read, and discussed. Born into a prominent and wealthy family, Eliot enjoyed a privileged education. After finishing two degrees at Harvard, he studied in Germany, at the Sorbonne in Paris, and at Merton College, Oxford. He settled in London, where he worked for Lloyds Bank, and in 1927 he became a British citizen.

Eliot is often associated with the American artists and writers who, dissatisfied with what they perceived as a decline in American cultural values, moved to Europe during and shortly after World War I. These expatriates transformed the senseless slaughter of the war and its socially disruptive aftermath into a metaphor for the general breakdown of civilization, fueled by the loss of a common cultural heritage and threatened by political destablization.

The poetry and criticism of T. S. Eliot has been deeply influential; he has also been attacked as an anti-Semite and as an elitist. (The Nobel Foundation)

Eliot's poetry reflects this view, often describing what he considered the decadence of contemporary life, plagued by a decay in spiritual values, a disregard for tradition, and the inability of government and religious institutions to provide significant order and meaning in life. His poems describe privileged men of culture displaced by the alienating effects of modern society; his poems also tell of victims, psychologically damaged products of a society in which transience has replaced any sense of community and the desire for novelty is purchased at the expense of quality. His characters are desperate for transcendence but impotent to effect any remedy for their spiritual malaise.

Eliot's poetry specifically depicts the point of view of an educated, white European male alienated by cultural values he does not respect or understand. He writes from a narrow ideological base, having once described himself as "a classicist in literature, a royalist in politics, an Anglo-Catholic in religion." The technical mastery of his poetry and the acute intellectual insight of his criticism have had an enormous influence on the history of literature. Eliot was awarded the Nobel Prize in Literature in 1948.

SUGGESTED READINGS

Ackroyd, Peter. *T. S. Eliot: A Life*. New York: Simon & Schuster, 1984.

Bergonzi, Bernard. *T. S. Eliot*. Macmillan, 1972.

Kenner, Hugh. *The Invisible Poet*. New York: McDowell, Obolonsky, 1959.

Spender, Stephen. *T. S. Eliot*. New York: Viking Press, 1976.

Wagner, Linda W. *T. S. Eliot: A Collection of Criticism*. New York: McGraw-Hill, 1974.

—Jeff Johnson

See also Existentialism; Expatriate identity; Literary standards; "Love Song of J. Alfred Prufrock, The"; *Waste Land, The*

Elitism

DEFINITION: Elitism is the belief that a select group—usually defined by class, wealth, or natural ability—is superior to other groups.

The belief in the superiority of an elite (the word "elite" comes from a French word for "select" or "chosen" and is related to the English word "elect") affects nearly every type of group identity. Sexism, racism, and ethnocentrism, for example, may be considered subcategories of elitism that are based on sex, race, or ethnicity. In its usual sense, however, elitism is a function of class identity. A sense of elitism usually occurs when an aristocratic or noble class regards itself as deserving special privileges or influence because of its exalted status. In North America, elites may also be defined in terms of wealth (the business elite), power (the political elite), or natural ability (the intellectual or cultural elite). Elitism in literature involves the portrayal of the merits or personality of a character as deriving primarily from that character's membership in a privileged class.

Early history

Elitism is a part of literary identity. Until literacy became common, for example, literature was largely written by and for the social elite. Authors thus tended to reflect the self-image of the aristocracy, rarely providing alternative points of view. For example, Homer's epic poems the *Iliad* and the *Odyssey* (both c. 800 B.C.) originated as songs composed for presentation in courts. For this reason, the principal characters in both poems are kings or members of the nobility. When Homer does not ignore commoners, he tends to depict them unflatteringly. Anyone who stands outside the social elite, such as Thersites in the *Iliad*, is usually said to be ugly, vain, uncivilized, lame, or stupid. Even among the ranks of the gods, characters who do not have elite status among the gods, such as craftsman god Hephaestus, are mocked. Occasionally a member of the lower classes, such as the swineherd Eumaeus in the *Odyssey*, is described favorably. These occurrences are rare, however, and the lower-class character is always praised for his subservient attitude to the elite.

The concept of the elite occurs in much of classical literature. In the *Republic* (between 388 and 366 B.C.), Plato proposes a utopian society that will be ruled by an elite class of philosopher-kings. Aristotle believed that the elite was naturally suited to rule others because of its superior virtue (*Politics*, c. 335-323 B.C.). The "harmony among social classes" (*concordia ordinum*) advocated by the Roman orator Cicero was an elite composed of the senatorial aristocracy and members of the wealthy middle class. Plebeians were expected to remain content and obedient to these "best people."

Influence of classical ideas

As Greek and Roman values spread throughout Europe, the belief in the innate superiority of an elite became common. During the Middle Ages, kings and aristocrats constituted an elite believed to rule through divine right. Characters displaying heroic traits in medieval literature—including Beowulf, Charlemagne, Siegfried, Arthur, and Roland—were almost always members of the social elite. Even individuals who protected the disfranchised, such as Robin Hood, tended to be kings in disguise or from an aristocratic background. As late as the Renaissance, in *Il libro del cortegiano* (1528; *The Book of the Courtier*, 1561) by Baldassare Castiglione, an aristocratic elite is depicted as possessing talents and virtues not found in other social groups.

In England, where the tradition of a stratified society was very strong, literary identity is influenced by elitism in all periods. Several of the Barsetshire novels written by Anthony Trollope during the 1850's and 1860's concern the possibility of marriage between a person who is a member of the elite and a person who is not. Although Trollope's novels usually have happy endings, class identity is established so firmly that the characters act as if even social interaction were impossible except between equals. An extreme example of this attitude appears in *Tom Brown at Oxford* (1861), the sequel to Thomas Hughes's popular novel *Tom Brown's Schooldays: By an Old Boy* (1857). When the title character of the novel flirts with a barmaid, he nearly loses his best friend, who later refers to the incident as "this folly, this sin." Readers of the novel are intended to view Brown as guilty of a major transgression and his friend's attitude as the norm. Identities based on membership in an elite also may be found in the novels of Jane Austen, Sir Walter Scott, and William Makepeace Thackeray. Charles Dickens and George Bernard Shaw wrote works that are sharply critical of elitism and of the values of privileged classes.

Elsewhere in Europe, writers frequently assumed that an individual's habits and identity were determined by membership in an elite. In the twentieth century, the superiority of the elite, as well as the idea that great civilizations are fostered by elitism, continued to be taken for granted. Karl Marx, for example, in *The German Ideology* (1846), notes that "the ideas of the ruling class are in every age the ruling ideas." In literature as well, Alexander Dumas *père*, Honoré de Balzac, Gustave Flaubert, Conrad Ferdinand Meyer, Leo Tolstoy, and others described elites, sometimes adopting and sometimes criticizing the values of the elites.

In 1776, the Declaration of Independence affirmed that "all men are created equal." The United States government, based on representative democracy, was constituted soon after. The goal of the founders of the United States was to minimize the influence of social, religious, and governmental elites. To some extent, these efforts were successful. Alexis de Tocqueville notes in *De la démocratie en Amérique* (1835, 1840; *Democracy in America*, 1835, 1840) that citizens of the United States rarely denigrated "peasants." Americans, he notes, did not live in a society in which the coarse habits and simple graces of rural laborers were distinctly different from those of a literate urban class. Several decades later, Henry James affirms in *Life of Hawthorne* (1880) that Americans lacked such things as sovereigns, courts, aristocracies, country gentlemen, palaces, castles, manors, old country-houses, and the sporting class: all the physical manifestations of elitism in its European form.

Elitism in North American literature

Select groups are still seen in North American literature. As the political philosopher Herbert Marcuse indicates in *One-Dimensional Man* (1964), the rich and poor in America share many tastes and experiences. Marcuse does not mean, however, that elites had vanished from society, but that the values of the elite had come to dictate those of other social groups, as Marx also indicates. One reason that elitism remains a factor in the New World is that many North American values and educational approaches have been borrowed from Europe. More important, elitism arose in North America because a new class, distinguished from others by its greater wealth and education, began to fill the role that the aristocracy occupied in other parts of the world. Frequently in North American literature wealth alone influences identity by its ability to admit characters to an elite, thus altering their status, outlook, and values.

Money, then, and ethnic background, are typically key elements for membership in the elite in North America. The narrator in F. Scott Fitzgerald's short story "The Rich Boy" says that the very rich are different, and an unnamed character in Ernest Hemingway's "The Snows of Kilimanjaro" says that the rich are different in that they have more money. Fitzgerald's statement and Hemingway's answer present two fundamentally different views of elitism. Fitzgerald, like a number of other authors, believed that wealth could, in and of itself, confer an elite status upon those who possessed it. By becoming wealthy, one automatically began to adopt certain values, elegance, taste, and a manner of life. Other authors, such as Hemingway, believed that class distinctions were obsolete in American society and held that genuine virtue—consisting primarily of courage, but also including intelligence, refinement, and self-assurance—was the property of individuals, not social groups. For Hemingway, membership in an elite was a matter of character, completely unrelated to questions of class, status, and power.

In *The Great Gatsby* (1925) Fitzgerald sets forth his views about the relationship among elitism, wealth, and the American Dream. Fitzgerald's character Jay Gatsby attains great wealth but finds that it is not sufficient evidence of his "success." He also wishes to be accepted into (or to have people believe that he had been accepted into) an elite social stratum representing the ultimate in beauty, taste, and refinement. Opposing views may be found, however, not only in the novels and short stories of Ernest Hemingway but also in the writings of American populists, including Mark Twain. In chapter 25 of *A Connecticut Yankee in King Arthur's Court* (1889), Twain summarizes this view with the words: "The master minds of all nations, in all ages, have sprung in affluent multitude from the mass of the nation, and from the mass of the nation only—not from its privileged classes."

**Antielitism in
literature**

As Twain's and Hemingway's writings indicate, there has been a strong tendency in North American literature to argue that the true elite is something other than the aristocracy. This point of view has a long heritage. Servant characters, such as the slaves Palaestrio and Pseudolus in the comedies of the Roman playwright Plautus, the factotum Figaro in *Le Barbier de Séville: Ou, La Précaution inutile* (1775; *The Barber of Seville: Or, The Useless Precaution*, 1776) by Pierre-Augustin Caron de Beaumarchais, the gentleman's gentleman Jeeves in the novels of P. G. Wodehouse, and the title character of Sir James M. Barrie's *The Admirable Crichton* (1902), all form a servant elite. These servants prove to be smarter and more capable than their aristocratic superiors. Likewise, the novels of John Steinbeck frequently suggest that the compassion and innate heroism of the marginal classes are superior to the shallow lives of the social elite.

SUGGESTED READINGS

Bachrach, Peter. *The Theory of Democratic Elitism*. Boston: Little, Brown, 1967. A social scientist analyzes the phenomenon of elitism in democratic societies.

Field, G. Lowell. *Elitism*. London: Routledge & Kegan Paul, 1980. The best general study of elitism as a social, artistic, and intellectual phenomenon. An excellent starting place in the study of elitism.

Fiske, John. *Power Plays, Power Works*. New York: Verso, 1993. Discusses the relationship between elitism and popular culture in twentieth century American society.

Henry, William A. *In Defense of Elitism*. Garden City, N.Y.: Doubleday, 1994. Argues that elitism should not be defined as the possession of undeserved privileges and respect but as the appropriate reward received for hard work and intellectual superiority. Highly controversial but informative.

Kadushin, Charles. *The American Intellectual Elite*. Boston: Little, Brown, 1974. Argues that the intelligentsia in America fills the same role as the aristocracy in Europe when it establishes tastes and values for all social classes.

Lasch, Christopher. *The Revolt of the Elites and the Betrayal of Democracy*. New York: Norton, 1995. The author examines the new social elites in American society and suggests that they are having a destructive effect upon a shared system of values.

Miles, Peter, and Malcolm Smith. *Cinema, Literature and Society*. New York: Croom Helm, 1987. Although focusing primarily on Britain in the period between World Wars I and II, this work provides a fascinating discussion of the relationship between high culture, as defined by the elite, and mass culture in literature and film.

Sontag, Susan. *Under the Sign of Saturn*. New York: Farrar, Straus & Giroux, 1980. In such essays as "Fascinating Fascism," Sontag suggests that the tastes and values acceptable in an elite would be destructive if accepted by the mass culture.

Sowell, Thomas. *The Vision of the Anointed: Self-Congratulation as a Basis for Social Policy*. New York: BasicBooks, 1995. A conservative analysis of the "new elites" (intellectuals, the media, politicians) and their influence in American society.

Taylor, Roger. *Beyond Art: What Art Is and Might Become If Freed from Cultural Elitism*. New York: Barnes & Noble Books, 1981. A philosophical study of the destructive impact of elitism upon the arts.

—*Jeffrey L. Buller*

See also Canon; Class and identity; Economics of identity; Popular culture; School; Stereotypes and identity

Elkin, Stanley

BORN: Brooklyn, New York; May 11, 1930
DIED: St. Louis, Missouri; May 31, 1995
PRINCIPAL WORKS: *Boswell: A Modern Comedy*, 1964; *Criers and Kibitzers, Kibitzers and Criers*, 1965; *A Bad Man*, 1967; *The Dick Gibson Show*, 1971; *Searches and Seizures*, 1973; *The*

Franchiser, 1976; *The Living End*, 1979; *Stanley Elkin's Greatest Hits*, 1980; *George Mills*, 1982; *Early Elkin*, 1985; *Stanley Elkin's "The Magic Kingdom"*, 1985; *The Rabbi of Lud*, 1987; *The Six-Year-Old Man*, 1987; *The McGuffin*, 1991; *Pieces of Soap: Essays*, 1992; *Van Gogh's Room at Arles: Three Novellas*, 1993; *Mrs. Ted Bliss*, 1995

IDENTITIES: Jewish

SIGNIFICANT ACHIEVEMENT: Through dark humor and inventive use of language, Elkin captures a unique Jewish American identity.

Stanley Elkin is admired for his ironic, humorous stories. (Miriam Berkley)

Stanley Elkin writes darkly humorous works. About half of his characters are Jewish, mostly secular Jews. Many of them, however, resist assimilation into mainstream American life. In his short stories and novels, Elkin establishes Jewish identity in two major ways. He captures Jewish humor through the unique intonations of Jewish American speech, and he casts his characters in professions often entered by Jewish men.

A consummate stylist, Elkin often presents his characters as caught between their religious heritage, which they consider anachronistic and from which they have distanced themselves, and late twentieth century American society, into which they refuse to integrate. To repair a tattered self-image, the gentile protagonist in *Boswell: A Modern Comedy* forms a club for famous and successful people; he then cannot sacrifice his individuality by joining.

Although Elkin considered himself a novelist, *Criers and Kibitzers, Kibitzers and Criers*, which clearly established his identity as a Jewish writer, caused many readers and some critics to consider Elkin essentially as a short-story writer. Elkin clearly established his identity as a novelist, however, by producing more than ten novels.

Aside from *Criers and Kibitzers, Kibitzers and Criers*, about half of whose stories treat Jewish subjects, Elkin deals with Jews and Jewish themes in a number of his other books. *A Bad Man* focuses on Leo Feldman, a department store owner hemmed in by a crazy father and a tedious son. In "The Condominium," a novella in *Searches and Seizures*, Elkin focuses on shiva, the Jewish funeral rite.

In *The Franchiser*, Elkin puts Ben Flesh, adopted by Julius Finsberg during the Depression, into an unbelievable family of eighteen twins and triplets, all afflicted with degenerative diseases. In *George Mills*, however, in which the protagonists are gentile, Elkin sacrifices ethnic identity for universality.

SUGGESTED READINGS

Bargen, Doris G. *The Fiction of Stanley Elkin*. Bern: Lang, 1980.

Charney, Maurice. "Stanley Elkin and Jewish Black Humor." In *Jewish Wry: Essays on Jewish Humor*, edited by Sarah Blacher Cohen. Bloomington: Indiana University Press, 1987.

Guttmann, Allen. *The Jewish Writer in America*. New York: Oxford University Press, 1971.

—*R. Baird Shuman*

See also Jewish American identity

Ellison, Ralph

BORN: Oklahoma City, Oklahoma; March 1, 1914

DIED: New York, New York; April 16, 1994

PRINCIPAL WORKS: *Invisible Man*, 1952; *Shadow and Act*, 1964; *Going to the Territory*, 1986; *The Collected Essays of Ralph Ellison*, 1995; *Flying Home and Other Stories*, 1996

IDENTITIES: African American

SIGNIFICANT ACHIEVEMENT: In his writings, Ellison emphasizes his belief in integration and pluralism in American society.

A native of rural Oklahoma, Ralph Ellison moved to New York City in 1936, where he met fellow black writer Richard Wright. Wright helped Ellison begin his writing career. In 1938, Ellison joined the Federal Writers' Project, which launched his educational and literary life, which was dedicated to exploring social and personal identities as defined by racial lines.

In 1945, Ellison, who was then exploring and espousing leftist views, began work on *Invisible Man*, a novel based on his post-World War II interest in racial identity, ethnic unity, and social justice. *Invisible Man* won the National Book Award and the Russwarm Award in 1953, catapulting Ellison into national prominence as an important black author. *Invisible Man* traces the life of a young African American male who is attempting to define his identity in the context of his race and of society as a whole. Ellison received numerous honors, including the 1969 Medal of Freedom Award for his leadership in the black literary community.

*Ralph Ellison,
author of* Invisible
Man *(1952).*
(National Archives)

Shadow and Act and *Going to the Territory* are considered his spiritual and literary autobiographies. They are collections of essays, criticism, and reviews advocating integration and plurality. Describing "geography as fate," Ellison wrote much about growing up in Oklahoma and about his deep interest in the creative process, in black folklore and myth, in vernacular and popular styles versus traditional and elite cultures, in jazz, in the blues, in literary modernism, and particularly in the dynamics of race.

Ellison frequently focuses on the complexity of these dynamics, which, for him, impose the obligation to question and challenge codified portrayals of African American life and to embrace the promise of American democracy despite its historic betrayals of the black community. Ellison's individualism often moved against the grain of public opinion; for example, his essay "The Myth of the Flawed White Southerner" defends Lyndon Johnson, then president of the United States, against the attacks of anti-Vietnam War protesters. He claimed he was an integrationist of the imagination, where ideas are difficult to control by social, economic, and political processes. Such ideas made him a target of black nationalists during the 1960's and early 1970's. Ellison is often compared to Mark Twain, William Faulkner, and Ernest Hemingway, all of whom Ellison spoke of as literary mentors.

SUGGESTED READINGS

Bloom, Harold, ed. *Ralph Ellison*. New York: Chelsea House, 1986.

Busby, Mark. *Ralph Ellison*. Boston: Twayne, 1991.

Hersey, John, ed. *Ralph Ellison: A Collection of Critical Essays*. Englewood Cliffs, N.J.: Prentice-Hall, 1973.

—Wesley Britton

See also African American identity; *Invisible Man*; Underground man: a literary archetype

Emergence of Green, An

AUTHOR: Katherine V. Forrest (1939-   )

FIRST PUBLISHED: 1986

IDENTITIES: Gay, lesbian, and bisexual; women

An Emergence of Green is a contemporary story of two women's lives as they meet and fall in love and struggle with the reality of their experience. The novel is set in suburban Los Angeles during the 1980's. One of the women, Val, is a struggling artist with an eight-year-old son. Carolyn is a neighbor who lives with her husband of eight years.

Katherine Forrest writes the story from a lesbian perspective, which creates strong women characters. Val is the stereotypical lesbian; she is tall, big, and strong in stature and presents an alarming persona to the straight world, especially Carolyn's husband. The women become good friends, and as they acknowledge their physical attraction to each other, they become lovers, which creates additional problems for the relationship and marriage of Carolyn and Paul.

As an artist, Val is most aware of the color of things in nature, at home, and the colors that people do or do not wear. The book's title is a reference to Val's explanation that moving to a more green place signifies more life, a different life, a life potentially filled with more growth. As the story continues, the women become victims of Paul's violence and hatred of Val. He is insistent that Carolyn is his property, that he has given her all the material comforts possible, and that she has no reason to no longer belong to him. Carolyn has over the years given her life away, changed jobs, changed houses, changed her entire being to please Paul. Finally, when she realizes that what she has called love for Paul is based on pity and wanting to have his life as important to her as it is to Paul, she begins to understand that somewhere she has lost most of her identity, and is functioning only as an object in Paul's life. From this awareness, she moves toward Val in a loving, sexual relationship that is more satisfying for her than any other previous relationship she has had. The dilemma then begins when she realizes that she must separate from Val and Paul to find her identity. In an effort to control Carolyn, Paul rapes her. Carolyn goes to Val for support and assistance.

Forrest uses the story of Val and Carolyn to remind readers that people fall in love with others with whom they would not expect to fall in love. The world continually changes, people's lives continually change, and as a result people's loves can change. The story contains humor, suburban reality, sexuality, passion, erotica, violence, and strength of character.

SUGGESTED READINGS

Boutelier, Nancy. "Breathing the Rarified Air of Freedom." *Lambda Book Report* 4, no. 8 (January-February, 1996): 6.

Brownworth, Victoria A. "No Mystery." *The Advocate* 655 (May 17, 1994): 50.

—Sandra J. Parsons

See also Feminism; Lesbian identity; Rape; Women and identity